THE CHRIST CONSPIRACY

The Greatest Story Ever Sold

Revised Edition

D. M. Murdock
a.k.a. Acharya S

Adventures Unlimited Press

Design and layout by D.M. Murdock (a.k.a. Acharya S). The cover image is a ninth-century reproduction of the zodiac by Claudius Ptolemy (c. AD 90–c. 168) from his work Tetrabiblos with Helios (the sun) at the center, identified as the Christ by the cross; twelve female figures representing the hours; and twelve apostles representing the twelve months, all surrounded by the twelve zodiac signs. Held today by the Vatican (Vaticanus graecus 1291).

ALSO BY D.M. MURDOCK (A.K.A. ACHARYA S)

Suns of God: Krishna, Buddha, and Christ Unveiled
Who Was Jesus? Fingerprints of the Christ
Christ in Egypt: The Horus-Jesus Connection
The Gospel According to Acharya S
Did Moses Exist? The Myth of the Israelite Lawgiver
The Astrotheology Calendar Serie

THE CHRIST CONSPIRACY

The Greatest Story Ever Sold

Revised Edition

Adventures Unlimited Press

The Christ Conspiracy
Revised Edition

ISBN 978-1-948803-22-9

Library of Congress Cataloging in Publication Data
Murdock, D.M./Acharya S
The Christ Conspiracy: The Greatest Story Ever Sold – Revised Edition
1. Jesus Christ—Historicity 2. Christianity—Origin
ISBN13: 978-1-948803-22-9

Published by:
Adventures Unlimited Press
One Adventure Place
Kempton, Illinois 60946 USA
auphq@frontiernet.net

AdventuresUnlimitedPress.com

10 9 8 7 6 5 4 3 2 1

Editorial Preface by Dr. Robert M. Price

Several years ago, I wrote a harsh review of a book called *The Christ Conspiracy* by one Acharya S. The book set forth the Christ myth theory, of which I am also an adherent, but it took a very different approach. I felt the need to distance myself from her work lest I be painted with the same broad brush that tarred her in many quarters—and still does. This review, I am sorry to say, caused Acharya considerable sorrow and trouble.

A few years later, I happened to get in contact with her via an e-mail we both received from a mutual acquaintance. Actually, Acharya contacted me, commenting that she was surprised I seemed somewhat open to changing my mind on a certain point that had also come up in my review of her book. I took advantage of this friendly feeler to join in conversation with her, to clear up a couple of misunderstandings, and, most of all, to apologize for the anguish I had caused her. I did not retract any critical judgments I had made of her work, but I was very sorry to have caused her such pain. Acharya was quite forgiving, and we became good friends. Since that time, a number of people, some of whom hold critical opinions closer to mine, have expressed astonishment, even anger, that I removed my review of her *The Christ Conspiracy* from my website. I withdrew from the chorus of denunciations of my new friend. Why? And have I come to recant my criticisms?

I disliked what I deemed the militantly anti-Christian tone of the book and considered it a sign of adolescent, village atheist behavior (not that my own writings are always without it!). Now I think such things are utterly beside the point. It is the content that matters. I neither chafe at the reverent piety of biblical critics like Joachim Jeremias nor bristle at the sarcasm of atheist polymath Frank Zindler. Besides, she soon put such understandable rage behind her.

There were a number of issues she mentioned in a kind of too-encyclopedic survey approach, speculations about the Masons, ancient civilizations (à la Colin Wilson, whom I also knew and much respected), and the like. I still think these matters did not belong in the same book with her Christ myth arguments. They are entirely unrelated questions, and I have no expertise at all in evaluating them. Still don't. I should have ignored them in my review. All such issues are absent from her subsequent, much more tightly focused books such as *Suns of God* and *Christ in Egypt*. And now they are conspicuous by their absence from the pages of this new version of *The Christ Conspiracy*.

Astrotheology of the Ancients

To me, the most interesting aspect of Acharya's work is her pursuit of old, now ignored theories by comparative religionists and mythologists suggesting that Christianity embodies a perennial theology of the heavenly bodies, their motions, and the common reflection of this astrotheology in the myths of all nations. The implications of this theory led its advocates to draw parallels between New Testament mythemes and those gathered from much farther afield (e.g., Hindu, Mexican, Egyptian and Chinese religion). This was the approach taken by the Christ mythicists of past generations, including James M. Robertson, Arthur Drews, and Kersey Graves. I feel that such multiplication of supposed parallels reaped from so wide a field tends to deflate the value of closer, more easily demonstrable parallels between Christianity and historically, geographically adjacent phenomenon like Gnosticism and the Mystery Religions. Acharya's approach seems to me to make everything tantamount to everything else. I still have this hesitancy and prefer to argue from within a narrower framework. But this isn't much of a criticism. And if it is, let me mitigate my criticism in two ways.

First, Acharya made me rethink the astrotheology business. Ignaz Goldziher (*Mythology Among the Hebrews*) had already convinced me of the propriety of F. Max Müller's (now unfashionable) "solar mythology" hermeneutic: that many Old Testament (and maybe even New Testament) figures began their narrative lives as fictive personifications of the heavenly bodies. Samson, Elijah, Enoch, Esau, and Moses were plainly, like Hercules, Mithras and Apollo, sun gods. So, it is no great leap to trace at least some prominent features of the Jesus myth to solar faith.

And how else do we explain the occurrence of the cross as a religious symbol all over the ancient world unless it was based on something all races had access to: the phenomena of the night sky? Makes sense!

I took issue with some of her older sources, where she found claims of icons and effigies of crucified gods or heroes, alleged to be Krishna or Indra. Yes, the evidence is sketchy, but it has to be explained *some* way. There must be *something* going on there, as when we discover nearly identical bas reliefs featuring a horned man in the lotus position, surrounded by forest animals—in both India and Ireland! Just coincidence? I cannot think so.

Primary Sources

Second, my criticisms and others in the same vein sent Acharya back to the drawing board, determined to unpack and display the evidence for parallel cases of solar symbols and mythology shared between

Christianity and other religions. She delved into the arguments of the old Mythicists to ferret out their sources and how they formed their opinions. I love this history of scholarship approach, and the most interesting part of my original review to write was a similar investigation of the alleged parallels and the evidence cited by these old scholars. The variety of old, now-ignored sources, on the fringe of the better-known Higher Criticism, was fascinating, too, and it was Acharya's use of them that introduced me to much of this material. I am grateful.

I find the books of Acharya S/D.M. Murdock to be researched in amazing depth, comprehensive with a scope that fairly makes my head spin, and written blessedly without the stuffy technical jargon present in much mainstream scholarship. Was she "reduced" to publishing her own books? So what? So was Hume.

But she didn't have to publish *this* one herself. She had planned this new edition of *The Christ Controversy*, but her fatal diagnosis took the task out of her hands. She placed it in mine, a great honor and a job I and others (Robert Tulip, David Deley, and N.W. Barker) have taken up gratefully and upon which we have done our best. It is still her book, not a hijacked vehicle for promoting our own pet theories. Like righteous Abel, being dead she still speaks. And the echoes of her work will long be heard.

—Dr. Robert M. Price
May 2019

Preface

"[It] was in the early twentieth century that disbelief in the existence of Jesus seems to have reached its peak. This is shown by the popularity of works from this period like *Die Christus Mythe* by Arthur Drews, which underwent three editions between 1910 and 1911, and the critical responses it inspired."

—Dr. Alice Whealey, *Josephus on Jesus* (172)

"The Egyptians, Greeks, and Romans were masters of such man/god fiction and the creation of such characters as Osiris, Dionysus, Asclepius, Hercules, Orpheus and the like, as the works of Hesiod, Euripides, Virgil, Ovid, Petronius, Seneca, Apuleius, et. al, demonstrate. Why not consider all of this literature simply part of this man-God personification literature, in this instance incorporating the new Jewish concept of 'Salvation'— 'Yeshu'a'?"

—Dr. Robert H. Eisenman, "Redemonizing of Judas: Gospel Fiction or Gospel Truth?"

"Jewish artisans and Jewish fishermen are your teachers and your saints, with countless statues carved in their image and innumerable cathedrals raised to their memories. A Jewish maiden is your ideal of motherhood and womanhood. A Jewish rebel-prophet is the central figure in your religious worship. We have pulled down your idols, cast aside your racial inheritance, and substituted for them our God and our traditions. No conquest in history can even remotely compare with this clean sweep of our conquest over you."

—Marcus Eli Ravage, *Century Magazine*, 1928

"It is, of course, a well-known fact that no one has yet succeeded in giving authentic evidences to establish the truth of all the stories that we read in the synoptic Gospels regarding the life of the Christ. On the contrary, the historic personality of Jesus has been denied over and over again by the most able scholars and higher critics of Europe and America."

—Swami Abhedānanda, *Great Saviors of the World* (1.39)

Revisiting the Conspiracy

Since this book was first published in 1999, many things have transpired, including the ability to search through millions of books quickly in order to find the most up-to-date research as well as the best primary sources. Readers of that first edition may be surprised to know how it was constructed, without benefit of large sums of money or all that privilege entails: In a word, I used my relatively small library of books I had bought over the years. Thus, I did not drill down as deeply as I could have, but time was of the essence as was the near utter lack of resources. Yet, despite its flaws—and there were a few—the book has stood the test of time, and I am now in a better position than ever to validate its main theses (and many of its minor ones as well) using the best possible sources. Hence, this second edition.

Substantially, nothing has changed since that first edition, although much has happened in the world at large, including a summary of my work being viewed by some 300 million as of 2013 in the hit internet documentary *Zeitgeist*. Since then, this book and much of the rest of my work has been vetted by all manner of critics, but the continued interest merely serves to highlight both the ongoing fascination with the subject matter and the efficacy of this particular analysis. In brief, what I am presenting in this book may be called "mythicism," the "mythicist position" or the "case for mythicism."

From the reaction to this book, it's clear that the "Characters" chapter poses the greatest threat to the notion that Jesus Christ was a historical figure. The various lists included there of characteristics in common with the Christ figure have been gone over with a fine-toothed comb by countless Christian apologists and assorted others such as New Testament scholars, theologians, historians and mythologists. That chapter has now been completely revised, with language tweaked for accuracy and all-new sources. I have been able to draw more often directly from primary sources, often in their original languages, as well as the writings of the most credentialed authorities in relevant fields, published by the best academic and scholarly publishers in the world.

Because of the contentiousness of this issue, I consciously chose to make this book "quote heavy," so that others could see exactly where the information was coming from and that I was not alone in my assessments. In using my own library, I had no thought for "credentialism" and the logical fallacy of "appeal to authority" when quoting these various authors. Instead, I simply relied on the content of what they said and judged their remarks on their own merit, rather than appealing to some imagined authority of "big names." This should have been obvious if only from the fact that many of these older scholars have been ignored or forgotten. Their (unknown) names do not carry much clout, but I think their arguments do, as you will see.

Some reviewers complained that such older scholarship was "outdated." While it is always desirable to incorporate the most modern research available, including various archaeological discoveries, the fact remains that the field of comparative religion and mythology is not one subject to wild vicissitudes based on new finds or theories. Indeed, what was said about Christianity and its origins during the second century remains the basis for the debate. But, in order to present a comprehensive survey of evidence for the mythicist thesis, one needs to incorporate sources from the earliest times to the most modern, including all those in between now deemed "outdated."

Breaking with the tradition established in the first edition of *The Christ Conspiracy* and *Suns of God*, but falling in line with my publications since then, I have transferred the footnotes from the end of the chapters to the bottom of the pages for the reader's ease of reference. These annotations often include suggestions for further reading.

Since my book was published in 1999, it has been read by many tens of thousands in English as well as thousands in Spanish. Among these have been fans and critics, from all walks of life, including professional scholars and clergymen. The reviews have been decidedly mixed, for obvious reasons. The overall thesis of Jesus as a mythical figure, representing largely a solar hero, has been both praised and assailed, but in the main it is only the detractors who have dared to speak loudly. Although many people have jumped on the Jesus myth bandwagon over the past 20 years since I first posted my "Origins of Christianity" essay online, only a handful have provided the evidence and data to demonstrate or, indeed, *prove* the case. I have consistently done so over the years, in books, articles, videos, forum posts, groups, emails, social networking sites and so on. My numerous efforts in this regard have included voluminous images, some of which are included here.

Unless otherwise noted, all Bible quotes here are from the Revised Standard Version ("RSV").[1]

The Inside Stuff on Conspiracies

As concerns the word "conspiracy" in the title of this book, despite the hysterical kneejerk reactions, it is perfectly valid to describe the events that shaped Christianity as conspiratorial. What is a "conspiracy"? They do exist, you know, though some think they can refute a hypothesis that displeases them by simply sneering, "conspiracy theory!" Have there never been conspiracies? Of course, and conspiracies need not be nefarious. The secret schemers on *The X-Files* would be conspirators, but the Constitutional Congress was a conspiracy, too. They were charged with merely revamping the Articles of Confederation, but, on their own initiative, threw the Articles out and created the Constitution

1 Copyright © 1946, 1952 and 1971 National Council of the Churches of Christ in the United States of America.

to replace it. The word "conspiracy" needn't imply something like the Protocols of the Elders of Zion.

Nevertheless, I have pruned a few remarks here and there in keeping with the object of this revision, which is to make this important information more readily available not only to the public at large but also through the educational system.

One objection lodged by various, more sober, scholars has been the bit about Masons having a hand in the creation of Christianity. These objections have been addressed in my book *Suns of God*, and further development of this thesis of a number of brotherhoods being involved in Christianity's creation can be found in the extensive chapter in my book *Christ in Egypt* entitled, "The Alexandrian Origins of Christianity."

In the last chapter of this book, considered one of the most controversial, I included much new material because of numerous discoveries since this book was first written. Needless to say, even though the sources may have been "outdated" or slightly inaccurate here and there, the overall thesis of global astrotheologically based religion and mythology is actually better established than ever before.

Some of these more controversial parts, such as the one dealing with Pygmies, have been widely overlooked or ridiculed, but if viewed without prejudice they provide some very interesting information and food for thought. I have trimmed down some of the sketchier ideas, although they remain of interest, in a speculative fashion.

Alas, despite my best solo efforts at research, writing, editing and proofreading the original edition, several mistakes crept in that have now been corrected.

Massey Effect

One of the sources I have used in this book somewhat frequently is the work of lay Egyptologist Gerald Massey. Because of the popularity of the first edition of this present work and the film *Zeitgeist*, Massey came under broad fire from all directions for a number of overt weaknesses, the biggest of which was that he was not a professional Egyptologist. Nevertheless, it is evident that his critics themselves are not experts on him or his work, which means that by this same credentialism they should not be making commentary upon him or it. Indeed, after one studies the issue in depth, it becomes apparent that Massey is far more qualified than the vast majority of his critics to discuss the matters of Egyptian religion and Christianity. His erudite work is itself the only relevant "credential."

In my book *Christ in Egypt*, I relate that Massey could read several languages, including not only English but also French, Latin, Greek and evidently Hebrew and Egyptian to a certain degree. In his intensive and meticulous efforts, Massey studied the work of the best minds of the time—all towering figures within Egyptology, especially during Massey's era, when most of them were alive and some were familiar with his work. These celebrated authorities in Egyptology whose works Massey studied and utilized include:

> Sir Dr. Budge; Dr. Brugsch-Bey; Jean-François Champollion; Dr. Eugene Lefébure; Dr. Karl Richard Lepsius; Sir Dr. Gaston Maspero; Dr. Henri Edouard Naville; Sir Dr. William Flinders Petrie; Dr. Thomas Joseph Pettigrew; Sir Renouf; le vicomte de Rougé; Dr. Samuel Sharpe; and Sir Dr. John Gardner Wilkinson, among many other scholars in a wide variety of fields.

Massey also used the work of Sir Dr. J. Norman Lockyer, the physicist and royal English astronomer who was friends with Budge and knew Egypt well, along with that of Dr. Charles Piazzi Smyth, royal Scottish astronomer and professor of Astronomy at the University of Edinburgh. Massey further studied the work of Reverend Dr. Archibald Sayce, professor of Comparative Philology at Oxford, as well as that of famous mythologist Sir Dr. James George Frazer, although he did not agree with their conclusions. He likewise cited the work of Francois Lenormant, Professor of Archaeology at the National Library of France, as well as that of comparative theologian and Oxford professor Dr. Max Müller, philosopher and Jesus biographer Dr. Ernest Renan, and Christian monuments expert Rev. Dr. John Patterson Lundy.

Gerald Massey was very much influenced by the work of Dr. Samuel Birch (1813–1885), archaeologist, Egyptologist and Keeper of the Department of Oriental Antiquities in the British Museum. The creator of the first alphabetically arranged Egyptian dictionary, Dr. Birch also was the founder of the prestigious and influential Society of Biblical Archaeology, to which belonged many other notables in the fields of archaeology, Assyriology, Egyptology and so on. Much more about Massey's long-term personal relationship with Birch can be found in my article, "Who is Gerald Massey?" Massey was likewise personally friendly with Sir Lockyer (1836–1920) as well as Dr. Birch's protégé Assyriologist Dr. Theophilus Goldridge Pinches (1856–1934). Massey's work was peer-reviewed by several renowned scholars of the day, including Birch, Lockyer and Dr. Richard Pietschmann, professor of Egyptology at the University of Göttingen.

In his scholarly works on Egypt, in addition to the available Egyptian sources, Gerald Massey utilized numerous other ancient texts, including Judeo-Christian writings such as the Bible and early Church fathers such as Justin Martyr, Irenaeus, Clement of Alexandria, Origen, Tertullian, Hippolytus, Eusebius, Epiphanius and Jerome. Massey also cited non-Christian, Jewish, and Gnostic writers such as Herodotus, Philo, Pausanias and Valentinus, along with writings such as the Talmud and the Hindu Puranas. Having taught himself to read not only English but also several other languages including Egyptian hieroglyphs as well as Sanskrit, facilitating an extensive comparison between these two languages, Massey scrutinized and interpreted the texts and monuments for himself, such as the Book of the Dead, as well as the famous zodiacs in the Temple of Dendera and the "Nativity Scene" at the Temple of Luxor.

The only reason Gerald Massey did not become a professional, degreed scholar is that he was born into extreme poverty and had to do hard, physical labor as a child, rather than attending school, which was not free to commoners in England at that time. Indeed, there was no public school system like we have today. Massey accomplished all of this scholarship without benefit of a formal education and should be afforded respect, even if one does not agree with his conclusions. Once again, we are faced with rabid credentialism and religious bias.

As concerns the oft-laid charge that Massey was engaged in mysticism and is therefore either "diabolical" or dismissible, here is a quote from him in response to his association with the movement of Theosophy and others:

> I cannot join in the new masquerade and simulation of ancient mysteries manufactured in our time by Theosophists, Hermeneutists, pseudo-Esoterics, and Occultists of various orders, howsoever profound their pretensions. The very essence of all such mysteries as are got up from the refuse leavings of the past is pretence, imposition, and imposture. The only interest I take in the ancient mysteries is in ascertaining how they originated, in verifying their alleged phenomena, in knowing what they meant, on purpose to publish the knowledge as soon and as widely as possible.[2]

Much has been made by Christian apologists of my own use of the writings of Theosophist Madame Blavatsky, cited a handful of times in all of my books, in order to cast my entire thesis and body of work into a bad light using the logical fallacy of guilt by association. The facts are that Jesus mythicism long predated Blavatsky and had issued in a great body of scholarship independent of Blavatsky's work. Indeed, she is not even a mythicist in the strictest sense, devising a "historical" Jesus of her own. The brief quotations I used from her work presented pertinent facts related to germane subjects; I did not reproduce her mystical claims and

2 Massey, *GML*, 247.

have no interest in such. None of my work rests on any of hers.

As concerns the use of works by Gnosticism expert G.R.S. Mead, it should be noted that Mead's work has been taken seriously by many sober scholars and is cited in thousands of other books, including many hundreds by such important publishers as E.J. Brill and various university presses, as well as in numerous books by Christian scholars and theologians. His close association with Theosophy, therefore, has not destroyed his reputation or prevented his work from being utilized.

While every attempt has been made to go to the originals where appropriate—in their original languages as well as superior translations—it remains important to include the opinions of older generations as part of the review of Jesus mythicism, since they represent continuity of a school of thought dating back centuries to millennia. Without them, our survey would not be complete. Indeed, it is important that the reader be struck by the centuries-long continuity of thought demonstrated here. If mythicism were an invention of yesterday, that may count against it, but in fact it has a long pedigree.

Why has my inclusion of the views of older scholars—some dating to the seventeenth century in English—proven controversial? In the spirit of Robertson Smith, quoted just above, we might ask why many important ancient texts have been lost to history, and the answer would be that scribes lost interest in them or came to disapprove of them—and simply stopped making new copies of them for future generations to read. (One might call it "passive-aggressive book-burning.") The same thing happens when modern scholars just stop discussing the theories of scholars they don't agree with. When someone like me rediscovers such a forgotten author and calls attention to his work, those with short scholarly memories object: if *they* have not heard of him, he must be a quack and a crack-pot, and so must the one who dared let the old voice be heard again. Maybe one of the most important "credentials" a scholar can have is an indifference to the "consensus" of the moment. As C.S. Lewis famously said, seek out the *old* books. Often they provide a healthy corrective to the new.

One critic complained that I did not deal with evemerism (or euhemerism) very much; however, my entire book is designed to show how evemerism is not the most satisfying explanation when the supernatural attributes are stripped away and the Jesus story is taken at face value. There's simply no core to the onion.

The Historical Method

In the criticisms of the first edition of *The Christ Conspiracy*, I heard just about everything imaginable, from shrills cries of "heretic!" to almost equally hysterical rants about "historical method." This latter phrase was held over the head of the unsuspecting layman like some mystical mumbo-jumbo that only the high priests of academia could understand, requiring triple PhDs and assorted other alphabet soup after one's name. It is not enough to hide behind such a shibboleth, pulling rank on the basis of it. One must exercise it, whether one uses the term or not.

William Robertson Smith on the historical method:

> Ancient books coming down to us from a period many centuries before the invention of printing have necessarily undergone many vicissitudes. Some of them are preserved only in imperfect copies made by an ignorant scribe of the dark ages. Others have been disfigured by editors, who mixed up foreign matter with the original text. Very often an important book fell altogether out of sight for a long time, and when it came to light again all knowledge of its origin was gone; for old books did not generally have title-pages and prefaces. And, when such a nameless roll was again brought into notice, some half-informed reader or transcriber was not unlikely to give it a new title of his own devising, which was handed down thereafter as if it had been original. Or again, the true meaning and purpose of a book often became obscure in the lapse of centuries, and led to false interpretations. Once more, antiquity has handed down to us many writings which are sheer forgeries, like some of the Apocryphal books, or the Sibylline oracles, or those famous Epistles of Phalaris which formed the subject of Bentley's great critical essay. In all such cases the historical critic must destroy the received view, in order to establish the truth. He must review doubtful titles, purge out interpolations, expose forgeries; but he does so only to manifest the truth, and exhibit the genuine remains of antiquity in their real character. A book that is really old and really valuable has nothing to fear from the critic, whose labours can only put its worth in a clearer light, and establish its authority on a surer basis.[3]

While much credentialism is batted about in this field in order to discredit independent scholars, the fact will remain that I do have appropriate research and writing skills for this effort. Indeed, a degree in history, no matter how advanced, will not suffice when dealing with ancient texts that require language skills, particularly in this instance Greek and Latin. My educational background in Classics includes not

3 Smith, W. The Old Testament in the Jewish Church, 17.

only the study of history—especially that of Greece and Rome, two very important centers for this quest—but also the appropriate languages of ancient Greek and Latin. My detractors have often been lacking in a degree even in history, much less the needful expertise in languages. Therefore, in my writings I am able to include in many instances various texts and passages in their original languages, whereas others are not. I am aware even of biblical scholars and theologians who, oddly, have few if any language skills. Certainly, they do not research in ancient Greek or even Latin on a regular basis, as I have been doing for the past decades.

Furthermore, my lack of association with an organization only enhances my position of neutrality in not being tied to an institutional or "official" viewpoint. I am, in effect, not bound by any external authority to skew the data in favor of a mainstream perspective.

In their quest to shore-up the faith at all costs, we have seen Christian fathers and later apologists forge numerous documents and artifacts. Even in this day and age, we have witnessed a Christian apologist and New Testament scholar forge a birth certificate for Jesus Christ simply as a joke, but there is no guarantee that subsequent readers will not think it real. Bored scholars have famously cooked up outright hoaxes to see if anyone could detect them, so we continue to see new secret gospels, gospels of Mrs. Jesus, and boxes of biblical bones. Such behavior shows the lengths to which apologists will go when they have no real, credible scientific evidence or even a cogent argument.

In my wide ranging for sources, I have encountered some that do not have or deserve the academic stamp of approval. These are occasionally useful to track down little-known data or better discussions of same. Thus they deserve inclusion in my bibliography. It doesn't mean I second everything on every one of their yellowed pages. And, besides, there's no excuse for not knowing the history of research, even the false leads.

When we apply the historical method to the four canonical gospels and the canonical epistles as depiction of a historical Jesus, we find that these texts fail miserably. Major scholars admit this freely. But that seems not to bother many New Testament scholars and theologians, as they endlessly throw obfuscating clouds of special pleading on behalf of Jesus and the gospel story.

This quest for a perfect historical Jesus has many times failed because of *a priori* assumptions and stubborn biases. For example, whole mythologies have arisen regarding the alleged persecution of a "vast multitude" of Christians by Nero, whom he purportedly blamed for the burning of Rome. Much scholarship rests on these notions, even down to such things as Nero being the identity of the Beast marked with the number 666 in the Book of Revelation. But where is any credible scientific evidence for a "vast multitude" of Christians at Rome during Nero's time or of any persecution under this emperor? By the standards of the historical method, this "event" clearly should be marked unlikely at best. But, since the story seems to provide a much-needed link between the later, more clearly marked Church history and the alleged advent of Jesus Christ, it does not occur to most scholars to apply real scrutiny. You don't want "skeptic" popping up on your resume.

It only gets worse when it comes to the subject of whether or not Jesus was a historical figure. This claim is usually accepted a priori, forgoing proper investigation of the evidence. In very few other subjects would a trained scholar or scientist accept matters "on faith"; yet this lack of scientific investigation is precisely what has happened when it comes to Christian origins—very little hard evidence is required for entire generations of scholars to assume that Christ existed and to work from there.

In many instances, the older scholars were better educated and qualified in these particular subjects, ironically, because they were *not* as specialized as their successors today. They had a broader scope of the many disciplines needed to analyze the data properly. However, many of the clergymen who made critical analyses tended to soft-peddle their results, leaving it to the canny reader to draw out the more serious implications. The attempts by modern apologists to minimize these researchers and their work seem either disingenuous or undiscerning. It is hardly uncommon to see today's geniuses reinventing wheels crafted centuries before them or even misrepresenting the views of those whose works they would supersede.

In many instances where we are citing "older scholarship," the subject necessitates such sources because they come from the hands of the travelers, scholars and missionaries who first contacted or communicated with the cultures whose traditions we are relating. For example, when we are discussing the gods of Central America or Polynesia, we must rely on the writings of scholars from the centuries during which the first contact occurred. These often European Christian sources frequently admit, against their own interest, the existence of startling and detailed parallels between biblical stories and the myths and traditions of isolated groups and tribes. Nevertheless, these chroniclers piously insisted that no possible outside influence upon the Christian religion could have occurred. Thus, it is imperative to utilize their writings, even though they represent "older scholarship," since they are nonetheless primary sources of an important sort. Some of these older writers were the last Westerners to observe and record these various previously uncontacted cultures intact, prior to their contamination by outside influences. Too bad we have no such "front line coverage" of American Indian or ancient Norse mythology before missionary beliefs rubbed off on them. Then we might know whether the Happy Hunting Ground was a recycled Christian heaven or if Ragnarok was derived from the biblical Armageddon. Too late now.

The superior scholarship expressed in the nineteenth century continued into the twentieth century, when it appears to have been squelched, not necessarily by direct argumentation that proved it incorrect, but by a massive redirect towards other subjects. While the scientific methods in numerous fields have most definitely produced a greater and improved understanding, with countless discoveries that have added tremendously to our knowledge, the fact is that these methods have largely been needed in the *hard* sciences. The subjects of comparative religion and mythology were not in need of much improvement in methodology, and the discoveries that have been made since that time have only *added to* our confidence in this earlier scholarship. Indeed, the improvements in the sciences of archaeology, linguistics and astronomy, to name but an important few, have served to *verify* this older scholarship quite astonishingly.

Fortunately, since the original edition of this book was published, a number of significant studies have appeared by professional scholars via academic presses that validate much of the information here, such as: Dr. Bart D. Ehrman's *Forged*; Dr. William O. Walker, Jr.'s *Interpolations in the Pauline Letters*; Dr. Marguerite Rigoglioso's *Virgin Mother Goddesses of Antiquities*; Dr. Bojana Mojsov's *Osiris: Death and Afterlife of a God*; Dr. Tryggve Mettinger's *The Riddle of the Resurrection*; Dr. Israel Finkelstein and Neil Silberman's *The Bible Unearthed*; Rev. Dr. J. Glen Taylor's *Yahweh and the Sun: Biblical and Archaeological Evidence for Sun Worship in Ancient Israel*; Dr. Robert M. Price's *The Pre-Nicene New Testament*; Dr. Dennis R. MacDonald's *The Homeric Epics and the Gospel of Mark*, Dr. Zacharias P. Thundy's *Buddha and Christ*, Dr. Payam Nabarz's *The Mysteries of Mithra* and Dr. Michael Lockwood's *Buddhism's Relation to Christianity*. In these instances, as well as in significant works from lay scholars such as Earl Doherty's *Jesus: Neither God Nor Man*, important contentions from the older scholars have essentially been *proved* using the most modern methods by skilled and credentialed modern scholars.

Myth and Match

Because of the fascination with the "Characters" chapter in particular, which was picked apart all over the internet, spawning entire articles on Wikipedia, for instance, I have expanded that section as well as reworded my contentions for accuracy and meticulously cited primary sources and/or the works of credentialed authorities, while expunging a very few unsupportable contentions.

Like the common mythical motif of the descent into the underworld or *katabasis*,[4] which was shared by the Jesus story in the apocryphal text *The Gospel of Nicodemus* or *Acts of Pilate*, many aspects of the gospel story can be found in pre-Christian religions and mythologies. Here I will demonstrate that fact and show how the gospel story was woven from Pagan motifs and biblical scriptures, along with other religious ideation and countless texts, some extant but most long perished.

There are many differences between the accounts of various gods; these exist because of the era and location in which the basic archetypical myths were amended, changed and expanded. These differences provide fascinating illustrations of cultural variety in the making. However, they are somewhat irrelevant in our quest to determine which religious ideas and mythological motifs influenced Christianity, although we must have as broad a perspective as possible, and these variances reveal much about the cultural milieu and the goals of Christianity's creators. In some instances, there may be more than one influence in the creation of a motif. Any given motif may have resulted—as did the Christian effort—from a combination of Paganism and Judaism (or Hinduism and Buddhism!).

I have no desire to attack so-called sacred texts. On the contrary, I hope that as many people as possible will become as educated as possible in all religious notions available, some of which are not only fascinating but also abundant in truth. This latter contention may seem shocking to some, but, in the first place, I view religious, spiritual and mythological ideas as highly important—if not the most important—cultural artifacts devised by humanity. Of course, much has been highly deleterious as well, and it is this religious pathology that I critique, even while drawing attention to the positive, such as the nature worship and astrotheology. These

4 In its article "Descent to the underworld," Wikipedia lists the following figures from antiquity around the world who were said to have made the trip into what the Greeks called "Hades": Osiris, Adonis/Tammuz, Dionysus, Heracles, Hermes, Orpheus, Persephone, Demeter, Psyche, Odysseus, Aeneas, Theseus, Pirithous, Enkidu, Gilgamesh, Inanna, Baldr, Hermod, Helreið Brynhildar, Lemminkäinen, Izanagi, Izanami, Hunahpu, Xbalanque, Kuan Yin, Ushas, Yudhisthira, Pwyll, Kaknu, Obatala, the latter specifically designated "the rising and dying god of Ile Ife, the Yoruba cultural centre." As we can see, this motif is common, as, we shall further see, are many other details recorded in the gospel story, page 181.

have led mankind to record a plethora of scientific observations of the natural world, albeit couched in anthropomorphized tales.

It is therefore not my intent to create atheists or theists of anyone; what one does in the privacy of one's own mind is entirely up to the individual and is none of my or anyone else's business, until it spills out onto others in a harmful fashion. In my criticisms I am simply pointing out the dangers and follies of blind belief. I want to do my small part in preventing the divisiveness caused by religious fanaticism and megalomania. The sharing of various religious ideas is wholesome, but conversion is not necessary. Forced conversion is positively evil. Insofar as one is educated re the world's religious, spiritual and mythological traditions, one is in a better position to choose to believe or to disbelieve. If one wishes to engage in "fantastic" or "wishful" thinking, that is one's prerogative.

In any event, such thorough religious education must include a detailed record of all aspects of religion, especially including the (unfortunately abundant) bad parts. To politely suppress and ignore the dark side of various religions, such as the Abrahamic faiths of Judaism, Christianity and Islam, represents the complete opposite of real piety and religiosity, since it is not only utterly dishonest but also contributes to endless suffering.

Blessed Are You When All Men Revile You

Generally speaking, the response to *The Christ Conspiracy* from many in the academic community has been ridicule, along with the rehearsal of the same hackneyed handful of ancient references "proving" Christ's historicity. Those who have examined this purported evidence, as well as the religion and mythology of the day, but remain unconvinced, have been dismissed as "insane" and their arguments ignored, after having been subjected to "withering criticism" that usually consists of nitpicking and *ad hominems*.[5] In order to incite their readers, critics of Mythicist scholarship repeatedly use words and phrases like "attacks Jesus" or "attacks Christianity,"[6] blatantly appealing to religious sentiment and fanning the flames of sectarian hatred. No one "argues" this way if they are able to mount a cogent rebuttal.

Nor would anyone with the facts on his side take cowardly refuge under the umbrella of "consensus," as if the truth were to be settled by

5 See, for example, Van Voorst, 8, 11.

6 For example, Christian theologian Van Voorst uses the word "attack" some dozen times in describing scholarship revealing the flaws in Christian doctrine and tradition, several times describing this investigation as an "attack on the historicity of Jesus," an "attack on Christianity" or an "attack against Jesus" (e.g., 11, 12, 60, 61, 64, 65, 66, 68, etc.).

majority vote. No one who felt he could soundly refute Mythicist Earl Doherty would try to short circuit the process by haughtily objecting that Doherty has no official degree in the field.

Why is there not even more evidence to pick through? Over the past two thousand years, Europe has been subjected to repeated destructions, including constant warfare and being overrun by savage invaders slaughtering and annihilating whole cultures. Both Mythicists and Historicists are hampered by the scarcity of evidence, but what shall we do? Blithely pretend that the position we happen to prefer is true simply because there is not a definitive preponderance of evidence?

The impression is given to schoolchildren that when the Lord God of the cosmos came to Earth, people all around knew it, and that, because of his astounding miracles, Jesus was famous around the known world during his lifetime—as is asserted in the New Testament—after which Christianity spread like wildfire, as is appropriate for such a supernatural and enlightening event. However, when pressed about the utter lack of a historical or archaeological record for Christ's existence, the common excuse is: "Why would anyone record him? He was just an obscure Jewish preacher in an isolated backwater." Obviously, the two opposing scenarios cannot be accurate, and Christian tradition from the earliest times, including, again, the Bible itself, contends for the former account of Christian origins, that Jesus was world famous, not the latter, that he was completely unknown.

In this edition, I have expanded considerably the earlier sections, especially as concerns purported non-biblical evidence for Christ's existence as a historical figure. In the earlier edition, this section was very short, because I had read so many impressive scientific analyses on the subject, I believed that the issue had been settled. I have included here a fairly thorough but succinct survey of claims regarding these various texts. In this regard, I have essentially *proved* the main contentions in my earlier book regarding these sources.

For space considerations, I have removed the chapters "Etymology Tells the Story," "The Bible, Sex and Drugs," "Out of Egypt or India?", and "Evidence of an Ancient Global Civilization."

The use of non-Latin scripts has been kept to a minimum in the text itself, while more appears in the footnotes, for the same reason that I have excluded repeated use of diacritical marks such as umlauts and those used in the International Alphabet of Sanskrit Transliteration ("IAST"): To simplify the experience for the lay reader, who may find such textual emendations to be intimidating.

—D.M. Murdock (a.k.a. Acharya S)

Introduction

"Believe not because some old manuscripts are produced, believe not because it is your national belief, believe not because you have been made to believe from your childhood, but reason truth out, and after you have analyzed it, then if you find it will do good to one and all, believe it, live up to it and help others live up to it."

—The Buddha[7]

"Whether Jesus ever actually existed has long been debated. The argument (very well documented) is that there is absolutely no corroborating evidence of his existence in documents other than highly suspect Christian sources. Analysts also note that practically all the events of Jesus' life, as well as many of his teachings, appear in the lives and utterances of mythical figures of other religions. This would indicate that Jesus was manufactured from borrowings from elsewhere to serve the purposes of early church leaders."

—Dr. Riane Eisler, *The Chalice & the Blade* (122)

"The Jesus of Nazareth who came forward publicly as the Messiah, who preached the ethic of the Kingdom of God, who founded the Kingdom of Heaven upon earth, and died to give His work its final consecration, never had any existence.

"He is a figure designed by rationalism, endowed with life by liberalism, and clothed by modern theology in an historical garb."

—Rev. Dr. Albert Schweitzer, *The Quest of the Historical Jesus* (20)

The history of religious belief on Earth is long and varied, with concepts, doctrines and rituals of all sorts designed to propitiate and beseech any number of gods and goddesses, dating back thousands of years. Although many people believe religion to be a good and necessary thing, little is more divisive than religion. It rends humanity in a number of ways through extreme racism, sexism and even speciesism.[8] Religion, in fact, is dependent on division, because it requires an enemy, whether it be earthly or in another dimension. Religion dictates that some people

7 This title "Buddha" appears in quotes because the "historical" Buddha represents a composite figure to whom were attributed many mythical miracles and wisdom sayings of other people. For more information, see my book *Suns of God: Krishna, Buddha and Christ Unveiled.*

8 Although religion is not a "race," and being critical of religion does not constitute "racism," the faces ascribe to "God" or the divine over the millennia most certainly often have occurred along racial lines, creating divisions between peoples based on race and ethnicity.

are special or chosen while others are immoral and evil, and it too often insists that it is the duty of the "chosen" to destroy the others. And organized religion puts a face on the divine itself that is sectarian, sexist and racist, portraying a male god of a particular ethnicity. The result is that, over the centuries, humankind has become utterly divided among itself and disconnected from nature, so that it stands on the verge of chaos.

More horrors have been caused in the name of God and religion than can be chronicled, but some examples can be provided, as well as an assessment of how religions function:

> The fires of Moloch in Syria, the harsh mutilations in the name of Astarte, Cybele, Jehovah; the barbarities of imperial Pagan Torturers; the still grosser torments which Roman-Gothic Christians in Italy and Spain heaped on their brother-men; the fiendish cruelties to which Switzerland, France, the Netherlands, England, Scotland, Ireland, America, have been witnesses, are none too powerful to warn man of the unspeakable evils which follow from mistakes and errors in the matter of religion, and especially from investing the God of Love with the cruel and vindictive passions of erring humanity, and making blood to have a sweet savor in his nostrils, and groans of agony to be delicious to his ears. Man never had the right to usurp the unexercised prerogative of God, and condemn and punish another for his belief. Born in a Protestant land, we are of that faith. If we had opened our eyes to the light under the shadows of St. Peter's in Rome, we should have been devout Catholics; born in the Jewish quarter of Alepp, we should have condemned Christ as an impostor; in Constantinople, we should have cried "*Allah il Allah*, God is great and Mahomet is his prophet!" Birth, place and education give us our faith. Few believe in any religion because they have examined the evidences of its authenticity, and made up a formal judgment, upon weighing the testimony. Not one man in ten thousand knows anything about the *proofs* of his faith. We believe what we are taught; and those are most fanatical who know least of the evidences on which their creed is based.[9]

Even today, when humankind likes to pretend it has evolved, battles go on around the world over whose god is bigger and better, and religious fanatics of any number of faiths repeatedly call for and receive the blood of "unbelievers" and "infidels." Few religions of any antiquity have escaped unspotted by innumerable bloodbaths, and, while Islam is currently the source of much fear in the world, Christianity ranks in the

9 Pike, 164–5.

same league as concerns its body count:

> [The] briefest glance at the history of the Christian churches—the horrible rancours and revenges of the clergy and the sects against each other in the fourth and fifth centuries AD, the heresy-hunting crusades at Beziers and other places and the massacres of the Albigenses in the twelfth and thirteenth centuries, the witch-findings and burnings of the sixteenth and seventeenth, the hideous science-urged and bishop-blessed warfare of the twentieth—horrors fully as great as any we can charge of the Aztecs or the Babylonians—must give us pause.[10]

Defenders claim that Christianity ended human sacrifice. This may be true, but to do so, Christianity had to sacrifice millions of humans. Christians also claim Christianity ended slavery, an assertion that is not true. Not only did Christians widely practice slavery,[11] but the ideology itself serves oppression and soul-enslavement: "Believe or go to hell. Submit your will to God or suffer eternally." As American anthropologist Dr. Jules Henry remarked, "Organized religion, which likes to fancy itself the mother of compassion, long ago lost its right to that claim by its organized support of organized cruelty."[12]

Communism and Nazism

To deflect the horrible guilt they bear, religionists have pointed to supposedly secular ideologies such as Communism and Nazism as oppressors and murderers of the people. However, few realize or acknowledge that the originators of Communism were born into Jewish families (Marx,[13] Lenin,[14] Hess,[15] Trotsky[16]) and that the most overtly violent

---

10 Carpenter, 118. If both World Wars are included in figure as "Christian" aggressions, it has been estimated that some 250 million people worldwide have perished in the name of Christianity. (See "Have 250 million been killed in the name of Christianity?") One estimate for the murders in the name of Islam is 270 million, as outlined in "Tears of Jihad." (See "Bibliography" here.)

11 See, for example, Patrick Gray (415): "The use of Paul's letters in the ideological justification of slavery is well-documented." Here Gray evidently refers to Ephesians 6:5; 1 Timothy 6:1; cf., 1 Peter 2:18.

12 Henry, 422.

13 Born into a Jewish family, the grandson of two rabbis, Marx was converted to Christianity at age six. (Manuel, 4; Wheen, 9)

14 The fact of Lenin's Jewish ancestry was well hidden, after his biographer Marietta Shaginian "had managed to find documents proving that Lenin's maternal grandfather, Blank, was a Jew." (Ioffe, 43)

15 *Universal Jewish Encyclopedia* (1943), "Hess, Moses"; "Soviet Russia."

16 "Leon Trotsky" was born Lev Davidovich ("David") Bronstein. (Linde-

leaders of both bloody movements were raised Roman Catholic (Hitler, Mussolini, Franco) or Eastern Orthodox Christian (Stalin), despotic and intolerant ideologies that too often breed fascistic dictators.[17] In other words, these movements were not "atheistic," as religionists maintain. Indeed, Hitler proclaimed himself a "Christian" and fighter for "his Lord and Savior," using the famous temple scene with Jesus driving out the "brood of vipers and adders" as a motivation for his evil deeds.[18] Said Hitler:

> It is of no matter whether or not the individual Jew is decent. He possesses certain characteristics given to him by nature, and he can never rid himself of those characteristics. The Jew is harmful to us.
>
> My feeling as a Christian leads me to be a fighter for my Lord and Savior. It leads me to the man who, at one time lonely and with only a few followers, recognized the Jews for what they were, and called on men to fight against them.... As a Christian, I owe something to my own people.[19]

As late as 1941, Hitler remarked to one of his generals, Gerhard Engel: "I am now as before a Catholic and will always remain so."[20] Whether or not Hitler was a "true" Christian is debatable, as he also reputedly considered Christianity a Jewish invention and part of their

mann, 430) See also *Jewish Encyclopedia* (1905), 418.

17 For more information and citation concerning these contentions, see my book *The Gospel According to Acharya S*, 129–131. There I argue that Stalin's hostility in particular towards religion may have been caused by religiously induced abuse he received from childhood onward. As I say there: "Josef Stalin's 'very religious' mother named him after St. Joseph, and wanted him to become a priest. Stalin himself supposedly claimed that his father had been a priest, and he was purportedly 'damaged by violence' while being 'raised in a poor priest-ridden household.' As a youth, Stalin spent five years in an Orthodox seminary, after which he purportedly renounced his religion. In his later years, Stalin apparently embraced Christianity once more."

18 Walker, B. (1983), 474. In *Mein Kampf* (1.11), Hitler said: "the Founder of Christianity made no secret indeed of His estimation of the Jewish people. When He found it necessary He drove those enemies of the human race out of the Temple of God." (Murphy translation.)

19 Snyder, 28–29; Dawkins, 275; Prange, 72, from a speech in 1922. In his autobiography *Mein Kampf* (1.2), Hitler stated: "Hence today I believe that I am acting in accordance with the will of the Almighty Creator: by defending myself against the Jew, I am fighting for the work of the Lord." (Dawkins, 275)

20 Atlantic Monthly, 292.24.

purported conspiracy for world domination. According to rumors over the decades, Hitler's paternal grandfather was Jewish, a much disputed contention that was given renewed traction in 2010, when headlines worldwide screamed, "Hitler Jewish? DNA Tests Show Dictator May Have 'Had Jewish and African Roots.'"[21] But Hitler himself was raised a Roman Catholic, and he was very much impressed by the power of the Church hierarchy.[22] He pandered to it and used it and religion as a weapon. All during his regime, Hitler worked closely with the Catholic Church, quashing thousands of lawsuits against it and exchanging large sums of money with it.[23] In addition, thousands of Nazis were later given safe passage by the Vatican, as well as by multinational governmental agencies, to a number of locales, including North and South America, via the "Ratline" from Germany through Switzerland and Italy.[24]

In reality, Hitler was only building on a long line of vilification of the Jews as "Christ killers," a charge used numerous times over the centuries whenever the Catholic Church wanted to hold a pogrom against common Jews and seize their assets.[25] The events of WWII, it is alleged, represent the grisly culmination of a centuries-old policy, started by the Church and continued by Martin Luther, as was well-known by Hitler.[26] Indeed, Hitler was embraced as a Christian instrument:

> The rise of Hitler's Germany provides an interesting case in point, showing a nation swept by militaristic sentiment coupled with a sense of divine mission. The churches accepted Hitler's warmongering with religious joy. In April 1937, a Christian organization in the Rhineland passed a resolution that Hitler's word was the law of God and possessed "divine authority." Reichsmin-

---

21 See, for example, the article by that name at Huffington Post. This news item was also carried by many other mainstream media outlets.

22 In *Mein Kampf* (1.1), Hitler remarked: "In my freetime I practised singing in the choir of the monastery church at Lambach, and thus it happened that I was placed in a very favourable position to be emotionally impressed again and again by the magnificent splendour of ecclesiastical ceremonial. What could be more natural for me than to look upon the Abbot as representing the highest human ideal worth striving for, just as the position of the humble village priest had appeared to my father in his own boyhood days? At least, that was my idea for a while." (Murphy translation)

23 Regarding Hitler's protection of the Catholic Church, renowned archivist Dr. Max Domarus (439) says: "The Führer had quashed no less than seven thousand indictments of Catholic clergymen."

24 Aarons and Loftus, xiii.

25 See, for example, Salsitz, 231; Gitelman, 209.

26 See Oberman (81ff) for a discussion of this contention.

ister for Church Affairs Hans Kerrl announced: "There has arisen a new authority as to what Christ and Christianity really are—that is Adolf Hitler. Adolf Hitler … is the true Holy Ghost." And so the pious gave him their blessing, and the churches gave him God's.[27]

But Hitler and the Church's behavior was not an aberration in the history of Christianity, the religion was intolerant, zealous and violent, with its adherents engaging in terrorism. For example, while blessing peacemakers and exhorting love and forgiveness of enemies and trespassers, the "gentle Jesus" also paradoxically declares:

> Do not think that I have come to bring peace on earth; I have not come to bring peace, but a sword. For I have come to set a man against his father, and a daughter against her mother, and a daughter-in-law against her mother-in-law; and a man's foes will be those of his own household. (Matt. 10:34)

Jesus further states that "nation will rise up against nation, and kingdom against kingdom" (Matt. 24:7); hence, with a few sentences, Jesus has seeded extreme division, sedition and enmity wherever Christianity is promulgated. In thus exhorting his followers to violence, however, Jesus himself was building on centuries-old Jewish thought that called for the "extermination" of non-Jews (i.e., "unbelievers") in Christian parlance.[28] As an example of this Judeo-Christian fanaticism, the apostle Paul was a violent zealot who as a Jew first persecuted the Christians and as a Christian subsequently terrorized the Pagans. As Joseph Wheless says in *Forgery in Christianity*:

> And [Paul], the tergiversant slaughter-breathing persecutor-for-pay of the early Christians, now turned for profit their chief apostle of persecution, pronounces time and again the anathema of the new dispensation against all dissenters from his superstitious, tortuous doctrines and dogmas, all such "whom I have delivered

27 Walker, B. (1983), 1061; Langer, 56.

28 See numerous Old Testament scriptures in which the "chosen people" are depicted as rampaging through Canaan/Palestine, slaughtering the peoples and taking their virgin girls as booty. As but one example, at Numbers 31, Moses tells his men to kill all the Midianites, including the women who have "known men." In addition to the many thousands of Syrian and Edomite soldiers he is depicted as killing, at 1 Chronicles 20:3 King David tortures and kills the people of Rabbah, Ammon's capital, along with the rest of the Ammonites: "And he brought forth the people who were in it, and set them to labor with saws and iron picks and axes; and thus David did to all the cities of the Ammonites." (For many more examples, see *The Dark Bible* by James Walker.)

unto Satan" (I Tim. 1:20), as he writes to advise his adjutant Timothy. He flings at the scoffing Hebrews this question: "He that despised Moses's law died without mercy.... Of how much sorer punishment, suppose ye, shall he be thought worthy, who hath trodden under foot the Son of God?" (Heb. x, 28, 29). All such "are set forth for an example, suffering the vengeance of eternal fire" (Jude 7); "that they might all be damned who believed not the truth" (2 Thess. ii, 12); and even "he that doubteth is damned" (Rom. xiv, 23). This Paul, who with such bigoted presumption "deals damnation 'round the land on all he deems the foe" of his dogmas, is first seen "consenting to the death" of the first martyr Stephen (Acts viii, 1); then he blusters through the country "breathing out threatenings and slaughter against the disciples of the Lord" (Acts ix, 1), the new converts to the new faith. Then, when he suddenly professed miraculous "conversion" himself, his old masters turned on him and sought to kill him, and he fled to these same disciples for safety, to their great alarm (Acts ix, 23–26), and straightway began to bully and threaten all who would not now believe his new preachments. To Elymas, who "withstood them," the doughty new dogmatist "set his eyes on him," and thus blasted him with inflated vituperation: "O full of all subtilty and all mischief, thou child of the devil, thou enemy of all righteousness, wilt thou not cease to pervert the right ways of the Lord?" (Acts xiii, 8–10). Even the "meek and loving Jesus" is quoted as giving the fateful admonition: "Fear him which is able to destroy both soul and body in hell" (Matt. x, 28)—here first invented and threatened by Jesus the Christ himself, for added terror unto belief. Paul climaxes the terror: "It is a fearful thing to fall into the hands of the living God' (Heb. x, 31)."[29]

The Myth of Massive Martyrdom

Along with the tale that Christianity began with a "Prince of Peace" comes the myth that the early Christians were gentle "lambs" served up in large numbers as "martyrs for the faith" by the diabolical Romans. The myth of martyrdom starts with the purported passage of the Roman historian Tacitus in which he excoriated Nero for killing a "great multitude" of Christians at Rome in 64 AD/CE; however, this passage appears to be a forgery, one of many interpolations made in the works of ancient authors, and other than this passage, there is little evidence of such a persecution under either Nero or Domitian. As British scholar Dr. George A. Wells says in *Did Jesus Exist?*:

29 Wheless, *IIGW*, 12.

> [The] earliest unambiguous Christian reference to persecution under Nero is a statement made by Melito, bishop of Sardis, about AD 170. It would be surprising if a "great multitude" of Christians lived at Rome as early as AD 64.... The evidence for persecution under Domitian is [also] admitted to be very slight indeed.[30]

What persecutions the Christians did suffer were not as gross as portrayed by propagandists in either number or severity:

> These punishments [of Christians] lacked the public finality of the death sentence: until, 180, no governor in Africa was known to have put a Christian to death. In the late 240s, Origen insisted with rare candour that "few" Christians had died for the faith.... They were "easily numbered," he said.[31]

English theologian Rev. Dr. Andrew Louth, editor of Eusebius's *The History of the Church*, adds:

> In fact, up to the persecution under the Emperor Decius (250–51) there had been no persecution of Christians ordered by the Emperor on an imperial scale.[32]

To bolster their claims of massive martyrdom, pious Christians began around the ninth century to forge the martyrdom traditions:

> The martyrs of the famous Roman "persecutions" under such emperors as Nero and Diocletian, seven centuries earlier, were largely invented at this time, since there were no records of any such specific martyrdoms. Names were picked at random from ancient tombstones, and the martyr-tales were written to order. In reality, it was the Christian church that did much more persecuting and made many more martyrs than Rome had ever done, because religious tolerance was the usual Roman policy.[33]

To weave their martyr-tales, the conspirators used the Jewish apocryphon the *Fourth Book of Maccabees*, which describes gruesome torture: "The tale told in the *4 Maccabees* was widely read by Greeks and early Christians and served as a model for Christian martyrdom stories."[34]

> [The] guards had produced wheels, and joint-dislocators, and racks, and bone-crushers, and catapults, and cauldrons, and braziers, and thumb-screws, and iron claws, and wedges, and

30 Wells, *DJE*, 41.

31 Fox, 434.

32 Eusebius, xxvi.

33 Walker (1988), 271-2.

34 Barnstone, 154.

branding irons.[35]

The author of Fourth Maccabees goes on to describe the most foul torture imaginable, including the infamous "racks" used to tear limbs from the body, as well as people getting skinned alive, their tongues and entrails ripped out, along with the obligatory death by burning. These techniques were later adopted with tremendous enthusiasm by the Christians themselves, who then became the persecutors:

> When the Christians were weak and powerless and subjected to occasional persecutions as "enemies of the human race," they were vocal and insistent advocates of liberty of conscience and freedom to worship whatever God one chose; the Christian "Apologies" to the Emperors abound in eloquent pleas for religious tolerance; and this was granted to them and to all by the Edict of Milan and other imperial Decrees. But when by the favor of Constantine they got into the saddle of the State, they at once grasped the sword and began to murder and despoil all who would not pretend to believe as the Catholic priest commanded them to believe.[36]

The melodramatic portrayal of early "Mom and Pop" Christians being driven underground and ruthlessly persecuted is not reality, nor are the stories of massive martyrdom. What is reality is that, from the fourth century onward, *it was the Christians who were doing the persecuting*. See, "*The Myth of Persecution: How Early Christians Invented a Story of Martyrdom*" by Candida Moss and "*The Darkening Age: The Christian Destruction of the Classical World*" by Catherine Nixey.

The Myth of the Rapid Spread of Christianity

It is widely believed that Christianity spread because it was a great idea desperately needed in a world devoid of hope and faith. It is further maintained that Christianity spread because of the "martyrdom" of its adherents, which purportedly so impressed a number of the early Church fathers that they cast off their Pagan heritage to join the "true faith." In reality, Christianity was not a new and surprising concept, as the ancient cultures possessed every bit of wisdom, righteousness and practically everything else found in Christianity.[37]

Furthermore, by the middle of the third century, there were at Rome—the hotbed of Christianity—only *one* bishop, "forty-six presby-

35 The Forgotten Books of Eden, 187.

36 Wheless (1990), 303.

37 For more information, see my books Suns of God, Christ in Egypt and The Astrotheology Calendar Guide.

ters, seven deacons, as many sub-deacons, forty-two acolytes and fifty readers, exorcists and porters."[38] From this fact, concludes noted historian Dr. Edward Gibbon, we "may venture to estimate the Christians at Rome, at about fifty thousand," among a total populace of no less than a million.[39]

The Rev. Dr. Robert Taylor—whose own persecution included two years in a British jail for preaching Jesus mythicism—remarks:

> It should never be forgotten, that miraculously rapid as we are sometimes told the propagation of the gospel was, it was first preached in England by Austin, the monk, under commission of Pope Gregory, towards the end of the seventh century. So that the *good news* of salvation, in travelling from the supposed scene of action to this favoured country, may be calculated as having posted at the rate of almost an inch in a fortnight.[40]

And as Oxford historian Dr. Robin Lane Fox says:

> [In] the 240s, Origen, the Christian intellectual, did admit that Christians were only a tiny fraction of the world's inhabitants.... If Christians were really so numerous, we could also expect some evidence of meeting places which could hold so many worshippers. At this date, there were no church buildings on public ground.[41]

If the rest of the Empire is factored in, it is estimated that by the middle of the third century Christians constituted only perhaps two percent of the total population.[42]

Also, as noted, there were in fact few martyrs, and the great attraction of Christianity was evidently not the courage of the (alleged) martyrs, but rather the position of power one might earn by one's "conversion." In actuality, Christianity did not spread because it was a great idea or because it was under the supernatural guidance of the resurrected "Lamb of God." Were that so, he would have to be held accountable, because Christianity was promulgated by the sword, with a bloody trail thousands of miles long, during an era called a "shameless age."

Like so much else about Christianity, the claims of its rapid spread are largely mythical. In reality, in some places it took many blood-soaked centuries before its opponents and their lineage had been sufficiently slaughtered so that Christianity could usurp the crown of reigning ideology. Pagan Europeans and others fought it tooth and nail, in an epic and

38 Gibbon, 1.589.
39 Gibbon, 2.301.
40 Taylor, R., 82–3.
41 Fox, 269.
42 Fox, 317.

heroic effort to maintain their own cultures and autonomy, in the face of an onslaught by those whom the Pagans viewed as "idiots" and "bigots." As independent comparative mythologist Barbara G. Walker says:

> Christian historians often give the impression that Europe's barbarians welcomed the new faith, which held out a hope of immortality and a more kindly ethic. The impression is false. The people didn't willingly give up the faith of their ancestors, which they considered essential to the proper functioning of the earth's cycles. They had their own hope of immortality and their own ethic, in many ways a kinder ethic than that of Christianity, which was imposed on them by force. Justinian obtained 70,000 conversions in Asia Minor by methods that were so cruel that the subject populations eventually adopted Islam in order to rid themselves of the rigors of Christian rule.
>
> As a rule, heathen folk resisted Christianity as long as they could, even after their rulers had gone over to the new faith for its material rewards.
>
> Certain words reveal by their derivation some of the opposition met by missionaries. The pagan Savoyards called Christians "idiots," hence *crétin*, "idiot," descended from *Chrétian*, "Christian." German pagans coined the term *bigot*, from *bei Gott*, an expression constantly used by the monks.[43]

43 Walker, B. (1983), 760; Potter/Sargent, 202; Chisholm, 15.600. The etymology of the word "cretin" as derived from "Christian" is accepted by mainstream scholarship. Under its entry for "cretin," *Websters II New College Dictionary* (274) states: "Fr. *crétin* < Swiss Fr. *crestin*, Christian, deformed idiot." In its article on "Insanity," *The Encyclopedia Britannica* (13.98) remarks: "*Crétin* probably comes from *Chrétien*, either from the idea that the person was innocent in the sense in which that word is employed occasionally to imply a person who cannot sin, or from the religious respect in which cretins were held." The etymology of "bigot" has been disputed, but the contention here did not originate with Walker, as its origin has been commonly depicted as such beginning centuries ago. Regarding "bigot," *The Secular Review and Secularist* (January 19, 1878, p. 44) states: "The following derivation of the word 'bigot' may be useful: Bigot means simply a worshipper (Anglo-Saxon, *bigan*, to worship, whence *begine*, a religious woman). M. Bescherelle insists that the English word is a corruption of the oath '*By-God*;' and the German *Bei Gott*, he says, confirms it." Moreover, John Eliot Hodgkin relates: "The word *bigot*, in its modern sense, is alluded to by Etienne Pasquier … who died in 1615, as being in his day in common usage in France; so that we must conceive its origin (which he explains as arising from the old German or old French oath, *bey-got*) to be at least as ancient as the middle of the sixteenth century. He further relates, on the authority of Guillaume de Nangy [+1302], that the Normans, who, under

Christianity was thus fervently resisted wherever it invaded, as nation after nation fell under the sword fighting it off, disdaining its doctrines and proponents as repugnant and blasphemous. As Walker also relates:

> Radbod, king of the Frisians, refused to abandon this faith when a Christian missionary informed him that Valhala was the same as the Christians' hell. Where were his own ancestors, Radbod wanted to know, if there was no Valhala? He was told they were burning in hell because they were heathens. "Dastardly priest!" Radbod cried. "How dare you say my ancestors have gone to hell? I would rather—yes, by their god, the great Woden, I swear—I would ten thousand times rather join those heroes in their hell, than be with you in your heaven of priests!"[44]

Some of the "barbarians" who resisted Christianity were actually far more advanced than those who followed what the Pagans considered a vulgar ideology. For example, "The Irish Fenians, whose rule was never to insult women, were said to have gone to hell for denying Christian anti-feminist doctrines."[45]

Christianity as State Religion

When the "great idea," threats of hell, and other sweet talk failed to impress the Pagans, the Christian conspirators began turning the screws by banning Pagan priests, holidays and "superstitions." Pagans were barred from being palace guards or holding civil and military office. Their properties and temples were destroyed or confiscated, and people who practiced "idolatry" or sacrifices were put to death. As Charles Waite says in *History of the Christian Religion to the Year Two Hundred*:

> Under Constantine and his sons, commissions had been issued against heretics, especially against the Donatists, who were visited with the most rigorous punishment.... The decrees for the extirpation of heathenism were even more severe. Jerome and Leo the Great were in favor of the death penalty.[46]

Under the "great Christian" Constantine, the "followers of Mithra

---

the reign of Charles the Simple, desired to be admitted into the Christian church, ran about crying *bigot! bigot! bigot!* that is, 'for the love of God' baptise us." (*Notes and Queries* (Aug. 29, 1863), 171)

44 Walker, B. (1983), 1039.

45 Walker, B. (1983), 771.

46 Waite, 528.

were hounded with such pertinacity that no one even dared to look at the sun, and farmers and sailors dared not observe the stars for fear of being accused of the heresy."[47] And where hellfire, repressive laws and bribery did not work, force was used. Leaders who were tolerant of religions other than Christianity, such as Emperor Julian "the Apostate" (331/2–363 AD/CE), were murdered.[48]

In *Bible Myths and Their Parallels in Other Religions*, T.W. Doane cites Gibbon relating how this "great faith" was in reality propagated by the most atrocious methods, remarking:

> In Asia Minor the people were persecuted by orders of [Christian emperor] Constantius.... [As Gibbon says:] "The rites of baptism were conferred on women and children, who, for that purpose, had been torn from the arms of their friends and parents; the mouths of the communicants were held open by a wooden engine, while the consecrated bread was forced down their throats; the breasts of tender virgins were either burned with red-hot egg-shells, or inhumanly compressed between sharp and heavy boards." ... Persecutions in the name of Jesus Christ were inflicted on the heathen in most every part of the then known world. Even among the Norwegians, the Christian sword was unsheathed. They clung tenaciously to the worship of their forefathers, and numbers of them died real martyrs for their faith, after suffering the most cruel torments from their persecutors. It was by sheer compulsion that the Norwegians embraced Christianity. The reign of Olaf Tryggvason, a Christian king of Norway, was in fact entirely devoted to the propagation of the new faith, by means the most revolting to humanity.... the recusants were tortured to death with fiend-like ferocity, and their estates confiscated. These are some of the reasons "why Christianity prospered."[49]

These "conversion" methods by Catholics against men, women and children, Christians and Pagans alike, included burning, hanging and all manner of torture, using tools such as described in Fourth Maccabees. Women and girls had hot pokers and sharp objects shoved up their vagi-

---

47 Larson, 191; Jackson, S.M., 7.423.

48 Julian's death was reputed to have been at the hand of Persian enemies, rather than his own soldiers. However, Christians *had* been involved in a previous attempt on his life, and Christian tradition contends that his death was "predicted in a dream" and that "St. Mercurius" struck him down at Christ's command. (See Acharya, *SOG*, 67)

49 Doane, 448–9.

nas, often after priests had raped them. Men and boys had their penises and testicles crushed or ripped or cut off. Both genders and all ages had their skin pulled off with hot pincers and their tongues ripped out. They were subjected to diabolical machinery designed for the weakest parts of the body, such as the knees, ankles, elbows and fingertips, all of which were crushed. Their legs and arms were broken with sledgehammers, and, if there was anything left of them, they were hanged or burned alive. Nothing more evil could possibly be imagined, and from this absolute evil came the "rapid" spread of Christianity.

The official excuse for this vile behavior was that Christian proponents had the right to purge the earth of "evil" and to convert the "heathen" to the "true faith." Over a period of more than a millennium, this "purification" and "conversion" to the religion of the "Prince of Peace" via the most horrendous torture methods ever devised, resulted in the slaughter of tens of millions worldwide.[50]

So far this despicable legacy of crime against humanity remains unavenged and its main culprit unblamed, inexplicably receiving the undying and unthinking support of hundreds of millions, including the educated, such as doctors, lawyers, scientists, etc. This acquiescence is the result of the centuries of destruction and degradation of their ancestors' cultures, which demoralized them and ripped away their spirituality and heritage. In annihilating these cultures, the Christian conspirators also destroyed countless books and much learning, prizing the subsequent illiteracy and ignorance, which made it even easier for Christianity to spread. Wheless recounts the state of the world under Christian dominance:

> With the decline and fall of the Roman Empire the Christian religion spread and grew, among the Barbarian destroyers of Rome. The Dark Ages contemporaneously spread their intellectual pall over Europe. Scarcely any but priests and monks could read. Charlemagne learned to wield the pen only to the extent of scrawling his signature. The barons who wrested Magna Carta from John Lackland signed with their marks and seals. The worst criminals, provided they were endowed with the rare and magic virtue of knowing how to read even badly, enjoyed the "benefit of clergy" (i.e., of clerical learning), and escaped immune or with greatly mitigated punishment. There were no books save painfully-written manuscripts, worth the ransom of princes, and utterly unattainable

50 See, for example, *Holy Horrors* by James Haught. See also Heinrich Kramer and James Sprenger's *The Malleus Maleficarum* (1487), a handbook of torture aimed at "witches."

> except by the very wealthy and by the Church; not till about 1450 was the first printed book known in Europe. The Bible existed only in Hebrew, Greek, and Latin, and the ignorant masses were totally ignorant of it other than what they heard from the priests, who told them that they must believe it or be tortured and killed in life and damned forever in the fires of hell after death. It is no wonder that faith flourished under conditions so exceptionally favorable.[51]

Such is the disgraceful history of the religion of the "gentle Prince of Peace." Yet there are those today who not only support its monstrous edifice, built on the blood and charred bones of tens of millions, as well as on the death of learning in the Western world, but, unbelievably, wish it to be restored to its full "glory," with the whole bloody works, witch-burnings, persecution, annihilation of unbelievers and all. The fact is that, so much trauma and bloodshed have been caused throughout the millennia strictly on the basis of unfounded faith and excessive illogic, and too much knowledge and wisdom have been lost, that human history has been burdened with ignorance and misunderstanding. It is high time for the oppressive and exploitative conspiracy behind religion in general and Christianity in particular to be exposed. As George Santayana warned, those who cannot remember the past are condemned to repeat it, and humans as a species are prone to amnesia.

---

51 Wheless, *IIGW*, 18.

The Quest for Jesus Christ

"This is the controversial question, Did Jesus really exist? Some readers may be surprised or shocked that many books and essays—by my count, over two hundred—in the past two hundred years have fervently denied the very existence of Jesus."[52]

—Dr. Robert E. Van Voorst, *Jesus Outside the New Testament* (6)

"[In] my conversations with newspaper writers and book editors who have asked me at various times to write about the historical Jesus, almost invariably the first question that arises is: But can you prove he existed?"

—Dr. John P. Meier, *A Marginal Jew* (1.68)

"Apart from the New Testament writings and later writings dependent on these, our sources of information about the life and teaching of Jesus are scanty and problematic."

—F.F. Bruce, *New Testament History* (163)

"The only definite account of his life and teachings is contained in the four Gospels of the New Testament, *Matthew, Mark, Luke* and *John*. All other historical records of the time are silent about him."

—*The Universal Jewish Encyclopedia* (6.83)

"The gospels are not primarily works of history in the modern sense of the word."

—Dr. John P. Meier, *A Marginal Jew* (1.41)

"One would naturally expect that the Lord Jesus Christ would be sufficiently important to receive ample notice in the literature of his time, and that extensive biographical material would be available. He was observed by multitudes of people, and his own followers numbered into the hundreds (1 Cor. 15:6), whose witness was still living in the middle of the first century. As a matter of fact, the amount of information concerning him is comparatively meager. Aside from the four Gospels, and a few scattered allusions in the epistles, contemporary history is almost silent concerning him."

—Dr. Merrill C. Tenney, *New Testament Survey* (203)

In exploring the origins of Christianity, our focus naturally turns to its purported founder and object of worship, Jesus Christ, whose story is told in the New Testament. So much interest and fascination have circulated around this wonderworker over the centuries that numerous and sizable tomes have been composed to fill out the New Testament

52 Since Van Voorst's book was published in 2000, there have been dozens more books and articles propounding that Jesus Christ is a mythical figure, including several of mine.

tale by digging into the few clues as to Jesus's nature and historical background, in order to produce a biographical sketch that either bolsters faith or reveals a more human side of this godman to which all can relate. Nevertheless, little has come of all these efforts, as the "real" Jesus remains a phantom, mutating to suit the needs of the era and the beholder.

Which Jesus?

It has been said that Jesus is all things to all people. This assertion is certainly true, as from the earliest times his nature and character have been interpreted and reinterpreted to fit the cultural context of his proponents and representatives. As Dr. Burton L. Mack, a professor of Early Christianity at Claremont School of Theology, says in *The Lost Gospel: The Book of Q and Christian Origins*:

> In the course of Christian history, to take one example of a series of social and cultural shifts, the Christ has been refigured many times over. In the period before Constantine, when bishops were taking their place as the leaders of the churches, the Christ was commonly depicted as the good shepherd who could guide the flock to its heavenly home. After Constantine, the Christ was pictured as the victor over death and the ruler of the world. During the medieval period, when the church was the primary vehicle of both social and cultural tradition, the story of Christ's ascent from the cross (or the tomb) to the seat of sovereignty, judgment, and salvation in heaven focused the Christian imagination on a Christ of a truly comprehensive, three-decker world. Somewhat later we see the Gothic Christ appear, and then the Christ of the crucifix, the man of Galilee, the cosmic Christ, the feminine Christ, and so on. In every case, the rearrangements were necessary in order to adjust the mythic world to new social constraints and cultural systems of knowledge.[53]

Jesus began his omnipotent reign when sons of God and sacred kings were all the rage. After the shocking and bloody turmoil of the Middle Ages, however, he became in the minds of the desperate a compassionate yet human teacher of morality, since it was obvious he could not possibly have been supernaturally in charge of the church in his name, which was torturing and slaughtering by the millions.

During the political upheavals of the twentieth century, Jesus was considered a heroic revolutionary striving against oppression, as well as a communist. When various Indian gurus and yogis with their magic tricks became famous, it was fashionable to locate Jesus in India and/

53 Mack, 210.

or Tibet. At that time, too, was the psychedelic explosion, so Jesus soon became a magic mushroom.

Within the "New Age" movement that began with the renaissance of spiritualism last century, he has become the "Cosmic Christ" and "Christ Consciousness." He has also of late become a black militant, a white supremacist, a gay activist, a woman, a heretic, a "Mediterranean peasant," an orthodox butcher whose name wasn't Jesus, a "Cynic-sage," an Arab, as well as the husband of Mary Magdalene and father of many children, from whom are descended at least one European royal family.

Now, with the popular subject of UFOs and extraterrestrials, Jesus is an alien with extraordinary powers because he is of a superior race, with any number of "alien" groups laying claim to his parentage. As commander of an enormous spaceship, this alien Jesus is waiting in the wings to rapture true believers off the earth in the nick of time during the coming earth changes. In a sense, Jesus *is* an alien, in that people are so alienated from the actual history of the planet they cannot grasp his true nature.

Wells adds to the list of "biographies" of Jesus:

> In the past generation, the "real" Jesus has been variously a magician (Smith), a Galilean rabbi (Chilton), a marginal Jew (Meier), a bastard (Schaberg), a cipher (Thiering), a Qumran dissident (Allegro, et al.), a gnosticising Jew (Koester), a dissident Jew (Vermes), a happily married man and father of sons (Spong), a bandit (Horsley), an enthusiastic (possible Zealot?) opponent of the Temple cult (Sanders). Perhaps most remarkable of all is the "real" Jesus of the Westar Project/Jesus Seminar whose existence has been pinned on just over thirty "authentic" sayings, derived from an eclectic application of biblical-critical axioms and confirmed by vote of the seminar members.[54]

Despite all of this literature continuously being cranked out, it is obvious that we are dealing not with biography but with speculation, and there remains in the public at large a serious and unfortunate lack of education regarding religion and mythology, particularly that of Christ. Indeed, the majority of people are taught in most schools and churches that Jesus Christ was an actual historical figure and that the only controversy regarding him is that some people accept him as the Son of God and the Messiah, while others do not. However, whereas this is the raging debate most evident today, it is not the most important. Shocking as it may seem to the general populace, *the most enduring and*

54 Wells, *JL*, viii.

profound controversy in this subject is whether or not the biblical Jesus Christ ever really existed.

History and Positions of the Debate

One might never guess there *was* any debate over the historical existence of Jesus from the publications readily found in popular bookstores; however, beginning over two centuries ago, a significant number of scholars started springing up to challenge long-held beliefs. In more recent times, this controversy erupted when G.A. Wells published *Did Jesus Exist?* and *The Historical Evidence for Jesus*, among others, arguing that Jesus is a non-historical character. *Jesus: The Evidence*, on the other hand, was an entire (slim) volume written to establish that Jesus did exist. Since that time and the initial publication of the present work, several more books have been added to the Mythicist library, and the debate has continued to rage, with many articles, radio programs and online videos. Both, the response and the Christian defense have been aggressive and sustained.

It should be noted that no such centuries-long defense would be needed if the existence of Jesus Christ as a historical figure were a well-attested fact, like the existence of Alexander the Great or Julius Caesar. In addition, it is not uncommon to hear someone say something like "Don't get me wrong—I believe he existed," a strange declaration, since, according to popular belief, "Everybody knows he existed." But does not such an assertion presuppose a state of uncertainty or debate? Why *say* it otherwise? No one discussing Abraham Lincoln, for example, needs to clarify her/his position by expressing the belief that Lincoln existed.

Indeed, it is such doubt, which has existed since the beginning of the Christian era, that has led many seekers of truth over the centuries to research thoroughly this important subject from an independent perspective and to produce an impressive volume of literature. While hidden, suppressed, or ignored, this body of scholarship nevertheless has demonstrated logically and cogently that Jesus Christ is a mythological character along the same lines as the gods of Egypt, England, Greece, India, Phoenicia, Rome, Sumer and elsewhere, entities presently acknowledged by mainstream scholars and the masses alike as myths rather than historical figures. Delving deeply into this large body of work, one uncovers evidence that the Jesus character is in fact *based upon* these much older myths and heroes. One discovers that the gospel story is not, therefore, a historical representation of a Jewish rebel carpenter who had physical incarnation in the Levant 2,000 years ago. In other words, it has been demonstrated repeatedly for centuries that the story of Jesus Christ was invented and did not depict a real person who was either a superhuman "son of God" or a man who was "evemeristically" built up into a superhuman fairytale by enthusiastic followers.

Within this debate regarding the nature and character of Jesus Christ, then, there have been three main schools of thought: the *believers* and the *evemerists*, both of which are *historicizers*, and the *mythicists*.

The Believers

The believers take the Judeo-Christian Bible as the literal "Word of God," accepting "on faith" that everything contained within it is historical fact infallibly written by scribes "inspired by God." As we shall see, this position is untenable and requires blind and unscientific devotion, since, even if we discount the countless mistakes committed over the centuries by scribes copying the texts, the so-called infallible "Word of God" is riddled with inconsistencies, contradictions, errors and yarns that stretch credulity to the point of non-existence.[55]

In order to accept the alleged factuality of the Christian tale (i.e., that a male God came down from the heavens as his own son through the womb of a Jewish virgin, worked astonishing miracles, was killed, resurrected and ascended to heaven), we are not only required to suspend critical thinking and integrity, but also we must be prepared to tolerate a rather repulsive and generally false portrayal of the ancient world and peoples. In particular, we must be willing to believe fervently that the "gentle Jesus"—who was allegedly the all-powerful God—was mercilessly scourged, tortured and murdered by Romans and Jews, the latter forever bearing the ignominious stigma as "vipers," "serpents," "spawn of Satan" and "Christ killers" who gleefully shouted "Crucify him!" and "Let his blood be on us and our children!" (Matt. 3:7, 12:34, 23:33; Luke 3:7; John 8:44; Mark 15:13–14; Luke 23:21; John 19:6, 15; Matt. 27:25)

In addition to this hideous notion, we are also expected to believe that the omnipotent and perfect God could fix the world, which he had created badly in the first place, only by the act of blood-atonement, specifically with his own blood. This notion of blood-atonement is rooted in the ancient custom of sacrificing humans and animals, a barbaric scapegoat ritual.[56] Indeed, the sacrifice of God seems far worse than that of either animals or humans, yet this deicide is supposed to be one of the

---

55 For a detailed discussion of the contradictions and illogic, etc., of the New Testament, see my book *Who Was Jesus? Fingerprints of The Christ.*

56 For more on the subject of human sacrifice and the sacred king ritual, see my book *Suns of God.*

highest "religious" concepts. In fact, it is "God's plan!" Concerning this Christian doctrine of human sacrifice, one critic remarks:

> And hereafter, when they laugh at the Jewish superstition of a scape-goat, let them bear in mind that the more sensible and intelligent people may laugh in turn at their superstitious doctrine of a scape-God.... The blood of God must atone for the sins of the whole human family, as rams, goats, bullocks and other animals had atoned for the sins of families and nations under older systems.... Somebody must pay the penalty in blood, somebody must be slaughtered for every little foible or peccadillo or moral blunder into which erring man may chance to stumble while upon the pilgrimage of life, while journeying through the wilderness of time, even if a God has to be dragged from his throne in heaven, and murdered to accomplish it.... Whose soul—possessing the slightest moral sensibility—does not inwardly and instinctively revolt at such a doctrine? ... We hold the doctrine to be a high-handed insult to the All-Loving Father—who, we are told, is "long suffering in mercy," and "plentiful in forgiveness"—to charge *Him* with sanctioning such a doctrine, much less originating it.[57]

In embracing Christianity as reality, we are also required to assume that, in order to get "his" important message across, "God" came to Earth in a remote area of the ancient world and spoke the obscure language of Aramaic, as opposed to the more universally spoken Greek or Latin. We must also be prepared to believe that there is now an invisible man of a particular ethnicity omnipresently floating about in the sky. In addition, we are asked to ridicule and dismiss as fiction the nearly identical legends and tales of many other cultures, while happily receiving the Christian fable as fact. Think about it: doesn't this dogmatic stance in effect amount to cultural bigotry and prejudice? All in all, in blindly believing we are faced with what can only appear to be an abhorrent and ludicrous plan on the part of "God."

The Evemerists

It is because of such irrational beliefs and prejudicial demands that many people have rejected Christian claims as incredible and

---

57 Graves, K., 161. For a discussion of Kersey Graves's work *The World's Sixteen Crucified Saviors*, please see my book *Suns of God*. Although it may provide a starting point for deeper research, that book suffers from the limited extent of comparative religion data then available. None of my major contentions is reliant on his work, and I cite Graves only sparingly.

unappealing. Nevertheless, numerous such dissidents have maintained that behind the fabulous fairy tales found in the gospels there *was* a historical Jesus Christ somewhere. This opinion usually has no firmer basis than that most people take it for granted, having been culturally acclimated to believe it. Its proponents have never even thought to study the matter, much less seen clear evidence to that effect. But surely better can be said of scholarly Christian apologists and mainstream scholars? This "meme" of a historical Jesus has been pounded into the heads of billions of people for nearly 2,000 years, such that it is assumed *a priori* by many, including scholars who have put forth an array of clearly speculative hypotheses dangling from highly tenuous threads regarding the "life of Jesus." Such speculators often claim that a historical Jewish master named Jesus was deified or "evemerized" by his zealous followers, who added to his mundane "history" a plethora of supernatural qualities and aspects widely found in more ancient myths and mystery religions.

This school of thought, called "Evemerism"[58] or "Euhemerism," is named after Evemeras (Euhemeros), a Greek philosopher of the fourth century BCE who developed the idea that, rather than being altogether mythical creatures, as the reigning intellectuals held, the gods of old were in fact historical characters, kings, emperors and heroes whose exploits were later inflated till these individuals were deified. I ask: how does the mainstream "historical Jesus" scholarship not count as evermerism? Why do we never seem to run across this term in critical discussions of Jesus? What distinguishes the approach of John Dominic Crossan, Rudolf Bultmann and Norman Perrin from that of the ancient evemerists other than that the latter were discussing Zeus and Apollo, whereas the former is applying the same methodology to the Christian god Jesus? It is yet another instance of special pleading. The avoidance of the term "evemerism/euhemerism" must be that this approach to the ancient gods has long been discredited and dismissed. I am of course arguing that it is no more viable when applied to Jesus Christ, who proves to be as fanciful as Zeus and Apollo.

Of the various evemerists "biographies" of Jesus, the two most popular are that Jesus was a compassionate teacher who irritated the

58 The transliteration "evemerism," as opposed to "euhemerism," dates back at least to 1856, when it was used in *The London Quarterly* (6.350ff). It is translated from the Greek along the same principles as "e*u*angelism" becomes "e*v*angelism," for ease of pronunciation and based on modern Greek pronunciation as well. As another example, the Greek verb for "to thank," *eucharisto*, is pronounced in modern Greek as *evcharisto*, with a "v" or "f" sound.

Romans with his goodness, and that he was a political rebel who annoyed the Romans with his incitement of discord, for which he was executed. Wells comments upon the theory *du jour*:

> As political activism is today à la mode, it is widely felt that a revolutionary Jesus is more "relevant" than the Jesus of the nineteenth century liberal theologians who "went about doing good" (Acts, 10:38). Both these Jesuses simply reflect what in each case the commentators value most highly rather than the burden of the texts. If Jesus had been politically troublesome, his supporters would have been arrested with him. But there is no suggestion of this in any of the gospels.[59]

He further states:

> There are ... three obvious difficulties against the supposition that a historical Jesus was actually executed as a rebel:
>
> (i) All Christian documents earlier than the gospels portray him in a way hardly compatible with the view that he was a political agitator ...
>
> (ii) If his activities had been primarily political, and the evangelists were not interested in—or deemed it inexpedient to mention—his politics, then what was the motive for their strong interest in him? How did they come to suppose that a rebel, whose revolutionary views they tried to suppress in their gospels, was the universal saviour?
>
> (iii) If such an episode as the cleansing of the temple was not a religious act (as the gospels allege) but an armed attempt to capture the building and to precipitate a general insurrection, then why does Josephus say nothing of it? As Trocmé has observed ... a military attack on the temple would not have been ignored by this writer who was so concerned to show the dangers of revolt and violence. Josephus' silence is corroborated by the positive affirmation of Tacitus that there was no disturbance in Palestine under Tiberius (AD 14–37), whereas the preceding and following reigns were characterized by rebellion and unrest there.[60]

Of these various "lives of Jesus," Wells also says:

> It is now customary to dismiss with contempt many nineteenth-century lives of Jesus on the grounds that their authors simply found in him all the qualities which they themselves

59 Wells, *WWJ*, 137.
60 Wells, *DJE*, 160.

> considered estimable. But the wide circulation today of books which portray him as a rebel seems yet another illustration of the same phenomenon.[61]

In the PBS *Frontline* program "From Jesus to Christ," evemerist scholar Dr. Shaye Cohen, professor of Hebrew Literature and Philosophy at Harvard University, admits the desperate situation of trying to find this "historical" reformer/rebel under the accreted layers of miracles:

> Modern scholars have routinely reinvented Jesus or have routinely rediscovered in Jesus that which they want to find, be it rationalist, liberal Christianity of the 19th century, be it apocalyptic miracle workers in the 20th, be it revolutionaries, or be it whatever it is that they're looking for, scholars have been able to find in Jesus almost anything that they want to find. Even in our own age scholars are still doing this. People are still trying to figure out the authentic sayings of Jesus … all our middle-class liberal Protestant scholars … will take a vote and decide what Jesus should have said, or might have said. And no doubt their votes reflect their own deep-seated, very sincere, very authentic Christian values, which I don't gainsay for a moment. But their product is, of course, bedeviled by the problem that we are unable to have any secure criteria by which to distinguish the real from the mythic or what we want to be so from what actually was so.

These various theories in the end constitute wheel-spinning in a futile effort to rescue historicity, *any* historicity, for the gospel tale. Because of the dearth of personality in the gospels and the irrationality of the tale, historicizers must imbue the character with their own personalities and interpretations of reality, such as: "When Jesus said, 'Blessed are the poor,' he surely didn't mean that poverty is a blessing but that those who lived with poverty are good, because they are not resorting to robbery."[62] And in order to pad out the "real" Jesus after most of his "life" is removed, scholars must resort to reasoning of the most tortured kind:

> While the miracles of Jesus could easily be created and multiplied by the credulity of His followers, [the followers] could never have devised ethical, speculative, or soteriological doctrines, which, although *in no instance original*, presented new combinations of established religious concepts and ethical principles.[63]

Thus, we have an admission that Jesus brought nothing new, but an

61 Wells, *DJE*, 176.

62 Larson.

63 Larson, 352.

insistence nevertheless that he deserved merit because he combined his unoriginal concepts in a novel mix. In reality, this type of eclecticism also was not new but quite common long before the Christ character arose. In *The Historical Jesus and the Mythical Christ*, Gerald Massey says of these scholars' efforts:

> It is pitiful to track the poor faithful gleaners who picked up every fallen fragment or scattered waif and stray of the mythos, and to watch how they treasured every trait and tint of the ideal Christ to make up the personal portrait of their own supposed real one.[64]

In *Ancient History of the God Jesus*, French writer Edouard Dujardin (1861–1949) remarks of evemerism:

> This doctrine is nowadays discredited except in the case of Jesus. No scholar believes that Osiris or Jupiter or Dionysus was an historical person promoted to the rank of a god, but exception is made only in favour of Jesus.... It is impossible to rest the colossal work of Christianity on Jesus, if he was a man.[65]

Indeed, evemerist scholars will admit that this humanized Jesus stripped of all miracles would not have "made a blip on Pilate's radar screen," being insignificant as one of the innumerable rabble rousers running about Palestine during this time. If we were to take away all the miraculous events surrounding the story of Jesus to reveal a human, we would certainly find no one who could have garnered huge crowds around him because of his preaching.[66] And the fact is that this crowd-drawing preacher finds his place in "history" only in the New Testament, completely overlooked by the dozens of historians of his day, an era considered one of the best documented in history.[67] Such an invisible character, then, could never have become a god worshipped by millions.

The standard Christian response to the evemerists has been that no such Jesus, stripped of his miracles and other supernatural attributes, could ever "have been adored as a god or even been saluted as the Messiah of Israel."[68] This response is quite accurate: No mere man could

64 Massey, *HJMC*, 170.

65 Dujardin, 3.

66 In some two dozen biblical scriptures, Jesus Christ is claimed to have been famed far and wide: Matt. 4:23–25, 5:1, 8:1, 8:18, 9:8, 9:31, 9:33, 9:36, 11:7, 12:15, 13:2, 14:1, 14:13, 14:22, 15:30, 19:2, 21:9, 26:55; Mark 1:28, 10:1; Luke 4:14, 4:37, 5:15, 14:25, etc.

67 Jackson, 186. For a discussion of the list of first- and second-century historians and other writers in my book *Who Was Jesus?*, see my article, "Rebuttal to Dr. Chris Forbes."

68 Dujardin, 3.

have caused such a hullabaloo and produced such hellish fanaticism, the product of which has been the unending spilling of blood and the enslavement of the spirit. The crazed "inspiration" that has kept the Church afloat merely confirms the mythological origins of this tale. Furthermore, the theory of evemerism has served the Catholic Church:

> [That] the gods of the ancients were nothing but the heroes or benefactors of mankind, living in very illiterate and remote ages, to whom a grateful posterity paid divine honors … appears at first sight to be probable; and as it has served the purpose of the Christian priests, to enable them to run down the religion of the ancients, and, in exposing its absurdities, to contrast it disadvantageously with their own, [Evemerism] has been, and continues to be, sedulously inculcated, in every public and private seminary.… Although the pretended worship of Heroes appears at first sight plausible, very little depth of thought or learning is requisite to discover that it has not much foundation in truth.[69]

In *Pagan Christs*, John M. Robertson (1856–1933), a British journalist and Member of Parliament, states of evemerism:

> It is not the ascription of prodigies to some remarkable man that leads us to doubt his reality. Each case must be considered on its merits when we apply the tests of historical evidence. We must distinguish between what the imagination has added to a meager biography, and those cases in which the biography itself has been added to what has grown out of a ritual or doctrine.[70]

The bottom line is that when one removes all the elements of earlier myths and motifs that evidently contributed to the formation of the Jewish godman, along with Old Testament "messianic prophecies" used as a blueprint, there remains no one and nothing historical left to which to point. As Walker says, "Scholars' efforts to eliminate paganism from the Gospels in order to find a historical Jesus have proved as hopeless as searching for a core in an onion."[71] Massey remarks that "a composite likeness of twenty different persons merged in one … is not *anybody*."[72] And, it is clear that, in their attempts, evemerist scholars have added their own likenesses to the composite.

Concerning the evemerist perspective, Kenneth Humphreys comments:

> Yet would, could a world-faith have arisen from a nonentity

69 Higgins, 2.44.
70 Robertson (1966), 96.
71 Walker, B. (1983), 469.
72 Massey, *HJMC*, 170.

who failed in his own lifetime to have been noticed by anyone? How creditable is it that a wandering rabbi, who wrote nothing himself, an also-ran in a world full of fakirs, soothsayers and exorcists, could have cast such a spell as to have reverberated through the ages?

A "minimalist" Jesus is actually less satisfactory than no Jesus at all because it still requires a search elsewhere for the roots of the new religion. And if the roots are to be found elsewhere what need is there for the obscure personage anyway?[73]

There were in reality comparatively few evemerized kings, heros and so on, and most deities were indeed mythical and allegorical. Discussing Babylonian mythology, theologian Dr. G. Johannes Botterweck (1917–1981) notes, "Deified men are rare; outside Gilgamesh and Tammuz (which is questionable), there are only a couple of examples of little significance."[74] He is being generous, as no scholar imagines there was a historical Gilgamesh or Tammuz, either. It follows that, if Babylonian religion is largely based on *myth*, and does not reflect evemerized "history," any religious concepts that emanated from the region were likewise *mythical*, not historical.

The Mythicists

This absence of a core to the onion has been recognized by many individuals over the centuries who have thus been unable to accept the historical nature of Jesus Christ, because not only is there no proof of his existence, but virtually all evidence points to a mythological character. As stated, this "Mythicist School" began to flourish a few hundred years ago, propelled by archaeological and linguistic discoveries and studies, as well as by the reduction of the Church's power and vicious persecution of its critics.[75] A number of erudite and daring individuals have overcome the conditioning of their culture to peer closely and with clear eyes into the murky origins of the Christian faith. Massey elucidates the mythicists' perspective:

> The general assumption concerning the canonical gospels is that the historic element was the kernel of the whole, and that the fables accreted round it; whereas the mythos, being preextant, proves the core of the matter was mythical, and it follows that the history is incremental.... It was the human history that accreted

73 Humphreys, "The End is Nigh—for Jesus, That is."

74 Botterweck, 1.271.

75 For more information on the mythicist school, see my articles "What is a Mythicist?" and "What is Mythicism?"

round the divinity, and not a human being who became divine.[76]

While the mythicist school has made real inroads only in the past couple of centuries, and even though its brilliant work and insight have been ignored by mainstream "experts" in both the believing and evemerist camps, the mythicist arguments have been built upon a solid basis of Bible criticism. Indeed, this controversy has existed from the very beginning as evidenced by the writings of the Church fathers themselves. They were forced by the "Pagan" intelligentsia to defend what the nonChristians and other Christians ("heretics") alike apparently saw as a preposterous and fabricated yarn. As Rev. Robert Taylor says in *The Diegesis*: "And from the apostolic age downwards, in a never interrupted succession, but never so strongly and emphatically as in the most primitive times, was the existence of Christ as a man most strenuously denied."[77] In this regard, Taylor also asserts:

> Those who denied the *humanity* of Christ were the first class of professing Christians, and not only first in order of time, but in dignity of character, in intelligence, and in moral influence.... The deniers of the humanity of Christ, or, in a word, professing Christians, who denied that any such man as Jesus Christ ever existed at all, but who took the name Jesus Christ to signify only an abstraction, or prosopopoeia, the *principle of Reason* personified; and who understood the whole gospel story to be a sublime allegory ... these were the first, and (it is not dishonour to Christianity to pronounce them) the best and most rational Christians.[78]

Again, this denial of Christ in the flesh is found numerous times in the writings of the day, including the New Testament itself (1 John 4:2; 2 John 1:7);[79] yet it is ignored by historicizers, believers and evemerists alike. Indeed, in their "exhaustive" research into this all-important subject, it seems as if historicizers have either willfully and unreasonably ignored the great minds of the mythicist school or have never come across them. If we assume that the historicizers' disregard of these scholars is deliberate, it may be because the mythicists' arguments have been too intelligent and penetrating to do away with. Before the internet

76 Massey, HJMC, 180.

77 Taylor, R., 253.

78 Taylor, R., 372.

79 The Epistle to the Romans speaks about Christ and Abraham as "according to the flesh." The Greek word "flesh," in fact, appears some 69 times in the Pauline epistles and 147 times in the canonical gospels, evidently reflective of the Gnostic atmosphere in which the New Testament was composed.

revolution—the true omniscient god—the works of the mythicists had not been readily available to the public, possibly fearfully suppressed because irrefutable, so we cannot completely fault the "experts" for having never read them. The contentions of these particular mythicists are, however, the most important work done in this field to date, so one could argue that any refutation which has not dealt with them properly is neither exhaustive nor convincing.

Some claim that mythicists make too much of the Pagan origins and ignore the Jewish aspects of the gospel tale. The Jewish elements, argue historicizers, must be historical and, therefore, Jesus existed. This is specious and sophistical reasoning, since anyone can interpolate quasi-historical data into a fictional story, and many people have done so, from the composers of *The Iliad* to those of the Old Testament and any number of other novels.

The fact is that it is historicizing scholars themselves who do not pay enough attention to the Jewish aspects, because if they did, they would discover that these elements are frequently erroneous, anachronistic and indicative of a lack of knowledge about geography and other details. This would scarcely have been so, had the writers been indigenous to the era and eyewitnesses to the events.

Massey summarizes the mythicist position:

> It can be demonstrated that Christianity pre-existed without the Personal Christ, that it was continued by Christians who entirely rejected the historical character in the second century, and that the supposed historic portraiture in the Canonical Gospels was extant as mythical and mystical before the Gospels themselves existed.[80]

And he further states, "Whether considered as the God made human, or as man made divine, this character never existed as a person."[81] Moreover, the claim of preexistence of the gospel portraiture was repeatedly confirmed by Christians, as shall be seen. According to the mythicist school, then, the New Testament could rightly be called, "Gospel Fictions"[82] and the Christian religion could be termed the "Christ Conspiracy."

---

80 Massey, *GHC,* 2.

81 Massey, *GHC,* 22.

82 Helms.

The Holy Forgery Mill

J'Accuse!

"[A] graver accusation than that of inaccuracy or deficient authority lies against the writings which have come down to us from the second century. There can be no doubt that great numbers of books were then written with no other view than to deceive the simple-minded multitude who at that time formed the great bulk of the Christian community."

—Rev. Dr. John A. Giles, *Hebrew and Christian Records* (2.19)

"It's important to acknowledge that strictly speaking, the gospels are anonymous."

—Dr. Craig L. Blomberg in Lee Strobel's *The Case for Christ* (26)

"Most of the apostles were illiterate and could not in fact write.... They could not have left an authoritative writing if their souls depended on it. Another problem is that writings started to appear that claimed to be written by apostles, but that contained all sorts of bizarre and contradictory views. Gospels were in circulation that claimed to be written by Jesus's disciples Peter, Phillip and Mary, and his brothers Thomas and James. Letters appeared that were allegedly written by Paul, Peter and James. Apocalyptic writings describing the end of the world or the fate of souls in the afterlife appeared in the names of Jesus's followers John, Peter and Paul. Some writings emerged that claimed to be written by Jesus himself.

"In many instances, the authors of these writings could not actually have been who they claimed to be, as even the early Christians realized."

—Dr. Bart D. Ehrman, *Forged: Writing in the Name of God—Why the Bible's Authors Are Not Who We Think They Are* (8)

"Matthew probably did not write Matthew, for example, or John, John."

—Dr. Bart D. Ehrman, *Forged: Writing in the Name of God* (10)

"In short, there were long, protracted and even heated debates in the early church over forged documents. Early Christians realized that there were numerous forgeries in circulation, and they wanted to know which books were written by their alleged authors and which were not."

—Dr. Bart D. Ehrman, *Forged: Writing in the Name of God* (22)

From the very beginning of our quest to unravel the Christ conspiracy, we find ourselves in suspicious territory: looking back in time, we discover that the real foundation of Christianity appears nothing like the image provided by the clergy and mainstream authorities. Indeed, those with vested interests in the origins of the Christian religion paint a far more rosy and cheerful picture than the reality. They offer us a miracle-making founder and pious, inspired apostles who faithfully and infallibly recorded his words and deeds shortly after his advent, and then went about promulgating the faith with great gusto and success in "saving souls." Contrary to this popular delusion, the reality is that, in addition to the enormous amount of bloodshed which accompanied its foundation, Christianity's history is rife with forgery and fraud. So rampant is this treachery and chicanery that any serious researcher must immediately begin to wonder about the story itself. In truth, the Christian tale has always been as difficult to swallow as the myths and fables of other cultures; yet countless people have been able to put rationality on the shelf out of little more than religious "brand loyalty."

Indeed, the story of Jesus as presented in the gospels is[83] so difficult to believe that even the fanatic Christian "doctor" and saint, Augustine (354–430), admitted, "For my part, I should not believe the gospel except as moved by the authority of the Catholic Church."[84] Nevertheless, this "monumentally superstitious and credulous Child of Faith" cannot have been *too* resistant, because he already accepted "as historic truth the fabulous founding of Rome by Romulus and Remus, their virgin-birth by the god Mars, and their nursing by the she-wolf."[85]

Apparently unable to convince himself rationally of the validity of his faith, early Church father Tertullian (c. 160–200) allegedly made the notorious statement, "*Credo quia absurdum est*—I believe because it is absurd."[86] In arguing against the Docetism of the "heretic" Marcion, who contended that Christ never came in the flesh, the ex-Pagan Tertullian (*De carne Christi*, 5) sought to defend his new faith against Pagan

83 See my book *Who Was Jesus?* for many examples of miracles, impossibilities, implausibilities; failed prophecies; contradictions and inconsistencies; errors in time and place; chronological problems; translation errors and language problems; illogic and irrationality; character issues; and repellant deeds, sayings and doctrines.

84 *Against the Epistle of Manichaeus Called Fundamental* (5.6); Augustine/Stothert, 131.

85 Wheless, *FC*, 163. See *City of God* (18.21); Augustine/Dods, 371.

86 Runia, 539. This phrase or *credo quia incredibile est*—"I believe because it is incredible"—has been ascribed widely to both Tertullian and Augustine, in neither of whose extant works can it be found; however. Runia notes that the original in Tertullian (*De carne Christi* 5.4) is *credibile est, quia ineptum est*—"It is credible because it is inept (silly)."

objections of falsification and fabrication by acknowledging that Christianity *was* "shameful" and "absurd":

> The Son of God was born—I am not ashamed, for the very reason that this is shameful: and the Son of God died—it is wholly credible, for the very reason that it is absurd; and, buried, rose again—it is certain, for the very reason that it is impossible.[87]

In addition to confessions of incredibility by Pagans and Christians alike, we also encounter repeated accusations and admissions of forgery and fraud.

The Anonymous Gospel Truth

None of the canonical gospels were written by its purported author[88] and, indeed, no mention of any New Testament text can be found in writings prior to the beginning of the second century of the Common Era (CE), long after the purported events. Since traditional author ascriptions turn out to be arbitrary and spurious, and since it is in them that we find the story of Christ, we must be doubtful as to its validity as well. Regarding the canonical gospels, Wheless concludes:

> The gospels are all priestly forgeries over a century after their pretended dates.[89]

Expounding upon this contention, French archaeologist Dr. Salomon Reinach (1858–1932) remarks:

> With the exception of Papias (c. 120), who speaks of a narrative by Mark, and a collection of sayings of Jesus, no Christian writer of the first half of the second century quotes the Gospels or their reputed authors.... It is true that St. Justin (c. 150) mentions the Memoirs of the Apostles, but the extracts he gives from these are never textually identical with passages in our Gospels. Some of them come from unrecognised gospels, called apocryphal, others from unknown sources.[90]

In *A Short History of the Bible*, Bronson C. Keeler[91] concurs with

87 Ryan, 95–6. The original Latin provided by the *American Catholic Quarterly Review* (24) is: *Natus est Dei Filius; non pudet, quia pudendum est: et mortuus est Dei Filius; prorsus credibile est, quia ineptum est: et sepultus, resurrexit; certum est, quia impossibile [est].*

88 For more information, see Murdock, *Who Was Jesus?*, 59–83.

89 Wheless, *FC*, 94.

90 Reinach, 218.

91 University of Michigan graduate Bronson C. Keeler, a newsman, was a "quite prominent member" of the professional and educational circles of St. Louis, Missouri, in the late 1800s. (*Michigan Alumnus*, 3.187; Hyde, 4.2072) He became prominent nationally as the chairman of the committee of the St. Louis Single Tax League, who caused the U.S. Congress to investigate Amer-

this assessment of the lack of literary evidence for the existence of the canonical gospels before the last half of the second century:

> They are not heard of till 150 AD, that is, till Jesus had been dead nearly a hundred and twenty years. No writer before 150 AD makes the slightest mention of them.[92]

Despite claims to the contrary, the early Church father and saint Justin Martyr (100–165 CE) does not quote any of the canonical gospels verbatim:

> At the very threshold of the subject, we are met by the fact, that nowhere in all the writings of Justin, does he once so much as mention any of these gospels. Nor does he mention either of their supposed authors, except John. Once his name occurs; not, however, as the author of a gospel, but in such a connection as raises a very strong presumption that Justin knew of no gospel of John the Apostle.[93]

It appears that, rather than representing the four canonical gospels, Justin's "Memoirs" refers to a single text, like "Acts," possibly the Gospel of the Hebrews, which was also called the "Gospel of the Apostles."[94]

In *The Christ: A Critical Review and Analysis of the Evidences of His Existence*, John E. Remsburg (1848–1919) elucidates:

> The Four Gospels were unknown to the early Christian Fathers. Justin Martyr, the most eminent of the early Fathers, wrote about the middle of the second century. His writings in proof of the divinity of Christ demanded the use of these Gospels had they existed in his time. He makes more than three hundred quotations from the books

---

ican farm mortgage indebtedness. (Miller, J.D., 10.40) Regarding Keeler's book, famed freethinker Colonel Robert G. Ingersoll remarks: "I have read Mr. Keeler's book with great pleasure and profit. He gives, in my opinion, a clear and intelligent account of the growth of the bible. He shows why books were received as inspired, and why they were rejected. He does not deal in opinions, but in facts; and for the correctness of his facts, he refers to the highest authorities ... Mr. Keeler must have spent a great deal of time in the examination of a vast number of volumes, and the amount of information contained in this book could not be collected in years. Every minister, every college professor, and every man who really wishes to know something about the origin and growth of the bible, should read this book." (Ingersoll (1888), front matter)

92 Keeler, 23.

93 Waite, 307. In *Dialogue with Trypho* (81), Justin mentions this "John" in the context of his "revelation," rather than his gospel. (Justin/Falls, 127) For more on the value or lack thereof of Justin Martyr in establishing the existence of the four canonical gospels of Matthew, Mark, Luke and John, see Acharya, *SOG*, 419ff, and Murdock, *WWJ*, 67–8.

94 See my discussion in *Suns of God* (420ff).

of the Old Testament, and nearly one hundred from the Apocryphal books of the New Testament; but none from the four Gospels.[95]

Concerning Justin, Oxford theologian Rev. Dr. John Allen Giles remarks, "The very names of the evangelists Matthew, Mark, Luke and John, are never mentioned by him—do not occur once in all his works."[96]

Regarding evidence of early Christian history, Waite concludes:

> No one of the four gospels is mentioned in any other part of the New Testament.... No work of art of any kind has ever been discovered, no painting, or engraving, no sculpture, or other relic of antiquity, which may be looked upon as furnishing additional evidence of the existence of those gospels, and which was executed earlier than the latter part of the second century. Even the exploration of the Christian catacombs failed to bring to light any evidence of that character.... The four gospels were written in Greek, and there was no translation of them into other languages, earlier than the third century.[97]

Waite says, "Nearly everything written concerning the gospels to the year 325, and all the copies of the gospels themselves to the same period, are lost or destroyed."[98] The truth is that very few early Christian texts exist because the autographs, or originals, may have been destroyed after the Council of Nicea and the "retouching" of 506 AD/CE under Emperor Anastasius, which included "revision" of the Church fathers' works.[99] Such redaction tampering would be inconceivable if these "documents" were truly the precious testaments of the very apostles themselves regarding the "Lord and Savior." Repeating what would appear to be utter blasphemy, a variety of church officials in the eleventh and twelfth centuries again "corrected" the "infallible Word of God."[100]

---

95 Remsburg, 52. The author's name is at times erroneously spelled "Remsberg."

96 Giles, 2.122.

97 Waite, 346.

98 Waite, 461.

99 Lardner (128) relates: "Victor Tununensis, an African bishop, who wrote a Chronicle ending at the year 566, says 'that when Messala was consul, that is, in the year of Christ 506, at Constantinople, by order of the emperor Anastasius, the holy gospels being written by illiterate evangelists, were censured and corrected.'"

100 Concerning this period in Europe, the *Catholic Encyclopedia* states: "The period of the eleventh and twelfth centuries may be considered as the golden age of monastic manuscript writing.... The Bible remained the book which was copied by preference." (Herbermann, 9.618) Regarding the Codex Vaticanus edition of the Bible, New Testament scholar Dr. Philip W. Com-

In addition to these major "revisions," there have been many others, including copying and translation mistakes and deliberate mutilation and obfuscation of meaning.

Pious Fraud

It has never been only nonbelieving detractors who have made such allegations of falsification and deceit by the biblical writers. Indeed, those individuals who concocted some of the hundreds of "alternative" gospels and epistles circulated during the first several centuries even admitted that they forged the texts. Of these numerous manuscripts, the *Catholic Encyclopedia* acknowledges:

> When, therefore, enterprising spirits responded to this natural craving by pretended Gospels full of romantic fables and fantastic and striking details, their fabrications were eagerly read and largely accepted as true by common folk who were devoid of any critical faculty and who were predisposed to believe what so luxuriously fed their pious curiosity. Both Catholics and Gnostics were concerned in writing these fictions. The former had no motive other than that of a pious fraud.[101]

Forgery during the first centuries of the Church's existence was thus admittedly rampant, so common in fact that this phrase, "pious fraud,"[102] was coined to describe it. Furthermore, while admitting that the Catholics were engaged in fraud, the *Catholic Encyclopedia* is also implying that the Gnostics were truthful in regard to the fictitious and allegorical nature of their texts. Regarding this Catholic habit of fraud, in *The Truth about Jesus: Was He a Myth?*, Rev. Dr. Mangasar Magurditch Mangasarian (1859–1943) states:

> The church historian, Mosheim, writes that, "The Christian Fathers deemed it a pious act to employ deception and fraud." Again, he says: "The greatest and most pious teachers were nearly all of them infected with this leprosy." Will not some believer tell us why forgery and fraud were necessary to prove the historicity of Jesus?
>
> Another historian, Milman, writes that, "Pious fraud was admitted and avowed" by the early missionaries of Jesus. "It was

fort (80) says that it is "generally recognized as one of the most trustworthy witnesses to the New Testament text [and] is the work of two scribes." He likewise relates that "two correctors worked on the New Testament," including a "tenth- or eleventh-century corrector, who retouched the writing and added accents and marks of punctuation." (Comfort, 80)

101 Herbermann, 1.606.

102 The phrase "pious fraud" was first used in the English language in 1678, according to the *Oxford English Dictionary*. (*OED* (1999), "fraud.")

an age of literary frauds," writes Bishop Ellicott, speaking of the times immediately following the alleged crucifixion of Jesus. Dr. Giles declares that, "There can be no doubt that great numbers of books were written with no other purpose than to deceive." And it is the opinion of [Rev.] Dr. Robertson Smith that, "There was an enormous floating mass of spurious literature created to suit party views."[103]

So fundamental to "the faith" was fraud that Wheless remarked:

The clerical confessions of lies and frauds in the ponderous volumes of the *Catholic Encyclopedia* alone suffice ... to wreck the Church and to destroy utterly the Christian religion.... The Church exists mostly for wealth and selfaggrandizement; to quit paying money to the priests would kill the whole scheme in a couple of years. This is the sovereign remedy.[104]

According to Christian father and Church historian Eusebius (260?-340?), Bishop of Corinth Dionysius (fl. 170) lashed out against forgers who had mutilated not only his letters but also the "word of the Lord" itself:

When my fellow-Christians invited me to write letters to them I did so. These the devil's apostles have filled with tears, taking away some things and adding others.... Small wonder then if some have dared to tamper even with the word of the Lord Himself, when they have conspired to mutilate my own humble efforts.[105]

In this regard, Dr. William O. Walker, Jr. Professor Emeritus of Religion at Trinity University, comments:

The addition of Christian interpolations was clearly not confined, however, to non-Christian documents. For example, Dionysius, Bishop of Corinth in the middle of the second century, claimed that "heretics" had both added materials to and deleted materials from his letters. Similarly, Irenaeus (late-second cen-

103 Mangasarian, 65–66. Mangasarian is for the most part (accurately) paraphrasing the following: Mosheim, 1.225, 1.321; Milman, 3.472; Giles, 2.19; *Enc. Brit*, 3.557. Interestingly, Old Testament scholar and professor of Hebrew at Aberdeen University, Rev. Dr. William Robertson Smith (1846–1894), was tried for "heresy" for his "Bible" article in the *Encyclopedia Britannica*, which was critical of the text as "history." Although cleared on all charges, Smith was subsequently excommunicated and "removed from his posts within the church because of his exegetical ideas." (Lemche, 303) Many of Smith's criticisms are now part of mainstream scholarship.

104 Wheless, xxxi.

105 Eusebius, 132.

tury) "express[ed] the greatest apprehension that his writings against heretics would be 'altered,' and the late-fourth-century writer Rufinus claimed that many of the Greek patristic writings had been interpolated. Other examples could be cited.[106]

In addition, a number of the fathers, including Eusebius, were deemed by their own peers to be untrustworthy liars who regularly wrote their own fictions about what their Lord said and did during his alleged sojourn upon the earth. According to historian Gibbon, Eusebius in one of his works, *Evangelical Preparation* (12.31), provides a handy chapter entitled: "How it may be Lawful and Fitting to use Falsehood as Medicine, and for the Benefit of those who Want to be Deceived."[107] Of Eusebius, Waite writes, "Not only the most unblushing falsehoods, but literary forgeries of the vilest character, darken the pages of his apologetic and historical writings."[108]

Wheless also calls Justin Martyr, Tertullian and Eusebius "three luminous liars."[109] Keeler states, "The early Christian fathers were extremely ignorant and superstitious; and they were singularly incompetent to deal with the supernatural."[110] Dr. Martin A. Larson (1897–1994) concludes that many early bishops "like Jerome, Antony, and St. Martin, were definitely psychotic. In fact, there was scarcely a single Father in the ancient Church who was not tainted with heresy, mental aberration, or moral enormity."[111] Thus, according to these stark assessments, it was deceptive, mentally ill individuals who originated Christianity. Yet, it should be kept in mind that these fathers were not

---

106 Walker, W., 30–31., quoting Walter Bauer, *Orthodoxy and Heresey in Earliest Christianity.* Trans. Team from Philadelphia Seminar on Christian Origins (Philadelphia: Fortress Press, 1971), 166.

107 Gibbon, *MWEG*, 766. Citing "Page 356, edit. Graec. Rob. Stephani, Paris, 1544," Gibbon includes the original Greek: "Οτι δεησει ποτε τω ψευδει αντι φαρμακου χρησθαι επι ωφελεια των δεομενων του τοιουτου τροπου." *The Southern Review* (IV, 4) comments, "The passage in Eusebius is in p. 356, Edit. Graec. Rob. Steph. Paris, 1544, and lib. xii. ch. 31, p. 607 of vol. i. edit. Franc. Vigeri. Paris, 1628." Indeed, Eusebius's original Greek passage can be found in Migne's edition of *Prepar. Evang.* (Lib. XII, Caput XXXI), with the Latin translation: "Falso nonnunquam, veluti pharmaco, ad corum utilitatem, qui hoc loquendi genere ovus habeant, utendum esse." (Migne, 21.1009–10) Naturally, this quote has been disputed and picked apart to absolve Eusebius of deceit; yet, we can see it is evidently authentic.

108 Waite, 328.

109 Wheless, *FC*, 105.

110 Keeler, 48.

111 Larson, 506.

altogether ignorant. Their familiarity, not only with Jewish writings but also with Pagan literature, is evident from their acute awareness of the comparisons between Christianity and Pagan religion.[112]

Addressing the issue of "pseudepigraphy," the scholarly term for forgery in another's name, Dr. Bart Ehrman remarks:

> It is often said—even by scholars who should know better—that this kind of "pseudonymous" (i.e., falsely named) writing in the ancient world was not thought to be lying and was not meant to be deceitful … this view is flat-out wrong.… Ancient authors who talked about this practice of writing a book in someone else's name said that it was both lying and deceitful and that it was not an acceptable practice.[113]

Of these "pseudonymous" (forged) products, Wheless further remarks:

> If the pious Christians, confessedly, committed so many and so extensive forgeries and frauds to adapt these popular Jewish fairytales of their God and holy Worthies to the new Christian Jesus and his Apostles, we need feel no surprise when we discover these same Christians forging outright new wondertales of their Christ under the fiction of the most noted Christian names and in the guise of inspired Gospels, Epistles, Acts and Apocalypses.[114]

He continues:

> Half a hundred of false and forged Apostolic "Gospels of Jesus Christ," together with more numerous other "Scripture" forgeries, was the output, so far as known now, of the lying pens of the pious Christians of the first two centuries of the Christian "Age of Apocryphal Literature."[115]

The editors of the Protestant *Encyclopedia Biblica* state, "Almost every one of the apostles had a gospel fathered upon him by one early sect or another."[116]

On the subject of biblical forgery, University of Cambridge librarian Rev. Dr. Conyers Middleton (1683–1750) remarks:

> For there never was any period of time in all Ecclesiastical History, in which so many rank *Heresies* were publicly professed, nor in which so many *spurious books* were forged and published by

112 See, for example, Louis Thomassin's La méthode d'étudier et d'enseigner Chrétiennement.

113 Ehrman (2011), 9.

114 Wheless, *FC*, 67.

115 Wheless, *FC*, 101.

116 Cheyne, 1.259.

> the Christians, under the names of Christ, and the Apostles, and the Apostolic writers, as in those primitive ages; several of which forged books are frequently cited and applied to the defense of Christianity, by the most eminent Fathers of the same ages, as true and genuine pieces.[117]

Wheless demonstrates how low the fathers and *doctors* of texts were willing to stoop:

> If the Gospel tales were true, why should God need pious lies to give them credit? Lies and forgeries are only needed to bolster up falsehood: "Nothing stands in need of lying but a lie." But Jesus Christ must needs be propagated by lies upon lies; and what better proof of his actuality than to exhibit letters written by him in his own handwriting? The "Little Liars of the Lord" were equal to the forgery of the signature of their God—false letters in his name, as above cited from that exhaustless mine of clerical falsities, the *Catholic Encyclopedia*.[118]

Indeed, Christian tradition pretends that Christ was extremely renowned even during his own time, having exchanged correspondence with King Abgar of Syria, also called Abgarus, who was most pleased to have the Christian savior take refuge in his country. Of course this story and the silly letters alleged to have been exchanged between the two are as phony as three-dollar bills,[119] illustrating the ridiculous mendacity to which historicizers had to resort to place their invented character and drama in a specific historical context.

Furthermore, the forgers were not very skilled or conscientious; they left many clues as to their underhanded endeavors. As Wheless states, "the Hebrew and Greek religious forgers were so ignorant or careless of the principles of criticism, that they 'interpolated' their fraudulent new matter into old manuscripts without taking care to erase or suppress the previous statements glaringly contradicted by the new interpolations."[120]

We have established the atmosphere of the foundation of Christianity: conspiracy, forgery and fraud, the result of which are its sacred texts, falsely alleged to be infallible accounts by eyewitnesses to the most extraordinary events in human history. Let us now examine the "evidence" left to us by these pious forgers as to the historicity of the great savior and godman Jesus Christ.

---

117 Middleton, lix.

118 Wheless, *FC*, 109.

119 See, for example, Bromiley (1979) 181), who labels the Abgar correspondence and other such texts as "Romantic and Novelistic Forgeries."

120 Wheless, *FC*, 178.

Biblical Sources

"In essence, if His words were not accurately recorded [in the Gospels], how can anyone know what He really taught? The truth is, we couldn't know. Further, if the remainder of the New Testament cannot be established to be historically reliable, then little can be known about what true Christianity really is, teaches or means."

—Dr. John Ankerberg and Dr. John Weldon, *Handbook of Biblical Evidences* (351)

"With all the differences between Matthew, Mark, Luke and John, and with numerous other gospels existing, we have an obvious problem. Each gospel has a particular way of seeing Jesus. How close to the historical facts are they?"

—Dr. John Dominic Crossan, *Who Is Jesus?* (4)

"If you take the gospels as a factual account of the life of Jesus, they're not all in sync … there are what we might identify as contradictions in the account.… If we want to read the gospels as eye witness accounts, historical records and so on, then not only are we in for some tough going, I think there's evidence within the material itself that it's not intended to be read that way. [The gospels] don't claim to be eyewitness accounts of his life … we're concerned about the gospel literature as being shot through with all kinds of tendencies and all kinds of biases and exaggerations."

—Dr. Allen D. Callahan, "From Jesus to Christ: What Are the Gospels?"

"The crucial question is this: Is it possible that any of the early Christian forgeries made it into the New Testament? That some of the books of the New Testament were not written by the apostles whose names are attached to them? That some of Paul's letters were not actually written by Paul, but by someone claiming to be Paul? That Peter's letters were not written by Peter? That James and Jude did not write the books that bear their names? Or … that the Gospels of Matthew, Mark, Luke and John were not actually written by Matthew, Mark, Luke and John? Scholars for over a hundred years have known that in fact this is the case."

—Dr. Bart D. Ehrman, *Forged: Writing in the Name of God* (9)

"[Much] recent Gospel scholarship … has concluded that the Gospels were written more than forty years after Jesus by unknown authors who were not eyewitnesses to him."

—Dr. Robert E. Van Voorst, *Jesus Outside the New Testament* (13)

"We should not expect to find in Scripture full scientific accuracy or complete historical precision."

—The Catholic Truth Society, *The Gift of Scripture* (18)

The story of Jesus Christ can be found only in the forged books of the New Testament, an assortment of gospels and epistles that required many centuries and hands to create. The biblical canon (authorized set and order of books) was not established even by the sixth century, as noted by English theologian Rev. Dr. Nathaniel Lardner (1684–1768), in his chapter (148) about the Christian writer Cosmas of Alexandria (fl. 535): "The canon of the New Testament had not been settled in the time of this writer, by any authority that was decisive and universally acknowledged."[121] Gnostic text expert George R.S. Mead (1863–1933) describes the confused compilation of the "infallible Word of God":

> The New Testament is not a single book but a collection of groups of books and single volumes, which were at first and even long afterwards circulated separately.... the Gospels are found in any and every order.... Egyptian tradition places Jn. first among the Gospels.[122]

In fact, it took well over a thousand years to canonize the New Testament, and the Old Testament canon remains different to this day between the Catholic and Protestant versions.[123] This canonization also required many councils to decide which books were to be considered "inspired" and which "spurious." Contrary to the impression usually given, these councils were not peaceful gatherings of the "good shepherds of Christ" but raucous free-for-alls between bands of thugs and their arrogant and insane bishops. As Keeler says:

> The reader would err greatly did he suppose that in these assemblies one or two hundred gentlemen sat down to discuss quietly and dignifiedly the questions which had come before them for settlement. On the contrary, many of the bishops were ignorant ruffians, and were followed by crowds of vicious supporters who stood ready on the slightest excuse to maim and kill their opponents.[124]

At the Council of Ephesus in 431, mobs consisting of the dregs

121 Lardner, 5.270–1.

122 Mead, *GG*, 59, 123. Interestingly, from both internal and external evidence, such as its apparent provenance, the gospel of John is clearly the most Egyptian of the canonical texts. For more information about the Egyptian nature and likely origin of John, see my book *Christ in Egypt*.

123 As stated in the article "Development of the New Testament Canon": "[F]ull dogmatic articulations of the canon were not made until the Council of Trent of 1546 for Roman Catholicism, the Thirty-Nine Articles of 1563 for the Church of England, the Westminster Confession of Faith of 1647 for Calvinism, and the Synod of Jerusalem of 1672 for the Greek Orthodox."

124 Keeler, 101.

of society and representing the warring factions of the Syrian city of Antioch and the Egyptian city of Alexandria broke out in riots and killed many each of the other.[125] This melee was merely one of many, and this shedding of blood by Christians was only the beginning of a hideous centuries-long legacy. Church historian Eusebius (8.1) describes the chaotic atmosphere prevailing in the early days of Christianity:

> But increasing freedom transformed our character to arrogance and sloth; we began envying and abusing each other, cutting our own throats, as occasion offered, with weapons of sharp-edged words; rulers hurled themselves at rulers and laymen waged party fights against laymen, and unspeakable hypocrisy and dissimulation were carried to the limit of wickedness.... Those of us who were supposed to be pastors cast off the restraining influence of the fear of God and quarreled heatedly with each other, engaged solely in swelling the disputes, threats, envy, and mutual hostility and hate, frantically demanding the despotic power they coveted.[126]

Such were the means by which the New Testament was finally canonized. Concerning the New Testament as it stands today, Wheless says:

> The 27 New Testament booklets, attributed to eight individual "Apostolic" writers, and culled from some 200 admitted forgeries called Gospels, Acts and Epistles, constitute the present "canonical" or acceptedly inspired compendium of the primitive history of Christianity.[127]

The various gospels, of which only four are now accepted as "canonical" or "genuine," are in actuality not the earliest Christian texts. The earliest canonical texts are demonstrably the Epistles of Paul, so it is to them that we must first turn in our investigation.

The Epistles

The various Pauline epistles contained in the New Testament form an important part of Christianity; yet, these "earliest" of Christian texts never discuss a historical background of Jesus, even though Paul purportedly lived during and after Jesus's advent and surely would have known about his master's miraculous life. Instead, these letters deal with a spiritual construct found in various religions, sects, cults and mystery schools for hundreds to thousands of years prior to the Christian era.

Aside from the brief reference to Pontius Pilate at 1 Timothy 6:13, an epistle widely rejected as post-Pauline, the Pauline literature "does

125 See, for example, Willard-Archer, 29.

126 Eusebius, 258.

127 Wheless, *FC*, 91.

not refer to Pilate, or the Romans, or Caiaphas, or the Sanhedrin, or Herod, or Judas, or the holy women, or any person in the gospel account of the Passion, and that it also never makes any allusion to them; lastly, that it mentions absolutely none of the events of the Passion, either directly or by way of allusion."[128] Other early "Christian" writings such as Revelation likewise do not mention any historical details or drama. Paul also never quotes from Jesus's purported sermons and speeches, parables and prayers, nor does he mention Jesus's supernatural birth or any of his alleged wonders and miracles, all of which one would presume would be very important to his followers, had such exploits and sayings been known prior to the apostle's purported time.

Mangasarian understandably asks:

> Is it conceivable that a preacher of Jesus could go throughout the world to convert people to the teachings of Jesus, as Paul did, without ever quoting a single one of his sayings? Had Paul known that Jesus had preached a sermon, or formulated a prayer, or said many inspired things about the here and the hereafter, he could not have helped quoting, now and then, from the words of his master. If Christianity could have been established without a knowledge of the teachings of Jesus, why, then, did Jesus come to teach, and why were his teachings preserved by divine inspiration? ...
>
> If Paul knew of a miracle-working Jesus, one who could feed the multitude with a few loaves and fishes—who could command the grave to open, who could cast out devils, and cleanse the land of the foulest disease of leprosy, who could, and did, perform many other wonderful works to convince the unbelieving generation of his divinity—is it conceivable that either intentionally or inadvertently he would have never once referred to them in all his preaching? ...
>
> The position, then, that there is not a single saying of Jesus in the gospels which is quoted by Paul in his many epistles is unassailable, and certainly fatal to the historicity of the gospel Jesus.[129]

Paul's First Letter to the Corinthians

One passage in the Pauline epistles cited by apologists as "proof" that Paul was familiar with an historical Jesus is 1 Corinthians 11:24–5:

> [And] when he had given thanks, he broke it, and said, "This is my body which is for you. Do this in remembrance of me." In the same way also the cup, after supper, saying, "This cup is the new covenant in my blood. Do this, as often as you drink it, in remembrance of me."

128 Dujardin, 33.

129 Mangasarian, 126–131.

Firstly, the context needs to be included, which is that Paul says in verse 23:

> For I received from the Lord what I also delivered to you, that the Lord Jesus on the night when he was betrayed took bread.

These verses are held up as evidence that Jesus really existed, because they are describing what has become known as the "Lord's Supper" or "Last Supper," which proponents claim is clearly a historical event, as depicted in the New Testament, as at Luke 22:7–30. In reading the pertinent passage in Luke, however, it should be kept in mind that biblical criticism has revealed several problems not only with these verses in Luke but also as concerns relevant passages in the other synoptic gospels (Matt. 26:17–30; Mark 14:12–26). Moreover, there simply is no evidence for the existence of the canonical gospels as we have them by the time Paul wrote this epistle, so he could not have been relating "facts" from them. The reality is that Paul was not in attendance at the Last Supper and would be relaying hearsay at best.

Regarding 1 Corinthians 11:23–26, in *Jesus: Neither God Nor Man*, Earl Doherty says:

> Here Paul attributes words to Jesus at what he calls "The Lord's Supper," words identifying the bread and wine of that "supper" with Jesus' body and blood. But is Paul recounting an historical event here? There are several arguments to be made that this is not the case, that Paul is instead describing something which lay in the realm of myth, similar to sacred meal myths, found in many of the Greek savior god cults, such as that of Mithras. In fact, the opening phrase of the passage points to Paul's reception of this information through revelation, not through an account of others who were supposedly participants at such an event.[130]

Doherty then goes on to produce an extensive analysis of the passage, including the Greek used to introduce it, which has Paul contending he received this knowledge "through revelation," not as a historical account. The word translated as "received" in the Greek is παραλαμβάνω or *paralambano*, which means, among other things, "to receive something transmitted," "to receive with the mind," as by oral tradition. We know that Paul never met the "historical" Jesus, so his reception of this transmitted information must have been psychic or spiritual, not physical. He is then "delivering" the "channeled" information to his audience, implying that *Paul* is the source of the

130 Doherty (2009), 18. For further analysis demonstrating that Paul's epistles do not reveal an "historical" Jesus, see Doherty's *The Jesus Puzzle* and *Jesus: Neither God Nor Man.*

Lord's Supper pericope later fleshed out by the evangelists.

Old Testament 'Prophecy' or Blueprint?

Secondly, as concerns 1 Corinthians 11:23, Dr. Robert M. Price discusses the Last Supper as a midrash of Psalm 41:9: "Even my bosom friend in whom I trusted, who ate of my bread, has lifted his heel against me." Hence, the "betrayal" related by Paul is likewise allegorical, based on Old Testament scripture or "messianic prophecy." (For details, see Price's article "New Testament Narrative as Old Testament Midrash.")

Isaiah 53:12 is likewise indicated as a source for the Last Supper:

> Therefore I will divide him a portion with the great, and he shall divide the spoil with the strong; because he poured out his soul to death, and was numbered with the transgressors; yet he bore the sin of many, and made intercession for the transgressors.

Earlier in 1 Corinthians (10:3–4), Paul refers specifically to the sacred meal shared by Moses and his followers in the desert:

> [And] all ate the same supernatural food and all drank the same supernatural drink. For they drank from the supernatural Rock which followed them, and the Rock was Christ.

Certainly, in referring to the Old Testament scripture (Exod. 17:6; Num. 20:11) Paul was speaking spiritually and allegorically, as he surely did not mean that a man named "Jesus of Nazareth" was following the Jews around during the Exodus, dressed as a rock. Clearly, here is a precedent upon which, some verses later, Paul could easily build a metaphorical "Lord's Supper," a concept he claimed to have received through "revelation," rather than depicting a historical event.

A Mithraic Ritual?

It is further interesting to note that the Greek word for "rock" is πέτρα or "petra," (same as "*petros*," as in "Peter"), which Paul (1 Cor. 10:4) equates with "*christos*" (ἡ πέτρα δὲ ἦν ὁ Χριστός) or "the anointed," a title held by several individuals in the Old Testament.[131] For example, there is the "anointed priest" at Leviticus 4:5 and 4:16: "ὁ ἱερεὺς ὁ χριστὸς." At Lamentations 4:20 we find reference to the "Lord's

131 *A Handy Concordance of the Septuagint* (261)lists some 43 scriptures that include the word χριστς or *christos*: Lev. 4:5, 16, 6:22, 21:10, 12; 1 Sam. 2:10, 35, 12: 3, 5, 16:6, 25:7, 7, 11, 26:9, 11, 16, 23; 2 Sam. 1:14, 16, 2:5-A, 19:21, 22:51, 23:1, 3a; 1 Chr. 16:22; 2 Chr. 6:42-B, 22:7; Pss. 2:2, 17:51, 19:7, 27:8, 83:10, 88:39, 52, 104:15, 131:10, 17; Isa. 45:1; Lam. 4:20; Ezek. 16:4+A; Dan. 9:25; Amos 4:13; Hab. 3:13. This list includes, as do all concordances, appearances of various forms of the word (e.g., singular, plural, nominative, dative, accusative, etc.). It is difficult to explain why the translators of the Septuagint rendered the Hebrew word as *christos*. The scripture, then, could read that the Lord "declares to man what is his *Christ*..."

Anointed" or χριστὸς κυρίου (Christos Kyriou). The equivalent Hebrew word is משיח, mashiyach or "messiah." Habakkuk 3:13 speaks of the Lord's anointed in the plural: To wit, τοὺς χριστούς, in the accusative plural. King Saul is named at 2 Samuel 1:14, 16 as "the Lord's anointed": τὸν χριστὸν κυρίου. 2 Samuel 19:21 likewise discusses τὸν χριστὸν κυρίου or "the Lord's anointed." 2 Samuel 22:51 and 23:1 name King David as the Lord's anointed or "χριστὸν θεοῦ" and so on. The very scripture in Daniel (9:25) used by apologists to claim that Christ's coming was predicted—ἕως χριστοῦ ἡγουμένου—includes the word "*christos*" to describe what is generally rendered "an anointed one." As we can see, readers or hearers of the Septuagint two to three centuries before the Common Era would have heard much about the very important Christos.

The Perso-Roman god Mithra, too, was the "*theos ek petras*" or "god of the rock," who was the god of the Persian king Cyrus, the latter likewise called "*christos*" in the Greek Old Testament/Septuagint (Isa. 45:1: "τῷ χριστῷ μου Κύρῳ"). (It should be noted, however, that some of the earliest codices, such as the Sinaiticus, often use the abbreviations XC, XN or XW for what is transliterated/translated as "Christos," etc. This same convention is utilized in the New Testament, where the abbreviations could in fact represent "Chrestos" in the autographs, here altered to create the impression of conformity based on a "historical" Jesus of Nazareth).

Moreover, the city of Tarsus, Paul's home town, was the Asia Minor center from which Mithraism spread during the first centuries BCE/CE. As New Testament scholar Dr. Jonathan A. Draper remarks:

> The first mention we have of the Mithraic cult in the Roman Orient is in Tarsus (Cilicia), the home of a number of Stoic philosophers and of the worshiping of Herakles Sandan, the bull-killer, and also the place where Saul of Tarsus started his strange path.[132]

What about 1 Corinthians 15:3–8?

Another passage used by apologists to demonstrate that Paul knew about an "historical" Jesus appears in the First Epistle to the Corinthians, attributed to Paul, in verses 15:3–8:

> For I delivered unto you first of all that which I also received, how that Christ died for our sins according to the scriptures; And that he was buried, and that he rose again the third day according to the scriptures: And that he was seen of Cephas, then of the twelve: After that, he was seen of above five hundred brethren at once; of whom the greater part remain unto this present, but some are fallen

132 Draper, 104.

asleep. After that, he was seen of James; then of all the apostles. And last of all he was seen of me also, as of one born out of due time.

As Ken Humphreys points out, when 1 Corinthians 15:3–4 makes Paul say that "Christ died for our sins," was buried, and "rose again on the third day" he clarifies—twice—that such contentions are "*according to the scriptures*."[133] In discussing scriptures, Paul is surely not referring to the canonical gospels or any other New Testament text; he is indicating *Jewish* scriptures (i.e., what we now call the Old Testament). Thus, he is evidently discussing a mystery ritual found in *Jewish* congregations at *synagogues/ecclesia* in the Diaspora. This figure of "the Anointed" could well be a reference to a mystical or gnostic figurehead, as in the Samothracian and Eleusinian mysteries (i.e., the classic "dying and rising" savior). If Paul can find this formula in the Jewish scriptures, we can be sure that the gospel writers could do it as well, decades later. The scriptures he refers to in verse 3 are Isaiah 53:1–12, the depiction of the "Man of Sorrows," raised up by the Lord and to whom the "arm of the Lord was revealed":

> He was despised and rejected by men; a man of sorrows, and acquainted with grief; and as one from whom men hide their faces he was despised, and we esteemed him not.
>
> Surely he has borne our griefs and carried our sorrows; yet we esteemed him stricken, smitten by God, and afflicted.
>
> But he was wounded for our transgressions, he was bruised for our iniquities; upon him was the chastisement that made us whole, and with his stripes we are healed.
>
> All we like sheep have gone astray; we have turned every one to his own way; and the LORD has laid on him the iniquity of us all.
>
> He was oppressed, and he was afflicted, yet he opened not his mouth; like a lamb that is led to the slaughter, and like a sheep that before its shearers is dumb, so he opened not his mouth.
>
> By oppression and judgment he was taken away; and as for his generation, who considered that he was cut off out of the land of the living, stricken for the transgression of my people?
>
> And they made his grave with the wicked and with a rich man in his death, although he had done no violence, and there was no deceit in his mouth.
>
> Yet it was the will of the LORD to bruise him; he has put him to grief; when he makes himself an offering for sin, he shall see his offspring, he shall prolong his days; the will of the LORD shall prosper in his hand;

---

133 Humphrey, 35.

he shall see the fruit of the travail of his soul and be satisfied; by his knowledge shall the righteous one, my servant, make many to be accounted righteous; and he shall bear their iniquities.

Therefore I will divide him a portion with the great, and he shall divide the spoil with the strong; because he poured out his soul to death, and was numbered with the transgressors; yet he bore the sin of many, and made intercession for the transgressors.

Commenting on 1 Corinthians 15, Rev. Dr. Matthew Henry remarks that the "apostle's business in this chapter [is] to assert and establish the doctrine of the resurrection of the dead, which some of the Corinthians flatly denied."[134] If the story of Jesus Christ having been resurrected from the dead a mere few decades previously were part of established Christian doctrine—based on testimony from hundreds of supposed eyewitnesses— It would seem ridiculous that these Corinthians could possibly deny the doctrine of the resurrection of the dead! This passage actually speaks *against* Christ's historicity.

Since Paul tosses himself into the mix with "Cephas," the twelve, the 500 and James, it would not be unreasonable to suggest that their experiences of the risen Christ were the same as that of these "brethren": To wit, mystical or gnostic, rather than historical. As we know, such mystical life-and-death experiences are common in various mystery traditions. There is little solid evidence to suggest that the experiences of these brethren were any more "real" than those of their Gentile compatriots. Indeed, it is obvious that Paul's Christ is a bridge between the mystical savior entities of the mysteries and the thoroughly historicized Christian messiah. It is further obvious that Paul's gnostic Christ has been given greater solid ground by a few tweaks here and there in his writings, along with entirely pseudonymous attributions to him.

The scripture verses to which Paul refers at 1 Corinthians 15:4 are from Jonah 1:17, which Jesus is made to cite at Matthew 12:40, comparing himself to the Old Testament prophet:

And the Lord appointed a great fish to swallow up Jonah; and Jonah was in the belly of the fish three days and three nights.

The motif of the sin-bearer dying and rising from the dead after three days is thus *pre-Christian* and was quite obviously well-known to Paul's congregations as having taken place centuries before, when the Old Testament was composed. This sacred-king scapegoat ritual was acted out repeatedly in numerous places, including especially the Near and Middle East, with kings or proxies for kings being sacrificed for the "sins" of the people. So, it would hardly be surprising if this

134 Henry, M., 3.1060.

expiatory sacrifice had occurred with any number of "Anointed" or *christed* individuals. Subsequently, in the Hellenistic world such bloody executions were transformed into symbolic initiation rites of spiritual rebirth. Hence, Paul could be referring not only to such actual past sacrifices of "Christs," but also to a mystery-school mystical and non-physical reproduction of such. He is therefore not referring to any "historical Jesus of Nazareth" at all.

Note that these Old Testament scriptures are, like Paul's summary thereof, in the past tense, indicating not a "prophecy" of someone who would be coming but of one who had already been, centuries before Christ's purported advent. It would seem that Paul is referring to the same *past* "Christ" of Isaiah 53. He is also obviously addressing individuals who were likewise familiar with Isaiah 53, not with a man from Galilee/Nazareth/Bethlehem who had suffered the "Man of Sorrows" treatment just a few decades earlier. This Pauline passage surely represents what is called "midrash," a figurative, narratized interpretation of Jewish scripture, not an account of a historical event.

In addition, even though the "Lord's Prayer" is clearly spelled out in the gospels as being given directly from Jesus's mouth, Paul confesses that he does not know how to pray (Rom. 8:26)! What, Jesus' own instruction was not good enough for him? Of course, he knew of nothing of the sort. Paul's Jesus is very different from that of the gospels. As Wells says:

> [These] epistles are not merely astoundingly silent about the historical Jesus, but also ... the Jesus of Paul's letters ... is in some respects incompatible with the Jesus of the gospels; [it is clear] that neither Paul, nor those of his Christian predecessors whose views he assimilates into his letters, nor the Christian teachers he attacks in them, are concerned with such a person.[135]

So it appears that Paul, even though he speaks of "the gospel"—from the Greek word εὐαγγέλιον or *evangelion*, which simply means "good news,"[136]—had never heard of the canonical gospels or even an orally transmitted life of Christ. The few "historical" references to an

135 Wells, *DJE*, 3.

136 The word εαγγλιον did not originate with the New Testament, of course, but can be found even in Homer's *Odyssey* (book 14, line 152, 166), dating to the ninth century BCE. In Homer, the word is translated as "news." (See, for example, Butler, S., 185.) The word "evangelion" is likewise used frequently in the Septuagint, as at at 2 Sam. 4:10, 18:19, 20, 22, 25, 27; 2 Kings 7:9. Regarding the word "euangelion," Dr. Stanley E. Porter states, "Initially the term referred to good news as 'glad tidings,' but in the second century it was used of a genre of literature."

actual life of Jesus cited in the epistles are demonstrably interpolations and forgeries, as are evidently the epistles themselves, not having been written by the Pharisee/Roman "Paul" at all, as evinced by Rev. Dr. Thomas K. Cheyne, et al., in the *Encyclopedia Biblica*:

> With respect to the canonical Pauline epistles, the later criticism here under consideration has learned to recognise that they are none of them by Paul: neither fourteen, nor thirteen, nor nine or ten, nor seven or eight, nor yet even the four so long "universally" regarded as unassailable. They are all, without distinction, pseudepigrapha [false writings].[137]

From this admission, Wheless concludes: "The entire 'Pauline group' … are thus all uninspired anonymous church forgeries for Christ's sweet sake!"[138]

Concerning forged Pauline epistles, Ehrman comments:

> There are thirteen letters in the New Testament that claim to be written by Paul, including two to the Thessalonians. In the Second Letter to the Thessalonians we find a most intriguing verse in which the author tells his readers that they are not to be led astray by a letter "as if by us" indicating that the "day of the Lord" is almost here (2:2). The author, in other words, knows of a letter in circulation claiming to be by Paul that is not really by Paul.
>
> But there is a terrifically interesting irony connected with this passage. Second Thessalonians, in which the passage appears, is itself widely thought among scholars not to be by Paul, even though it claims to be written by him.[139]

Regarding the canonical epistle to the Hebrews, Ehrman further remarks:

> The book of Hebrews was particularly debated [in antiquity]; the book does not explicitly claim to be written by Paul.… For centuries its Pauline authorship was a matter of dispute.[140]

Concerning two of the "Pastoral" epistles, Ehrman states, "Other Christian teachers disputed whether 1 and 2 Timothy were actually by Paul, some claiming that their contents showed that he did not write them."[141]

In "The Myth of the Historical Jesus," Hayyim ben Yehoshua evinces that the orthodox dates of the Pauline epistles (c. 49–70) cannot

---

137 *Encyc. Bib.*, 3.3625.
138 Wheless, *FC*, 231.
139 Ehrman (2011), 19.
140 Ehrman (2011), 22.
141 Ehrman (2011), 22.

be maintained, also introducing one of the most important individuals in the formation of Christianity, the Gnostic-Christian "heretic" Marcion of Pontus (c. 100–160), a well-educated "man of letters" who entered the brotherhood and basically took the reins of the fledgling Gnostic-Christian movement:

> We now turn to the epistles supposedly written by Paul. The *First Epistle of Paul to Timothy* warns against the Marcionist work known as the *Antithesis*. Marcion was expelled from the Church of Rome in c. 144 CE and the *First Epistle of Paul to Timothy* was written shortly afterwards. Thus we again have a clear case of pseudepigraphy. The *Second Epistle of Paul to Timothy* and the *Epistle of Paul to Titus* were written by the same author and date to about the same period. These three epistles are known as the "pastoral epistles." The ten remaining "non-pastoral" epistles written in the name of Paul, were known to Marcion by c. 140 CE Some of them were not written in Paul's name alone but are in the form of letters written by Paul in collaboration with various friends such as Sosthenes, Timothy and Silas.... The non-canonical *First Epistle of Clement to the Corinthians* (written c. 125 CE) uses the *First Epistle of Paul to the Corinthians* as a source and so we can narrow down the date for that epistle to c. 100–125 CE However, we are left with the conclusion that all the Pauline epistles are pseudepigraphic. (The semi-mythical Paul was supposed to have died during the persecutions instigated by Nero in c. 64 CE) Some of the Pauline epistles appear to have been altered and edited numerous times before reaching their modern forms.... We may thus conclude that they provide no historical evidence of Jesus.[142]

It is clear that the epistles do not demonstrate a historical Jesus and are not as early as they are pretended to be. Instead, they are the products of a number of hands over several decades during the second century, implying that the "historical" Jesus apparently was not known even at

142 The "Pauline" epistle 1Timothy 6:20 contains the Greek word ντιθσεις or "antithesis," which was the title of a Marcionite work. The pertinent passage with the word untranslated would read (my very literal translation): "avoiding the unholy empty-talk and antithesis of the falsely named Gnosis." The apparent clue has been disputed by suggesting that it was just a useful Greek word. However, the association of the antithesis with Gnosticism, along with the other proofs for a late date for this epistle, provides valid evidence that the author is indeed warning against Marcion's tract and/or movement. It is further important to note that no one before Irenaeus (c. 180) mentions this epistle.

that late point.[143] And, again, these texts were further mutilated over the centuries.

Regarding a non-Pauline canonical letter, the second Epistle of Peter, Classicist Rev. August Kampmeier (1856–1930) remarks:

> The second epistle of Peter in the New Testament pretends not only to have been written by Peter, the intimate disciple of Jesus, but it even says, referring to the story of the transfiguration of Jesus on the mount: "The voice: This is my beloved Son, in whom I am well pleased, we ourselves heard come out of heaven, when we were with him on the holy mount" (Chap. i. 18).
>
> It has long been known that this epistle is entirely spurious. Even in the fourth century it was believed by some to be spurious, and these doubts have again and again turned up, till now no unprejudiced Biblical scholar accepts it as authentic.[144]

Price also cites "the theory of Jerome D. Quinn that Luke wrote the Pastorals to follow Acts as volume 3 in a series."[145]

> Some scholars have argued that Luke wrote not only Acts but the Pastoral Epistles as well. There are striking similarities of ideas and vocabulary between Luke-Acts and the Pastorals beyond what one would expect even from books sharing the same milieu. Paul cannot have written them, as a surfeit of differences makes all too plain.[146]

In Price's review of William O. Walker's book, he says:

> Professor Walker devotes a chapter apiece to discussing the debates over and the case for seeing as interpolations 1 Corinthians 14:34–35 (silencing women);11:3–16 (the veiling of prophetesses); 2:6–16 (secret wisdom about the archons of this age and the deep things of God); 12:31b-14:1a (the "love chapter"); and Romans 1:18–2:29 (the sins of idolaters; the parity of righteous Jews and Gentiles). Then, more briefly, he presents the basics of the case for seeing another groups of texts as interpolations, skipping the refutations and counter-refutations: Romans 16:25–27 (the doxology); 2 Corinthians 6:14–7:1 (unequal yoking with unbelievers and Beliar); 1 Thessalonians 2:13–16 (God's judgment on persecuting Jews); Romans 13:1–7

143 For an in-depth analysis of the Pauline epistles vis-à-vis their lack of reference to a historical Jesus, see Earl Doherty's *The Jesus Puzzle* and *Jesus: Neither God Nor Man*.

144 Carus, 21.53.

145 Price, R. (2006), 490.

146 Price, R. (2006), 497.

(obey the authorities); 1 Corinthians 10:1–22 (idols are devils in disguise). And he says, in effect, that interpolations are like cockroaches: if you can spot some, there must be a lot more lurking somewhere. And he lists passages that have attracted scholarly stares of suspicion: 1 Corinthians 1:2; 4:17; 6:14; 7:29–31; 11:23–26; 15:3–11; 15:21–22; 15:31c; 15:44b-48; 15:56; Galatians 2:7–8; Philippians 1:1c; 2:6–7; 1 Thessalonians 4:1–8; 4:10b-12; 4:18; 5:1–11; 5:27. And of course J.C. O'Neill (whose views of Romans 1:18–2:29 he accepts) posited a number of other interpolations in Romans and Galatians.

The Gospels

Although they are held up by true believers to be the "inspired" works of the apostles, from the evidence or lack thereof, the canonical gospels appear to be forged at the end of the second century, all four of them probably between 170–180,[147] a date that just happens to correspond with the establishment of the orthodoxy and supremacy of the Roman Church. Despite the claims of apostolic authorship, the gospels were not mere translations of manuscripts written in Hebrew or Aramaic by Jewish apostles, because they were originally composed in Greek. As Waite relates:

> It is noticeable that in every place in the gospels but one (and the total number is nearly a hundred) where Peter is mentioned, the Greek name "Petros" is given, which is supposed to be used by Jews as well as others. This would indicate that all the canonical gospels, Matthew included, are original Greek productions.[148]

Of these Greek texts and their pretended apostolic attribution, Wells states:

> [A] Galilean fisherman could not have written what Kümmel calls such "cultivated Greek," with "many rhetorical devices," and with all the Old Testament quotations and allusions deriving from the Greek version of these scriptures, not from the Hebrew original.[149]

Furthermore, as the writer of Luke freely admits, there were numerous gospels in circulation prior to the composition of his gospel.[150] In fact, of the dozens of gospels that existed during the first centuries of the Christian era, several once considered canonical or genuine were

147 For more proofs concerning this late dating of the gospels, see my books *Suns of God*, 407–419, which includes a discussion of the order of the gospels, and *Who Was Jesus?*, 60–83.

148 Waite, 32.

149 Wells, *WWJ*, 198.

150 For more information see Murdock (2007).

later rejected as "apocryphal" or spurious, and vice versa.

Out of these numerous gospels the canonical texts were chosen by Church father and bishop of Lyons, Irenaeus (c. 120–c. 200), who claimed that the number four was based on the "four corners of the world."[151] It has been suggested that this comment is masonic and that these texts may represent the four books of magic of the "Egyptian Ritual,"[152] contentions that provide hints as to where our quest is heading.

The Canon Order

According to some early Christians, the Gospel of Matthew ranks as the earliest, which is why it appears first in the canon. However, as noted, the gospels have been arranged in virtually every order, and scholars of the past few centuries have considered Mark to be the earliest, used by the writers/compilers of Matthew and Luke. Going against this trend, Waite evinced that Luke was first, followed by Mark, John and Matthew. In fact, these gospels were written not from each other but from common source material, including the "narrative"— διήγησις or *Diegesis* in the original Greek (Luke 1:1). The first gospel of the "narrative" type appears to have been the proto-Lukan text, the "Gospel of the Lord," published in Rome by the Gnostic-Christian Marcion, as part of his "New Testament." As Waite relates:

> The first New Testament that ever appeared was compiled and published by Marcion. It was in the Greek language. It consisted of "The Gospel," and "The Apostolicon." No acts—no Revelation, and but one gospel. The Apostolicon comprised ten of Paul's Epistles, as follows: Galatians, 1st and 2nd Corinthians, Romans, except the 15th and 16th chapters, 1st and 2nd Thessalonians, Ephesians, Colossians, Philemon and Philippians; arranged in the order as here named. This canon of the New Testament was prepared and published shortly after his arrival in Rome; probably about 145 AD. Baring-Gould

151 *Adv. haer.* 3.11.8: "τεσσαρα κλιματα του κοσμου." (Irenaeus/Deane, 36) The Greek word "klimata" usually means "regions" or "districts," coming down to us as "climate." While a number of writers have rendered this phrase "four *corners*," the Greek word for "corners" is "goniais." However, it appears that this convention of describing the four "corner" or "regions" of the world interchangeably was used in antiquity as well, such as in Latin texts using the phrase *quattuor angulorum et cardinum mundi.* (Schneemelcher, 356) The word angulorum is plural for "angles" or "corners," while the word "cardinum" is plural for "regions" or "cardinal points." In any event, it seems clear that the four compass directions were meant. In antiquity until this day, these cardinal points have been very important in the placement of buildings, especially sacred sites, as part of masonry.

152 Massey, *HJMC*, 161.

> thinks he brought the gospel from Sinope.... [Marcion's] gospel resembles the Gospel of Luke, but is much shorter.[153]

It is interesting to note that the two missing chapters of Romans (15 and 16) imply a historicized Jesus, whereas the rest of the epistle does not. Furthermore, the gospel referred to by Paul in this epistle and others ("my gospel") has been termed the "Gospel of Paul," presumed lost but apparently in reality claimed by Marcion to be a book he found at Antioch, along with 10 "Pauline" epistles, and then edited, bringing it around 139–142 to Rome, where he translated it into both Greek and Latin.

The Gospel of the Lord (c. 145 AD/CE)

Originally in Syrian Aramaic or Samaritan Hebrew,[154] so goes the argument, Marcion's Gospel of the Lord, which predated the canonical gospels by decades, represents the basic gospel narrative, minus key elements that foster the Jesus-historicizing agenda. Although much the same as the later Gospel of Luke, Marcion's gospel was Gnostic, non-historical, and did not make Jesus a Jewish man. This Jesus was not born in Bethlehem and did not grow up in Nazareth, which evidently did not exist as a populated town at the time.[155] In Marcion's gospel there is no childhood history, as Marcion's Jesus was not born but "came down at Capernaum[156]" (i.e., appeared out of thin air) in "the fifteenth year of the reign of Tiberius Caesar" (27–8 AD/CE), the very sentence used in Luke to "prove" Jesus's historicity. This term "came down" or "descended"[157] was interpreted in antiquity to mean that "Jesus descended in a celestial adult body directly from heaven,"[158] a non-historical, Gnostic belief. Concerning Marcion's Docetic doctrine, in *Marcion and Luke-Acts*, Dr. Joseph B. Tyson, Emeritus Professor of Religious Studies at Southern Methodist University, comments:

> Roukema cites a seventh-century Syriac manuscript that appears to quote Marcion as saying, "Our Lord was not born from a woman,

153 Waite, 274–5.

154 "[This] language is sometimes called Chaldee, sometimes Syriac, sometimes Syro-Chaldaic; but most commonly by the writers of the New Testament, and the first Christians, Hebrew ... it was the language of Syria and Mesopotamia, and of Jerusalem and Galilee in our Savior's time.... Syriac and Chaldee are by the prophet Daniel synonymous languages" (Jones, J., 294).

155 See Acharya, *SOG*, 436–7. See also Zindler, Salm.

156 Capernaum is brought up because it supposedly "fulfills prophecy" (Isaiah 9:1-2)

157 Strong's (G2718) defines as: "1) to come down, go down; a) of one who goes from a higher to a lower locality; b) of those who come to a place by a ship."

158 Price, R. (2006), 268.

but stole the domain of the Creator and came down and appeared for the first time between Jerusalem and Jericho, like a human being in form and image and likeness, but without our body."[159]

Marcion's original, non-historicizing and non-Judaizing New Testament was apparently a thorn in the side of the "carnalizing conspirators," who were thus compelled to put a spin on the facts by claiming that the "heretic" had expurgated the Gospel of Luke, removing the genealogies and other "historical" and "biographical" details. But it was not Marcion who had mutilated the texts but the historicizers who added to his.[160]

In the practice of forgery or mutilating and editing earlier works, the tendency is for accretion and interpolation, rather than excision and reduction of text. This fact provides further reason to suggest that Marcion's gospel was earlier than Luke's.

The Gospel of Luke (170 AD/CE)

Irenaeus is the first person to name Luke as the author of the gospel attributed to him.

Charles H. Talbert (*Luke and the Gnostics*), though again without actually holding to a second-century date, showed that Luke shared the agenda and views of the second-century apologists Irenaeus, Justin Martyr and Tertullian.[161]

Luke has simply collected these various second-century Christian mores and retrojected them into the golden age of the apostles to give them added weight.[162]

Tertullian fought against the Gnostic idea of a spiritually resurrected Christ. Is it any accident that Luke has the same concern, as opposed to the presumably earlier view of 1 Corinthians 15:49–50 and 1 Peter 3:18?[163]

[There] is no better candidate than Polycarp as redactor of Ur-Lukas and author of Acts. It would certainly fit our information that Polycarp had publicly denounced Marcion as the first-born of Satan. He was someone with opportunity and motive to undo Marcion's work by co-opting his scriptures for the benefit of Catholicism. With the identification of Polycarp as our pseudonymous author, we receive another bonus in the possible identification of the

159 Tyson, 156.
160 For more information on Marcion, see Acharya, *Suns of God*, 425, etc.
161 Price, R. (2006), 489.
162 Price, R. (2006), 490.
163 Price, R. (2006), 490.

hitherto-mysterious Theophilus. Huller, following Alvin Boyd-Kuhn, plausibly suggests Theophilus of Antioch, a contemporary of Polycarp, as the recipient of the work.[164]

While it is currently dated by the mainstream to around 50 to 100 AD/CE, the Gospel of Luke is acknowledged by early Church fathers to be of a late date. As Waite states:

> Jerome admits that not only the Gospel of Basilides, composed about AD 125, and other gospels, admitted to have been first published in the second century, were written before that of Luke, but even the Gospel of Apelles also, which was written not earlier than AD 160.[165]

Concerning the date of Luke, Price remarks:

> The first time Luke's gospel is mentioned in the historical record is about 180 AD/CE, when Irenaeus listed it among four gospels he was willing to accept. Justin may have referred to Acts in about 150 CE, but the reference is too vague to be certain.[166]

He further states:

> Most scholars today posit a date for Luke of between 80–90 CE, but this is simply an attempt to push it back in time as far as possible while admitting that neither Mark nor Luke was written before the death of Paul in 62 CE or the fall of Jerusalem in 70 CE—and this in order to keep within the lifetime of a companion of Paul, which is who tradition says Luke was.
>
> The Tübingen critics (F.C. Baur, Franz Overbeck, Edward Zeller) dated Luke-Acts to the second century. More recently, Walter Schmithals, Helmut Koester and John C. O'Neill have maintained that second-century date.[167]

Citing several reasons the Gospel of Luke must have been written during the latter half of the second century, including anachronisms and doctrines that were clearly developing only at that time, Price offers the evidence that Luke was based on an "Ur-Lukas," which in fact was Marcion's Gospel of the Lord. This theory explains the differences and similarities between Luke and Acts, as well as the Pastoral Epistles (Titus and 1 and 2 Timothy), as it posits that the writer of Acts and the Pastorals was the redactor of Marcion's text. On stylistic grounds, this research demonstrates that the author of this "trilogy" of Luke,

---

164 Price, R. (2006), 498.

165 Waite, 80. See Murdock, *WWJ* (74–76), for the original texts of Jerome, Origen and Epiphanius identifying various second-century non-canonical and Gnostic texts as the "many narratives" that preceded Luke.

166 Price, R. (2006), 481.

167 Price, R. (2006), 483.

Acts and the Pastorals was possibly the early Church father Polycarp (69–155). Polycarp was not only hostile to Marcion, demonstrating his familiarity with the supposed "heretic," but he was also a contemporary of Theophilus.

The *terminus a quo* for Luke would be around 150, while the *teriminus a quem* would be 170, when first the text enters into the literary record. One wonders, of course, why there was a 15–year gap between its latest possible composition and its emergence into the historical record.

Confirming this association between Luke and Theophilus of Antioch, the *Catholic Encyclopedia* relates that fourth-century Antioch contained a "basilica called 'the ancient' and 'apostolic.'" This building, says *CE*, "was probably one of the oldest architectural monuments of Christianity; ancient tradition maintained that it was originally the house of Theophilus, the friend of St. Luke."[168] *The Catholic Encyclopedia* comments, "Theophilus ... wrote in the latter part of the second century an elaborate defense and explanation of the Christian religion."[169] Might this project have been prompted by its author's reception of Luke's gospel?

Like the rest of the gospels Luke fits into the time frame between 150–180. In this case, it would seem that Polycarp wrote Luke-Acts in order to fortify Theophilus's faith, and that the latter preserved and cherished it until his elevation to the office of bishop, at which time he released it to the public. In this regard, it is interesting to note that Theophilus also wrote a polemic against Marcion.

The identity of Luke-Act's Theophilus has been puzzling for those attempting to place the emergence of these texts before the end of the first century, since there is only one "Theophilus" in the historical record up to that point, the Jewish high priest briefly mentioned in Josephus (*Ant.*, 18.5.3; 19.6.2; Whiston, 382, 410). Recent attempts to identify this high priest as Luke's Theophilus also speculatively identify the "Johanna" in Luke (8:3, 24:10) as the granddaughter of the Jewish priest. It seems inconceivable, however, that in mentioning Theophilus, Josephus would not have mentioned what must have been a highly prominent conversion to Christianity.

Moreover, when Acts 4:6 discusses various other high priests, including Annas, cited by Josephus as being the priest Theophilus's father, as well as other family members, he does so in a manner implying that his reader—Theophilus—does not already know who they are. Furthermore, if the Jewish high priest Theophilus had been a very early

168 Herbermann, 1.568.
169 Herbermann, 1.568.

convert, one would think that Christians would have trumpeted that fact loudly at every opportunity. Such is not the case, however. No wonder few scholars have accepted this attempt to combine the two men named Theophilus.

But one might object, if we have eliminated one man named Theophilus as the man mentioned in Like and Acts, there must be a great number who shared the name to whom Luke wrote. But how many of them would have merited the honorific epithet *kratistos*, meaning "mightiest, strongest, noblest, most illustrious, best, most excellent" and used to address "men of prominent rank or office" (Strong's G2903)? Surely it best fits a person of high position, such as a priest or bishop.

Theophilus of Antioch (fl.c. 169–c. 183)

There is good reason to believe that Luke is addressing this Theophilus and that the bishop was possibly the very first person to comment on the canonical gospels, which by his time had supposedly been in circulation for several decades but nary a trace of which can be found before then. In the "Introductory Note" to an authoritative translation of *Ad Autolycum*, Rev. Marcus Dods remarks of Theophilus:

> He was one of the earliest commentators upon the Gospels, if not the first; and he seems to have been the earliest Christian historian of the Church of the Old Testament.[170]

Dods names Theophilus as the "founder of the science of Biblical Chronology among Christians," so one must ask why this important Church father has been largely forgotten or ignored?

Also, Theophilus himself says he converted to Christianity through reading the *Jewish* scriptures—if he were aware of the canonical gospels, which are surely the most effective proselytizing tools, why would he need to rely on the Old Testament scriptures?

As concerns Bishop Theophilus's three-part work *Apology to Autolycus*, Dr. Michael E. Hardwick remarks that "the main use of *Apology to Autolycus* was in the anti-Marcionite struggle."[171] One of the chapters (12) in book 1 of *Autolycus* is called "The meaning of the word 'Christian.'" It seems odd that someone would need to define the word "Christian" some 150 years after Christ purportedly died. Is it just a coincidence that Luke-Acts does not show up in the historical record until the last quarter of the second century, that Acts 11:26 explains that Jesus's followers were first called "Christians" at Antioch, where Theophilus served as the bishop, and that Theophilus's *Autolycus*

170 Roberts, A., 2.87.

171 Hardwick (1989), 7.

includes a chapter defining the word "Christian," as if it were novel to his readers? It would make sense if the author of the gospel sent that work to Theophilus first and the Book of Acts only subsequently, and that in the latter (11:26) he is actually referring to Theophilus's dubbing Jesus-believers "Christians" in the period between writing the two books. Nothing says Acts had to be an immediate second chapter instead of a subsequent sequel.

In the same chapter (12) Theophilus accuses his unbelieving adversary Autolycus of ridiculing and calling him "Christian," as if the label were a bad thing. The bishop defines the word by saying "that which is anointed is sweet and serviceable, and far from contemptible."[172] He is writing in Greek, in which the word "*christos*" means "anointed," but he is also playing on the word "*chrestos*," meaning "useful" or "serviceable."[173] Is it possible that to that point "Christians" were actually called "Chrestiani?"[174] Even the ridicule itself may be indicative of the newness of the name at that time. Neither the word "Christian" nor "Christians" is used anywhere else in the New Testament, except Acts 11:26, 26:28 and 1 Peter 4:16, two texts that do not show up clearly in the historical record until the latter half of the *second* century.

The Gospel of Luke is a compilation of dozens of older manuscripts, 33 by Friedrich Schleiermacher's count,[175] including the Marcionite Gospel of the Lord. This thesis holds that, using Marcion's gospel, the Lukan writer(s) interpolated and removed textual matter in order both to historicize the story and to Judaize Marcion's Jesus. In addition to lacking the genealogy and childhood found in the first two chapters of canonical Luke, Marcion also was missing nearly all of the third chapter,

---

172 Roberts, A., *ANF*, 2.92.

173 When referring to this chapter in Theophilus (1.12), Sir James Donaldson says: "The argumentation of this chapter depends on the literal meaning which Theophilus attaches to Christos, the Anointed One; and he plays on this meaning, and also on the similarity of pronunciation between χρηστς, 'useful,' and χριστς , 'anointed.'" (Roberts, *ANF*, 2.92)

174 For further discussion, see Acharya, *Suns of God*, 394, etc.

175 As I related in *Who Was Jesus?* (73), Waite notes that the German critic Schleiermacher determined Luke's gospel to have been compiled from 33 different manuscripts, showing the divisions upon which these texts are delineated (Waite, 379–380). Of the German scholar's book *A Critical Essay on the Gospel of St. Luke*, Waite (151) relates: "Dr. Frederick Schleiermacher, who is styled, in the Imperial Dictionary of Biography, 'the most influential theologian of Protestant Germany that has appeared during the present century,' in an able essay, has shown that the Gospel of Luke consists, almost entirely, of a compilation of manuscripts, older than the time of the compiler."

save the bit about Capernaum, all of which were interpolated into Luke to give Jesus a historical background and Jewish heritage. Also, where Marcion's gospel speaks of Jesus coming to Nazareth, Luke adds, "where he had been brought up," a phrase missing from Marcion that is a further attempt to make Jesus Jewish.

Another example of the historicizing and Judaizing interpolations into Marcion's gospel is the portrayal of Christ's passion, which is represented in Marcion thus:

Saying, the Son of Man must suffer many things, and be put to death, and after three days rise again.[176]

At Luke 9:22, the passage is rendered thus:

Saying, "The Son of man must suffer many things, *and be rejected by the elders and the chief priests and scribes*, and be killed, and on the third day be raised."

The inclusion of "elders and the chief priests and scribes" apparently represents an attempt to make the story seem as if it happened one time in history at a certain place, as opposed to the recurring theme in a savior-god cult and mystery school indicated by Marcion.

Of this Lukan creation, Massey says:

> It can be proved how passage after passage has been added to the earlier gospel, in the course of manufacturing the later history. For example, the mourning over Jerusalem (Luke xiii. 29–35) is taken verbatim from the 2nd Esdras (i. 28–33) without acknowledgement, and the words previously uttered by the "Almighty Lord" are here assigned to Jesus as the original speaker.[177]

The specific verses within these "mourning" passages that correspond to one another are 2 Esdras 1:30, 32 and Luke 13:34. Although these passages may not have been "verbatim" in the original languages—2 Esdras was composed in Hebrew and translated into Latin, while Luke was written in Greek—they are close enough in concept, and the fact that the words of God in Esdras are transferred into the mouth of Jesus in Luke is likewise significant. There is no evidence that 2 Esdras (also called 4 Ezra) Ezra relied upon Luke, and since the text is dated by most mainstream authorities to the end of the first century, Luke, apparently using this text or a common source, could not have been composed until after that time.

Regarding Luke, Schleiermacher states: "He is from beginning to end no more than the compiler and arranger of documents which he found in existence."

---

176 Waite, 294.

177 Massey, *GHC*, 19.

Regarding Marcion and Luke, Rev. Dr. Sabine Baring-Gould states:

> The Gospel he had he regarded with supreme awe; it was because his Gospel was so ancient, so hallowed by use through many years that it was invested by him with sovereign authority.
>
> The Gospel of our Lord, if not the original Luke Gospel—and this is probable—was the basis of Luke's compilation.
>
> The Gospel of our Lord contains nothing which is not found in that of St. Luke. The arrangement is so similar that we are forced to the conclusion that it was either used by St. Luke, or that it was his original composition.
>
> All these facts point to Marcion's Gospel as the original of St. Luke.[178]

It is impossible to believe that, if Baring-Gould's assessment is correct, Marcion would have mutilated a text he clearly held in high regard. Indeed, the evidence points in the opposite direction, that Marcion's gospel was mutated into the current "Luke," as well as, apparently, serving as the "Ur-Markus" used to compose the canonical gospel of Mark.

After discussing a possible root text for Luke, an "Ur-Lukas" that performed the same function as its more famous cousin "Ur-Markus," Price mentions research demonstrating the possibility of authorship by the early Church father Polycarp (69–155 AD/CE).[179]

One more note about Lukan sources: it has been contended more or less widely for centuries that the author of Luke-Acts utilized the works of Josephus to pad out the "history" in his gospel. The following pericopes look like borrowings from Josephus:

- The census under Quirinius/Cyrenius (Luke 2:1–2)
- The three Jewish rebel leaders (Acts 5:36–37; 21:38)
- The death of Herod Agrippa (Acts 12:20–23)
- Various aspects of Felix's life (Acts chapter 24)
- The tetrarch Lysanias (Luke 3:1)
- The "parable of the hated king" (Luke 19:11–12, 14, 27)
- The famine during the reign of Claudius (Acts 11:27–28)
- Pilate's aggressions (Luke 13:1–2)[180]

The Gospel of Mark (175 CE)

It is clear that the Gospel of Luke does not represent the faithful representations of eyewitnesses to the events it depicts. Were any of the

178 Baring-Gould, 275–6.

179 Price, R., (2006), 498.

180 Carrier, "Luke and Josephus."

other canonical gospels written by anyone close in time to the alleged advent of Christ? Mark's gospel is often portrayed as being the earliest; yet it, too, does not represent an eyewitness record, whether of Mark or of Peter, who tradition claims was Mark's mentor in detailing the gospel story. Ehrman comments:

> As for Mark, there is nothing about our Mark that would make you think it was Peter's version of the story.... In fact, there is nothing to suggest that Mark was based on the teachings of any one person at all, let alone Peter. Instead, it derives from the oral traditions about Jesus that 'Mark' had heard after they had been in circulation for some decades.[181]

So who really did write Mark, and when? Price opines:

> Like the other gospels, Mark seems to come from the mid-second century CE. Probably the crucial piece of evidence for dating the book is the Olivet Discourse, or the Little Apocalypse as Timothee Colani dubbed it, constituting chapter 13 of the gospel. It appears to have been an independent apocalyptic pamphlet circulating on the eve of the Roman destruction of Jerusalem and its temple. Mark picked it up and made it part of his text; but which destruction and which temple were portrayed? As Hermann Detering has shown, the warnings of dangers and dooms outlined in the text fit better the destruction of city and temple during the Roman campaign against the messianic King Simon bar-Kochba in CE 136 than in CE 70 as is usually assumed. This means that Mark has absorbed an earlier document that already stemmed from the first third of the second century CE.[182]

Thus, the suggestion arises that the Gospel of Mark must have been composed after the destruction of 135 AD/CE. In supporting this late dating of the canonical gospels, Price cites various anachronisms within Mark, such as "the depiction of synagogues scattered throughout Galilee when in fact they seem to have been largely confined to Judea before 70 CE."[183]

Dr. Price further makes the startling but logical connection between the "heretic" Marcion and the evangelist Mark. In his association of Marcion with Mark, Price comments:

> We may also note the clear Marcionite tendency of the gospel, with its unremittingly scathing portrayal of the disciples of Jesus as utter failures to carry on the Christian legacy. Indeed,

181 Ehrman (2011), 227.
182 Price, R., (2006), 69.
183 Price, R. (2006), 69–70.

it is not unlikely the subsequent choice of the ascription "Mark" reflects the name of Marcion, the early-to-mid second century champion of Paulinism.[184]

It is interesting that the Greek original for "Mark" is "Markos. In Latin it is "Marcus," the latter being the name of "three leading Gnostics," one of whom is depicted by Church father Adamantius (fourth cent.) as a defender of Marcionism. Moreover, in his *Dialogue* Adamantius concurred with the assertion of early Church father and bishop Papias (fl. c. 130 AD/CE) that the evangelist Mark had never heard or been a follower of Christ.[185]

After discussing the connection and confusion between the New Testament characters Simon Peter and Simon Magus, Price clarifies this suggestion of a Marcionite derivation for the Gospel of Mark:

> This need not mean that Marcion the Paulinist was himself the author of the present gospel, but it very likely does preserve the memory of the Marcionite/Gnostic milieu in which it was written. A better candidate for authorship would be Basilides, a Gnostic who claimed to be the disciple of Glaukias, interpreter of Simon Peter, unless this too was a confusion with Simon Magus/Paul.[186]

This theory of Mark being a product of the early Gnostic Basilides (fl. c. 120–140 AD/CE), rather than of Marcion himself, may explain why Marcion's Gospel of the Lord differs from that of Mark, possessing more of a connection to the gospel of Luke.

There are several reasons to suggest that the original Mark—Ur-Markus—was composed at Alexandria.[187] After the final destruction of Jerusalem and Judea by the Romans in 135, the Jerusalem church was taken over by non-Jews. Of this destruction and appropriation, Eusebius says:

> When in this way the city was closed to the Jewish race and suffered the total destruction of its former inhabitants, it was colonized by an alien race, and the Roman city which subsequently arose changed its name, so that now, in honour of the emperor then reigning, Aelius Hadrianus, it is known as Aelia. Furthermore, as the church in the city was now composed of Gentiles, the first after the bishops of the Circumcision to be put in charge of the Christians there was Mark.[188]

184 Price, R. (2006), 70.
185 Catholic Encyclopedia, "St. Mark"
186 Price, R. (2006), 70.
187 Price, R. (2006), 71.
188 Eusebius, 108.

This devastation and changeover occurred in the eighteenth year of Hadrian's rule (i.e., 135 CE); thus, we see that *this* Mark of whom Eusebius speaks could not have been the biblical character Mark. The date is, however, perfect for the Gnostic *Marcion*. Validating this notion of Marcion and Mark being confused, in *Dialogue with Trypho* (35.6), Justin Martyr calls Marcion's followers Μαρκιάνοι or "*Markianoi*."[189] Eusebius provides confirmation of this association of Mark with Marcion when he immediately follows his comment about Mark with a discussion of "Leaders at that time of *Knowledge* falsely so called" (i.e., Gnostics and *Gnosis*). Indeed, legend held that Mark wrote his gospel in Rome and brought it to Alexandria, where he established churches, while Marcion purportedly published his gospel in Rome and no doubt went to Alexandria at some point.

Like Waite, Mead also does not put Mark first: "It is very evident that Mt. and Lk. do not use *our* Mk., though they use most the material contained in our Mk."[190] In fact, all three canonical gospels apparently used Marcion—or, "Ur-Markus"—as one of their sources.

Like Marcion, Mark has no genealogy; unlike Marcion, he begins his story with John the Baptist, the hero of the Nazarenes/Mandaeans, added to incorporate that faction. The Gospel of Mark was admittedly tampered with, as the Revised Standard Version (RSV) of the New Testament notes at several verses (16:9–20) regarding the resurrected apparition and ascension added to the end. Here we have absolute proof of the gospels being changed to fit the circumstances, rather than recording history.

In discussing these interpolations in Mark and other texts, Ehrman pulls no punches in accusing "pseudepigraphical" forgers of plagiarism and deception in certain instances.

> A scribe who wanted a text to say something other than what it did may well have changed the text for just that reason. In some cases it is hard to imagine how else the resultant deception could have come about. Whoever added the final twelve verses of Mark did not do so by a mere slip of the pen.[191]

Mark also provides an example of how interpolation was used to set the story in a particular place:

> For instance, Mk. 1:16 reads: "And passing along by the sea of Galilee he saw Simon and Andrew." ... Almost all commentators agree that the words "by the sea of Galilee" were

189 Justin/Falls, 55.

190 Mead, *GRS*, 128.

191 Ehrman (2011), 250.

> added by Mark. They are placed quite ungrammatically in the Greek syntax.... Mark, then, has interpolated a reference to *place* into a report which lacked it.[192]

As to the authorship of Mark, ben Yehoshua avers that "the style of language used in *Mark* shows that it was written (probably in Rome) by a Roman convert to Christianity whose first language was Latin and not Greek, Hebrew or Aramaic." It would seem, possibly, that the compiler of Mark used the Latin version of Marcion's gospel, while Luke and Matthew used the Greek version, accounting for the variances between them. Indeed, the author of Mark was clearly not a Palestinian Jew, as Wells points out: Mark "betrays in 7:31 an ignorance of Palestinian geography."[193] The reason for geographical, topographical and anachronistic errors in the canonical gospels is that they were composed not by those who were actually familiar with the area and time in which the story was placed, but by writers who used the Greek *Septuagint* as the basis for their fictional accounts.

The Gospel of John (178 AD/CE)

The Gospel of John is thought by most authorities to be the latest of the four, but Waite provides a compelling argument to place it third and reveals its purpose not only as refuting the Gnostics but also as establishing the primacy of the Roman Church:

> So strong is the evidence of a late date to this gospel, that its apostolic origin is being abandoned by the ablest evangelical writers.... Both Irenaeus and Jerome assert that John wrote against Cerinthus. Cerinthus thus flourished about AD 145. [T]here is evidence that in the construction of this gospel, as in that of Matthew, the author had in view the building up of the Roman hierarchy, the foundations of which were then (about AD 177–89) being laid.... There is a reason to believe that both [John and Matthew] were written in the interest of the supremacy of the Church of Rome.[194]

Concerning John's gospel, Price writes, "As for the vexing question of gospel authorship, we may immediately dismiss the claim that it was

192 Wells, *DJE*, 71.

193 Wells, *DJE*, 78. This scripture reads: "Then he returned from the region of Tyre, and went through Sidon to the Sea of Galilee, through the region of the Decapolis."

194 Waite, 400–1. In *De Viris Illustribus* (ch. 9), Jerome remarks: "John, the apostle whom Jesus most loved, the son of Zebedee and brother of James, the apostle whom Herod, after our Lord's passion, beheaded, most recently of all the evangelists wrote a Gospel, at the request of the bishops of Asia, against Cerinthus and other heretics and especially against the then growing dogma of the Ebionites, who assert that Christ did not exist before Mary."

one of the twelve disciples of Jesus."[195]

That the Gospel of John served as a refutation of the Gnostics, or an attempt to usurp their authority and to bring them into the "fold," is obvious from its Gnostic style. It has been suggested that the author of John used the gospel of the Gnostic-Christian writer Cerinthus (c. 145?) to refute the "heresiarch."[196] As Waite relates:

> The history as well as the writings of Cerinthus are strangely blended with those of John the presbyter, and even with John the apostle.... A sect called the Alogi attributed to him [Cerinthus] (so says Epiphanius), the gospel, as well as the other writings of John.[197]

The tone of this gospel is anti-Jewish, revealing that it was written/compiled by a non-Jew or possibly an "exiled" Israelite of a different tribe, such as a Samaritan, who not only spoke of "the Jews" as separate and apart from himself but also was not familiar with the geography of Palestine. As Waite also says:

> There are also many errors in reference to the geography of the country. The author speaks of Aenon, near to Salim, in Judea; also of Bethany, beyond Jordan, and of a "city of Samaria, called Sychar." If there were any such places, they were strangely unknown to other writers. The learned Dr. Bretschneider points out such mistakes and errors of geography, chronology, history and statistics of Judea, as no person who had ever resided in that country, or had been by birth a Jew, could possibly have committed.[198]

In addition, as Keeler states:

> The Gospel of John says that Bethsaida was in Galilee. There is no such town in that district, and there never was. Bethsaida was on the east side of the sea of Tiberias, whereas Galilee was on the west side. St. John was born at Bethsaida, and the probability is that he would know the geographical location of his own birthplace.[199]

---

195 Price, R. (2006), 667.

196 Waite, 265. The contention by some that Cerinthus lived around 100 AD/CE is apparently based on the received Christian history, which states that the Gnostic "heretic" knew the evangelist John. However, there is no solid evidence that Cerinthus thrived at that time, and it appears that his period is decades later, lending credence to a late dating of John.

197 Waite, 265.

198 Waite, 397–8.

199 Keeler, 16. See also "Bethsaida" in *The International Standard Bible Encyclopedia* (*ISBE*): "As is the case with the other Bethsaida [a city east of the Jordan], no name has been recovered to guide us to the site..." (Orr, 451ff) The *ISBE* jumps through formidable hoops in attempting to explain away this apparent geographical error, which should not have been an

Furthermore, the writer of John relates several events at which the apostle John was not depicted as having appeared and does not record others at which he is said to have been present. Moreover, John is the only gospel containing the story of the raising of Lazarus from the dead, which is likely a version of an Egyptian myth.[200] Indeed, John's gospel seems to have an Egyptian provenance and to have been written for an Egyptian audience, likely at Alexandria.[201]

The earliest extant fragments of a New Testament text are some fragments of papyrus that appear to be from the Gospel of John, called P52. These have been dated conservatively from the first quarter to the end of the second century. Of these fragments, Dr. Philip W. Comfort remarks, "Though the amount of the text in P52 is hardly enough to make a positive judgment about its textual character, the text seems to be Alexandrian."[202]

P52 has been dated on paleographic grounds; however, paleography is not always entirely reliable. Commenting on the efforts of earlier scholars to date these fragments, Early Christian historian Dr. Brent Nongbri remarks:

> What emerges from this survey is nothing surprising to papyrologists: paleography is not the most effective method for dating texts, particularly those written in a literary hand. [C.H.] Roberts himself noted this point in his edition of P52. The real problem is the way scholars of the New Testament have used and abused papyrological evidence. I have not radically revised Roberts's work. I have not provided any third-century documentary papyri that are absolute "dead ringers" for the handwriting of P52, and even had I done so, that would not force us to date P52 at some exact point in the third century. Paleographic evidence does not work that way. What I have done is to show that *any serious consideration of the window of possible dates for P52 must include dates in the later second and early third centuries*. Thus, P52 cannot be used as evidence to silence other debates about the existence (or non-existence) of the Gospel of John in the first half of the second century. Only a papyrus containing an explicit date or one found in a clear archaeological stratigraphic context could do the work scholars

---

issue if the gospel of John were truly inspired and essentially written infallibly by God—a contention battled against even by various early Church fathers; hence, Irenaeus's long defense of the book.

200 See Murdock, *CIE*, 488–494, etc.

201 For more on this subject, see Murdock (2009).

202 Barret, 69.

want P52 to do. As it stands now, the papyrological evidence should take a second place to other forms of evidence in addressing debates about the dating of the Fourth Gospel.[203]

The Gospel of Matthew (173? 180? AD/CE)

Robert Price rejects the tradition of the apostolic authorship of the Gospel of Matthew:

> The mid-second century bishop Papias, together with some other not particularly credible sources, informs us that the apostle Matthew compiled the sayings of the Lord in Hebrew, possibly meaning the sister language Aramaic, and other unnamed persons translated the work with varying degrees of success. Many have supposed Papias to be talking about our Gospel according to Matthew, but there is no solid reason for thinking so.[204]
>
> [There] are two factors making it impossible for the apostle Matthew to have penned our gospel. First, we can scarcely imagine that an eyewitness of the historical Jesus, present to hear both his master's public proclamations and informal table talk, would have ignored his own fund of memories in favor of a third-hand account like Mark's. Matthew's gospel is essentially no more than a new and revised edition of Mark. Second, there is the matter of the Matthean character called "Matthew the tax collector" (Matt. 9:9; 10:3). This fellow is a combination of two distinct Markan characters: Levi the tax-collector (Mark 2:14) and Matthew the disciple (Mark 3:18).[205]

Price contends that Matthew was clearly composed or, rather, significantly redacted, from Ur-Markus, at Antioch.[206] His influences include not only Mark but also the Hebrew Tanakh/Old Testament, the Syriac Bible, the Septuagint and the translation of Theodotion.[207]

Although later Christian writers claimed it was a "translation" of a manuscript written in Hebrew by the apostle Matthew, the canonical Gospel of Matthew as we have it was originally written in Greek and evidently did not exist prior to the end of the second century. As Waite says:

> The Greek Gospel of Matthew was a subsequent production, and either originally appeared in the Greek language, or was a

203 Nongbri, Brent. "The Use and Abuse of P52: Papyrological Pitfalls in the Dating of the Fourth Gospel." *Harvard Theological Review* , 98:23–52; 2005. (Emph. added.)

204 Price, R. (2006), 113.

205 Price, R. (2006), 114.

206 Price, R. (2006), 116.

207 Price, R. (2006), 116.

translation of the Gospel of the Hebrews, with extensive changes and additions. There is reason to believe it to have been an original compilation, based upon the Oracles of Christ, but containing, in whole, or in part, a number of other manuscripts.[208]

Scholars usually date Matthew around 80–90 AD/CE in order to push it back as close as possible to the ostensible time of the historical Jesus, similarly pegging Mark at about 70 CE. That is, however, entirely too early for Mark as we have seen, and thus too early for Matthew as well.[209]

If Mark's gospel is already beset with such anachronisms as synagogues in the wrong locations and holy men being called "rabbi," Matthew mentions the Seat of Moses (21:2), a chair set aside in every synagogue for the presiding elder. Unfortunately, this was a second-century phenomenon. Everything considered, it seems that Matthew should be dated about as late as we can possibly date it. Irenaeus's list of four canonical gospels in 180 CE gives us an upper limit. But if, as some have suggested, Irenaeus's *Against Heresies* was pseudepigraphical, like the various pseudo-Justin and pseudo-Tertullian writings, then the sky is the limit. As Walter Schmithals has suggested, the gospels appear to have been all but non-existent for about 200 years. They are nowhere quoted or cited verbatim till very late in the second century.[210]

Providing potential evidence that Matthew is somewhat earlier than the 180 date, which is asserted by Waite, Keeler and others, Harvard theologian Rev. Dr. John White Chadwick (1840–1904) contended that the existence of Matthew is not clearly described in the historical record until 173, when the Bishop of Hierapolis, Apollinaris, first ascribed it to Matthew.[211]

The Gospel of Matthew is particularly noteworthy in that it contains the interpolation at 16:17–19 (not found in either Mark or Luke) that gives authority to the Roman Church: To wit, the statement by Jesus that Peter is the rock upon which the church is to be built and the keeper of the keys to the kingdom of heaven. The appearance of this gospel determining Roman dominance corresponds to the violent schism of 180–190 between the branches of the Church over the celebration of Easter, the "Easter Controversy" under Bishop and then Pope Victor of

208 Waite, 75.

209 Price, R. (2006), 115.

210 Price, R. (2006), 115.

211 Chadwick, J.W., 273.

Rome.[212]

It seems clear that the canonical gospels are of a late date, forged long after the alleged time of their purported authors. Such they appear to be, and, as Doane says, "In these four spurious Gospels ... we have the only history of Jesus of Nazareth."[213]

The Narrative

Despite all, some believers will continue to claim the gospels are inspired by the omnipotent God and represent an inerrant representation of the life of "the Lord." Far from being "inerrant," these spurious gospels contradict each other in numerous places.[214] As noted by Dr. Otto M. Schmiedel, considered one of the greatest authorities on the life of Jesus: "If John has the genuine tradition of the life of Jesus, then that of the Synoptics is untenable; if the Synoptics are right, then the fourth Evangelist is rejected as a source."[215]

Wheless says:

> The so-called "canonical" books of the New Testament, as of the Old, are a mass of contradictions and confusions of text, to the present estimate of 150,000 and more "variant readings," as is well known and admitted.[216]

In regard to these "variant readings," Waite states:

> Of the 150,000 variant readings which Griesbach found in the manuscripts of the New Testament, probably 149,500 were *additions and interpolations*.[217]

In this mess, the gospels' pretended authors, including two apostles, give conflicting histories and genealogies. The birth of Jesus is depicted as having occurred at different times, in Matthew about two years *before* and in Luke more than nine years *after* Herod's death (4 BCE). Jesus's birth and childhood are not mentioned in Mark, and although Jesus is said in Matthew and Luke to have been "born of a virgin," his lineage is also traced through Joseph to the house of David, so that he may "fulfill prophecy." Furthermore, the genealogies presented in Luke and Matthew are irreconcilable. Wheless says, "Both genealogies are false

212 See Eusebius, *Hist. Eccl.*, 5.23; Herbermann, 5.228.

213 Doane, 459.

214 See Murdock, *Who Was Jesus?*, 148–154.

215 My translation of Schmiedel's original German, which reads: "Wenn Johannes die ächte Ueberlieferung über das Leben Jesu hat, dann ist die der Synoptiker unhaltbar, haben die Synoptiker Recht, dann ist der 4. Evangelist als Quelle abzulebnen." (Schmiedel, 18–19)

216 Wheless, *FC*, 174. See also Wells, esp. *WWJ*.

217 Waite, 213.

and forged lists of mostly fictitious names."[218] A number of the names, in reality, appear to be not "patriarchs" but older gods.

Regarding the contradictory chronology found in the New Testament, ben Yehoshua states:

> The New Testament story confuses so many historical periods that there is no way of reconciling it with history. The traditional year of Jesus's birth is 1 CE. Jesus was supposed to be not more than two years old when Herod ordered the slaughter of the innocents. However, Herod died before 12 April 4 BCE. This has led some Christians to redate the birth of Jesus to 6–4 BCE. However, Jesus was also supposed have been born during the census of Quirinius. This census took place after Archelaus was deposed in 6 CE, ten years after Herod's death. Jesus was supposed to have been baptised by John soon after John had started baptising and preaching in the fifteenth year of the reign of Tiberias, i.e., 28–29 CE, when Pontius Pilate was governor of Judaea, i.e., 26–36 CE. According to the New Testament (Lk 3:1–2), this also happened when Lysanias was tetrarch of Abilene and Annas and Caiaphas were high priests. But Lysanias ruled Abilene from c. 40 BCE until he was executed in 36 BCE by Mark Antony, about 60 years before the date for Tiberias and about 30 years before the supposed birth of Jesus! … Also, there were never two joint high priests; in particular, Annas was not a joint high priest with Caiaphas. Annas was removed from the office of high priest in 15 CE after holding office for some nine years. Caiaphas only became high priest in c. 18 CE, about three years after Annas. Many of these chronological absurdities seem to be based on misreadings and misunderstandings of Josephus's book *Jewish Antiquities* which was used as reference by the author of *Luke* and *Acts*.[219]

Thus, the few incidents useful for dating are found mainly in Luke and evidently turn out to be false or inaccurate. Moreover:

218 Wheless, *FC*, 207.

219 A Christian apology for this seeming error of conflating the high priesthood of Annas, which extended from 6 to 15 AD/CE, with that of Caiaphas, who reigned from 18–36 AD/CE, runs as follows: "Luke's apparently anachronistic reference to Annas as 'high priest' … may reflect Luke's dependence on a group who refused to acknowledge Anna's deposition.… It is more likely that this language reflects the continued use of the title for Annas after his departure from the office." (Green, 635) Obviously, without concrete evidence for such a contention, it remains speculation. The simpler explanation is that the gospels represent not historical accounts from eyewitnesses but fictional compilations long after the supposed facts.

> Luke ii. 1, shows that the writer (whoever he may have been) lived long after the events related. His dates, about the fifteenth year of Tiberius, and the government of Cyrenius (the only indications of time in the New Testament), are manifestly false. The general ignorance of the four Evangelists, not merely of the geography and statistics of Judea, but even of its language—their egregious blunders, which no writers who had lived in that age could be conceived of as making—prove that they were not only no such persons as those who have been willing to be deceived have taken them to be, but that they were not Jews, had never been in Palestine, and neither lived at, or at anywhere near the times to which their narratives seem to refer.[220]

As we can see and will continue to see, the notion of "inerrancy" cannot be sustained.

> Virtually all gospel episodes, on close scrutiny, seem to bear such striking resemblance to this or that Old Testament narrative scene that the similarity cannot be coincidental. It seems rather that the gospel incidents have been retold or rewritten from scriptural prototypes, especially from the Septuagint (LXX), the Greek translation of the Tanakh, or Hebrew Bible. Why are the gospels filled with rewritten stories of Jonah, David, Moses, Elijah and Elisha rather than reports of the historical Jesus?[221]

Gospel Bloopers

As concerns Jesus's birthplace, while the synoptics Matthew (2:1) and Luke (2:15) place it in Bethlehem, so that he is from David's village, John says he is from Galilee and that the Jews rejected him because he was *not* from Bethlehem, whence the Messiah must come to "fulfill scripture" (John 7:41–42). Also, in the conflicting and illogical gospel account, Jesus's birth is heralded by a star (Matt. 2:2), angels (Luke 2:9) and Magi or wise men traveling from afar (Matt. 2:1), and represents such a danger to Herod that he takes the heinous and desperate act of slaughtering the male infants in Bethlehem (Matt. 2:16–18).[222] Yet, when Jesus finally appears in his hometown, the inhabitants are "astonished" (Matt. 13:53) and "take offense" (Matt. 13:57), as if they had never heard of their own messiah's miraculous birth with all the fanfare, or of Herod's dreadful deed, or of any of Jesus's "wisdom" and "mighty

---

220 Doane, 462.

221 Price, R. (2006), 66.

222 Christian tradition places the number of the "wise men" or kings at three. For a discussion of this motif of dignitaries approaching a divine child, see *Christ in Egypt* and "Rebuttal to Dr. Chris Forbes."

works," not even the purportedly astounding temple-teaching at age 12 (Luke 2:42, 46–7).

Even Jesus's own family, who obviously knew of his miraculous birth and exploits, rejects him, believing that he was "beside himself"[223] (Mark 3:21–31; cf., John 7:5). John's gospel contradicts the synoptists in portraying Christ's family as accepting him (John 2:12), although John 7:5 says that "even his brothers did not believe in him."

In addition, in the Christian tale, the wise men are represented as following the star until they arrive in Jerusalem and are summoned to Herod (Matt. 2), whereupon he tells them to continue following the star until they reach the place where the baby Jesus lies. The wise men then go off and find the baby, but Herod cannot, so he must put to death every infant boy born in Bethlehem since the initial appearance of the star (Matt. 2:16). One must ask, how is it that the "wise men" needed Herod's help to know that the star would lead them to the babe, when they were already following it in the first place? And why wouldn't Herod simply have followed the star himself and killed only Jesus, rather than all the boys? In reality, the terrible story of Herod killing the infants as portrayed only in Matthew is evidently based on ancient mythology, not found in any histories of the day, including that of the Jewish general Josephus, who does otherwise chronicle Herod's real abuses.

In the gospel story, practically nothing is revealed of Jesus's childhood, and he disappears completely from the age of 12 to about 30 (Luke 3:23), when he suddenly reappears to begin his ministry. After this dramatic and unhistorical appearance out of nowhere, Jesus is said in the synoptics to have taught for one year before he died, while in John the number is around three years (John 2:13; 6:4; 11:55). Furthermore, in Matthew, Mark and Luke, Jesus's career takes place in Galilee, except for the end in Jerusalem, while John places his story for the most part in Jerusalem and other sites in Judea, discrepancies that reveal two

223 In the original Greek, those at Mark 3:21 who "went out to lay hold on him" or "those close to him." The pertinent word here means "from, of at, by, besides, near." (Strong's G3844) This phrase has been rendered by various Bible translators as referring to Jesus's "friends" (KJV, YNG, WEB, HNV), "own people" (NKJV, RVR, NASB), "family" (NLT, NIV, ESV, RSV) and "relatives" (DBY). In any event, it is understood that Jesus's "own people," whether family, friends or both, rejected him, inexplicably despite his having been designated the messiah at birth by miraculous signs and wonders, including not only the extraordinary massacre of infants by Herod but also a visit by an angel of God to tell his relatives and the other townspeople about the son of God's very birth. (Matt. 1:20; Luke 1:35; 2:10–11) Paired with John 7:5, it is apparent that the evangelists are discussing Christ's own family as rejecting him.

important forces at work in the gospels (i.e., the northern kingdom of Israel and the southern kingdom of Judah).

Ben Yehoshua continues the critique as to the purported "history" of the New Testament:

> The story of Jesus's trial is also highly suspicious. It clearly tries to placate the Romans while defaming the Jews. The historical Pontius Pilate was arrogant and despotic. He hated the Jews and never delegated any authority to them. However, in Christian mythology, he is portrayed as a concerned ruler who distanced himself from the accusations against Jesus and who was coerced into obeying the demands of the Jews. According to Christian mythology, every Passover, the Jews would ask Pilate to free any one criminal they chose. This is, of course, a blatant lie. Jews never had a custom of freeing guilty criminals at Passover or any other time of the year. According to the myth, Pilate gave the Jews the choice of freeing Jesus the Christ or a murderer named Jesus Barabbas. The Jews are alleged to have enthusiastically chosen Jesus Barabbas. This story is a vicious antisemitic lie, one of many such lies found in the New Testament (largely written by antisemites).

Walker points out other errors of fact and perception about the part of the world in question during the era of Jesus's alleged advent:

> The most "historical" figure in the Gospels was Pontius Pilate, to whom Jesus was presented as "king" of the Jews and simultaneously as a criminal deserving the death penalty for "blasphemy" because he called himself Christ, Son of the Blessed.... This alleged crime was no real crime. Eastern provinces swarmed with selfstyled Christs and Messiahs, calling themselves Sons of God and announcing the end of the world. None of them was executed for "blasphemy."[224]

Mangasarian concurs that the story is implausible:

A Roman judge, while admitting that he finds no guilt in Jesus deserving of death, is nevertheless represented as handing him over to the mob to be killed, after he has himself scourged him. No Roman judge could have behaved as this Pilate is reported to have behaved toward an accused person on trial for his life.

In this same regard, Massey states:

> The account of Pilate's shedding the blood of the Galileans and mingling it with their sacrifices (Luke xiii. 1) has been added by some one so ignorant of the Hebrew history, that he has ascribed to Pilate an act which was committed when Quirinius was governor,

224 Walker, B. (1983), 470.

twenty-four years earlier than the alleged appearance of Jesus.[225]

In order to shore up their fallacious claims of Christ being crucified under Pilate, Christian forgers even went so far as to produce the "Acts of Pilate" (c. 150–200 AD/CE). After the New Testament canon was formalized, this book was deemed "spurious," thus demonstrating that it was merely an opinion as to what was "inspired" and what was "forged." *The Acts of Pilate* purports to relate the trial of Jesus before Pilate, in accordance with the canonical gospel accounts but in greater detail. Some of the scenes of this book appear to have been lifted from Homer's *Iliad*:

> Pilate has been turned into Achilles ... Joseph is the good old Priam, begging the body of Hector, and the whole story is based upon the dramatic passages of the twentyfourth book of the Iliad.[226]

The Gospel of Nicodemus (fifth cent. AD/CE), which comprises both the *Act Pilati* and *The Descent of Christ into Hades,*[227] even goes so far as to purport to be a record of the actual conversations of the astonished faithful and prophets of old, such as David and Enoch, who have been resurrected from the dead after Jesus's own resurrection and ascension! This "true" gospel also contains a ludicrous conversation between Satan and his "prince" in Hell. The fictitious nature of such writings is obvious, as is, ultimately, that of the gospels.

Furthermore, the gospel accounts of Jesus's passion and resurrection differ utterly from each other, and none states how old he was when he died. In fact, the early Church fathers were constantly bickering over how old "the Lord" was when he died, with Irenaeus—who was widely respected by his peers as a highly educated establisher of doctrine—fervently insisting that Jesus was at least 50 years old,[228] rather than the 30 or 33 held by other traditions, including the four gospels he helped canonize. Indeed, Irenaeus "flatly denied as 'heresy' the Gospel stories as to his crucifixion at about thirty years of age."[229]

If the gospel narrative as found in the canon had existed earlier than

225 Massey, *GHC*, 19.

226 Mead, DJL, 66. See also the work of Dr. Dennis R. MacDonald's The Homeric Epics and the Gospel of Mark and Does the New Testament Imitate Homer? Four Cases from the Acts of the Apostles.

227 New International Encyclopedia, 1.748.

228 *Heresies*, 2.22.6; Roberts, A. (1903), 1.392. Irenaeus based his argument on John 8:57: "The Jews then said to him, 'You are not yet fifty years old.'" The bishop of Lyons felt it made more sense that Jesus must have been approaching 50, or the Jews would have remarked that he was not yet 40, if he were still in his 30s.

229 Wheless, *FC*, 173.

170–80, and if it constituted a true story, there would be no accounting for the widely differing traditions of "the Savior's" death: To wit, "By the third century AD, there were no fewer than 25 versions of Jesus' death and resurrection! Some have him not being put to death at all, some have him revived back to life, and some have Jesus living on to an old age and dying in Egypt."[230] These various details of the lives of Christ and his apostles should have been "set in stone," had the story been true and these books been written by the apostles, or even had an orally transmitted "life of Christ" been widespread during the decades that followed.

Various other aspects of the gospel accounts reveal their non-historical nature, including faulty geography, as mentioned, and incidents such as Jesus's preaching in Galilee, which allegedly occurred precisely during the time Herod was building the city of Tiberias. Of this incident, Dujardin says:

> We should here note the total lack of historic verity as to facts and places in the gospels. With the methods then available a town was not built rapidly, and the work would not have been completed in AD 27 or even 30. The gospel writers were therefore unaware that they were placing in a countryside overturned by demolition and rebuilding the larger part of the teaching of Jesus.
>
> If the stories are historical, it is in the middle of timber-yards that one must picture the divine precepts delivered, with the accompaniment of the noise of pikes and mattocks, the grinding of saws, and the cries of the workers.[231]

Furthermore, in the gospels Jesus himself makes many illogical contradictions concerning some of his most important teachings. First he states that he is sent only "to the lost sheep of Israel" (Matt. 15:24) and forbids his disciples to preach to the Gentiles (Matt. 10:5). Then he is made to say, "Go ye therefore, and teach *all nations*" (Matt. 28:19).

Next, Jesus claims that the end of the world is imminent and warns his disciples to be prepared at a moment's notice (Mark 13:24–33; Matt. 24:34). He also tells them to build a church from which to preach his message, an act that would not be necessary if the end was near. This doomsday "prophecy" did not pan out; nor has Jesus returned "soon," as was his promise (Matt. 16:28). Even if Christ had been real, his value as a prophet would have been nil, as his most important "prophecies" have not been fulfilled, thus proving that he was no more prophetic than the average newspaper astrologer, no more divine than a palm reader.

230 Notovich, 6.

231 Dujardin, 100.

In reality, the contradictions in the gospels are overwhelming and irreconcilable by the rational mind. In fact, the gospel was not designed to be rational, as the true meaning of the word "gospel" is "God's Spell," as in magic, hypnosis and delusion.[232]

As Dr. Mack says:

> The narrative gospels can no longer be viewed as the trustworthy accounts of unique and stupendous historical events at the foundation of the Christian faith. The gospels must now be seen as the result of early Christian mythmaking.[233]

One of the more suggestive bloopers takes place in Acts 10:11–15, in which, after Jesus's death, Peter has a vision of a "great sheet" descending from heaven, upon which were "all kinds of animals and reptiles and birds of the air." A mysterious voice commands, "Rise, Peter; kill and eat." Appalled, Peter objects, "No, Lord; for I have never eaten anything that is common or unclean." He is chastised by the voice, which responds, "What God has cleansed, you must not call common." Informing his followers of this extraordinary experience (Acts 10:28), Peter is a changed man:

> You yourselves know how unlawful it is for a Jew to associate with or to visit any one of another nation; but God has shown me that I should not call any man common or unclean.

Analyzing this scene, Dr. Andrew P. Gould comments that it:

> demonstrates unequivocally that the whole "inclusivist message," which is directly attributed to Jesus via innumerable Gospel stories, was in fact completely foreign to Jesus. Otherwise, it would not have been necessary for Peter, one of his closest and "rockiest" supporters, to receive a vision about it well after Jesus's death. Thus, this story, by itself, tells us that vast portions of the

232 As I write in *The Gospel According to Acharya S* (4), the term "gospel" comes from the Old English "godspell," which combines "good" and "spell." The word "good" in turn derives from the Old English "god," which is precisely the same spelling, of course, as the OE term for "God." There is little doubt that the term "godspell" was viewed not only as a "good spell" but also a "*god* spell." In any event, for some entrancing reason *evangelion* was eventually translated into English as "good *spell*," rather than "good news" or "good tidings." In this regard, the New Testament tale thus has served as a *spell* that has kept humanity hypnotized for nearly 2,000 years. The word "*evangelion*," "*evangelia*" or other forms can be found in the Greek Old Testament or Septuagint at 2 Sam. 4:10; 18:19, 20, 22, 25, 27; 2 Kings 7:9. To bear "good news" or "glad tidings" is בשר or *basar* in the Hebrew (Strong's H1319), while the "good news" itself is בשורה or *bsowrah*.

233 Mack, 10.

Gospels, in which Jesus is pictured as associating and engaging in table fellowship with all kinds of forbidden persons (tax collectors, prostitutes, etc.) and dismissing Jewish dietary law in favor of a universalist, humanitarian message ("What goes into a man's mouth does not make him unclean but what comes out of his mouth, that is what makes him unclean." Matt 15:10), are just constructed from whole cloth. In fact, it is astonishing that anyone can remain a believing Christian after pondering this clumsy addendum to the Jesus Gospel stories.[234]

In reality, it seems much of the gospel story was designed to compel xenophobic and anti-Gentile Jews into accepting this path of "Catholicism" or universalism, rejecting the picky, harsh and bigoted Jewish law. Scripture after scripture hammers home this point. Yet, Peter—upon whose "rock" Jesus builds his church (Matt. 16:18)—acts as if he has never heard of such a notion, and must be told once more via a disembodied voice in the air. It seems as if Peter was completely oblivious of one of the central teachings of Christianity, as expressed by Paul (Gal. 3:28): "There is neither Jew nor Greek, there is neither slave nor free, there is neither male nor female; for you are all one in Christ Jesus."

The Acts of the Apostles (177 AD/CE)

The Book of Acts presents special problems. Where to begin?

> In the Greco-Latin codices D and E of Acts, we find a text widely differing from that of the other codices, and from the received text. By Sanday and Headlam … this is called the DELTA text; by Blass … it is called the BETA text. The famous Latin Codex now at Stockholm, from its size called the *Codex Gigas*, also in the main represents this text. Dr. Bornemann (Acta. Apost.) endeavoured to prove that the aforesaid text was Luke's original.… Dr. Blass (Acta Apost., p. vii) endeavours to prove that Luke wrote first a rough draft of Acts, and this is preserved in D and E. Luke revised this rough draft, and sent it to Theophilus; and this revised copy he supposes to be the original of our received text.… It seems far more probable that D and E contain a recension, wherein the copyists have added, paraphrased and changed things in the text, according to that tendency which prevailed up to the second half of the second century of the Christian era. (Herbermann, 1.122)

> The Acts of the Apostles bear a number of similarities to the ancient Hellenistic novels, whose height of popularity was … the

234 Gould, "Review of *The New Testament Code* by Robert Eisenman."

second century.[235]

> Luke fits best as a contemporary and kindred spirit of Papias, bishop of Hierapolis in Asia Minor about 140–50 CE. Papias collected traditions, many legendary, of the days of the apostles. His accounts and Luke's are strikingly similar at five points.... Papias does not mention Luke's gospel alongside Mark and Matthew, presumably because he did not know of it. It had not been written yet.[236]

Describing the unreal atmosphere of the clearly fictional Acts, Robert Price remarks:

> Note that Luke has every step of the fledging church carefully overseen by the vigilant eye of the twelve, who stay magically untouched in Jerusalem even when the whole church is otherwise scattered by persecution (Acts 8:1).[237]

This fictional device reflects the views of the apologists of the second half of the second century, whose main concern was to associate their doctrines with apostles in order to give them direct authority from Christ. Other additions by Luke to the Ur-Markus, Ur-Lukas, and Q sources include the lengthened speech by John the Baptist (Luke 3:10–14), which establishes essentially timeless edicts reflecting that the church at this point had begun to hunker down, rather than continuing to wait for the "end of the world" that was obviously not coming.[238]

As concerns the ascription of Luke and Acts to the same author, some scholarship has shown there are important problems with this thesis, such as vocabulary differences. The bulk of the text, however, evidently comes from the same individual, but these difference indicate that someone else has redacted the texts. As Price states:

> The solution to this dilemma lies with Marcion. We are told that his *Apostolicon* contained a shorter version of the Gospel of Luke. The Catholic fathers were quick to allege that Marcion had shortened our traditional Luke, trimming away portions that were doctrinally objectionable to him, especially parts that linked Christianity with Judaism or the Old Testament. Albrecht Ritschl ... made the suggestion later revived by John Knox and Joseph Hoffman, that it had been just the reverse: Marcion had instead possessed a shorter, earlier version of Luke which scholars call Ur-Lukas. The Catholic Church proceeded to expand Ur-Lukas by the addition of material that was anti-Marcionite.... This redactor

235 Price, R. (2006), 492.
236 Price, R. (2006), 493.
237 Price, R. (2006), 489.
238 Price, R. (2006), 488.

> would have gone on to write Acts to supplement Marcion's exclusive focus on Paul at the expense of the twelve. In fact, this is clearly the most natural explanation for the Peter-Paul parallelism in Acts: the particular Paulinists and Petrinists the book of Acts wants to reconcile are the Marcionites and Catholics.
>
> [The] Lukan Ecclesiastical Redactor edited Ur-Lukas, which in relevant passages was more like its Markan original. Thus the author of Acts was merely the redactor of Luke. This accounts for the thematic consistencies and vocabulary differences.[239]

In addition to the hundreds of epistles and gospels written during the first centuries, there were many "Acts" of this apostle or that. Although mainstream scholarship claims the book was written by Luke, the disciple of Paul, the canonical Acts of the Apostles as we have it does not show up clearly in the historical record earlier than the end of the second century, long after the purported events it depicts. Acts purports to relate the early years of the Christian church; yet in it we find a well-established community that could not have existed at the time this book was alleged to have been written (i.e., not long after the death of Christ). Taylor calls Acts "a broken narrative," and Higgins states that it was fabricated by monks, "devil-drivers" and popes, who wished to form an alliance by writing the book, "the Latin character of which is visible in every page."[240] The respected *Encyclopaedia Biblica* (1.57) relates the opinion of Protestant German theologians Dr. F.C. Baur and Dr. Eduard Zeller that Acts's contents are "untrustworthy."

The purpose of Acts was not to record the history of the early Church but to bridge the considerable gap between the gospels and the epistles. Like Matthew and John, Acts was also designed to empower the Roman hierarchy:

> It is plain that the Acts of the Apostles was written in the interest of the Roman Catholic Church, and in support of the tradition that the Church of Rome was founded by the joint labors of Peter and Paul.[241]

The author(s) of Acts used text from Josephus and, evidently, from the writings of Aristides, a Sophist of the latter part of the second century, to name a couple of its sources, which also purportedly included the life of Apollonius of Tyana, the quasi-mythical Cappadocian/Samaritan/Greek miracle-worker of the first century AD/CE.

The first time Luke's gospel is mentioned in the historical

239 Price, R. (2006), 496.
240 Higgins, 2.131-2.
241 Waite, 417–19.

record is about 180 AD/CE when Irenaeus listed it among four gospels he was willing to accept.[242]

Revealing once again how modern scholarship is catching up with and confirming the much-maligned scholars of the nineteenth century, Dr. Robert Price comments:

> The Tübingen critics of the nineteenth century (F.C. Baur, Franz Overbeck, Edward Zeller) dated Luke-Acts to the second century. More recently, Walter Schmithals, Helmut Koester and John C. O'Neill have maintained this second-century date. Baur placed Luke-Acts late on the historical time line because of its catholicizing tendency.[243]
>
> For Luke-Acts, it is the church that dispenses salvation through baptism, which requires faith in the name of Jesus and in the leadership of the apostles. This is not a work of the apostolic age.[244]

Bible Prophecy

Many people believe that the biblical tale of Jesus must be true because the Bible itself predicted his advent and because so many other Old Testament "prophecies" had come true, demonstrating that the book was indeed "God's word." First of all, much of the biblical "prophecy" was written after the fact—a practice called "post diction"—with merely an appearance of prophecy. Secondly, the book has served as a *blueprint*, such that people have deliberately followed to some degree its so-called prophecies, thus appearing to bring them to fulfillment. Thirdly, very few if any "prophecies," particularly of the supernatural kind, have indeed come true. Fourthly, biblical interpreters claim that records of events centuries in the past somehow refer to the future. As concerns purported prophetic references to Jesus in the Old Testament, Wells says:

> Nearly all New Testament authors twist and torture the most unhelpful Old Testament passages into prophecies concerning Christianity. Who, ignorant of Mt. 2:16–9, could suppose that Jeremiah 31:15 (Rachel weeping for her children) referred to Herod's slaughter of the Innocents?[245]

To demonstrate that their Messiah was predicted, Christians have also grabbed onto the brief reference made in Psalm 2 to "the Lord and his *Anointed*," a word that in the Greek translation of the Hebrew Bible, the Septuagint, is "Christos." In fact, the Septuagint, allegedly translated and redacted during the second and third centuries BCE at

---

242 Price, R. (2006), 481.
243 Price, R. (2006), 483.
244 Price, R. (2006), 486.
245 Wells, *HEJ*, 36.

Alexandria, Egypt, contains the word "Christos" at least 40 times.[246] This *title* "Christos" or "anointed," however, referred to a king or priest, not a superhuman savior. This Christian defense, in reality, proves that there were other Christs long before Jesus, including David (1 Sam. 26:9; 2 Sam. 1:14, 1:16), Zadok (1 Chr. 29:22) and Cyrus (Isa. 45:1). The title "Christ" or "Anointed" ("Mashiah") was in reality held by all kings of Israel, as well as being "so commonly assumed by all sorts of impostors, conjurers and pretenders to supernatural communications, that the very claim to it is in the gospel itself considered as an indication of imposture."[247]

In *Secular View of the Bible*, Constantine Grethenbach remarked that the Old Testament represented "a series of writings not a line of which has a known author, and but few incidents of which are corroborated by other testimony."[248] In reality, despite all the efforts by apologists to push the Bible's composition back to the time of Moses, Old Testament scholars have known for centuries that most of the Old Testament books were written after the so-called Babylonian Exile of the sixth century BCE, all the way up to the second century.[249]

As we have seen, the same can be said largely of the New Testament, especially as concerns the authorship of the canonical gospels as we have them. Thus, Christianity is apparently based upon a false proposition, and, without the inspired authorship of apostles under an infallible god, the Church is left with little upon which to base its claims. Regarding this state of affairs, Wheless declared:

> The Gentile Church of Christ has therefore no divine sanction; was never contemplated nor created by Jesus Christ. The Christian Church is thus founded on a forgery of pretended words of the pretended Christ.[250]

Regarding the gospel dates, Dr. Jay Raskin remarks:

> We need to stop dating the New Testament and [some] Epistles to the First Century and recognize them as late Second-Century creations, which all the scientific evidence points to.[251]

246 See, for example, 1 Kings 2:10; Psalms 2:2; 20:6; 27:8; 83:10; 88:52; 131:10; Leviticus 4:5; 6:15; 21:10; Amos 4:13; Daniel 9:26; Lamentations 4:20; Habakkuk 3:13.

247 Taylor, 7.

248 Grethenbach, 1.

249 See, for example, Spoer's discussion of pre-exilic and post-exilic texts and passages (6ff).

250 Wheless, *FC*, 224.

251 Comment on "World's Earliest Christian Engraving Shows Surprising Pagan Elements" by Owen Jarus.

Non-Biblical Sources

"The brief mentions of Jesus in the writings of Josephus, Tacitus and Suetonius have been generally regarded as not genuine and as Christian interpolations; in Jewish writings there is no report about Jesus that has historical value. Some scholars have even gone so far as to hold that the entire Jesus story is a myth."

—*The Universal Jewish Encyclopedia* (6.83)

"[There] are very few sources for knowledge of the historical Jesus beyond the four canonical Gospels. Paul and Josephus offer little more than tidbits. Claims that the later apocryphal Gospels and the Nag Hammadi material supply independent and reliable historical information about Jesus are largely fantasy. In the end, the historian is left with the difficult task of sifting through the Four Gospels for historical tradition."

—Dr. John P. Meier, *A Marginal Jew* (2.5)

"So we are right to assume that even the Gospels have no value as witnesses to the historicity of Jesus. The question remains: Are there are any historical proofs that Jesus existed?"

—Dr. Solomon Zeitlin, "The Halaka in the Gospels" (373)

"We may now proceed to examine directly the actual documentary evidence for the life of Jesus. This evidence may be divided into two classes: non-Christian and Christian. Of the former, next to nothing exists. In all, this evidence mounts up to some twenty-four lines, not a single one of which is of admitted authenticity."

—Dr. Harry Elmer Barnes, *The Twilight of Christianity* (391)

We have seen that the gospel accounts are unreliable as history and cannot serve as credible scientific evidence that Jesus Christ ever existed. Now we shall ask if there are any non-biblical, non-partisan records by historians during the alleged time of the astonishing events: To wit, a virgin-born "son of God" who was famed widely as a great teacher and wonderworker, miraculously healing and feeding multitudes, walking on water and raising the dead; who was transfigured on a mount into a shining sun; whose crucifixion was accompanied by great earthquakes, the darkening of the sun and the rising from their graves of numerous "saints"; and who himself was resurrected from the dead. Indeed, in the New Testament, Jesus's far-and-wide fame is recounted in some two dozen passages.[252] Of these alleged events, Eusebius (1.13.1) asserts:

252 Matthew 4:23–25; 5:1; 8:1, 18; 9:8, 31; 9:33, 36; 11:7; 12:15; 13:2; 14:1, 13, 22; 15:30; 19:2; 21:9; 26:55; Mark 1:28; 10:1; Luke: 4:14, 37; 5:15; 14:25, etc.

> Because of His power to work miracles the divinity of our Lord and Saviour Jesus Christ became in every land the subject of excited talk and attracted a vast number of people in foreign lands very remote from Judaea.[253]

Surely these extraordinary events known far and wide were recorded by one or more competent historians of the time? As noted, the centuries surrounding the beginning of the Christian era, the periods of Tiberias and Augustus, were, in fact, some of the best-documented in history, as admitted even by Christian apologists.[254] As Christian apologist, missionary and Anglican ex-priest Rev. Robert Keable (1887–1927) states:

> [Few] periods of the ancient world were so well documented as the periods of Augustus and Tiberius. But no contemporary writer knew of His existence. Even a generation later, a spurious passage in Josephus, a questionable reference in Suetonius, and the mention of a name that may be His in Tacitus, that is all.[255]

As an example of the prolificity of ancient historians, Livy (59 BCE–17 CE), the Roman historian under Augustus, alone composed 142 volumes, over a hundred of which were subsequently destroyed[256] (possibly by conspirators trying to cover their tracks).

Despite this fulsome historical documentation, there are basically *no nonbiblical references to a historical Jesus* by any known historian of the time during and after Jesus's purported advent. As Walker says, "No literate person of his own time mentioned him in any known writing."[257] Hellenistic Jewish historian and philosopher Philo (20 BCE–50 CE), alive at the ostensible time of Jesus, was silent on the subject of the great Jewish miracle-maker and rabble rouser who brought down the wrath of Rome on Judea, despite the facts that he wrote many volumes (including development of the concept of the Word or *Logos*) and that his works appeared to have been used freely in the creation of Christianity.[258]

Nor are Jesus and his followers mentioned by any of the dozens of additional philosophers, historians and others who wrote during the first and second centuries of the Common Era, at the same time and in the same place where the Christians were supposedly swarming. As stated

253 Eusebius, 30.
254 Jackson, 186.
255 Keable, 11.
256 von Albrecht, 837.
257 Walker, B. (1983), 465.
258 For more on the subject of Philo, see my books *Suns of God* (49–50, 379ff), *Who Was Jesus?* (228, etc.) and *Christ in Egypt* (466–469, etc.).

by John E. Remsburg:

> Enough of the writings of [these] authors … remains to form a library. Yet in this mass of Jewish and Pagan literature, aside from two forged passages in the works of a Jewish author, and two disputed passages in the works of Roman writers, there is to be found no mention of Jesus Christ.[259]

Even the books circulated by Christian apologists as providing "proof" of Christ's existence, such as *Jesus Outside the New Testament* by Dr. Robert E. Van Voorst, conclude that the nonbiblical references represent a "*small witness* to Jesus … found outside the New Testament in classical Roman, Jewish and Christian writings."[260] This "small witness" is quite easily picked apart and revealed to be valueless in providing evidence of a historical Jesus. Often cited as having refuted the Jesus-myth thesis, Van Voorst merely presents the same list of "proofs" previously dealt with by mythicists over the past several centuries, such as: Josephus, Suetonius, Tacitus, Pliny the Younger, Mara bar Serapion, Thallos, Lucian and Celsus. He tosses in the Dead Sea Scrolls and a text from the Middle Ages, the *Toledot Yeshu*, both of which sources have been shown to have little value as credible, scientific evidence of Christ's historicity.

Flavius Josephus (37–c. 95 CE), Jewish Historian

For many centuries, defenders of the faith have pointed proudly to a passage found in *Jewish Antiquities* by the historian Josephus. This man had been a rebel general in the war against Rome (66–73 CE), who, seeing inevitable defeat looming, switched sides and aided the Romans. For his service he was rewarded by Vespasian and Titus by being attached to their imperial household, the Flavians. Thus, did Joseph bar Matthias become Flavius Josephus. And thus, the favorite Josephus text of Christian apologists came to be dubbed the *Testimonium Flavianum* (TF). It reads as follows:

> About this time there lived Jesus, a wise man, if indeed one ought to call him a man. For he was one who performed surprising deeds and was a teacher of such people as accept the truth gladly. He won over many Jews and many of the Greeks. He was the Christ. And when, upon the accusation of the principal men among us, Pilate had condemned him to a cross, those who had first come to love him did not cease. He appeared to them spending a third day restored to life, for

259 Remsburg, 25. In the first edition of *The Christ Conspiracy*, this quote was erroneously attributed to McClintock and Strong.

260 Van Voorst, 3.

> the prophets of God had foretold these things and a thousand other marvels about him. And the tribe of the Christians, so called after him, has still to this day not disappeared.

Flavius Josephus: Antiquities of the Jews, Book 18, Chapter 3, *3*

When analyzing this passage, we need to keep firmly in mind all the forgery committed by Christian writers over the centuries. Imagine you were a Christian forger bent on proving the "truth" about Christianity, especially in the face of skepticism as to the very historicity of its central figure. Where would be the ideal place to put a fabricated testimony to Christ's historicity, if not in the works of a famed historian? And if you were canny enough to make it succinct so as to provide fewer clues to arouse suspicion, wouldn't the result be exactly like the *Testimonium Flavianum*?

The statement that "the tribe of Christians … has still to this day not disappeared" might imply a length of time that exceeds the several decades between Christ's alleged advent and Josephus's writing, especially if we accept the received history and mainstream dating for the canonical gospels. If these texts were in existence for some time, and—according to Tacitus and assorted Christian tales—there was a "vast multitude" of Christians at Rome, blamed for the burning of that city, why would Josephus need to clarify who they were and that they still existed?

Reflecting the consensus of the day, Dr. Gordon Stein comments:

> [The] vast majority of scholars since the early 1800s have said that this quotation is not by Josephus, but rather it is a later Christian insertion in his works. In other words, it is a *forgery, rejected by scholars*.

Since his time a mere couple of decades ago, a huge, concerted effort has been made to change that prevailing opinion of forgery to the "partial interpolation theory," which rescues some of the TF from the dustbin, thus maintaining Josephus's value in providing "evidence" of Christ's historicity. Based on the numerous contentions that the TF represents the "best evidence" of Christ's existence as a historical figure, the purpose behind this effort is transparent, and the same objections to the passage remain. Giving reasons for suspecting the TF as a forgery, Stein remarks:

> The whole passage reads as if it had been written by a Christian. Josephus is made to call the Christian religion "the truth." He would hardly have said that. Although Josephus reports the miracles of a number of other "prophets," he is silent about the

miracles attributed to Jesus.

Eusebius the Forger?

Several writers conclude that it was Eusebius himself who forged the passage.[261] As Dr. Alice Whealey remarks, "No other ancient writer knew Josephus' works anywhere near well enough to have crafted something so similar to Josephus' style."[262] Says Stein:

> We also know Eusebius to be the man who said that lying for the advancement of the church was quite acceptable. He was probably the one who inserted this suspect passage into Josephus' works.

Says Bartram:

> An argument used to support the claim that Josephus mentions Jesus Christ is that this was then mentioned by Origen, but the fact is we do not have any original text by Origen and no contemporaneous evidence for either Origen or works attributed to him.
>
> We do not have any original text by Josephus either, for the oldest are medieval. Even if he did write of Jesus, we do not know if he wrote *Christ* or *Chrest*.
>
> The Aramaic Josephus is missing. That is a warning.[263]
>
> [Authorship] and dissemination of publications was a very public business and the secret police of Rome were very effective. The emperors kept an eagle eye on philosophers, religious figures and authors.
>
> Though authors didn't need a printer, they needed the full panoply of marketing methods to gain a wide audience and this included gaining a publisher with the means to copy large numbers of books, hold launch parties and distribute copies across the empire.[264]

Regarding books in ancient Rome, Classics professor Dr. Mary Beard remarks:

> All reading material was laboriously copied out by hand. The ancient equivalent of the printing press was a battalion of slaves, whose job it was to transcribe one by one as many copies of Virgil, Horace or Ovid as the Roman market would buy.[265]

As concerns the demand, Beard conservatively estimates that, out of the million or so citizens at Rome, some 100,000 were literate, which

---

261 See, for example, Olson, "Eusebius and the *Testimonium Flavanium*," *CBQ* 61, 1999, 305–322.

262 Whealey in Böttrich, 74. Whealey provides an extensive analysis of whether or not Eusebius forged the TF.

263 Bartram, "Mani and Authorship of the Canonical Gospels."

264 Bartram, "Josephus as a primary source for the New Testament."

265 Beard, "Scrolling Down the Ages."

would constitute a substantial book market. These texts were not the codices we think of today, which did not come into popular usage until after the second century, but, rather, long and cumbersome rolls of papyrus. All in all, publishing a book at the time in question would be a costly and daunting task. Beard also reminds us of one reason we have few copies of texts from antiquity, as the mass-produced copies were cheaply fabricated, while those made to last longer were very expensive. Says Beard:

> A cut-price book roll would presumably have fallen to pieces as quickly as a modern mass-market paperback. But worse, the pressure to get copies made quickly meant that they were loaded with errors and sometimes uncomfortably different from the authentic words of the author.

In addition to all the errors that could transmit the wrong message to the masses about the writer's intentions, the Roman Empire was thick with censorship and spying, as sedition seemed to be all around. Few books would have a long shelf-life if not approved by Roman authorities. As is the case today, wealthy people could air their views through monopolizing the media—that is how politics and religion have often been spread throughout the ages, with might being right. For anyone's views—including those of Paul—to be published and to make it into the public eye would require wealth and political power.

Many have suggested that the writer of Luke used Josephus to flesh out his story, thus proving that Luke was writing later than the Jewish historian. Many attempts have been made to equate passages from Luke with those in Josephus, some of which appear to be successful.

The focus of the gospel writer on the sites of Capernaum, Bethsaida and Chorazin (Matt. 11:21–3) may also be explained by their significance in Josephus, as concerns journeys of Vespasian and Titus (*Wars*, 3.9.7, 3.10.8–9; *Life*, 72). These verses appear to look *back* on the destruction of these villages, explaining their eradication at the hands of Rome as divine punishment for having rejected the Christian gospel.

One of the more interesting parallels is Jesus, son of Shaphat, a rebel leader at the Sea of Galilee mentioned by Josephus (*Wars*, 3.9.7), comparable to the gospel Jesus, himself a leader of anti-establishment rebels whose movement gained momentum at the Sea of Galilee.

The parts of the New Testament for which we may look to Josephus or other history tend to be restricted to those which name historical individuals, particularly as in Acts as opposed to the gospels. These would include individuals such as Zacharias, son of Barachias (Matt. 23:35), who apparently is a reference to Josephus's Zacharias, son of Baruch

(*Wars* 4.5.4). Another figure that seems to be taken from Josephus is the Theudas mentioned at Acts 5:36, whose account can evidently be found in Josephus's *Antiquities* 20.5.1.

The identification of Saul/Paul of the New Testament with the Saulus of Josephus—both kinsmen of Herod(ion)—is also intriguing, as are several other identifications, such as James the brother of Jesus, fleshed out by Robert Eisenman. In some instances, no doubt, certain characters such as Paul and James quite likely did have a historical framework—after all, someone *was* writing letters and leading congregations. However, these are likewise fictional compilations, with characteristics of both historical and mythical figures or, at least, symbolic configurations, such as serving as part of "12 helpers" or "four brothers."

Another such instance occurs, of course, in the discussions of the census of Cyrenius/Quirinus (*Ant.* 17.2.4; 18.1.1; Luke 2:1–2), as is the discussion of other such known historical figures as Agrippa, Herod, Bernice, Pilate, et al. The gospel writers could easily have turned to Josephus in order to flesh out their stories—is it coincidental that at the point when Josephus clearly begins to emerge in Christian writings, so, too, do the canonical gospels as we have them, toward the end of the second century?

The parallel between the scourging of Jesus ben Ananus (*Ant.* 15.3.9) and Jesus of Nazareth (Matt. 27:26; Mark 15:15; John 19:1) is also intriguing, although scourging appears as a common part of the ancient sacred-king scapegoat ritual sacrifice that is archetypically recounted in the gospel story.

The "warning" at Matthew 24:19 about the "future" "desolating sacrifice spoken of by the prophet Daniel"—about which Jesus is made to say, "alas for those who are with child and for those who give suck in those days!"—may indeed reflect knowledge of what actually did happen in Josephus's time, as recounted in the story of nursing woman slaying her son. (*Wars* 6.3.4) Certainly, such traumatic events would stick in the minds of people decades later who were trying to recreate a fictional scenario of what would happen at such a time, when the temple was destroyed.

The discussion at Matthew 24:11 that "many false prophets shall rise" could certainly be a retrospective view of what happened—continually—in Judea, but the "prophecy" need not have come from Josephus, since it was a common occurrence.

The dramatic appearance of the Son of Man at Matthew 24:30–31 reflects the book of Daniel (7:13), Isaiah 27:13 and Zechariah 9:14.

The supernatural aspects of the gospel story, however, appear not to come from secular histories but from the Old Testament and pre-Christian mythology and philosophy. In some instances, we appear to have a combination of Egyptian religion with movements of historical individuals such as Titus, with these latter largely limited to place names used in the gospels. Acts and the epistles are, of course, more historical in the sense that they do not depict the supposed historical exploits of a supernatural savior. What they do appear to depict is a "low-magic" cult not much different from the various mystery cults of the Roman Empire and beyond, except that the Christian effort was densely concentrated, highly concerted and well-funded.

In some cases, there is an overlap of explanations, encompassing two or more possible sources, a situation that may have been understood and appreciated by the writers as well. In fact, these correlations between Jewish scripture and tradition, and Pagan religious, philosophical and mythological motifs, may explain their inclusion in the New Testament, which is, above all else, a syncretizing text designed to unify the various factions of the Roman Empire.

One such overlap may be in the story of the precocious Jesus teaching in the temple at the age of 12, much to the amazement of the religious doctors. Josephus tells a similar tale about his own childhood, in which he wowed the "high priests and principal men" with his knowledge of the law (*Life*, 2). This story of teaching in the temple of the Most High at 12 finds its parallel in the myth of the Egyptian god Horus, for example, who, as the morning sun, passes into his "father's temple" at noon. This motif seems to be reflected in the story of the precocious 12-year-old Sa-Osiris.

The precocity of the divine child is also found in the myths of Krishna, Hercules, Buddha and Dionysus as well. It may well be that the educated writer of Luke was aware of more than one of these parallels when he wrote his account.

Another pericope that might reflect more than one source is that of the crucifixion between two thieves. Josephus gives an account of three of his acquaintances crucified by Titus's troops (*Life*, 75), two of whom die, while the other recovers, much like the tale of Christ's crucifixion, wherein the two thieves surrounding him die, while he is revived. (Mark 15:43–5)

However, this theme of the divine figure between two others can be found in the symbolism of the popular god of the Roman Empire, Mithra, who is seen centrally poised between the two "torch-bearers," one pointing to heaven and one to hell, similar roles to those of the "good and bad thieves" of the gospel tale. Moreover, in the cross of the equinox in the circular zodiac we find the solar god Horus between the two "thieves" of the baboon and jackal.[266]

266 See Murdock, *CIE* page 357

How much of Josephus was used in the gospels remains uncertain. What we need is an in-depth study of the Greek phrases and terms shared by various New Testament texts and Josephus.

Gaius Plinius Caecilius Secundus/Pliny the Younger

One of the few "references" held up by Christian apologists as evidence of Jesus's existence is the exchange of letters (*Epistulae* 10.96–7) between the Roman emperor Trajan (53–117 AD/CE) and the Roman governor Pliny the Younger (c. 62–113 AD/CE), administrator of the Asian Minor province of Bithnya-Pontus (which happens to be where Marcion is from as well). In this earliest reference to Christian worship outside the New Testament, Pliny asks Trajan for help in dealing with what he views as treasonous cultists:

> [In] the case of those who were denounced to me as Christians, I have observed the following procedure: I interrogated these as to whether they were Christians; those who confessed I interrogated a second and a third time, threatening them with punishment; those who persisted I ordered executed....
>
> Soon accusations spread, as usually happens, because of the proceedings going on, and several incidents occurred. An anonymous document was published containing the names of many persons. Those who denied that they were or had been Christians, when they invoked the gods in words dictated by me, offered prayer with incense and wine to your image, which I had ordered to be brought for this purpose together with statues of the gods, and moreover cursed Christ—none of which those who are really Christians, it is said, can be forced to do—these I thought should be discharged. Others named by the informer declared that they were Christians, but then denied it, asserting that they had been but had ceased to be, some three years before, others many years, some as much as twenty-five years. They all worshipped your image and the statues of the gods, and cursed Christ.
>
> They asserted, however, that the sum and substance of their fault or error had been that they were accustomed to meet on a fixed day before dawn and sing responsively a hymn to Christ as to a god, and to bind themselves by oath, not to some crime, but not to commit fraud, theft, or adultery, not falsify their trust, nor to refuse to return a trust when called upon to do so. When this was over, it was their custom to depart and to assemble again to partake of food—but ordinary and innocent food. Even this, they affirmed, they had ceased to do after my edict by which, in accordance with your instructions, I had forbidden political associations. According-

> ly, I judged it all the more necessary to find out what the truth was by torturing two female slaves who were called deaconesses. But I discovered nothing else but depraved, excessive superstition....
>
> [The] contagion of this superstition has spread not only to the cities but also to the villages and farms. But it seems possible to check and cure it. It is certainly quite clear that the temples, which had been almost deserted, have begun to be frequented, that the established religious rites, long neglected, are being resumed, and that from everywhere sacrificial animals are coming, for which until now very few purchasers could be found.[267]

This letter features the three words "Christians," "Christian" and "Christ." This letter was supposedly written about 110 to 112 AD/CE; yet we are informed that the word "Christian" was first heard at Antioch, where it was defined some 70 to 80 years later by the Antiochene bishop Theophilus. Moreover, the rites to which Pliny is objecting are clearly those of Jews and possibly Essenes, such as filling temples and sacrificing animals, as well as hymn-singing to God at dawn. Indeed, these could very well be Messianic Jews who revered "the Anointed," as the concept had been developed throughout the Old Testament/Septuagint, into the apocryphal and intertestamental literature, etc.

It should also be noted that when this letter was purportedly written, "Christians" at Alexandria were evidently considered followers of the Greco-Egyptian hybrid god Serapis, as found in another letter purportedly from the emperor Hadrian (c. 134 AD/CE).[268] According to Drews, the original word in this letter is "*Chrestiani*," and the one whom they worship is "Chrestus."[269] Concerning the haphazardly exchanged terms, "Christos" and "Chrestos," or variants thereof, he remarks:

> Dr. Barr Mitchell, in his learned monograph on "χρηστος," has shown that in the so-called "Christian" epitaphs there is no instance earlier than the third century wherein the name-word is not written "Chrestos" or else "Chreistos." ... And in *Antiqua Mater*, professor

267 Lewis and Reinhold, 551-2.

268 See Murdock (2009), 443–4.

269 The English translation of Drews renders the passage in Hadrian's letter thus: "Those who worship Serapis are the Chrestians, and those who call themselves priests of Chrestus are devoted to Serapis. There is not a high-priest of the Jews, a Samaritan, or a priest of Chrestus who is not a mathematician, soothsayer, or quack. Even the patriarch, when he goes to Egypt, is compelled by some to worship Serapis, by others to worship Chrestus. They are a turbulent, inflated, lawless body of men. They have only one God, who is worshipped by the Chrestians, the Jews, and all the peoples of Egypt." (Drews (1972), 52.)

> Johnson … says that for the first *four* centuries it was the common practice of the Christians to write the name of their Master "Chrest" or "Chreist." On the whole, then, it seems pretty certain that not earlier than the third century did the term "Christian" come into use.[270]

It is interesting to note that these "Christians" at Alexandria appear to be the inheritors of the *Therapeutan* community at Lake Mareotis and elsewhere. The reference to "deaconesses" in Pliny's letter is indicative of the Therapeutan hierarchy that already existed in Philo's time.[271]

We hear from Cassius Dio (60.6.6) that it was *Jews* who "had again increased so greatly that by reason of their multitude it would have been hard without raising a tumult to bar them from the city."[272] Thus, Claudius "did not drive them out, but ordered them, while continuing their traditional mode of life, not to hold meetings."[273] Christian historian Paulus Orosius (*Hist.* 7.6.15–6) likewise remarks about Claudius expelling Jews from Rome.[274] He then cites Suetonius as having mentioned "Christus," which we know is a Christian error, as the word should be "Chrestus."

Christos or Chrestos?

Lactantius (*Divine Institutes*, 4.7) discusses the savior's name:

> CHAP. VII—OF THE NAME OF SON, AND WHENCE HE IS CALLED JESUS AND CHRIST.
>
> But although His name, which the supreme Father gave Him from the beginning, is known to none but Himself, nevertheless He has one name among the angels, and another among men, since He is called Jesus among men: for Christ is not a proper name, but a title of power and dominion; for by this the Jews were accustomed to call their kings. But the meaning of this name must be set forth, on account of the error of the ignorant, who by the change of a letter are accustomed to call Him Chrestus.[275]

The Latin words used by Pliny (or a redactor) in the received text are "*Christiani*" and "*Christo*." Moreover, it is possible that the original form of this letter—if it is genuinely from the hand of Pliny—may have

---

270 Foote, 429. For another discussion of the term "Chrestos" or "Chrestus," see my book *Suns of God*, 395, etc.

271 For a thorough discussion of the Therapeuts and their relationship to Christianity, see my book *Christ in Egypt*, 433ff, etc.

272 Cook, 15.

273 Cook, 15.

274 Cook, 15.

275 Roberts, 7.105–6.

read "Chresto," meaning "the Good One," as happened throughout the second and into the third centuries as concerns Jesus. If so, it could be referring to a number of other figures, including gods such as Serapis, who most assuredly was labeled "Chresto,"[276] if not "Christo," in antiquity. The use of this term to describe Egyptian gods as "the good" became popular in post-Ptolemaic times, being applicable not only to Serapis but also to Osiris, et al.[277]

The word χρηστός in the nominative singular can be found in the works of Sophocles (c. 496–406 BCE),[278] Euripides (c. 480–406 BCE),[279] Aristophanes (c. 448–380 BCE),[280] Isocrates (436–338 BCE),[281] Xenophon (c. 430–354 BCE),[282] Plato (c. 429–347 BCE)[283] and Chariton (c. first cent. BCE to first cent. AD/CE).[284] Philo uses the term θεό-χρηστος or "*theochrestos*," meaning "God-proclaimed."[285] Interestingly, in *Proptrepticus* (10.105.2.6), Clement of Alexandria (c.150–c. 215) writes, "ὁ χρηστός ἐστι πανταχοῦ σωτήριος"—"The Good is everywhere salvation."

If we factor in other cases and forms, such as the plural χρηστοὶ or *chrestoi*, we find many more instances in ancient writers.[286] In the play *Acharnians* by Aristophanes, for example, one of the main characters, Dicaeopolis, declares himself a πολίτης or *polites chrestos*, or "valuable citizen."[287] Concerning this development, Classics professor Dr. James F. McGlew relates, "For those in democratic Athens who were invested in making such distinctions, *chrēstoi* were citizens of high status with claims to special responsibilities and privileges; the *ponēroi*

276 Drews (1972), 49–50.

277 Foote, 429. Foote cites this "play on words" between "Christos" and "Chrestos" as occurring in Romans 16:18; 1 Peter 2:3, Justin Martyr, Clement of Alexandria and Tertullian.

278 For example, *Trachiniae*, lines 3, 452; *Antigone*, 520; 662, etc.

279 For example, *Alcestis*, line lll; *Heraclidae*, 999; *Hecuba*, 598; *Troiades*, 397; *Iphigenia Aulidensis*, 380, 984.

280 For example, *Acharnenses*, line 595; *Nubes*, line 8, etc.

281 For example, *Nicocles*, section 16, line 5.

282 For example, *Memorabilia*, 2.3.17.4, 2.4.5.4; *Anabasis* 1.8.1.3.

283 For example, *Apologia Socratis*, 33.b.4; *Theaetetus*, 161.a.7, 166.a.2, etc.

284 For example, *De Chaerea et Callirhoe*, 2.2.1.5, 2.11.6.4, 3.2.4.2, 5.9.3.2, etc.

285 Pape, 1.1086.

286 For example, Thucydides, *Historiae*, 1.91.2.3, 3.64.4.4; Xenophon, *Atheniensium respublica*, 1.9.4, 1.14.4, 1.14.8, 2.19.2; Plato, *Cratylus*, 386.b.5, 386.d.5, etc.

287 McGlew, 71, 78.

(the wretched) provided the amorphous human backdrop against which the *chrēstoi* stand out."[288] The *chrestoi* are thus generally the aristocracy,[289] noblemen,[290] elite or "socially prestigious men of wealth and good families,"[291] gentlemen of the upper classes, although, as we have seen, freedmen and slaves were often called "chrestos" as well.

> The dead as *chrêstoi*. On Attic grave-reliefs ... The expression *chrêste chaire*, sometimes couple with the title *hêrôs*, is found from the fourth century onwards, especially on epitaphs from Boeotia, Thessaly, Asia Minor and Cyprus, later spreading to all areas of the Greek world.[292]

Its usage in the classical Greek poets included describing a man who was "good, honest, upright,"[293] in other words, righteous. In consideration of its use by Philo to mean "proclaimed" or "declared," the word χρηστός appears to be related to the word χρηστήριος, meaning "prophetic," the accusative of which is χρηστήριον, referring to an oracle or sacrificial victim.[294] Indeed, according to Liddell & Scott a χρήστης or *chrestes* is a "prophet" or "soothsayer" who "expounds oracles."[295] Also according to Liddell & Scott, both terms, *chrestes* and *chrestos* are derived from the verb χράω or χράομαι,[296] meaning "give an oracle, pronounce; converse with."[297] It thus appears that this term "Chrestos" has a long tradition not only in common usage such as calling someone "good" or "useful" but also as a word employed within—indeed, evidently *derived from*—philosophy, religion and the mysteries.

The term χρηστός appears seven times in the New Testament, translated with the following meanings: "kind, easy, better, goodness, good, gracious." (G5543) At Ephesians 4:32, when Paul says, "Be ye kind to one another," the word for "kind" is χρηστοί or *chrestoi*, the plural of *chrestos*. This passage could be translated: "Become to one another *chrestoi*." Since "Christ" is indicated here only by the abbreviation Xω, the latter part of this scripture could also be rendered, "as God in *Chrest*."

The word Chrestos quite obviously existed before Christianity, in

288 McGlew, 71.
289 Ober, 251.
290 Ober, 281.
291 Lebow, 109.
292 Garland, 135.
293 Liddell & Scott, 2.1674.
294 *Pocket Oxford Classical Greek Dictionary*, 350. In Euripides (*Ion*, 1320) "oracular tripod" employed by the oracle/priestess of Delphi.
295 Liddell & Scott, 2.1674.
296 Liddell & Scott, 2.1674.
297 *POCD*, 350.

relation to religion, for one, and was co-opted by the Christian movement. It did not, therefore, describe Christians during the first century. In reality, its usage in Suetonius essentially proves this fact of pre-existence among *Jews*, rather than serving as any kind of evidence of Christ's existence as a historical character. Indeed, we see this co-opting of a popular religious term throughout the second century and onward, as instances of the word "chrestos/chrestus" and "chrestianoi/chrestianos," etc., were busily changed by Christian hands.[298] It is claimed that in the autographs or originals of works by Justin, Tertullian, Lactantius and Clement the word for "Christians" is, in reality, "Chrestians"; yet, since their time it has been rendered by enterprising scribes/copyists as "Christians."

In the highly popular Marcionite church, which so highly influenced the Christian tradition of the late second century, there was a noticeable division between the "evil" demiurge or ruler of this world and the "Good God" or *Chrestos*.[299] At the oldest known Christian church/synagogue in Syria, a Marcionite edifice at Deir Ali/Lebaba dated to 318/9 AD/CE, there appears an inscription to "the Lord and Savior Jesus the Good." It is interesting to note that this inscription calls the place of worship not an *ecclesia* or church but a *synagogue*, as further verified by the *Acts of Phillip* (*Acta Philippi*). Hence, the "savior" of Docetic-Gnostic Christianity is "Jesus the Chrestos." Thus, Clement's comment that the "Good One is salvation everywhere."

An example of this Greek word χρηστός or *chrestos* can be found at Matthew 11:30, where it is generally translated as "easy" (Strong's G5543): "For my yoke is easy, and my burden is light." It could, however, be rendered "For my yoke is Chrestos," wherein the word "yoke" here—ζυγός or *zugos*—refers to "troublesome laws" (i.e., Mosaic law) (Strong's G2218). This scripture, then, could be referring to a spiritual figurehead leading Jews out of the oppressive mosaic law.

The word χρηστός is used also at Luke 6:35: "you will be sons of the Most High; for he is kind." Here the "Most High" refers, of course, to God, who is "kind" or *chrestos*.

In the Epistle to the Ephesians (4:32), Christ's followers are exhorted to be χρηστοί or *chrestoi*. Romans 2:4 speaks of "the goodness of God," here as a neutral noun, "τὸ χρηστὸν τοῦ θεοῦ—"the *chreston* of

298 Commenting on the reference to "Christian" at 1 Peter 4:16, Canon Frederic William Farrar (1882), 1.171) notes: "Perhaps we should read the ignorant heathen distortion, *Chrestian* (see *Life and Work of St. Paul*, i. 301) with א" (Codex Sinaiticus).

299 McGowan, 199.

God." Even as late as the composition of 1 Peter (2:3), the Lord is called "Chrestos": εἴπερ ἐγεύσασθε ὅτι χρηστὸς ὁ κύριος. This scripture translates as, "Since you have tasted that the Lord [is] good/*chrestos*." The same phrase is used in the Septuagint translation of Nahum 1:7: χρηστὸς κύριος—"good lord"—and elsewhere in the Greek text.[300]

Since the Old Testament more readily associates majesty and condescension, it commonly uses *chrēstós* for God (Ps. 106:1; Jer. 33:11) or his name (Ps. 52:9) or mercy (Ps. 69:16). One can hope and trust in the Lord who is good (34:18). God is good and upright (25:8; cf. Dt. 32:4). Yet the severity that God shows in the law is the presupposition of this goodness; his ordinances are good (119:4, cf. 65ff).[301]

Thus, a reader or hearer of the Greek Old Testament during the few centuries prior to the Common Era, would be familiar with this phrase χρηστὸς κύριος or "Chrestos Kyrios" in describing their god. This contention could be logical especially when one factors in that Jews avoid using the sacred tetragrammaton YHWH to describe their deity. Perhaps, among many other epithets, such as the "Most High," these ancient Jews invoked God/Yahweh as "Chresto."

Philo also labels the "sayings proclaimed by God" as *logia theochresta*. This fact reveals a focus within Jewish mysticism on the word Chrestos. Considering the appearance of the phrase Chrestos kyrious—Good Lord—in the Septuagint/LXX, we can safely conclude that the Jewish god was invoked at times as Chrestos, possibly quite often during gatherings of Greek-speaking Jews, of whom there were many in the Roman Empire, including some 50 percent of the large and important Egyptian city of Alexandria.

> Philo uses *chrēstós* in the senses "serviceable," "helpful" and "good." He relates it to the goodness of God that the righteous seek to follow. Rulers are "gracious" and "friendly" or "kind" is implied when God is called *chrēstós*.[302]

The question remains, is there any extant artifact from before, say, the fourth century, in which the word "Christos" is used, as opposed to "Chrestos?"

Chrestos can also be found in Josephus to connote "morally good,"

300 According to *A Handy Concordance of the Septuagint* (261), the word χϱηστς appears in the following scriptures: Job 3:31; Psalms 24:8; 33:9; 51:11; 68:17; 85:5; 99:5; 105:1; 106:1; 108:21; 111:5; 118:39, 68; 135:1AS; 144:9; Prov. 2:21; Jer. 24:2, 3; 40:11; 51:17; 52:32; Ezek. 27:22; 28:13; Dan. 2:32; Nah 1:7. Not all of these are in reference to God, of course, but this exercise shows how abundantly the term appears in scripture.

301 Kittell (Bromiley 1985), 1320.

302 Bromiley (1985), 1321.

"kind," "gentle," "benevolent," "considerate" and "well disposed."[303]

These facts may explain why some of the earliest known "Christians," such as the followers of Marcion, were called "Chrestiani" who followed "Jesus the Good" or "Chrestos."

Concerning "Chrestus," Augustsson says it was a "common name in the Roman Empire, at least amongst slaves and freed men, as we learn from inscriptions in Latin."

Regarding some of these inscriptions, Dr. John Granger Cook remarks:

> In the 485 Latin inscriptions in one database with the masculine or feminine form (*Chrestus* or *Chreste* and several other variations such as *Chrestius*), the individuals are apparently pagan, with the exception of one Jewish woman named *Chreste*.[304]

In view of all the confusion in antiquity between Chrest and Christ, and considering his comment about "Chresto," it is not illogical to suggest that any purported mention of "Christians" in Suetonius was originally *Chrestiani*, also having nothing to do with followers of a historical Jesus of Nazareth.

In this regard, Justin Martyr (*First Apology*, 4) writes that "indeed, so far at least as one may judge from the name we are accused of [Christian], we are most excellent [Chrestian] people." Moreover, Clement of Alexandria (*Stromata*, 2.4) likewise mentions this confusion: "Now those who have believed in Christ both are and are called good [*Chrestoi*]."

This common name "Chrestos" is recorded on an ancient bowl from Pergamon dating between the late second century BCE and the early first century AD/CE, found off the coast of Alexandria by the team of French marine archaeologist Dr. Franck Goddio and now rests in the Alexandria Maritime Museum (C1_3557). While it was ballyhooed as the "earliest evidence for Christ," the bowl's inscription clearly says χρηστου or "chrestou." The context in which the bowl was found is evidently the early first century, while the bowl itself is thought to be from the first century BCE. This "Chrestos" artifact, however, is one of many, including hundreds of epitaphs found all around Greece for some centuries.

> For Pr. Bert Smith of Oxford University, it might be a dedication or a present made by a certain Chrestos belonging to an association (maybe religious) called Ogoistais. In this sense, Pr. Klaus Hallof, director of the Institute of Greek Inscriptions in the Berlin-Brandenburg Academy of Inscriptions believes that it is necessary to connect "ogostai" to known Greek denominations of religious associations

303 Bromiley (1985), 1321.

304 Cook, 17. See also Cook, 16.

> such as Hermaistai, Athenaistai, Isiastai which gathered worshippers of the god Hermes or the goddesses Athena and Isis. "Ogo," according to this hypothesis, would be a divine form of expressing the god Osogo or Ogoa of whom Strabon and Pausanias talk with regard to a divinity worshipped in Milas, in Caria.[305]

The inscription could read, "Through Chresto, the Magician." Based on other artifacts and texts of the Classical world in later centuries that reflect a strong interest in magic, the bowl could have been used for divination via the "Good God" or Chrestos.[306]

In the spells of the Greek Magical Papyri (e.g., PGM IV.1227–64) we also find reference to "Jesus Chrestos."[307]

A Manichean epistle from a Coptic papyrus codex reads:

> Mani, apostle of Jesus Chrestos and all the other brothers who are with me.... Peace through God the Father, and our lord Jesus Chrestos.[308]

Regarding this codex of Mani's epistles, Iain Gardner remarks, "The form 'Chrestos,' that is, 'Jesus the Good,' is found throughout the text."[309]

Manichaean churches and scriptures existed as far east as China and as far west as the Roman Empire. Although most of the original writings of the founding prophet Mani (c. 216–276 CE) have been lost, numerous translations and fragmentary texts have survived. Its beliefs are a synthesis of Christianity, Zoroastrianism and Buddhism.[310]

The most important Manichaean writings were in Syriac-Aramaic, since Marcion was likewise very engaged in Syria. This region, it should be recalled, was the source of much Gnosticism. In chapter 2 of "On the Manichaeans," Alexander of Lycopolis (fl. fourth cent. AD/CE) says of Mani: "God he called good, and matter he affirmed to be evil."[311] That is to say, Mani called God "Chrestos." It is further interesting to note that, according to Alexander, the Manichaeans "honor very especially the sun and moon, not as gods, but as the way by which it is possible to attain unto God."[312]

---

305 Bartram, "Chrest Magus."
306 See, for example, Bartram.
307 Kippenberg, 156.
308 Mirecki (2001), 96.
309 Mirecki (1997), 163.
310 Welburn, 68.
311 Roberts, 6.241.
312 "Of the Manichaeans" (5); Roberts, 6.242.

If Luke and Acts had only one author, why does the phrase "Jesus Christ" appear not one time in Luke but multiple times in Acts? It is obvious that whoever wrote Acts is not the author of Luke but merely the redactor, who didn't think to pepper the previously written work with the phrase "Jesus Christ." This phrase only appears three times in Matthew, all in the first chapter, and twice in John (1:17, 17:3): Ἰησοῦς Χριστός. It is therefore not in any of the other synoptics, and only in Matthew at the beginning, indicating that chapter may be interpolated, which is indeed a contention made by some scholars and researchers.

The verses in Luke that mention "Christ" may originally have had "Chrest" or they may have been interpolated by the redactor to Judaize the text. Indeed, these instances in which "Christ" is mentioned in Luke appear to be in those scriptures interpolated into Marcion's gospel, such as Luke 2:11, 26; 3:15. In his reconstruction of Marcion's gospel, Price indeed translates the equivalent of Luke 4:41 not as "they knew that he was the Christ" but as "they knew him to be the Good One,"[313] substituting "Chrest" in other instances of "Christ" in Luke as well. In the Codex Sinaiticus of Luke 4:41, the abbreviation XN, "CHN," which is generally rendered "Christos," occurs here in the accusative, "Christon." However, it could just as easily be "Chreston." The same can be said for the abbreviation XC, "CHS," transliterated as "Christos." It is simply assumed that these abbreviations in these manuscripts refer to "Christos," the "Anointed," rather than "Chrestos," the "Good." Price renders these abbreviations as Chrestos where the scripture is Marcionite and Christos where it is a Lukan interpolation meant to Judaize the text.

There are twelve instances rendered as "Christ" in Luke: 2:11, 26; 3:15; 4:41; 9:20; 20:41; 22:67; 23:2; 23:35, 39; 24:26 and 46. However, none of these actually has the word spelled out; each utilizes the abbreviation XC or XN. The same can be said for the other gospels in the Codex Sinaiticus. Nowhere is "christos" spelled out! Matthew 1:1, for example is abbreviated as XY, which is usually transliterated as "Christou" but which could just as easily—and more probably, perhaps—be rendered "Chrestou." The word for "Jesus" in this scripture is abbreviated as IY; hence, the Greek for "Jesus Christ" is rendered IY XY, the former of which looks like "iu" in the lower case. The same configuration occurs at Matthew 1:18, IY XY, and the same Greek abbreviation IY is used to describe the Israelite hero Joshua in the Sinaiticus Old Testament.

In the Codex Sinaiticus, the phrase "Jesus Christ" does not even appear at John 1:17: It is the abbreviation IY alone, meaning only "Jesus." The notation by the Codex's online transcriber says XY is omitted. The

313 Price, R. (2006), 269.

other instances in the gospels, Matthew 1:17 and Mark 1:1, in which the phrase is rendered "Jesus Christ" are IY XY in the CS. In Sinaiticus, at Acts 4:10 we find the phrase ιυ χυ του ναζοραιου, which is generally rendered "Jesus Christ of Nazareth," but which could be translated as "Jesus Chrest the Nazoraios," this latter word meaning "Nazarene," not "Nazareth."

The word usually transliterated as "Joshua" at Hebrews 4:8 is the same as that for Jesus: ιc or "IS."

All four instances transliterated as "Christ," 1:1, 2, 5 and 11:15, are abbreviated as IY in the Greek of Sinaiticus.

Sixteen instances of "Christ" in Matthew are 1:1, 16; 1:17, 18; 2:4; 11:2; 16:16, 20; 22:24; 23:10; 24:5, 23; 26:63, 68; 27:17, 22.

From these data, we can conclude that the Marcionite concept of the "Good God" and "Jesus the Good," not Jesus the Christ, reigned supreme for centuries, much longer than has been understood by mainstream scholarship, which has simply ignored all these facts and dismissed them in the same manner as the second- and third-century apologists and polemicists. If Jesus Christ were a real, historical person by whose earthly life and sacrifice early Christians were being convinced and converted, the fact that Docetic Marcionism became the dominant force—in which "Jesus Christ" was a disincarnate entity who was not Jewish—remains simply inexplicable. This development makes sense only if the Docetism was first, and carnalizers, historicizers and Judaizers usurped the effort, as the evidence shows, in order to create a "historical Jesus of Nazareth," in the second century, over 100 years after this figure was supposedly crucified.

Scholars and researchers at "History Hunters International" (HHI) have examined the Codices Vaticanus and Sinaiticus and found *no* instances in the New Testament of the use of the Greek word "Christos." *All* terms translated as "Christ" were abbreviations that originally could have been "Chrestos." In their studies of the subject, History Hunters researcher David remarks:

> HHI returns constantly to the archaeological record, or more accurately, the lack of an archaeological record containing any peer-reviewed evidence supporting a Jesus-centered Christianity for the first century of our era.
>
> HHI has been studying the historical and archaeological record tracing the origin of Christian papyri and artifacts back to the second century CE. We asserted that pushing the origin of a Jesus-centered Christianity further into the first century is, given

the state of the present evidence, not valid science.[314]

Although the details will be welcome, we can make a generalized conclusion that the secretive cult of the Chrestiani was both pre-Christian and proto-Christian. These Chrestians were "givers of oracles and money lenders" whose cult was co-opted to become followers of the "anointed" (i.e., Christians). Chrestos also means "a creditor, lender of money, usurer; a debtor, borrower," as well as "declarer of oracles, prophet." This mix undoubtedly included many Jews as well as Pagans.

The Chrestos or Chrestus may be the head(s) of a religious sect that practices divination, mysteries and other mystical arts, perhaps explaining the comment in the New Testament about others healing in "Christ's" name.

Were the tortured "deaconesses" mentioned by Pliny members of the *Chrestian* cult? This changeover may likewise explain why we find women involved in the early Church, whereas the usurpers, co-opters and conspirators of the latter half of the second century onward, increasingly squeezed the women out of leadership positions.

In investigating the Pliny letter from a "Chrestian" perspective, HHI's David points out that, if some of the "Christians" had recanted "many years ago," up to 20 years before, it demonstrates the existence of Chrestianity as a secret society some two decades before the Roman writer, during the time of Domitian (81–96 AD/CE). As a possible and plausible reason for the authorities to object to these Chrestians, David states:

> The Chrestians' activities diverted money away from the Panhellenic temples. Certainly whatever the trustee faction practiced by these Chrestians, disputes of a monetary nature arose. Those among the elites vested in the temple economies had reason to inform on this secret society and its members.[315]

Thus, Pliny and his superiors and peers would have objected because the Chrestians were competitors with the official temple cult, cutting into its popularity and profits.

> ... *chrest* as a lexeme is rooted in the practice of popular magic in the ancient world, particularly in association with secret societies.[316]

314 "Acts of the Chresmologoi: the Role of Oracles and Chronicles in the Creation of Divine Men." The word "chresmologia" is defined as "the delivery of an oracle, prophecy, divination, foretelling," while a "chresmologos" is a "practitioner of this form of divination."

315 "Acts of the Chresmologoi: the Role of Oracles and Chronicles in the Creation of Divine Men."

316 "Acts of the Chresmologoi: the Role of Oracles and Chronicles in the Creation of Divine Men."

> The archaeology we have for Chrest and Jesus Chrest is for a figure of Greek magic, a Jesus Aberamentho with the head of a cockerel. The Jesus Chrest in the earliest gospels is a fully-formed man, more in the tradition of Apollonius of Tyana than a deity to be commanded to perform an exorcism. He is not first or second century, but from the third at the earliest and probably the fourth.[317]
>
> There is no "Christ" in Vaticanus and Sinaiticus, the two oldest codices of the New Testament.
>
> We ... examined the earliest codices of the New Testament, Vaticanus and Sinaiticus, where we found no mention of "Christ" at all.
>
> Instead, we found "Chrest," various Greek titles such as Soter, and abbreviations.[318]

"Chrestos" appears to be the god or spiritual figurehead of the money/banker cult. Is the overturning of the money-changers' tables in the temple a story designed not only to Judaize the text but also to indicate the Christos faction at work? This notion is further validated by the fact that one of the words for "money" in Greek is χρήμα (*chrema*) or the plural χρηματα (*chremata*), from the root χρη, which means "useful."

Manuscript Tradition

As is typical, the manuscript tradition for Pliny's epistles is complicated and messy, reflecting Book 10 possibly as circulating separately and combined only in later centuries with Pliny's other letters. The earliest text that actually contains letter 10 is the Avanzi/Avantius edition, which was printed in 1502 in Venice, Italy, but which was purportedly discovered in France by one "Petrus Leander" or Pietro Aleandro, who made a "quick and partial" copy of Pliny's epistles from the *Codex Parisinus*.[319] It is assumed that this edition reflects what was originally in the earliest extant manuscript of Pliny's epistles, the "P" manuscript, M462 of the Pierpont Morgan collection, which evidently dates to the late fifth century but which no longer contains letter 10, as it purportedly did at St. Victor, Paris, in 1500. However, this association may represent mere wishful thinking in order to trace the letter's existence as far back as is possible.

The first time we encounter the pertinent material from Book 10 is in Tertullian (*Apologeticum*), who is subsequently quoted by Jerome and Eusebius.[320] The question needs to be asked, is there any other evi-

---

317 Bartram, "Mani and Authorship of the Canonical Gospels."

318 Bartram, "Pliny correspondence with Trajan: Christians or Chrestians?"

319 Sandy, 30.

320 Interestingly, Tertullian's "paraphrase" relates that these "Christians" gathered at daylight to sing to Christ *and* God, rather than Christ *as* God:

dence that Pliny tortured and killed Christians? That he made them curse Christ? That a policy of forcing Christians to curse Christ existed at this early date? Since we hear of complaints about cursing Christ from Polycarp towards the middle of the second century, it would seem that such a policy may be a mid-second century concern.

However, it has been suggested that the letter is worthless at best or spurious at worst. Regarding the Pliny letter, Dr. Arthur Drews comments:

> Of the younger Pliny it is hardly necessary to speak further in this connection. He was dragged into the discussion of the "Christ-myth" at a late stage, merely to enlarge the list of witnesses to the historicity of Jesus. No one seriously believes that any such evidence is found in Pliny....
>
> [The] genuinenesss of this correspondence of Pliny and Trajan is by no means certain. Justin does not mention it on an occasion when we should expect him to do so, and even Tertullian's supposed reference to it (*Apol.*, cap. ii) is very doubtful. The tendency of the letters [10.96–7] to put the Christians in as favourable a light as possible is too obvious not to excite some suspicion. For these and other reasons, the correspondence was declared by experts to be spurious even at the time of its first publication, at the beginning of the sixteenth century; and recent authorities ... have disputed its authenticity, either as a whole or in material points.[321]

As we consider the contention of this letter that Pliny tortured Christians, including two "deaconesses," and recommended their execution, it is imperative that we examine closely the letter's origin to be certain that it is genuine and that the Latin governor is not being libeled. The

"...coetus antelucanos ad canendum Christo et deo..." (Pliny/Hardy, 214) It is possible, of course, that Tertullian misquoted based on his memory, filtered through his Christian conditioning. On the other hand, if the Pliny letter is genuine, Tertullian's change may be reflecting a doctrinal endorsement, since the debate raged for decades to centuries as to Christ's "true nature," whether a god or a man, the second person of the trinity. This change might lend support to the mythicist contention that Christianity began with a mythical figurehead/god or a deified "anointed" from a Jewish cult.

321 Drews, A. (1972), 18–9. Drews cites these authorities: "Semler, Aubé (*Histoire des Persécutions de l'Église*, 1875, p. 215, etc.), Havet (*Le Christianisme et ses Origines*, 1884, iv, 8), and Hochart (Études au Sujet de la Persecution des Chretiens sous Neron, 1885, pp. 79–143; compare also Bruno Bauer, *Christus und die Casaren*, 1877, p. 268, etc., and the anonymously published work of Edwin Johnson, *Antigua Mater*, 1887).

fact that the book was apparently circulated separately and only combined later with the other nine books raises suspicion, as does the fact that its style is "much simpler" than these others.

However, even if the text is genuine, its value as credible, scientific evidence for the historicity of Jesus is basically nil, since it is too late to serve as anything but a witness to a certain group of rabble rousers who worshipped a "god" named *Christo*. Apologists automatically assume that the "god Christo" refers to "Jesus," but no such name appears anywhere in Pliny's writings. As we have seen, many people were titled "Anointed," including various Jewish heroes, as well as other gods, so it could be one of these others. There is no indication in the letter that this "Anointed" was a real person at any point in history.

Other modern scholars who have questioned whether or not Suetonius's "Chresto" refers to Jesus Christ include Howard Dixon Slingerland, Stephen Benko and Oskar Z. Augustsson. Says Augustsson: "Christians seem to *want* Suetonius' words to be a reference to Jesus, because they have yet another (alleged) evidence for his historical existence."

The contention at Acts 18:2 that "Claudius had commanded all the Jews to leave Rome," in which the author makes no attempt to insinuate that these outcasts were really Christians, further serves as evidence that this passage in Suetonius refers to *Jews*, not Christians, and therefore provides no proof of Christ's historicity.

As late as the third to fourth centuries, the terms "Christians" and "Chrestians" were being haphazardly interchanged.[322] Perhaps Pliny's letter is describing the same group disparaged in the notorious Hadrian letter, which appears in a text, the *Historia Augusta*, that evidently dates to the fourth century but which depicts well the milieu of the earlier day. Perhaps the compilers of the *Historia Augusta* used a genuinely ancient document? Could the words in this Hadrian letter be "Chrestian" and "Chrest," rather than "Christian" and "Christ"? The setting would fit these conjurers and money-lenders better than it would the later impression of Christians.

Bartram asks:

> The question arises, from our point of view: what is the primary source of this published correspondence? That is, are they based on the letters themselves? The short answer is 'no,' they are not based on his letters.[323]

322 See, for example, Gibson, Elsa. *The "Christians for Christians" Inscriptions of Phrygia*. Missoula, MT: Scholars Press, 1978.

323 Bartram, "Pliny correspondence with Trajan: Christians or Chrestians?"

According to Pliny translator Peter G. Walsh:

This translation is based on the text of the letters edited by R.A.B. Mynors (Oxford, 1963), which is faithfully reproduced in the Loeb edition (ed. B. Radice, 1969). It rests on three separate manuscript traditions, which Mynors labels α, β, γ and which are popularly known as the Nine-book, Ten-book and Eight-book versions....

The Ten-book tradition (β) provides the sole evidence for Book X; no manuscript survives after V 6, so that we are dependent on printed editions for the rest.... The existence of the letters as we have them is attributable to the heroic endeavours of the Italian and French humanists. They assembled them from widely dispersed texts of the three traditions.[324]

Bartram summarizes:

The earliest letters are medieval and we do not know what exactly Pliny may have written—Chrest or Christ.

Such is the case for all texts claimed in support for early Christianity: they either use Chrest, an abbreviation, or they do not exist—and belong to a Christian textual tradition, rather than history.

If we are to find any value in the Testimonia, the many texts for which no primary source material exists, such as Pliny and Justin amongst others, it is by studying them within their archaeological context.

The term used in the artefactual evidences of the early centuries is Chrest/Good—not messiah—and Jesus the Good, and that is the context within which the missing primary source material should be interpreted.

If the Pliny-Trajan correspondence is genuine, then we may consider the term used was not *Christian* but *Chrestian*. This method of interpretation applies also to the earliest codices of the New Testament.[325]

Publius/Gaius Cornelius Tacitus

Like Pliny, the historian Publius/Gaius Cornelius Tacitus (c 55–120 AD/CE) did not live during the purported time of Jesus but was born more than two decades after "the Savior's" alleged death. Thus, if there were any passages in his work referring to Christ or his immediate followers, they would be secondhand and must stem from long after the alleged

324 Walsh, xxxvi.

325 Bartram, "Pliny correspondence with Trajan: Christians or Chrestians?"

events. Tacitus's account represents the only Pagan "record" of Christ being put to death by Pontius Pilate, which is why this passage is crucial to "historical Jesus" studies and Christian apologetics. Indeed, Tacitus is held up by apologists as an "extremely rich source of data who confirms important aspects of Christian history," but is this true? Can we consider a late second-hand passage of some 200 to 300 words to be an "extremely rich source of data?" Is the information accurate, and does it date from the purported time?

There is a great historical irony in this text of Tacitus; it is the only time in ancient pagan literature that Pontius Pilate is mentioned by name—as a way of specifying who Christ is. Pilate's fate in the Christian creeds is already foreshadowed in a pagan historian.[326]

In a passage in *The Annals* (15.44) purportedly composed between 103 and 120 AD/CE, Tacitus supposedly related that the Roman emperor Nero (37–68 AD/CE) had blamed the burning of Rome during his reign (64 AD/CE) on "those people who were abhorred for their crimes and commonly called Christians." This holocaust resulted in the destruction of some two-thirds of the great city; yet, oddly enough, it is only in Tacitus that we read this story of Nero blaming the devastation on the Christian population:

Nero fastened the guilt and inflicted the most exquisite tortures on a class hated for their abominations, called Christians by the populace. Christus, from whom the name had its origin, suffered the extreme penalty during the reign of Tiberius at the hands of one of our procurators, Pontius Pilatus, and a most mischievous superstition, thus checked for the moment, again broke out not only in Judaea, the first source of the evil, but even in Rome, where all things hideous and shameful from every part of the world find their centre and become popular. Accordingly, an arrest was first made of all who pleaded guilty; then, upon their information, an immense multitude was convicted, not so much of the crime of firing the city, as of hatred against mankind. Mockery of every sort was added to their deaths. Covered with the skins of beasts, they were torn by dogs and perished, or were nailed to crosses, or were doomed to the flames and burnt, to serve as a nightly illumination, when daylight had expired. Nero offered his gardens for the spectacle, and was exhibiting a show in the circus, while he mingled with the people in the dress of a charioteer or stood aloft on a car. Hence, even for criminals who deserved extreme and exemplary punishment, there arose a feeling of compassion; for it was not, as it seemed, for the public good, but

326 Meier, J. (1991), 1.99.

to glut one man's cruelty, that they were being destroyed.[327]

Arguments for Authenticity

Was this passage original and integral to *The Annals*? Those who think it is contend, first, that the passage's tone is "anti-Christian;" second, there is a "scapegoat" motif in it; third, it has a certain Latin style; and, fourth, it is integrated well into the story.[328] But these arguments turn out to be shallow and easily addressed.

In the first place, if one were to imitate a Roman writer of the time, to make an interpolation realistic instead of simplistically reflective of Christian dogma (which after so many centuries of just such fraud was a real suspicion on people's minds), one would indeed make the Christians appear unsympathetic.

But suppose this passage were really from Tacitus's hand, and Christians were truly viewed thus, how could we account for this sociopathic loathing for the "gentle lambs of God?"

Secondly, the scapegoat motif is found in the Old Testament (Ps. 22; Lev. 16; Isa. 53)[329], as well as in the religious doctrines, myths, legends and rituals of other cultures, centuries before the Common Era.[330] Indeed, the gospel story represents one more version of this ancient archetype enacted in ritual form. A major reason for the creation of Christianity was to put an end to this bloody practice with the once-for-all sacrifice of Jesus. Was this sacrifice a historical event? Absolutely—it happened countless times in the centuries and decades prior to the ostensible death of Jesus. There is no need to find one "historical" Jesus, when this gospel *play* is understood as a literary *archetype* of the ancient sacred-king, human sacrifice/scapegoat ritual.

---

327 The Latin of the earliest extant manuscript is: "Ergo abolendo rumori Nero subdidit reos et quaesitissimis poenis adfecit, quos per flagitia invisos vulgus **Chrestianos** appellabat. auctor nominis eius **Christus Tibero imperitante per procuratorem Pontium Pilatum supplicio adfectus** erat; repressaque in praesens exitiablilis superstitio rursum erumpebat, non modo per Iudaeam, originem eius mali, sed per urbem etiam, quo cuncta undique atrocia aut pudenda confluunt celebranturque. Igitur primum correpti qui fatebantur." (Tacitus, *Annales ab excessu divi Augusti* , ed. C.D. Fisher, Cornelii Taciti Annalium (Oxford 1906); Linck, 61.)

328 Lowder, "Josh McDowell's 'Evidence' for Jesus."

329 Various scriptures in Psalms are seen as major "messianic prophecies" by which Jesus of Nazareth was deemed messiah. These passages were clearly used as a *blueprint* to create a *mythical* messiah.

330 See my book *Suns of God* for more information on the history of religiously related human sacrifice.

Thirdly, according to Latin scholar Polydore Hochart (1831–1916) and John Wilson Ross (1818–1887), who wrote on the subject of Tacitus's Latin, specifically vis-à-vis *Annals* 15:44, the Latin of this passage does *not* closely resemble Tacitus's style elsewhere. Some scholars call the Latin of Book 15 of the *Annals* inferior and coarse, not at all like Tacitus's style. Indeed, the text "bears a character of exaggeration, and trenches on the laws of rational probability, which the writings of Tacitus are rarely found to do."[331]

Next, if the controverted passage can even be considered "well integrated" into the surrounding text, it could just be that the skilled forger found a very good place to interpolate it and was smart enough to exploit it. However …

Protestant humanist scholars Joseph Scaliger (1540–1609) and Isaac Casaubon (1559–1614) "already had their own reasons for a remorseless treatment of the flaws of the *Annales*."[332] There are in fact many reasons to consider this passage a forgery, not the least of which is the consideration of abundant Christian interpolations and "pseudonymous" forgeries also attributed to ancient authors in order to lend authority and credibility to Christian doctrines and history. To ignore such a record, in the face of yet more suspicious circumstances, represents folly, shortsightedness and wishful thinking, possibly reflecting an agenda of one sort or another, but certainly not science.

Here are some of the reasons to suspect the Tacitus passage as a forgery, in toto:

1. [There] is no corroborating evidence that Nero persecuted the Christians;
2. There was not a multitude of Christians in Rome at that date;
3. "Christian" was not a common term in the first century;
4. Nero was indifferent to various religions in his city;
5. Nero did not start the fire in Rome;
6. Tacitus does not use the name Jesus;
7. Tacitus assumes his readers know Pontius Pilate;
8. The passage is present word-for-word in the Chronicle of Sulpicius Severus.[333]

---

331 Taylor, R. (1829), 396.
332 Whealey, 87.
333 This list represents a summary of Dr. Gordon Stein's arguments, created by J.J. Lowder.

Procurator or Prefect?

The term "procurator" is anachronistic. It was used in Tacitus's time, but not in Pilate's time. The passage assumes familiarity with Pontius Pilate, although it uses the term "procurator," rather than his proper title of "prefect," which Tacitus surely would have known and used. Indeed, he is familiar with both terms in other parts of *The Annals* and used both appropriately. But even if Tacitus actually wrote the passage, his dependence on Josephus would make the former's account worthless as corroboration.

Vast Multitudes of Christians at Rome?

Why would Tacitus need to clarify that these multitudes were "called Christians by the populace," unless he were addressing someone who did not know who Christians were? Surely by his time Christians must have been well-known, especially since Nero allegedly blamed them for a massively traumatic tragedy that must have killed thousands. It looks as if a Christian interpolator took for granted that a pagan writing for pagans would assume the Christian faith would be alien to them. He tacitly pictured the absolute ideological separation between the two faiths as a social separation, necessitating such an explanation to fellow outsiders.

The pertinent Latin is *multitudo ingens*, with *multitude* defined as "large number, multitude, crowd; common people; mob"[334] and *ingens* meaning "monstrous, vast, enormous."[335]

As I ask in *Who Was Jesus?* (95), if there was a vast multitude of Christians at Rome in the '60s, why would Suetonius write some 40 to 50 years later that Christianity was a "new" superstition? How could Suetonius fail to discuss such a scenario in his *Life of Nero*, especially when the historian does record the fire but blames it on Nero himself, making no connection between the fire and the alleged punishment of Christians?

If Nero had blamed Christians for burning Rome, where there purportedly had been a vast multitude of Christians, would we not expect Tacitus to discuss this alien belief system at least a bit more?

One apologist attempts to make relative the phrase "vast multitude," claiming that, under certain circumstances, such as a minor occurrence, a small number of people might be considered an "immense multitude." However, this special pleading does not suffice in the case of a massive situation wherein some two-thirds of a major city—the very capital of the Roman Empire—has been destroyed, resulting in many thousands of lives lost. In this instance, clearly a "vast/immense multitude" would

334 Cassell's Latin English Dictionary, 144.
335 Cassell's Latin English Dictionary, 117.

refer to thousands of people.

Even though Christians were allegedly accused of a heinous crime, purportedly constituting a "vast multitude" at Rome, and supposedly had been persecuted mercilessly, nowhere else does Tacitus mention them, Christ or Pilate, or even allude to their existence.

If Tacitus declares there was a "vast multitude" of Christians at Rome during this time, yet there is no evidence for such a contention, may we not logically conclude a) Tacitus was wrong, which is somewhat incomprehensible with such a major event and his access to Roman records, or b) the passage is an interpolation?

If we agree that "vast multitude" means precisely what it says, rather than some tortured illogic, and that Nero is hereby alleged to have persecuted many Christians, we next need to ask if large groups of people could have been thrown to the lions at Rome decades before the Colosseum was built.

Annals as Forgery?

While scholars like Dr. John P. Meier will assert that "there is no historical or archaeological evidence to support the argument that a scribe may have introduced the passage into the text,"[336] the reality is that there is no historical or archaeological evidence that the text existed prior to the eleventh century at all. The passage, however, is not recorded by any early Church father, and, indeed, was unknown to the world until the fifteenth century, when the manuscript apparently written at Monte Cassino in the eleventh century was allegedly discovered at the San Marco monastery in Florence, Italy.

When it is argued that the passage exists in all extant copies of *The Annals*, it should be noted that all of these copies come from the *same* medieval manuscript, found in the Laurentian library (no. 68.2).

The entire *Annals* itself has come under fire because of its suspicious "discovery" during the fifteenth century.[337] Suffice it to say that it needs to be kept in mind that the age when this manuscript suddenly surfaced was one of tremendous forgery, because the wealthy elite of Europe, including especially the pope, were clamoring for texts for their libraries, particularly those texts that upheld Christianity. In this regard, many destitute monks took advantage of this boon and provided many

336 "Tacitus on Christ." See Meier (1991), 168–171.

337 Interested readers are referred to the works of J.W. Ross and Herb Cutner, as well as Murdock (2004; 398ff), for further discussion of the subject of *The Annals* themselves representing a forgery. For example, Ross addresses the contention that the earliest manuscript containing book 10 dates to the eleventh century.

"long lost" and "discovered" manuscripts to their benefactors.

Chrestiani versus Christiani?

A very important fact concerning this debate is that the original Latin of Tacitus's *Annals* 15.44, the term widely translated as "Christians" is apparently *Chrestianos*, the term used to describe followers of "the Good One," or "Chrestos/Chresto/Chrestus." In the oldest extant manuscript of this passage, folio 38r of the "second Medicean," or M.II, housed at the Laurentian Library in Italy, where it is numbered 68.2, close examination reveals that the "e" in "Chrestiani" has been erased and replaced with an "i," with a marginal gloss clarifying the meaning as "Christiani." This manuscript has been examined by a number of experts who have deemed it clearly manipulated in this manner. Remember, this particular manuscript is the one from which all other extant copies of Tacitus have been reproduced; hence, again, the argument for authenticity based on all copies being the same is fallacious.

The passage has been suspected for many years to say "Chrestiani," after scholars noted the space between the "i" and the "s." Thus, in some printed Latin editions—notably the Fisher edition—the word was rendered "Chrestiani." Certain scholars, researchers and apologists denied this apparent fact, but an ultraviolet examination in modern times confirms it, showing that there was indeed an erasure of a letter underneath—clearly the letter "e." The individual who requested the most recent examination of the word using modern technology was Dr. Erik Zara, who concludes:

> I consider it now totally safe to say, in accordance with the examinations made by Andresen, Lodi and Rao, that the fourth letter in "Christianos" indeed has been changed from an "e" to an "i." Accordingly, the scribe originally wrote Chrestiani, "Chrestians."

Since the handwriting of the original word and that of the marginal gloss are different, and considering that the marginal gloss says "Christiani," it seems most likely that it was the glossator who "corrected" the manuscript. Others who had the opportunity to make this change include "humanist and Latin professor Zanòbi da Strada (1312–1361)," a friend of Giovanni Boccacio, the individual suspected of stealing the manuscript from the Monte Cassino monastery in the fourteenth century.[338]

The word "Christus" here, however, shows no evidence of tampering. We would submit that the entire passage about Christus, Pilate and Tiberius is an interpolation or marginal gloss that made its way into the text. In "Tacitus as a Witness to Jesus," Roger Viklund demonstrates

338 Zara, "The Chrestianos Issue in Tacitus Reinvestigated."

how this passage could have been interpolated, after having first appeared as a marginal gloss:

I have suggested that the sentence 'Auctor nominis eius Christus Tiberio imperitante per procuratorem Pontium Pilatum supplicio adfectus erat' ('Christ, from whom the name had its origin, was in the reign of Tiberius executed by procurator Pontius Pilatus') could have been a later addition.

Viklund reconstructs a hypothetical original using images from Dr. R. A. Daniel Pihl. This conclusion of interpolation is shared by Dr. Zara, who in "Tacitus' sentence about Christus—a marginal gloss?" lists several reasons for suspecting that "the sentence about Christus was a marginal gloss, later inserted to the text." This sentence being a later marginal gloss/interpolation explains why earlier Christians showed no interest in this Tacitean passage, since it was certainly not about them. This conclusion also explains why "Tacitus" refers to Pilate as a "procurator," rather than "prefect," since he clearly did not write this error.

The fact that the earlier word was "Chrestiani" would imply that, if a leader was mentioned at all, his name/title would be the same as in Suetonius (i.e., "Chresto"). Thus, the Tacitean passage would reflect the same story about *Jews* rabble rousing in the name (actually an epithet) of their God, יהוה/YHWH, and possesses no value whatsoever in establishing a "historical" Jesus. The fact that Tacitus evidently did not like Jews would explain the passage's negative tone.

Reasons for suspecting this passage to be a forgery include the fact that the original appears to have said "Chrestus," not "Christos." It should also be noted that, while the passage discusses a "Christus" or, possibly, "Chrestus," nowhere does it mention a figure called "Jesus" who purportedly lived a century earlier. Even if the entire passage is original to the text, it seems a safe bet that the sentence "auctor nominis eius Christus Tibero imperitante per procuratorem Pontium Pilatum supplicio adfectus erat" is an interpolation, especially since the word *Chrestiani* would logically be identified as being inspired by "Chrestus," not "Christus" as in the received text. With this change, we see that it is possible that Tacitus based his account on Suetonius, or vice versa, or that both used a similar or the same source text. If such is the case, the Tacitean account—minus the interpolated sentence about Christ being "afflicted with capital punishment"—could, like Suetonius, refer to *Jews* invoking their God/Yahweh as "Chresto"; hence, they are "Chrestiani." This suspicion is encouraged by the Latin phrase used by the Tacitean interpolator for "afflicted punishment" or *supplicio adfectus*.

In *Apology* (3.5), Tertullian comments upon the "mispronunciation" by non-Christians of "Christian" as "Chrestian." It is assumed that this "mispronunciation" was due to "vulgarity" on the part of those using the term,[339] when in fact it appears to be a pre-Christian title that was adopted by the influential sect of the Marcionites, for one.

Tacitus does express disdain for Jews, however, and if this passage is genuine to Tacitus, he could have been referring to a group of them rabble-rousing under their pre-Christian "anointed," unless, of course, the original word was "Chrestus," which could refer to any number of individuals deemed "the good" or "the useful," including slaves.

Augustsson says:

> Roger Pearse informs me that one manuscript of *Annales* 15:44 does indeed containing [sic] "Chrestus," which has been changed into "Christus." … In the *Annales* 15:44 translation by Mitchell, as in that by Schmid and Rohde, the text reads "Chrestus," and not "Christus," as Schmid informs me. So "Chrestus" is evident in manuscripts and has been changed during the Middle Ages …
>
> The conclusion is that Tacitus in no way is speaking of Jesus from Nazareth or about Christians, but rather about Chrestus and Chrestians …

Indeed, how likely is it that Tacitus is referring to an agitation at the time of Nero different from the one recorded by Suetonius, who clearly refers to *Jews* and to *Chrestus*?

The impression is given widely that all references to "Chrestiani" indicate *Christians*; therefore, any discussion of "Chrestus" must be referring to *Christ*. However, this contention is erroneous, because it is only applicable to any extent to the *second* century. Indeed, there is no evidence that any of the hundreds of inscriptions and references to "Chrestians" that date from the first century have anything to do with Christians at all. In fact, *all* inscriptions from the first century citing "Chrestians" apparently refer either to *Pagans* or *Jews*.

Hence, rather than referring to Christians, it appears there was a pre-Christian sect of some sort that followed Jewish rules to some extent, the members of which seem to have been largely among the elite. In fact, "Chrestianus" was a Roman *cognomen*,[340] referring to the third name of a male citizen, originally often a "nickname" that eventually was passed from father to son. For example, a Pagan inscription (CIL VI, 24944) cites someone called "Iucundi Chrestiani," while another (CIL VI 1056. 2 1. 3) mentions "Agid[ius] Chresti(anus)."[341] This missing piece of the

339 Tertullian/Arbesmann, 16.

340 Cappelletti, 75.

341 Cappelletti, 75.

puzzle sheds tremendous light on the subject of Christian origins, as it appears that Christianity began not with a "historical Jesus of Nazareth" but with a sect of Chrestiani, whose religion was coopted during the second century, when it was historicized and Judaized.

If non-Jews/Greeks were the ones who confused "Christos" with "Chrestos," because they rarely used the former term, as it was favored by Jews, would this not prove its pre-Christian use? In reality, it seems hardly scientific to claim that non-Jews were "confused," when the name clearly was common as a Roman cognomen.

Interestingly, it seems that the one time the word "Christians" is used in the New Testament, at Acts 11:26, it originally appeared as "Chrestians," as evidenced by the Codex Sinaiticus. In that text, dating to the fourth century, the word is clearly written with a capital eta or H: "XPHCTIANOY." Since the original Latin Vulgate New Testament of Jerome evidently transliterated the word as "Christiani," it is possible that the term "Christian" came into popular usage after the Codex Sinaiticus was written, but before or with Jerome, between the fourth and fifth centuries. The same development can be seen in the Codex Sinaiticus version of Acts 26:11, which clearly reads XPHCTIANON—"Chrestianon." This manuscript was changed or "corrected" by at least seven different hands from the fourth to twelfth centuries, amassing some 14,800 "corrections" by Tischendorf's estimate.

The same rendering of "χρηστιανους" at Acts 11:26 occurs in the Codex Augiensis,[342] which dates to the ninth century, demonstrating that even at that late date there remained manuscripts with "Chrestiani."

The online searchable Codex Sinaiticus even lists the word at Acts 11:26 as χρηcτιανουc—"*chrestianous*"—not "*christianous*."[343] The searchable Sinaiticus does likewise for the word at Acts 26:28—χρηcτιανον—"*chrestianon*," not "*christianon*." The same can be said for 1 Peter 4:16—χρηcτιανοc—"*chrestianos*," not "*christianos*."

In this regard, there is a marble inscription (CIL VI 24944) from the first century that cites one "Iucundus Chrestianus" or, as it is in the accusative "Iucundi Chrestiani"—Iucundus the Chrestian. This inscription is dedicated to the "Gods of the Underworld," reflecting a religious purpose and clearly a *Pagan* monument.

This inscription also mentions "Antoniae Drusi," an apparent reference to Antonia Minor, mother of Claudius (10 BCE–54 AD/CE), sister-in-law of Tiberius and associate of Alexandrian Jew and Roman citizen

342 Scrivener, 428.

343 codexsinaiticus.org/en/manuscript.aspx?book=51&chapter=11&lid=en&side=r&verse=26

Tiberius Julius Alexander Major (15/10 BCE–69 AD/CE), also known as "Alexander the Alabarch," a wealthy patron of several important figures of antiquity, including Nero and Vespasian.

John Bartram comments, "We now see that Chrest and Chrestian refer to members of an axis of power between Rome and Alexandria, whose two prime movers are Antonia Minor and Alexander Lysimachus (the Alabarch)."[344]

The "Iucundus" of the inscription is apparently Lucius Caecilius Jucundus (c. 20–69 AD/CE), a Roman banker who lived at Pompeii, Italy. It is important to recall that "*chrestos*" referred not only to diviners and assorted "good folks" from slaves to nobility but also to gods, including the Jewish one. It is also important to note that *chrestes* referred to both a creditor and a debtor (i.e., someone involved in a monetary transaction). All of these terms come from the same verb, χράω or *chrao*, which means to divine, to lend, and to be useful. (Money, after all, is useful and good.)

It is clear that many "Chrestiani" were members of the wealthy elite, including both Jews and Pagans, apparently building on the "*chrestoi*" of past eras, creating an actual organized brotherhood, sect or cult following an idealized "Chrestos." This "Chrestos" may have been the "Good God," represented by a person or persons, perhaps, since pre-Christian times. No "historical" founder is thus necessary to explain this movement, which was obviously co-opted in the second and third centuries by "enterprising spirits" who historicized and Judaized what had become the Gnostic effort.

Alexander the Alabarch had loaned a sizable sum to the wife of Jewish king Herod Agrippa I, whose daughter Berenice is the "Bernice" mentioned at Acts 25:13 who was Titus's mistress. Other players include: Alexandrian prefect Tiberius Julius Alexander (20 AD/CE to late first cent.), son of the Jewish magnate Alexander the Alabarch and Philo's nephew; and Josephus, the Jewish general who surrendered to Vespasian and Titus.

It is rumored that these figures belonged to a secret society called "the sons of the Sun"; could they also have been *Chrestiani*? What was their relationship to the Therapeuts? Since Philo was the greatest explicator of the Therapeuts, and since his brother was the Alexandrian alabarch who sponsored Vespasian, there is an obvious connection.

Bartram tells us:

> The history of conspiracy and assassination in the first century—but beginning with that of Julius Caesar in the century before—

344 Bartram, "Chrestians and the lost history of Classical Antiquity."

is driven by the Rome-Alexandria axis.

> Theology was but one tool in their armoury and without the resources of the Alexandrian Library to be mined by a brother of the Alabarch [Philo], these thugs would have stayed in the first century as a footnote.[345]

We thus submit that this *conspiracy* extended to the creation of Christianity. Episkopos, bishop, deacon, ecclesia, pontifex—these are all pre-Christian titles. The Roman college of priests or Collegium Pontificum was the "most illustrious" of four priestly colleges in Rome at the time and was headed by the pontifex maximus.

If "Chrestian" is a term used only by ignorant Pagans to describe Christians, why does the original scribe of the Codex Sinaiticus use it? Because, perhaps, the gospel story was not originally about "Jesus the Christ" but "Jesus the Chrest," the pre-Christian and proto-Christian mystical savior?

Does Acts 16:16 reflect a battle between *Chrestians* and Paulinists? Competition because of the lucrative nature of the religion business?

"First century Chrestianity ran afoul of both Roman law (*lex superstitio illicita*) and Neoplatonist morality on a variety of grounds."

According to Roman law, magic or *Magia* constituted a criminal offense when performed with evil intent to either physically harm or defraud a person. Magia was a broad term encompassing many possible types of magic practices: sorcery, nocturnal sacrifices, numerology, astrology, spell-casting, etc.[346]

It seems from the evidence—which includes inscriptions apparently with the word "Chrestian" mutilated[347]—part of the conspiratorial censorship that accompanied the rise of Christianity included the expunging of Chrestianity from the historical record.

Tacitus (*Annals*, 3.60):

> A license and an unrestrained practice of establishing sanctuaries was growing common throughout the cities of Greece. Temples were filled with the vilest slaves. By the same expedi-

345 Bartram, "Chrestians and the lost history of Classical Antiquity."

346 "Acts of the Chresmologoi: the Role of Oracles and Chronicles in the Creation of Divine Men."

347 See Bartram, "The vacuum of evidence for pre-fourth century Christianity": "Arycanda (Lycia). In 311-312 delegates from one province asked the emperor to make those 'atheists,' the _ _ _ _ _tians, stop violating the rules of piety. To that end, they were to be forbidden from engaging in their execrable practices and ordered to worship the gods. (Museum of Istanbul) Note that the letters—along the left edge—which would have spelt either *Chres* or *Chris* have been destroyed."

> ent, debtors took shelter against creditors, and men suspected of capital offences [sought an asylum]. No authority was sufficiently strong for checking the seditions of a people that protected the crimes of men as the ordinances of the gods.[348]

> Given the available hard archaeological data, we may posit that the early Christians were in a fundamental sense *chresmologoi*, some comprising secret societies encompassing the functions of a *chrestis*. That is to say, they engaged in the business of declaring oracles for money and perhaps lending money on the basis of influence of such pronouncements. At least a portion of their clientele derived from this trade.[349]

It appears that the Paul character represented a *chresmologos* who was successful in destroying his competitors. This "chresmologue" is a diviner, singer and/or interpreter of oracles and signs: "The apostles are diviners, declarers of oracles, interpreters of signs." Obviously, in order to ply one's trade most profitably, one would wish to attach oneself to an ancient god or prophet, known by such epithets as "Chrestos" or "Christo," perhaps.

> [The] texts that flesh this Christ out were written in the second century, for chresmological purposes, to enhance the authority, allure and market share of the secret society brought to light by Pliny circa 112 CE.[350]

> In the first century of this era, Chrestians are the elite, "the great and the good," and not until the reign of Domitian, when Hadrian first takes public office, or perhaps a little later, with his [boy toy] Antinous, is Chrest associated with those outside the elite circles of imperial power.[351]

What Neronian Persecution?

As I relate in *Suns of God*, the Neronian persecution of Christians is unrecorded by any other historian of the day and supposedly took place at the very time when Paul was purportedly freely preaching at Rome

348 Ussher, 801. Tactitus's original Latin is as follows: "Graecas per urbes licentia atque impunitas asyla statuendi; complebantur templa pessimis servitiorum; eodem subsidio obaerati adversum creditores suspectique capitalium criminum receptabantur. Nec ullum satis validum imperium erat coercendis seditionibus populi, flagitia hominum ut caerimonias deum protegentis." (Tacitus/Allen, 251.)

349 David, "Acts of the Chresmologoi."

350 "Acts of the Chresmologoi: the Role of Oracles and Chronicles in the Creation of Divine Men."

351 Bartram, "Pliny correspondence with Trajan: Christians or Chrestians?"

(Acts 28:30–31), facts that cast strong doubt on whether it actually happened. Drews concludes that the Neronian persecution is likely "nothing but the product of a Christian's imagination in the fifth century."[352] Referring, perhaps, to Severus?

In reality, the purported passage in Tacitus regarding Christians being persecuted under Nero appears likely to be yet another of the many interpolations and forgeries, as previously discussed. Zealous defender of the faith Eusebius never mentions the Tacitus passage, nor does anyone else prior to the fifteenth century AD/CE:

> This passage, which would have served the purposes of Christian quotation better than any other in all the writings of Tacitus, or of any Pagan writer whatever, is not quoted by any of the Christian fathers.... It is not quoted by Tertullian, though he had read and largely quotes the works of Tacitus.... There is no vestige or trace of its existence anywhere in the world before the 15th century.[353]

Moreover, nowhere else does Tacitus discuss Pontius Pilate at all.

Eusebius contends that Nero was hateful of Christians; yet, he never mentions the emperor blaming them for the burning of Rome or his subsequent persecution of them. He could therefore not have been aware of any such testimony, whether in Tacitus or elsewhere. Again, before we simply accept this calumny against Nero, even if deserved, we must be certain this text is genuine. Its history and composition are not encouraging in this regard, however.

Nero was allegedly targeted by a conspiracy engineered by Gaius Calpurnius Piso, who was arrested in 65. The person who ratted him out was a Greek freedman (*chestos*?) and imperial chamberlain named "Epaphroditus," which is the same name at Philippians 2:25, 4:18 and 4:23. Were the congregations of the churches to which the Pauline epistles were addressed *Chrestiani*? Certainly, these cities in the main were seats of pre-existing brotherhood organizations, including the various collegia and religious associations such as that of Dionysus and Orpheus, as well as many other religions, such as Mithraism. Could the Chrestiani be one of these pre-Christian brotherhood organizations or a title for one elite or select group among them? Could they be related to the Therapeutae at Alexandria? All of these questions are suggested by the evidence.

Bartram identifies the underlying "historical" Paul as the "Saulus" of Josephus, who was related to one Costobarus. We would add that "Paul's" life is oddly intertwined with that of Apollonius of Tyana as well. It seems more likely that, while some elements of Paul's life appear

352 Drews (1998), 231.
353 Taylor, R., 395–6.

to have been based on Saulus, the stories of his travels and letter-writing, missionary activities, etc., are borrowed from those of Apollonius.

Was the destruction of the Jerusalem temple revenge for *Jews* burning Rome? The anti-Jewish sentiment is clear from Seneca to Tacitus and beyond—people did not like Jews. Nero hated the Jews, Claudius hated the Jews, Caius hated the Jews, the Greeks hated the Jews. Some very wealthy Jews had great clout and power, such as Tiberius Alexander. Seneca was an advisor of Nero.

Greeks—including those in Syria (i.e., Syrians)—and Jews were constantly battling each other in Palestine and Egypt, among others. One of these riots in 66 at Caesarea, in fact, led to the Jewish War that eventually destroyed the temple. (Josephus, *Ant.*, 20.173–84; *Wars* 1.284–92).

Sources/Influences: Sulpicius Severus

Stein says that the Tacitean passage is "present almost word-for-word in the *Chronicle* of Sulpicius Severus (died in 402 AD), where it is mixed in with obviously false tales." He contends that, rather than Severus having copied this passage from Tacitus, since no one else up to that time seems to have known about it, it is more likely that "copyists working in the Dark Ages from the only existing manuscript of the *Chronicle* simply copied the passage from Sulpicius into the manuscript of Tacitus which they were reproducing." It seems that the apparent forger of this Tacitus passage used Suetonius, Tertullian, Josephus, Sulpicius Severus, et al., to create his interpolation.

If Tacitus wrote this passage, including that Christ had allegedly been put to death during the reign of Tiberius, why doesn't he include this important event in his books on Tiberius in *The Annals*?

The emphasis of this short passage on Christ being crucified under Pontius Pilate represents a clue to the forces at work here, since that motif is central to the Apostles' Creed, an early Christian statement of faith with 12 articles, including: "He suffered under Pontius Pilate, was crucified, died, and was buried." Tacitus's forger here stops short of the real purpose of the Apostles' Creed, which is to ensure domination by the Catholic Church.[354]

354 The Apostles' Creed appears to have been written by the Church father Ambrose around 390. Constituting 12 articles of faith, the Creed reads as follows: "1. I believe in God, the Father almighty, creator of heaven and earth; 2. I believe in Jesus Christ, his only Son, our Lord; 3. He was conceived by the power of the Holy Spirit and born of the Virgin Mary; 4. He suffered under Pontius Pilate, was crucified, died, and was buried; 5. He descended to the dead. On the third day he rose again; 6. He ascended into heaven and is seated at the right hand of the Father; 7. He will come again to judge the living and the dead; 8. I believe in the Holy Spirit; 9. the holy catholic Church, the com-

Absence from Early Christian Literary Record

Like Josephus's *Testimonium*, this (purported) Tacitus passage is not cited by the early Church fathers, including Tertullian, who does otherwise cite the Roman historian's works. In his *Apology* (16.1), for example, Tertullian complains about Tacitus having sowed the seed of ridiculing Christians for supposedly worshipping an ass. No, says Tertullian, it was the *Jews* who deified the "head of an animal of this kind."[355] If the passage about Nero crucifying Christians is genuine, saying such horrendous things about Christians, why would this Church father not become irate over it, too?

After asserting in his *Apology* (5) that the emperor Tiberius had been a Christian who had attempted to get the Roman Senate to recognize Christ as a god—a fallacious contention— Tertullian says:

> Consult your histories: you will find in them that Nero was the first to rage with the imperial sword against this religion, which was just at that particular time coming to life at Rome.[356]

Since the first part of Tertullian's contention is clearly erroneous, we may suspect the rest of it as well.

Calumny and Libel?

As we should do with the contentions regarding Pliny torturing and executing harmless and peaceful Christian lambs, we need to proceed cautiously about libeling Nero for words he may not have spoken and deeds he may not have done. Since we have no independent corroboration from the appropriate time, this passage may represent unfounded calumny and should therefore not be so casually and uncritically accepted as genuine, perhaps a "willing suspension of disbelief" stemming from the desire to find historical documentation for the Christian savior's historical existence. To rest the existence of the world's most famous man upon this *Pagan* writer's meager and suspicious passage appears preposterous.

It has been suggested that this "blood-curdling story about the frightful orgies of Nero reads like some Christian romance of the dark ages, and not like Tacitus."[357] Indeed, it has been pointed out that this Tacitean martyrdom story resembles later fictional Christian martyrdom tales. Says New Testament scholar Dr. Darrell J. Doughty (1936–2009):

---

munion of saints; 10. the forgiveness of sins; 11. the resurrection of the body; 12. and life everlasting. Amen." ("English translation of the Apostles' Creed in the Catechism of the Catholic Church." Va. 1997-03-25.

355 Tertullian/Sider, 35.

356 Tertullian/Sider, 16–7.

357 "Is Tacitus Reference an Interpolation?"

> [It] is highly remarkable that no other ancient source associates Christians with the burning of Rome until Sulpicius Serverus in the late fourth century.... The dramatic and fantastic description of the tortures suffered by the scapegoats resembles the executions portrayed in the later legendary Acts of Christian Martyrs.

If, on the other hand, we are to accept this passage as genuine, the question needs to be asked why Tacitus—a Roman *senator*—himself would make such derogatory remarks about Rome, calling it the city "to which all that is horrible and shameful floods together and is celebrated?" Would a respected Roman senator and historian truly state that a multitude of people were hideously tortured and killed not for the crime of burning the city—for which they were "falsely accused and executed"—but in reality, because they hated the human race? Why does Tacitus first say that the Christians were *falsely* accused and then conclude that they were "clearly guilty," yet they were not killed for the "public good" but because of the "fierceness of one man" (i.e., Nero)? Why is Tacitus so vicious towards the Christians, if they were not guilty of burning Rome? This passage is confused and hardly seems to reflect the thinking of "Rome's greatest historian."

Gaius Suetonius Tranquillus

Christian apologists also hold up as evidence of Jesus Christ the minuscule and possibly interpolated passage from the Roman historian Gaius Suetonius Tranquillus (c. 69/75–c. 130–140 AD/CE) referring to someone at Rome named "Chrestus" or "Chrestos," the Greek for "good" or "useful." In Suetonius's *Life of Claudius* (c. 113 AD/CE) we find the following passage (25.4):

> Iudaeos impulsore Chresto assidue tumultuantis Roma expulit.[358]

> [Those] Jews impelled by Chrestos to assiduously cause tumult, [Claudius] expelled out of Rome.

It is argued that Christ was not alleged to have been at Rome, so this passage is not applicable to him. However, the counter claim is that these "Jews" or, rather, Christians, could have simply been *inspired* by Jesus of Nazareth. Yet, the title "Chresto," meaning "good" and "useful," is not the same as "Christo," and was frequently held by freed slaves, among others, including various gods. Thus, these Jews—for they are not described as "Christians"—could have been stirred up by an ex-slave or some other figure revered as "the Good One" or, as we have seen from the Septuagint, the Most High or *God*. (E.g., Nah. 1:7)

Dr. Robert Eisenman also suggests that the incident may record

358 Smallwood, 210.

Jews agitating over the appointment of Herod Agrippa I as King of Judea by his friend Claudius in 41 AD/CE.[359] In this regard, this king is called "*chrestos*" by Josephus. In any event, Jews impelled by God to rabble-rouse would not be an uncommon occurrence at the time, and this passage very well could refer to them. No knowledge of Christians or Christ is therefore necessary at all.

In his *Life of Nero* (16.2; c. 110 AD/CE), Suetonius also mentions "Christians" as involved in a "new and mischievous superstition" and being punished by Nero:

> afflicti suppliciis Christiani, genus hominum superstitionis nouae ac maleficae[360]
>
> He afflicted capital punishment on the Christians, a class of men of a new and mischievous superstition.

It seems odd that a movement over 80 years old would be considered "new," particularly since both Peter and Paul were said to have proselytized at Rome. Indeed, the Book of Acts claims Paul was such a known rabble-rouser that he was arrested and hauled before Roman authorities, even appealing to Caesar himself (Acts 26:32). Paul not only purportedly spent two years in prison in Rome, but it was there that he allegedly later experienced martyrdom in the arena "before a jeering crowd" during Nero's reign.

Strangely, despite his noteworthy life, Paul appears nowhere in the historical record. Moreover, this passage in Suetonius may have been another Christian interpolation, breaking the narrative in an unnatural manner. In any event, these brief mentions of "Chrestos" and "Christians" do not provide credible scientific evidence of the historicity of the gospel story; nor do they add anything to our quest to find out who Jesus was.

The use of the term "mischievous superstition" and the punishment by Nero are reminiscent of the Tacitean passage, which appears to have been created at least in part from Suetonius, perhaps via Serverus. The word *supplicium* means not only punishment but especially capital punishment, indicating that Nero executed these "Christians."

Regarding these "historical references," Taylor says, "But even if they are authentic, and were derived from earlier sources, they would not carry us back earlier than the period in which the gospel legend took form, and so could attest only the legend of Jesus, and not his historicity." In any case, these scarce and brief "references" to a man who supposedly shook up the world, can hardly serve as proof of his existence,

359 Eisenman (1997), 624.

360 C. Suetonius Tranquillus, *Nero*, ed., Maximilian Ihm.

and it is absurd that the purported historicity of the Christian religion is founded upon them.

There were indeed at the time of Christ's alleged advent dozens of relatively reliable historians and other writers who generally did not color their perspectives with a great deal of mythology, cultural bias and religious bigotry—where are *their* testimonies to such amazing events recorded in the gospels? As Mead relates,

> It has always been an unfailing source of astonishment to the historical investigator of Christian beginnings, that there is not a single word from the pen of any Pagan writer of the first century of our era, which can in any fashion be referred to the marvelous story recounted by the Gospel writer. The very existence of Jesus seems unknown.[361]

The silence of these historians is, in fact, deafening testimony against Christ's historicity.

Talmudic and Other Jewish References

One might think that there would at least be reference to the "historical" Jesus in the texts of the Jews, who were known for record-keeping. Yet such is not the case, despite the resort to the references to "Jesus ben Pandera," who purportedly lived during the first century BCE, or other "Jesuses" mentioned in Jewish literature. Unfortunately, these characters do not fit either the story or the purported timeline of the gospel Jesus, no matter how the facts and numbers are fudged.

The story of Jesus ben Pandera, for example, related that, a century before the Christian era, a "magician" named "Jesus" came out of Egypt and was put to death by stoning or hanging. However, ritualistic or judicial executions of this kind were common, as were the name "Jesus" and the magicians flooding out of Egypt. In addition, there is in this story no mention of Romans, among other oversights. Even if ben Pandera were real, it is definitely *not* his story being told in the New Testament.

Massey explains the difficulty with the ben Pandera theory:

> It has generally been allowed that the existence of a Jehoshua, the son of Pandira … acknowledged by the Talmud, proves the personal existence of Jesus the Christ as an historical character in the gospels. But a closer examination of the data shows the theory to be totally untenable.… Jehoshua ben Pandira must have been born considerably earlier than the year 102 BC.… The Jewish writers altogether deny the identity of the Talmudic Jehoshua and the Jesus of the gospels.… The Jews know nothing of Jesus

361 Mead, *DJL*, 48.

as the Christ of the gospels.[362]

Of the Pandira/Pandera story, Larson states, "Throughout the middle ages, the legend of Pandera and Yeshu, *considered by most scholars a Jewish invention*, continued to persist."[363] This Jewish invention may have been created in order to capitulate to the Christian authorities, who were persecuting "unbelievers." It is further surmised that this tale itself is a historicized version of a motif in the myth of Dionysus, who, raised by panthers as his nursemaids, could be deemed "son of a Panther," or *panthera* in Latin. Hence, Dionysus/Bacchus/Iacchus—who bore the epithet ῾ΥΗΣ or IES[364]—is "ben Panthera."

In any event, the tale in the Talmud does not appear until decades to centuries after the Christ myth already existed and does not serve as evidence of a "historical" Jesus.

Wells summarizes the Talmudic material and examines its value:

> Klausner's very full survey of the relevant material in [the Talmud] led him to the conclusion that the earliest references to Jesus in rabbinical literature occur not earlier than about the beginning of the second century.... If there had been a historical Jesus who had anything like the career ascribed to him in the gospels, the absence of earlier references becomes very hard to explain. When Rabbis do begin to mention him,

362 Massey, *HJMC*, 186–197.

363 Larson, 281.

364 See, for example, Taylor, R. (1829), 213. Of Dionysus, Forlong (1.544) says: "Over his shrine was the mystic I.H.S. which became the Christian emblem for 'Iesus hominum salvator.'" Taylor traces the term ΥΗΣ—which would ordinarily be transliterated as UES—to the Christian Hesychius of Miletus (fl. sixth cent. AD/CE). Concerning the "moist or fertilising god" Hyes, citing Hesychius (l.c.) and Strabo (p. 471), Dr. William Smith iterates that "Hyes was also a surname of Dionysus, or rather of the Phrygian Sabazius, who was identified sometimes with Dionysus and sometimes with Zeus." (Smith, W. (1846), 533–4) The original Greek for "Hyes" is ῾ΥΗΣ, beginning with an aspirated υ or upsilon. While the letter y/υ is often transliterated as "y" or "u," it is pronounced (in modern Greek, at least) as somewhere between a short "i" and a long "e," the latter like the final "y" in English words, such as "really" and "truly." Modern Greek has also lost the initial aspirant found in antiquity, such as occurred with the particle ό, pronounced in antiquity "ho" and in modern Greek as "o." In his *Theol., Scr. Eccl. et Lexicogr.*, (Lexicon (Ε—Ω); p. 616, ln. 11), Bishop Photius writes: "Yes: epithet of Dionysus." Photius (p. 616, l. 19) also defines "the surname of Sabazios" or "Sabazius," the name of a Phrygio-Thracian god closely related to and serving as an epithet for Dionysus and Zeus. (For the edition of Photius, see: R. Porson, Φωτίου το πατριάρχου λέξεων συναγωγή, 1-2. Cambridge: Cambridge University Press, 1822; 1:10–367; 2:367–659.)

they are so vague in their chronology that they differ by as much as 200 years in the dates they assign to him.... It is clear from this that they never thought of testing whether he had existed, but took for granted that this name stood for a real person.... But let us see what modern Jewish scholarship, as represented by Sandmel and Goldstein, has to say about Jesus' historicity. Sandmel concedes that what knowledge we have of him "comes only from the NT," "since he went unknown in the surviving Jewish and pagan literature of his time"; and that passages about him in the ancient rabbinical literature reflect NT material and give no information that is independent of Christian tradition. That the Talmud is useless as a source of reliable information about Jesus is conceded by most Christian scholars.[365]

Other Talmudic references to Jesus, cloaked by the name "Balaam," are derogatory condemnations written centuries after the purported advent, thus serving as commentary on the tradition, not testimony to any "history."

Concerning the Talmudic "evidence," Stein remarks:

> [The] present Talmud contains virtually no mention of Jesus. This is because there was much persecution of the Jews during the Middle Ages, and many Jews were afraid that the presence of the numerous unfavorable references to Jesus which existed in the Talmud of the time would bring down the additional wrath of the Christians. These references were gradually eliminated, by agreement, during the many subsequent recopyings of the Talmud which occurred over the years. However, most of these references to Jesus have not been lost to our view, since they have been collected by scholars from ancient copies of the Talmud and republished several times.... If we look at the materials concerning Jesus which had been removed from the later copies of the Talmud, we can see that they say that he was a bastard and a magician who learned magic spells in Egypt or else stole the secret name of God from the temple and used it to work magic or miracles. The father of Jesus is also claimed to be a soldier named Pantera. At any rate, authorities are agreed that most of this Talmudic material derives from the period from 200 to 500 AD, and represents Jewish attempts to deal with the growing strength of Christianity. It makes no attempt to be historically accurate and, in fact, is of no use in determining if Jesus was an historical person.

Wells further states:

Now that so much in the NT has fallen under suspicion, there is a natural tendency to exaggerate the importance of non-Chris-

365 Wells, *DJE*, 12.

tian material that seems to corroborate it—even though Christian scholars past and present have admitted that, on the matter of Jesus' historicity, there is no pagan or Jewish evidence worth having.[366]

Catholic scholar and monsignor Dr. John P. Meier concurs with the assessment that the Talmudic accounts are worthless in establishing an "historical" Jesus:

[Scholars] of rabbinic tradition do not agree among themselves on whether even a single text from the Mishna, Tosefta or Talmud really refers to Jesus of Nazareth.[367]

He also concludes, "Jesus of Nazareth is simply absent from the Mishna and other early rabbinic traditions" and that "apart from Josephus, Jewish literature of the early Christian period offers no independent sources for the inquiry into the historical Jesus."[368]

To reiterate, "The forged New Testament booklets and the foolish writings of the Fathers, are the sole 'evidence' we have for the alleged facts and doctrines of our most holy Faith," as, adds Wheless, is admitted by the *Catholic Encyclopedia* itself.[369]

Concerning another major Jewish source of information for the precise era in which Christ allegedly walked the earth, as previously noted, the philosopher Philo is entirely silent on the subject:

> Much as Josephus would, a half century later, Philo wrote extensive apologetics on the Jewish religion and commentaries on contemporary politics. About thirty manuscripts and at least 850,000 words are extant. Philo offers commentary on all the major characters of the Pentateuch and, as we might expect, mentions Moses more than a thousand times.
>
> Yet Philo says not a word about Jesus, Christianity nor any of the events described in the New Testament. In all this work, Philo makes not a single reference to his alleged contemporary "Jesus Christ," the godman who supposedly was perambulating up and down the Levant, exorcising demons, raising the dead and causing earthquake and darkness at his death.
>
> With Philo's close connection to the house of Herod, one might reasonably expect that the miraculous escape from a royal prison of a gang of apostles (Acts 5.18,40), or the second, angel-assisted, flight of Peter, even though chained between soldiers and guarded by four squads of troops (Acts 12.2,7) might have occasioned the

366 Wells, *DJE*, 207.
367 Meier, J. (1991), 1.95.
368 Meier, J. (1991), 1.98.
369 Wheless, *FC*, 125.

> odd footnote. But not a murmur. Nothing of Agrippa "vexing certain of the church" or killing "James brother of John" with the sword (Acts 12.1,2).[370]

The passage about Jesus Barabbas and Christ's scourging at Matthew 27:26–29 seems to be a convoluted account lifted from Philo's story (*Flaccus*, 6) about the "madman named Carabbas" who is "dressed and adorned like a king" and paraded through the streets to the shouts of the multitudes, who called him by the name reserved for "kings among the Syrians."[371] In Philo's works, in fact, there are numerous "Christian" concepts, including a development of the Logos or "Word of God." The term "*logos*" (including plural, all cases and derivatives such as *logia*) appears hundreds of times in the Septuagint,[372] frequently in the context of "Word of God" (e.g., Hebrew: אמרה—*'imrah*),[373] and it is obvious that Philo was developing his concept based on this Jewish notion, combined with the Platonic logos. This logos development by one of the most powerful and wealthy individuals of the Roman Empire coincided with the precise era when Christ was supposedly walking the earth—the very logos of Philo's devising. Yet, the Jewish philosopher has not one word about what would be a most astonishing development with incredible divine timing that would indicate the Jewish god was indeed in charge and favoring his chosen people at last in their continual struggles against the heathens.

Thallus, Phlegon, Mara bar-Serapion. Lucian

Gordon Stein aptly summarizes the situation regarding a few other ancient sources often, but falsely, cited as evidence for a historical Jesus.

> The testimony (supposed, as the work in question is now lost) of Thallus is also worthless on the historicity question. Julius Africanus, in a surviving fragment, states that Thallus in the period before 221 AD, wrote that the darkness which supposedly covered the earth at the time of the Crucifixion was due to the death of Jesus. He is merely telling *what the Christians of the time believed....*

370 Humphreys, "Philo of Alexandria."

371 For more information on parallels between Christianity and Philo, see Humphreys, "Philo of Alexandria."

372 Carl F. Henry (177) asserts that the word "logos" in some form appears 1147 times in the LXX. For hundreds of instances, see *A Handy Concordance of the Septuagint*, 153–4. See, for example, Psalm 105:19; LXX 104:19: "...until what he had said came to pass the word of the LORD tested him." (KJV).

373 This Hebrew word אמרה is also translated in the LXX as μα or *rhma.*

> We have no way of dating the fragment quoting the letter of Mara Bar-Serapion. It doesn't mention Jesus or Christ, but merely says that the Jews of the time (which time is uncertain) killed their "wise King." We do not know to what this refers.... It is, again, worthless as evidence for a historical Jesus. Likewise, Lucian's sarcastic comment, written in the second century, is worth nothing except as evidence that he was aware that the Christians of his time ... felt or thought that there was a man who was crucified in Palestine as the basis of their sect. This was written far too late to be used as historical evidence, nor is it offered by Lucian as such.
>
> When you add up all of the following facts, the case for the existence of Jesus as an historical person becomes rather remote: 1) there are no proven, legitimate references to the existence of Jesus in any contemporary source outside of the New Testament ... 2) There is no evidence that the town of Nazareth, from which Jesus' mother supposedly came, ever existed at the time he was supposedly living there, 3) the existence of Jesus is not necessary to explain the origin or growth of Christianity (were the Hindu gods real'?), 4) the New Testament accounts do not provide a real "biography" for Jesus until you look at the Gospels. The earlier Pauline epistles imply only that he was a god, and 5) the biblical accounts of the trial and death of Jesus are logically self-contradictory and legally impossible.

Concerning the non-biblical evidence for the life of Christ, Dr. John P. Meier remarks:

> With Josephus and Tacitus we exhaust the early independent witnesses to Jesus' existence, ministry, death and ongoing influence. Suetonius, Pliny the Younger and Lucian are often quoted in this regard, but in effect they are simply reporting something about what early Christians say or do; they cannot be said to supply us with independent witness to Jesus himself.[374]

While we certainly concur that Suetonius, Pliny the Younger and Lucian are worthless in establishing any independent witness to Jesus, so, too, are Josephus and Tacitus, since neither of these writers was an eyewitness to any of the events they are purported to record, and since we are given no solid evidence as to whence they are receiving their information. Indeed, they are in the same boat, so to speak, with Suetonius, Pliny the Younger and Lucian in "simply reporting something about what early Christians say or do."

---

374 Meier, J. (1991), 1.91.

Further Evidence of a Fraud

> "And when we say also that the Word, who is the first-birth of God, was produced without sexual union, and that He, Jesus Christ, our Teacher, was crucified and died, and rose again, and ascended into heaven, we propound nothing different from what you believe regarding those whom you esteem sons of Jupiter."[375]
>
> —Justin Martyr, *First Apology* (21)

"As well as the danger of relying on texts which do not exist, there is the massive problem of known texts which have been 'lost' (such as the declarations of loyalty to Diocletian from every town and city in the empire) and the enormous quantity of texts which Christian scholars and the Christian Church admit to being forgeries. Between the destruction of important texts and inscriptions, and the admitted dishonesty for Christian texts, a scholar is faced with the unedifying task of investigating a religion which, down to its roots, is riddled with lies and fakery."

—John Bartram, "Mani and Authorship of the Canonical Gospels"

"According to these men, neither was the Word made flesh, nor Christ, nor the Saviour (Soter).... For they will have it, that the Word and Christ never came into this world; that the Saviour, too, never became incarnate, nor suffered.... But according to the opinion of no one of the heretics was the Word of God made flesh."[376]

—Bishop and Saint Irenaeus, *Against Heresies* (3.11.2–3)

There is basically no credible and scientific textual evidence proving the existence of Jesus Christ, since the biblical books and apocryphal literature are better explained as fraud and fiction. In our quest we will now examine what proponents and opponents of the Christian religion were claiming beginning in the second century, during which the "new faith" actually arose. Little of the actual works of most opponents survives, unfortunately, because the Christian conspirators went on a censorship rampage for centuries, with possession of heretical literature a capital crime from the time of the late Roman Empire. However, in their refutations the Christians themselves preserved many of their opponents' main points of contention, the most important of which for the present examination was that the gospel story and Christian doctrine were false,

375 Roberts, A. (1885), 1.170.

376 Roberts, A., 1.426–7. (Emph. added.)

whether in whole or in part, written as exercises in symbolic imagination rather than historical record. In fact, from their polemics it is clear that the early Christians were incessantly under criticism by scholars of great repute whom the Christians at first viciously impugned[377] and later murdered by the thousands.[378] Yet it was not only the dissenters and Pagans who apprehended the truth; a number of Church fathers themselves disclosed that they knew the story and religion of Jesus Christ were not original but were founded upon or equivalent to more ancient myths and ideologies throughout the known world.

Confessions of the Church Fathers

For example, influential Church doctor Augustine ("Of True Religion," *Retractiones* 1.13) readily confessed that Christianity was a rehash of what already existed long prior to the Christian Era:

> For what is now called the Christian religion existed of old and was never absent from the beginning of the human race until Christ came in the flesh. Then true religion which already existed began to be called Christian.[379]

In addition, in the face of criticism that Christianity was fabricated, Eusebius (*Eccl. Hist.* 1.4) sought to demonstrate it was not "novel or strange" by claiming it was based on older ideas. Says he:

> The Religion proclaimed by him to All Nations was neither New nor Strange.
>
> [Although] it is clear that we are new and that this new name of Christians has really but recently been known among all nations, nevertheless our life and our conduct, with our doctrines of religion, have not been lately invented by us, but from the first creation of man, so to speak, have been established by the natural understanding of divinely favored men of old.[380]

Eusebius thus admitted not only that Christianity was built upon earlier ideologies but also that the name "Christian" was still "undeniably new" by his time, 300 years after the purported beginning of the Christian era, in spite of the New Testament tales that Jesus had been famed

377 See the writings of the Church fathers of the second and third centuries, especially.

378 See, for example, Kelso, "Victims of the Christian Faith," for a long list of the "heretic" and non-Christian "ethnic cleansing" engaged in by Christian fanatics for centuries. Among these hundreds of thousands of casualties beginning in the early fourth century were many intellectuals. We are all familiar, of course, with the infamous treatment of Galileo and Copernicus, to name but two.

379 Augustine/Burleigh, 218.

380 Schaff (1890), 1.87.

far and wide, that the gospel had been "preached to all the nations,"[381] that a vast church network had sprung up during the first century, and that Christians were notorious rabble-rousers responsible for burning Rome and being thrown to the lions in the Colosseum and other arenas. This contention validates the notion that the word "Christian" came into wide usage at Antioch only during the second century. This fact in turn calls into suspicion earlier writings that use the term, such as Josephus and Pliny, as opposed, say, to *Chrestiani*.

Regarding these Christian admissions, Doane states:

> Melito (a Christian bishop of Sardis), in an *apology* delivered to the Emperor Marcus Atoninus, in the year 170, claims the patronage of the emperor, for the *now*-called Christian religion, which he calls "*our philosophy*," "on account of its *high antiquity*, as having been *imported* from countries lying beyond the limits of the Roman empire, in the reign of his ancestor Augustus, who found its *importation* ominous of good fortune to his government." This is an absolute demonstration that Christianity did *not* originate in Judea, which was a Roman province, but really was an exotic oriental fable, *imported* from India.[382]

As this exotic oriental fable settled in, the story goes, it was placed in Judea and based on Old Testament tales as well, as is affirmed by Tertullian in his *Against Praxeas* (16), in which he gives the following ludicrous argument, when confronted with the similarities between Christ and a number of Old Testament characters, such as Joshua, or *Jesus*, as his name is in Greek:

Early Manifestations of the Son of God, as Recorded in the Old Testament; Rehearsals of His Subsequent Incarnation.

> Thus was He ever learning even as God to converse with men upon earth, being no other than the Word which was to be made flesh. But He was thus learning (or rehearsing), in order to level for us the way of faith, that we might the more readily believe that the Son of God had come down into the world, if we knew that in

381 Some Christians have believed that what Matthew (24:9ff) described about the end of the world, which could only happen after the gospel had been preached to all the nations, was fulfilled by Paul's statement at Colossians 1:5–6, 23: "For the hope which is laid up for you in heaven, whereof ye heard before in the word of the truth of the gospel; Which is come unto you, as [it is] in all the world … provided that you continue in the faith, stable and steadfast, not shifting from the hope of the gospel which you heard, which has been preached to every creature under heaven." (See, for example, Virginian pastor David B. Curtis's "Gospel Preached to all the World? (Matthew 24:4–14).")

382 Doane, 409.

times past also something similar had been done.[383]

It is more than a little odd that the "omniscient" God would need to learn how to be a human, especially when humans themselves do not receive such an opportunity to "rehearse." In reality, Tertullian's pitiful "excuse" sounds more as if "God" is acting in a *play* (and as if Tertullian has a screw loose).

In his *First Apology* (21), Christian father Justin Martyr (c. 100–165) acknowledged the similarities between the older Pagan gods and religions and those of Christianity, when he attempted to demonstrate, in the face of ridicule, that Christianity was no more ridiculous than the earlier myths:

> ANALOGIES TO THE HISTORY OF CHRIST.
>
> And when we say also that the Word, who is the first-birth of God, was produced without sexual union, and that He, Jesus Christ, our Teacher, was crucified and died, and rose again, and ascended into heaven, we propound nothing different from what you believe regarding those whom you esteem sons of Jupiter. For you know how many sons your esteemed writers ascribed to Jupiter: Mercury, the interpreting word and teacher of all; Aesculapius, who, though he was a great physician, was struck by a thunderbolt, and so ascended to heaven; and Bacchus too, after he had been torn limb from limb; and Hercules, when he had committed himself to the flames to escape his toils; and the sons of Leda, and Dioscuri; and Perseus, son of Danae; and Bellerophon, who, though sprung from mortals, rose to heaven on the horse Pegasus. For what shall I say of Ariadne, and those who, like her, have been declared to be set among the stars? And what of the emperors who die among yourselves, whom you deem worthy of deification, and in whose behalf you produce some one who swears he has seen the burning Caesar rise to heaven from the funeral pyre?[384]

Justin (*First Apol.* 22) reiterates the similarities between his godman and the gods of other cultures:

> [If] any one objects that He was crucified, in this also He is on a par with those reputed sons of Jupiter of yours, who suffered as we have now enumerated.... And if we even affirm that He was born of a virgin, accept this in common with what you accept of Perseus. And in that we say that He made whole the lame, the paralytic and those born blind, we seem to say what is very similar to

383 Roberts, A., 3.611-2.

384 Roberts, A. (1885), 1.170.

the deeds said to have been done by Æsculapius.[385]

In making these comparisons between Christianity and its predecessor Paganism, however, Justin sinisterly spluttered:

> It having reached the Devil's ears that the prophets had foretold the coming of Christ, the Son of God, he set the heathen Poets to bring forward a great many who should be called the sons of Jove. The Devil laying his scheme in this, to get men to imagine that the *true* history of Christ was of the same character as the prodigious fables related of the sons of Jove.[386]
>
> But those who hand down the myths which the poets have made adduce no proof to the youths who learn them; and we proceed to demonstrate that they have been uttered by the influence of the wicked demons, to deceive and lead astray the human race. For having heard it proclaimed through the prophets that the Christ was to come, and that the ungodly among men were to be punished by fire, they put forward many to be called sons of Jupiter, under the impression that they would be able to produce in men the idea that the things which were said with regard to Christ were mere marvellous tales, like the things which were said by the poets.[387]

In his *Dialogue with Trypho the Jew* (69), Justin again admits the pre-existence of the Christian tale and then uses his standard, irrational and self-serving apology (i.e., "the devil got there first").

> Be well assured, then, Trypho … that I am established in the knowledge of and faith in the Scriptures by those counterfeits which he who is called the devil is said to have performed among the Greeks; just as some were wrought by the Magi in Egypt, and others by the false prophets in Elijah's days. For when they tell that Bacchus, son of Jupiter, was begotten by [Jupiter's] intercourse with Semele, and that he was the discoverer of the vine; and when they relate, that being torn in pieces, and having died, he rose again, and ascended to heaven; and when they introduce wine into his mysteries, do I not perceive that [the devil] has imitated the prophecy announced by the patriarch Jacob, and recorded by Moses? And when they tell that Hercules was strong, and travelled over all the world, and was begotten by Jove of Alcmene, and ascended to heaven when he died, do I not perceive that the Scripture which speaks of Christ, "strong as a giant to run his race," has been in like manner imitated? And when he [the devil] brings forward Æsculapius as

385 Roberts, A. (1905), 1.170.

386 Wheless, *FC*, 32.

387 Roberts, A. (1885), 1.181.

> the raiser of the dead and healer of all diseases, may I not say that in this matter likewise he has imitated the prophecies about Christ? … And when I hear, Trypho, that Perseus was begotten of a virgin, I understand that the deceiving serpent counterfeited also this.[388]

This "devil did it" response became *de rigeur* in the face of persistent rational criticism. Nowhere does Justin contend that *humans* plagiarized Christianity to create these gods *after* Christ's alleged advent. Clearly, these gods and their relevant attributes *preceded* Christ, and Justin is well aware of this fact.

Christian author Lactantius (240–330), in his attempts to confirm the emperor Constantine in his new faith and to convert the "Pagan" elite, also widely appealed to the Pagan stories as proof that Christianity was not absurd but equally viable as they were, even though naturally he dismissed these earlier versions as works of the devil. As Wheless says, "In a word, Christianity is founded on and proved by Pagan myths."[389]

Since it is clear that early Christian apologists themselves made these comparisons of Christ to other gods, why should we not do likewise? Moreover, the comparison implies that those rationalists within the Pagan world or the Jewish religionists, both of whom who viewed the Greeks and Roman gods as mythical figures, would do likewise with the Christian version. Perhaps Trypho was among these, which is why Justin has him remarking that the Christians have "made a Christ of your own."

Other Christians were more blunt in their confessions as to the nature and purpose of the Christian tale, making no pretense to being believers in higher realms of spirituality, but demonstrating more practical reasons for fanatically adhering to their incredible doctrines. Illustrating this contention, in his play from 1564, Bishop of Ossory John Bale (1495–1563) appears to be suggesting that Pope Leo X (1475–1521) was privy to the truth based on his high rank, when the bishop recounts an alleged exchange between Cardinal Bembo (1470–1547) and the pope, with the latter supposedly exclaiming, "What profit has not that fable of Christ brought us!"[390]

Even if the Pope himself did not express such a sentiment, Bale—a high-ranking Church official—certainly is acknowledging *someone's*

---

388 Roberts, A. (1905), 1.233.

389 Wheless, *FC*, 152.

390 *Encyclopedia Britannica*, XXIII, 87. (Emph. added.) See also Walker, 471; Taylor, 35. Bale's original Latin is as follows: "Quantum nobis nostrisque ea de Christo fabula profuerit, satis est omnibus saeculis notum." (Roscoe, III, 339.)

viewpoint, which means that at that time there were those who dismissed the gospel story as a *fable*. Since I have been online, beginning in 1995, many individuals have written to me about having been ministers, seminarians, Catholic clergymen, Jesuits, Presbyterians, et al., relating that, in the higher levels of the Church educational institutions, "they know it is all myth." As Wheless also says, "The proofs of my indictment are marvelously easy."[391]

The Gnostics

Although the Christian conspirators were quite thorough in their criminal destruction of the evidence, especially of ancient texts, resulting in the loss of much irreplaceable information on Christian origins, from what remains we can see that the scholars of other schools and sects never gave up their arguments against the historicizing of a very ancient mythological character. This group of critics included many Gnostics who strenuously objected to the carnalization and Judaization of their allegorical texts and ideas by the Christians.

The standard version of Church history fosters the impression that the philosophy or religion of Gnosticism began only during the Christian era and that Gnosticism was a corruption of literal orthodoxy. However, Gnosticism is far older than Christianity, extending back thousands of years. The term Gnosticism, in fact, comes from the Greek word *gnosis*, which means "knowledge," and "Gnostic" simply means "one who knows," rather than designating a follower of a particular doctrine. It has been suggested that, from time immemorial, those who understood "the mysteries" were considered "keepers of the gnosis." In this sense, conveying the deeper mystical meaning, the Greek philosophers Pythagoras and Plato were "Gnostics," as was the Jewish philosopher Philo, whose works influenced the writer of the Gospel of John and other Christian texts and doctrines.

Nevertheless, during the early centuries of the Christian era, "Gnosticism" became more of a monolithic movement, as certain groups and individuals began to amalgamate the many religions, sects, cults, mystery schools and ideologies that permeated the Roman Empire and beyond, from England to Egypt to India and China. This latest infusion of Gnosticism traced its roots to Syria, oddly enough the same nation in which Christians were first so called, at Antioch. Of this development, Massey says:

> We are told in the Book of Acts that the name of the *Christiani* was first given at Antioch; but so late as the year 200 AD no canonical New Testament was known at Antioch, the alleged

391 Wheless (1930), xxi.

birth-place of the Christian name. There was no special reason why "the disciples" should have been named as Christians at Antioch, except that this was a great centre of the Gnostic Christians, who were previously identified with the teachings and works of the mage Simon of Samaria.[392]

These Antiochan Gnostic-Christians were followers of "Simon the Magus," who was impugned as the "heresiarch" or originator of all Christian heresies. Yet this Simon Magus appears to have been a mythical character derived from two mystical entities, Saman[393] and Maga, esteemed by the Syrians prior to the Christian era. This religion could be called Syro-Samaritan Gnostic Christianity. Syro-Judeo-Gnosticism, on the other hand, was originally a Jewish heresy, starting with what became called "Mandaeism" or "Mandaeanism,"[394] a highly astrological ideology purported by some to date to the fourth century BCE. that tried to bridge between Judaism and Zoroastrianism, and that was very influential on Christianity, contentions debated by mainstream scholars. Certainly, any later sect by that name had its roots in the pre-Christian astral religion pervasive in the area for thousands of years, dating to Sumero-Babylonian times.

The Mandaeans

There can be little doubt that the baptism for which the Mandaeans are famous represents a continuation of ritual bathing from great antiquity, having significantly to do with the ancient Sumero-Babylonian fish god Oannes. The Sumero-Babylonian-Mandaean focus on water is understandable in a land surrounded by important rivers such as the Tigris and the Euphrates. This ancient lineage was included as part of the "star

392 Massey, *GHC*, 12.

393 Discussing Simon in his *First Apology* (26), Justin asserts: "He was considered a god, and as a god was honoured with a statue, which statue was erected on the river Tiber, between the two bridges, and bore this inscription, in the language of Rome: 'Simoni Deo Sancto'—To Simon the holy God." (Roberts, A., 1.171) Regarding an inscription in the Vatican about the "god Semo," Roberts, et al. (1.187) state: "The explanation is possibly this: Simon Magus was actually recognized as the God *Semo*, just as Barnabas and Paul were supposed to be Zeus and Hermes (Acts xiv. 12.), and were offered divine honours accordingly." Interestingly, in Indian religious tradition, the word *saman* refers to both a god and religious hymns. (See, for example, Obeyesekere, 153; te Nijenhuis, 1.) In consideration of the Indian presence in the Middle East and its evident philosophy incorporated into Gnosticism, this contention about Simon and Saman may possess merit.

394 It is noteworthy that this fascinating ancient sect has survived to this day in Iraq but is seriously endangered.

worshippers" called "Sabians" in pre-Islamic Arabia. These Sabians may have been influenced at an early age by the same Abrahamic strain of thought that passed through "Ur of the Chaldees" on its way to what became Israel. Indeed, in ancient texts such as the Talmud Abraham is considered the first and greatest star-gazer or *astrologer*, reflected the *astrotheological* religion.

It is very telling that the word "mandaean" comes from the Aramaic , meaning "knowledge," translated in Greek as *gnosis*. Although this sect may not have been labeled as such in the pre-Christian era, it is clear that it represents a combination of pre-Christian religious movements, including Jewish, Zoroastrian and "Sabian" or pre-Islamic star worship/astrotheology. Moreover, in consideration of the fact that these Gnostics are not Christians, yet they supposedly revere a "Christian" character, John the Baptist, we would submit that this figure is not truly a "Christian" character at all but represents a combination of Oannes, the ancient Mesopotamian fish god and the Egyptian god Anubis the Purifier. Indeed, the Mandaeans themselves relate that, on their way to settling in Mesopotamia, they passed through Israel from Egypt. An examination of all the data indicates that the Baptist was incorporated into the gospel story in order to subordinate the Mandaean sect under Christ's authority.

The Gnostic tree of thought thus had many branches; it was not uniform and was colored by the variety of cultures and places in which it appeared, a development that created competition. Professor of Religion at Princeton University Dr. Elaine Pagels says, "These so-called Gnostics, then, did not share a single ideology or belong to a specific group; not all, in fact, were Christians."[395] Indeed, the various Gnostic "Christian" texts from Chenoboskion were found in non-Christian, Pagan tombs.[396] Thus, we find in the ancient world Syrian or Samaritan Gnosticism, Jewish Gnosticism, Christian Gnosticism and Pagan Gnosticism, with a variety of often overlapping subsects.

Yet, as stated, Gnosticism was eclectic, gathering together virtually all religious and cultic ideologies of the time, constituting a combination of "the philosophies of Plato and Philo, the Avesta and the Kabbala, the mysteries of Samothrace, Eleusis and of Orphism."[397] Buddhism and Osirianism were major influences as well. The Gnostic texts were multinational, using terms from the Hebrew, Persian, Greek, Syriac/Aramaic, Sanskrit and Egyptian languages.

Although there now seems to be a clear-cut distinction between

395 Pagels, *AES*, 60.
396 Doresse, 133–5.
397 Doresse, 2.

Gnostics and Christians, that was not the case at the beginning of the Christian effort, which truly commenced during the *second* century, and the fact is that Gnosticism *was* proto-Christianity. The distinction was not even very great as late as the third century, when Neoplatonic philosopher and fierce Christian critic Porphyry attacked "Gnostics," whom he considered to be Christians, as did Plotinus (205–270), both of whom indicted the Christians/Gnostics for making up their texts. Pagels describes the murky division between the "Gnostics" and the "Christians":

> [One] revered father of the church, Clement of Alexandria ... writing in Egypt c. 180, identifies himself as orthodox, although he knows members of gnostic groups and their writings well: some even suggest that he was himself a gnostic initiate.[398]

It has been contended that, despite the claim he was raised a Christian, Bishop Irenaeus himself was in reality a Gnostic and had a zodiac on the floor of his church at Lugdunum/Lyons, France.[399] Furthermore,

---

398 Pagels, *GG*, 67.

399 Higgins, 2.129: "Irenaeus was Bishop of Lyons. He was one of the first fathers of the church who suffered martyrdom.... He was an Asiatic, but was sent as bishop to Gaul. He founded or built a church in that country. This church is yet remaining at Lyons, though in the course of almost 2000 years no doubt it has undergone many alterations. On the floor, in front of the altar, may be seen a Mosaic pavement of the Zodiac, though a considerable part of it is worn away." Irenaeus's Gnostic involvement is indicated by his detailed knowledge of Gnostic doctrines. As an "Asiatic" it is possible Irenaeus was specifically chosen for his bishopric because he was very familiar with Gnosticism, which largely emanated out of Asia Minor. As Higgins (2.129) says: "Irenaeus was evidently a Gnostic. If he were not, how came he to place the Zodiac on the floor of his church, a part of which, not worn away by the feet of devotees, is yet remaining? He was of the sect of the Christ not crucified.... St. Paul preaches, in a very pointed manner, Christ crucified; this was in opposition to the Christ not crucified of the Gnostics.... Gnosticism was the secret religion of the conclave.... Most fortunately the church has been guilty of the oversight of letting the passage of Irenaeus escape. One of the earliest, most celebrated, most respected, and most quoted authorities of its ancient bishops, saints and martyrs, tells us in distinct words, that Jesus was not crucified under Herod and Pontius Pilate. This he tells us on the authority of his master Polycarp, also a martyr, who had it from St. John himself, and from all the old people of Asia." This sect of "Christ not crucified" is Gnostic, and Irenaeus's view in this regard is illustrated by his remarks (2.22.5) that Jesus lived until he was more than 50, accusing of "forgery" or "false opinion" those writers who contended Christ died one year after beginning his ministry. In Harvey's Latin edition of Against Heresies, this section appears at 1.33.3. (Irenaeus/Harvey, 1.330.) See also Higgins, 2.121. However, in context, it is clear that

the great "Christian" saint Augustine was originally a Manichaean, i.e., a *Gnostic*, before he was "converted" (i.e., promised a prominent place in the newly formed Catholic Church), whereupon he then excoriated his former sect.[400]

Concerning this confusion between the Christians and Gnostics, Waite relates, "Most of the Christian writers of the second century who immediately succeeded the apostolic fathers, advocated doctrines which were afterward considered heretical."[401] Yet the orthodox Christians used whatever doctrine they could to benefit their cause, exalting these same "heretics," including Origen (c. 185–254) and Tertullian, as founding fathers.

Many "Christian" concepts are in fact "Gnostic," such as the disdain for the flesh and for matter in general. In actuality, the Gnostic-Christian ideology deemed as "evil" both matter and the god of the material world, the "Demiurge," also called "the god of this world," or "the prince of this world," as well as "Ialdabaôth," the jealous god. Jesus's own Gnosticism is revealed at John 7:7: "The world cannot hate you, but it hates me because I testify of it that its works are evil." And Paul's Gnostic thought appears where he reveals his abhorrence of the flesh, as at Galatians 5:19–21:

> Now the works of the flesh are plain: fornication, impurity, licentiousness, idolatry, sorcery, enmity, strife, jealousy, anger, selfishness, dissension, party spirit, envy, drunkenness, carousing, and the like. I warn you, as I warned you before, that those who do such things shall not inherit the kingdom of God.

At 2 Corinthians 4:2–4, Paul speaks gnostically about the "god of this world" being evil. In this passage, the apostle also reveals that the scriptures were tampered with and, by the use of the word "renounced" (rather than, say, "shunned") suggests that he and his cohorts themselves were at some point guilty of "underhanded ways," apparently including such mutilation of texts, which they were thereafter giving up:

> We have renounced disgraceful, underhanded ways; we refuse to practice cunning or to tamper with God's word.... And even if our gospel is veiled, it is veiled only to those who are perishing. In

---

Irenaeus did believe Jesus was crucified, albeit at age 50, during the reign of Claudius Caesar.

400 Bart Ehrman kindly pointed out my anachronistic error in including the words "until after the Council of Nicea" in the original edition (60). I also specified Augustine as a "Mandaean," whereas he was a *Manichaean*, although the two have been interchanged since antiquity.

401 Waite, 251.

their case *the god of this world* has blinded the minds of the unbelievers, to keep them from seeing the light of the gospel of the glory of Christ …

Concerning these sentiments, Massey comments:

> Speaking from his Gnostic standpoint, Paul declared to the historic Christians who followed John and Peter, that God had sent them a working of error, that they should believe a lie, because they rejected the truth as it was according to his spiritual Gospel![402]

Not only was Paul propounding a "veiled" or "spiritual" gospel, here he is a classic Gnostic, called the "Apostle of the Gnostics,"[403] in that, according to careful analysis, he appears not to have acknowledged a carnalized or historical Jesus Christ.[404] As Massey further says:

> Paul opposed the setting up of a Christ carnalized, and fought the Sarkolaters [carnalizers] tooth and nail.… If the writings of Paul were retouched by the carnalizers, that will account for the two voices heard at times in his Epistles and the apparent *duplicity* of his doctrine.… Paul passed away and his writings remained with the enemy, to be withheld, tampered with, reindoctrinated, and turned to account by his old opponents who preached the gospel of Christ carnalized.[405]

The Gnostic Christ of Paul is also reflected at Galatians 3:27–8: "For as many of you as were baptized into Christ have put on Christ. There is neither Jew nor Greek, there is neither slave nor free, there is neither male nor female; for you are all one in Christ Jesus." Regarding this concept, Massey says:

> The Christ of the Gnostics was a mystical type continued from mythology to portray a spiritual reality of the interior life. Hence the Christ in this human phase could be female as well as male; for such to become historical, or be made so, except by ignorantly mistaking a mythical Impersonation for a Hermaphrodite in Person![406]

The Gnostic focus on attaining gnosis, or the "kingdom of God within," is also a concept that made it into the Christian religion and Bible, but that is widely ignored in favor of "a-gnosis" or ignorance, and "*pistis*" or blind faith.

---

402 Massey, *GHC*, 25–26.

403 See, for example, Dunlap, 544; McGiffert, 617; Moreschini, 229.

404 The reader is again referred to the work of Earl Doherty and others preceding him as concerns the lack of references to a historical "Jesus of Nazareth" in the Pauline epistles.

405 Massey, *HJMC*, 193–7.

406 Massey, *GHC*, 21.

The fact is that "Gnosticism" of some sort existed first and was eventually changed into orthodox Christianity by 220 AD/CE. or so. As time went on, the carnalizing Christians created distance between themselves and their Gnostic roots by rewriting texts for their own benefit. As Classicist Dr. John Jackson says, "It will be noticed that generally speaking the earlier Epistles show signs of Gnostic influence, while the later show signs of anti-Gnostic bias."[407]

In turn, the Gnostics likened the orthodox Christians to "dumb animals" and stated that it was the orthodox, not the Gnostics themselves, who were the blasphemers, because the orthodox did not know "who Christ is."[408] As Pagels relates, "Gnostic Christians … castigated the orthodox for making the mistake of reading the Scriptures—and especially Genesis—literally, and thereby missing its 'deeper meaning.'"[409] In fact, "Historic Christianity originated with turning the Gnostic and Esoteric teachings inside out and externalizing the mythical allegory in a personal human history."[410]

As stated, many of the Gnostics were fervently "anti-material." When the historicizing Christians appeared and began to insist that their savior had indeed "come in the flesh," the Gnostics equally zealously held that *their* Christ could never take human form. These, in fact, were the Christian "heretics" characterized by Taylor as the "first class of professing Christians."[411]

Docetism and the Mystical Christ

The denial of Christ "come in the flesh" (1 John 4:3; 2 John 1:7) was called "Docetism," a term used by the historicizers to gloss over the disbelief in the incarnation by saying it meant that Christ existed but had never taken a material body. This enabled them to bury the issue of whether any Christ had ever appeared on earth. Reframing the issue in this fashion made it appear that no one was denying the events of the gospel story, only that some claimed the historical Jesus was something like a hologram. While later Gnostics may have followed this opinion, the pioneers evidently did not, nor did the Pagans, who were more blunt in their assessment as to the historical nature of Christ. Of Docetism,

407 Jackson, 119.

408 Pagels, *GG*, 102-3. See, for example, *The Second Treatise of the Great Seth* (7.2), in which the Gnostic author refers to Christians as "unknowingly empty, not knowing who they are, like dumb animals." (Meyer, N.W. (1977), 334)

409 Pagels, *AES*, 63.

410 Massey, *GHC*, 25.

411 Taylor, R., 372.

Massey says:

> The Docetae sects, for example, are supposed to have held that the transactions of the gospel narrative *did occur*, but in a phantasmagoria of unreality. This, however, is but a false mode of describing the position of those who denied that the Christ could be incarnated and become human to suffer and die upon the cross. The Christians who report the beliefs of the Gnostics, Docetae and others, always *assume the actual history and then try to explain the non-human interpretation as an heretical denial of the alleged facts*. But the docetic interpretation was first, was pre-historical.[412]

As Humphreys says:

> The evidence of Jesus's "human existence," far from being confirmed and agreed by early Christians, was a matter of ferocious contention. Many Christians between the 1st-4th [centuries] had NO belief in a flesh and blood Jesus; it was offensive to their particular interpretation of the divine.[413]

In *Against Heresies* (1.9.3), Irenaeus speaks of the followers of the Gnostic-Christian Valentinus (second cent.), who preceded Irenaeus and was so orthodox that he was nearly elected bishop of Rome:

> For, according to them, the Word did not originally become flesh. For they maintain that the Saviour assumed an animal body, formed in accordance with a special dispensation by an unspeakable providence, so as to become visible and palpable.[414]

Elsewhere (1.6.1), Irenaeus says of these Gnostics:

> At the same time, they deny that He assumed anything material [into His nature], since indeed matter is incapable of salvation.[415]

Irenaeus (4.33.5) further complains about the Docetics, while acknowledging them as followers of the Master (i.e., Christians):

> He shall also judge those who describe Christ as [having become man] only in [human] opinion. For how can they imagine that they do themselves carry on a real discussion, when their Master was a mere imaginary being? Or how can they receive anything steadfast from Him, if He was a merely imagined being, and not a verity? And how can these men really be partaking of salvation, if He in whom they profess to believe, manifested Himself as a merely imaginary being?[416]

---

412 Massey, *HJMC*, 177.

413 Humphreys, "Circus Circus! The Jesus Parade is Always in Town."

414 Roberts, A., 1.329.

415 Roberts, A., 1.324.

416 Roberts, A., 1.508. This paragraph appears in the Latin version at 4.52.2:

It is clear that the Docetics viewed Jesus Christ—or, rather, Jesus the *Chrest*—as an "imaginary being" (i.e., *mythical*, rather than historical). How can we explain such a situation, if Christianity depends on a historical Christ having lived a century before?

It needs to be reiterated that Irenaeus specifically addresses the Docetics' Christ as an "imaginary being." The word "imaginary" surely denotes a Jesus who existed not in the perceptions of witnesses (whatever the consistency of his form), but only in the fanciful speculations of daydreamers. In other words, not an *illusion* but rather a *delusion*.

In addition to denying that Christ came in the flesh, the early followers were extremely confused as to the "history" of their savior, depicting his death, for example, in dozens of different ways, even though such astounding events should have been seared into memory. Irenaeus recounts other Gnostic-Christian "heresies," beginning with the Samaritan belief that it was not Christ who had died on the cross but "Simon," a peculiar development if Jesus's "history" had been based in fact and widely known from the time of his alleged advent.

In his diatribe against the Gnostics Valentinus, Marcion, Basilides, and Saturninus, Irenaeus (3.11.2–3) recapitulates their diverse beliefs and doctrines:

> But according to Marcion, and those like him, neither was the world made by Him; nor did He come to His own things, but to those of another. And, according to certain of the Gnostics, this world was made by angels, and not by the Word of God. But according to the followers of Valentinus, the world was not made by Him, but by the Demiurge.... For they say that he, the Lord and Creator of the plan of creation, by whom they hold that this world was made, was produced from the Mother; while the Gospel affirms plainly, that by the Word, which was in the beginning with God, all things were made, which Word, he says, "was made flesh, and dwelt among us."
>
> But, according to these men, neither was the Word made flesh, nor Christ, nor the Saviour (*Soter*).... For they will have it, that the Word and Christ never came into this world; that the Saviour, too, never became incarnate, nor suffered, but that He descended like

"Judicabit autem et eos qui putativum inducunt. Quem admodum enim ipsi vere se putant disputare, quando magister eorum putativus fuit? Aut quemadmodum firmum quid habere possunt ab eo, si putativus et non veritas erat? Quomodo autem ipsi salutem vere participare possunt, si ille, in quem credere se dicunt, semetipsum putativum ostendebat?" (Harvey, 2.260.) The pertinent Latin word here is *putativus*, which *Entick's Latin-English Dictionary* (436) defines as "supposed, imaginary."

a dove upon the dispensational Jesus; and that, as soon as He had declared the unknown Father, He did again ascend into the Pleroma. Some, however, make the assertion that this dispensational Jesus did become incarnate.... *But according to the opinion of no one of the heretics was the Word of God made flesh.*[417]

Here Irenaeus makes distinctions between the Word/Logos, the Christ, the Savior/Soter and the "dispensational Jesus." According to these *Christian* "heretics," none of the former became incarnate, in other words, walked the earth, although the Savior did "descend upon the dispensational Jesus," a strange manner of describing the main (supposedly historical) figure of Christianity. Moreover, only "some" claimed that even the "dispensational Jesus" became incarnate, which means that others did *not* claim so, leaving even the "dispensational Jesus" disincarnate or nonhistorical. All these distinctions, of course, represent fancy footwork to cover up the fact that many early followers of "Christ" or, rather, "Chrest," did not know any historical Jesus.

Other sects, such as the followers of Apelles, held that Christ's body was made of "star stuff,"[418] and the Ebionites claimed that Christ was a "type of Solomon" or "type of Jonah,"[419] appropriate designations, as we shall see. Obviously, the Gnostics were not uniform in their beliefs and doctrines, despite their attempts at harmonization, mainly because Gnosticism encouraged creativity and freedom of expression. The most

417 Roberts, A., 1.426–7. (Emph. added.) The Latin version appears at 3.11.7–8, the latter part of which reads: "Secundum autem illos, neque Verbum caro factum est, neque Christus, neque qui ex omnibus factus est Salvator. Etenim Verbum et Christum nec advenisse in hunc mundum volunt: Salvatorem vero non incarnatum neque passum; descendisse autem quasi columbam in eum Jesum qui factus est ex dispositione, et cum annuntiasset incognitum Patrem, iterum ascendisse in Pleroma.... Secundum autem nullam sententiam haereticorum, Verbum Dei caro factum est." (Irenaeus/Harvey, 41-2.)

418 Regarding this Gnostic-Christian "heretic," *Encyclopaedia Metropolitana* remarks: "Apelles, without supposing that the body of Christ was a mere phantasm, denied that He was born of the Virgin Mary; maintained that in His descent from Heaven, He borrowed a kind of aerial form from the substances of the upper world and sidereal regions.... This ethereal body of Christ, on His ascension to Heaven, returned to the stars and the elements from which it had been derived" (Smedley, et al., 11.145).

419 In *A Dictionary of Christian Biography* (2.25), Smith, et al., remark upon "the tendency of this class of Ebionites to exalt the Old at the expense of the New, to magnify Moses and the Prophets, and to allow Jesus Christ to be "nothing more than a Solomon or a Jonas." (Tertull. *de Carne Christi*, c. 18)."

disturbing of these heresies, of course, was the denial of Christ's historicity.

The Docetists continued for many decades, well into the third century. In his "Twelve Topics of the Faith," Gregory Thaumaturgus (205–265), head of the Alexandrian school, wrote:

> If any one says that the body of Christ is uncreated, and refuses to acknowledge that He, being the uncreated Word (God) of God, took the flesh of created humanity and appeared incarnate, even as it is written, let him be anathema.[420]

As Topic I, this subject was obviously the most important and once again reveals that the fathers were engaged in an ongoing program of presenting Jesus Christ as a carnalized or historical personage who truly walked the earth in the flesh. Gregory gives as a major reason for the necessity of Christ existing in the flesh that "Christ, on rising from the dead, showed His disciples the print of the nails and the wound made by the spear, and a body that could be handled."[421] As we can see, it is paramount to the orthodox Christian faith that Christ be historical, or he could not have resurrected, and "if Christ has not been raised, then our preaching is in vain and your faith is in vain," says Paul (1 Cor. 15:14).

Gnosticism scholar Dr. Jean Doresse reveals the ultimate "heresy" of the Gnostics, although he is interpreting it as if the history were first: "Firstly, a flood of light is thrown upon the strange figure that the Gnostics made of Jesus.... For them, his incarnation was fictitious, and so was his crucifixion."[422] In other words, they denied Jesus Christ ever existed "in the flesh," carnalized and, therefore, *historical*, by the definition of the word as: "having once existed or lived in the real world, as opposed to being part of legend or fiction or as distinguished from religious belief."[423] In fact, the earliest Gnostic-Christians appear not to have been aware of the claims that Christ had "existed or lived in the real world." As noted, others were revolted by the concept of Christ appearing in the material world, claiming his appearances were essentially phantasmagoric, unreal, allegorical and mystical—in a word, mythical. Speaking for one of the most widespread and influential Gnostic-Christian sects, Manichaeism, the Manichaean Christian Bishop Faustus remarked:

> Do you receive the gospel? (ask ye). Undoubtedly I do! Why then, you also admit that Christ was born? Not so; for it by no means follows that believing in the gospel, I should therefore believe that

420 Roberts, A. (1888), 6.50.
421 Roberts, A. (1888), 6.50.
422 Doresse, 305.
423 Random House Unabridged Dictionary.

Christ was born! Do you think that he was of the Virgin Mary? Manes hath said, 'Far be it that I should ever own that Our Lord Jesus Christ [descended by scandalous birth through a woman].[424]

Faustus's gospel was apparently the same in concept as Paul's "spiritual gospel" and Marcion's non-historicizing Gospel of the Lord. Like Marcion, Faustus expresses an extreme manifestation of the Gnostic distaste of "flesh" and "matter" (i.e., misogyny, the contempt for women). The word "matter" or "mater," as in "material," was also the word for "mother," and matter was deemed female. Thus, the absolute separation of spirit and matter found within the Christian religion has its roots in Gnosticism, as does the attendant sexism. Yet other Gnostic sects were more balanced and addressed the feminine aspect of the divine.

The Manichean perspective has been summarized thus:

One of the most primitive and learned sects … were the Manicheans, who denied that Jesus Christ ever existed in flesh and blood, but believed him to be a God in spirit only.[425]

These "heretics" were so common that the historicizers had to forge two Epistles "of John" to combat and threaten them: "every spirit which confesses that Jesus Christ has come in the flesh is of God, and every spirit which does not confess Jesus is not of God." (1 John 4:2–3) And again at 2 John 7: "For many deceivers have gone out into the world, *men who will not acknowledge the coming of Jesus Christ in the flesh*; such a one is the deceiver and the antichrist." Of these canonical Johannine passages, Doane says:

> This is language that could not have been used, if the reality of Christ Jesus's existence as a man could not have been denied, or, it would certainly seem, if the apostle himself had been able to give any evidence whatever of the claim.[426]

Concerning this development, Massey comments:

> We see from the Epistle of John how mortally afraid of Gnostic Spiritualism were the founders of the historical fraud. "Many deceivers are gone forth into the world that confess not that Jesus Christ cometh in the flesh." These words of John state

424 Doane, 512. The original Latin is as follows: "Accipos avengelium? Et maxime. Proinde ergo et natum accipis Christum? Non ita est. Neque enim sequitur, ut si evangelium accipio, idcirco et natum accipiam Christun. *Faust. l. 3. in*.... Ergo non putas, eum ex Maria virgine esse? *Manes dixit*: Absit, ut Dominum nostrum Jesum Christum per naturalia pudenda mulieris descendisse consitear. *ap. Arch. c. 47. p. 85. Vid. et cap. 5. p. 8.*" (Lardner (1745), 6.277–8.)

425 Graves, *WSCS*, 101.

426 Doane, 512.

> the Gnostic position. Their Christ had not so come, and could not be carnalized. These Gnostics were in the world long before they heard of such a doctrine; but when they did they denied and opposed it. This, says John, is anti-Christ.[427]

For example, a commentator on the works of Church father St. John Chrysostom (c. 347–407) remarks, "The Docetae, as their name denoted, considered that our blessed Lord did not actually exist on earth, or suffer upon the cross, but that all was a phantasy."[428] In discussing the various "heretics" of the second century and onward, the author first addresses the Valentinians, who "were of opinion that our Lord had passed through the Blessed Virgin as water through a conduit."[429] He then says, "Others asserted that the incarnation of Christ was a myth."

St. Ignatius, Bishop of Antioch

It was evidently the purpose of Antiochan bishop and saint Ignatius (c. 50–98/117) to convince those inclined to Docetism that "Christ really and truly lived," by way of writing letters to the churches of Asia Minor and Rome. Of Ignatius, Wheless says:

> He was the subject of very extensive forgeries; fifteen Epistles bear the name of Ignatius, including one to the Virgin Mary, and her reply; two to the apostle John, others to the Philippians, Tarsians, Antiocheans, Ephesians, Magnesians, Trallians, Romans, Philadelphians, Smyrnaeans, and to Polycarp, besides a forged *Martyrium*; the clerical forgers were very active with the name of Saint Ignatius.[430]

As Waite says: "It is now established that the only genuine writings of Ignatius extant, are the Cureton Epistles. These consist of about twelve octavo pages. They were written AD 115."[431] By a few decades later, some 100 pages had been forged in his name. The Cureton epistles comprised the three Syriac texts: the Epistles to Polycarp, to the Romans and to the Ephesians. The other epistles, then, are late forgeries, and those that were "original," not necessarily from the hand of Ignatius but of the early second century, were evidently interpolated after the beginning of Roman dominance at the end of that century. The older elements reflect Gnosticism, which, as noted, preceded orthodox, historicizing Christianity and which emanated out of Syria, in particular

427 Massey, *GHC*, 24–5.

428 St. Chrysostom's Picture of the Religion of His Age, 107.

429 *St. Chrysostom's Picture*, 108, citing Chrysostom's "*In Matt. Homil.* viii. § 1."

430 Wheless, *FC*, 133.

431 Waite, 212.

Antioch, where Ignatius was alleged to have been a bishop.

For example, the gnosticizing Ignatius makes reference to the delusion-inducing "prince of this world," such as in Ephesians (17), in which he says, "So you must never let yourselves be anointed with the malodorous chrism of the *prince of this world*'s doctrines."[432] The "malodorous chrism" of which Ignatius speaks is apparently the mystery of the lingam or phallus, evidently practiced in a variety of mystery schools for centuries prior to the Christian era, including by Old Testament characters.[433] By the term "malodorous," Ignatius is also evidently addressing the highly esoteric chrism or anointing that used semen.

Regarding Ignatius's epistles, Dr. Richard H. Popkin (1923–2005), a professor of philosophy, remarks:

> The letters were published at the end of the fifteenth century along with four spurious ones, but generally it may be said that Catholic scholars championed the testimony of Ignatius as being a useful near-apostolic support of the episcopal church, while Protestants tended to reject the entire body of documents as false.[434]

From the repeated emphasis that Christ really lived and died, "according to the flesh," etc., the purpose of many of the later epistles attributed to Ignatius was evidently to deal with those "blasphemers" who denied his Lord "ever bore a real human body" (Smyrnaeans) and to program his followers into believing Jesus's "history."

Clearly, these epistles were created in the era when Docetism reigned and was being written against by Church fathers,[435] during the middle to the latter half of the second century, at the earliest. If Christianity started with a historical Jesus of Nazareth, and if his followers were converted specifically because of his example, summarized in proselytizing texts such as the Apostle's Creed, it is inexplicable that, in the first place, Docetism would ever have existed and, secondly, even at this late date

432 Staniforth, 65.

433 Walker (1983), 793–4: "Patriarchal Semites worshipped their own genitals, and swore binding oaths by placing a hand on each other's private parts, a habit still common among the Arabs. Words like testament, testify and testimony still at*test* to the oaths sworn on the testicles. Abraham's servant swore by placing his hand 'under the thigh' of his master (Genesis 24, 9) because 'thigh' was a common euphemism for 'penis'..." Lingam worship in India is well-known, reflected also in the black stone at Mecca, which is evidently the remains of an ancient shiva lingam. See, for example, Leeming (2005), 239.

434 Popkin, 144.

435 Walter Bauer, *Orthodoxy and Heresey in Earliest Christianity*. Trans. a team from The Philadelphia Seminar on Christian Origins (Philadelphia: Fortress Press, 1971), p. 67.

there would be Christians who would need to be reminded of these various supposed facts as to Christ's purported life.

In the (forged) Epistle to the Magnesians (11), "Ignatius" exhorts his followers to resist such "heresies":

> I want you to be unshakably convinced of the Birth, the Passion and the Resurrection, which were the true and indisputable experiences of Jesus Christ, our Hope, in the days of Pontius Pilate's governorship.[436]

And again, in the letter to the Smyrnaeans (1) "Ignatius" begins by emphatically protesting:

> [Our] Lord … is truly of the race of David according to the flesh, but Son of God by the divine will and power, truly born of a virgin and baptized by John that all righteousness might be fulfilled by him, truly nailed up in the flesh for our sakes under Pontius Pilate and Herod the tetrarch.[437]

Further in Smyrnaeans (2, 3), he reiterates:

> And suffer He did, verily and indeed; just as He did verily and indeed raise Himself again. His Passion was no unreal illusion, as some sceptics aver who are all unreality themselves.... For my own part, I know and believe that He was in actual human flesh.[438]

In his Epistle to the Trallians (9), "Ignatius" repeats the conditioning of his "flock":

> Close your ears, then, if anyone preaches to you without speaking of Jesus Christ. Christ was of David's line. He was the son of Mary; He was verily and indeed born, and ate and drank; He was verily persecuted in the days of Pontius Pilate, and verily and indeed crucified.... He was also verily raised up again from the dead.[439]

And in his Epistle to Mary at Neapolis (5), "Ignatius" does continue to protest too much, and reveals how prevalent were the denials of the history:

> Avoid those that deny the passion of Christ, and His birth according to the flesh: and *there are many at present* who suffer under this disease.[440]

Next, Pseudo-Ignatius programs the Philippians against the unbelievers and Gnostics, ironically using a Gnostic concept to threaten

436 Staniforth, 73.
437 Haase, 26.2017,
438 Staniforth, 101.
439 Staniforth, 81.
440 Roberts, A. (1903), 1.123.

them, and sets the stage for centuries-long persecution with his calumny against the Jews:

> Christ was truly born, and died, for there is but One that became incarnate … the Son only, [who became so] not in appearance or imagination, but in reality. For "the Word became flesh." … And God the Word was born as man, with a body, of the Virgin, without any intercourse of man.… He was then truly born, truly grew up, truly ate and drank, was truly crucified, and died, and rose again. He who believes these things, as they really were, and as they really took place, is blessed. He who believeth them not is no less accursed than those who crucified the Lord. For *the prince of this world* rejoiceth when any one denies the cross, since he knows that the confession of the cross is his own destruction.… And thou art ignorant who really was born, thou who pretendest to know everything. If any one celebrates the Passover along with the Jews, or receives the emblems of their feast, he is a partaker with those that killed the Lord and His apostles.

In all his protestation, Pseudo-Ignatius offers no proof whatsoever of his claims and heinous accusations except his word that "Jesus the Lord was truly born and crucified." This utterly unscientific habit occurs repeatedly throughout the Christian fathers' works, without a stitch of tangible proof and hard evidence. It is upon this fanatic protestation and not factual events that Christianity's "history" is founded.

Obviously, if everyone in the early Christian movement had known and/or believed that Jesus Christ had existed "in the flesh," the authors of the Ignatian epistles would not have needed continually to press home their historicizing contentions. Regarding "Ignatius's" assorted historicizing elements, Earl Doherty states in "The Jesus Puzzle—Part 1: A Conspiracy of Silence":

> Before Ignatius, not a single reference to Pontius Pilate, Jesus' executioner, is to be found. Ignatius is also the first to mention Mary; Joseph, Jesus' father, nowhere appears. The earliest reference to Jesus as any kind of a teacher comes in 1 Clement, just before Ignatius, who himself seems curiously unaware of any of Jesus' teachings. To find the first indication of Jesus as a miracle worker, we must move beyond Ignatius to the Epistle of Barnabas.[441]

---

441 Doherty, jesuspuzzle.humanists.net/partone.htm. This "argument from silence" represents only one aspect of Jesus mythicist studies. Indeed, it is the mere starting point, and a crucial criterion and analysis that constitutes an aspect of good scientific examination. Indeed, without examining what elements are not only present but also absent, we are not being thorough in our scholar-

Despite "Ignatius's" attempts, by Irenaeus's time, around 170—which is probably the era in which these pseudepigraphical letters actually were composed—the Gnostics were still so powerful that Irenaeus felt compelled to spend a great deal of effort refuting them, even though he himself may have engaged in Gnostic initiation at some point. In his attacks Irenaeus was forced to take on the most influential of all Gnostics, Marcion.

Marcion of Pontus

The Cappadocian/Syrian/Samaritan Marcion of Sinope, Pontus, (c. 85–160), was the son of a Christian bishop, possibly a bishop himself and a wealthy shipowner. He had an enormous impact on Christianity, publishing the first New Testament, upon which the familiar Catholic canon was eventually based. Although he was considered a Christian even by his adversaries, Marcion was one of those "heretics" who vehemently denied that Christ had come in the flesh, died and been resurrected. Marcion was "anti-matter," and his Gnostic god was not the same as the violent, angry YHWH of the Old Testament, a book Marcion rejected. Like others before and after him, Marcion viewed as evil the "god of this world," a notion reflected in the works of Paul, whom Marcion considered the truest apostle.

Undoubtedly largely due to his wealth, Marcion was able to establish syngagogues/churches in a variety of places, and Marcionism enjoyed a widespread following around the Roman Empire, especially in Syria and Palestine. By the time he arrived at Rome, around 142/3 AD/CE, Marcion had already successfully founded several churches. So effective was Marcion that, by Epiphanius's time, Marcionites constituted a "vast number of men" who could be found in numerous places, including "not only in Rome and Italy but in Egypt, Palestine, Arabia, Syria, Cyprus and the Thebaid and even in Persia."[442] Marcionism continued to increase, such that even by the fifth century there were so many Marcionites that the Bishop of Cyrus, one Euphrates, was compelled to convert (forcibly, no doubt) over 1,000 of them. This bishop is the same who burned some 200 copies of the *Diastessaron*, purportedly written by Tatian, which therefore may have been a Marcionite/Docetic text. Tatian, though a disciple of the anti-Marcionite Justin Martyr, was, like Marcion, an ascetic and is said to have founded the sect of the Encratites

---

ship or presenting all the data. Wave-of-the-hand dismissals of the significance of these data will not suffice to reduce it. Special pleading aside, this silence/absence is, indeed, highly significant in many instances. As Jacob Neuser says, "What we cannot show, we do not know."

442 Herbermann, 9.648.

who, like the Marcionites, required celibacy for salvation. Some have drawn a parallel between Marcion and Tatian, too, in that both adopted a single gospel, Marcion's being a shorter version of Luke, Tatian's *Diatessaron* a combination of Matthew, Mark, Luke, and John.

In any event, it is obvious that the Docetic/Marcionite church was more widespread and dominant than was the "orthodox/catholic" Church that began to attain notoriety only toward the end of the second century. Why is this important fact not widely known?

The one "historical" fact from Marcion's gospel used by the later historicizers was: "In the fifteenth year of the reign of Tiberius Caesar, Jesus came down to Capernaum, a city of Galilee, and taught them on the sabbath days." This "coming down at Capernaum" was not considered a historical event by Marcion, who denied the incarnation, so it was interpreted by Christian historicizers as meaning that Marcion claimed "the Lord" had been a "phantom" or spiritual being who literally "came down from the heavens" at that time.

Interpreting this passage in its proper mythological, allegorical and Gnostic context, Massey observes:

> Tertullian [*Against Marcion*, 1.19.2] says, "According to the gospel of Marcion, in the fifteenth year of Tiberius, Christ Jesus *deigned to emanate from heaven, a salutary spirit*." But, he also says, according to this "Great Anti-Christian," the Christ was a phantom, who appeared suddenly at the synagogue of Capernaum in the likeness of a full-grown man for the purpose of protesting against the law and the prophets! But it is certain that the Lord or Christ of Marcion is entirely non-historical. He has no genealogy or Jewish line of descent; no earthly mother, no father, no mundane birthplace or human birth.[443]

In his "On the Flesh of Christ" (1, 2), Tertullian repeats his charges that Marcion expurgated Luke by removing historicizing and Judaizing elements:

> Marcion, in order that he might deny the flesh of Christ, denied also His nativity, or else he denied His flesh in order that he might deny His nativity; because, of course, he was afraid that His nativity and His flesh bore mutual testimony to each other's reality, since there is no nativity without flesh, and no flesh without nativity.
>
> He will not brook delay, since *suddenly* (without any prophetic announcement) did he bring down Christ from heaven. "Away," says he, "with that eternal plaguey taxing of Caesar, and the scanty inn, and the squalid swaddling-clothes, and the hard stable. We

443 Massey, *GHC*, 18. See Tertullian/Evans, 1.49.

do not care a jot for that multitude of the heavenly host which praised their Lord at night. Let the shepherds take better care of their flock, and let the wise men spare their legs so long a journey; let them keep their gold to themselves. Let Herod, too, mend his manners, so that Jeremy may not glory over him. Spare also the babe from circumcision, that he may escape the pain thereof; nor let him be brought into the temple, lest he burden his parents with the expense of the offering; nor let him be handed to Simeon, lest the old man be saddened at the point of death. Let that old woman also hold her tongue, lest she should bewitch the child." After such a fashion as this, I suppose you have had, O Marcion, the hardihood of blotting out the original records (of the history) of Christ, that His flesh may lose the proofs of its reality.[444]

Although couched in mystical terms like "Docetism," the bottom line for orthodoxy is that Marcion and other early *Christians* "blotted out," denied, ignored or never knew about "the original records (of the history) of Christ" and the purported "proofs of its reality." But in actuality Marcion did not "do away with" these various historicizing and Judaizing elements, as apparently, they were not attached to the story until after Marcion's death.

Tertullian continues his fact-bending and illogical diatribe about a subject that was obviously very important and required a great deal of attention, which was that denial of Christ come in the flesh:

Chapter V.—Christ Truly Lived and Died in Human Flesh. Incidents of His Human Life on Earth, and Refutation of Marcion's Docetic Parody of the Same. There are, to be sure, other things also quite as foolish (as the birth of Christ), which have reference to the humiliations and sufferings of God.... But Marcion will apply the knife to this doctrine also, and even with greater reason.... Have you, then, cut away all sufferings from Christ, on the ground that, as a mere phantom, He was incapable of experiencing them? *We have said above that He might possibly have undergone the unreal mockeries of an imaginary birth and infancy.* But answer me at once, you that murder truth: Was not God really crucified? And, having been really crucified, did He not really die?

Here Tertullian is relating again that Docetists took Christ as a "mere phantom" who did not possess all the typical biographical and historical details. It is inexplicable that so many people—Christians, who had either been baptized or otherwise initiated or converted into Christianity—could get it so wrong! Why would they be professing Christians, yet

444 Roberts, A. (1903), 1.521-2.

deny the most basic tenets of a "historical" faith laid out by a "historical" founder, whom they nevertheless believed was the messiah and God?

It makes more sense that the Gnosticizing Docetist effort existed first and was co-opted by historicizers and Judaizers, turning the mystical and mythical savior into a historical personage, than it does for those indoctrinated into a movement purportedly founded in the previous century, allegedly based on the teachings and example of an astounding historical and (super)human savior, to simply deny the whole of the historical and biographical material!

The rule of thumb for stories passed along over decades and centuries is that they *accrete* details, rather than lose them, just as the original gospel of Mark or Ur-Markus served as the core of much of Matthew and Luke. These texts were *accreted*, as it would appear it was Marcion's gospel which was turned into Luke's.

To repeat, the Gnostic texts were non-historicizing, allegorical and mythological. In other words, they did not tell the story of a "historical" Jewish master. Several other Gnostic texts were non-historicizing and non-Judaizing, such as the *Diatessaron* of Tatian (fl. 170), of which 200 copies were in use in Syrian churches as late as the time of "church superintendent" Theodoret (fl. 435 AD/CE), who removed them, no doubt violently, because they had no genealogies and did not declare Jesus to be "born of the seed of David."[445] Thus there is no reason to assume Tatian believed that Jesus Christ was a carnalized or historical person, or even that "the Savior" was Jewish. If 200 texts were still in use in the Syrian churches in Theodoret's time, this implies that well into the fifth century there were still plenty of Christians who did not believe in the incarnation.

Marcionite churches possessed characteristics, such as "abstaining from marriage, flesh and wine,"[446] vegetarianism, celibacy and female priests and deacons,[447] in common with both the Essenes and Therapeuts, who were alike in monkishness but differed in some details.

The Pagans

In addition to the non-carnalizing Gnostics, there were many non-Gnostic "Pagan" detractors, although "Pagan" was a pejorative term used to describe illiterate country folk ("hicks") and applied by Christians in a fraudulent attempt to demonstrate that they were more learned than their critics. These "Pagan" critics were, in fact, highly erudite in their own right, much more scientific than their adversaries and,

445 Theodoret, *De fab. Haer*; Harris, J.R., 13.

446 Mead (1906), 248.

447 See, for example, *Acta Philippi*.

as noted, frequently more moral.

As non-Christians, the Pagans were less euphemistic than the Gnostics in their denial of Christ's appearance in the flesh, calling it a blatant fabrication and subjecting the Christians to endless ridicule, such that a number of Christian apologists were forced to write long, rambling and illogical rants in attempts to silence their critics.

Celsus

One of the harshest critics of Christianity was the Epicurean and Platonist philosopher Celsus (second cent. AD/CE), who was so potent in his arguments in his work *The True Word* or *True Discourse* (c. 177) that Gnostic-Christian Origen was compelled to compose his refutation *Against Celsus*. Regarding Celsus's opinions of the Christian religion and its adherents, Lydia Maria Child relates:

> Celsus, in common with most of the Grecians, despised Christianity as a blind faith, that shunned the light of reason. He says: "They are forever repeating, Do not examine. Only believe, and thy faith will make these blessed. Wisdom is a bad thing in life; foolishness is to be preferred." He jeers at the fact that ignorant men were allowed to preach. He says: "You may see weavers, tailors, fullers and the most illiterate and rustic fellows, who dare not speak a word before wise men, when they can get a company of children and silly women together, set up to teach strange paradoxes among them.... This is one of their rules: Let no man that is learned, wise or prudent come among us; but if any be unlearned, or a child, or an idiot, let him freely come. So they openly declare that none but the ignorant, and those devoid of understanding, slaves, women and children, are fit disciples for the God they worship."[448]

Doane also relates Celsus's general impression of Christianity, one reflected by many others and admitted by Christians: "The Christian religion contains nothing but what Christians hold in common with heathens; nothing new, or truly great."[449] Celsus also "charged the Christians with being unphilosophical and credulous, fancying that they were the center of interest in the universe. He ridicules the miracles."[450] Regarding Celsus's indictment of Christianity, Doresse remarks:

> In this he asserts that the teaching of the Gospel derives, in part, from Plato, from Heraclitus, from the Stoics, the Jews, from the Egyptians' and Persians' myths and the Cabiri![451]

448 Child, 2.363–4. See Origen, *Contra Celsus*, 2.

449 Doane, 411.

450 Bellamy, 50.2.723.

451 Doresse, 62.

His remarks are confirmed by the following summary of Celsus by Dr. Don Allen, a professor at Johns Hopkins University:

> In his *Book of Truth* Celsus had asserted that almost all Christian doctrines were warped versions of Platonic idealism, but in addition Christians had certain other dogmas and rites eclectically put together of borrowings from the philosophy of the Stoics, the Jewish tradition, the mysteries of Mithra, the myths of Typhon, Osiris and the Cabiri. The story of Christ is no more than a concatenation of various old myths plus the remembrances of various wandering Greek and barbarian wonder-workers who had plagued antiquity.[452]

Being educated in such philosophies, Celsus had no difficulty recognizing the biblical narratives as fiction. In *Fiction as History*, professor of Classics and Ancient History Dr. Glen W. Bowersock comments:

> The fiction and mendacity that Celsus wished to expose in his *True Discourse* were nothing less than the Christian representation of the life and death of Jesus Christ.[453]

Bowersock continues:

> Origen strained every nerve in the third century to confute Celsus's elaborate attempt to expose the Gospel narratives as fiction.... For any coherent and persuasive interpretation of the Roman empire it becomes obvious that fiction must be viewed as a part of its history.[454]

Fiction as History

Under Nero fiction thrived, as the emperor had an insatiable appetite for Greek and Roman literature, such that he sparked a renaissance, no doubt with numerous poets, playwrights and novelists vying for imperial favor and patronage. Such was the atmosphere into and out of which Christianity was born. Bowersock also states:

> Parallels in form and substance between the writings of the New Testament and the fictional production of the imperial age are too prominent to be either ignored or dismissed as coincidental. Both Celsus, in his attack on the Christians, and Origen, in his defense of them, recognize the similarities, particularly ... where apparent miracles—such as the open tomb or resurrection

---

452 Allen, D., 11. Allen cites *Contra Celsum* in Migne's *Patrologiae Graecae*, vol. 11, cols. 1287–1503 and 951-54. These sections correspond roughly to books/chapters 6.1-7.59 and 3.26–27, respectively, in the English translation by Crombie.

453 Bowersock, 3.

454 Bowersock, 9–12.

of the dead—were at issue.[455]

Over the centuries, ancient texts were reworked in order to explain the founding of nations and other auspicious events, as was the case with the Roman book *The Aeneid*, which is a rewriting of *The Iliad* designed to glorify the foundation of the Roman state.[456] Every culture and nation had its heroic epics and legendary foundations, including Greece and Rome. Israel was no exception, and its legendary foundation related in the Old Testament is as fictitious as the tale of Romulus and Remus, the mythical founders of Rome. The foundation of Christianity is no less fictitious, except in the minds of the people who have always been told otherwise.

Celsus was not the only vocal and erudite critic of "the new superstition," as Christianity was called.[457] Another detractor was Ammonius Saccas (third cent. AD/CE), a Greek philosopher and founder of the Alexandrian Neoplatonic school of the third century. Saccas taught that "Christianity and Paganism, when rightly understood, differ in no essential points, but had common origin, *and are really one and the same thing*."[458] Another group of "Pagan" critics could be found in India: "Brahmins constantly tell [Christian] missionaries that [the Christian] religion is only corrupted Brahminism."[459]

So widespread was the criticism and ridicule that Christian elder Arnobius (fourth cent.) complained, "The Gentiles make it their constant business to laugh at our faith and to lash our credulity with their facetious jokes."[460] In fact, as Massey states, "The total intelligence of Rome [treated] the new religion as a degrading superstition founded on a misinterpretation of their own dogmas."[461] Indeed, in his "On the Incarnation" (7), Saint and Alexandrian Bishop Athanasius (c. 293–373) fretted endlessly about being mocked, particularly for believing that Jesus Christ was historical:

> We come now to the unbelief of the Gentiles; and this is indeed a matter for complete astonishment, for they laugh at that which is no fit subject for mockery, yet fail to see the shame and ridiculousness of their own idols.... First of all, what is there in our belief that

455 Bowersock, 124.

456 Bowersock, 60ff.

457 See, for example, Suetonius, *Life of Nero* (16): "Afflicti suppliciis Christiani, genus hominum superstitionis novae ac maleficae" (Suetonius/Rolfe, 2.110).

458 Doane, 411.

459 Higgins, 2.663.

460 Doane, 275.

461 Massey, *HJMC*, 180.

is unfitting or ridiculous? *Is it only that we say that the Word has been manifested in a body?*[462]

Another vocal critic of Christianity was the Emperor Julian, an apostate from Christianity and convert to Paganism, who, coming after the reign of the fanatical and murderous "good Christian" Constantine, returned rights to Pagan worshippers, for which he may have been murdered. In the seventh charge in *Julian apud Cyril.* (bk 2), Julian expressed his objections to the Christian religion thus:

If anyone should wish to know the truth with respect to you Christians, he will find your impiety to be made up partly of the Jewish audacity, and partly of the indifference and confusion of the Gentiles, and that you have put together not the best, but the worst characteristics of them both.[463]

Christianity as Criminality

In fact, the Christians were not just mocked, they were considered criminals. As Pagels relates:

> In an open letter addressed to "rulers of the Roman Empire," Tertullian acknowledges that pagan critics detest the movement: "You think that a Christian is a man of every crime, an enemy of the gods, of the emperor, of the law, of good morals, of all nature."

The early Christians were thus accused of heinous behavior, including infanticide and orgies, imputations that Christians themselves later used against their enemies. In the face of such charges, Justin Martyr (10) was forced to say, "Do you also … believe that we eat human flesh and that after our banquets we extinguish the lights and indulge in unbridled sensuality?"[464] And Tertullian was compelled to write: "We are accused of observing a holy rite in which we kill a little child and then eat it … after the feast, we practice incest.… This is what is *constantly* laid to our charge."[465] Here we see, as previously contended, that Christians were under constant criticism during the first couple of centuries of Christianity's creation.

Pagels also relates:

> The Christian group bore all the marks of conspiracy. First, they identified themselves as followers of a man accused of magic and executed for that and treason; second, they were "atheists," who denounced as "demons" the gods who protected the fortunes of the Roman state.… Besides these acts that police could iden-

462 Athanasius/Lawson, 75.
463 Taylor, R. (1829), 258–9.
464 Larson, 298.
465 Larson, 298.

> tify, rumor indicated that their secrecy concealed atrocities: their enemies said that they ritually ate human flesh and drank human blood.[466]

Another of the Pagan criticisms, as we have seen, was that the Christians were plagiarists (and degraders) of old ideologies and concepts, an accusation that the later Christians were compelled to confirm as they attempted to gain respectability for their "new superstition." Thus did the Christians admit the superlative nature and morality of those "Pagan" ideologies, by attempting to raise Christianity's esteem, comparing the new faith to these earlier revered religions and philosophies. In his *First Apology* (20–1), Justin aligned himself with several ideologies that existed long prior to the Christian era:

> For in our saying that all things were fashioned and came into being through God we will seem to speak the opinion of Plato. And in saying that there will be a conflagration, we will seem to speak the opinion of the Stoics. And in our saying that the souls of the wicked are punished after death, remaining in consciousness, and that the souls of the virtuous remain free from punishment and live happily, we will seem to say the same things as the poets and philosophers. And in saying that human beings should not worship inferior things, we announce the same as the comic poet Menander and those saying these things, for they declared the artisan to be greater than the thing crafted.
>
> And when we say that the Logos, which is the first offspring of God, was born without sexual intercourse as Jesus Christ our teacher, and that after his crucifixion, death and resurrection he went up to heaven, we introduce nothing stranger than those you call the sons of Zeus.[467]

In fact, Plato was widely studied by the Christian fathers/forgers, as is obvious from their writings, particularly those pontificating about "the Word," an ancient concept refined by the Greek philosopher (*Timaeus* 29d7–30a6).[468] Indeed, Justin Martyr was originally a Platonist or, specifically, a Middle Platonist.[469] As to the purported difference between "Pagans" and "Christians," Doane states:

466 Pagels, *GG*, 76.

467 Justin/Minns, 131.

468 For an extensive discussion of the pre-Christian logos concept, as developed by Plato and Philo, see Runia, *Philo of Alexandria and the Timaeus of Plato.*

469 Allert (68) remarks: "Justin was not a Platonist in the pure sense of that school of thought. He was a Middle Platonist, and his understanding of Plato was an interpretation."

> The most celebrated Fathers of the Christian church, the most frequently quoted, and those whose names stand the highest were nothing more or less than Pagans, being born and educated Pagans.[470]

These celebrated Pagan-Christian fathers included Pantaenus (d. c. 200), Origen, Clement of Alexandria, Gregory Thaumaturgus and Tertullian.

The Jews

Naturally, orthodox Jews also denied the reality of Christ, although, like other cultures, they were eventually forced through violence to grant that the tale had at least some historicity, as exemplified in the Talmud, for example. In his debate with Trypho the Jew, Justin depicts Trypho as saying:

> If, then, you are willing to listen to me (for I have already considered you a friend), first be circumcised, then observe what ordinances have been enacted with respect to the Sabbath, and the feasts, and the new moons of God; and, in a word, do all things which have been written in the law: and then perhaps you shall obtain mercy from God. *But Christ—if He has indeed been born, and exists anywhere—is unknown, and does not even know Himself, and has no power until Elias come to anoint Him, and make Him manifest to all.* And you, having accepted a groundless report, invent a Christ for yourselves, and for his sake are inconsiderately perishing.[471]

Trypho's remarks indicate not only that the Jews did not accept Christ as a historical person but also that they recognized Christ's true nature as a *solar deity*. The name of his "anointer," Elijah or Elias (Matt. 11:14), is not only a title for John the Baptist based on the Old Testament prophet, but also *Helios*, the sun.[472] Indeed, the name Elijah or Elias is rendered in the Greek Old Testament/Septuagint (LXX) as Ηλιου—essentially the same as *Helios*, the sun god. Is Elijah yet another "midrashic" attempt to refashion a popular foreign god, Helios the Sun, into a "Jewish prophet" to humanize and Judaize yet another mythical figure?

To such accusations, Justin attempts to respond in a chapter titled, "The Christians Have Not Believed Groundless Stories," but he offers no proof at all, merely groundless protestations. It is difficult to imagine that, when Trypho says Justin has "made a Christ for himself," he is

470 Doane, 412.

471 Roberts, A. (1885), 1.198–9.

472 See below for more information about Elijah/Elias's solar nature. See also Keary, 424, et al. The original Greek at Matthew Ēlias, spelled with an unaspirated eta and alpha, rather than an aspiration eta and an omicron, as in Helios.

referring to anything other than the creation of a myth, especially since at one point (ch. 67), Justin portrays the Jew as comparing Jesus with the Greek hero Perseus, who is clearly a mythical figure. According to Justin:

> And Trypho answered, "The Scripture has not, 'Behold the virgin shall conceive, and bear a son,' but, 'Behold, the young woman shall conceive, and bear a son,' and so on.... But the whole prophecy refers to Hezekiah, and it is proved that it was fulfilled in him, according to the terms of the prophecy. Moreover, in the fables of those who are called Greeks, it is written that Perseus was begotten of Danae, who was a virgin; he who was called among them Zeus having descended on her in the form of a golden shower. And you ought to feel ashamed when you make assertions similar to theirs ... do not venture to tell monstrous phenomena, lest you be convicted of talking foolishly like the Greeks."[473]

As to the origins of Christianity, Massey spells it out:

> Christianity began as Gnosticism, refaced with falsehoods concerning a series of facts alleged to have been historical, but which are demonstrably mythical. By which I do not mean mythical as exaggerations or perversions of historic truth, but belonging to the pre-extant Mythos.... It is obvious that the Roman Church remained Gnostic at the beginning of the second century, and for some time afterwards. Marcion, the great Gnostic, did not separate from it until about the year 136 AD. Tatian did not break with it until long after that. In each case the cause of quarrel was the same. They left the Church that was setting up the fraud of Historic Christianity. They left it as Gnostic Christians, who were anathematized as heretics, because they rejected the Christ made flesh and the new foundations of religion in a spurious Jewish history.[474]

Thus, we can see that the truth of the gospel story and the existence of its main character, Jesus Christ, have been called into question since the tale was released upon an unsuspecting public.

Physical Evidence

> "We do not yet have first-century papyri discussing Jesus of Nazareth....
>
> "For the balance of the first century and the first third of the second, not a single archaeological artifact attests to the existence of the Jesus-centered Christianity in the whole of the empire. During

473 Roberts, A. (1905), 1.231.

474 Massey, *GHC*, 12-13.

this same period no evidence for any of the higher religious offices dedicated specifically to the Christian church are to be found in either the archaeological or historical record. We are therefore justified on the basis of these conclusions to dispense for the moment with both an historical first-century Jesus and his church."

—David, *History Hunters International*, "Acts of the Chresmologoi:

The Role of Oracles and Chronicles in the Creation of Divine"

"Not a single artefact of any medium—including textual—and dated reliably before the fourth century can be unambiguously identified as Christian....

"There are very many texts claimed to be Christian and composed before the fourth century, though the documents themselves are not dated to that early period. We have found no text before the fourth century which mentions either Jesus Christ, or the term 'Christian.'

"The earliest fragments and codex of the New Testament predate the fourth century, though nowhere in them have we found the key word Christ. Many biblical scholars claim that they do, but our visual inspection of them fails to find a single such usage of this term. We have been unable to find a single text transliterated correctly in this regard....

"As there are gospels and other texts of a religious character, so there is archaeology for places of worship and many artefacts: none spell Christian. Claims that any are Christian are, in fact, a matter of opinion only and we disagree with all such opinions."

—John Bartram, "The Vacuum of Evidence for Pre-4th Century Christianity"

"When Hadrian invented the cult of his Antinous, he created masses of good archaeology for us to find: an entire city, temples, very many statues and even the obelisk describing how Antinous was made a god. Thought Christianity claims to be empire-wide and with many adherents belonging to the Greco-Roman elite, it has nothing."

—John Bartram, "Mani and Authorship of the Canonical Gospels"

It has been demonstrated that there is no reliable textual evidence for the existence of Jesus Christ and that, in fact, his physicality and the historicity of the gospel tale were denied from the earliest times by Pagans and Christians ("heretics") alike. What about the physical remains? What does archaeology tell us about the historicity of the Christian story? In order to determine the evidence, we must look to architecture, monuments, coins, medals, inscriptions, pottery, statues, frescoes and mosaics, among other artifacts. Unfortunately, much of the evidence has been completely destroyed, mostly due to "religious" fervor; however, there remains enough to reveal the conspiracy and fraud.

Jesus's Physical Appearance

There is no physical description of Jesus in the New Testament, other than that which resembles the sun, such as at his transfiguration at Matthew 17:2: "And he was transfigured before them, and his face shone like the sun, and his garments became white as light," a fitting description for the "light of the world" who is "coming in the clouds" and whom "every eye will see" (John 8:12; 9:5; Rev. 1:7). The androgynous character at Revelation 1:13–15 has also been interpreted to refer to Jesus: "And in the midst of the seven candlesticks, one like unto the Son of Man, clothed in a garment down to the foot, and girt about his paps [breasts]. His head and his hair were white as white wool, white as snow." A number of people have claimed that the "wooly" hair reference means Christ was a black man, and they cite black crucifixes and bambinos as evidence.[475] As can be seen, the scriptural "evidence" of Jesus's physicality creates more problems than it solves.

In fact, early Christian fathers admitted that Jesus's appearance was unknown, which is appropriate in consideration of the Docetic belief that he had never appeared "according to the flesh." For example, St. Augustine related that "in his time there was no authentic portrait of Christ, and that the type of features was still undetermined, so that we have absolutely no knowledge of His appearance."[476] This deficiency would appear to be very strange, particularly since it was claimed that Jesus was "known throughout the world." How, pray tell, did anyone recognize him?

This lack of monumental documentation has been explained as an extension of the Jewish prohibition against idol worship; however, no such proscription would need to be followed, since, according to Paulinist doctrine, Christ's fulfillment of the law freed Christians from its observance. Later Christians maintained no such prohibition; indeed, from the third century onward the Alexandrian Gnostics and Coptic Christians in particular made many representations of various aspects of the

475 See, for example, Ben-Jochannan, 4, 375.

476 Lecky, 223. Augustine's original Latin in *De Trinitate* (7.4, 5) is: "Qua fuerit ille [Christ] facie nos penitus ignoramus: Nam et ipsius Dominicae facies carnis innumerabilium cogitationum diversitate variatur et fingitur, quae tamen una erat, quaecumque erat." (Milman (1840), 3.505.)

gospel tale and Christian doctrines.

Despite the lack of any gospel description, Jesus was alternately described by the early Christian fathers as either "the most beautiful of the sons of men" or "the ugliest of the sons of men"—another highly strange development, if this character were real. But, as Augustine admitted, this debate existed before the "type of features" was determined (i.e., fabricated and standardized). Dr. Fox relates the ambiguity of Christ's appearance:

> Nobody remembered what Jesus had looked like. Citing Isaiah, one wing of Christian opinion argued that he had chosen a mean and ugly human form. By c. 200, he was being shown on early Christian sarcophagi in a stereotyped pagan image, as a philosopher teaching among his pupils or a shepherd bearing sheep from his flock.[477]

It is beyond belief that, had Jesus existed and been seen by "the multitudes," no one would remember what he looked like. The authors of the gospels, pretending to be the apostles, professed to remember Jesus's exact deeds and words, verbatim; yet, they couldn't recall what he looked like!

Many people think that the standard image with the long, dark hair is how Jesus's early followers saw him. In reality, the earliest images of Christ portray a young, beardless boy, at times with blond hair:

> The Christian art of [the first three to four centuries] remained delightfully pagan. In the catacombs we see the Saviour as a beardless youth, like a young Greek god; sometimes represented, like Hermes the guardian of the flocks, bearing a ram or lamb round his neck; sometimes as Orpheus tuning his lute among the wild animals.[478]

In his *Christian Iconography* Dr. Adolphe Napoléon Didron states:

> [He] was almost constantly represented at that period, under the figure of a beautiful and adorable youth of about fifteen or eighteen years of age, beardless, with a sweet expression of countenance, and long and abundant hair flowing in curls over his shoulders: his brow is sometimes encircled by a diadem or a *bandeau*, like a young priest of the Pagan gods; this is, in fact, the favorite figure.[479]

Didron further remarks:

> The youthfulness of Christ, which is remarked on the most ancient Christian monuments, is a predominating and very curious fact. On sculptured sarcophagi, in fresco paintings and

477 Fox, 392.

478 Carpenter, 180–1.

479 Didron, 1.239.

> Mosaics, Christ is thus represented as a young man of twenty years of age, or a graceful youth of fifteen, without any beard, the shape of his face round, the expression gentle, resplendent with divine youth, just as Apollo was figured by the Pagans, and as angels are represented by Christians.[480]

According to the gospel story, Jesus disappeared between the ages of around 12 and 29 before he began his ministry, so this depiction of him at "about fifteen to eighteen years of age" certainly would be odd, since his followers never saw him at that age. These depictions demonstrate that Jesus's appearance was arbitrary, allegorical, unhistorical and not based on a single individual. Dujardin says:

> As to archaeological evidence, the oldest paintings in the Catacombs not only display no features that confirm the gospel legend, but represent Jesus under forms that are inconsistent with it.[481]

Christ as Lamb and Fish

Furthermore, the Christian crucifix originally held the image of a lamb instead of a man, up until the eighth to ninth centuries, at which time Christ was depicted as a young, pagan god:

> The earliest artists of the crucifixion represent the Christian Saviour as *young and beardless*, always without the crown of thorns, alive, and erect, apparently elate; no signs of bodily suffering are there.[482]

As theologian Rev. Dr. Richard R. Viladesau relates:

> In one of the earliest depictions [of the crucifixion], on a fifth-century ivory now in the British museum, Jesus is shown both carrying the cross and crucified.... In both scenes, Christ is young, long-haired and beardless: the Apollonic "beautiful Christ" favored by the period.

Moreover, some of the earliest images associated with Christ include not only a lamb but also a fish, rather than a man:

The fish, in the opinion of antiquaries in general, is the symbol of Jesus Christ.... A fish is sculptured upon a number of Christian monuments, and more particularly upon the ancient sarcophagi.... It is also upon medals bearing the effigy of our Saviour, and upon engraved stones, cameos and intaglios. The fish is also to be remarked upon the amulets worn, suspended from the neck by children, and upon ancient glasses and sepulchral lamps.[483]

480 Didron, 1.249–50.

481 Dujardin, 2.

482 Doane, 203.

483 Didron, 344–5.

Didron further states:

> Baptismal fonts are more particularly ornamented with the fish....
>
> To conclude, in sculptured or paint monuments, representing the Lord's Supper, the last repast of Jesus Christ, the fish is figured amongst the meats; it accompanies the Paschal Lamb amongst others.... In manuscriptures with miniatures, on painted glass and enamels of the thirteenth and fourteenth centuries, the first is constantly exhibited, placed upon a dish in the middle of the table at the Last Supper, among the loaves, knives and glasses, which are used at the repast.[484]

The fish motif apparently is representative of the astrological age of Pisces, symbolized by the two fishes, an icon found in pre-Christian monuments such as the circular zodiac at Dendera, Egypt (c. 50 BCE). This symbol was adopted into Christianity and became widely popular. This fact alone suggests that those who devised Christian icons, both physical and literarily, were aware of the precessional ages. We submit that, some five or six centuries earlier, those who devised or finalized those stories in the Old Testament were likewise aware of this important astronomical/astrological milestone.

Jesus or Serapis?

In addition, the archaeological evidence reveals the existence of the dark-haired and bearded "Jesus" image long *before* the Christian era. In this regard, Higgins describes a medal of "the Savior" purportedly found in pre-Christian ruins with the image of a bearded man with long hair, with an inscription in Hebrew on the other side. He then exclaims:

> And now I wish to ask any one how a coin with the head of Jesus Christ and a legend, *in a language obsolete in the time of Jesus Christ*, should arrive in Wales and get buried in an old Druidical monument? ... Whether this medal represents the son of the Virgo Paritura, found in the Western countries long before the Christian era, or Jesus Christ, cannot be reduced to a demonstration.[485]

The image held today of a white man with long, dark hair and a beard is also that of Serapis, the syncretic god of the Egyptian state religion in the third century BCE, who was by the fourth century CE the most highly respected god in Egypt. According to the purported letter from the emperor Hadrian to his friend Servianus, Serapis was considered to be the "peculiar god of the Christians."[486] As Classicist, Plutarch trans-

484 Didron, 346–7.

485 Higgins, 2.154. The image is found at 2.527.

486 For a discussion of this alleged correspondence between Hadrian and

lator and world-renowned expert on antique engraved gems, Dr. Charles W. King (1818–1888) concludes:

> There can be no doubt that the head of Serapis, marked as the face is by a grave and pensive majesty, *supplied the first idea for the conventional portraits of the Saviour.*[487]

Coins

Coin evidence is one of the more underrated methods of archaeology; yet it provides a superior dating system for a number of reasons, especially since coins do not disintegrate over time. Unfortunately for Christian claims, the numismatic evidence for early Christianity is nil. Speaking about how coin discoveries can overturn historical descriptions, numismatist and archaeologist Dr. P.J. Casey says:

> [The] close consideration of coin evidence may shake the foundations of the literary narrative. This is because coins are produced with immediacy in response to events, whereas the literary record is composed after the event, often much after, and can suffer from bias if not outright distortion or suppression of facts.[488]

It therefore needs to be asked why there is no coin evidence for Christianity from the first, second or third centuries of the Common Era. As Rev. Dr. Lino Sanchez suggests: "Because the 'events' were literary events (Fiction!)—only!"

Birth Caves, Tombs, Sundry Sites

Many people point to "Calvary Hill," Jesus's tomb, the stations of the cross, and other tourist spots in Jerusalem and Israel as evidence that there must have been *somebody* there and *some* drama must have taken place. It is an unfortunate fact that, because of this belief, hundreds of unstable people have been running about these so-called sacred sites trying to get themselves "crucified" even to this day. It is this same religious madness that has given rise not only to the Christian myths, but also to the booming business of relics, holy sites, etc. Of these purported sacred sites, Wells remarks:

> There is not a single existing site in Jerusalem which is mentioned in connection with Christian history before 326, when Helena (Mother of Constantine) saw a cave that had just been excavated, and which was identified with Jesus' tomb.[489]

Indeed, it is reported that when Helena's representative inquired in

---

Servianus, the authenticity of which has been questioned, see Murdock, *CIE*, 279–80.

487 King, C.W., 69.

488 Casey, P.J., 43.

489 Wells, *HEJ*, 194.

Jerusalem as to the "Lord and Savior Jesus Christ," no one had ever heard of him except, reputedly, one old man, who promptly showed Helena's envoy a field of buried crucifixes, which was apparently evidence sufficient for these great minds to settle the matter: they had found the "true cross."[490]

Doherty addresses the problem of these so-called sacred sites:

> In all the Christian writers of the first century, in all the devotion they display about Christ and the new faith, not one of them expresses a desire to see the birthplace of Jesus, to visit Nazareth his home town. No one talks about having been to the sites of his preaching, the upper room where he held his Last Supper, the hill on which he was crucified, or the tomb where he was buried and rose from the dead. Not only is there no evidence that anyone showed an interest in visiting such places, they go completely unmentioned. The words Bethelehem, Nazareth and Galilee never appear in any of the epistles, and the word Jerusalem is never used in connection with Jesus.
>
> Most astonishing of all, there is not a hint of pilgrimage to Calvary itself, where humanity's salvation was presumably consummated. How could such a place not have become the center of Christian devotion, how could it not have been turned into a shrine?[491]

Elsewhere, Doherty remarks:

> Is it conceivable that Paul would not have wanted to run to the hill of Calvary, to prostrate himself on the sacred ground that bore the blood of his slain Lord? Surely he would have shared such an intense emotional experience with his readers! Would he not have been drawn to the Gethsemane garden, where Je-

490 Regarding the story of Helena's alleged discovery of the "True Cross," Dr. Annabel Jane Wharton (20–1) comments: "The familiar story of Helena's discovery of the True Cross first appears where the story was most needed: in the West. In 395, Saint Ambrose of Milan told the earliest recorded version of the narrative of Helena's discovery of the three crosses near Golgotha. The dowager empress Helena, Constantine's mother, traveled to Jerusalem in 325; Bishop Eusebius of Caesarea provides a rich account of her journey and pious activities. He indicates that she was involved in the dedication and endowment of the Church of the Nativity in Bethelehem and a church on the Mount of Olives. He makes no mention of the cross. Only at the very end of the fourth century, nearly four hundred years after the Crucifixion and some seventy years after Helena's pilgrimage, did a remote Latin bishop first associate the empress with the discovery of the True Cross. The tradition of Helena's excavations was generally accepted by ecclesiastics and laymen as historical reality in the Middle Ages and, more surprisingly, by some scholars in modernity."

491 Doherty (1999), 73–4.

sus was reported to have passed through the horror and the self-doubts that Paul himself had known? Would he not have gloried in standing before the empty tomb, the guarantee of his own resurrection? Is there indeed, in this wide land so recently filled with the presence of the Son of God, any holy place at all, any spot of ground where that presence still lingers, hallowed by the step, touch or word of Jesus of Nazareth? Neither Paul nor any other first century letter writer breathes a whisper of any such thing.

It is in reality inconceivable, particularly in consideration of the religious fanaticism evident even today, that if Jesus actually existed such zealots as Paul and the other early Christians who were purportedly "dying for the faith" in droves were completely uninterested in such sacred sites and relics. The complete absence of such records indicates that the entire story was fictional.

Jesus in India?

Surprising at it may seem, Christians are not the only ones who point proudly to sacred Jesus sites. The Kashmir vale in India lays claim to the grave sites of both Moses and Jesus. Jesus, as the wandering prophet Yuz Asaf, allegedly lived there for many years following his deliverance from the Cross. This story is a favorite of Ahmadiyya Islam, which asserts that the "prophet" Jesus did not die on the cross but ended up at Srinigar, India, where he lived until the age of 120, fathering children.[492] Thus, many Kashmiri Muslims claim Christ as their ancestor.

The evidence may seem convincing to the uninitiated; however, "Yuz Asaf" has been taken as a corruption for "Johasaphat," originally "Bodhisattva" (Arabic "Yūdhasaf"), which could indicate a Buddhist priest. "Yuz Asaf" is also basically the same as "Joseph," which is יוסף or *Yowceph* in the Hebrew and which may have been a title of a priest or brotherhood member and not necessarily a name. If "Yuz Asaf" is not a local Buddhist saint, it may be that this individual, who is not buried in the direction of a Muslim burial, was a wandering Jewish or Christian priest/missionary from "Palestine." Obviously, genetic testing by a reputable and neutral agency would be desirable, as would carbon dating for the tomb.[493]

Prior to the Ahmadiyya movement, others attempted to place not only his death but also Jesus's "lost years" in India and/or Tibet, where Russian traveler Nicholas Notovitch (b. 1858) purportedly received a

492 See, for example, Houtsma, 206; Schäfer and Cohen (1998), 306.

493 For more on this subject, see my article, "Jesus in India? The Myth of the Lost Years."

text by Tibetan monks recording Jesus's life and times. In his book *The Unknown Life of Jesus*, Notovich claimed that the contents of this text were written "immediately after the Resurrection." The manuscript itself was purported to date from the second or third century after the Christian era and was certainly not composed "immediately after the Resurrection." Moreover, the text has been widely assailed as a forgery, most notably in *Famous Biblical Hoaxes* by Dr. Edgar J. Goodspeed, who related:

> Notovitch's writings were immediately controversial. The German orientalist Max Mueller, professor of Indian philosophy in Oxford who'd never been to India himself, published a letter he'd received from a British colonial officer J. Archibald Douglas, which stated that the presence of Notovich in Ladakh was "not documented." The head of the Hemis community signed a document that denounced Notovitch as an outright liar.[494]

Goodspeed surmised that the author used the Gospel of Luke as one source text. Notovitch's claims were championed by Indian swami Sri Abhedananda in the 1920s and continue to receive support to this day. Ehrman sums up the contemporary critical view thus: "Today there is not a single recognized scholar on the planet who has any doubts about the matter. The entire story was invented by Notovitch, who earned a good deal of money and a substantial amount of notoriety for his hoax ."[495]

Even if genuinely dated from the early centuries, the text itself says at the beginning, "*This is what is related on this subject by the merchants who have come from Israel*,"[496] thus demonstrating not that "Jesus"—or "Issa," as he is called there—lived in India but that the Jesus *tradition* was brought to India and Tibet by the extensive trading and brotherhood network that readily allowed for such stories to spread. The Notovitch text has a cheery view of the Jews, throws the entire onus of the crucifixion on Pilate and the Romans, and was apparently written as not only Jewish but Buddhist propaganda, as evidenced by the following passage, designed to elevate Buddha above Jesus: "Six years later, Issa, whom the Buddha had chosen to spread his holy word, could perfectly explain the sacred rolls."[497] One notable aspect of the text, however,

494 Goodspeed (1956), from the chapter "The Unknown Life of Jesus."

495 Ehrman (2011), 254.

496 Notovitch (1916), 99.

497 For a more detailed, critical look at the "Jesus in India" theory, as well as his purported appearance in Great Britain, see my article "Jesus in India? The Myth of the Lost Years."

is its pro-women exhortations, which differ markedly from Jewish and Christian traditions.

Furthermore, it should be noted that there were innumerable "traveling prophets" throughout the ancient world, spouting the same parables and platitudes and doing the standard bag of magic tricks as Jesus, as do the countless Indian yogis of today. It is difficult to believe that the Indians or Tibetans would be very impressed by such stories, as if new to them. Nor is it possible that the Hindus would not have recognized in the "life of Christ" that of Christna/Krishna; indeed, they did.

In addition, concerning the Indian "grave of Moses," the name "Mousa," or Moses, is common in Kashmir, as also on graves. Along with the Moses and Jesus graves, there are also at least *two* tombs of the apostle "Thomas" in India.

The Japanese, British or American Jesus?

In fact, over the millennia, the establishment of such revered tombs has been routine. Japan also lays claim to the tombs of both Moses and Jesus. The villagers of Shingo insist that Jesus and his brother were buried there, and they have the graves to prove it. As do the Indians and Tibetans, the Shingoese assert that Jesus was educated by religious masters in Japan during his "lost years." The Japanese tale goes further than the Indian and maintains that, after escaping crucifixion when his brother was mistakenly executed in his place, Jesus fled with the remains of his brother and with followers to Shingo, where he married a Japanese woman, fathered three daughters and lived to be 106.[498] Although some locals will swear the story is true, it turns out that the Shingo graves are those of Christian missionaries dating from the sixteenth century.

Jesus the Druid?

While the "Jesus in India" theory asserts the Jewish sage spent his entire early period there, the British tale of Jesus has him travel in his youth to Glastonbury in order to learn from the Druids. The story goes that many of the tin miners in Britain at the time of Jesus's alleged advent were Jewish, which is sensible since British tin-mining was evidently highly valued by the Jews' Phoenician predecessors and cousins. One such miner was purportedly Jesus's "uncle" Joseph of Arimathea, who, along with Jesus, allegedly founded the first Christian church at Glastonbury. However, the fact that Glastonbury was a "great Pagan sanctuary" in pre-Christian times makes this story suspicious as myth-making and propaganda.[499]

498 See, for example, "Shingō, Aomori."

499 For more information about this subject, see my article "Jesus the Druid?"

God, Priest or King?

Confusion between the gods and their messengers is behind many of the tales about this or that god or godman having been real, and having walked or lived here or there. Often the person who is preaching about the foreign or "alien" god is called by the same name as the god; hence, his exploits are confused with the mythology he is presenting. For example, a "priest of Apollo," becomes "priest Apollo" and may then be shortened to "Apollo." Egyptian pharaohs, who represented the god Horus on Earth, were frequently named for the gods, such as the Setis, and rulers in central America were likewise named for gods, such as Quetzalcoatl.

In cases of culture clash or tribal warfare, an entire culture, tribe or place may be called by the name of a god. When there are migrations, tradition may be garbled such that it seems to be the name of an individual rather than of a whole culture. Confusion occurs as well when a number of individuals hold the same name or title, as in Buddhism, where the exploits and sayings of many Buddhas, mythical and historical, are rolled into one.[500]

The Jesus Family Tomb, James Ossuary, etc.

The founding of tombs of godmen has been popular since antiquity, as exemplified by the numerous Osirians in Egypt, where legend had pieces of the god buried here and there. This pursuit continues to this day, as "tombs of Jesus" pop up every once in a while, such as the latest popularized in the late 2000's, with the "Jesus Family Tomb" affair, yet another discredited claim for a supposedly Christian artifact. In this same regard, the tomb of St. Peter has likewise been discovered at least two times, while still another fraudulent artifact was proposed to be the resting place of James the brother of Jesus, the so-called James Ossuary.[501]

The existence of "tombs" or other sacred sites proves little in itself, since it is a common practice to set up symbolic sites, the symbolism of which over time becomes lost to the masses. Sacred site-making is also great business—imagine owning the piece of property where God himself was born, walked and died! Providing an example of this type of profiteering, Fox states:

> [Just] outside [Athens], they claimed, was the very cave in which the infant Zeus had been nursed. Claiming the infant Zeus, the city gained honour, visitors and a temple of particular design. The claim, naturally, was contested by other cities that had caves:

500 See Acharya, *Suns of God.*

501 See my article, "Bone Box No Proof of Jesus."

> Zeus's birthplace, like his tomb, became a topic of keen intercity rivalry.[502]

The island of Crete also laid claim to both Zeus's birth and death caves. At Delphi, Greece, there are purported graves of Dionysus[503] and Apollo,[504] and Osiris had his tomb at Sais in Egypt and elsewhere. Orpheus had his tomb in Thrace, where also Dionysus was torn to shreds and buried.[505] There are also several places where the Virgin Mary rested and/or died, including the Mount of Olives,[506] Ephesus and Gethsemane, the latter of which did not even exist at the time.[507] Nepal lays claim to being "Buddha's birthplace," as does the Indian village of Kapileswara in Bhubaneswar, Orissa.[508] Are we to suppose these deities were really born or buried in these places? The pillars of Hercules are celestial; yet they were assigned geographical location: Does this mean Hercules was a real man? In the case of the various gods and their locations, the abstract is first, the historical second.

Holy Footprints

Again, sites where a god allegedly walked are found around the world, attesting a trend not monopolized by and not originating with Christianity. As Walker states:

> All over India the "footprints of Buddha" are still worshipped at holy shrines; but some of these Buddhist feet were originally worshipped as the feet of Vishnu. Even earlier, some may have been the red, henna-dyed feet of the Goddess. In antiquity, stones dedicated to Isis and Venus were marked with footprints, mean-

---

502 Fox, 69.

503 Frazer (1912), 7.14.

504 Frazer, 1.1.34; Farnell, 4.129.

505 Frazer (1912), 7.14.

506 Tavard, 24.

507 Regarding John the Evangelist and the Virgin, Fleetwood (548) says: "It is thought that he took her along with him in Ephesus, where she died in an extreme old age; that there is a letter of the oecumenical council of Ephesus, importing that in the fifth century it was believed she was buried there. Yet this opinion was not so universally received but that some authors of the same age think the Virgin Mary died and was buried at Jerusalem; or, rather, in the sepulchre at Gethsemane, near that city, where to this day, it is shown as a magnificent church dedicated to her name." The site of Gethsemane appears to have been part of an olive processing region, but no archaeological evidence of a "garden" or "town" by that name has been discovered. (Rousseau, 110–1.) In fact, nowhere in the New Testament is the place of Christ's agony named as a "garden"; hence, the "Garden of Gethsemane" is a fictional motif.

508 Tripathy, "The Real Birth Place of Buddha."

ing "I have been here." The custom was copied later on Christian tombs, where the footprint bore the legend *In Deo*.[509]

Such footprints are found over the purported grave of Jesus in Srinagar, India, as well.

If proof of the historicity of a god lies in graves, birthplaces and such, then all of these gods must also have been historical, which would mean that Jesus is a Johnny-come-lately in a long line of historical godmen. In reality, this relic- and site-fabrication is standard behavior in the world of mythmaking and is no indication or evidence of historicity. As noted, these birthplaces, graves and relics of gods, godmen and saints have been hyped for purposes of tourism (i.e., for money).

The Shroud of Turin and Other "Holy Relics"

In its quest to create a religion to gain power and wealth, the Church forgery mill did not limit itself to mere writings but for centuries cranked out thousands of phony "relics" of its "Lord," "Apostles" and "Saints." Although true believers desperately keep attempting to prove otherwise, through one implausible theory after another, the Shroud of Turin is counted among this group of frauds:

> There were at least 26 "authentic" burial shrouds scattered throughout the abbeys of Europe, of which the Shroud of Turin is just one.... The Shroud of Turin is one of the many relics manufactured for profit during the Middle Ages. Shortly after the Shroud emerged it was declared a fake by the bishop who discovered the artist. This is verified by recent scientific investigation which found paint in the image areas. The Shroud of Turin is also not consistent with Gospel accounts of Jesus' burial, which clearly refer to multiple cloths and a separate napkin over his face.[510]

Regarding the shroud, Biblical history and archaeology professor Dr. Gerald Larue relates:

> Carbon-14 dating has demonstrated that the Shroud is a 14th-century forgery and is one of many such deliberately created relics produced in the same period, all designed to attract pilgrims to specific shrines to enhance and increase the status and financial income of the local church.[511]

Carbon dating of the shroud revealed that it dates from the fourteenth century, but proponents claim the tested piece was contaminated by a fire at that time. They also claim to have found pollen from plants in the Middle East on the shroud, but critics respond that the pollen may

509 Walker, *WDSSO*, 309.

510 "Freethought Datasheet #5," Atheists United.

511 Leedom, 164.

have been picked up in more recent times, by being carried to the Middle East.

Studies have also revealed that the elegant herring-bone weave of the shroud is anachronistic compared with the crude weave of the time and place where Jesus was said to have been buried.

Walker comments on the holy relic mill:

> About the beginning of the 9th century, bones, teeth, hair, garments, and other relics of fictitious saints were conveniently "found" all over Europe and Asia and triumphantly installed in the reliquaries of every church, until all Catholic Europe was falling to its knees before what Calvin called its anthill of bones.... St. Luke was touted as one of the ancient world's most prolific artists, to judge from the numerous portraits of the Virgin, painted by him, that appeared in many churches. Some still remain, despite ample proof that all such portraits were actually painted during the Middle Ages.[512]

And Wells states:

> About 1200, Constantinople was so crammed with relics that one may speak of a veritable industry with its own factories. Blinzler (a Catholic New Testament scholar) lists, as examples: letters in Jesus' own hand, the gold brought to the baby Jesus by the wise men, the twelve baskets of bread collected after the miraculous feeding of the 5000, the throne of David, the trumpets of Jericho, the axe with which Noah made the Ark, and so on.[513]

At one point, a number of churches claimed the one foreskin of Jesus, and there were enough splinters of the "True Cross" that Protestant reformer John Calvin said, "In truth, if all the pieces that could be found were collected into a heap, they would form a good ship load."[514] The disgraceful list of absurdities and frauds goes on, and, as Pope Leo X was satirized as having said, the Christ fable has been enormously profitable for the Church. Again, it must be asked why force, forgery and fraud were needed to spread the "good news" brought by a "historical son of God."

The relic business was not limited to the Christian faith, however, as there have always been relics associated with other luminaries of the vast pantheon found around the world. As Hislop says:

> If, therefore, Rome can boast that she has sixteen or twenty holy coats, seven or eight arms of St. Matthew, two or three

512 Walker, B. (1983), 880–1.

513 Wells, *HEJ*, 184.

514 Gordon, B., 189.

> heads of St. Peter, this is nothing more than Egypt could do in regard to the relics of Osiris. Egypt was *covered* with sepulchres of its martyred god; and many a leg and arm and skull, all vouched to be genuine, were exhibited in the rival burying-places for the adoration of the Egyptian faithful.[515]

As regards other "evidence" of Christianity, such as weeping or bleeding statues, so much in vogue these days, or visions, voices, or miracles, etc., these too have their Pagan predecessors:

> False prophecies and miracles and fraudulent relics were the chief reliance among the Pagans, as among the Christians, for stimulating the faith, or credulity, of the ignorant and superstitious masses. The images of the gods were believed to be endowed with supernatural power. Of some, the wounds could bleed; of others, the eyes could wink; of others, the heads could nod, the limbs could be raised; the statues of Minerva could brandish spears, those of Venus could weep; others could sweat; paintings there were which could blush. The Holy Crucifix of Boxley, in Kent, moved, lifted its head, moved its lips and eyes; it was broken up in London, and the springs exposed, and shown to the deriding public; but this relation is out of place—this was a pious Christian, not Pagan, fake. One of the marvels of many centuries was the statue of Memnon, whose divine voice was heard at the first dawn of day.... Other holy relics galore were preserved and shown to the pious: The Aegis of Jove... the very tools with which the Trojan horse was made ... the Cretans exhibited the tomb of Zeus, which earned for them their reputation as Liars. But Mohammedans show the tomb of Adam and Christians that of Peter! There were endless shrines and sanctuaries at which miracle-cures could be performed.... The gods themselves came down regularly and at the fine feasts spread before their statues.[516]

In establishing their "holy relics," the Catholics were merely carrying on a long line of priestly hoaxing. If such "relics" are "evidence" of the reality of Jesus and Mary, are they not also "evidence" of the reality of Venus, whose statue also wept, or of the Indian elephant-headed god Ganesha, whose images drink milk by the bucket? A truly pious person, then, would do well to worship them all and not just these meager few from Palestine.

Doane sums up the quest thus:

---

515 Hislop, 179.
516 Wheless, *FC*, 11-12.

> In vain do the so-called disciples of Jesus point to the passages in Josephus and Tacitus; in vain do they point to the spot on which he was crucified; to the fragments of the true cross, or the nails with which he was pierced, and to the tomb in which he was laid. Others have done as much for scores of mythological personages who never lived in the flesh. Did not Damis, the beloved disciple of Apollonius of Tyana, while on his way to India, see, on Mt. Caucasus, the identical chains with which Prometheus had been bound to the rocks? Did not the Scythians say that Hercules had visited their country? And did not they show the print of his foot upon a rock to substantiate their story? Was not his tomb to be seen at Cadiz, where his bones were shown? Was not the tomb of Apollo to be seen at Delphi? Was not the tomb of Achilles to be seen at Dodona … ? Was not the tomb of Aesculapius to be seen in Arcadia … ? Was not the tomb of Deucalion—he who was saved from the Deluge—long pointed out … in Athens? Was not the tomb of Osiris to be seen in Egypt … ? … Of what value, then, is such evidence of the existence of such an individual as Jesus of Nazareth?[517]

Basically, after nearly 2,000 years of seeking, there remains no physical evidence for the existence of Jesus Christ as a historical figure. In addition, since there are sacred sites all over the globe, for practically every culture, it is merely cultural bias that allows so many to claim that theirs are the only true ones, that their land is *the* "Holy Land."

The Bible as History?

Furthermore, if we look to the archaeological evidence to support the Old Testament, we will find much less than expected. Although the texts make the Jewish people appear to have been a force to be reckoned with in the region, there is no evidence of grand buildings, navies or militaries of the Jews. In fact, during the centuries prior to the Christian era, the Greeks barely noticed the Jews, and the famous historian Herodotus could not find the "great" kingdom of Judah: "Solomon, *whose magnificent empire was invisible to Herodotus*, when searching for kingdoms in Judea."[518] As Higgins remarks:

> Where is the empire of Solomon the Magnificent first read of in the works of the Gentiles? It is not noticed by Herodotus, Plato or Diodorus Siculus. It is a most extraordinary fact that the Jewish nation, over whom … the mighty Solomon had reigned in all his glory, with a magnificence scarcely equaled by the greatest

517 Doane, 511.

518 Higgins, 1.668.

> monarchs, spending nearly eight thousand millions on a temple, was overlooked by the historian Herodotus, writing of Egypt on one side and of Babylon on the other—visiting both places, and of course almost necessarily passing within a few miles of the splendid capital of the nation, Jerusalem. How can this be accounted for?[519]

Hazelrigg adds:

> Suleyman was a Persian title equivalent to the Greek *Aiolos*, and meant "universal emperor." Like Pharaoh, it was not a name, but a designation of rank. The Jews, aiming at universal empire, feigned that one of their kings bare this name; and it is with this petty pilfered thane (for in a little place like Judea he could be no other), that the mighty Suleymans of the Orient are confounded alike by the civilized European and the ignorant Bedoween.... One need not search very diligently in order to find similar disparities between biblical statement and the inferences of historical evidence.[520]

This dearth of evidence for such an empire was noticed at least 2,000 years ago, and eventually provoked the Jewish historian Josephus to write his *Antiquities of the Jews* to demonstrate that the Hebrew culture was very old. While the Hebrew culture may have been old, the "nation of Israel" in fact was not a "great empire" but a group of warring desert tribes with grandiose stories "borrowed" from other cultures. Out of this fertile imagination and opportunism came an even more grandiose tale to end all tales: the Christian myth.

The Myth of Hebrew Monotheism

"The Israelites, who at first were as polytheistic as the other nations of the ancient Near East, in the end merged the gods of their progenitors and ended up worshipping one God, Yahweh, who remained closely related to the *elohim*, 'the gods' or ancestors of their progenitors."

—Dr. Temba L.J. Mafico, *The Bible in Africa* (488)

"As a rule, ancient Near Eastern religions were polytheistic, and the religions of Judah and Israel were no exception....

"Since life in Syria-Palestine depended on rainfall, the most important role within the panthea was held by the weather god, who was responsible for the lives of human beings, animals and vegeta-

519 Higgins, 1.772.

520 Hazelrigg, 178.

tion.... Well-known names of the weather god included Baal, Addu/Haddu and also YHWH. The female companion of the weather god was conceived as a mother goddess: here the goddesses Hepat, Shala and Asherah can be named.

"Other important deities included Dagan, a god of the underworld and of grain; Rashpu, who was responsible for pestilence and also for protecting against pestilence; the sun god or sun goddess, who was the god of justice and righteousness; and the moon god, who was responsible for all aspects of fertility. Deities of minor rank included artisan gods, messenger gods, spirits and demons, and also the kings who underwent divinization after their death.

"The king was believed to be the son of the highest god and, as such, functioned as the deity's earthly governor."

—Dr. Francesca Stavrakopoulou and Rev. Dr. John Barton, *Religious Diversity in Ancient Israel and Judah* (28)

"And he received the gold at their hand, and fashioned it with a graving tool, and made a molten calf; and they said, 'These are your gods, O Israel, who brought you up out of the land of Egypt!'"

—Exodus 3:24

"The LORD will bring you, and your king whom you set over you, to a nation that neither you nor your fathers have known; and there you shall serve other gods, of wood and stone."

—Deuteronomy 28:36

"And the LORD said to Moses, 'Behold, you are about to sleep with your fathers; then this people will rise and play the harlot after the strange gods of the land, where they go to be among them, and they will forsake me and break my covenant which I have made with them.'"

—Deuteronomy 31:16

"They stirred him to jealousy with strange gods; with abominable practices they provoked him to anger.

"They sacrificed to demons which were no gods, to gods they had never known, to new gods that had come in of late, whom your fathers had never dreaded."

—Deuteronomy 32:16–7

"Now therefore fear the LORD, and serve him in sincerity and in faithfulness; put away the gods which your fathers served beyond the River, and in Egypt, and serve the LORD."

—Joshua 24:14

"And yet they did not listen to their judges; for they played the harlot after other gods and bowed down to them; they soon turned aside from the way in which their fathers had walked, who had obeyed the commandments of the LORD, and they did not do so."

—Judges 2:17

As demonstrated, the historical and archaeological record fails to provide any credible, scientific evidence that the New Testament story is true. Nor does it bear out important Old Testament tales; hence the religion that Christianity is purportedly based on is unsubstantiated as well. In fact, the very notion of the monotheistic Hebrew God, as allegedly depicted in the Old Testament, who could produce a son, is baseless.

It is a common belief that the Hebrew people, beginning with Moses, were monotheists whose one god, Yahweh, was the only true god, as revealed exclusively to Hebrew prophets. These original monotheists, it is believed, were superior to and had the right to destroy the polytheistic cultures around them by killing their people and stealing their towns, booty and virgin girls, which is what "God's chosen" are recorded as doing throughout the Old Testament.[521] This monotheist versus polytheist scenario represents the common perception, but it is incorrect, as the Hebrews were latecomers to the idea of monotheism and were originally themselves polytheists.

The Dawn of Monotheism?

In actuality, the Hebrews were by no means the originators of the concept of monotheism, as the Egyptians, for one, had the One God at least a thousand years before the purported time of Moses, by orthodox dating. As Wheless says:

> This finally and very late evolved monotheism is neither a tardy divine revelation to the Jews, nor a novel invention by them; it was a thousand years antedated by Amenhotep IV and Tut-ankh-amen in Egypt—nor were even they pioneers. We have seen the [Catholic] admission that the Zoroastrian Mithra religion was "a divinely revealed Monotheism" (*CE*. ii, 156).[522]

The monotheism of the Persian religion of Zoroastrianism, in fact, is virtually identical to that of Judaism, or Yahwism, which is, in part, an offshoot of Zoroastrianism. In the Zoroastrian text the Bundahishn, the main Zoroastrian god Ahura-Mazda or Ormuzd tells Zoroaster:

521 See, for example, Numbers 25:1-9, 31:17–18; Joshua 8:1-29; Judges 21:10–2; Ezekiel 9:5–7: "'Pass through the city after him, and smite; your eye shall not spare, and you shall show no pity; slay old men outright, young men and maidens, little children and women, but touch no one upon whom is the mark. And begin at my sanctuary.' So they began with the elders who were before the house. Then he said to them, 'Defile the house, and fill the courts with the slain. Go forth.' So they went forth, and smote in the city."

522 Wheless, *FC*, 70.

> I am he who holds the star-spangled heaven in ethereal space; who makes this sphere which once was buried in darkness a flood of light. Through me the Earth became a world firm and lasting—the earth on which walks the lord of the world. I am he who makes the light of sun, moon and stars pierce the clouds. I make the corn-seed, which perishing in the ground sprouts anew, multiplying endlessly, etc. I created man whose eye is light, whose life is the breath of his nostrils; I placed within him life's unextinguishable power.[523]

Prior to the intrusion of monotheistic Yahwism, the Hebrews were not monotheists separate and apart from their polytheistic "Gentile" neighbors, either before or after Moses.

The Polytheism of 'the Chosen'

The Hebrew polytheism explains why in the Old Testament "the chosen" are constantly depicted as "going after" other gods and why "the LORD God" himself changes from hero to hero, king to king and book to book. As to the polytheism of the Hebrews and the supposed superiority of monotheism, John Robertson says:

> There is overwhelming testimony to the boundless polytheism of the mass of people even in Jerusalem, the special seat of Yahweh, just before the Captivity. Monotheism did not really gain a hold in the sacred city until a long series of political pressures and convulsions had built up a special fanaticism for one cult....
>
> Monotheism of this type is in any case morally lower than polytheism since those who held it lacked sympathy for their neighbors....
>
> Most of the Jewish kings were polytheists....
>
> What I am concerned to challenge is the assumption—due to the influence of Christianity—that Jewish monotheism is essentially higher than polytheism, and constitutes a great advance in the progress of religion....
>
> If the mere affirmation of a Supreme Creator God is taken to be a mark of superiority, certain primitive tribes who hold this doctrine and yet practice human sacrifice must be considered to have a "higher" religion than the late Greeks and Romans.[524]

523 Mackay, 2.289. We ought to note that the chaotic state of Zoroastrian sources makes it difficult to trace the evolution of Zoroastrian theology, which may never have been simply monotheistic. Likewise, it now seems that the Egyptian Akhenaten (Amenhotep IV) may not have been a strict monotheist either.

524 Robertson, J.M. (1966), 17–9.

The Hebrew polytheism is reflected in the various biblical names for "God," the oldest of which were the plural Elohim, Baalim and Adonai, representing both male and female deities. In order to make the Hebrews appear monotheistic, the biblical writers and translators obfuscated these various terms and translated them as the singular "God" (Elohim), "the Lord" (Adonai), "the LORD God" (YHWH Elohim) or "the LORD" (YHWH/IEUE). As Higgins states:

> In the original, God is called by a variety of names, often the same as that which the Heathens gave to their Gods. To disguise this, the translators have availed themselves of a contrivance adopted by the Jews in rendering the Hebrew into Greek, which is to render the word.... *Ieue* [YHWH], and several of the other names by which God is called in the Bible, by the word ... Lord.... The fact of the names of God being disguised in all the translations tends to prove that no dependence can be placed on any of them. The fact shows very clearly the temper or state of mind with which the translators have undertaken their task. God is called by several names. How is the reader of a translation to discover this, if he finds them all rendered by one name? He is evidently deceived. It is no justification of a translator to say it is of little consequence. Little or great, he has no right to exercise any discretion of this kind. When he finds God called Adonai, he has no business to call him Jehovah or Elohim.... The fact that Abraham worshipped several gods, who were, in reality, the same as those of the Persians, namely, the creator, preserver, and the destroyer, has been long asserted, and the assertion has been very unpalatable both to Jews and many Christians; and to obviate or disguise what they could not account for, they have had recourse, in numerous instances, to the mistranslation of the original.[525]

The Biblical Writers

Although many people still believe that the Bible is a monolithic product of the Almighty himself, infallibly recorded by the authors purported, the reality is that "Moses" did not write the Pentateuch, or first five books, and that the other Old Testament texts are, like those of the New Testament, pseudepigraphical (i.e., not written by those in whose names they appear). Also like the New Testament, over the centuries the various texts of the Old Testament were "redacted" many times, which is a scholarly way of saying they were interpolated, mutilated and forged. As Wheless remarks of the Old Testament books:

> It may be stated with assurance that not one of them bears the name of its true author; that every one of them is a composite

525 Higgins, 1.62.

> work of many hands "interpolating" the most anachronistic and contradictory matters into the original writings, and often reciting as accomplished facts things which occurred many centuries after the time of the supposed writer.[526]

The Pentateuch, for example, had at least four authors or schools of writers. Even though they are from different authors, these separate segments, some of which were written centuries apart, were interwoven in a confusing yet clever manner. The oldest section of these books is the "Yahwist/Jahwist" or "J" account wherein God is called "Yahweh," designated by the Hebrew Tetragrammaton יהוה or "YHWH." The next section is called "E," for "Elohist," so-named because the writer mostly uses the word "Elohim" for "God," although it should be rendered "Gods." The major portion of the Pentateuch was created by "P," for the Priestly Writer, who refers to God mostly as Elohim and less often as Yahweh. The next discernible influence is "D," the Deuteronomist, who apparently cobbled together portions of J and E, along with the laws of Deuteronomy, then wrote the "history" books that follow, including Joshua, Judges, 1 and 2 Samuel, and 1 and 2 Kings. The Deuteronomist is a fanatical Yahwist and writes his "histories" of the kings from a biased perspective, judging their reigns based on whether or not they had "done right in the sight of Yahweh." Finally, someone (or a school) called by scholars the Redactor ("R"), possibly the author of "Ezra," pulled together the various works during or after the "Babylonian Captivity" (586–538 BCE).

Concerning the dates when these texts were composed, in *The Bible Unearthed* archaeologist Dr. Israel Finkelstein comments:

> In the last few decades scholarly opinions about the dates and authorship of these individual sources have varied widely. While some scholars argue that the texts were composed and edited during the existence of the united monarchy and the kingdoms of Judah and Israel (c. 1000–586 BCE), others insist that they were late compositions, collected and edited by priests and scribes during the Babylonian exile and the restoration (in the sixth and fifth centuries), or even as late as the Hellenistic period (fourth-second centuries BCE).[527]

One of the oldest portions of the Bible is the "song of Moses," which comes at Exodus 15:1–19. Yet even this section appears not to be scientifically datable to earlier than the first half of the tenth century BCE.[528]

526 Wheless, 69.

527 Finkelstein, 13.

528 Botterweck, 1.69.

These various texts and their authors represent different schools of thought and influences, as well as competing priesthoods, explaining why the harried folk of the Levant were constantly falling out of favor with their God(s). The Elohist's stories are often silly and nonsensical, when taken literally, because they actually represent the mythologies of a variety of cultures from Canaan/Phoenicia to Egypt, Persia and India. The Yahwist, who portrays some of the same anthropomorphic myths as E, is, of course, very concerned with the Jealous God, Yahweh, as opposed to the various Elohim. P dispenses with the tall tales and portrays his Elohim, now a unified entity, as very cosmic and impersonal, rather than walking about in the Garden of Eden, for example. D and R are, of course, Yahwistic.

As stated, in order to represent the polytheistic Hebrews as monotheists, the biblical writers mutilated texts and reinterpreted history, while the translators used the trick of rendering these many gods and goddesses as the singular "God," "Lord," or "LORD." For example, the word YHWH, transliterated as "Jehovah," appears over 6,700 times in each of the Darby and Young's Literal (YLT) translations, while it is used only four times in the King James Version (KJV) and not once in the most modern versions such as the RSV and NIV. Of these versions, only the Darby retains the word "Elohim" for "God(s)," and this word almost always is accompanied by "Jehovah," even though "the LORD God" was not called YHWH until the time of Moses (Exod. 6:3). In this way, translators have given the appearance of uniformity where there was none.

The Elohim, El and Ayil

El introduces himself biblically at Genesis 31:13, in which he is made to address Jacob: "I am the God of Bethel, where you anointed a pillar and made a vow to me." The "God of Bethel" in Hebrew is אל–בית אל or "El Beth-El," meaning "God House [of] God. The Hebrew word here for "anointed" is משח or *mashach*, the primitive root of the word for "messiah." An alternative form, אלוה or *'elowahh*, likewise meaning "God" or "false god" (H433), appears 52 times in the Bible, 42 of which are in the Book of Job, considered to be a later usage post-dating the Babylonian Exile.[529]

The plural term Elohim or אלהים appears over 2,500 times in the Old Testament but is falsely translated in most versions. Strong's first definition of Elohim (H430) is plural, including "rulers, judges, divine ones, angels, gods." Etymologically, the word *elohim* is the plural of אלוה or *'elowahh*, which Strong's (H433) defines as "God" and "false

529 Spoer, 6.

god." In turn, *'elowahh* is said to be from the word אל or *'el*, which, per Strong's (H410) also is the singular "god, god-like one, mighty one," as well as "god, false god (demons, imaginations)" and "God, the one true God, Jehovah." It is interesting to note that the word from which *'el* is shortened, according to Strong's from אַיִל or *'ayil* (H352), which in turn means "ram," as in food, sacrifice and "skin dyed red, for tabernacle."

This fact of the ram being associated with the word for "god" and with the sacrifice and tabernacle is interesting in view of the suggestion that the Judean tribal god Yahweh achieved monotheistic dominance during the Age of Aries, represented by a ram or lamb. Surely, the Hebrew priests were aware of these correspondences, and this fact explains much about the presence of the ram/lamb motif in the Old Testament. This word *'ayil*, in fact, whence comes the word *el* or "god," is the same used to describe the ram caught in the thicket which Abraham substitutes as a sacrifice for his son Isaac (Gen. 22:13).

Our hypothetical history includes not only the changeover from the age of the bull to the age of the ram, but also from the Indian god Brahma to the Hebrew patriarch Abraham, who here is basically discontinuing the ritual sacrifice of his lineage as a burnt offering to the sacred ram, whose shortened name means "God" in Hebrew.

In the Old Testament, *elohim* is rendered 246 times as referring to "gods," while it is translated nearly 10 times more, 2,346 instances, as the singular and capitalized "God" or "Lord God," depending on the translation. This fact of plurality explains why in Genesis (1:26) "Gods" said: "Let *us* make man in *our* image." As it is here, the word *elohim* appears throughout the rest of Genesis as well, indicating its pre-Yahwistic usage and the polytheism of the early Israelitish people.

As stated, Elohim refers to both "gods" and "goddesses," and its singular form, El, served as a prefix or suffix to names of gods, people and places, whence EmmanuEl, GabriEl, Beth-El, etc. Even "Satan" was one of the Elohim, as Walker relates:

> In the original wording, Satan was one of the *bene ha-elohim*, sons of "the gods"; but Bible translators always singularized the plurals to conceal the facts that the biblical Jews worshipped a pantheon of multiple gods.[530]

Of the Elohim, Taylor contends:

> The Jewish *Elohim* were the decans of the Egyptians; the same as the genii of the months and planets among the Persians and Chaldeans; and Jao, or Yahouh, considered merely as one of the beings generically called Elohim or Alehim, appears to have

530 Walker, B. (1983), 895; McDonald, H., 38.

been only a national or topical deity.[531]

The Elohim were in reality a number of "El" gods, such as: El/Elohim Chay, the "Living God" (Jer. 10:10); El De'ah, the "God of Knowledge" (1 Sam. 2:3); El 'Elyown , the "God Most High" (Gen. 14:18); El 'Emeth, the "God of Truth" (Ps. 31:5); El 'Emuwnah, the "God of Faithfulness" (Deut. 32:4); El Gĕmuwlah, the "God of Recompense" (Jer. 51:56); El Kabowd, the "God of Glory" (Ps. 29:3); El Ma'al, the "God Above"; El Neqamah or Neqamoth, the "God of Vengeance" (Ps. 94:1); El *'Owlam*, the "Everlasting God" (Gen. 21:23); El Ro'iy, the "God of Seeing" (Gen 16:13); El Sabaoth,[532] the "God of the Heavenly Hosts" (1 Chr. 17:24); El Shaddai, the "Almighty God" (Exod. 6:3); El Simchah, "God of Joy" (Ps. 43:4); El Yeshua, "God of Salvation" (Isa. 12:2),[533] and so on.

El Shaddai or אל שדי was the name of the god of Abraham, or the "God of the fathers," who was replaced by Yahweh in the sixth chapter of Exodus:

> And God spake unto Moses and said unto him, I am Yahweh: and I appeared unto Abraham, unto Isaac, and unto Jacob, by the name of El Shaddai, but by my name Yahweh I was not known unto them.[534]

Interestingly, El Shaddai was later demonized in Deuteronomy 32:17 and Psalm 106:37, condemned as one of the "devils" or שדים—the Canaanite *Shedim*, to whom the Israelites sacrificed their sons and daughters.[535] Psalm 106, in fact, provides a concise chronicle of how the "chosen people" "whored after" other gods (i.e., were polytheistic).

At Exodus 20:5, the Hebrew reads: יהוה אלהים אל קנא. Transliterated this phrase says, *YHWH elohim el qanna*—"Yahweh Gods [the] god jealous/zealous." Here we see that Yahweh is one of the Elohim, El Qanna, the Jealous or Zealous God. Other verses in which Yahweh is the Jealous God appear at Exodus 34:14; Deuteronomy 4:24, 5:9, 6:15; Joshua 24:19.

531 Taylor, R. (1829), 21.

532 This Hebrew word for "hosts," צבא or *tsaba'* (H6635), appears to be the root of the name for the Arab followers of astral religion called Sabians or Sabeans, having as one definition the "army" or "host" of "sun, moon and stars" and of the "whole creation." In this regard, Alexander Waugh (35) deems the stars as "sub-gods" in Israelite religion.

533 Botterweck (1.275) notes that the "God of Salvation" appears in some form or another 13 times in the Old Testament—clearly, "God Jesus" was a significant focus long before Jesus of Nazareth ever purportedly existed.

534 Potter, 42.

535 Potter, 44.

It is contended that these *el* gods were simply different titles and aspects of the one God, and that the plural *Elohim* equates to the *pluralis majestaticus* or "royal we" usage, as is also found in the Koran. However, this "royal we" usage seems to be a relatively modern development, not evidenced in antiquity. Moreover, the fact is that the plural Elohim existed before the henotheistic development with Yahweh, and that they were clearly gods, angels and "sub-gods," so to speak, this latter demotion developing especially as Yahweh came to prominence. The fact that the oldest parts of the Bible maintain this word *elohim* for "God(s)" is indicative of this contention of priority, as is all the evidence regarding Canaanite deities and the "whoring after" them by the Israelites, as well as the pre-Israelitish Semitic and Sumerian/Mesopotamian gods.

In the Ugaritic, "gods" is *ʾlm*[536] or *elim*, and the singular word for god, El, also represents a proper name. In East Semitic, such as Old Akkadian, the word for "god" is *ilu*, while "gods" is *ilū*.[537] Dr. Botterweck states that "in the Canaanite pantheon ʿIl was the proper name of the god par excellence, the head of the pantheon,"[538] while the Phoenicians likewise invoked El, who "among the gods" was he "who sacrifices his own children."[539] This same word has been passed down through Old Arabic *ʿilāh*, meaning "god." The Egyptian gods are likewise described in the Bible as אלהים or Elohim, as at Exodus 12:12, as are the gods of the Amorites (Josh. 24:15; Jdg. 6:10) and of "Syria, Sidon, Moab, the Ammonites and the Philistines," as at Judges 10:6.[540] At 1 Kings 11:33, the great Sidonian goddess Astoreth, the Moabite god Chemosh and the Ammonite god Milcom are likewise deemed "Elohim."

While it is clear that the term originated as a plural concept of "gods," in a somewhat common development of the human mind, which allows for polytheism, pantheism, monotheism and atheism at once, the Elohim did eventually become perceived as one, dominant "El." The word El also represented a deity both male and female, but the later Jews generally interpreted it exclusively as male.

---

536 Botterweck, 1.271.

537 Botterweck, 1.242.

538 Botterweck, 1.242.

539 Botterweck, 1.248: "[The] popularity of child sacrifice in Carthage depended on an El cultus." We also discover that Carthage's chief god is Baal-hammon or El-hamman, who was identified with Saturn or Kronos.

540 Botterweck, 1.276.

El as Solar Deity and Saturn, Elohim as Stars

Also meaning "strength, power" and "mighty things in nature,"[541] among other things, אל or "El" possesses both lunar and solar attributes, and it has been contended variously that he was the moon, the sun, or the "day star on high,"[542] as reflected in עליון—El 'Elyown or Elyon, the "Most High God." Botterweck remarks that "we can say that the OT still shows knowledge of a Canaanite god named 'ēl *'elyôn*," who "represents a hypostatic embodiment of an attribute or ... of a 'particular aspect of El.'"[543] Although in Ugaritic mythology the two were separate and conflicting entities,[544] in later times the Canaanite or West Semitic god El or Al, who is equivalent to Yahweh, is, like the latter, basically the same as the Phoenician god Baal, whose aspect Baal Shamēm or Beelsamēn is equated by Herennius Philo of Byblos (c. 64–141 AD/CE) with both the sun and the Greek god Zeus.[545] As Dr. Javier Teixidor remarks, "El, the god of the Canaanite pantheon, was given the epithet *Baal Hamon*; later on, the epithet became a divine name, hence a divine being to be equated with Kronos or Saturnus."[546]

According to Philo of Byblos, the Phoenican El was also associated with the planet Saturn,[547] which at one point was considered the "central and everlasting sun" of the night sky. In antiquity the sun thus was often associated with the planet Saturn, as it was with so many other celestial bodies and terrestrial elements.[548] El/Saturn's worship is reflected in the fact that the Jews still consider Saturday as the Sabbath or "God's Day." Furthermore, El is Elias, "the sun god Helios to whom Jesus called from the cross."[549]

Since El is significantly solar, it is logical that the many Elohim of

541 Strong's H410.

542 See, for example, the works of Ditlef Nielsen and René Dussaud. See also Mitchell, L., 107. The phrase "day star" is often associated with the "morning star" (i.e., Venus), but it would also represent the solar orb or sun, which is indeed the *day star*. See, for example, Ogilvie (1.669), re "Daystar": "2. The sun, as the orb of day."

543 Botterweck, 11.129.

544 See, for example, Oldenburg, The Conflict between El and Baal in Canaanite Religion.

545 Pope, M.H., 57. On the scholarship showing El to be solar, Pope (82ff) argues that various contentions regarding El's solar nature, such as by Rene Dussaud, are inconclusive.

546 Teixidor, 12.

547 See, for example, Baumgarten (1981), 198ff.

548 See, for example, Jastrow, "Sun and Saturn."

549 Walker, B. (1983), 84, 125, 271-2.

the Bible also represent the stars. Indeed, in the Assyro-Babylonian system the *elohim* are the "gods of the night," in other words, the stars.[550] In this regard, the Sumerian word *dingir*, meaning "god," is "written with the sign of a star, which can also be read as *an*, 'heaven.'"[551] Importantly, the Akkadian *ilu* is "usually written with *AN* as in Sumerian."[552] It is interesting to note that the Greek word ἄνω or *ano* means "up," "on high," and "above," and can be combined with the Greek word *ouranos* ("heaven, the sky"), as at Psalm 113:11 in the Septuagint.

El and Archon

It is important to note that "El" is translated in the Septuagint as ἀρχων or "*archon*," at Ezekiel 31:11, in which the "mighty one of the heathens," אל גוי or El Gowy, is rendered ἄρχοντος ἐθνῶν or "ruler of the people." Used numerous times in the LXX, "archon" is the same term later employed in Gnosticism to describe the "ruler of this world" or "prince of this world." At Genesis 25:16 in the Septuagint, we find reference to δώδεκα ἄρχοντες, the "twelve princes." And some Gnostics counted twelve archons (personifying the houses of the Zodiac or months of the year), though most numbered them as seven (based on the five known planets and the sun and moon).

At Genesis 34:2, a reference appears to ὁ ἄρχων τῆς γῆς or "the prince of the earth," which sounds much like the later "prince of this world." The same phrase ἄρχων τῆς γῆς is used at Genesis 42:6 to describe Joseph as the "governor over the land." It appears that the Gnostics were practicing the time-honored tradition of midrash or allegorical interpretation of various biblical scriptures.

The disparagement of the "calf images of Samaria" (Hos. 8:6) is suggestive of the change in ages from Taurus to Aries. Contrary to the common claim that there is no evidence for the knowledge of such ages by the Jews, they can scarcely have avoided familiarity with the concept during their exile in Babylon, where astronomy, astrology and the zodiac were highly developed by at least the eighth century and, in significant details, for some ages before. (And of course, a great number of Jewish scholars continued to dwell there even after the 50 or so years of the Exile.)

At Psalm 115:3, the biblical God is described thus: "Our God is in the heavens; he does whatever he pleases." The word rendered here for "God" is *elohim*, "gods," while "heavens" is שמים or *shamayim*, defined by Strong's (H8064) as "heaven, heavens, sky," as well as "visible heav-

550 Botterweck, 1.271.

551 Botterweck, 1.269.

552 Botterweck, 1.270.

ens" and "abode of the stars" and "the visible universe, sky, atmosphere, etc." This combination of the divine with the celestial environs and bodies represents clear astrotheology.

The subsumption of various gods under one god has occurred many times in history. When the more numerous Sumerian gods were absorbed into the Semitic pantheon, they were reduced in number, with their various god-names becoming epithets for individual gods such as Marduk, who received 50 divine "epithets" from the Sumerian pantheon.[553]

Baalim and Adonai

It is clear that Baal and El were eventually identified, from the fact that they are both considered the supreme god of the Canaanites and Phoenicians.

Appearing in the Ebla texts around 2400 BCE,[554] the god בעל or "Baal" and gods בעלים "Baalim" are mentioned some 80 to 90 times in the Old Testament (H1168), as the Israelites are frequently castigated (or even murdered!) by "their own" priests for "going after Baal."[555] Like the Elohim, the plural Baalim or Baals were often represented by the singular "Baal," an Egyptian term combining "Ba," the symbol of the planet and goddess Venus, with "al" or "el," the designation of the sun. Thus it has been contended that Baal was the name for the sun in the Age of Taurus (the Bull), which was ruled by Venus.

The Taurean age is one of 12 ages representing the astronomical cycle called the "precession of the equinoxes," whereby the sun rising at the vernal or spring equinox is backdropped by a different constellation every 2,150 years. The precession takes nearly 26,000 years to move through the 12 constellations, a cycle called the "Great Year."

The knowledge of the precession goes back thousands of years and is found around the globe from China to Mexico,[556] reflecting that the so-called primitive ancients were in reality extraordinarily advanced. It is commonly claimed the precession was only discovered by the Greek astronomer Hipparchus, from his reading of Babylonian star records in the second century BCE, but, beginning about 6,500 years ago, when the sun passed the spring equinox in the constellation of Taurus, the sacred bull motif sprang up in many parts of the world, including the Levant, where it symbolized Baal. Curiously, there's a "slaying of Arishta the bull" in the *Vishnu parva* of the Indian text the *Harivamsa* (21).

553 Botterweck, 1.271.
554 Van der Toorn, 113.
555 For example, Jdg. 2:11-13; 3:7; 6:25–30; 8:33, Jdg. 10:6–10; 1 Sam. 7:4; 12:10; 1 Kings 18:18, etc.
556 Jackson, 183–4.

Another indication of the knowledge of the precession predating Hipparchus by centuries appears in the *Brahmanas*, which "emphasize the Krittikas or the Pleiades as the first of the *Nakshatras*, reflecting an astronomical era of the Taurus equinox."[557] The fact is that the bull motif and the ram/lamb motif do indeed receive much attention during these eras.

The worship of Baal demonstrably pervaded the entire area inhabited by the Canaanites. During the period of the Middle Kingdom, if not earlier, the cult was adopted by the Egyptians, along with the cult of other Canaanite gods.[558]

Like the other epithets for "God," Baal is a title meaning "Lord," "master" or "husband."[559] In one form or another it appears to be a very old appellation for the Deity, found not only in Egypt but also in India as Bala.[560] In the ancient languages of Ireland and Sri Lanka, "Baal" means "sun."[561] Baal is in reality the earlier name of the character later known as Yahweh, as is stated at Hosea 2:16: "'And in that day,' says YHWH, 'you will call me, "My husband," and no longer will you call me "My Baal."'"

Walker relates that Baal was

"The Lord" among ancient Semites; consort of the goddess Astarte.... Every god was a Baal. The title was introduced into Ireland via Phoenician colonies from Spain.... Old Testament Jews worshipped many *baalim* as past or present consorts of the Goddess Zion (Hosea 2:2–8). Yahweh shared these other gods' temples for a long time, until his priesthood managed to isolate his cult and suppress the others.[562]

The status of Yahweh and his godly compatriots may be summed up thus:

The *Baal* of the Israelites (the Shemesh of the Moabites and the Moloch of the Ammonites) was the identical "Sun-Jehovah," and he is till now "the King of the Host of Heaven," the Sun, as much as Astoreth

557 Frawley.

558 Van der Toorn, 133.

559 *Zondervan Illustrated Bible Dictionary*, "Baal": "This Hebrew word appears in the OT with a variety of meanings.... Sometimes it is used in the primary sense of "master" or "owner" (as in Exod. 21:28, 34; Jdg. 19:22; Isa. 16:8). Since the Hebrew husband was regarded as the literal owner of his wife, *ba'al* was the common term for "husband" (as in Exod. 21:3; 2 Sam. 11:26; Hos. 2:16)."

560 Higgins, I, 238.

561 Higgins, II, 289.

562 Walker, B. (1983), 84.

[Astarte] was the "Queen of Heaven"—or the moon.[563]

The other Baalim worshipped by the Israelites included: "Baal Peor," the "Lord of the Gap" (Num. 25:3); and "Baal Berith," "Lord of the Covenant" (Judg. 8:33). As there was an "El Yeshua," there was also a "Baal Yehoshua," also transliterated Jehoshua, Joshua or Jesus—Ba'al-yiš'a—the "Lord of Salvation,"[564] long before the Christian era. Various other *baals* or aspects of Baal mentioned in the Bible include: Baal-berith, Baal-gad, Baal-hamon, Baal-hazor, Baal-hermon, Baal-judah, Baal-meon, Baal of Peor, Baal-perazim, Baal-shalisha, Baal-shamem, Baal-tamar, Baal-zaphon and Baal-zebub.[565]

Another word basically the same in meaning as "Baal" is אדון—"Adon" or *'Adown* (H113)—from which comes "Adonai" (אדני) a term used for "Lord" (H136) some 449 times in the Hebrew Bible, 315 times in connection with the Tetragrammaton YHWH.[566] So closely related were Baal and Adonai, in fact, that we see references by scholars to "BaalAdon."[567] Concerning the relationship between Adonis and Adonai, Jacqueline R. Isaac comments, "It has also long been recognized that the name of Greek Adonis is from the Semitic root *'dn*, meaning 'lord.'"[568] Isaac also notes that the "connection of Ba'al with the underworld provides support for the connection of Baal with Adonis and the tradition of Adonis in the underworld."[569]

Like "Baal" and "El," evidently, "Adonis" is an epithet for the sun, held by the Greco-Syrian god by the same name: "Adonis or Adonai was an Oriental (Phoenician and Hebrew) title of the sun, signifying Lord."[570] In his *Saturnalia* (1.21.1–4), ancient Latin writer Macrobius (c. fourth–fifth centuries AD/CE) identifies Adonis as the sun: "That Adonis too is the sun will be clear beyond all doubt if we examine the religious practices of the Assyrians."[571] Professor of Classical Languages and Cultures Dr. R.M. van den Berg summarizes Macrobius's comments:

563 Blavatsky, *SD*, 1.397fn.

564 Zondervan Illustrated Bible Dictionary, "Baalis."

565 van der Toorn, XXXIII. See the *Zondervan Illustrated Bible Dictionary* for discussions and biblical citations for these various *baals*.

566 Botterweck, 1.62.

567 van der Toorn, 8.

568 Wood, J.R., 243.

569 Wood, J.R., 243.

570 Knight, R.P., 85.

571 Macrobius/Davies, 141. For the Latin text, see Kaster (277ff), who renders the passage thus: "You will not doubt that Adonis, too, is the sun, once you've considered the beliefs of the Assyrians." Davies's translation here is the more literal.

> Macrobius … gives the following interpretation of the myth: the boar that kills Adonis is a symbol of the winter. The winter "wounds" the sun, which thus gives less warmth and light to us, and in this way causes the death of living beings. For the half of the year that the sun traverses the six lower signs of the zodiac Adonis is temporally dead. He is with Proserpina/Persephone. At that time of the year, Venus/Aphrodite mourns for Adonis: the days are shorter. When the sun traverses the six higher signs of the zodiac, he is with Venus: the days are longer and there is more light.[572]

Macrobius's explanation—which represents stories about the seasons that predates his era by many centuries, as evidenced by its presence in the pre-Christian Persephone myth—perfectly demonstrates the astrotheological nature of much important ancient religion and mythology. This astronomical, astrological and astrotheological knowledge was not limited to non-Jewish Gentile/Pagan cultures, obviously, and can be found abundantly within the often hidden meanings of Jewish scriptures and as part of the true nature of Hebrew, Israelite and Jewish tribal gods such as El, Baal, Adon and Yahweh.

As van den Berg comments: "Adonis, like Dionysus and Attis, dies but is then brought back to life again."[573]

Even though the biblical writer mentions the god, by the time of Hosea in the eighth century BCE. Baal worship among the Israelites appears to have waned considerably, with the rise of Yahwism in its place.[574] The Egyptian god Seth was identified with Baal.[575]

Yahweh, the Lord Sun

As Dr. Ulf Oldenburg says:

> Yahweh is also called El. That El is a proper name and not only an appellative, meaning "god," is proven by several passages in the Bible. According to the Genesis account, El revealed himself to Abraham and led him into Canaan where not only Abraham and his family worshipped El, but also the Canaanites themselves.[576]

The attempted changeover from Elohim/Baalim/Adonai to יהוה or Yahweh "coincided" with the prominence of the Levitical priesthood, as Moses, to whom Yahweh purportedly first appeared, was said to have

---

572 Berg, R.M., 174.

573 van den Berg, 174.

574 Kelle, 144ff.

575 van der Toorn, 110.

576 Oldenburg, 1-2.

been a "son of Levi" (Num. 26:59). The Levites were fanatic priests who, according to the biblical tale, seemed obsessed with moving Israel from the age of bull sacrifice ("Taurus") into that of the sacrifice of the ram/lamb ("Aries"). In Exodus 12 Moses appears to reset the precessional clock by changing the beginning of the year and instituting the Passover and "the feast of the lamb and the salvation of Israel by the *blood* of the lamb."[577]

The Precession of the Equinoxes

This development of the Levitical priesthood emphasizing the ram over the bull after the sun had moved from the age of Taurus into that of Aries might be viewed as mere coincidence, since Moses purportedly lived over 1,000 years before the purported discovery of the equinoctial precession by Hipparchus (c. 190–c. 120 BCE). But the story of Moses does not appear in the historical record until several centuries later, perhaps as late as the sixth century BCE or later, after the Babylonian Exile. It was during this period that the Jewish priesthood learned much Babylonian culture, including religion, mythology and philosophy. Babylonian astronomy and astrology were significantly developed by this time, and there are indications that knowledge of the precession of the equinoxes precedes by centuries to millennia the "discovery"—or, rather, reportage—by Hipparchus.

The *Brihat Samhita* (3.1–2) seems aware of the precession of the equinox:

> There was indeed a time when the Sun's southerly course [summer solstice] began from the middle of the star [*nakshatra*, constellation/lunar mansion] Āśleṣā and the northerly one [winter solstice] from the commencement of the star Dhaniṣṭhā. For, it has been stated so in ancient works.
>
> At present the southerly course of the Sun starts from the beginning of Cancer and the other from the initial point of the sign Capricorn.[578]

Frawley (see below) places this passage around 1300 BCE.

We must ask the same question about the Babylonians that we asked concerning Hipparchus: did they suddenly come up with all the concepts depicted in the zodiac and astrological lore? Just as the Egyptians did not come up with the perfect pyramid, without experimental stages and improvements over hundreds to thousands of years, so too did the "perfected" Greco-Babylonian zodiac and general archaeo-astronomical knowledge develop over a period of time. Many ancient stories preserve

577 Anderson, 79.
578 Bhat, 23.

bits and pieces from earlier stages of astronomical, astrological and astrotheological knowledge.

The fact that the god-name/divine epithet "El" derives from the term *ayil*, meaning, "ram," suggests Canaanite/Phoenician knowledge of the age of Aries, as does the Abrahamic sacrifice of the "ram in the thicket" and other details examined here.

Since 1999 when *Christ Conspiracy* was first published, new credible evidence further substantiating the astrotheological origins of many of our most cherished religious concepts demonstrates that the ancients had knowledge of precession of the zodiac as far back in time as 40,000 years ago:

> This knowledge, it seems, enabled them to record dates, using animal symbols to represent star constellations, in terms of precession of the equinoxes. Conventionally, Hipparchus of Ancient Greece is credited with discovering this phenomenon. We show here that this level of astronomical sophistication was actually known at least 36 thousand years earlier. Evidence accumulated from many ancient archaeological sites, representing dates from at least 38,000 BC to the middle of the Neolithic, overwhelmingly supports this view.
>
> • The Lion Man of Hohlenstein-Stadel, southern Germany circa 38,000 BC
> • Chauvet, northern Spain circa 34,000 BC
> • Lascaux, southern France circa 15,000 BC
> • Altamira, northern Spain circa 14,000 BC
> • Göbekli Tepe, southern Turkey circa 10,000 BC
> • Çatalhöyük, southern Turkey circa 7000 BC

From "*Decoding European Palaeolithic Art: Extremely Ancient Knowledge of Precession of the Equinoxes*" by Martin B. Sweatman, Alistair Coombs, *Athens Journal of History*, 2019, athensjournals.gr/history/2019-5-1-1-Sweatman.pdf

Age of the Zodiac

Moreover, scholars who place the development of the 12-division zodiac/solar circle in Babylon in the seventh to eighth centuries BCE do not appear to have factored in the advanced astronomy and astrology of the Indians, as reflected in the earliest known Indian texts, the Vedas. In "Vedic Origins of the Zodiac" Dr. David Frawley says concerning the RigVeda, conservatively dated to around 1500 BCE, that:

> there are clear references to a chakra or wheel of 360 spokes placed in the sky. The number 360 and its related numbers like 12, 24, 36, 48, 60 72, 108, 432 and 720 occur commonly in Vedic

symbolism. It is in the hymns of the great Rish Dirghatamas (RV 1.140–164) that we have the clearest such reference.

The hymns of Dirghatamas speak clearly of a zodiac of 360 degrees, divided in various ways, including by three, six and twelve, as well as related numbers of five and seven.... The symbols we ascribe to these twelve divisions is a different factor that can vary to some degree. The actual stars making up the constellation that goes along with the sign is yet a third factor....

What is important about the hymns of Dirghatamas is that he shows the mathematical basis of such harmonic divisions of a zodiac of 360 degrees.

For Dirghatamas, as was the case for much of later Vedic astronomy, the main God of the zodiac is the Sun God called Vishnu. Vishnu rules over the highest heaven and is sometimes identified with the pole star or polar point. [579]

At RV 1.155.6, concerning Vishnu we read:

> He causes, by his gyrations, ninety and four periodical revolutions, like a circular wheel, vast of body, and evolving in many forms, through the praises (addressed to him); ever young, though not infantile, he comes at our invocations.

Other inferences of the zodiacal wheel may appear at RV 1.164, called *Asya Vāmasya* or the "Riddle of the Sacrifice" or the famous hymn describing the "lord of men with seven sons" and the "seven (horses)" yoked to the "one-wheeled car" (*ekacakram*) with three axles. The "lord of men" is said to be the son, while the "one-wheeled car" represents the solar orb, the annual path of the sun or the year. The seven sons or seven horses may symbolize the seven rays of the sun or the days of the week, named after the sun, moon and five visible planets. The next verse mentions the "seven sisters," who are likewise speculated to be the same as the sons or horses; however, it may also be that these represent the Pleiades, whose number at the time was seven and who were deemed in antiquity the "Seven Sisters."[580]

Dr. Frawley interprets this passage thus: "The zodiac is the single-wheeled chariot or circle yoked to the seven planets, which are all forms of the sun or sunlight. It is the wheel of time on which all beings are placed." The three axles may represent three divisions/seasons of the year, as in Egypt, for one.

579 Frawley, "Vedic Origins of the Zodiac: The Hymns of Dirghatamas in the Rig Veda."

580 The seventh sister in the Pleiades is no longer visible; hence, iconography today shows their number as six.

At RV 1.164.11, we read that the "twelve-spoked wheel of the true (sun) revolves round the heavens, and never (tends) to decay; seven hundred and twenty children in pairs, Agni, abide in it."[581] Frawley renders this passage: "The wheel of law with twelve spokes does not decay as it revolves around heaven. Oh Fire, here your 720 sons abide."

Furthermore, the Vedic/Sanskrit word *gṛihá* or *gRha* means "assistant, servant" in the RV (10.119.13), as well as "house" (RV 7.89.1).[582] It later appears in the Bṛhat-Saṃhitā by Varāhamihira or "Var-BrS" (vci, civ) and Var-Br (1.4f; 1.16) as "sign of the zodiac" and "astrological mansion."[583] Interestingly, *gṛihákāraka* is defined as "a house-builder, mason, carpenter (kind of mixed caste), Yājñ. iii, 146."[584] The term *gṛhakarmakara* means "domestic servant."[585] The word *gṛihá* is also used to connote a temple, as in *kandikAgriha* or "temple of Durga."[586] Within it are collected 360 (spokes), which are, as it were, moveable and immoveable."[587]

Griffith renders the passage thus:

> Twelve are the fellies, and the wheel is single; three are the naves. What man hath understood it?
>
> Therein are set together spokes three hundred and sixty, which in nowise can be loosened.[588]

In the same RV verse (1.164.43) appears a reference to *viṣūvatā/vaiSuvata/vishuvat* or "equinox."[589]

The great astronomer and mathematician Varahamihira (505–587 CE) calls the "entrance of the sun into a sign of the zodiac" the *Praveśa*.[590]

In addition to meaning "solar," "divine," "celestial" and "son of the

---

581 The original Vedic is: dvādaśāraṃ nahi tajjarāya varvarti cakraṃ pari dyāṃ ṛtasya | ā putrā aghne mithunāso atra sapta śatāni viṃśatiśca tasthuḥ. The word dvādaśāraṃ means "having 12 spokes (as the wheel or cycle of the year)." (Monier-Williams, 504.)

582 Monier-Williams, 361. English translations of the Rigveda such as Griffith and O'Flaherty render this term at RV 10.119.13 as "house" or "dwelling," rather than "assistant" or "domestic servant." The connection between the house and servitude remains evident.

583 Monier-Williams, 361.

584 Monier-Williams, 361.

585 www.SpokenSanskrit.de

586 Monier-Williams, 91.

587 www.srivaishnava.org/scripts/veda/rv/rvbook1.htm

588 Griffith, 1.293.

589 Monier-Williams, 998; Vemuri, 443.

590 Monier-Williams, 692.

sun,"[591] among others, the word *saura* represents "a solar month (consisting of 30 risings and settings of the sun or the period during which the sun is in one sign of the zodiac)."[592] Keep in mind that the Indian months follow the same lines as the zodiacal divisions, as opposed to the Western calendrical system.

Moreover, the names of several zodiacal signs can be found in the Vedas, which means these terms are clearly not foreign intrusions but exist in the indigenous language. In this same vein, Vedic religion also contains a "tradition of assigning animals to constellations," as at *Shatapatha Brahmana* 10.2.1.

Frawley concludes:

> Clearly the Vedas show the mathematics for an early date for the zodiac as well as the precessional points of these eras long before the Babylonians or the Greeks supposedly gave them the zodiac.

The Gold Calf and Calf of Samaria

Prior to being labeled "Yahweh," the Israelite god was called "Baal," signifying the sun in the Age of Taurus. The Israelites were bull-worshippers, exemplified by Exodus 32, the story of Moses and the Egyptian Golden Calf—Horus, the son of Hathor the Cow Goddess—as well as the ongoing biblical discussion of the "two calves of gold … the gods who brought Israel up out of Egypt" (1 Kings 12:28) and the "graven calves of Samaria," artifacts of Molech worship among others. It is against Baal and the "calf of Samaria" that Hosea rails in the biblical book attributed to him, as at 8:5–6: "I have spurned your calf, O Samaria. My anger burns against them. How long will it be till they are pure in Israel? A workman made it; it is not God. The calf of Samaria shall be broken to pieces." At Hosea 10:5, the people and priests mourn and wail over the "calf of Beth-aven," destroyed after Hosea's thugs went after all the Baal-worshippers. The "shame of Samaria" is again addressed at Amos 8:14, obviously an ongoing problem for the Yahwists, continuing to be mentioned as the "sin of Samaria" as late as the Book of Daniel (c. second cent. BCE).

Yahweh, Iao and Ieou/Ieuo

When the equinox passed into Aries, the theory goes, "the Lord's" name was changed to the Egyptian "Iao,"[593] a name associated by the

---

591 Monier-Williams, 1254; Macdonell, 361;

592 Monier-Williams, 1254.

593 Higgins, 1.259. Spoer (8) remarks that "Egypt, more than any other country, has been considered the land in which the name Yahweh originated." Spoer (9–10) argues against Egyptian origin, and then looks at the case for

Greek writer Diodorus Siculus (fl. 60–30 BCE) and others with the Jewish god YHWH, IEUE, Yahweh, Jahweh, Jehovah and Jah.[594] In the Gnostic text the *Pistis Sophia* (5.128/358), Jesus is depicted as using this ancient name "IAO/Iao," which represents the totality of "God," as the "I" symbolizes the universe/unity, the "a" is the "alpha" or beginning, while the "o" is the "omega" or end.[595]

Thus, the sacred name or Tetragrammaton of God יהוה/YHWH/IEUE/IAO can be etymologically linked to numerous gods, even to "Jesus," or "Yahushua," whose name means "salvation" or "Iao/YHWH saves." As Higgins says:

> The pious Dr. Parkhurst … proves, from the authority of Diodorus Siculus, Varro, St. Augustin, etc., that the Iao, Jehovah, or *ieue*, or *ie* of the Jews, was the Jove of the Latins and Etruscans.… he allows that this *ie* was the name of Apollo.… He then admits that this *ieue* Jehovah is Jesus Christ in the following sentences: "It would be almost endless to quote all the passages of scripture wherein the name … (*ieue*) is applied to Christ … they cannot miss of a scriptural demonstration that Jesus is Jehovah." But we have seen it is admitted that Jehovah is Jove, Apollo, Sol, whence it follows that Jesus is Jove, etc.[596]

According to the Jewish kabbalistic text the Zohar (70), יהו or *ihu/ieu* represents *chessed* or "kindness" also rendered "mercy" and "lovingkindess" (e.g., Ps. 17:7).[597] Indeed, these three letters are the same used as the suffix for the name "Elijah" or אליהו (1 Ki 17:1), meaning "my God is Jehovah" or "Yah(u) is my God."[598] Here יהו is rendered "Yah" or "Jah," minus the second and last ה/*he* or "h." The first letter of this triad, י or *yodh*, is pronounced "y" but is often transliterated as "i." The last letter of *yah/jah*, ו or *waw* or *vau*, is transliterated as a "w," "v" and "o" or "u," since it serves as a "placeholder" for these vowels. Thus, this shortened *yah* appears to be the source of Diodorus's transliteration of

India as the origin of Yahweh, identified with the Vedic god Agni, or China, as the god of the "Old Man," Lao Tzu. Spoer (11) concludes that the origin for the Tetragrammaton is Babylon. He (12) gives reason to equate "Ya" with the Babylonian god Ea.

594 Diodorus (*Library of History*, 1.94.1-2): "among the Jews Moyses referred his laws to the god who is invoked as Iao." (Diodorus/Oldfather, 321.)

595 Mead, G.R.S. (2003), 295–6.

596 Higgins, I, 327.

597 Strong's H2617. Says Zion Nefesh: "The letters יהו help to connect to Chokmah," this latter being the anthropomorphized, female entity Wisdom, also known as "Sophia."

598 Strong's H452

the Jewish god as IAΩ or "IAO."

The standard rendering of "Elijah" or אליה without the letter *waw/vau*, the same as with the name "Adonijah" or אדניה (e.g., 2 Sam. 3:4), reveals that the word yah/jah as a name of God could also be indicated merely by the two letters יה or *yh/ye/ih/ie*. This "bigrammaton" יה or IE can be found at Exodus 15:2, where it is rendered as *Yahh* and translated as "Lord." The word יה is Strong's H3050, defined as "Jah (Jehovah in the shortened form)" and the "proper name of the one true God." Found by itself 49 times in the Old Testament, יה is also part of compound words beginning with "Je" and ending with "iah" or "jah."

Various scholars have asserted that this abbreviated form יה or IE was used "more ordinarily" than the Tetragrammaton,[599] but such usage was evidently a later development and not very common.[600] The fact remains, however, that this bigrammaton was indeed used as a sacred name within Hebrew religion.

Eusebius cites Porphyry as saying: "The history of the affairs of the Jews is told most truthfully, because most in accordance with their places and names, by Sanchuniathon of Beirut, who had received the records from Hierombalos [Jerome-Baal], the priest of the god 'Ieuo.'"[601]

Oldenburgy also says:

> *Yw* is probably identical with *'Ieuo* (Greek Ἰευώ), the name of an important god at Beirut, from whose priest Sanchuniathon received his records (PE i. 9).... Just as *Yw-El* was the name of Yamm, so *'Ieuo* may also have been the name of the Phoenician Yamm.... For a discussion of the name *Yw* and its connection to Yahweh cf. O. Eissfeldt, *Sanchunjaton von Berut*.[602]

This god Ἰευώ has been associated with Ἰάω or IAO, famously depicted by Diodorus as the god of the Jews, also known as YHWH. The correspondence between Ἰευώ or "Ieuo" and Ἰησοῦς or "Jesus" was likely noticed in antiquity as it has been since then. Moreover, the existence of this god name lends credence to the contention that, over the doorway of the temple of Apollo at Delphi and elsewhere could be found the mystical letters IE. For the original Greek, see Eusebius (*Praepar. Evang*. 10.9, 485B) in Migne (21.808). Van Kooten states that "Philo of Byblos indeed appears to have known the Jewish God not only as 'Ieuo'

599 For example, Friedrich Delitzsch, *Iesaia*.
600 Spoer, 14.
601 Oldenburg, 4.
602 Oldenburg, 126.

… but also as 'Iao.'"[603] Interestingly, the word "ieou" is used in the Pistis Sophia, in a Gnostic invocation.[604]

The word "Ieou" is used abundantly in other Gnostic texts, called the *Books of Ieou*.[605] Ieou is described in these Gnostic texts as the "Overseer of the Light,"[606] the "First Man,"[607] the "father of My father,"[608] the "providence of all the rulers and gods and powers which are in the matter of the Light of the Treasure,"[609] "Lord over the whole Treasure,"[610] the "Great King of the Light-treasure," the "Great Man himself," the "King of the whole Light-realm,"[611] the "Great Light,"[612] the "Emanator of the Middle Light-world"[613] and "God of the Middle-Light World."[614]

Concerning this name "Ieou," Mead remarks:

> The authentic name of the supernal Demiurgos is translated as the True God or God of Truth, and is given in Greek transliteration as Ieou, which Schmidt transliterates into German as Jeû.
>
> I would suggest that Ieou is a transliteration of the four-lettered mystery name of the creator according to Semitic and Chaldaean tradition, the tetragrammaton of the Kabalah. Theodoret tells us that the Samaritans pronounced this name Iabe (Iave) and the Jews Iaō. Since the sixteenth century, by adding the vowels of Adonai to the unpronounceable YHVH, it has been pronounced Jehovah. It is now generally written Yahweh; but there is no certainty in the matter, beyond the fact that Jehovah is absolutely wrong. Ieou or Iaō are probably attempts in Greek transliteration at the same Semitic name, which contained letters totally unrepresentable in Greek. [615]

In one speech, "the Savior"—Jesus—refers to "the mysteries which are in the Books of Ieou, which I made Enoch write down in Paradise." The resemblance between Ieou and Iesous (Jesus) is obvious, especially

603 van Kooten,127.
604 Mead (2003), 295.
605 Mead (1906), 465, etc.
606 Mead (1906), 465.
607 Mead (1906), 498.
608 Mead (1906), 510.
609 Mead (1906), 512.
610 Mead (1906), 524.
611 Mead (1906), 529.
612 Mead (1906), 530.
613 Mead (1906), 533.
614 Mead (1906), 540.
615 Mead (1906), 534.

in light of the genitive of Iesous, which is Ἰησοῦ or Iesou. The resemblance between "Iave" and "Iove" or Jove also needs to be considered.

Commenting upon the "two great Lights," Mead states: "It appears that Ieou and Melchizedek are powers behind or symbolized by the sun and moon."[616]

Another form of the Jewish god's sacred name can be found in the Jewish magical papyri, as ιαωουηε, along with the oft-appearing *Iave* and Ιαβα or *Iaba*/*Yaba*. Here we can see the name "Jove" as well. An Ethiopic Christian manuscript (Bodleian MSS. Aeth. 9.5) depicts the savior giving to his disciples the various "magical names of Jesus," including *Yâwê*.[617]

Interestingly, the Sanskrit word *yahu* means, among other things, "strong," "swift" and "mighty."[618]

(For more variants and further discussion of the name Yahweh, see my book *Suns of God*, 119–20.)

The Androgynous Yahweh

Yahweh had yet another aspect to "his" persona, as at some early stage the "sacred Tetragrammaton" of "God" was bi-gendered. As Walker states:

> Jewish mystical tradition viewed the original Jehovah as an androgyne, his/her name compounded as Jah (*jod*) and the pre-Hebraic name of Eve, Havah or Hawah, rendered *he-vau-he* in Hebrew letters. The four letters together made the sacred tetragrammaton, YHWH, the secret name of God.... The Bible contains many plagiarized excerpts from earlier hymns and prayers to Ishtar and other Goddess figures, with the name of Yahweh substituted for that of the female deity.[619]

Thus, even Yahweh was at one time plural, but "he" eventually became a he-man sky god. This singular Yahweh was a warrior god, apparently representing the sun in Aries, which is ruled by the warlike Mars and symbolized by the Ram—the same symbolic ram "caught in a thicket" by Abraham and used by him as a replacement sacrifice for his son Isaac.

The Jealous/Zealous God

The warrior god Yahweh was not only Jealous but also *Zealous*, as his name is rendered in Young's Literal Translation:

> [For] ye do not bow yourselves to another god—for Jehovah,

---

616 Mead (1906), 512, 513.

617 Driver, 20.

618 www.SpokenSanskrit.de

619 Walker, WDSSO, 202.

whose name [is] *Zealous*, is a *zealous* God. (Exodus 34:14)

In fact, the same word in Hebrew, קנא or *qanna'*, is used for both "jealous" and "zealous," although it is transliterated differently, *qanna* (H7067) being "jealous" and *qana* (H7065) meaning "to envy, be jealous, be envious, be zealous."

As El Elyon was but one of the Canaanite Elohim, the Most High God, so apparently was "Yahweh," as "El Qanna," the Jealous/Zealous God, which is why in the Old Testament he keeps sticking his nose in and shouting at everyone. The title "Jealous/Zealous" is also appropriate for a god represented by a volcano, as was Yahweh by the smoky and fiery Mt. Sinai. Hence, Yahweh's fanatical followers themselves were intolerant and hot-headed zealots.

The Volcano God

As we have seen, Yahweh represented not only the sky but also the sun, the heat, energy and fire, all of which were localized on the earth in the Jewish Yahweh, whose priests claimed dominance over all other gods and priests by using a volcano to frighten the Hebrews into submission. The word Yahweh or Yahveh in the Sanskrit means "everflowing,"[620] an apt description for a volcano god. In describing the volcanic mountain of God, revealing Yahweh's volcanic nature, the Bible (Exod. 19:16) states:

On the morning of the third day there were thunders and lightnings, and a thick cloud upon the mountain, and a very loud trumpet blast, so that all the people who were in the camp trembled.

Exodus 20:18–19 also relates:

And Mount Sinai was wrapped in smoke, because the LORD descended upon it in fire; and the smoke of it went up like the smoke of a kiln, and the whole mountain quaked greatly. And as the sound of the trumpet grew louder and louder, Moses spoke, and God answered him in thunder.

Deuteronomy 9:21 relates that Moses took the idolatrous golden calf, ground it into dust and threw it "into the torrent that flowed down the mountain." Moreover, Numbers 11 and Psalm 11, 18 and 97 speak of the Lord's fire and volcanic activity. The "most vivid description" of Yahweh as a volcano can be found at Psalm 18:7–8, 11–14.

Then the earth reeled and rocked; the foundations also of the mountains trembled and quaked, because he was angry. Smoke went up from his nostrils, and devouring fire from his mouth; glowing coals flamed forth from him.... He made darkness his covering

620 Stone, 124.

around him, his canopy thick clouds dark with water. Out of the brightness before him there broke through his clouds hailstones and coals of fire. The LORD also thundered in the heavens, and the Most High uttered his voice, hailstones and coals of fire. And he sent out his arrows, and scattered them; he flashed forth lightnings, and routed them.

As Stone observes, "The imagery is hard to ignore."[621]

In *Moses and Monotheism*, Sigmund Freud concluded, "Jahve was undoubtedly a volcano god." Indeed, if Yahweh were not a volcano god, his violent and angry persona would be doubly repulsive:

> Sometimes he is described as roaring like a lion, at others as hissing like a snake, as burning with rage, and unable to restrain his own passions, as kicking, smiting, cursing, swearing, smelling, vomiting, repenting, being grieved at his heart, his fury coming up in his face, his nostrils smoking, etc.[622]

As stated, Yahweh the volcano god made his entrance at the same time as Moses and Aaron, brothers and "sons of Levi."

The Indo-European Levites?

It appears that Moses and Aaron may have been made only to *appear* to be Levites, a tribe that, were actually "Indo-Europeans invaders" who took over the desert tribes and forced a centralized religion on them in order to gain power and wealth. These zealots, however, need not have been "invaders" as such, since Indo-European/Aryans already dwelled among the Semites. Although the "house of Levi" is purported to descend from the "sons of Shem" (i.e., to be Semites), it appears that at least some of the Levites may have been described as "sons of Japheth," known as Assyrians, Persians, Babylonians and assorted other "Chittim," "Kittim" or "Kittaeans," a generic Jewish term for Aryans.

Both of these groups, Semites and Aryans, are claimed in the Bible to have been "sons of Noah" who were to "share the same tent" and to enslave the descendants of Noah's third son, the Hamites; thus, at some point their distinction could not have been very pronounced. In fact, the Aryans and Semites are more intermingled than suspected, as some of the "sons of Japheth" became Ashkenazi, (or European Jews), as stated at Genesis 10:2–3. Indeed, the distinction was made long afterwards, when the Yahwists were compiling their books and attempting to promote themselves as strict segregationists. Furthermore, these Yahweh zealots incorporated Egyptian mythology, making them "Indo-Aryan-Egyptians," precisely the mix found in the Levant. Wherever they

621 Stone, 123.
622 Taylor, R. (1829), 22.

were from, the Levites certainly represented a break from the old, polytheistic Semitic/Hebrew tribes.

Egypt, Samaria, India, Babylon and Syria

This break is thus reflected in the story of Moses, where the Hebrews are portrayed as having a difficult time turning from their ancient worship of the Egyptian god Horus as the golden calf, son of the Egyptian mother goddess Hathor, who was represented as a cow. As Walker states:

> Egypt revered Mother Hathor as the heavenly cow whose udder produced the Milky Way, whose body was the firmament, and who daily gave birth to the sun, Horus-Ra, her Golden Calf, the same deity worshipped by Aaron and the Israelites: "These be thy gods, O Israel, which brought thee up out of the land of Egypt" (Exodus 32:4).[623]

Even though Yahweh was also identified with the sun, the Golden Calf was so horrifying to the Judean Levites that they wrote diatribes against its worship, such as the book of Hosea, whose author rails against the Baals and the "calf of Samaria" (the nation also called Israel, as well as Ephraim, after the "son of Joseph").[624]

Moses's Levitical/Yahwist law, however, evidently didn't stick, as even the exalted Hebrew patriarch Solomon set up for his foreign wives altars to the Moabite sun god Chemosh and the Tyrian sun and fire god Moloch, (1 Kings 11:7–8). Although he was purportedly vilified by "the Lord," Chemosh was, as Walker relates:

> Hebrew form of Shamash, the sun god of Sippar and Moab, worshipped in the temple of Solomon (1 Kings 11:7). Because Chemosh was one of Yahweh's rivals, called an "abomination" by later priests attempting to suppress all cults but their own, he was adopted into the still later Christian pantheon of hell as a demon.[625]

Like that of India and Egypt, the Levantine pantheon of the first millennium BCE. was in fact burgeoning with deities, as is evidenced by the numerous Canaanite and Phoenician deities alone. As noted, even Yahweh himself was not a single god, nor is "he" found in any one culture. At one point, Yahweh was associated with the Indian elephant-headed god Ganesha, whose name means "Lord of Hosts,"[626] also a biblical epithet for Yahweh (1 Sam 1:3). As Yahweh is essentially purported to have done in the gospel story, in Indian mythology Ganesha "impregnated

623 Walker, B. (1983), 180–1.

624 Strong's H669.

625 Walker, B. (1983), 163.

626 Bolle, 30.

the Virgin Goddess Maya, who subsequently gave birth to Buddha."[627] If Yahweh is the monotheistic father god who gave birth to Jesus, he must also have given birth to Buddha. However, as the Hebrew god בהמות or Behemoth (Job 40:15), Ganesha was later demonized by the Christians.[628]

Yahweh also took many of his attributes from the Babylonian god Marduk, who "created the world by separating the celestial and the abyssal waters."[629] In fact, Marduk and Ishtar were worshipped by the Jews at Elam.[630] Among these many gods revered by the Hebrews was also the Sumero-Babylonian goddess Aruru, who was worshipped in the Jewish temple.[631]

Furthermore, the Hebrew word ישראל or Israel itself is an interesting compound, etymologically traced to the roots שרה or *Sarah* and אל or *el*.[632] It has been claimed "Isra-el" or "Issa-ra-el" is not a Jewish appellation but comes from the combination of three different reigning deities: Isis, the Egyptian goddess revered throughout the ancient world; Ra, the Egyptian sun god; and El.[633] Standard etymologies, however, recognize only the *el* part of this equation, as the accepted prefix *sarah* means "contend, have power, persist"; thus, "Israel" signifies "God prevails" or, rather "*El* prevails" as dominant god.

Genesis 33:20 features a strange appellation that confirms this declaration of El's supremacy: "There he erected an altar and called it

627 Walker, *WDSSO*, 372.

628 Walker, *WDSSO*, 236. In defining this term *behemowth* (H930) the BlueLetterBible.org relates, "Some translate as elephant or hippopotamus but from the description in Job 40:15–24, this is patently absurd." The description is not necessarily "patently absurd," however, if it concerns the fantastical Indian elephant god Ganesha. What *is* absurd is the definition given to *behemowth* by Brown-Driver-Briggs Hebrew Dictionary of "perhaps an extinct dinosaur." How would a Hebrew scribe know what an extinct dinosaur ate? What the "sinews of its stones" looked like? How it roared? As Walker says, "Various biblical scholars argued about whether Behemoth was an elephant or a hippopotamus.... However, most of his "portraits" were modeled on Indian pictures of Ganesha with his man-shaped body and elephant head."

629 Walker, B. (1983), 581.

630 Walker, B. (1983), 829.

631 Walker, B. (1983), 815.

632 Strong's H3478, H8280 and H410, respectively.

633 See, for example, Hazelrigg (20–21): "...Israel, meaning a belt or land of the heavens, the twelve tribes of which compare to the number of constellations that environ the ecliptic, and through which the Sun makes his annual circuit.... Issa-ra-el, the kingdom of the moon (Isis), Sun (Ra), and stars (El)."

El-El'ohe-Israel." This hyphenated word אל אלהי ישראל or "El-El'ohe-Israel" is defined (H415) as "the mighty God of Israel."

In addition, the Syrian savior Tammuz was the god or genius of Jerusalem, where also the Greek god Dionysus was worshipped "under his Phrygian name of Zeus Sabazius."[634] In fact, Jewish coins have been found with the images of Dionysus on one side and the word YHWH on the other. Walker relates that "Jews living in Asia Minor said their Jehovah was another form of Zeus Sabazius."[635] As Princeton University Professor of Jewish Studies and Religion Dr. Peter Schäfer (b. 1943) states:

> Sabazius was a Phrygian god whose orgiastic cult came to Athens as early as the fifth century BCE and who is very well attested in the imperial period. He was identified with Dionysus and, in Asia Minor, with Zeus-Jupiter. The equation of the Jewish God with Jupiter Sabazius no doubt was facilitated by the similarity of "Sabazius" with either "Sabaoth" or "Sabbath."[636]

The Hebrews are also reported to have sacrificed rams to Jupiter,[637] who himself was often represented as a ram, called "Ammon" or "Hammon," possibly reflecting the worship of the Egyptian god Amon/Ammon and the Phoenician god Baal Hammon.

As we can see from these numerous examples of Hebrew, Israelite and Jewish polytheism, including the usurpation of attributes from other figures in neighboring religions, to put it bluntly, "The Hebrew-Christian One-God is a patent Forgery and Myth."[638]

Concerning the nature of the biblical god, van der Toorn, et al., remark:

> God can be said to 'shine forth' (*hôpîa*', Deut 33:2), to 'flash up' (ZRH, Isa 4:5), verbs usually connected with the sun. Like the sun, God is all-seeing and all-knowing; his eyes bring "hidden sins" to the light (Ps 19:13). This solar imagery may have favoured the development of the concept of God's invisibility: just as no one can look at the midday sun for a sustained period of time, so no one can see God and not lose his sight.[639]

Indicating the time of his possible entry into the region's pantheon, "there is no extrabiblical reference to Yahweh prior to the Mesha stele

634 Walker, B. (1983), 236–7.
635 Walker, B. (1983), 874.
636 Schäfer (1997), 51.
637 Carpenter, 47.
638 Wheless, *FC*, 78.
639 Van der Toorn, 363.

(KAI 181:18)."[640]

In addition to his solar and volcanic nature, the monotheistic Jewish tribal god took on the attributes of the moon as well, and the Hebrews were early moon-worshippers, as reflected in many Jewish traditions, such as the lunar calendar and various rituals as highlighted by Theodor Reik in *Pagan Rites in Judaism*, which I have excerpted in my book *Suns of God* (117–9). Indeed, we discover that "Yahweh has been identified with the Egyptian moon-god."[641]

In conclusion, all these attributes and associations thoroughly demonstrate that the Jewish religion has not been monolithic but has been significantly astrotheological, and has resembled that of its "Gentile" neighbors and relatives much more than is widely acknowledged.

The Imposition of Monotheism

The myth of Hebrew monotheism comes from the Yahweh propagandists who set about to formulate "the" Jewish religion. While the Elohim were the special gods of the northern tribes and kingdom of Israel, the Levitical Yahweh was the local god of the southern kingdom of Judah. As such, Yahweh is made to elevate Judah above all the other tribes by making it the progenitor of the kings of Israel. Yahweh and Judah are basically the same word, as Judah is יהודה or *Yĕhuwdah, Yahuda*, etc., meaning "Yahweh, I will praise." In this name we find the sacred trigrammaton יהו or IHU/IEU/IAO/YAH/JAH, etc.

This name "Judah" is also the same as "Judas," which is Ἰούδας in Greek and "Iudas" in Latin, and which was thus likewise the name of the tribal god. Under Strong's G2455, Blue Letter Bible defines "Judah or Judas" as "he shall be praised." In the Douay-Rheims Catholic Bible, Judah is called "Juda," the same as the Septuagint's Ἰούδα, which is likewise in the Greek textus receptus of the New Testament (e.g. Matt. 2:6). The Catholic Bible includes various apocryphal texts such as 2 Esdras (11:9), which mentions "Judas the son of Senua," and 1 and 2 Maccabees, in which appears the Maccabean hero Judas Maccabeus. It seems obvious that the "Judas" of the New Testament is a fictional character based on *this* Judas, among other figures, as well as the land of Judah/Judas.

In any event, it was these Jews and not all Hebrews and Israelites who were Yahweh-fanatics. The other nations, in reality, were frequently both uninterested in and repulsed by the violent, angry, jealous, zealous god that Yahweh became.

In this regard, Knight and Lomas say:

640 Smith, M.S. (1994), 151.
641 Spoer, 8.

> For many, Yahweh was no more than the Israelite war god, useful in time of battle but a fairly lowly figure when viewed against the full pantheon of the gods. The names given to notable Israelites down the ages shows a strong respect for Baal, and even the most ardent Yahwist would not pretend that the Jews of this period believed in only one god.[642]

The Queen of Heaven and Jezebel

From the biblical texts, the Yahwists were a rude bunch of marauders who pretended to speak for their "Lord" and who then spent centuries destroying the ancient Hebrew polytheism so they could hold total power over the people. Their favorite targets were the local followers of the Great Goddess, who were ubiquitous in the ancient world. Larson illustrates how prevalent and long-lived was the worship of the Canaanite goddess and how great the zeal to destroy it:

> The Old Testament contains at least forty passages in which the Yahweh prophets denounce the temple groves of Ashtoreth (Ishtar) with their sacred prostitution; and it is obvious that the Israelites celebrated her ritual almost universally until the middle of the seventh century.[643]

In addition to these 40 in which appears the name עשתרת or *'Ashtoreth/'Ashtarowth* (H6252-3), in many others the goddess is described simply as the "Queen of Heaven," appropriate in consideration of the fact that Astoreth means "star" or "stars." At 1 Kings 11:5, 33; 2 Kings 23:13), Astoreth is deemed the "goddess of the Zidonians" and the "abomination." The Hebrew word for "goddess" in 1 Kings is, interestingly, אלהים or *'elohiym*. The goddess's name is also transliterated as Ashtaroth, Astaroth, Astarte, Ashratum/Ashratu, Asherdu(s), Ashertu(s), Aserdu(s), Asertu(s) and Ishtar, this last in the Assyro-Babylonian pantheon. She has been identified as well with the Ugaritic goddess Athirat and with Isis, the Egyptian "Queen of Heaven," a title likewise held by the Christian figure of the Virgin Mary.

The much-vilified biblical character Jezebel was in reality a refined priestess of Baal and Astoreth, the Goddess, while her main nemesis, Elijah, a Yahweh zealot, as evidenced by his name, was a crude, dirty and hairy wildman. Except in the eyes of the Yahwists, Jezebel was considered Hebrew royalty, and her worship of the Great Goddess was consistent with what had existed prior to the Yahwist invasion.

In the Old Testament, the Yahwist priests are depicted as virtually foaming at the mouth in describing "their" people as worshipping Baal

642 Knight and Lomas, 166.

643 Larson, 210.

and Astoreth, but many of "their" people at this time were virgin girls who had been the only ones spared as the Yahwist thugs captured town after town, slaughtering the inhabitants, stealing their property and raping their young (Num. 31:17–18, et al.). These surviving girls continued their ancient tradition of worship, including that of the Goddess and assorted Baals, much to the constant frustration and outrage of the sexist, patriarchal and virgin-enslaving Yahwists.

In order to establish their supremacy, the creed and duty of the Yahwists were as follows (Deut. 12:2–3):

> You shall surely destroy all the places where the nations whom you shall dispossess served their gods, upon the high mountains and upon the hills and under every green tree; you shall tear down their altars, and dash in pieces their pillars, and burn their Asherim with fire; you shall hew down the graven images of their gods, and destroy their name out of that place.

The Yahwist goal is described at 1 Samuel 7:4: "So Israel put away the Baals and the Ashtaroth, and they served the LORD only." The word for "Lord" here is יהוה or *Yĕhovah*.

Part of the Hebrews' ancient worship included the establishment of "high places" where they set up altars and other religious accoutrements, including the אשרים or *asherim* (2 Chr. 14:3; Isa. 27:9), singular אשרה or *'asherah* (Deut. 16:21). This word *'asherah* is the same term used to describe the goddess herself but is transliterated 40 times in the Bible as "grove." *'Asherah* (H842) also refers to the "sacred trees or poles set up near an altar," representing "the stylized multibranched tree symbolizing the Great Goddess of Canaan."[644] Sacred groves were erected by Hebrews including the patriarch Abraham, who established one in Beer-Sheba. In this instance the word "grove" is אשל or *'eshel*, which has been transliterated as *ashre*;[645] yet, later Yahwist fanatics destroyed them. These *asherim* in sacred groves served as "astronomical instruments," reflecting the connection between trees and the stars, which possessed the names of trees.[646]

The High Places

Sacred high places were specially constructed all over the Levant as sites of sacrifice, both animal and human, by non-Semites and Semites alike. Semites were in fact, the last people of the region to maintain human sacrifice, into Hadrian's time, when it was banned.[647] These sac-

644 Walker, *WDSSO*, 196.

645 Landseer, 312.

646 Higgins, 2.193.

647 Walker, B. (1983), 464.

rifices on high places, however, served not only for the propitiation of the Gods but also to provide *food*, and this was the major reason the monopolizing Yahwists went after the high places: so that they could control the Hebrews down to the food they ate, giving the priests tremendous power.

Obviously, it is more than unreasonable to insist that, in order to eat, the people of a nation must all go to a centralized place, where they would have to pay a priest to slaughter their food animals; thus, the people relentlessly rebuilt the high places and ignored the centralizing priests. When the threats and destruction of the high places failed to end the polytheism, however, the Yahwists repeatedly butchered "their own" people (Num. 25, Ezek. 9), demonstrating that the repressive, despotic monotheism is no more "moral" than other religious or secular ideologies and governing systems. In the face of such unbearable oppression as having their food controlled, the people not only rebelled against the imposed Jealous/Zealous God, YHWH, they turned to other gods to get rid of him.

Dividing the Kingdoms

According to the biblical story it was this oppression that split the kingdom in two after Solomon's death (1 Kings 12:16), at which time the northern kingdom of Israel returned to the old polytheism under the Ephraimite king Jeroboam (1 Kings 12:32). Jeroboam (tenth cent. BCE), it should be noted, was appointed by Solomon to be the foreman over the *slaves* of the "house of Joseph" (i.e., Ephraim/Manasseh (1 Kings 11:28), who had originally inhabited the northern lands but whom the genocidal tribe of Judah had been unable to exterminate (1 Kings 9:20)). The division actually occurred after the people, including Jeroboam, asked Solomon's son Rehoboam to "lighten the yoke" of his father.

Jeroboam then made two golden calves at the Hebrew sacred sites of Dan and Beth-El and said to the northern Israelites, "*You have gone up to Jerusalem long enough.* Behold your gods, O Israel, who brought you out of the land of Egypt." Jeroboam was thus expressing the frustration of the people, "Jews" and "Gentiles" alike, who had been slaves to the Jerusalemite priests. The king was also stating that it was the golden calf of Horus/Baal, as opposed to the volcanic Yahweh, who brought Israel out of Egypt.

Hezekiah, Josiah, Hilkiah and the Book of the Law

According to the story, Jeroboam's efforts were doomed to failure, because a couple of centuries later two "reformer" kings, Hezekiah and Josiah, arose to reinstate the repressive and exploitative centralized worship. Hezekiah (715–687 BCE), in fact, "purged" Judah and Ephraim of their high places and Asherim in a frenzied rampage that destroyed centuries-old religious sanctuaries. Jewish Studies professor Dr. Richard Friedman says of this purge:

> The religious reform meant more than breaking idols and cleansing the Temple. It also meant destroying the places of worship of *Yahweh* outside of the Temple in Jerusalem. In addition to the Temple, there had been various local places where people could go to sacrifice to God. These places of worship in the local communities were called "high places." Hezekiah eliminated them. He promoted the centralization of the religion at the Temple in Jerusalem.[648]

The high priest of Jerusalem, therefore, came to hold enormous power, as Jerusalem was the only "Jewish" religious center left. At 2 Kings 18:4, King Hezekiah (fl. 715/6–687) is depicted as destroying even the bronze serpent of Moses—a 500-year-old religious relic called "Nĕchushtan" (Num 21:9)—striking a blow at the Levitical priesthood traced through Moses ("Mushites"), an act that leaves one to wonder how Hezekiah could represent a "great" exemplar of the Mosaic law and religion.

After Hezekiah's death, his son Manasseh (fl. 687–642 BCE) returned the local "pagan" worship to the people (2 Chr. 33:1–10), but the reformers struck back with their favorite king Josiah (c. 649–609 BCE), who was even more vehement than Hezekiah in his assaults on the old religion. In order to explain why the Hebrews kept going after other gods, the biblical writers pretended that the "book of the Law" of Moses had been "lost" and found 600 years later (622 BCE) by Josiah's high priest, Hilkiah, a "son of Zadok" or Sadducee (2 Kings 22:8). After reading/hearing the law (2 Kings 23:4–20)—or before (2 Chr. 34:3–7), depending on which of the contradictory accounts in the "infallible word" one reads—Josiah goes on a rampage and purges the high places.

The tale is obviously fictitious, as, in reality, it cannot be explained why, if Moses had been real and had such a dramatic and impactful life, his Law would have been "lost" in the first place. And if it had been lost, how did Hezekiah know to follow it when he made his purges and reforms? It is also inexplicable why "the Lord" would have gone to so much trouble to talk regularly with Moses and Aaron, give them an enormous amount of detailed instructions, and then just let "his chosen" put it all away for 600 years. Where was "the Lord" during this time? He was purportedly involved in every little detail of Israelite life; yet he never reminded them of the long-lost law?

648 Friedman, 91–92.

The truth is that Hilkiah's book of law was created in his time or afterward in order to consolidate the power of the priesthood, in particular that of the Judean Levites. Shortly thereafter, Jerusalem was destroyed because it was considered troublesome, an oppressive atmosphere that may have been one of the reasons the majority of "Jews" did not return to Palestine after the end of the "Babylonian captivity."

This important incident of Josiah and the new law provides an example of how the Old Testament was not produced in the manner commonly portrayed but represents the work of several hands or schools. The early stories basically constitute ancient myths mixed with the tribal "histories," with a number of people over the centuries re-writing them for propagandistic purposes, long after their purported era. The fact is that the Hebrews/Israelites were polytheists before and after the supposed finding of the law, and that the law itself was variously interpreted by the different tribes/nations.

In addition to the variety of gods and doctrines represented by the biblical writers we must factor in the various tribes, with the Elohist, for example, affiliated with the kingdom of Israel and the Jahwist with Judah. The differing accounts, then, were combined in an attempt to unify the kingdoms, and the tribe/god whose scribes wrote the stories was elevated above the rest. As Robertson says, "Yahweh (or Yah, or Yaha) was simply a local worship aggrandized by the [tribal] king and imposed on the fictitious history of the Hebrews long afterwards."[649]

The state of Israel during biblical times can be summed up thus:

> It is supposed by many—in fact, we have heard it asserted by those who should know better—that the Israelites were always *monotheists*, that they worshiped One God only—*Jehovah*. This is altogether erroneous; they were not different from their neighbors—the Heathen, so-called—in regard to their religion. In the first place, we know that [the Israelites] revered and worshiped a *Bull*, called *Apis*, just as the ancient Egyptians did. They worshiped the *sun*, the *moon*, and the *stars* and all the host of heaven. They worshiped *fire*, and kept it burning on an altar, just as the Persians and other nations. They worshiped *stones*, revered an *oak tree*, and "bowed down to *images*." They worshiped a "Queen of Heaven" called the goddess *Astarte* or *Mylitta*, and "burned incense" to her. They worshiped *Baal*, Moloch, and *Chemosh, and offered up human sacrifices to them*, after which in some instances, *they ate the victim.*[650]

The Hebrews were thus not distinct from their polytheistic neigh-

649 Robertson, J.M., 17.

650 Doane, 108.

bors, except after centuries of programming and conditioning that eventually caused them to become a "race separate and apart from the rest of the world." As George E. Mendenhall asserts:

> Ancient Israel can no longer be treated as an isolated independent object of study; its history is inseparably bound up with ancient oriental history, whether we are concerned with religion, political history or culture.[651]

The Levant, in fact, was a melting-pot of ideologies and gods of all sorts from around the known world, out of which would arise a "king of kings" and "lord of lords" to beat them all.

The Characters

> "Scholarly doubt about the historicity of Jesus in the early twentieth century seems to have been related to the late nineteenth century's fascination with comparative mythology. This in turn had probably been encouraged by the archaeological recovery of previously unknown Near Eastern sources dating from Biblical times during the nineteenth century. For example, parallels between the flood story contained in the Epic of Gilgamesh, which was first brought to light in the 1870s, and the flood story in Genesis suggested that Noah was not a real person, but rather a mythical figure drawn from a common fund of Near-Eastern lore. Given this, it is hardly surprising that some should assume the same of Jesus as well. The short-lived but influential History of Religions school of late nineteenth century German seminaries had shown that many non-Christian Hellenistic religions shared such elements with early Christianity as a belief in redemption through the sacrifice of a god."
>
> —Dr. Alice Whealey, *Josephus on Jesus* (172–3)
>
> "By the way, it is quite a big question, whether Jesus Christ has ever lived."[652]
>
> —Napoleon Bonaparte, as related by Christopher Martin Wieland
>
> "I feel no hesitation to state that the Christos of the Gospels is an imitation of Krishna. It is my honest opinion—nay my belief too—that the story of the life of *Krishna* went to Alexandria with the Buddhist Missionaries. History tells us that in the time of Emperor Asoka, the preachers of Buddhism were sent to

651 Wright, G., 35.

652 Bietenholz, 326.

> different parts of the world, and some of them went to the city referred to above. Philo, the greatest Jewish historian, testifies to the above statement when he says in one of his works that "there were men of all religions in this monastery; Brahmans from the East who believed in *Krishna*."[653]
>
> —Thakur Kahanchandra Varma, *The Historicity of Christ Proving That the Christ of the New Testament is a Myth and the Gospels Spurious*

We have seen that there is no credible evidence for the historicity of the Christian founder, that the earliest Christian proponents of the literal Gospel were as a whole either utterly credulous or astoundingly deceitful. We have seen that these "defenders of the faith" were compelled under incessant charges of fraud to admit that Christianity was a revision of older religions. It has also been demonstrated that the world into which Christianity was born was filled with assorted gods and goddesses, as opposed to a monotheistic vacuum. In fact, in their fabulous exploits and wondrous powers many of these gods and goddesses are significantly the same as the Christ character, as attested by the Christian apologists themselves. In further inspecting this issue we discover that "Jesus Christ" appears to be a compilation of various of these gods and goddesses, who were worshipped and whose dramas were regularly played out by ancient peoples long before the Christian era.

Although many people have the impression that the ancient world consisted of unconnected nations and tribes, the truth is that during the era Jesus allegedly lived there was a network of international trade and another of esoteric brotherhoods stretching from Europe to China. The resulting information network included the library at Alexandria and provided access to numerous oral traditions and manuscripts that told a similar basic narrative and many motifs portrayed in various lands with different place names and ethnicities for the characters. In actuality, the legend of Jesus parallels the story of Krishna, for example, in important details, with many features of Indian mythology centuries or millennia prior to the Common Era, as far back as the earliest Indian text, the Rig Veda. Even greater antiquity can be attributed to the detailed Horus myth of Egypt, which also is practically identical to certain aspects of the Christian version but which preceded it by thousands of years.[654]

---

653 Dīkshita, v.

654 For a fairly thorough analysis of the primary source material and scholarship regarding the parallels between Horus and Jesus, see my book *Christ in Egypt*.

From the most credible scientific evidence, the Jesus story apparently incorporated elements from the tales of other deities in the ancient world, including several of the following world saviors, most or all of whom predate the Christian myth. We need not suggest that all of these characters were necessarily used in the creation of the Christian myth, as some of them are found in parts of the world purportedly unknown at the time; however, it is likely that a fair number of these deities were conscripted. Thus, we find the same tales around the world about a variety of godmen and sons of God, a number of whom also had virgin or otherwise miraculous births or were of divine origin; were born on or near December 25 or the winter solstice, in a cave or underground; were baptized; worked miracles and marvels; held high morals, were compassionate, toiled for humanity and healed the sick; were the basis of soul-salvation and/or were called Savior, Redeemer, Deliverer; had eucharists; vanquished darkness; were hung on trees, crucified or otherwise killed; and were resurrected or revived, returning to heaven, whence they came.

As concerns the specious claim that the analogies between the Christ myth and those outlined below are "non-existent" because they are not found in "primary sources," let us return to the words of the early Church fathers, who acknowledged that major important aspects of the Christ character are indeed found in the stories of earlier, Pagan gods, but who asserted that the reason for these similarities was that the evidently prescient devil "anticipated" Christ and planted "foreshadowing" of his "coming" in the heathens' minds. The Church fathers are clear that the devil had done this trickery in order to "get men to imagine that the true history of Christ was of the same character as those prodigious fables and poetic stories."[655]

Here is a clear admission that these mythical motifs long pre-dated the Christian era and that the gods' "lives" were very similar to that alleged of Jesus. This contention is backed up by numerous artifacts from the ancient world, including books, inscriptions, statuary, wall carvings and paintings, as well as oral traditions and so on.

The list of these saviors and sons of God includes the following[656]:

655 Taylor, R. 244. Taylor includes in the footnote the original Greek of Justin, referencing it as "*Justini Apolog.* 2."

656 This list has been pruned of a few unsupportable contentions based on unconvincing modern speculation. For example, the character "Issa/Isa of Arabia," who was born of the Virgin Mary and was the "Divine Word" of the ancient Arabian Nasara/Nazarenes around 400 BCE (Lockhart, 116) is obviously just Jesus as he appears in the Koran. Also, the character of "Beddru of Japan" appears to be a misprint of "Beddhu," another translitera-

- Adad (Hadad) and Marduk of Assyria, the latter considered "the Word" (Logos)[657]
- Adonis, Aesclepius, Apollo, Dionysus, Heracles/Hercules and Zeus of Greece
- Agni, Krishna and Indra of India and Tibet
- Attis of Phrygia
- Baal or Bel of Babylon/Phoenicia
- Balder and Odin/Wodin/Woden/Wotan of the Scandinavians, "wounded with a spear."[658]
- Bali of Afghanistan[659]
- Buddha/Beddhu of India, China and Japan
- Caesar Augustus and Julius Caesar of Rome
- Chu Chulainn of Ireland
- Codom and Deva Tat (Buddha) of Siam[660]
- Dahzbog of the Slavs
- Dumuzi or Tammuz of Sumeria and Babylonia
- Fo-hi, Lao-Kiun, Tien, and Shang-Ti of China, the "Lord on High," brought into the world through divine, miraculous birth.[661]
- Hermes of Egypt/Greece, who was born of the Virgin Maia and called "the Logos" because he was the Messenger or Word of the Heavenly Father, Zeus.
- Hesus of the Druids and Gauls
- Horus, Osiris, Serapis and Isis of Egypt[662]
- Jao/Iao of Nepal
- Jupiter/Jove of Rome
- Mithra of Persia/India
- Perseus of Greece, who was born of the immortal Father God, Zeus, and the virgin Danae.
- Prometheus of Caucasus/Greece

---

tion of "Buddha." (See my article, "Beddru is Beddou is Buddha." Also, it is unclear who are characters like "Crite of Chaldea" or "Zoar of the Bonzes"; hence, these have been removed. In addition, the contention that there was an "Ieo of China," who was "the great prophet, lawgiver and savior" with 70 disciples came from Higgins (2.421), whose sources are unclear.

657 Carus, 35.341; Boman, 58.

658 Lindow, 248.

659 Apparently, this god is a manifestation of the Hindu deity Balarama. (See Perry, 17.)

660 Acharya, *SOG*, 367–368; Garnier, 103.

661 Leeming (1992), 54.

662 For more information on these gods, see Christ in Egypt.

- Quetzalcoatl of Mexico
- Quirinius of Rome
- Salivahana of southern India, who was a "divine child, born of a virgin, and was the son of a carpenter," himself also being called "the Carpenter," and whose name or title means "cross-borne" ("Salvation")[663]
- Tammuz of Syria, the savior god worshipped in Jerusalem[664]
- The Mikado of the Shintos
- Thor of the Gauls
- Universal Monarch of the Sibyls
- Wittoba of the Bilingonese/Telingonese
- Xamolxis/Zalmoxis of Thrace, the savior who "promised eternal life to guests at his sacramental Last Supper. Then he went into the underworld, and rose again on the third day."[665]
- Yahweh of Israel
- Zarathustra/Zoroaster of Persia

This list does not pretend to be complete, nor is there adequate room here to go into detail about all these mythological characters. It should be noted that, as with Jesus, a number of these characters have been considered historical persons, but today almost none of them is considered as such.

The Major Players

Some of the more prominent figures whose alleged lives and/or teachings bore a striking resemblance to those of Jesus Christ in several germane details highlighted as follows. It should be noted that some of these figures, such as the Indian god Agni and Egyptian gods Horus and Osiris, long predate the Common Era, revealing the precedence of these motifs for centuries or millennia prior to the supposed advent of Jesus. The stories of Horus and Osiris, however, remained popular into the so-called Christian era, while others such as Asclepius likewise were widely popular when Christianity was forming. Hence, these motifs and rituals had been known in the Pagan world for many centuries and con-

663 Higgins, I, 662-9. In his original work, Kersey Graves depicted this god as coming from "Bermuda." After ridicule for naming a Caribbean island, Graves responded that he was speaking of a "Bermuda," which is a "small province as appears in ancient Burmah." (Perry, 76.) For more on Salivahana, see *Suns of God*.

664 Walker, 468.

665 Walker, B. (1983), 1099.

tinued for hundreds of years into the Common Era.

Adonis of Greece, Syria and Phrygia

Pre-Christian mention of the resurrection of Adonis can be found in the fifteenth Idyll of Theocritus (250 BCE). Annual festivals, called Adonia, were held in his honour at Byblus, Alexandria, Athens and other places. Although there were variations in the ceremony itself and in its date, the central idea was the death and resurrection of Adonis. A vivid description of the festival at Alexandria is given by Theocritus in his fifteenth idyll, the *Adoniazusae*:

You only (Adonis) of the demi-gods,
Do visit both this world and the stream of Acheron (The Underworld)
For Agamemnon had no such lot, nor Aias,
That mighty lord of the terrible anger, nor Hector,
The eldest born of the twenty sons of Hecuba, nor Patroclus,
Nor Pyrrhus, that returned out of Troy land,
Nor the heroes of yet more ancient days,
The Lapithai and Deucalion's sons,
Nor the sons of Pelops, and the chiefs of Pelasgian Argos.
Be gracious now, dear Adonis, and propitious
Even in the coming year.
Dear to us has your advent been, Adonis,
And dear shall it be when you come again.[666]

It is now generally agreed that Adonis is a vegetation spirit, whose death and return to life (Easter) represent the decay of nature in winter and its revival in spring.

Agni of India

The fire and solar god Agni are prominently featured in the Rig Veda. The word "Agni" itself is interesting for its possible relationship with the Latin word "*agnus*," meaning "lamb," as in "Agnus Dei," the "Lamb of God," an important epithet for Jesus Christ. In the Gospel of John (1:29), Christ is called "Lamb of God," which is ὁ ἀμνὸς τοῦ θεοῦ in the Greek, the "*amnos* of God," an interesting title in consideration of Christ's Greek and Roman counterparts Zeus and Jupiter *Ammon*. Agni is not only fire: he is also considered the rising sun,[667] the morning ball of fire. Concerning Agni, Wheeler states:

[The] conception of the god of fire was Agni, and Agni was not only the flame which burns upon the hearth or altar, but also the

666 www.cartage.org.lb/en/themes/BookLibrary/books/bibliographie/T/Theocritus/theocritus.html

667 O'Flaherty, 178.

lightning which manifests itself in the clouds, and even the light of the sun, moon and stars. Yet both the sun and moon appear as separate and individual deities, the former under the name of Surya, and the latter under the name of Soma or Chandra.[668]

As described in the Rigveda, Agni the Fire God shares the following in common with Christ:

- Agni's father is a carpenter.[669]
- Agni symbolically represents the spiritual fire of life and the processes of transformation.
- Agni is "born in a manger."[670]

668 Wheeler, 1.8.

669 See the sections on the carpenter-god or carpenter-priest motif here and in my book *Suns of God* and ebook *Krishna, the Indian Christ: Parallels between Hinduism and Christianity*. The Greek word used in the New Testament, τέκτων or *tekton* (G5045) appears some two dozen times in the Septuagint, as at 1 Samuel 13:19. In the Hebrew of that verse, the word translated as *tekton* is חרש or *charash* (H2796), used 33 times in the Old Testament and defined as "craftsman, artisan, engraver, graver, artificer; graver, artificer." This notion of craftsmen guilds can be seen in 1 Chronicles (4:14), which speaks of the residents of the Valley of Charashim (i.e., carpenters). *Tekton* is also translated as "carpenter," as at 2 Samuel 5:11. Here the Greek is τέκτονας ξύλων or "craftsmen of wood," followed by τέκτονας λίθων or "craftsmen of stone," translated as "masons." The role of carpenters, builders and masons was an important one in antiquity, as it was they who built the Temple of the Lord (2 Kings 22:6). At Isaiah 40:19–20, we read about the *tekton* who casts gold for an idol and sets up a graven image; likewise it is a *tekton* who creates the "calf of Samaria" (Hosea 8:6). The oddest passage, perhaps, in which the word *tekton* is used is Zechariah 1:20: "And the LORD showed me four *tektons*," here translated variously as "carpenters" (KJV), "craftsmen" (NIV), "smiths" (RSV) or "blacksmiths" (NLT). This vision occurred after "the word of the Lord" "came unto" Zechariah, to whom it is explained that the four tektons are the "horns which scattered Judah, so that no man raised his head; and these have come to terrify them, to cast down the horns of the nations who lifted up their horns against the land of Judah to scatter it." There is a very interesting passage in this regard at Hebrews 11:10, which states: ἐξεδέχετο γὰρ τὴν τοὺς θεμελίους ἔχουσαν πόλιν ἧς τεχνίτης καὶ δημιουργὸς ὁ θεός. The RSV renders this scripture: "For he looked forward to the city which has foundations, whose builder and maker is God." Of interest to us are the word τεχνίτης or *technits*, which, like *tekton*, means "artificer" or "craftsman," and the phrase δημιουργὸς ὁ θεός or "demiurge [is] [the] God." In other words, the builder or demiurge of the holy city (sought by Abraham) is God.

670 This concept of "birth in a manger" reflects the creation of fire in a nest of kindling or bundle of wood.

- Agni is a purifier and "baptizer with fire."[671] (Matt. 3:11–2; 13:49–50)
- He dispels darkness with his light.
- Agni is the divine mediator between heaven and earth.[672]
- Agni is a priest and divine messenger.[673]
- He is the "source of light throughout the universe."[674]
- He "abides on earth like a prince surrounded by faithful friends."[675]
- Agni is the Supreme and Absolute God.[676]
- Agni is the "ruler of the universe, the lord of men, the wise king, the father, the brother, the son, the friend of men."[677]

Agni's relationship to Krishna is evident from BG 10.23, in which Krishna says that, of the "eight Vasus," he is *pāvakaḥ*, an epithet for "Agni the fire god." It is with good reason that early peoples deemed fire not only a "gift from God" but also a divine entity in its own right, as it provided so much of what makes mankind human, including not only warmth and light, protection against the terrors and dangers of the night, but also a central focus of hearth and home, where families, tribes and clans found community and safety.

Apollo of Greece

One of the most obvious of the sun gods, Apollo replaced the god Helios as the solar hero in later Greek poetry, centuries before the Common Era. The Greek sun god shares the following with Jesus Christ:

- Apollo is the son of the Most High God, who in this case is Zeus, whose name in the genitive is "Dios," meaning "God."
- Apollo is a healing god, depicted with long, flowing hair.[678]
- Apollo was called *Soter* or "Savior," centuries before Christ.
- Apollo was resurrected at the vernal equinox.[679]

The contention that Apollo is called *Soter* is not unexpected, especially when it is considered that the word *soter* or other form such as

671 Wheeler, 1.18.

672 This role comes in part from the ability of fire to consume sacrifices to the gods, taking humanity's propitiation via the smoke to the heavenly abode. (Wheeler, 1.18.)

673 Wheeler, 1.18.

674 Wheeler, 1.18.

675 Wheeler, 1.19.

676 Wheeler, 1.19, citing RV 1.73.

677 Wheeler, 1.20, citing RV 1.1-2.

678 Apollonius of Rhodes, *Argonautica* 2; Coleridge, 76.

679 Mackey, 398.

"soteria" and "soterios" is used hundreds of times in the Bible.[680] For example, at Deuteronomy 32:15 the word *soteros* appears as "salvation," rendered by *yĕshuw'ah* in the original Hebrew.

Asclepius of Greece

One of the gods whose "life" and appearance most certainly inspired the creators of the gospel story is the Greek god Asclepius, also commonly transliterated as "Aesculapius" or "Asklepious," among other permutations. The son of the Greek sun god Apollo and the Lapith princess Coronis, Asclepius was the god of medicine and healing, a characteristic shared with the later "Divine Physician," Jesus Christ. Asclepius's worship predates the Christian era by centuries, extending into and beyond the second century AD/CE, when his syncretistic Egyptian counterpart Serapis was purportedly worshipped by both Christians and Jews at Alexandria.[681]

Asclepius shares the following with the Christ myth, parallels found in Pindar, Apollonius Rhodius and elsewhere:

- Asclepius was the son of a god and a mortal woman whose birthplace on Earth was a sacred site.
- He was exposed to grave danger after his birth.[682]
- Asclepius healed the sick, cured the blind and resurrected his faithful from the dead.[683]

680 The Greek word σωτῳ or *soter* can be found in the LXX at Deut. 32:15; Jud. 3:9, 15; 12:3; 1 Sam. 10:19; 1 Chr. 16:35; Neh. 9:27; Pss. 23:5; 24:5; 26:1, 9; 61:3, 7; 64:6; 78:9; 94:1; Prov. 29:25; Isa. 12:2; 17:10; 45:15, 31, 33; 62:11; Mic. 7:7; Hab. 3:18. (*A Handy Concordance of the Septuagint*, 235.)

681 In a letter purported to be from the emperor Hadrian (76–138), the Roman ruler calls Serapis the "peculiar god of the Christians." For a discussion of this letter, see my book *Christ in Egypt*, 279–80. It is possible that this letter originally read "*Chrestians*."

682 Penny Cyclopedia, 1.154.

683 Apollodorus (*The Library*, 3.10.3) cites the resurrections by Asclepius of half a dozen men, reputed from several centuries prior to the common era. (Apollodorus/Frazer, 2.17) See also *Penny Cyclopedia*, 1.154. Per Pausanias (*Description of Greece,* 2.27.2-5), Asclepius is depicted as raising Hippolytus from the dead, hundreds of years before Jesus's similar miracles. (Pausanias/Jones, 393.) Indeed, Asclepius's resurrections were so abundant that in some tales he is killed by Zeus because he is on the verge of emptying out the underworld. It is interesting to note that the vengeance of Asclepius's death by Apollo represents an astrotheological motif, in that Zeus subsequently bans the sun god from the night sky. (Apollonius Rhodius, *Argonautica*, 4.610ff) It is clear that the son of the sun god—Asclepius—is also solar in nature, and this motif of death and resurrection is likewise solar, as it is in

- Asclepius was called Σωτὴρ or *Soter*, "Savior" and *Paean*, "Healer," centuries before Christ held the same titles.[684]
- As happened with Jesus, the Father God, Zeus, caused the death of Asclepius, after which the healing god was resurrected to become a major deity.[685]
- After his death, Asclepius ascended to heaven, where Zeus made him into the constellation of Ophiuchus, the "serpent-holder."[686]
- From heaven Asclepius interacted with mortals and interceded on their behalf, securing their release from death.
- Asclepius convinced a doubter, the blind woman Ambrosia, of his miraculous powers.[687]
- Asclepius is depicted with long, dark hair and a dark beard, wearing a white robe.[688]
- He was associated with the cock, a symbol of vigilance,[689] as was Jesus (Mark 14:30) and Gnostic/Christian tradition.[690]
- As Christ carries the shepherd's rod, so too does Asclepius bear his "snake-entwined staff."[691]

---

many other cultures, including and especially the Egyptian. (See my book *Christ in Egypt*.)

684 MacMullen, 48, 84, 167.

685 Lucian/Sheldon, 67; Littlewood, 215, Ovid (Hyg. *Astr.* 2.14).

686 Littlewood, 215, citing Ovid (Hyg. *Astr.* 2.14). Ophiuchus is an interesting mythological character whose life has been compared to both Jesus and Paul of Tarsus.

687 Van der Loos, 415.

688 See, for example, the bust of Asclepius at the Antiquarium of the Palatine at Rome and the statue of the god at the National Archaeological Museum of Athens.

689 Penny Cyclopedia, 1.154.

690 In a Coptic fragment that may be part of the Gnostic text *The Gospel of the Twelve*, Christ is portrayed at the Last Supper, at which a cock is served on a platter. The server, Matthias, tells Jesus that the Jews who saw him killing the cock threatened to kill Christ in the same manner. Jesus concurs that they will kill him, but he predicts that this particular cock will "give the signal before the light dawns" and be "like John the Baptist who heralded me in advance." The Savior then states, "I am the true light which has no darkness in it. When this cock died, they said of me that I would die.... However, this cock will rise." Jesus then touches the cock and bids it to live, resurrecting it, whereupon it flies away. Christ next says: "Behold the cock you sacrificed three hours ago is risen. They shall crucify me, and my blood will be the salvation of the nations (and I will rise on the third day)." (Hastings, 1.501-2.)

691 See, for example, the mosaic from Palmyra (c. 160–260 AD/CE), with Asclepius on a throne, holding a snake-entwined staff. (Patton, 99.)

- Like Jesus with the serpent (ὄφις/*ophis*) of Moses (John 3:14), Asclepius is associated with the snake or serpent.[692]

One of Asclepius's daughters was named "Iaso" or "Ieso,"[693] meaning "Healing," which bears a striking resemblance to the various permutations of Yahweh and Jesus, including "Iao" or "Iesous," this latter said to come from the same Greek root, *iasthai*, "to heal."

Asclepius provides another good example of how several figures can become intertwined to produce one mythical figure: "Agreeably to the intricacy and confusion which prevails on that subject, several Aesculapii are said to have existed."

The similarity between Asclepius and Jesus was striking enough that early Church father Justin Martyr saw fit to include the Greek god in his *First Apology*, comparing Christ to earlier gods: "Æsculapius, who, though he was a great physician, was struck by a thunderbolt, and so ascended to heaven."[694] In that pithy sentence, in fact, are three motifs nearly identical to elements in the Christian story: A "great physician," a tragic, violent death, and an ascension to heaven. This comparison alone is enough to warrant suspicion of the Christian tale as no less mythical than the myths of the "sons of Jove."

Diodorus Siculus (*Library of History* 4.7.1.1–2):

> Asclepius was the son of Apollo and Coronis … he healed many sick whose lives had been despaired of, and … he brought back to life many who had died.

Attis of Phrygia

The story of Attis, the "crucified" and resurrected Phrygian son of God, predates the Christian savior by centuries, in roughly the same region as the gospel tale. Attis is especially important in our quest because his worship not only predates Christianity but also continued well into the Christian era, recorded for example in the fifth century by Augustine.

Attis shares the following characteristics with Jesus:

- Attis was born on December 25 of the Virgin Nana.[695]
- He was a shepherd, as Christ was called the "Good Shepherd."[696]

692 *Penny Cyclopedia*, 1.154; van der Loos, 226: "The deity Aesculapius was very closely connected with the snake."

693 Depending on the dialect, this demigoddess's name is spelled either ασώ or iησώ, the latter especially resembling ησος or "Jesus." She had a cult of followers called the "sons of Ieso.

694 Roberts, A., *ANF*, I, 170. (Emph. added.)

695 Leeming, *MVH*, 25. Frazer ((1919), 263) says: "His birth, like that of so many other heroes, is said to have been miraculous. His mother Nana was a virgin who conceived by putting a ripe almond or a pomegranate in her bosom."

696 Lane, 39.

- He was considered the "only begotten son,"[697] the Logos/Word,[698] and the savior slain for the salvation of mankind.[699]
- His cult had a sacrificial meal, at which, it is contended, his body as bread was eaten by his worshippers.[700]
- His priests were "eunuchs for the kingdom of heaven" (Matt. 19:12).[701]
- Attis served as both the Divine Son and the Father.[702]
- On "Black Friday,"[703] he was "crucified" on a tree,[704] from which his holy blood ran down to redeem the earth.[705]

---

697 Although it is unclear whether or not Attis was ever called "monogenes" or "only begotten," his role is archetypically that of a monogenic character. (See, for example, King, C.W., 258; Knight, R.P., xxii.) That "monogenes" was an important title shared by more than one figure in antiquity is indicated by its presence as a Gnostic figure, particularly associated with the Valentinians.

698 In his *Hymn to King Helios* (179c), Julian asks, "But is not this Logos Attis ?" (Julian/Wright, 1.501.)

699 Leeming (1998), 231. As have many other scholars, Guignebert ((1961) 72) likewise considered Attis a "savior and interceding god." Davutoğlu (19) remarks: "Pagans and members of mystery religions within the syncretic atmosphere of the *Pax Romana* believed in gods—Osiris, Attis, Dionysus—who died to redeem mankind with such titles as *Soter* (Savior) and *Eleutheriom* (Deliverer)." Since we know that Dionysus and others such as Asclepius were called Soter, this contention concerning Attis does not surprise us.

700 Guignebert (1961), 73. The nature of the sacrificial meal has been discussed numerous times, with uncertainty over whether this ritual constituted part of the mysteries. In consideration of other instances of the sacred-meal ritual including this motif, this speculation may be merited. For example, it is noted that in "the Liturgy" Attis is called the "cornstalk," indicating his role as a grain and fertility god, common attributes of the sun god. (Farnell, *Hibbert Journal*, 11.317; 1904.)

701 See, for example, Bremmer, 285.

702 Says Frazer (1906), 200: "[The] resurrection of Attis, who combined in himself the characters of the divine Father and the divine Son, was officially celebrated at Rome on the same day" (i.e., March 25, the vernal equinox culmination and the date upon which Christ's resurrection was placed in antiquity).

703 Speaking of Attis's spring celebration, Berry (20) remarks: "The festival began as a day of blood on Black Friday and culminated after three days in a day of rejoicing over the resurrection. Note the extremely close parallel between the Attis festival and the festival of Easter adopted by the Christian Church about three centuries later." See also Browne, 106.

704 Tacey, 110.

705 Zorach, 72. Frazer ((1914) 1.268) states: "On the twenty-secnd of March, a pine-tree was cut in the woods and brought into the sanctuary of Cybele,

- He descended into the underworld.[706]
- After three days, Attis was resurrected on March 25 (as tradition held of Jesus) as the "Most High God."[707]

Providing a summary of the mythos and ritual of Attis, along with parallels to Christian tradition, Professor of Classics and Ancient History at the University of Manchester Dr. Andrew T. Fear states:

> The youthful Attis after his murder was miraculously brought to life again three days after his demise. The celebration of this cycle of death and renewal was one of the major festivals of the metroac cult. Attis therefore represented a promise of reborn life and as such it is not surprising that we find representations of the so-called mourning Attis as a common tomb motif in the ancient world.
>
> The parallel, albeit at a superficial level, between this myth and the account of the resurrection of Christ is clear. Moreover Attis as a shepherd occupies a favourite Christian image of Christ as the good shepherd. Further parallels also seem to have existed: the pine tree of Attis, for example, was seen as a parallel to the cross of Christ.
>
> Beyond Attis himself, Cybele, too, offered a challenge to Christian divine nomenclature. Cybele was regarded as a virgin goddess and as such could be seen as a rival to the Virgin Mary ... Cybele as the mother of the Gods, mater Deum, here again presented a starkly pagan parallel to the Christian Mother of God.
>
> There was rivalry too in ritual. The climax of the celebration of Attis' resurrection, the Hilaria, fell on the 25th of March, the

---

where it was treated as a great divinity.... The trunk was swathed like a corpse with woolen bands and decked with wreaths of violets, for violets were said to have sprung from the blood of Attis, as roses and anemones from the blood of Adonis; and the effigy of a young man, doubtless Attis himself, was tied to the middle of the stem.... The third day, the twenty-fourth of March, was known as the Day of Blood: the Archigallus or high-priest drew blood from his arms and presented it as an offering." Much frantic and vulgar behavior ensues, drowning the shrieks of the tortured proxy for the god, considered by Frazer as part of the "mourning for Attis" that "may have been intended to strengthen him for the resurrection." Some of these elements, such as the blood producing violets, are related by Arnobius (*Against the Heathen*, 5.7).

706 Bleeker, 1.517. The descent is called in Greek the κατάβασις or *katabasis*, "going down," which is the opposite of the *anastasis*, or "standing up," the term which was used to describe Christ's resurrection, as well as that of the Egyptian god Horus by Diodorus in the first century BCE.

707 Lane, 39.

date that the early church had settled on as the day of Christ's death.[708]

As we can see, according to this scholar, Attis is killed, fixed to a tree, and resurrects after three days, while his mother is "regarded as a virgin goddess" comparable to the Virgin Mary.

Attis's Virgin Mother

The Phrygian god Attis's mother was variously called Cybele and Nana. Like Isis and Mary, Nana/Cybele is a perpetual virgin, despite her status as a mother. The scholarly term used to describe virgin birth is "parthenogenesis," while many goddesses are referred to as "Parthenos," the Greek word meaning "virgin." This term is applicable to the Phrygian goddess Cybele/Nana as well.

The diverse names of Attis's mother and her manner of impregnation are explained by Dr. David Adams Leeming, Professor Emeritus of English and Comparative Literature at the University of Connecticut:

> Attis is the son of Cybele in her form as the virgin, Nana, who is impregnated by the divine force in the form of a pomegranate.[709]

Attis Born on December 25

The "December 25" or winter-solstice birth of the sun god is a common theme in several cultures around the world over the past millennia, including the Egyptian. As it is for Mithra, Horus and Jesus, this date has likewise been claimed for Attis's nativity as well. For example, Barbara G. Walker writes:

> Attis's passion was celebrated on the 25th of March, exactly nine months before the solstitial festival of his birth, the 25th of December. The time of his death was also the time of his conception, or re-conception.[710]

In this same regard, Shirley Toulson remarks:

> In the secret rites of this Great Mother the young god Attis figured as her acolyte and consort.... Each year he was born at the winter solstice, and each year as the days shortened, he died.[711]

The reasoning behind the myth of the vegetative and solar god Attis's birth at the winter solstice is sound enough, in that it echoes natural cycles, with the god's death at the vernal equinox also representing the time when he is conceived again, to be born nine months later. As an example of scholarly extrapolation of this date, in discussing the winter-solstice orientation of a tomb in the Roman necropolis at Carmona,

---

708 Lane, 39–40.

709 Leeming, *MVH*, 25.

710 Walker, B. (1983), 77.

711 Toulson, 34.

Spain, which possessed an image of Attis,[712] archaeologist Dr. Manuel Bendala evinced the birth of the god at that time:

> [The] peculiar orientation of a chamber, into which the first rays of the morning sun would directly penetrate on the day of the winter solstice, led me to deduce that this would be a kind of *sanctum sanctorum* of the sanctuary, where the devotees of Attis celebrated the *Natalis Invicti*.[713]

The *Natalis Invicti* is the "Birth of the Unconquered One," referring to the sun. This contention is reasonable when one considers that Attis himself was evidently a sun god, as related by Brandeis University Professor of Classical Studies Dr. Patricia A. Johnston:

> G. Thomas ... traces the development of the idea of resurrection with regard to Attis, [which] seems to be firmly established approximately by the time of Firmicus Maternus and the Neo-Platonists, i.e., the fourth century AD. By this time, "Attis is now conceived of as a higher cosmic god, even the Sun-god.... At the solstice ... symbolically Cybele is seen to have paled before the ascendant Attis."[714]

Moreover, at times the young Attis was merged with Mithra,[715] whose birthday was traditionally held on December 25 and with whom, in graphic representations, he shared the same Phrygian attire. As we have seen, the *Natalis Invicti* was traditionally the birth of Mithra and Sol Invictus.

In this regard, as Dr. Fear relates:

> Allegorical readings of metroac mythology allowed the cult to be integrated into the popular cult of *Sol Invictus*. Attis became emblematic of the sun god, and Cybele of the mother earth.[716]

To summarize, as Sol Invictus or the Unconquered Sun—again, who is likewise identified with Mithra—Attis, too, would have been depicted as having been born on December 25 or the winter solstice, the time of the *Natalis Invicti*.[717]

The myths of Attis's death include him being killed by a boar or by castrating himself under a tree, as well as getting hanged on a tree or "crucified." Indeed, he has been called the "castrated and crucified

---

712 Vermaseren, *CCCA*, 62.
713 Vermaseren, *CARC*, 408.
714 Vermaseren, *CARC*, 108.
715 Vermaseren, *CARC*, 108.
716 Vermaseren, *CARC*, 43.
717 Halsberghe, 159.

Attis."[718] Again, it should be noted that the use of the term "crucified" of gods like Horus and Attis does not connote that he or they were literally nailed to a cross, as we commonly think of crucifixion, based on the Christian tale. As we have seen, there have been plenty of ancient figures who appeared in cruciform (suspended, spread-eagled, impaled, etc.), some of whose myths specifically have them punished or killed through crucifixion, such as Prometheus.

Attis's Crucifixion

The crucifixion in solar mythology represents the circle of the year with a cross in the center, symbolizing the solstices and equinoxes. Hence, as a sun god, Attis would logically have been said to be "crucified," as have been his solar counterparts in the esoterica of the solar cultus. As a nature god as well, he would be described as being hung on a cross at the vernal equinox, when the days and nights are equal, until he rises to bring the resurrection of the spring from the death of winter, as well as the day triumphing over the night as the days increase in length.

Moreover, Attis is said to have been "crucified" to a pine tree,[719] while Christ, too, was represented as both crucified and *hung on a tree* (Acts 5:30; 10:39; 1 Peter 2:24). As stated by La Trobe University professor Dr. David John Tacey: "Especially significant for us is the fact that the Phrygian Attis was crucified upon the tree."[720] In antiquity, these two concepts were obviously similar enough to be interchangeable in understanding.

As we know from rituals that have continued into relatively recent times (e.g., among the Khonds of India), when the sacred-king victims of their human sacrifice rituals are hung on a tree, the arms of the sacrifice were often extended onto branches on either side, or in *cruciform*.[721] Indeed, some of these cults/tribes use movable crossbars, so it can very accurately be stated that they hang their victims on a tree that is also a cross—a cross-shaped tree, in fact. Hence the two are essentially the same. The wood upon which a crucified victim is hung need not be a hewn cross but can be a tree, and Attis's hanging upon a tree is thus considered a "crucifixion." "It was an ancient custom to use trees as gibbets for crucifixion, or, if artificial, to call the cross a tree."[722]

In fact, in the biblical book of Deuteronomy (21:22), the writer speaks of hanging criminals upon a tree, as though it were a general

718 Harari, 131.
719 Price, R. (2000), 87.
720 Tacey, 110.
721 Acharya, *SOG*, 281.
722 Higgins, 2.499.

custom:

> And if a man has committed a crime punishable by death and he is put to death, and you hang him on a tree: His body shall not remain all night upon the tree, but thou shalt in any wise bury him that day; (for he that is hanged [is] accursed of God).

Furthermore, Paul seems to refer to the above Deuteronomy quote in the correct context when he says: "Christ hath redeemed us from the curse of the law, being made a curse for us; for it is written, 'Cursed is every one that hangeth *on a tree*'" (Gal. 3:13).

Again, in the Book of Acts, Christ is specifically said to have been hung on a tree:

> The God of our fathers raised up Jesus, whom ye slew and hanged on a tree. (Acts 5:30)

And we are witnesses of all things which he did both in the land of the Jews, and in Jerusalem; whom they slew and hanged on a tree. (Acts 10:39)

Concerning Attis's death, Doane remarks:

> Attys, who was called the "Only Begotten Son" and "Saviour," was worshipped by the Phrygians.... He was represented by them as a man tied to a tree, at the foot of which was a lamb, and, without doubt, also as a man nailed to the tree.[723]

In his book *Divine Institutes* (4.11), Christian writer Lactantius (c. 240–c. 320) relates that, according to his oracle, the sun god Apollo of Miletus was "mortal in the flesh, wise in miraculous deeds, but he was made prisoner by the Chaldean lawgivers and nailed to stakes, and came to a painful death."[724] If the oracle really had recounted a genuinely ancient account of Apollo's passion, then we have a pre-Christian mythical precedent for that of Jesus. Moreover, the identification of Attis with Apollo is apt, since both were taken in antiquity to be sun gods and were discussed together, as by Macrobius and the Emperor Julian "the Apostate" (331/332–363 AD/CE). Julian said that both Apollo and Attis were "closely linked with Helios,"[725] the older Greek sun god.

The Passion of Attis

In *Christianity Before Christ*, Dr. John Jackson relates:

> In the Attis festival a pine tree was felled on the 22nd of March and an effigy of the god was affixed to it, thus being slain and hanged on a tree.... At night the priests found the tomb illuminated from within but empty, since on the third day Attis had

723 Doane, 190–191.

724 Lactantius, 245.

725 Athanassiadi, 204.

arisen from the grave.[726]

In his *Against the Heathen* (4.42), Christian apologist Arnobius (d. c. 330) acknowledges that Attis is perceived as the sun, but wonders about the story told of him that he was born in Phrygia and "suffered certain things, [and was said] to have done certain things also, whom all the theatres know in the scenic shows, to whom every year we see divine honours paid."[727] He further wonders whether or not "this name [was] made to pass from the sun to a man, or from a man to the sun?"

The drama or passion of Attis took place in what was to become Galatia, and it was the followers of Attis to whom Paul addressed his Epistle to the Galatians at 3:1: "O foolish Galatians! Who has bewitched you, before whose eyes Jesus Christ was publicly portrayed as crucified?" Since the Galatians presumably were not in Jerusalem when Christ was purportedly crucified, we may sensibly ask just who this was who was "publicly *portrayed* as crucified" before their eyes? This "portrayal" certainly suggests the recurring passion of the cult of Attis, and some of Attis's most ardent followers were called "Galli," as in Gaul and Galatia.

In his *Exhortation to the Heathens* (2), Clement of Alexandria relates that "Dionysus was called Attis, because he was mutilated."[728]

Attis was popular not only in Phrygia/Galatia but also in Rome, where he and Cybele, the Great Mother of the Gods, had a temple on Vatican Hill for six centuries.[729] So similar was the Attis myth to the Christian story that the Christians were forced to resort to their specious argument that the devil had created the Attis cult first to fool Christ's followers.

Three Days in a Tomb and Resurrected

We have already seen Dr. Fear's commentary that Attis was dead for three days and was resurrected, worth reiterating here:

> The youthful Attis after his murder was miraculously brought to life again three days after his demise. The celebration of this cycle of death and renewal was one of the major festivals of the metroac cult. Attis therefore represented a promise of reborn life and as such it is not surprising that we find representations of the so-called mourning Attis as a common tomb motif in the ancient world.[730]

The death and resurrection in three days, the "Passion of Attis," is

726 Jackson, J., 67.
727 Roberts, A. (1890), 6.505.
728 Roberts, A. (1885), 2.176.
729 Walker, B. (1983), 77.
730 Lane, 39

also related by professor Merlin Stone:

> Roman reports of the rituals of Cybele record that the son … was first tied to a tree and then buried. Three days later a light was said to appear in the burial tomb, whereupon Attis rose from the dead, bringing salvation with him in his rebirth.[731]

There is a debate as to *when* the various elements were added to the Attis myth and ritual. Contrary to the apologetic tactic of dismissing all correspondences between Christianity and Paganism, the fact that Attis was at some point a "dying and rising god" is confirmed by Dr. Tryggve Mettinger, a professor of Old Testament Studies at the University of Lund and author of *The Riddle of the Resurrection*: "Since the time of Damascius (sixth cent. AD/CE), Attis seems to have been believed to die and return."[732] By that point, we possess clear discussion in writing of Attis having been resurrected, but when exactly were these rites first celebrated and where? Attis worship is centuries older than Jesus worship and was popular in some parts of the Roman Empire before and well into the Christian era.

It is important to remind oneself that simply because something occurred after the year 1 AD/CE—which was not the dating system used at that time—does not mean that it was influenced by Christianity, as it may have happened where Christianity had never been heard of. In actuality, not much about Christianity emerges until the second century, and there remain to this day places where Christianity is unknown; hence, these locations can still be considered, in effect, pre-Christian.

It is probable that the Attis rites were celebrated long before Christianity was recognized to any meaningful extent. Certainly, since they are mysteries, they could have been celebrated but not recorded previously, especially in pre-Christian times, when the capital punishment for revealing the mysteries was actually carried out.

In the case of Attis, we possess a significant account in Diodorus (3.58.7) of his death and mourning, including the evidently annual ritual creation of his image by priests. Hence, these noteworthy aspects of the Attis myth are clearly pre-Christian. Although Diodorus does not specifically state that Attis was resurrected, the priests parading about with an image of the god is indicative that they considered him risen, as this type of ritual is present in other celebrations for the same reason, such as in the Egyptian festivities celebrating the return of Osiris or the rebirth of Sokar.

Regardless of when these attributes were first associated specifically

731 Stone, 146.

732 Mettinger, 159

with Attis, the dying-and-rising motif of springtime myths is verified as pre-Christian by the fact of its appearance in the story of Tammuz as well as that of the Greek goddess Persephone, also known as Proserpina, both of whose "rise" out of the underworld was celebrated in the Greco-Roman world. That the festivals celebrating the Attis myth represent spring celebrations and not an imitation of Christianity is the most logical conclusion. Indeed, the presence of such a ritual in springtime festivals dating back to the third millennium BCE, as Mettinger relates, certainly makes the case for borrowing by Christians, rather than the other way around.[733]

Buddha

Although most people think of "the Buddha" as one person who lived during the fifth or sixth centuries BCE, like Jesus the Buddha character can also be demonstrated to be a compilation of godmen, legends and sayings of various holy men both preceding and succeeding the period attributed to *the* Buddha (i.e., Siddhartha, Gautama or Gotama).[734] The dates of Buddha's alleged advent continue to be changed, and there have been many eras suggested since antiquity, a reflection of the non-historical nature of the tales about him.

> Gotama was only one of a long series of Buddhas who arise at intervals and who all teach the same doctrine. The names of twentyfour of such Buddhas who appeared before Gotama have been recorded.... It was held that after the death of each Buddha, his religion flourishes for a time and then decays. After it is forgotten, a new Buddha emerges and preaches the lost Dhamma, or Truth.
>
> It seems quite probable in the light of these facts that any number of teachings attributed to "the Buddha" may have been in existence either before or at the time when Gotama was believed to have lived....
>
> The name Gotama is a common one; it is also full of mythological associations. There was admittedly *another* Gotama known to the early Buddhists, who founded an order. So what proof is there that the sayings and doings of different Gotamas may not have been ascribed to one person?[735]

The belief in a historical Buddha is not based on solid and credible scientific evidence but on tradition and surmise. Instead, "the Buddha" is a compilation of characters that share the following in common with

733 Murdock, *RZC*, 15–16, For a discussion of the dating of various aspects of the Attis myth, see *Christ in Egypt*, 392ff.

734 See my book *Suns of God* for more on this subject.

735 Robertson, 75–6.

the Christ figure:

- Like Jesus, Buddha was a divine being, pre-existent in "heaven" before taking birth.[736]
- As at Matthew 1:18–21, 24–25, heavenly beings announce to the Buddha's future stepfather that his wife has conceived miraculously.[737]
- Buddha was born of the virgin Maya,[738] who was considered the "Queen of Heaven."[739]
- He was of royal descent, a prince.[740]
- As at Luke 2:13–14, Buddha's birth was "accompanied by music of the heavenly hosts"[741] and a "marvelous and powerful light."[742]
- After Buddha was born, a "slaughter of the infants was ordered by the tyrant Bimbasara."[743]
- When Buddha was a babe, a saint prophesied he would be great, as did Simeon concerning Christ (Luke 2:25–35).[744]
- As a child he taught his teachers.[745]
- Buddha was presented in the temple, where "the idols fell down before him."[746]
- He began his quest for enlightenment at age 29.[747]
- He crushed a serpent's head.[748]
- As Jesus was tested by the devil (Luke 4:1–13), Buddha was

736 Hopkins, 127–128; Thundy, 80; Lockwood, 17.

737 Lockwood, 22, citing the *Lalitavistara* (6).

738 Lockwood, 19; Thundy, 84ff.

739 Coomaraswamy, 73; Lillie, *BB*, 26. See *Suns of God* and below for a discussion of Buddha's mother as a virgin.

740 Thundy, 81.

741 Lockwood, 3, citing the story of the Bodhisattva in the Tusita Heaven, which is represented in a carving from the eighth century AD/CE (Lockwood, 17.).

742 Thundy, 107.

743 Del Mar, 124; Kloppenborg, 76.

744 Hopkins, 128; Lockwood, 3. Lockwood (30) cites a limestone carving of "The visit of Asita," from the second century AD/CE, found at Amarāvatī and now in the British Museum, London. Lockwood (31) further cites a carving found at NāgājunakoṇDa from the third century AD/CE with the same pericope of the sage Asita visiting the newborn Bodhisattva and declaring that the babe would become a "perfectly accomplished Buddha."

745 Carpenter, J.E., "Obligations of the New Testament to Buddhism," 973.

746 Hopkins, 128.

747 Thundy, 54.

748 Dameron, 53.

tempted by Mara, the evil one, who offered him "universal dominion."[749]

- Buddha is surrounded by animals and attended by "angels" (*devas*),[750] while Jesus goes among wild animals and is ministered to by angels (Mark 1:13).
- He reformed religion and prohibited idolatry,[751] as a "sower of the word,"[752] and preached "the establishment of a kingdom of righteousness."[753]
- He performed miracles and wonders, healed the sick,[754] fed 500 men from a "small basket of cakes."[755]
- Buddha walks on water[756] and inspires a disciple to walk on water, too.[757]
- His apparition is witnessed by a Buddhist disciple, Kasyapa who, traveling with 500 monks, encounters an unknown personage from whom he learns of the death of Buddha. Likewise, Luke has the (similarly named) disciple Kleopas encounter an unknown personage on the road to Emmaus." (Humphreys)
- He preached a "sermon on the mount"[758] and taught chastity, temperance, tolerance, compassion, love, and the equality of all.[759]

---

749 Carpenter, J.E., "ONTB," 974; Lockwood, 3, citing a carving/stupa from Sāṇchī, dating to the first century BCE (Lockwood, 36.).

750 Lockwood, 3, citing the *Majjhima-Nikaya* 36 (Mahāsaccakasutta) and a carving/stupa from Sāṇchī, dating from the first century BCE (Lockwood, 39.).

751 Dobbins, 212; Wallbank, 172.

752 Mead, *GG*, 133.

753 Carpenter, J.E., *CRW*, 48.

754 Carpenter, J.E., "ONTB," 974.

755 Carpenter, J.E., *FTG*, 89.

756 Lockwood, 3, citing the Sanchi stupa from the first century BCE. Lockwood (40) concludes: "In India, accounts of the paranormal ability of walking on water are as old as the ancient epic, *Mahabharata*—long before the time of the Buddha.

757 Whitney, 8, 361; Aśvaghosha/Beal, 222; Garbe, *IC*, 56. Lockwood (41) cites the text *The Silnishasa-Jataka.* A "careful and comparative study of the Indian and Christian miracles of walking on the water" was produced by W. Norman Brown, who concluded that the two stories were not devised independently and noted that the Buddhist pericope can be found on the Sanchi stupa/stone monument, built around 250 BCE, thus predating the Christian story by centuries. (Lockwood, 41.)

758 Carpenter, J.E., "ONTB," 975.

759 Carpenter, J.E., "ONTB," 977–978.

- Buddha was received in his native city with a triumphal welcome.[760]
- Buddha has a "last supper" before his death,[761] which, like Christ, he predicts three times.[762]
- He was betrayed by a disciple, who led others to kill him.[763]
- "Buddha dies between 2 trees."
- Some of his persecutors became his disciples.[764]
- A tremendous earthquake occurred upon Buddha's death.[765]
- Buddha died,[766] suffered for three days in hell,[767] and was resurrected.[768]
- "The dead Buddha is burned and it is the smoke of his corpse which rises– the true 'resurrection.'" (From a second/first century BCE play 'Samghabhedavastu' (*Mahâparinirvâna sûtra*)[769]
- At his birth, he was pronounced ruler of the world and presented with "costly jewels and precious substances."[770]
- Buddha was baptized in water, with the "Spirit of God" or "Holy Ghost" present.[771]
- His followers were obliged to take vows of poverty and to renounce the world.[772]
- He was transfigured on a mount, when it was said that his face "shone as the brightness of the sun and moon."[773]
- In some traditions, he died on a cross,[774] and he is depicted in cruciform, with arms outstretched.
- He was resurrected, as his coverings were unrolled from his

760 Carpenter, J.E., "ONTB," 976.
761 Humphreys: "The death episode begins for Buddha crossing the Ganges at Magadha, from whence he goes on to Kusinagari for a last meal."
762 Humphreys
763 Carpenter, J.E., "ONTB," 976.
764 Carpenter, J.E., "ONTB," 976.
765 Carpenter, J.E., "ONTB," 977.
766 See also my book *Suns of God*, 357ff, as to a discussion of whether or not Buddha was "crucified." See also below concerning "Buddhist Crucifixion."
767 Thundy, 102; Del Mar, 124.
768 Paine, 102.
769 Humphreys (2005), 105–6.
770 Doane, 290.
771 Doane, 292.
772 Doane, 294.
773 Doane, 292.
774 Pike, 290; Higgins, I, 159, 444.

body and his tomb was opened by supernatural powers.[775]

- His death is accompanied by darkness. (Humphreys)
- Buddha ascended bodily to Nirvana or "heaven."
- He was called "Lord," "Master," the "Light of the World," "God of Gods," "Father of the World," "Almighty and All-knowing Ruler," "Redeemer of All," "Holy One," the "Author of Happiness," "Possessor of All," the "Omnipotent," the "Supreme Being," the "Eternal One."[776]
- He was considered the "Sin Bearer," "Good Shepherd,"[777] the "Carpenter,"[778] the "Infinite and Everlasting,"[779] and the "Alpha and Omega."[780]
- He came to fulfill, not destroy, the law.[781]
- Buddha is to return "in the latter days" to restore order and to judge the dead."[782]

Concerning the dates of various Buddhist inscriptions that contains a number of these parallels, in *Buddhism's Relation to Christianity*, Dr. Michael Lockwood, a professor at Madras Christian College in India for over three decades, remarks:

> [There are] several stone inscriptions of King Aśōka, who, in the third century BCE, ruled over most of India, and beyond, into what is now Afghanistan. These inscriptions reveal the spreading abroad of the Buddhist doctrine (Dharma), as far as Egypt and other countries around the Mediterranean. There are many parallels between Buddhist doctrine and Christian doctrine.[783]

Buddha's Birth

According to ancient Buddhist legend, the sage's mother was a "chaste wife, into whom miraculously entered in the shape of a white elephant the future Buddha, who subsequently came out of her right side."[784] Sanskrit scholar Dr. Edward W. Hopkins states that this miraculous birth story undoubtedly dates to "as early as the third century BC and perhaps earlier."[785] Indeed, the miraculous birth of Buddha, as well as

775 Doane, 293.
776 Doane, 116.
777 Blavatsky, IU, II, 209, 537–538.
778 Massey, HJMC, 150.
779 Mead, 134.
780 Doane, 292.
781 Doane, 294.
782 Doane, 293.
783 Lockwood, 3–4.
784 Hopkins, 129.
785 Hopkins, 130.

his temptation, are carved on monuments that date to 150 BCE or older.[786]

In the fourth century of the Common Era, Church father St. Jerome (*Adversus Jovinianum* 1.42) discussed Buddha specifically as having been born through the side of a *virgin*:

> Among the Gymnosophists of India, the belief has been handed down from generation to generation as authentic that a virgin gave birth to Buddha, the founder of their religion, out of her side.[787]

Jerome's words—"handed down from generation to generation" and "*opinionis auctoritas traditur*"—indicate not that the motif had been recently copied from Christianity by Indian monks or priests but that it was a tradition of some age.

Regarding the Buddhist birth tradition, Dr. Thundy comments:

> Virginal conception or *virginitas ante partum*, in the physical sense, means that the divine child is conceived in the mother's womb without the agency of a male progenitor, that the divine child descends directly into the mother's womb, and that she should not have had any children before. The canonical account of the miraculous conception of Buddha is given in the Discourse on the Wondrous and Marvelous Events (*Acchariyabhutadhammasutta*), in which Ananda, the favorite disciple, recites to Buddha the events of conception and birth.

In the *Majjhimanikaya*, we read:

> [When] the future Buddha is descending into his mother's womb, she is pure from sexuality, has abstained from taking life, from theft, from evil conduct in lusts, from lying, and from all kinds of wine and strong drink, which are a cause of irreligion.[788]

The story of Buddha's birth revealing the purity of his mother can also be found in the Buddhist text the *Lalitavistara* (3). Edmunds asserts the date to be unknown, "but the cycle of legends therein was known in China in the first century, from a Buddhist source."[789]

Buddhist Crucifixion

In the texts, we find the curious motif of a Buddhist figure having been "crucified." In this regard, concerning the Buddhist influence on the gospel story, scholar of Buddhism and Sanskrit Dr. Christian Lindt-

786 Hopkins, 137.

787 Hanna, 166.

788 Edmunds, 1.173.

789 Edmunds, 1.174. Edmunds points out that some Buddhists perceive Christ's birth not as "virginal" but more like the immaculate conception. See Thundy for a scholarly distinction wherein *parthenos* is appropriate, as in *virginitas ante partum*.

ner writes:

> The Sanskrit manuscripts prove:
>
> • Everything that Jesus says or does was already said or done by the Buddha.
>
> • Jesus, therefore, is a mere literary fiction.
>
> • The Last Supper was the Last Supper of the Buddha.
>
> • Baptism in the name of the Father, the Son and the Holy Spirit was baptism in the name of the Buddha, the Dharma and the Samgha.
>
> • All the miracles performed by Jesus had already been performed by the Buddha.
>
> • The twelve disciples of Jesus were, in fact, the twelve disciples of the Buddha.
>
> • It was king Gautama—not Jesus—who was crucified.[790]
>
> • It was Tathâgata—not Jesus—who was resurrected.
>
> • There is nothing in the Gospels, no person, no event, that cannot be traced back to cognate persons, events or circumstances in the Buddhist gospels.
>
> • Jesus is a Buddha disguised as a new Jewish legislator, teacher, Messiah and king of Israel.
>
> • The Gospels, forming the foundation of Christianity, are, therefore, typical Buddhist literature, fiction, designed for missionaries whose language was Greek.

Concerning this purported "crucifixion" or impalement of an important Buddhist figure, related in, among others, a Buddhist text dating to the first century BCE—the *Samghabhedavastu/ Mahâparinirvâna sutra*[791]—Dr. Zacharias P. Thundy states:

> This is the story of Gautama, a holy man, who was wrongfully condemned to die on the cross for murdering the courtesan Bhadra. Gautama is impaled on the cross, and his mentor Krishna Dvapayana visits him and enters into a long dialogue, at the end

790 Lindtner, 87ff. In private correspondence, Dr. Lindtner informed me that there were three sources for the crucifixion story of Buddha: the *Lotus Sutra*, the *Mahaparinirvana Sutra* and the *Samghabhedavastu*, of which the MPS is a part. He specifies that the episode is in the *Mûlasarvâstivâdavinaya recension* of the MPS.

791 Concerning this episode, Thundy specifically states: "We have been able to identify two major Sanskrit sources for the trial narratives. A. Sangabhedavastu of the Mahaparinirvanasutra: Professor Lindtner has identified the Sangabhedavastu section of the Mahaparinirvanasutra of the Vinayapitaka of the Mulasarvastivadins. I have studied this text carefully and have arrived at some significant conclusions." Again, Lindtner specifies that the episode is in the Mûlasarvâstivâdavinaya ("MSV") *recension* of the MPS.

of which he dies at the place of skulls after engendering two off-spring, the progenitors of the Ikshavaku Dynasty.[792]

As is evident from the remarks of Dr. Burkhard Scherer, a Classical Philologist, Indologist and Lecturer in Religious Studies (Buddhist and Hindu Studies) at Canterbury Christ Church University, the fact that there is "massive" Buddhist influence in the gospels has been well-known among scholars for a long time. Says Dr. Scherer:

> Just recently, Duncan M. Derrett published his excellent *The Bible and the Buddhists* (Sardini, Bornato [Italy] 2001). With Derrett, I am convinced that there are many Buddhist narratives in the Gospels.

Because of this non-historicity and of the following characteristics of the Buddha myth, which are not widely known but which are very old, we can see that Buddha is yet another personification of the ancient, universal mythos.

In addition to the characteristics of the "teaching/savior god" as outlined above, the Buddhistic influence in Christianity includes: Renouncing the world and its riches, including sex and family; the brotherhood of man; the virtue of charity and turning the cheek; monasticism and conversion. That Buddhism preceded Christianity is undeniable, as is its influence in the world long prior to the beginning of the Christian era. As Walker relates:

> Established 500 years before Christianity and widely publicized throughout the Middle East, Buddhism exerted more influence on early Christianity than church fathers liked to admit, since they viewed Oriental religions in general as devil worship.... Stories of the Buddha and his many incarnations circulated incessantly throughout the ancient world, especially since Buddhist monks traveled to Egypt, Greece, and Asia Minor four centuries before Christ, to spread their doctrines.... Many scholars have pointed out that the basic tenets of Christianity were basic tenets of Buddhism first; but it is also true that the ceremonies and trappings of both religions were more similar than either has wanted to acknowledge.[793]

792 "The Sanskrit Sources of the Gospel Narratives of the Trial and Death," jesusisbuddha.com/PDF/Thundy.pdf See also Lindtner, 87–97. Although there are many "Buddhas," a number of whom appear to make up the composite character of "the Buddha," this figure is evidently not one of them. The point, however, is that evidently pre-Christian Buddhist texts contain a crucifixion scene which parallels that found in the gospels.

793 Walker, B. (1983), 123.

As to Buddhistic influence in the specific area where the Christ drama purportedly took place, Larson contends:

> Buddhist missionaries penetrated every portion of the then known world, including Greece, Egypt, Baktria, Asia Minor, and the Second Persian Empire. Palestine must have been permeated by Buddhist ideology during the first century.... The literature of India proves that Jesus drew heavily upon Buddhism, directly or indirectly, to obtain not simply the content of His ethics, but the very form in which it was delivered. Both Gautama and Jesus found parable effective.[794]

Indeed, it seems that a number of Jesus's parables were direct lifts from Buddhism; for example, that of the prodigal son, the Buddhist version of which appears in chapter 4 of the *Saddharmapundarika-Sutra* (the *Lotus Sutra*).[795]

The existence of Buddhism in the Middle East during the Christian era is acknowledged by Christian apologists themselves such as Cyril and Clement of Alexandria, who said the Samaneans or Buddhists were priests of Persia.[796]

Black Buddhas

Furthermore, a number of scholars have pushed back the origins of Buddhism centuries to millennia prior to the alleged advent of Gautama Buddha. True "Buddhism" is much more ancient than the legends of *the* Buddha, since ancient Indian temples long predating the era of "Gautama" contain depictions of the Buddha as a *black* man, not only in color but in feature.[797] In Higgins's opinion, Buddhism has been the most widespread religion on the planet, also found in England, where it was the religion of the Druids. He also states that the "Hermes of Egypt, or Buddha, was well-known to the ancient Canaanites" (i.e., the people who preceded and in large part became the Israelites). Therefore, Buddhism was no doubt an early influence on Hebrew thought and religion.

Buddhism in the West

Long before the word "missionary" came to be synonymous with Christianity Buddhist monks ('*dharma-bhanakas*') were traipsing across Asia. Travelling the Silk and Spice Routes they spread their doctrines all the way from Khotan in central Asia to Antioch, Athens and Alexandria in the west.

One such visit is documented in 20 BC in Athens. A Buddhist philos-

---

794 Larson, 142-8.

795 Acker, 316. See *Sacred Books of the East*, 21, p. 98ff.

796 Higgins, I, 163.

797 Higgins, I, 161.

opher, Zarmarus, part of an embassy from India, made a doctrinal point by setting himself alight. His tomb became a tourist attraction and is mentioned by several historians.

Clearly, the evangelists of Buddha were committed to their cause. Is it simply coincidence that the hero of the Buddhist tale is just a tad similar to the Christian superman?[798]

In the *Bhagavad Gita* (10:4), the phrase "spiritual intelligence" is transliterated as *buddhir* and *buddhiḥ*.[799] Elsewhere (10.8), "the spiritually intelligent" is rendered *budhāḥ*. At 10.10, the "spiritual intelligence" is rendered *buddhi*. There is little reason to suppose that in antiquity this correspondence with *buddha* went unnoticed. Indeed, from such motifs as both figures having mothers named "Maya" or "Maia," it appears that the myth of Buddha was "confounded" or, as so often happens, deliberately merged with stories of *Budha* (i.e., Mercury/Hermes). This sort of synthesis has happened continually in religions around the world since time immemorial; hence, it would be unsurprising in this instance as an explanation for some of these correlations.

Dionysus/Bacchus

Dionysus or, as he was later known, Bacchus, Bacchos, Iacchos or Iacchus, is perceived as Greek, but he is clearly an older "foreign" god. There is evidence that Dionysus was related to, or significantly a remake of, the Egyptian god Osiris, whose cult extended throughout a large part of the ancient world for thousands of years. Dionysus's religion was well-developed in Thrace, northeast of Greece, and Phrygia, which became Galatia, where Attis also later reigned. The son of Zeus and the Father or Helios the Sun,[800] Dionysus is best remembered for the rowdy celebrations in his name, the Bacchanalia,[801] but he had many other functions and evidently contributed several attributes to the Jesus character.

- Dionysus was born of a virgin[802] on "December 25" or the winter solstice[803]

798 Humphreys (2005), 98.

799 *Bhagavad Gita*, www.bhagavad-gita.org/Gita/verse-10-04.html

800 The emperor Julian (*Orat.* 4.152c-d; 5.179b) held that Dionysus was the son of both Helios and Zeus, respectively. (Julian/Wright, 419, 501.)

801 Hence his depiction as the Otis Campbell of Olympus in Disney's *Fantasia*.

802 Campbell (1991), 4.27; Rahner, 139–140; Campbell, Mythic Image [fix], 34; Diodorus; Minucius, Commodius 12; Hugh-Jones, 108; Rigoglioso (2009), 95; White, 183; Rigoglioso (2010), 111.

803 Macrobius, 1.18; Rahner, 139–140, 141.

- Bacchus is the son of the heavenly Father.[804]
- Like Jesus and the biblical God (John 10:30), Dionysus and his father are one, the son representing the father incarnate.[805]
- As the Holy Child,[806] he was placed in a cradle/crib/manger "among beasts."[807]
- At his birth, Dionysus is approached by groups of three individuals each.[808]
- He was a traveling teacher who performed miracles.[809]
- He was the God of the Vine, and turned water into wine.[810]
- Dionysus rode in a "triumphal procession" on an ass.[811]
- Like Jesus during his passion, Dionysus was a "man of suffering."[812]
- He was a sacred king killed[813] and eaten in a eucharistic ritual for fecundity and purification.[814]
- The god traveled into the underworld to rescue his loved one, arising from the land of the dead after three days.[815]
- Dionysus rose from the dead on March 25[816] and ascended into

---

804 Dionysus's father, the god of the sky/heaven, Zeus, bears the epithet *Pater* or "Father." See, for example, Aeschylus, *Seven Against Thebes* 512; Kerenyi, 77.This divine title evolved from the Vedic sky father Dyaus Pita through Zeus Patera to Jupiter and the Christian Deus Pater.
805 Kerenyi, 119, 114.
806 Meyer, M., 19.
807 Clasby, 51. The Greek word for "manger" in the New Testament to describe where Jesus was placed is φτνη or *phatne*, which means not only "manger" but also "crib." (Strong's G5336; *The Pocket Oxford Classical Greek Dictionary*, 338) Dionysus is styled "Liknites," or "he of the cradle," the word *liknon* referring to a basket or cradle, in which babes are often placed. (Kerenyi, 44; Macnicol, 274; Clausen, 230; Horstmanshoff, 203.)
808 See the image of Dionysus's birth, where he is held by Hermes and handed to an unidentified goddess, in the Museum of Naples. While the wise men or kings in the gospel story are not numbered, they are said to bear *three* gifts, and Christian tradition for many centuries has numbered them at three.
809 Pliny,
810 Pliny, 2.103; Pliny/Holland, 1.140.
811 For example, Hobgood-Oster, 27.
812 Kerenyi, 70.
813 Kerenyi, 110, 116.
814 Campbell (1991), 4.23.
815 Classical Journal, 29.92.
816 This contention is evidently based on the fact of the Dionysia or Mysteries of Dionysus around the vernal equinox, beginning about March 25 and ending on March 30. (Hastings, C., 10) Regarding the Dionysian spring

heaven.[817]

- Bacchus was deemed "Father,"[818] "Liberator"[819] and "Savior."[820]
- Dionysus was evidently considered the "Only Begotten Son,"[821] "King of Kings,"[822] "God of Gods,"[823] "Sin Bearer,"[824] "Redeemer,"[825] "Anointed One"[826] and the "Alpha and Omega."[827]
- He was identified with the Ram or Lamb.[828]

---

festival of Anthesteria, Burkert (241) remarks: "The rhythm of the three-day festival is easy to discern; a certain similarity with the sequence of Good Friday and Easter cannot be overlooked."

817 Justin, *First Apology*, 21; Roberts, A. (1879), 2.25.

818 Macrobius 1.18.1; Macrobius/Kaster, 1.245.

819 Adrados, 327.

820 One of Bacchus's epithets is Soter or "savior, deliverer." (Taylor, B., 528)

821 Like Attis and others, Dionysus appears to have been μονογενής, *monogenes* or "only begotten." See, for example, Knight, R.P., xxii. See also Müller (1893), x.

822 Bonnefoy, 163; Frazer, *GB*, 451. Frazer cites Proclus as saying: "Dionysus was the last king of the gods appointed by Zeus. For his father set him on the kingly throne, and placed in his hand the sceptre, and made him king of all the gods of the world."

823 See note 861 above.

824 Hardwicke, 217. This contention appears to come from an analysis by Rev. Alexander Hislop of the name "Dionysos," which he contends signifies "sin bearer." (Hislop, 71-2) In view of Dionysus's salvational function, such a role would be expected.

825 Dupuis, 135; Stoyanov, 30.

826 Although Dionysus may not have been called explicitly "Christos" or "Anointed One" in Greek, his corpse as "Osiris-Dionysus" was anointed in myrrh, making him *christed*. (Freke and Gandy, 56, 61) Bacchus was perhaps also a "Chrestos" or "Good One," as were Isis and others in the pantheon around the Mediterranean. Here it should be recalled that Osiris, Isis's husband, was Dionysus's Egyptian counterpart.

827 This notion may derive from the fact that Dionysus worship became ubiquitous, spreading wherever the vine and wine became popular. See Kerenyi, xxiv, etc. Doane (193) comments: "Beausobre quotes the inscription on a monument of Bacchus, thus: 'C'est moi, dit il, qui vous conduis, C'est moi, qui vous conserve, ou qui vous sauve; Je sui Alpha et Omega.'" Beausobre (55–56) explains this inscription as having to do with the Gnostic "Abraxas," a name he breaks down into two words. One of these, *Abros*, is an epithet of the sun and signifies the god/theonym IAO spelled *Iota Alpha Omega*, to whom was assimilated Bacchus, both representing solar aspects, per Macrobius and others. Hence, the inscription would be applicable to Bacchus: "It is me, says he, who guides you; it is me, who protects you, or who saves you; I am Alpha and Omega."

828 William Smith (1850a:1.1046) relates that in order to protect his son,

- As Jesus was the sacrificial lamb, Dionysus's sacrifice is represented by the goat.[829]
- His sacrificial title of "Dendrites"[830] or "Young Man of the Tree" indicates he was hung on a tree or crucified.[831]

One with the Sun

Citing "Orpheus" (*PEG*r fr. 542–43), Macrobius (1.18.18) identifies Dionysus as a sun god: "The sun, whom they call with the surname Dionysus."[832] He also cites another Orphic verse: "Zeus is one, Hades is one, the sun is one, Dionysus is one."[833] According to Church father Eusebius, Pagan writer Porphyry (c. 235–c. 305 AD/CE) wrote of the sun that "the fiery power of his revolving and circling motion whereby he ripens the crops, is called Dionysus."[834]

Moreover, since (Sabazian) Zeus and Dionysus essentially were "different names of the same character, the Son of Rhea,"[835] Bacchus and his father shared many attributes and epithets. Also, as Robert Graves says, "Dionysus Sabazius was the original Jehovah of the Passover," identified with Yahweh by Plutarch. [836]

The True Vine

Dionysus's role as the god of wine is echoed in the later Christian story of Jesus multiplying the jars of wine at the wedding feast of Cana (John 2:1–9). Concerning this miracle, biblical scholar Dr. A.J. Mattill remarks:

> This story is really the Christian counterpart to the pagan legends of Dionysus, the Greek god of wine, who at his annual festival in his temple of Elis filled three empty kettles with wine—no water needed! And on the fifth of January wine instead of water gushed from his temple at Andros. If we believe Jesus' miracle,

---

Zeus changes Dionysus into a ram. In addition, Dionysus is depicted in ancient texts—for example, *Dionysalexandros* by Athenian comic poet Cratinus (519–422 BCE)—as otherwise assuming the appearance of a ram as a disguise, also described as a "sheep." (Bakola, 262-3.)

829 Kerenyi, 80.

830 Dyer, 106, 159, 176.

831 Walker, B. (1983), 237.

832 Kaster, 255.

833 Kaster, 255. "*PEGr*" is the *Poetae Epici Graeci*, ed. A. Bernabé, Stuttgart, 1996.

834 Eusebius, *Evangelicae Praeparationis* ("The Preparation or the Gospel"), III, XI, 112d-115a; Eusebius/Gifford, 122-125.

835 Graves, R., 335.

836 Graves, R., 335.

why should we not believe Dionysus's?[837]

The Virgin Birth

According to the most common Theban tradition, Dionysus was the son of the god Zeus and the mortal woman Semele, who apparently was originally a goddess.[838] In the more archaic Cretan version of the story, which the pre-Christian Greek historian Diodorus Siculus (6.75.4) relates, Dionysus was the son of Zeus and Persephone,[839]the daughter of Demeter also called Kore ("Maiden"), who is styled a "virgin goddess."[840] Joseph Campbell explicitly calls Semele a "virgin":

> While the maiden goddess sat there, peacefully weaving a mantle on which there was to be a representation of the universe, her mother contrived that Zeus should learn of her presence; he approached her in the form of an immense snake. And the virgin conceived the ever-dying, ever-living god of bread and wine, Dionysus, who was born and nurtured in that cave, torn to death as a babe and resurrected.[841]

In *The Cult of the Divine Birth in Ancient Greece* Dr. Marguerite Rigoglioso concludes: "Semele was also likely a holy parthenos by virtue of the fact that she gave birth to Dionysus via her union with Zeus (Hesiod, *Theogony* 940)."[842] The fact that Persephone is associated with parthenogenesis, the scholarly term for "virgin birth," lends credence to the notion that Dionysus was virgin-born. As related further by Rigoglioso in *Virgin Mother Goddesses of Antiquity*:

Persephone's connection with the parthenogenetic pomegranate is attested in text and iconography. In speaking directly about the Eleusinian Mysteries, Clement of Alexandria (*Exhortation to the Greeks* 2:16) informs us that the pomegranate tree was believed to have sprung from the drops of the blood of Dionysus.[843]

The later Christian apologist Athenagoras depicts the impregnation of Persephone by Zeus as a snake as an act of "rape," which Kerenyi says is "no doubt coarsening its style."[844] Indeed, from Rigoglioso's

837 Leedom, 125.

838 Kerenyi, 107.

839 See also Firmicus Maternus, *De errore profanarum religionem* 5.5. [chck] Kerenyi, 110.

840 Kerenyi (111) relates that the Cretans claimed both Kore and Demeter as Dionysus's mother.

841 Campbell (1991), 4.27.

842 Rigoglioso (2009), 95.

843 Rigoglioso (2010), 111.

844 Kerenyi, 112.

survey and conclusions, it appears that earlier myths were made misogynistic as the patriarchy increased its influence. It must be recalled that Persephone/Kore was indeed a *virgin* goddess,[845] reflecting a nature myth, and not a real person who could be "raped" by anyone, whether Zeus or another. The fact that Kore was considered the virgin mother of Aion well into the Common Era depicts the maintenance of this old nature myth concerning the pristine state of *spring*. In this nature myth, the father god (Zeus) "visits his hidden daughter (Kore) in a cave, and she bears him to himself as his own son,"[846] a myth similar to the biblical nativity story.

Born on December 25

As with Jesus, December 25 and January 6 are both traditional birth dates in the Dionysian myth and simply represent the period of the winter solstice. Indeed, the winter-solstice date of the Greek sun and wine god Dionysus was originally observed in early January but was eventually placed on December 25, as related by Latin writer Macrobius (c. 400 AD/CE). Rahner (141) states:

> As to the dates, Norden has shown that the change from January 6 to December 25 can be explained as the result of the reform introduced by the more accurate Julian calendar into the ancient Egyptian calculation which had fixed January 6 as the date of the winter solstice.

Regardless, the effect is the same: the winter sun god is born around this time, when the shortest day of the year begins to become longer.

The Church father Epiphanius (fourth cent.) discussed the birth of the god Aion, son of the Greek goddess Persephone or Kore, at the time of the winter solstice. Christian theologian Rev. Dr. Hugo Rahner remarks:

> We know that Aion was at this time beginning to be regarded as identical with Helios and Helios with Dionysus ... because [according to Macrobius] Dionysus was the symbol of the sun.... He is made to appear small at the time of the winter solstice, when upon a certain day the Egyptians take him out of the crypt, because on this the shortest day of the year it is as though he were a little child.... Macrobius transfers [this feast] to the day of the winter solstice, December 25.[847]

Miracles

The miracles of Dionysus are legendary. As the god of the vine, Dionysus is depicted in ancient texts as traveling around teaching ag-

845 Kerenyi, 114.
846 Kerenyi, 114.
847 Rahner, 139–140.

riculture, as well as doing various other miracles, such as in Homer's *Iliad*, dating to the ninth century BCE, and in *The Bacchae* of Euripides, the famous Greek playwright who lived around 480 to 406 BCE.

Riding the Ass

Historian of Christianity Dr. Laura Hobgood-Oster remarks:

> [The] ass connects Christianity to Roman traditions. As Thomas Matthews states: "Early Christian art is rich with Dionysiac associations." He also points out that in "classical art the ass is common in Dionysiac processions.... In addition, a mule, offspring of an ass and a horse, is the common transport of Dionysus himself." Thus just as visual portrayals show Jesus and Mary riding on an ass in the flight to Egypt (Matthew 2:14–15), so Dionysus mounts an ass ... making even more interesting connections to Christianity.[848]

Death, Journey into the Underworld, Resurrection and Ascension

Dionysus's death and resurrection were famous in ancient times, so much so that Christian father Origen (c. 184–c. 254) felt the need to address them in his *Contra Celsum* (IV, XVI-XVII), comparing them (unfavorably, of course) to those of Christ. By Origen's time, these Dionysian mysteries had already been celebrated for centuries.

Dionysus/Bacchus's resurrection or revival after having been torn to pieces or otherwise killed earned him the epithet of "twice born." The journey into the underworld is deemed *katabasis*, while the ascension out of it is the ἀνάστασις or *anastasis* (G386), the very term used in the New Testament (Matt. 22:23, etc.) and elsewhere to describe Jesus's resurrection. It was said that Dionysus/Bacchus "slept three nights with Proserpine [Persephone]," evidently referring to the god's journey into the underworld to visit his mother.[849] Like Jesus, the god was supposed to have "ascended to heaven," as Justin Martyr and others mention.[850] Note that Dionysus is depicted here as an adult, rising out of the underworld after death, with a horse-driven chariot so typical of a sun god. One major astrotheological meaning of this motif is the sun's entrance into and exit from the cave (womb) of the world at the winter solstice.

The Eucharist

As Campbell points out:

> Dionysus-Bacchus-Zagreus—or, in the older, Sumero-Babylonian myths, Dumuzi-absu, Tammuz ... whose blood, in this chalice to be drunk, is the pagan prototype of the wine of the

848 Hobgood-Oster, 27.

849 Classical Journal, 29.92.

850 *First Apology*, 21; Roberts, A., 2.170.

sacrifice of the Mass, which is transubstantiated by the words of consecration into the blood of the Son of the Virgin.[851]

Kerenyi describes the "great Dionysian sacrifice, where the sacrificial animal represents the suffering, dismembered god."[852]

Divine Epithets and Roles

Dionysus is called *Soter* or "Savior" in various inscriptions, including a bronze coin from the Thracian city of Maroneia dating to circa 400–350 BCE.[853]

On Dionysus/Bacchus being labeled the "Alpha and Omega," Rev. Isaac de Beausobre discusses an ancient inscription in which the mysterious figure of Abraxas, whom Beausobre equates with Dionysus/Bacchus, says, "I am the Alpha and Omega."[854]

In an Orphic hymn, Phanes-Dionysus is styled by the Greek title *Protogonos* or "first-born" of Zeus, also translated at times as "only-begotten son," although that term is really the translation of μονογενής (*monogenes*) as in, for example, John 1:14. The Greek word μονογενής appears at: Judges 11:34, where it is translated "only child"; Psalm 21:21 (Masoretic 22:20), translated as "my darling," "my precious life"; Psalm 24:16, rendered "I am desolate," "I am alone"; and Psalm 34:17, translated "my darling, "my precious life" and "my only life," etc. The corresponding Hebrew term is יחיד or *yachiyd* (H3173), which means "only," "only one," "solitary," "one" or "only begotten son." It is also a word used by pre-Christian writers such as: Hesiod (*WD*, 376; *Theo.*, 426), referring to an "only son," "only member of a kind"; Herodotus (*Hist.*, 7.221), "only son";[855] and Plato (*Timaeus*, 31b, 92c), in reference to the "one-generated" or "sole of its kind" Heaven.[856]

Like Jesus in his unity with the Father, Dionysus is called *Pater*, or "father" in Greek.

"The image of the Maenads dancing around Dionysus Dendrites on the vessel in Berlin, SM F 2290, belongs among the most impressive of

---

851 Campbell (1991), 4.23.

852 Kerenyi, 116.

853 Wright, F., 30. See also Adrados, 327.

854 Lardner, 8.379; Beausobre, 56.

855 Herodotus, tr. A. D. Godley (Cambridge, MA: Harvard University Press. 1920).

856 Liddell and Scott, "μονο-γενής," www.perseus.tufts.edu/hopper/text?doc=Perseus:text:1999.04.0057:entry=monogenh/s; *Plato in Twelve Volumes*, v. 9. tr. W.R.M. Lamb (Cambridge, MA: Harvard University Press, 1925); London, William Heinemann Ltd. 1925.

those relating to the cult of the wine god left to us."[857] Chisholm, et al., remark: "His earliest images were of wood with branches still attached in parts, whence he was called Dionysus Dendrites, an allusion to his protection of trees generally."[858] The hanging of a god on a tree (actually a sacrificial proxy) was a common motif of ritual sacrifice in antiquity.

Again, while it is difficult to tell if Dionysus himself was ever actually *called* "anointed" ("Christos"), Lactantius (*Div. Inst.* 1.21.45) tells us that during the festival of Dionysus "the people … prance about in dance naked, oiled and garlanded."[859] Since the solar-vegetative god Dionysus was known to bestow upon his followers the miracle of producing not only wine but also olives/oil (Ovid, *Metamorphoses*, 13.780),[860] and since Greeks frequently oiled up during sacred rites, Dionysus, too, could be considered "oiled" or "anointed." Moreover, the famed "navel of the world," the stone *omphalos*, which was used to hold the anointing oil in many sacred sites, has specifically been associated with Dionysus, as at his tomb at Delphi.[861]

Hjelde says that "the reborn Dionysus is called *luseus*—redeemer or saviour."[862] In the Orphic hymns, Dionysus is called *Luseus* or "Liberator."[863]

Regarding Dionysus and Jesus, Dr. Miguel Herrero de Jáuregui states that "the similarities … between Dionysian and Christian spiritual experience explain their similar roles as savior gods and the shared conception of them as sons of a divine Father."[864]

As Walker states, Dionysus was "a prototype of Christ, with a cult center at Jerusalem," where during the first century BCE he was worshipped by Jews.[865] One of Dionysus/Bacchus's symbols was ΙΗΣ—"IHS" or "IES," which became identified with Jesus. With the Latin terminus "–us" becomes "Iesus" or "Jesus," as prominently used in

857 Cancik, et al., 8.54.

858 Chisholm, 8.287.

859 Lactantius/Bowen, 113.

860 Ovid/Lombardo, 371.

861 *Janus*, 18: "An ancient vase painting shows Dionysos seated on a circular concave seat, called the omphalos ('navel'), one of the conical or pyramidal stones, revered in the Greek world, which he brought along with him from Delphi."

862 Hjelde, 149

863 Graves, R. (1978), 366.

864 Herrero de Jáuregui, 334.

865 Walker, B., 236. Diyagi-Mendels (107) remarks: "The cult of Dionysus was also one of the most popular… in the land of Israel," having become thus with the arrival of Alexander in the third century.

Catholic liturgy and iconography.[866]

Concerning Dionysus and his influence on Christianity, Larson concludes:

> Dionysus became the universal savior-god of the ancient world. And there has never been another like unto him: the first to whom his attributes were accredited, we call Osiris; with the death of paganism, his central characteristics were assumed by Jesus Christ.[867]

Like Jesus the Nazarene, Dionysus is the "true Vine," and the grape imagery is important to both cults. As Walker says:

> [The grapevine] was preeminently an incarnation of Dionysus, or Bacchus, in his role of sacrificial savior. His immolation was likened to the pruning of the vine, necessary to its seasonal rebirth.... In Syria and Babylon the vine was a sacred tree of life. Old Testament writers adopted it as an emblem of the chosen people, and New Testament writers made it an emblem of Christ (John 15:1, 5). When accompanied by wheat sheaves in sacred art, the vine signified the blood (wine) and body (bread) of the savior: an iconography that began in paganism and was soon adopted by early Christianity.[868]

On Crete, Dionysus was called Iasius,[869] a title also of the son of God/Zeus associated with the Orphic mysteries of Samothrace,[870] who has been identified with Dionysus and who was promulgated by the

---

866 Many older scholars and researchers contended for this etymological development, such as Kavanagh (2.192): "As to the well-known monogram of both Jesus and Bacchus, and which is, in Roman characters, equal to IES, and also of JESUS; but it is not the root of either, More recent writers who contend for the same are Dr. Robert Lima (2005, 114), citing George Ryley Scott (1949, 169). Let us recall the Hebrew abbreviation for Yahweh of the "sacred bigrammaton" יה or *ie*.

867 Larson, 82.

868 Walker, *WDSSO*, 456.

869 Mackay, 2.111.

870 Lewis, N., 28, translating Maurus Servius Honoratus's commentary on Vergil's *Aeneid*, book 3, commline 167, where Iasius is depicted as a Samothracian ruler. In his entry "Iasius or Iasion" in *Who's Who in Classical Mythology*, historian Dr. Michael Grant (241) says: "The historian Diodorus Siculus indicated that Iasion, after being instructed by Zeus in the Mysteries of Samothrace, married the goddess Cybele—who bore him Corybas—and was made immortal." Dixon-Kennedy (171) also asserts: "Diodorus Sicilus names Iasion as the originator of the Mysteries of Samothrace, a god in his own right, and then the husband of Cybele. He is yet another example of a young consort god associated with a fertility goddess."

"apostle" Orpheus[871] in his missionary work, as he took essentially the same basic route later purportedly traveled by Paul.[872] Iasius, Iesius or Jason is in fact equivalent to Jesus.

Hercules/Heracles

The Greek demigod Heracles, or Hercules, is well-known for his 12 labors, which correspond to the 12 signs of the zodiac and are demonstrations of his role as "Savior." Born of a virgin, he was also known as the "Only Begotten" and "Universal Word."[873] The virgin mother of Heracles/Hercules was called Alcmene, whose name in Hebrew was "almah," the "moon-woman," who, as Walker says, "mothered sacred kings in the Jerusalem cult, and whose title was bestowed upon the virgin Mary. Parallels between earlier myths of Alcmene and later myths of Mary are too numerous to be coincidental. Alcmene's husband refrained from sexual relations with her until her god-begotten child was born."[874]

- Hercules was born at the winter solstice of the mortal (virgin) mother[875] and God the Father.
- When his time had ended, he was dressed as a sacred king in a scarlet robe and killed.
- Hercules was sacrificed at the vernal equinox or "Easter."
- The Greek son of God was resurrected as "his own divine father."
- Hercules ascended to heaven, where he became a god.[876]
- Hercules was a "Prince of Peace," "Sun of Righteousness," and "Light of the World."[877]

Walker summarizes the story of Hercules and its relationship to the Christian tale:

> His Twelve Labors symbolized the sun's passage through the twelve houses of the zodiac.... The influence of Heracles's cult on early Christianity can hardly be overestimated. St. Paul's home town of Tarsus regularly reenacted the sacred drama of Heracles's death by fire, which is why Paul assumed there was

871 Apollonius Rhodius (*Argonautica*,1.916ff) tells us that Orpheus introduced the Samothracian mysteries to the Argonauts. (Apollonius/Rieu, 61.)

872 All of the areas whose citizens were addressed in Paul's epistles represented significant seats of mystery schools and brotherhoods, which were more or less loosely networked around the Mediterranean. These include Thessalonica, Corinth, Galatia, Rome, Ephesus, Philippi and Colosse.

873 Doane, 193.

874 Walker, B. (1983), 22.

875 Smith, R. Scott, 27; Rank, 140.

876 Ovid, *Metamorphoses* (9); Ovid/Miller, 22-24.

877 Walker, B. (1983), 393–4.

> great saving virtue in giving one's body to be burned, like the Heracles-martyrs (1 Corinthians 13:3).... He was the same sun greeted daily by the Persians and Essenes with the ritual phrase, "He is risen." The same formula announced Jesus's return from the underworld (Mark 16:6).... He was born at the winter solstice (Christmas), when the sun reaches his *nadir* and the constellation of the Virgin rises in the east. As Albert the Great put it centuries later, "The sign of the celestial virgin rises above the horizon, at the moment we find fixed for the birth of our Lord Jesus Christ."[878]

The Virgin Mother

Hercules's own birth follows the pattern of the more ancient virgin births, with a divine being descending from heaven to fecundate a mortal woman. The tryst between Zeus and Alcmene is mentioned as far back as the *Iliad* (14.315–28) and close in proximity to Christ's purported advent (Diodorus, 4.81.1–3).[879] In fact, like that of Dionysus, Perseus and others, Hercules's birth is similar to the later Christian traditions concerning the birth of Christ.

The story tells of a virgin daughter, Alcmene, being kept under lock and key until she marries, at which point she informs her husband that she will not consummate the marriage until he avenges her murdered brothers. At this point, Zeus is lying in wait, presumably eying the maiden for the specific reason that she is a virgin. Concerning Alcmene, Alexander William remarks:

> She lived with her spouse together, in consent of abstinence, from the first ... till he should have avenged the slaughter of her brother; and it was during his absence, she being yet a virgin, that Zeus intervened.[880]

As is the case with those ancient female figures of myth, there is more here than meets the eye. When inspecting the fascinating subject of miraculous, divine and virgin births, the bigger picture must be painted first, that of the parthenogenesis of the earlier Mother Goddesses that evidently permeated human religious thought.

Considering how old and widespread the virgin-mother concept was, as applied (e.g., to Hercules's fellow Greek hero Perseus, born of the virgin Danae—as noted by early Church fathers), we should not be surprised that Hercules may also have been perceived as virgin born, especially in view of the fact that he is largely a solar hero and the vir-

878 Walker, B. (1983), 393–4.

879 Levine, et al., 80.

880 William, A., 56.

gin-mother motif is significantly astrotheological, playing a great role in the mythology of the sun.

Horus/Osiris of Egypt

W.R. Cooper, unlike many today, does not underestimate the Egyptian factor in early Christianity:

> the works of art, the ideas, the expressions and the heresies of the first four centuries of the Christian era cannot be well studied without a right comprehension of the nature and influence of the Horus myth.[881]

In his *Hymn to the King Helios* (148D), Emperor Julian says: "Why should I go on to speak to you of Horus and of the other names of gods, which all belong to Helios?"[882]

The legends of Osiris/Horus go back thousands of years, and many people over the millennia have thought Osiris to be a real person, some claiming he lived up to 22,000 years ago, a piece of farfetched evemerism. The cult of Osiris, Isis and Horus was widespread in the ancient world, including Rome. In the Egyptian myth, Horus and his onceand-future Father, Osiris, are frequently interchangeable, as in "I and the Father are one" (John 10:30). In this regard, it is significant that Horus and Osiris are sun gods, as related by Egyptologist Dr. Erik Hornung:

> Many Egyptian gods can be the sun god, especially Re, Atum, Amun, and manifestations of Horus. Even Osiris appears as the night form of the sun god in the New Kingdom. It is often not defined which particular sun god is meant in a given instance.[883]

As sun gods or aspects of the sun, Ra, Horus and Osiris are frequently identified or interchanged with each other, as the sun moves through the sky during the day and the underworld at night. So interchangeable are Osiris and Horus, in fact, that there is even a hybrid god Osiris-Horus or Asar-Heru.[884]

Osiris, Lord of Lords

Concerning Osiris, Walker says:

> Of all saviorgods worshipped at the beginning of the Christian era, Osiris may have contributed more details to the evolving

881 Cooper, W.R., 49.

882 Julian/Wright, 407. The original Greek of Julian's is as follows: "τί ούν έτι σοι τόν Ὥρον λέγω καί τάλλα θεων ονόματα τά πάντα Ηλίω προσήκοντα;" Julian's editor Wilber Cave Wright calls Horus "The Egyptian sun-god, whose worship was introduced first into Greece and later at Rome."

883 Hornung (1982), 283. For more information about Horus as a sun god, see Murdock, *CIE*, 28–66.

884 Budge, (1991), 60. See also Campbell (1995), 142.

Christ figure than any other. Already very old in Egypt, Osiris was identified with nearly every other Egyptian god and was on the way to absorbing them all. He had well over 200 divine names.[885]

Egyptologist Sir Dr. E.A. Wallis Budge remarks:

> The cult of Osiris is as old as Dynastic Egyptian civilization, and, from the earliest to the latest times, he was regarded as the god-man who suffered, died, rose again, and reigned eternally in heaven. He was the "King of eternity, lord of the everlastingness, prince of the gods and men, the god of gods, king of kings, lord of lords, prince of princes, the governor of the world, whose existence is everlasting" (*Papyrus of Ani*, Plate 1). To the Egyptians Osiris was the god who "made men and women to be born again" … who made them to rise from the dead, and bestowed upon them everlasting life; he was, in all times, the cause of their resurrection, and was also the resurrection itself. He was both god and man, and could sympathize with them in sickness and death, and the idea of his human personality brought them comfort.[886]

Budge goes on:

> [From] first to last, Osiris was to the Egyptians the god man who suffered, and died, and rose again, and reigned eternally in heaven. They believed that they would inherit eternal life, just as he had done.[887]

Concerning Osiris, Walker says:

> Osiris's coming was announced by Three Wise Men: the three stars Mintaka, Anilam, and Alnitak in the belt of Orion, which point directly to Osiris's star in the east, Sirius (Sothis), significator of his birth….
>
> Certainly Osiris was a prototypical Messiah, as well as a devoured Host. His flesh was eaten in the form of communion cakes of wheat, the "plant of Truth." … The cult of Osiris contributed a number of ideas and phrases to the Bible. The 23rd Psalm copied an Egyptian text appealing to Osiris the Good Shepherd to lead the deceased to the "green pastures" and "still waters" of the nefernefer land, to restore the soul to the body, and to give protection in the valley of the shadow of death (the Tuat). The Lord's Prayer was prefigured by an Egyptian hymn to OsirisAmen beginning, "O Amen, O Amen, who are in heaven." Amen was also

885 Walker, B. (1983), 748–754.

886 Budge (1909), 139.

887 Budge (1904), 2.126.

invoked at the end of every prayer.[888]

A list of Osiris's numerous titles by Egyptologist Dr. Edourd Naville includes "Osiris the living," "lord of life," "inviolate god," "creator of millions of men," "in heaven," "lord of eternity," "the begetter," "the prince" and "the great god everlasting."[889] He is also called "Osiris in the monstrance,"[890] a monstrance representing in Roman ritual a "transparent vessel in which the host or victim is exhibited." Commenting on this intriguing title, Massey provides other details as to the similarity between Osirianism and Christianity:

> Osiris in the monstrance should of itself suffice to show that the Egyptian Karast (Krst) is the original Christ, and that the Egyptian mysteries were continued by the Gnostics and Christianized in Rome.[891]

In my book *Christ in Egypt*, in the section "Osiris the Christ?" I examine the evidence for this interesting contention concerning a relationship between the word "Christ," and the Egyptian term "Karast" or "KRST." Osiris is called *nb qrs.t*, "lord of the tomb," transliterated as "KRST" or *karast* and meaning "tomb," "embalmment," "burial," "funeral" and "sarcophagus."[892]

Like Dionysus, Osiris was a god of the vine and a great traveling teacher who civilized the world. He was the ruler and judge of the dead. Osiris was plotted against and killed by Set and "the 72." Like the passion of Jesus, Osiris's resurrection served to provide hope to all that they may do likewise and become eternal.

Osiris's "son" or renewed incarnation, Horus, shares the following in common with Jesus:

- Horus was born of the virgin Isis-Meri on December 25 in a cave/manger, with his birth announced by a star in the East and attended by dignitaries or "wise men."[893]
- He was a child teacher in the Temple or "House of the Father" and was baptized when he was 30 years old.[894]
- Horus was baptized by "Anup the Baptizer,"[895] who becomes "John the Baptist."

888 Walker, B. (1983), 748–754.
889 Naville, 24.140–1.
890 Proceedings of the Society of Biblical Archaeology, 141.
891 Massey, *EBD*, 54–5.
892 Murdock (2009a), 314–6.
893 Murdock, *CIE*, 79–209.
894 Murdock, *CIE*, 210ff.
895 Murdock, *CIE*, 233ff.

- He had 12 companions, subjects or "disciples."[896]
- He performed miracles and raised one man, El-Azar-us, from the dead.[897]
- The Egyptian god walked on water.[898]
- Horus was transfigured on the Mount.[899]
- He was also the "Way, the Truth, the Light, the Messiah, God's Anointed Son, the Son of Man, the Good Shepherd, the Lamb of God, the Word," etc.[900]
- He was "the Fisher," and was associated with the Lamb, Lion and Fish ("Ichthys").[901]
- Horus's personal epithet appears to have been "Iusa," the "ever-becoming son" of "Ptah," the "Father."[902]
- Horus (or Osiris) was called "the KRST," long before the Christians duplicated the story.[903]
- His earthly father was named "Seb" ("Jo***seph***").
- He was of royal descent.[904]
- He delivered a "Sermon on the Mount" and his followers recounted the "Sayings of Iusa."[905]
- He was crucified between two thieves, buried for three days in a tomb, and resurrected.
- He came to fulfill the Law.[906]
- Like Jesus, "Horus was supposed to reign one thousand years."[907]

Furthermore, inscribed about 3,500 years ago on the walls of the Temple at Luxor were images of the Nativity Scene of the pharaoh Amenhotep III, which include an "Annunciation," along with what has been described as an "Immaculate Conception, Birth and Adoration of Horus," whom the living pharaoh was said to represent.[908] Regarding

896 Murdock, *CIE*, 261ff.
897 Murdock, *CIE*, 298ff, et al.
898 Murdock, *CIE*, 293–297.
899 Massey, *AELW*, II, 911.
900 Murdock, *CIE*, 309ff.
901 Massey: "Horus in Egypt had been a fish from time immemorial, and when the equinox entered the sign of Pisces, Horus, was portrayed as *Ichthys* with the fish sign over his head." (Massey, *HJMC*, 25.)
902 Murdock, *CIE*, 324ff, 424, et al.
903 Murdock, *CIE*, 313ff.
904 Doane, 163.
905 Jackson, 118.
906 Massey, *EBD*, 126.
907 See Murdock (2009a), 420ff.
908 In the first edition of this present work, I described this scene as represent-

this scene, Egyptologist Dr. Samuel Sharpe (1799–1881) comments:

In this picture we have the Annunciation, the Conception, the Birth, and the Adoration, as described in the First and Second Chapters of Luke's Gospel; and as we have historical assurance that the chapters in Matthew's Gospel which contain the Miraculous Birth of Jesus are an after addition not in the earliest manuscripts, it seems probable that these two poetical chapters in Luke may also be unhistorical, and be borrowed from the Egyptian accounts of the miraculous birth of their kings.[909]

In addition, in the catacombs at Rome are pictures of the baby Horus being held by the virgin mother Isis—the original "Madonna and Child." As Massey says: "It was the gnostic art that reproduced the HathorMeri and Horus of Egypt as the Virgin and childChrist of Rome." Referring to the passage at Acts 4:13, in which the proselytizing Peter and John are taken to be ἄνθρωποι ἀγράμματοί and ἰδιῶται—"unlearned men" and "ignorants" or "idiots"—Massey comments: "*You poor idiotai*," said the Gnostics [to the early Christians], "*you have mistaken the mysteries of old for modern history, and accepted literally all that was only meant mystically*."[910]

Iasion/Iasios/Iasius of Samothrace

First found in Homer's *Odyssey* (ninth cent. BCE), followed by a discussion in the seventh or eighth century BCE in Hesiod (*Theog*. 969–974), Iasion of Samothrace, also called Iasios, Iasius, Iasus, Jason,[911] Aetion

ing the Egyptian god Thoth announcing to the Virgin Isis that she will conceive Horus; with Kneph, the "Holy Ghost," impregnating the virgin; and with the infant being attended by three kings, or magi, bearing gifts. The scene may warrant such "Christian" language but needs to be explained in greater detail, such as discussing how the mother of a pharaoh—the living Horus—was considered to represent Isis. Further details are in my book *Christ in Egypt*, 167–94.

909 Sharpe, *EMEC*, 19. (Emph. added.)

910 Massey (1883), 2.485.

911 In his translation of Clement of Alexandria's second reference to "Iasion" (*Exhort. Heath.*, 2), Rev. Alexander Roberts (2.180) renders the name as "Jason" in English. In discussing "men who have taken part in the mysteries," Diodorus (5.49.6) specifically names the Argonautic hero Jason as one of the most famous ancient heroes and demigods to be initiated. (Meyer, M., 41) Jason's association with Iasion is clear from the great significance given to the Samothracian mysteries as being vital to sea faring. Moreover, Astour (276) calls Iasion "the hero who bore an almost identical name to that of Jason: *Iasiôn*, or Iasios." He then remarks: "The significance of the name does not rouse the slightest doubts: it derives from *iaomai*, "to heal," *iasis* "healing, recovery." Any earlier source for this precise contention is renowned scholar of myth and language Dr. Jacob Bryant (1715–1804), who remarked: "Jason was certainly a title of the Arkite God, the

and Eëtion,[912] is the legendary founder of the famed Samothracian mysteries, in which many Greek notables participated over the centuries, beginning hundreds of years before the Common Era. As is clear from references in ancient writers such as Ovid (*Metamorphoses*, 9.682), reverence for Iasion and the Samothracian mysteries lasted for centuries, into the Common Era, with many Roman dignitaries partaking in initiation as well. Indeed, Virgil (*Aeneid*, 3.246) proudly claims "old Iasius" as originating in Italy.

In one variant, as the son of Zeus and Electra whose brother Dardanus was the legendary founder of Troy, Iasion mated with the earth mother goddess Demeter/Cybele, producing *Qarûb-ba'al*[913] or Korybas, whose name contributed to the Korybantes, Cybele's followers.

Iasion—again, whose name is also represented as *Jason*, meaning "healer," that has been associated since pre-Christian antiquity with the name "Jesus"[914]—shares a number of significant attributes with the Christ figure.

- Iasion is born of a virgin mother[915] and God the Father ("Zeus Pater").[916]

---

same as Arcas, Argus ... and the temples were not built by him, but erected to his honor.... *He was concealed and shut up in an Ark, as if he had been dead.* Justin places him in the same light as Hercules and Dionysus; and says, that by most of the people in the east he was looked up to as the founder of their nations, and had divine honours paid to him.... I suspect that Æson, Jason, Jasion and Jasius were originally the same title" (Bryant, 3.412–3).

912 Church father Clement of Alexandria (*Exhort. Heath.*, 2) uses the name "Eëtion" to describe Iasion. (Clement/Butterworth, 31).

913 Hellenosemitica, 276.

914 One such example occurred when the Hellenizing Jewish priest Jesus (fl. 175 BCE), brother of Onias, changed his name to Jason. (Josephus, *Ant.*, 12.5.1/239; Whiston, 256) Morton Enslin remarks: "That Jews often had gentile names as well as Jewish—and that these often resembled each other: Jason-Joshua (Jesus)—is too well-known to need argument." (Aune, 142) For more information on the Jason/Jesus connection, see my book *Suns of God*, for example, pp. 115–6.

915 Rigoglioso (2009), 163–5.

916 Hock, 524. The name "Zeus," which is "Dios" in the genitive, means "God," while "Pater" signifies "Father." The epithet "Zeus Pater" is "Jupiter" in Latin and "Dyaus Pitar" in Sanskrit/Vedic, meaning "Sky Father." Indeed, the Greek word διος or "dios" means "shining, brilliant, excellent, noble; divine." (*Pocket Oxford Classical Greek Dictionary*, 87) Citing Suidas (John. Malal., 32), Herbert (70) contends that "Iasius" or "Iasion" means "son of Iasus" and that Iasus is "Jupiter Picus," in other words Zeus Pater, and equates him with Jason, captain of the Argo.

- He is a healer[917] who performs miracles.
- He brought "divine revelation to mankind," which, if believed, will "provide a pleasant life with dignity for all eternity."[918]
- Iasion is killed, his death occurring by the will of the Father in Heaven,[919] and is resurrected.[920]
- As does Jesus in Revelation 21:
- Iasion attains immortality in the heavenly city, where he is associated with 12 immortal figures.[921]
- As in the Wedding Feast of Cana, Iasion is associated with wine and marriage.
- Like Jesus and his "twin" Thomas,[922] Iasion is identified as one of a pair of twins.[923]

As concerns Iasion's miraculous birth, Dr. Marguerite Rigoglioso argues that, as one of the seven Pleiades, Electra was a *parthenos* or virgin, a special category in the ancient Greek "cult of the divine birth."[924] She notes that six of these figures give birth to heroes, citing her research demonstrating that the "purported purpose of virgin conception was to generate divine children/heroes." Rigoglioso further remarks: "Diodorus states outright that these seven women were considered human ancestors who were immortalized simultaneously on account of (1) their "chastity," and (2) their birthing of gods' children."[925] In consideration of the plethora of pre-Christian virgin-born gods, goddesses, heroes and

917 Astour, 276–7, 280.

918 This parallel refers to the revelation of the mysteries, just as Christ revealed the Christian mysteries. As Diodorus (8.15.3) points out, if the mysteries are believed, the gods will provide eternal life. (Schuddeboom, et al., 47) For more on the subject of Christian mysteries, see my book *Suns of God*, for example, pp. 518ff.

919 In *The Odyssey* (5.116), Homer states that Zeus, jealous of Iasion's tryst with Demeter, "quickly punished him with a fiery thunderbolt." (Eickhoff, 117) In some later accounts, Iasion's death is caused by his brother, Dardanus, or his own horses. (Smith, W., 552)

920 The bodily resurrection is indicated by Ovid's account that "Ceres bewailed the age of her Iasion, grey and stricken old…" (Ovid, *Metam.*, 9.682)

921 Diodorus (5.49.2) recounts that Iasion was welcomed into the "circle of the gods" (i.e., Olympus). The home of the gods in Greek mythology is traditionally placed on the top of Mt. Olympus, high up in the sky/heavens.

922 Thomas is named specifically as Jesus's twin in the apocryphal *Book of Thomas the Contender* (138), found at Nag Hammadi: "The savior said, 'Brother Thomas … Now, since it has been said that you are my twin and true companion."

923 *Poet. Astr.* II.22.

924 Rigoglioso (2009), 163–5.

925 Rigoglioso (2009), 163.

rulers, it would not be surprising to find the founder and main figure of the important Samothracian mysteries likewise to possess this characteristic.

Not only do we have yet another example of a pre-Christian figure who is killed and resurrects—a *dying-and-rising* god—but there is also reason to suggest that death and resurrection were central themes of ancient mysteries.

As Strabo (*Geo.*, 7.149) tells us, Iasion and Dionysus both possessed the epithet of "Iacchus," one of several indications that the two were identified in antiquity. Orpheus, who was said to have been initiated into the Samothracian mysteries, is depicted as proselytizing both Iasion, and Dionysus/Bacchus.

It appears that, like Dionysus, Jason and so many others, Iasion is significantly a solar hero or sun god. After speaking of Dardanus, Max Müller remarks:

> The name of the other brother, Îăsion, varies between Îăsion, Îăsios, Îăsos and Iăson. These names seem to have had the same origin.... The name of Îăson or Îăsion corresponds strictly to Vivasvân, the sun ... and this ... might account for his marriage with Demeter on the thrice-plowed field, and for the birth of Ploutos (wealth) as their child.[926]

Inanna/Inana of Sumeria

One of the female archetypes whose legend resembles that of Christ in pertinent details is the Sumerian goddess Inanna or Inana, also known as Ninnar and Nana, among other names possibly derived from "Ninana," meaning "lady of the sky" or "Queen of Heaven." From cuneiform texts, Inanna is a very ancient goddess, dating to possibly as early as 7,000 years ago if not more.[927] Among other symbolism, Inanna represents the planet Venus, and her stories largely represent astral myths or astrotheology. In this same regard, she is portrayed as the daughter of the moon goddess Nanna. Her later Akkado-Babylonian counterpart is the goddess Ishtar, virgin mother of Tammuz. In poems from around 2000 BCE, Inanna is depicted as follows:

- Like the much later Christian virgin mother Mary and other goddesses, such as the one followed by the Canaanites and repeatedly discussed in the Bible, Inanna was the "Queen of Heaven."[928]

926 Müller, 2.246.

927 "Inanna." en.wikipedia.org/wiki/Inanna

928 See, for example, "Aratta's Reply: First Counterchallenge" in *Emmerkary and the Lord of Aratta* (220–1), one of the epics of Sumerian kings, in which reference is made to the "Queen of Heaven and Earth, the goddess of

- Like Jesus (Rev. 22:16), Inanna is the "morning star" or Venus.[929]
- Like Christ, who is tempted by Satan and harassed by demons, so too is Inana menaced by demons, big and small.[930]
- As Christ is depicted doing in apocryphal texts, Inanna descends into the underworld.
- Inanna is murdered and her body hung on a stake.[931]
- After three days, she is resurrected.[932]
- Her religion has the "bread of life," used to restore her from death.[933]
- Like Christ, Osiris and the Egyptian pharaohs with their shepherd crooks, or Moses with his magical stick, Inanna carries a "measuring rod."[934]
- Like many gods and goddesses, including Jesus, Inanna is associated with love, war, rain and storms,[935] and is a civilizing deity.[936]
- Like Christ,[937] Inanna demanded supremacy of worship.[938]
- Similar to the gospel story, in which the son pleads with the Father to spare his life (Matt. 26:39), Inanna instructs her devotees to lament before her father Nanna: "Father Nanna, don't let anyone kill your daughter in the underworld."[939]
- As is the case in the gospel story with Jesus, it is Inanna's father

---

the myriad powers, Holy Inana." (Vanstiphout, 69)

929 Shipp, 68.

930 "Inana's descent," 290–294.

931 Astour, 272. It should be recalled that the Greek word used to describe Jesus's "cross," *stauros* (Strong's G4716), also means "stake."

932 In the Sumerian myth, Inanna is resurrected by the god Enki, who sends into the underworld two creatures to sprinkle her body with "water of life" and "food of life." (James, E.O. (1996), 9.) This motif is reminiscent of the role of Osiris in the afterlife, including a purifying baptism with the "water of life" and the consumption of sacred bread.

933 Leeming (2005), 197.

934 Winter, 292.

935 van der Toorn, 453.

936 Vanstiphout, 174.

937 Revelation 22:13 has Jesus stating, "I am the Alpha and the Omega, the first and the last, the beginning and the end." At John 14:6, he also says, "I am the way, and the truth, and the life; no one comes to the Father, but by me."

938 This supremacist motif appears in the myth about Inanna's destruction of Mount Ebih, "which has refused to recognize her superiority."

939 "Inana's descent," 48–56.

who resurrects her from the dead.[940]

Although Inanna is not specified in extant texts as a mother, maternity is suggested by the fact that she is identified with the Babylonian goddess Ishtar,[941] among others, who is depicted as the mother of Tammuz, the equivalent of Dumuzi. As van der Toorn, et al., say: "Inanna-Ishtar seem already to be identified early in Mesopotamian history."[942] The name "Dumuzi" means "faithful son"[943] or "true son,"[944] indicative that he did indeed occupy the same role of son/consort not only in the Babylonian myth but also in other myths of the region and beyond. In this regard, Dr. William W. Hallo (b. 1928), a professor of Assyrian and Babylonian literature at Yale University, remarks:

> Dumuzi was the son of Duttur (or Ninsu), the husband of Inanna.... These goddesses (and others) figured prominently as reciters of lamentations designed to assure the return of the deceased deity to the world of the living. Even Inanna who, according to the mythology, had consigned Dumuzi to the netherworld in the first place, participated in these appeals. The "Death of Dumuzi" is recounted in a moving Sumerian lament and incorporated in a number of other compositions of a mythological character, such as "The Descent of Inanna."[945]

The Old Testament book of Ezekiel 8:14–15 depicts Jewish women in Jerusalem mourning the death or underworld descent of Tammuz in much the same manner that Inanna is lamented when she enters the netherworld. This lamentation occurred at the summer solstice, when the heat and drought signaled the death of vegetation, thus contributing the name to the Jewish summer month of Tammuz.[946] Hence, it is clear that this god was not only vegetative but also astrotheological, given his association with the summer solstice, which is a solar observance.

---

940 In "Inana's descent" (65–67) the goddess laments: "Father Enki, the lord of great wisdom, knows about the life-giving plant and the life-giving water. He is the one who will restore me to life."

941 van der Toorn, et al., 452ff.

942 van der Torn, et al., 453.

943 James (1961a), 237.

944 Stray, 32.

945 Hallo, 228.

946 The fact that Jews named one of their summer months after a Pagan god seems remarkable; yet, it indicates how important was that god to the supposed "monotheistic" Jews and how nature worship and astrotheology crossed ethnic boundaries.

Descent into the Underworld

The Sumerian poem titled "Inanna's Descent to the Underworld" is found on a cuneiform tablet, in which she is also depicted as having "seven powers," and she must pass through the "seven gates" and by "seven judges" (*Anunnaki*), the number seven obviously being sacred as early as this time, if not much earlier. The poem also mentions masons and carpenters. Inanna beseeches the Sumerian father god, Enki, the "lord of great wisdom," to restore her to life, with his knowledge of the "life-giving plant and the life-giving water." The "life-giving water" is a common theme in Egyptian mythology and many others in which baptism, sprinkling with water or immersion into water, is considered a sacred purification rite.

Since it is clear from ancient texts that Dumuzi dies or enters the underworld, subsequently to be resurrected, it is likely that along with Tammuz's death/underworld entrance comes his eventual resurrection as well. In an Akkadian text, Tammuz's resurrection is predicted by his sister Belili. Hence, in Jerusalem several centuries before the Common Era Ezekiel says Jewish women were lamenting and celebrating the death and resurrection of a god with many attributes similar to those of the much later Jesus.

Her shepherd-king husband Dumuzi/Tammuz[947] rescues her from the underworld, much like the later Greek myth of Orpheus and Eurydice, as well as the Christian apocryphal tale of Jesus's descent into the underworld to rescue various Old Testament figures. In turn, like Persephone/Kore of Greek myth, Dumuzi must agree to stay in the underworld for six months, while his sister must remain the rest of the year.[948] This dual six-month period of "siblings" also appears in the New Testament, applied to John the Baptist and Jesus, whose births are celebrated at the June and December solstices.

Although some writers attempt to create distinctions between the

947 It is significant that Inanna and Dumuzi's "*hieros gamos*" or sacred marriage occurred at the vernal equinox, a time associated with the planet Venus. Inanna's eight-pointed star or rosette is also a symbol for Venus, as well as resembling the common "Buddhist" wheel, which in turn may represent the sun wheel, with its double cross signifying the solstice, equinoxes and cross quarter days. The single-cross solar wheel symbolizes the solstices and equinoxes.

948 The descent's astral mythology has been explained in recent scholarship by Clyde Hostetter as representing "an allegorical report of related movements of the planets Venus, Mercury and Jupiter; and those of the waxing crescent Moon in the Second Millennium, beginning with the Spring Equinox and concluding with a meteor shower near the end of one synodic period of Venus." ("Inanna," en.wikipedia.org/wiki/Inanna)

myths of the older gods and that of Jesus, such as claiming that those who descend into the underworld are not really dead, and thus they are not really resurrected, the fact is that in "Inanna's descent" (246–253) the goddess is clearly depicted as having *died* and being restored or *resurrected* to life. Indeed, not only does she herself wish for Father Enki to *restore her to life* but she is also depicted as a "corpse hanging on the hook," who "arises" after being sprinkled with the *life*-giving plant and water. Literature professor Dr. Evans Lansing Smith summarizes the Inanna cycle:

> Inanna descends into the underworld for three nights, during which time her body is hung up to rot on a peg (the first crucifixion on record, but of a female divinity!), before being revived by the water and bread of life.[949]

Sometimes, as Mettinger shows, a god's resurrection was celebrated, not mere days subsequent to the commemoration of his death, but some months later. Thus the pious celebrated each portion of the story at its proper spot on the calendar, waiting till Spring to celebrate the Springtide resurrection. Some modern scholars call attention to texts like Ezekiel 8:14, a ritual of mourning for Tammuz, with no mention of a resurrection celebration, and from this they conclude there was no resurrection sequel. But in fact, there is a good reason for one not being noted in the same reference: it was yet months away.

Julius Caesar

The only individual in this present analysis who is clearly a historical person is the Roman emperor Julius Caesar, whose life remarkably "foreshadowed" that of Christ, a mere few decades prior to Jesus's purported advent, showing a continuation of these *mythical* motifs from remote antiquity to the time of interest, the first and second centuries AD/CE.

- Julius Caesar was believed to be the product of a miraculous or "virgin" birth and was considered the "son of God."
- He was murdered and upon his death the sun darkened, and the city was shaken by earthquakes, whereupon "shades of the silent dead walked abroad."[950] (Matt. 27:52)
- Caesar was resurrected and ascended into heaven to be with the gods.
- Caesar was worshipped as God.

Concerning Caesar's birth, Dr. Frederick Cornwallis Conybeare re-

949 Smith, E.L., 392.

950 Ovid, *Metamorphoses* (15); Ovid/Miller, 421. Also Virgil Georgics Book 1

marks:

> [The] mother of Julius Caesar conceived him miraculously in a temple of Apollo, so that this first of the emperors was son of a god. The emperor Alexander likewise was conceived by a virgin.[951]

In The Paganism in Our Christianity, Arthur Weigall writes:

> The Egyptian writer, Asclepiades, states that Julius Caesar was miraculously conceived by Apollo in the womb of his mother when she was in the temple of that god. The famous hero, Perseus, was the son of the god Zeus by a virgin princess named Danae, a fact which caused Justin Martyr, one of the Christian Fathers in the middle of the Second Century, to write: "When I hear that Perseus was begotten of a virgin, I understand that the deceiving serpent (Satan) counterfeited this.
>
> According to one legend, the father of the philosopher Plato was warned in a dream of the child's coming birth, his wife, who was still a virgin, having been divinely fertilized.[952]

Theologians Dr. Thomas G. Long and Rev. Dr. Cornelius Plantinga (b. 1946) remark that "Pythagoras was called virgin born, and Plato, and Augustus Caesar, and many more."[953]

In Ovid's *Metamorphoses* (15), published in 8 AD/CE, the Roman poet says of Julius Caesar: "Caesar is god in his own city … changed to a new heavenly body, a flaming star; but still more his offspring deified him."[954]

Krishna of India

> The Bhāgavata [Purana], along with the Bhagavad Gita, are the main sources of scriptural authority used by Gaudiya Vaishnavas for demonstrating the pre-eminence of Krishna over other forms of God. An oft-quoted verse from the Bhāgavata is used as a representational statement by Krishna sects to show that Krishna is "Bhagavan Svayam," or God himself: "These [other incarnations] are amsha, or kala, partial incarnations, but krishnas tu bhagavan svayam, 'Krishna is Bhagavan, God himself.'"(1.3.28).[955]

In discussing the comparisons between Krishna and Christ, Christian apologists have claimed either that there are no real parallels or

---

951 Conybeare, 192.

952 Weigall, 42.

953 Long and Plantinga, 248.

954 Ovid/Miller, 2.417. The original Latin (745–749) is as follows: "Caesar in urbe sua deus est; quem … rerum in sidus vertere novum stellamque comantem, quam sua progenies" (Ovid/Miller, 2.416.).

955 "Bhagavata Purana," en.wikipedia.org/wiki/Bhagavata_Purana.

that these "exact counterparts"—as the *Catholic Encyclopedia* calls them[956]—were copied from Christianity.[957] However, Indian and other scholars contend that the Krishna story is uninfluenced by Christianity, many averring that any borrowing must have been by Christianity from Hinduism. Moreover, the similarities between the Christian and Indian saviors number in the hundreds, particularly when the early Christian

---

956 *CE*, "Brahmanism" (2.734).

957 See, for example, the anonymous writer in *The Athenaeum* who falsely contended that "the history of Krishnah has been borrowed by the Brahmans from the Gospel." (Robertson, *CM* (1900), 149.) In a text called *Record of Christian Work* (39.266–7), under a subsection entitled, "Brahmanical Borrowings from the Gospel," the author(s) discusses the "knowledge of Christ" arriving in India via the churches in Syria. He then says: "the Gospel, instead of being passed on to the masses, merely filtered into Hindu literature in a debased and legendary form. Modern rationalism has repeatedly attempted to trace Christianity back to Hindu sources but this is the reversal of what actually happened. The Brahmins got from Christian sources, presumably Syrian, the life of Christ and borrowed various episodes from it, introducing them into the Mahabharata." Weber, Garbe and Hopkins's work attempting to show Christian origins for numerous elements confirms with reams of scholarship that these various parallels not only exist but that they were so startlingly similar that, it was concluded, one must have copied from the other. Since they thought Christianity was a "divine revelation," it had to be the Brahmans who plagiarized the story of Christ and biblical doctrines. However, although in much later centuries some Christian elements certainly were incorporated into Indian religion, it has never been shown that the Krishna mythos is anything but Indian. Indian religion from centuries to millennia prior to the Common Era contains many of these characteristics, motifs, episodes and rituals, such as the Rigveda texts on Agni, Indra and others. Some claim that these many parallels have been "stolen from the spurious gospels attributed to St. Thomas," as well as "all the adulterated theory, professed by the Nestorians, the Manichees and other Eastern sects of Christians." (Hamilton, A., 2.226.) In this same regard, Abhedānanda (1.36) remarks: "Oriental scholars and Christian missionaries have often compared [Krishna's] life and teachings with those of Jesus the Christ. Some of them have denied the historical personality of Krishna; while others have tried to prove that He was a mythical god of ancient India, and that He did not exist at all. Again, after noting the wonderful similarity that exists between the lives of Krishna and Christ, many have come to the conclusion that the whole story of Krishna's life and teachings is based upon the life and sayings of Jesus the Christ, and that the Krishna-cult of the Hindus did not exist before the first invasion of that country by the early Christian missionaries. Furthermore, some of the followers of the Christ were so astonished at finding in India a religion so near like their own, that they could only account for it by supposing that the devil, foreseeing the advent of the Savior, originated a system of religion in advance of His, and just like it."

texts now considered apocryphal are factored in. It should be further noted that, as with Jesus, Buddha and Osiris, many people have believed and continue to believe in a historical Krishna whose true adventures are faithfully recorded in Indian sacred texts.[958] This fact is important to keep in mind, because it means that millions of devout Hindus sincerely believe that the *entire* Krishna story occurred as *history*, many centuries before the Common Era and Christ's purported advent. They therefore do not believe that Krishna's "myth" could have been copied in any part from Christianity.

The following represents a partial list of the correspondences between Jesus and Krishna:

- Krishna was a divinely conceived "son of God,"[959] the deity incarnate, an incarnation of the sun god, who rises or awakens at the winter solstice.[960]
- His birth and divine mission having been foretold, Krishna was born of the "virgin" Devaki ("Divine One")[961] in a prison, a "stable"[962]

958 As Abhedānanda (1.39) says, "The life of Krishna, to the Hindu mind, is as historical as the life of Jesus the Christ to the Christian." For non-Hindus, of course, it is difficult to believe the supernatural tales of the Krishna myth, including, for example, that the blue-skinned god was "born with four hands and five weapons, wearing all kinds of ornaments." ("Narada's cleverness," *The Hindu*. Sep 07, 2009; www.hindu.com/2009/09/07/stories/2009090755381200.htm.)

959 In addition to being the "son" or incarnation of Vishnu, Krishna is the son of Devaki, the "Divine," considered to be the "Mother goddess." (Chandra, 70.) In the Harivamsa (2.4.2), Devaki is called *devatopama* or "goddess-like."

960 Davis, S., 3.166, evidently based on Jones (1793:258).

961 *Indian Studies* (108) states that Krishna's "mother's name, Devaki... can also be interpreted as meaning 'the divine one.'"

962 Hopkins (1901), 163. In discussing what many scholars of the day were certain was Christian influence on the Krishna tale and Hinduism, Hopkins cites several parallels that reflect a typical evolution in myth-making as tales accrete and change, as in Krishna's birth story: "The scene too of Krishna's nativity is not only like that of Christ's, but in becoming so, it has altered all the old inherited features of the Krishna tradition, which has been renounced in favor of this new presentation. Krishna is no longer heroic in birth as in life. The place of his nativity has become a stable, *gokula*, and his birth, which in the older tradition occurred in prison at a time of fear and danger, is now of peaceful character.... The especial weight laid upon the Child-cult in this worship of Krishna, so utterly opposed to that of the older Krishna-worship, makes it impossible to doubt that at least this form of Krishnaism derives from a Christian source." In some texts (e.g., "The Nectar of Instruction, 9"), Krishna is called *gokula-pateha*—"master of

or, like the cave-born Christ of tradition,[963] a "cave-like dungeon."[964]

- Krishna was of royal descent, a prince,[965] who became "King of the Yadus."[966]
- As was Christ with his cousin John the Baptist, Krishna was preceded by a "precursor," his brother Balarama.[967]
- Upon birth, the baby Krishna was placed in a "basket for winnowing corn; *in other words, a manger.*"[968]

Gokula." Concerning the Krishna birth legend, Emile Senart (391) tells how the "confusion, in certain sources, of the *sûtikâ-griha* (lying-in room) with a *gokula*, a stable, contrary to the strict details of the recital, seems to him [scholar A. Weber] one more sign of Christian imitation. But it must be remembered that the sûtikâ-griha must, in the terms of the ritual, contain not only Devaki with her son and Vasudeva, but also, and all together, the images of the shepherds, of the servants of Kansa, the guards of Devaki.... The intention then was not to give a faithful picture of the facts reported in the legend, but to group in a single frame all the personages included in it. How, on that footing, could separation be made of the new-born and the mother, or distinction between the prison and the dwelling of the shepherd?" (tr. Robertson, *CM*, 192.) The birth of Krishna in a *griha* or "room" is interesting, in light of the fact that in Sanskrit *griha* also means "house" as in "houses" or "signs" of the zodiac.

963 In *Dialogue with Trypho* (78), Justin Martyr states that "when the child was born in Bethlehem, since Joseph could not find a lodging in that village, he took up his quarters in a certain cave near the village; and while they were there Mary brought forth the Christ and placed Him in a manger, and here the Magi who came from Arabia found him." (Dods (1867), 195.) For a survey of the apocryphal texts and other Church fathers discussing Christ's birth in a cave, see Donehoo, 50–1.

964 Knapp, 199.

965 Thundy (1993), 132. See also Sheridan, 11. Krishna's mother, Devaki, was the princess of Mathura, sister of the king. (Vitsaxis, 41) Thundy (1993:96) comments: "We find the following reference to Krishna in the Chinese version of the 'plowing match' found in the *Abhinishkramanasutra*: 'The Rishis, looking downwards, beheld the prince underneath the tree, sitting with his legs crossed.... Then the Rishis began to consider—'Who can this be?' 'Is it Brahma, Lord of the world?—or is it Krishna Deva, Lord of the Kama Loka?' ... 'Is he the image of Krishna?'"

966 Barth, 174; Abhedānanda, 1.64. The "Yadus" or "Yadavas" were the descendants of the hero Yadu, living in the area near Mathura and Vrindavana, where the Krishna cult thrived. (Monier-Williams, 845.) Krishna became their king when he killed the previous monarch, Kamsa. (Jackson, S.M., 1889:405.)

967 Thundy (1993), 98.

968 Robertson, *CM* (1900), 150. See also Bhattacharya, 27, citing the earliest known bas-relief sculpture of Krishna (c. first cent. CE), which depicts a "stout person carrying a winnowing basket on his head. The child Krishna is

- Great signs and wonders occurred at Krishna's birth,[969] including the appearance of a bright star.[970]
- His birthplace was filled with a "marvelous and powerful light."[971]
- The heavenly hosts danced and sang at his birth.[972]
- His birth was attended by angels,[973] wise men[974] and shepherds.[975]
- He was presented with gifts, including gold and incense.[976]
- Krishna's foster father (Nanda) was in the city to pay taxes when the god was born.[977]

---

supposed to be in the basket, though owing to the angle at which the basket is shown on the condition of the relief we do not see him."

969 O'Flaherty, 212. See the *Harivamsa/Vishnu Purana* (2.4.15–20).

970 Bryant, *KS*, 119; Robertson, *CM* (1900), 175. The story of the star, which is called "Rohini" (Aldebaran), is found in the *Bhagavat Purana* (10.3.1). See also the *Harivamsa/Vishnu Parva* (2.4.16).

971 Thundy, 107. The *Vishnu Purana* (5.3) records the birth of Krishna as accompanied by "the quarters of the horizon," being "irradiate with joy, as if moonlight was diffused over the whole earth." (Wilson, H.H., 502).

972 In the *Vishnu Purana* (5.3), the "spirits and nymphs of heaven," we are told, "danced and sang," and at midnight, "when the support of all about to be was born, the clouds emitted low pleasing sounds and poured down rain of flowers." (Wilson, H.H., 502)

973 The word "angels" is used to describe the "spirits and nymphs of heaven" who "showered flowers on the spot," as in the *Vishnu Purana* (5.3) (e.g., Sen, 1.325.). These "angels" or *devas* at Krishna's birth are described in the *Harivamsa/Vishnu Parvan* (2.4.18).

974 Abhedānanda, 1.59; O'Flaherty, 212. Abhedānanda describes the renowned wise man or "high sage" Maharishi Nārada Muni as appearing at Krishna's birth "before the wise men, sages, saints and innocent shepherds, heralding, like the morning star, the advent and glorious rise of the divine Sun, the Savior of mankind." The sages or madhusUdanam at Krishna's birth are described in the *Harivamsa/Vishnu Purana* (2.4.19).

975 Garbe (1914), 41.

976 Abhedananda, 1.59.

977 Hopkins (1901), 166; Dahlquist, 13; Abhedānanda, 1.55; Thundy, 99. Thundy (142) states: "It is a fact that no Roman census for tax assessment was held in Judea before that of Quirinius in AD 6–7. So there is neither Jewish nor Greco-Roman literary evidence to support a tax-related circumstance surrounding the birth of Jesus except the Indian parallel in which Krishna was born when his parents went to pay taxes." In the first edition of the present work (116), I related the contention that Krishna's "earthly father was a carpenter," citing Leedom (185) and Taylor (1829: 173). Krishna's earthly stepfather is Vasudeva, while his foster father, Nanda, is portrayed as a cow-

- Krishna was persecuted by a tyrant who ordered the slaughter of infants.[978]
- He was pursued by evil spirits or demons, whom he destroyed.[979]
- As was Jesus in the tradition of Christopher or "Christ-bearer,"

---

herd. For a discussion of this carpenter-god motif within Indian religion and elsewhere, see my book *Suns of God* (366ff). The Hindu god Tvastar is represented as a carpenter, and as "first-born creator of the universe," son of Aditi and father of Agni, the Vedic fire and sun gods, whose ancient tale so resembles the Christ myth. Mentioned some 65 times in the *Rigveda* and in the Mitanni tablets (c. 1500 BCE), Tvashtar's name "characterises him simply as a modeller (world-modeller) or work-master, divine artist, skilful smith, or 'carpenter.'" (Drews, 1910:114) Thus, again, as in the Christ myth the god's father is a carpenter. Also, since Tvaṣṭṛ is a "solar deity in the epic of Mahābhārata and the Harivaṃśa," and since "Tvashtar" is an epithet of Surya, it is apparent that this carpenter god is, like Krishna, also a sun god and that in India sun gods were considered "carpenters." (Acharya (2004), 368) Since it is neither Vasudeva/Basudev nor Nanda but the god Vishnu who is essentially Krishna's "father" or progenitor, and since Vishnu is a sun god, it could be said that Krishna's "father" is a "carpenter," as he himself would also be, as a sun god. Adding to this carpenter-guild motif with a carpenter god at the head, in "On some Festivals to Village Goddesses," F. Fawcett describes how certain rituals at the annual festival to the Indian goddess Mariamma or Maryamma are conducted by the ritual/*puja* priest or *pujari*, "who is by caste a carpenter." (Fawcett, 264–5.) "Maryamma" or "Mariama" represents a divine epithet applied to the goddess, including, it is contended, to Krishna's mother, Devaki; interestingly, the name "Mary" is Μαρία or Μαριάμ—"Mariam"—in the Greek and "Miriam" or "Miryam" in the Hebrew. (Strong's G3137, H4813) As an example of this carpenter motif, the Indian god Viśvákarma (Sanskrit: viśvá-karman "all-accomplishing; all-creator…") is the "Hindu presiding deity of all craftsmen and architects. He is believed by Hindus to be the 'Principal Universal Architect,' the architect who fabricated and designed the divine architecture of the Universe, the Lord of Creation." ("Vishvakarman," en.wikipedia.org/wiki/Vishvakarman) We further discover that "the divine smith Tvastar originates from Vishwakarma." This "carpenter god" and Indian "Great Architect of the Universe" Vishwakarma is found in the Rigveda and is thus a very early example of this motif. Viśvákarma is described in the *Mahabharata* as the "Lord of the Arts, Executor of a thousand Handicrafts, the Carpenter of the Gods, the most eminent of Artisans, the Fashioner of all ornaments … and a great and immortal God." (Dowson, 364.)

978 Doniger, 477.

979 In the *Bhagavad Gita* (10.14), where Krishna is called *kesava*, here meaning "Lord Kṛṣṇa destroyer of the Kesi demon" or "one who destroyed the asura or demon Kesi in the Krishna avatar." ("Kesava," en.wikipedia.org/wiki/Keshava)

the infant Krishna was carried across a river.[980]

- While the young Christ is depicted as fleeing to a place called "Maturea,"[981] Krishna is said to have been born in the city of Mathura.[982]
- As a young boy, the Indian god worked miracles and wonders, and was hailed as a divine incarnation.[983]
- Also, as a youth, Krishna outstripped his teachers with his intelligence and knowledge.[984]
- Like Jesus teaching in the temple as a youth, as a boy Krishna was a "zealous reformer of religion" who "warred upon vested priestly or rather priest-crafty interests and pretensions."
- Krishna was "tempted" in the wilderness by "various fiends," before crushing the serpent's head.[985]
- As an adult, Krishna became the master to many disciples.[986]

980 Bryant, *KS*, 6; Hopkins (1901), 166; Robertson, (1900), 194. This scene appears on the earliest known bas-relief representation of Krishna, which was discovered in the Gayatri mount near Mathura, India, and dating to the first century AD/CE (Bhattacharya, 9, 27).

981 The motif of Christ's flight to Egypt is fleshed out in the *Infancy Gospel of Thomas* or *Arabic Infancy Gospel*, representing an episode clearly included in the gospel story in order to "fulfill prophecy" from the Old Testament, in which God called his "son out of Egypt" (Hosea 11:1). This verse is in the past tense, however, and refers to Israel, not Jesus. This instance serves to illustrate how the composers of the New Testament took Old Testament scriptures and reworked them to create the fictional Christ character. See, for example, Jeremy Taylor (58), for the name of "Matarea" or "Maturea," also transliterated "Matariyeh," an ancient moniker for the city of Heliopolis. Chapter 24 of the gospel reads: "From there they went to that sycamore tree which today is called Matarea, and the Lord Jesus made to gush forth in Matarea a spring, in which the lady Mary washed his shirt." (Schneemelcher and Wilson, 460. See also Roberts, A. (1903), 8.409.)

982 In the *Harivamsha* (2.22.7), Kamsa is named as the king of Mathura, while Krishna's birth, destined to overthrow Kamsa, is related in the *Vishnuparva* part of the *Harivamsa* (HV 2.4). The ancient center of Krishna worship, Mathura was "sacked and many of its temples destroyed by [the Muslim invader] Mahmud of Ghazni in 1018 and again by Sikandar Lodhi, who ruled the Sultanate of Delhi from 1489 to 1517."

983 Abhedananda, 1.62. See the *Protevangelion* and infancy gospels for Christ's similar childhood.

984 Vetterling, 1058.

985 Robertson, *CM* (1900), 150; O'Flaherty, 221-6. This story appars in the *Vishnu Purana* (5.7). In Christian tradition, Christ is said to be the one who puts enmity between the woman (Eve) and the snake. (Gen 3:15), building on texts such as Rom 16:20 and 2 Cor. 11:3.

986 The most famous of these disciples is Arjuna, the recipient of Krishna's

- Like Christ the Shepherd, Krishna the Cowherd was worshipped by shepherds as a god.[987]
- He is depicted among shepherds, holding a shepherd's crook,[988] and is the "Shepherd God."[989]
- Krishna preached faith "in God's love to man and in his mercy and forgiveness of sins."[990]
- He raised a child from the dead[991] and healed lepers, the deaf

---

teachings in the Bhagavad Gita.

987 Garbe (1913a), 345–6, citing the "Krishna part" or Vishnuparvan of the Indian text the Harivamsha, as well as the "fifth book of the Vishnu-purâna and the tenth of the Bhâgavatapurâna." The Harivamsa is a "later appendix to this epic [Mahabharata] [that] contains the earliest detailed version of Krishna's childhood and youth.

988 In describing a miniature painting of Krishna "having a meal with the shepherds on an island on the Yamuna," Bhattacharya (111-2) remarks: "In the centre of the composition Krishna, the dark one, is sitting on green grass surrounded by the other seven young shepherds.... This is a scene from Krishna's pastoral life.... Krishna is holding some delicacy in his right hand, and in his left hand he holds a crook. The other young shepherds also carry crooks." (The scene represents *Bhagavata Purana/ Srimad Bhagavatam* 10.13.8–11 and can be found at the Museum der Volker Kunst in Berlin, Germany (M.V.D. IC 5617).

989 Abhedananda (1.38) calls Krishna the "Shepherd of mankind." Thundy (99) remarks upon the "resemblances between Krishna and the Christ of the Gospel of John," stating also that the latter "presents Christ as a good shepherd with his religion of love—a trait shared by Krishna himself."

990 Garbe (1913), 508, citing the *Bhagavad Gita*.

991 In the *Mahabharata* (*Adi Parva*), Krishna/Vasudeva is depicted as resurrecting the child of Uttara and Abhimanyu, the sole successor of the Pandavas. (Ganguli, 287, citing "Section LXLIV.") Also see Robertson, *CM* (1900), 151. Describing another episode from the Mahabharata, Wheeler (1.414–5) names the young man as the "dead son of Duhsalá and Jayadratha miraculously restored to life by Krishna." Citing a passage in the *Mahabharata* as "XVI.—The Horse Sacrifice," Wheeler (1.414–5) relates the narration thus: "And when his mother Duhsalá saw that her son was dead, she uncovered her head, and ran out of the palace until she came to Arjuna; and she said to him:—'O Arjuna, you slew my husband, and now my son has expired at the mention of your name: I am your sister.'... And Arjuna had compassion on her, and said:—'O my sister, whatsoever I can possibly do for you, I will.' And Krishna and Arjuna, and the daughter of DhritarAshtra then went to the dead body of the son of Jayadratha; and Krishna laid hold of the dead man's hand, and said:—'Arise!' And by the will of the Almighty the dead man immediately arose; and when he beheld those around him, his mother said to him:—'O my son, this new life has been given to you by reason of

and the blind.[992]

- Krishna miraculously fed the multitudes.[993]
- He gave his disciples the ability to work miracles.
- His path was "strewn with branches."
- A fig tree figures prominently in Krishna's myth,[994] in which the god says, "Among trees, I am the sacred fig-tree"[995] and is depicted also as approaching one, where he "utters a sort of parable."[996]
- Krishna used parables to teach the people about charity and love.
- His teachings were compiled in a book as "revealed scripture."[997]
- "He lived poor and he loved the poor,"[998] humbly washing the feet of guests.[999]
- Krishna was anointed with oil by a woman bearing a jar of ointment.[1000]
- Like Jesus, Krishna continually manifested his divinity and then denied it.[1001]
- He was transfigured in front of his beloved disciple.[1002]
- Krishna had a "beloved disciple" named Arjuna, Arjun, Arjoon[1003] or "Ar-jouan."[1004]

Krishna; pay respectful obeisance to him.' So her son threw himself at the feet of Krishna."

992 Abhedananda, 1.63.

993 Abhedananda, 1.69.

994 Chandra, 190.

995 BG 10:26; Stoler Miller, 92.

996 Robertson, *CM* (1900), 150.

997 Krishna's teachings are presented in the Hindu sacred text the *Bhagavad Gita*, part of the epic *Mahabharata* and considered an *upanishad* or philosophical text.

998 Jacolliot, 250. In the story of Krishna and Garuda, Krishna is made to describe the town in which he was raised, Vrindavan, as a "poor, dusty village," where he lived with his "poor mother." (Dalal-Clayton, 63; "Krishna and the Cowherd.") At *Bhagavata Purana* 10.60.14, Krishna remarks: "We are poor, and we are dear to those who are poor."

999 Abhedananda, 1.69.

1000 Abhedānanda, 1.64.

1001 Robertson, *CM* (1900), 150.

1002 Abhedananda, 1.63–64. In the Bhagavad Gita (11.9), Krishna is depicted as having revealed his Supreme Godhood to his disciple Arjuna.

1003 Reynolds, L.J., 113.

1004 In order to illustrate the point of comparison with the "beloved disciple" John, Doane (247) adds a hyphen to this older transliteration of "Arjuna." The original of "John" is "Ioannes," which does not have a "j" sound. Hence, this etymological connection is not indicated, although the coincidence remains intriguing

- Tradition holds that Krishna died after being shot in the foot while under a (fig) tree, leading to the suggestion he was pinned against the tree by an arrow or "crucified."[1005]
- At Krishna's death, the sun darkened.[1006]
- Krishna descended into hell to rescue others.[1007]
- After he was killed, Krishna appeared alive again and forgave his killer, sending him to heaven, like Christ with the penitent thief and his forgiving those who "know not what they do" (Luke 23:39–43, 34).[1008]
- After his death, the alive-again Krishna ascended to heaven,[1009] where he lives on and blesses his followers.
- Both Christ and Krishna claimed, "I am the Resurrection."[1010]

---

and has been noticed in the past. Speaking of John the Baptist, Higgins (2.137) remarks: "the fish Oannes was in name the same as John.... Now, I think, there can be no doubt that Arjoon of the Indians is the same as John of the Christians.... John is the cousin of Christ, Arjoon of Cristna." It is possible that Christ's beloved disciple and his cousin were modeled in part after Krishna's beloved disciple, regardless of whether or not their names are etymologically related.

1005 Abhedānanda (1.80): "His feet were shot through with the arrow of an unknown barbarian hunter." See the discussion "Krishna Crucified?" below and in my book *Suns of God*. See also "Was Horus Crucified?" for a discussion of the meaning and use of the term "crucify."

1006 Jackson, 80: "The light of the sun was blotted out at noon on the day of Krishna's death." This contention makes sense in consideration of the thesis that Krishna is a solar hero, sun god or aspect of the sun; hence, his death would represent the extinguishing of the sun.

1007 Abhedananda, 1.67. See the similar story about Jesus as found in the apocryphal text the *Gospel of Nicodemus* or *Acts of Pilate*"

1008 Wilson, H.H., 612. This story is recorded in the *Vishnu/Bhagavata Purana* (5.37). As Thomas L. Strange (238) remarks: "He translated his slayer to heaven, as Jesus gave a passport to heaven to the thief dying at his side."

1009 MBh 16.4: "The high-souled one comforted him and then ascended upwards, filling the entire welkin with splendour." (Ganguli/Rāya, 13.12) See also Vyasa, 304; Gupta, 871.

1010 In the Gita (10.34), Krishna says, "I am all-grasping death; and I am the resurrection of those who are about to be." (Wilkins, 63.) The original Sanskrit of this latter clause is: *udbhava ca bhaviyatam*, also transliterated as *udbhavashcha bhavishyataam. Udbhava* is translated as "generation," "orientation," "appearance" "creation," "arising from such things," "birth" and "taking birth." *Ca* means "also," "and" and "as well," while *bhavisayatam* is "of future manifestations." So, "generation of future incarnations" would constitute a reasonable rendering. Yogi Ramacharaka (90) renders the complete passage: "also am I Death from whose visits none are exempt. And, likewise, am I the Re-birth, which dissolves Death." Charles Johnston (84) translates

- Krishna is "a personal savior, a messianic deliverer who will bring all men and women salvation if only they choose to give Him their devotion."[1011]
- As Vishnu, Krishna is the god "who incarnates himself when sin threatens to take the upper hand in the world, and destroys it."[1012]
- As God having taken birth to interact with humanity as a teacher and savior, Krishna is both "fully human and fully divine."[1013]
- Krishna is the "Creator,"[1014] the "Divine One,"[1015] "Lord of creation,"[1016] "Lord of the god of gods,"[1017] "Lord of all gods"[1018] "Lord of

---

this passage as: "I am all-consuming Death; I am the birth of things that shall be." Purohit and Burroughs (85) prefer: "I am all-devouring Death; I am the Origin of all that shall happen." Prabhupada (173) renders 10.34 thus: "I am all-devouring death, and I am the generator of all things yet to be" or "I am the generating principle of all that is yet to be." Edwin Arnold's poetic rendition is: "And bitter Death which seizes all, and joyous sudden Birth, Which brings to light all beings that are to be on earth." (Arnold, E., 103) Other translations of the phrase specifying Krishna as the "resurrection" include: "the birth of those who are to be" (Judge, W.Q.); "the source of things to be" (Gandhi); "prosperity of those who are to be prosperous" (Sivananda, 2000); "the origin of future beings" (Prasad); "the origin of things that come to be" (Beck). This "origin" or "source" of all things to be/future beings follows Krishna stating that he is "death." Such a juxtaposition indicates a cycle of death and rebirth or reincarnation. The concept of reincarnation is highly important within Hinduism and represents a rebirth or resurrection from the death experienced in the previous cycle of mortality. Krishna is saying he is the source of eternal life bringing forth innumerable souls who continuously take rebirth/are reincarnated. He is thus the source of their resurrection into this world.

1011 Blank, 252.

1012 Dahlquist, 77. In the Vishnu Sahasranama or "Thousand Names of Vishnu," the name or epithet "Krishna" is listed as the fifty-seventh.

1013 See Subhamoy Das for further examination of Krishna-Christ parallels.

1014 At BG 10.32, Krishna says, "I alone am the creator."

1015 In the Bhagavad Gita (e.g., 10.17), Krishna is repeatedly called "Bhagavan/Bhagwan," which, along with "Bhagavad" or "Bhagavat," means "God" or "Divine One."

1016 In the *Bhagavad Gita* 10.14, Krishna is called *kekava*, which means, among other things, "lord of creation." *Kekava* also means "one who is endowed with the rays of light spreading within the orbit of the sun" and "Lord Krsna destroyer of the Ke*l*i demon" or "one who destroyed the asura or demon Kesi in the Krishna avatar."

1017 Bryant, *KLBG*, 308.

1018 BG 10.12. The Sanskrit reads adi-devam, translated as "original Lord of all gods."

lords"[1019] and "king of the gods,"[1020]

- He was perceived as the "Redeemer,"[1021] "Firstborn,"[1022] "Sin Bearer,"[1023] "Anointed,"[1024] "Liberator"[1025] and "Universal Word."[1026]
- Krishna is "Supreme among Men, Sustainer and Lord of Creatures, God of Gods, Master of the Universe."[1027]
- As Vishnu, the godman/avatar is the second person of the Trinity,[1028] considered the "Beginning, the Middle and the End,"[1029] ("Alpha and Omega"), the "source of all spiritual and material worlds,"[1030] as well as being omniscient,[1031] omnipresent[1032] and omnipotent.[1033]

1019 Abhedananda, 1.60: "Krishna [is] the Lord of all." He also calls him "the most beloved Lord and Savior of all." (Abhedananda, 1.38.)
1020 BG 10.22; Stoler Miller, 92.
1021 Abhedananda, 1.77.
1022 Walker, 515. In the *Mahabharata* (Drona Parva 7.183), Krishna is deemed the "foremost of beings." (Ganguli, 7.597; Joseph, 2.52)
1023 Abhedananda, 1.81.
1024 BG 11.11. The Sanskrit word *anulepanam* is generally translated as "anointed" or "wore ointments."
1025 Bryant, *KS*, 98.
1026 Walker, 515. At BG 10.34, Krishna identifies himself as *vak* or "perfect speech."
1027 BG 10.15; Stoler Miller, 91.
1028 Abhedānanda, 1.56. Thundy (130) states that "the Christian idea of the incarnation of the Second Person of the Trinity has no better parallel in the Old Testament or Hellenistic sources than in the Indian religions, where Vishnu, the Second Person of the Hindu Trinity, became incarnate in Krishna and the divine Bodhisattva became man in Siddhartha Gautama."
1029 BG 10.20; Campbell, 315.
1030 BG, 10.8. Barbara Stoller Miller's rendition of this part of 10.8 is: "I am the source of everything, and everything proceeds from me." (Stoler Miller, 90) At BG 10.2, Krishna says, "I am the source of all the gods and great sages." (Stoler Miller, 89.) AT BG 10.3, he is also the "beginningless great lord of the worlds." (Stoler Miller, 89.)
1031 Dhavamony, 96. In his commentary on BG 9.11, Ramanuja says that "Lord Krishna is the Supreme omniscient, omnipresent and omnipotent Lord of all creation." (Bhagavad-Gita: Chapter 9, Verse 11," www.bhagavad-gita.org/Gita/verse-09-11.html
1032 BG 9:15 says: "Still other people worship and wait upon Me through knowledge of My unique, various and innumerable, omnipresent forms." (Bryant, 2007:84) See also Stoler Miller (85), where the term is rendered "universal presence."
1033 BG 10.12. Arjuna calls Krishna "supreme, the infinite spirit, the highest abode, sublime purifier, man's spirit, eternal, divine, the primordial god, unborn, omnipotent." (Stoller Miller, 90.)

- His disciples shout the words "Jai Shri Krishna" or "Jishnu Krishna," meaning "Victory to Lord Krishna" or "Victorious Krishna," respectively.[1034]
- As Christ was the "lion of the tribe of Judah," Krishna is the lion (of the tribe of Yadus).[1035]
- He was perceived as the "Son of God" and "our Lord and Savior,"[1036] who came to earth for man's salvation.[1037]

1034 Knott, 40. This particular Sanskrit word for "victory," is also transliterated as *jaya*. In *The Bible in India*, French advocate Louis Jacolliot, who lived in India for some 20 years, asserted that Krishna's disciples bestowed upon him the title "Iezeus," "Jezeus" or "Jeseus," meaning "pure essence." While there is a Sanskrit word for "essence" that might be part of such a compound, sar or *sAra*, this claim was assailed by Max Müller, among others, and it may be that Jacolliot's transliteration was hampered by his native French language. Rather than casting aspersions on the Frenchman, others such as Sanskrit scholar Sir Monier-Williams have suggested he was relating an epithet for the god Shiva, Isa or Issa. "Jezeus" may be "a corruption of the Sanskrit word *I'sa*, Lord.' *I'sa* properly belongs as a title to Siva; but it is sometimes used of Krishna (or Vishnu), as, for example, in the Vishnu Purana (Wilson, Hall's ed. vol. v, p. 43)." (*Journal of the Transactions of the Victoria Institute*, 21.179.) Furthermore, there are thousands of religions and sects in India, dating back millennia, as well as thousands of languages and dialects, and it is impossible to say for sure that people Jacolliot knew locally in South India were not shouting something that sounded to him like "Jezeus," "Jeseus" or, since he was French, "Jezeu." One strong possibility is that his devotees were making the traditional greeting of "Jai Krishna" or "Jai Shri Krishna." In Bengal, for instance, this cry might sound more like "Jai Shri Kriston," as the latter is how Bengalis pronounce "Krishna." The resemblance between "Kriston" or "Kristo" and "Christos" has struck not a few people over the centuries. Hopkins (1901:162) cites one epithet for Krishna as "Jishnu," meaning "Victorious," appearing in Indian literature as early as the *Rigveda*. He then says "hence the form Jishnu Krishna is only a chance collocation and of chance likeness with the name Jesus Christ." An epithet deeming Krishna "pure essence" would certainly be appropriate, since such a characteristic represents one of the "eight qualities of God." (Popley, 90)

1035 At BG 10.30, Krishna says that, of all the animals, he is the lion. In the original edition of this present work, I related Jacolliot's contention that Krishna was called the "lion of the tribe of Saki." I have been unable to confirm this specific appellation.

1036 Krishna is frequently called "Lord," and his salvation role is evident: "Krishna introduced the important concept of God's entry into the world as a beneficent savior." (*Numen*, v. 28–30, 42.)

1037 BG 4.8: *Paritranaya sadhunam vinasaya ca duskrtam dharma-samsthapanarthaya sambhavami yuge yuge*—"For the protection/deliverance/salvation of devotees/pious men and the annihilation/de-

- Krishna's religion teaches that followers can attain spiritual salvation through a personal relationship with God in the form of the godman.[1038] Both Christ and Krishna are said to be eternal and preexistent, coming down to earth or incarnating as humans for a variety of reasons.[1039]
- A future incarnation of Vishnu, Lord Krishna as the Kalki avatar, will arrive riding a white horse and destroy the wicked,[1040] including the "prince of evil,"[1041] the "destroyer of all things."[1042]

As we can see, there are numerous detailed parallels between the stories of Krishna and Christ. Summarizing a few of these correspondences, Thundy remarks:

> The similarities between the Krishna-Jesus stories are obvious. For instance, both infants are born in mangers or rather in the homes of cowherds/shepherds; both infants are born when their parents go to pay taxes (go to register to vote); both infants escape the murderous wrath of tyrants who massacre innocent children; both go into exile.[1043]

Thundy goes on to point out a difference, that of the purportedly non-virginal state of Krishna's mother, to be discussed below.

What's in a Name

Part of the controversy concerning commonalities between Krishnaism and Christianity has revolved around the Indian and Christian godmen's respective names. A common earlier English spelling of Krishna was "Christna," which reveals a possible relation to "Christ." This suggestion is logical, since in Bengali the name for Krishna is "Krista," "Kristo" or "Christo," while in Pali it is "Christos," likewise the Greek for "Christ."[1044] As Bhavan states: "We know that the Bengali pronunci-

---

struction of evil-doers/miscreants, and to establish righteousness/sacred duty/principles of religion, I appear from age/millennium to age/millennium."

1038 See the *Bhagavata Purana*, which is "primarily a bhakti text, with an emphasis on achieving moksha through cultivating a personal relationship with Vishnu in the form of Krishna."

1039 See, for example, Yogananda, xxviii.

1040 Turner, 258; Bryant (2007), 18. At Revelation 19:11, it is said that Jesus will return in his Second Coming riding on a white horse.

1041 Abbott, J.K., 4. The "prince of evil" is named as either Kali or Kāla, the "Shining One" and the goddess's male counterpart, elsewhere named as a "demon." (Donaldson, 12.3.1075)

1042 Sykes, 121.

1043 Thundy, 100.

1044 Dīkshita, v. It has been contended that, centuries prior to the supposed

ation of the word 'Krishna' is 'Kristo.' Christo or Christ is only a matter of spelling."[1045]

As another Indian scholar asserts: "In Bengali, in India, there are many people who are named Christo. It is a form of *Krishna*."[1046] "Christ" is often rendered as *Khrist* when transliterated in Indian languages. Sri Ramakrishna Mathah relates that the names "Krishna" and "Christ" became "a focal point in such debates: 'But despite decades of two-way arguments, it was eventually determined that the name *Christ* was taken from the Greek *Christos*, which is derived from the Sanskrit Krishta, or Krishna.'"[1047]

Indologist Dr. Richard Garbe was so struck by the parallels between the "lives" of Christ and Krishna that he wrote several articles attempting to prove that the Indian priesthood borrowed numerous elements from Christianity, noting at one point for example, "In some localities of India the word Krishna is pronounced Krishta."[1048]

Concerning this parallel and the possible influence of Krishnaism on Christianity, one Indian writer, Thakur Kahanchandra Varma of Lahore, concludes:

> I feel no hesitation to state that the Christos of the Gospels is an imitation of Krishna. It is my honest opinion—nay my belief too—that the story of the life of *Krishna* went to Alexandria with the Buddhist Missionaries. History tells us that in the time of Emperor Asoka, the preachers of Buddhism were sent to different parts of the world, and some of them went to the city referred to above. Philo, the greatest Jewish historian, testifies to the above statement when he says in one of his works that "there were men of all religions in this monastery; Brahmans from the East who believed in *Krishna*.[1049]

Christian missionaries in India themselves were so struck with the similarities between the names of the two gods that they explained "Krishna" as the "*nomen ipsum corruptum Christi*,"[1050] or a "corruption

time of Jesus, the soldiers of Alexander the Great called Krishna "Christos," or "Anointed," not an illogical or unreasonable conclusion, considering that Krishna was called "Anointed" in Sanskrit. However, there appears to be no extant evidence from antiquity for this contention.

1045 Bhavan, 38.53.

1046 Osho, 351.

1047 Mathah, 311.

1048 Garbe, "CELK," 36.

1049 Dīkshita, v.

1050 Hopkins, 166. Jesuit missionary Giorgi or Georgius, who traveled extensively throughout Asia, related: *Est Krishna...nomen ipsum corruptum Chris-*

of the very name of Christ."

Krishna's Solar Nature

As in many religious systems, there have been mysteries within Indian religion as well. Several Indian texts discuss such mysteries, as RV 1.164.45, which refers to the four "levels of speech," three of which are "hidden in secrecy."

Much of the *Mahabharata* is taken up with a battle between the solar and lunar races. The Rajas of Bharata were said to be descended from the moon, while the Pandavas emanated from the sun. Krishna stands for the dark half of the month, from full moon to new moon (Macdonell, 73) (i.e., waning).

Concerning the Adityas or "sons of Aditi," the goddess identified with the universe, the direction of east and the dawn,[1051] Wheeler comments:

> [At] a later period they were represented as being twelve in number, and were apparently identified with the twelve signs of the zodiac, or rather with the sun in twelve different characters, each character corresponding to the sign through which it passed in succession. The most important fact connected with this circle of divinities is that the god Vishnu, so prominent in the later mythology, appears in the Rig-Veda merely as one of the Adityas.[1052]

Here we see not only an important astrotheological motif within Indian religion but also an example of the process by which deities achieve dominance, as in the evolution of Vishnu worship.

As Wheeler states:

> Súrya, or the Sun, is another Vedic deity; and indeed seems under different names to have always held a high place amongst the primitive gods of every nation, by virtue of its prominence in the heavens, and the extent to which its influence is felt upon earth.... it seems extremely probable that one of the earliest efforts of poetical genius was to personify the Sun as the deity of light,

---

ti Servatoris—"Krishna" is a corruption of the "very name of Christ the Savior."

1051 Aditi is spoken of as "that far-distant East" and "more than" or "beyond" the dawn, which is styled *aditer anakam* or the "face of Aditi." (Müller, 1869:1.231; RV 1.113.19.) Griffith renders the phrase "Aditi's form of glory," while Aurobindo (131) prefers "form (or, power) of Aditi," and Muir (1865:1.64) translates it "manifestation of Aditi." In that hymn too, the Dawn is called *mata devanam*—"mother of the gods," the same epithet shared by Aditi, who is styled "Deva-mâtri." Muir (1878:13–14) cites "Nirukta (iv. 22)" as describing Aditi as the "mighty mother of the gods (*adîna deva-mata*)."

1052 Wheeler, 1.24.

travelling through the blue ether in a golden chariot.[1053]

A study of the term *raví* is quite revealing as to the solar nature of various aspects of Indian religion, as it connotes "a particular form of the sun (sometimes regarded as one of the 12 Adityas ... the sun (in general) or the sun-god."[1054] Thus "Surya" is not the only name of the sun god; on the contrary, numerous Indian gods or divine names symbolized the sun, including Vishnu and, apparently, Krishna.

The reverence for the sun and its identification as the supreme lord and with many other deities and heroes can be found in the Vedas, as well as the commentaries known as the Upanishads and Vedanta literature. For example, in the *Akshi Upanishad*, associated with the *Yajurveda*, as part of the "science of the wise," there appears a salutation to the sun by the "blessed Samkriti," one of the followers of Vishnu traditionally held to have "composed Vedic hymns or incantations"[1055]:

> Then the blessed Samkriti repaired to the solar world. Bowing down to the Sun, he glorified the Sun by means of the science of the Wise:
>
> Om, Salutation to the blessed Lord, the glorious Sun, to the Power of the eye.
>
> Om, Salutation to the Sky-Wanderer.
>
> Om, Salutation to the Commander of the Army (of light).
>
> Om, Salutation to darkness (excess of light).
>
> Om, Salutation to Energy.
>
> Om, Salutation to Light.
>
> Lead me from the unreal to the Real; lead me from darkness to Light; lead me from death to Immortality.
>
> Of the essence of Purity, the blessed One scorches (the sins of the sinful) ...
>
> Here rises the Sun, thousand-rayed, existent in myriad ways, the life of all animate beings. (I meditate on Him who is) omniform, compassionate, omniscient, ambrosial, of the essence of light, the Scorcher.
>
> Om, Salutation to the blessed Lord, the Sun, the Offspring of the Infinite, the Power of the eye. The flood of days! The flood!! All Hail!
>
> Thus, glorified by means of the science of the Wise, the-Lord-in-the-form-of-the-Sun was highly gratified. He said: Whichever Brahmana studies without break this science of the

1053 Wheeler, 1.22.

1054 See, for example, Monier-Williams, 869.

1055 Mullick, 282.

> Wise never contracts any eye-disease. None is born blind in his family. Teaching this to eight Brahmanas one becomes perfect in this science. Whosoever knows this is magnified.[1056]

This teaching discourse between the sun and "his" devotee/disciple Samkriti continues at some length. From the last paragraph, the "science of the wise" sounds to be not only sun worship but also sun gazing, which purports to provide the practitioner with health, happiness and enlightenment.

While millions of people globally believe in a "historical" Krishna who "really and truly walked the earth," others aver that his story has all the hallmarks of not only a mythical character but also of a solar hero. Concerning this debate, in *Essays on Indo-Aryan Mythology*, Narayan Aiyangar remarks:

> The Mahabharata and the Puranas are unanimous in saying that the god Krishna was an incarnation of the god Vishnu, born as the son of Vasudeva and Devaki.... His story is made up of marvellous legends. From them scholars have tried to eliminate his godhood and all that is extravagant and physically impossible, and reduce him to a human being who, born as the son of one Vasudeva, made his name as a great Kshatriya hero, but who subsequently was deified for the purpose of hero-worship. But in the case of Krishna, instead of a man being deified, the contrary seems to me to be the case, viz., that god Vishnu is anthropomorphized and made man—god-man—as Krishna Vasudeva.... Likewise, Krishna [is] identical with Vishnu, the God of Sacrifice.[1057]

Like so many Indians, the Yadavas were worshippers of the sun, along with other forms of deity. This fact alone suffices to demonstrate that Krishna, as their "king" and head deity, is a solar hero, the sun god anthropomorphized and historicized, a very common development within religion and mythology dating back thousands of years.

As revealed in the *Mahabharata* (5.2563, 14.1589ff) and in the *Harivaṃśa* (2359, etc.), Krishna is identified or equated with Vishnu, an aspect or epithet of the sun, a solar hero or sun god. At *Bhagavad Gita* 10.21, Krishna is depicted as saying: "I am Vishnu striding among sun gods, the radiant sun among lights."[1058] Another translation of the full passage is: "Of the twelve Adityas I am Visnu, of all the luminaries the radiant sun, of the seven Maruts [storm deities] I am Marici ["ray of

---

1056 Warrier, 1-2.
1057 Narayan, 478.
1058 Stoler Miller, 92.

light"] and of the constellations I am the moon." Thus, like several of the Egyptian gods, such as Osiris, Krishna is both solar and lunar. Similar to the Egyptian sun god or solar hero Horus, in the *Bhagavad Gita* (11.15) Krishna is said to have "eyes like the sun and the moon."

Under "Krishna" in his *Sinhalese English Dictionary*, Rev. Benjamin Clough states that "in Hindu mythology Krishna is considered the most celebrated form of Vishnu or rather Vishnu himself; in that form he is however distinct from the ten avatars or incarnations of Vishnu, being always identified with the deity himself."[1059] Clough additionally relates that "Krishna" is also "one of the names of Arjuna the charioteer of the sun."[1060] Indeed, Vishnu is a solar deity or epithet/aspect of the sun, while, as his incarnation—"being always identified with the deity himself"—Krishna likewise is solar in nature.

Krishna also says, "I dispel darkness born of ignorance with the radiant light of knowledge" (BG 10.11; Stoler Miller, 90). Among other connotations, Krishna's epithet *keśava* means "one who is endowed with the rays of light spreading within the orbit of the sun."

Revealing the astrotheological nature of the Krishna myth, in the *Rigveda* (63.6, etc.) the word *aruṇá* is defined as "reddish-brown, tawny, red, ruddy (the color of the morning opposed to the darkness of night)."[1061] It is also defined as: "the dawn (personified as the charioteer of the sun)," as found in the Buddhist text the *Majjhima Nikāya*.[1062] The Sinhalese word for "sun charioteer" is *Śúrasúta*, likewise an epithet for Krishna's charioteer Arjuna;[1063] hence, we can see the patently obvious connection between *aruna* and *arjuna*. Indeed, some characters in the Krishna cycle appear to be personifications of the Vedic Aruna and Surya, with Arjuna replacing the former and Krishna the latter. Later, in the *Bhagavat Purana*, Aruna is named as one of Krishna's sons. Hence, the darkness gives birth to the tawny dawn. Once again, we find an apparent germ of the later Krishna-myth motif in the Vedas, as well as the blatantly solar nature of Krishna.

Ushas, the Vedic dawn goddess and "daughter of heaven," is a "vision of early morning, of the first pale flush of light, imaged as a pure and lovely maiden awakening a sleeping world as a young wife awakens her children."[1064] Concerning Ushas, the Rigveda (1.48.7) states: "This

1059 Clough, 144.
1060 Clough, 144.
1061 Monier-Williams, 88.
1062 Monier-Williams, 88, citing "Mn. x, 33, &c."
1063 Clough, 705.
1064 Wheeler, 1.26.

auspicious Ushas has harnessed her vehicles from afar, above the rising of the sun, and she comes gloriously upon man with a hundred chariots."[1065] The fact that Krishna is not only an incarnation of the sun god but also a deity himself who possesses many solar attributes should be kept in mind when investigating the Krishna-Christ parallels.

Slaughter of the Innocents

The story of the king Kamsa or Kansa slaughtering a series of infants in order to prevent his predicted opponent—Krishna—from growing to adulthood is well-known, and its correspondence to the gospel story of King Herod's massacre of the innocents (Matt. 2) has been noted many times over the centuries. This motif is also found in the myths of Moses and the Babylonian king Sargon, as well as the Sumerian god-king Etana.[1066] The slaughter of the innocents is depicted in the *Vishnu Parva* section of the *Harivamsa*, an appendix to the *Mahabharata* composed around the fourth century CE.

After discussing the similarities between the births of Buddha and Christ, Dr. Zacharias Thundy remarks:

> Some other details surrounding the birth of Jesus in both Matthew's and Luke's narratives seem to have been derived from another Indian birth story, the story of the birth of Krishna.[1067]

Speaking of the story of King Kamsa slaughtering the innocents, Thundy comments:

> It is possible that Matthew incorporated elements from the Krishna story into the Buddhist story and Judaized his version in order to proclaim the superiority of Jesus as the leader and king of the new religious movement.[1068]
>
> Thundy gives many good reasons to think that the gospel of Matthew was composed based significantly on Buddhist texts.

'Virgin' Birth?

The parallels between Krishna and Jesus include the miraculous births of both gods. It is debated whether or not Krishna's mother, Devaki—deemed "chaste" in the *Srimad Bhagavatam* (10.3.43) and said to be a "chaste lady"[1069] and "chaste mother"[1070]—could also be called a "virgin," since she traditionally had given birth to seven children prior to Krishna. But of course, a miraculous conception need not be a virgin-

1065 Wheeler, 1.27.
1066 Leeming (2005), 149.
1067 Thundy, 96.
1068 Thundy, 123.
1069 Vallabhācārya, 512, 552.
1070 Vallabhācārya, 513.

al conception, though they are parallel, practically equivalent, conceptions. Krishna is depicted as conceived via an immaculate, miraculous or sexless conception via the chaste Devaki. The *Srimad Bhagavatam*/BG (10.3.17) also says: "You never entered the womb of Devaki; rather, You existed there already."[1071]

The "baby" Nidra whom Kamsa kills is revealed to be a form of the "moon-faced" goddess, who "remained kanyā forever" (HV 2.4.38–9). At HV 2.4.47, the Goddess is called *yogakanyā* or "virgin union," who appears in order to protect *keshava* or Krishna.

In the *Vishnu Parva* part of the *Harivamsha*, an appendix to the *Mahabharata*, Krishna's conception is graphically described, after his mother, the "goddess-like" Devaki, is depicted as appearing like "Rohini," the "wife of the moon" (HV 2.4.5, 7) Devaki conceives six times, which conceptions (*shaDgarbhA-s*, lit. "wombs") were "smashed against a rock" by King Kamsa, like the six older siblings of Zeus who were eaten by Kronos. (HV 2.4.2) The *Vishnu Parva* relates that "she"—the goddess of magic, Yogamāyā, according to K.S. Ramachandran[1072]—"transferred the seventh conception to Rohiṇī," meaning that Vishnu as Krishna was placed into Devaki's womb by the Goddess. This "conception," too, was destroyed, after which Krishna is placed into Devaki's womb in the same fashion. At the same time, the cowherd's wife Yasoda conceives the girl Nidrā, "who carries out the instructions of Vishnu and who manifested from Vishnu's body."[1073] When both women give birth at the same time in their eighth month, the two children are swapped, whereupon Nidra is killed in Krishna's place.

At HV 2.4.47, the Goddess is called *yogakanyā* or "virgin (divine) union." Since there is a word for "virgin violator" or "girl calumniator"—*kanyā'-dūṣaka*—it is clear that one important meaning of *kanya* is "virgin." Indeed, it is further evident that the *kanya* or maid's sexual "purity" is implied in using this term. As says the Bhavishya Purana, Krishna was born as a result of "mental transmission" from Vasudeva's mind to Devaki's womb.[1074]

Aditi the Vedic Virgin

According to the myth, Devaki is an incarnation of the dawn god-

1071 Prabhupāda (1977), 1.220.

1072 HV 2.4.1-2; mahabharata-resources.org/harivamsa/vishnuparva/hv_2_004.html

1073 HV 2.4.10, translated by K.S. Rmachandran, mahabharata-resources.org/harivamsa/vishnuparva/hv_2_004.html

1074 Banerjee, "When Lord Krishna Was Born."

dess Aditi,[1075] who was the "Vedic virgin," "divine "virgin," "eternal virgin" or "celestial virgin,"[1076] despite the fact that she, too, gave birth to eight children, including the sun: "Aditi is the divine Virgin. She has unruptured hymen. She gives birth to the sun by immaculate conception."[1077] Devaki is "represented as being a new birth or manifestation of Aditi."[1078]

In Christian scripture (Mark 6:3), the Virgin Mary is likewise said to be the mother of at least seven children, but this claim does not negate her supposed perpetual virginity, as is not uncommon with *myths*. If Mary can give birth even one time yet remain a virgin,[1079] then she can also give birth seven or more times and remain a virgin. The same can be said of Devaki, as it was of Aditi and many other goddesses.

In this regard, the description of Krishna's birth in the *Vishnu Purana* (*Bhagavat Purana* 5.3), is suggestive, as we are told that on this day the "sun of Achyuta rose in the dawn of Devaki to cause the lotus petal of the universe to expand."[1080] The term "Achyuta" is explained by *Vishnu Purana* translator Dr. Horace H. Wilson (1786–1860) as "a common name of Vishnu," interpreted in one place in the *Mahabharata* as meaning, "he who is not distinct from final emancipation."[1081] *Achyuta* is defined in the *Sanskrit Dictionary for Spoken Sanskrit* as meaning "permanent," "steadfast," "solid" and "imperishable," also translated as "infallible" and used frequently in a religious context.[1082] The germane point here is that it is the "sun of Vishnu" who rises in the "dawn of Devaki," a perfectly comprehensible notion when explained in astrotheological terms with Krishna representing the new-born *sun*, much as in the myth of Osiris and Horus; while Devaki symbolizes the dawn whence he comes.

At RV 1.89.10, Aditi is glorified:

1075 Parmeshwaranand, 1; Vallabhacarya, 3517, citing the Rig Veda, 1.89.10.

1076 See, for example, Sankarananda, 2.107, 1.138; Agrawala, 59; Turner, 15.

1077 Sankarananda, 1.138; Shashi, 178.

1078 Dowson, 3.

1079 Of course, no New Testament text speaks of the perpetual virginity of Mary. The doctrine is a later development of the myth. But we are comparing whole myth-cycles, not restricting our discussion to "canonical" sources.

1080 Wilson, H.H., 502.

1081 Wilson, H.H., 8.

1082 See, for example, BG 1.21, 11:41-2; SB 1.4.31, 1.5.12, 3.18.25, etc. (vedabase.net/a/acyuta). Interestingly, *achyuta* or *acutya* serves as a prefix for several words, including *acyutavasa* or "sacred fig-tree," the Latin name of which is *Ficus Religiosa*

aditirdyauraditirantarikṣamaditirmātā sa pitā sa putraḥ
viśve devā aditiḥ pañca janā aditirjātamaditirjanitvam

Ralph T.H. Griffith renders this passage thus:

Aditi is the heaven, Aditi is mid-air, Aditi is the Mother and the Sire and Son.

Aditi is all Gods, Aditi five-classed men, Aditi all that hath been born and shall be born.[1083]

Furthermore, the solar hero Krishna himself is a "son of Aditi," which means that he is born of the virgin dawn. Citing the "*Mahābhārata, Vanaparva*, vv. 484 ff," Christian missionary Dr. John Muir translates the passage as: "And thou, Krishna, of the Yādava race, having become the son of Aditi, and being called Vishnu."[1084]

In *Durgā as Mahiṣāsuramardinī: A Dynamic Myth of Goddess*, concerning Aditi, whom he names as "a very ancient goddess," Dr. Indira Shankar Aiyar states:

> Aditi was needed only to mother the Adityas and she took their characteristics of light and might. The Aryans also patterned their lives according to these divinities. She is said to be a virgin goddess, that is, after Indra's birth. Her virgin godhead could be seen as the Kanya Kumari aspect of the later Goddess. The myth states that, after the hero's birth, she should die or get her spouse killed, so that no more conception can take place in that womb. There are other epithets which also point to her virgin status like "yuvati."[1085]

Elsewhere, Aiyar says, "Aditi, in the HV, is born as Devaki, the mother-goddess Devagarbhā."[1086] "Devagarbha" means "Divine Womb." A "divine womb" would be a "pure womb" or "virgin womb" (i.e., *kanyagarbha*).

Citing the *Vedangas* ("limbs of the Vedas") and the "Pourourava" or *Pururava*, Jacolliot relates the following verses:

> It is in the bosom of a woman that the ray of the divine splendor will receive human form, and she shall bring forth—being a virgin—for no impure contact shall have defiled her.
>
> The lamb is born of an ewe and a ram, the kid of a goat and a buck goat, the child of a woman and a man; but the divine Paramatma (soul of the Universe) shall be born of a virgin, who shall

1083 Griffith, 115.
1084 Muir, 118; Roy, P.C., 2.29. See also Bryant (2007), 61, who cites the Mahabharata 3.13.23.
1085 Aiyar, 115.
1086 Aiyar, 212.

be fecundated by the thought of Vishnu.[1087]

knya or Kanyā

Virginity was so important to ancient Indians that there are many words conveying "virgin" in Sanskrit, such as: *kanyakā*, *kanyā*, *kanīnakā*, *kumārikā*, *mālatī*, *nivarā*, *kumārī*, *akṣatayoni*, *akṣatā*, *ananyapūrvā*, *agrū*, *asprṣṭamaithunā*, etc. Some of these terms, such as *akṣatayoni* and *asprṣṭamaithunā*, clearly refer to genitals and sexual activity. There are many additional compound words reflecting the esteem for virginity, such as *nāgakanyā* or "serpent-virgin."[1088]

The Sanskrit word for "virgin," *kanyā*, along with its many variants, is used hundreds of times in Indian texts such as the *Mahabharata*.[1089] The word *kanyagarbha/kanyāgarbhaḥ* or "virgin womb" can be found at MBh 1.126.3,[1090] book 1, section 138 of Ganguli's translation: "That far-famed destroyer of hostile hosts, the large-eyed Karna, was born of Pritha in her maidenhood."[1091]

One or another form of the word *kanya* is used in the *Rigveda* as well, generally translated as "maid" or "maiden."[1092] The status of *kanya* as a virgin is clear from such terms as *kanyātva* and *kanyābhāva*, which mean "virginity" and "maidenhood," and *kanyādūṣaṇa*, which refers to "defilement of a virgin" or "deflowering."[1093] RV 1.123.10 is a comparison of the Goddess—Dawn—with "a maid," the term used here is *kanyeva*, prior to which appears the word *kR^iShNAd* or *kṛṣṇād*, translated as "darkness." Hence, the dawn newly breaking through the darkness is virginal. When the translation "maiden" is used (e.g., RV 1.161.5), the Kanya reference here is to the constellation of Virgo.

MBh 1.1.82 says: "*Samavāye tato rājñāṃ kanyāṃ bhartṛsvayaṃvarām prāptavān arjunaḥ kṛṣṇāṃ kṛtvā karma suduṣkaram.*" Ganguli

1087 Jacolliot (1870), 222. Pururava was a mythical king, the "ancient chief of the Lunar race," associated in the *Rig Veda* (10.95.1-18) and elsewhere with Surya the sun and Ushas the dawn. Son of the planet Budha or Mercury/Hermes, Pururava is claimed to be the first progenitor of Krishna's line.

1088 A study of how the serpent virgin is used to describe characters in Indian texts would be of interest.

1089 See, for example, book 5, chapter 187; *Mahabharata online*, fiindolo.sub.uni-goettingen.de/gretil/1_sanskr/2_epic/mbh/sas/b05/b05c187.htm

1090 *Mahabharata online*, fiindolo.sub.uni-goettingen.de/gretil/1_sanskr/2_epic/mbh/sas/b01/
b01c126.htm#b01c126v003. Monier-Williams has this term *kanyAgarbha* listed as appearing at "MBh, xii, 49."

1091 Ganguli, 1.287.

1092 For example, RG 1.123.10.

1093 Monier-Williams, 249.

renders this passage: "After a while, Arjuna obtained the virgin Krishna at the *swayamvara*, in the midst of a concourse of Rajas, by performing a very difficult feat of archery."[1094]

Again, we read that "the mother of Krishna was reputedly a virgin, and the incarnate god is sometimes designated as 'the virgin's son' (*kanyakājāta, kānīnagarbha*)."[1095]

The word *kanya* also means "chaste and undefiled," qualities of virgins.

Is Krishna called "Kaniya" or "Kaneya"—"Kanya"—to signify "virgin born?" Although he is said to be the father of many children, Krishna, too, shares the epithet *kanya* or "virgin." Surely, the epithet of "virgin" for the gopi-loving Krishna would otherwise be ridiculous? Or yet another example of how gods/goddesses are both sexually active and virginal at once?

Virgin Mothers in the Epics

Yet another virgin birth appears in the *Ramayana*, in the story told by Jambavan about Anjana's mother, "a maiden among the goddesses above":

> One day, while she was wandering care-free on a mountain slope, Vaayu saw her beauty and fell in love with her and embraced her. She was wroth. "Who are you, O wicked one" she asked, "who dares insult me?" The Wind-God answered: "Be not angry, your body is not tainted by my touch and loses not its virgin purity. Not in body but in my heart's desire did I embrace you, and out of this ethereal embrace, a child will be born to you, equal to me in strength and vigour. He will be the mightiest and most intelligent amongst the *Vaanaras*."[1096]

Addressing this recurrent theme in the epics of "born-again virgins," so to speak, Dr. Krishna Chandra Mishra remarks:

Draupadi is stated to have become virgin (*kanyā*) afresh even after her union with any of the five brothers whom she was married with, M90.14; Madhavi is said to have become virgin after several issues V.1 14.11. Satyavatī and Kuntī became *kanyā* after giving

1094 Ganguli, 1.7

1095 Śudraka, 62. Monier-Williams translates *kanyakajata* as "son of an unmarried woman," while *kananagarbha* or *kanyagarbha* is rendered "offspring of an unmarried woman," meaning "virgin womb." Hence Krishna *kanyagarbha* would denote "Krishna of the virgin womb." It should be noted that in antiquity virgins and unmarried women were generally deemed the same, so the term translated as "unmarried woman" is meant to convey "virgin."

1096 Rajagopalachari, 210.

birth to Vyīsa and Karṇa respectively.[1097]

He also states: "It appears that the meaning of virginity had somewhat changed in a definite perspective. Many girls like Kali (Satyavati), Kunti, Madhavi and Draupadi, who had been polluted for one or other reasons, are treated as virgins (*kanyā*) worthy of marriage."[1098] As Mishra further states, "Chastity was no essential condition for a virgin."[1099]

Krishna's paternal aunt Kunti herself is depicted as a virgin mother in the *Mahabharata*.

Krishna Vyasadeva, Son of a Virgin

The scribe Vyasa, legendary classifier of the Vedas and composer of the Mahabharata—also called "Krishna," evidently a reflection of his skin color—was said to be *kānīna* or "son of a virgin."[1100] Like "the" Krishna, Vyasa has been considered an avatar of Vishnu.[1101]

Suggestively, at BG 10.37, Krishna identifies himself as the sage Vyāsadeva or "Veda Vyasa," traditional divider of the Vedas, author of the Puranas and Brahmana Sutras, and compiler of the *Mahabharata*, said to have been virgin-born.[1102] If the god Krishna identifies himself as the sage Krishna, the former must possess the attributes of the latter, including the status of having been born of a virgin. This contention is especially valid in consideration of the rest of the evidence brought forth here and elsewhere.

According to Jacolliot, the Vedanta says, "In the early part of the Kali Yug shall be born the son of a virgin," another passage showing the pre-Christian virgin-birth motif, this one seemingly referring to Krishna.

Devaki Virgin Claims

Since the eighteenth century, numerous writers have used the term "virgin" to describe Devaki, including Indian authors. Abhedānanda, for one, calls Krishna's mother, Devaki, a "holy virgin."[1103]

Virgin Mother Goddess

Evoking the scholarly concept of an ancient goddess—often the Great Mother—also being *parthenos* or a virgin in Indian folklore, Dr. Prithvi Kumar Agrawala, a professor at Banaras Hindu University, remarks: "When the folk goddesses are … known as 'maidens,' they are

1097 Mishra, 347.
1098 Mishra, 347.
1099 Mishra, 348.
1100 Garbe (1913), 331. The story is recounted in the Mahabharata, in the Adi Parva (63) and Sambhava Parva (105); Ganguli, 1.176–7, 1.317–8.
1101 Mahābhārata 12.350.4–5
1102 See "Sridhara Swami's Commentary," www.bhagavad-gita.org/Gita/verse-10-35.html.
1103 Abhedānanda, 1.50.

believed to be a group of the virgins or kindred mother goddesses of virgin nature."[1104]

Concerning the goddess or divine epithet Umā, Dr. Daniel C. Gilman, et al., remark:

> In Hindu mythology, one of the principal names of the consort of the god Siva … also called Durga, Devi, Kali, Parvati…. The myths relating to this goddess, who is worshiped in various parts of India, but especially in Bengal, are recounted in the great epic poems and Puranas…. According to the *Harivanśa* … in another life she was born as the daughter of Yasoda, and exchanged for Vishnu … when, in his incarnation as Krishna, he was born as a son of Devaki. On that occasion she was killed by Kansa, and became a divine virgin, to whom the gods addressed their praises, when she was called Kanya, or Kumari, the virgin.[1105]

We find a very pointed *parthenos* or "divine virgin" motif in this very myth, in the precise pericope in which the Indian hero is born, the birth narrative.

Interestingly, another word in Sanskrit for "virgin" is *pārtha* or *pārthona*, meaning "Virgo of the zodiac" and equivalent to the Greek *parthenos*.[1106] This fact does not mean necessarily that the signs were adopted from the Greek zodiac or that there were not 12 divisions earlier than contact with the Greek culture, as the term *kanya* also represented the constellation of Virgo and the 12-division zodiacal wheel.

Yet another character in the *Mahabharata* —the earliest layers of which evidently date from the fifth to eighth centuries prior to the Christian era—by the name of "Kunti," is likewise claimed to have been a virgin mother.

Mango Conception

In addition, Krishna's mother earlier had given birth as a "newly wed" and possibly *virginal* teenager, after becoming pregnant from eating half a mango. As professor of Religion Dr. Alf Hiltebeitel states:

> Devaki and Rohini are sisters of sixteen and fifteen distraught at their bridegroom's great age. All three newlyweds join Kamsa (the girls' brother) on a forest hunt. There the girls tease Kamsa into shooting down a mango tree's single fruit, from which each eats half and gets pregnant…. The griping about Vasudeva's "great age" may be indicative of a suggestion of nonconsummation of the recent marriage. In any event, it must be kept in mind that these are quite

1104 Agrawala, 69.
1105 Gilman, 19.620–1.
1106 Monier-Williams, 621.

obviously *myths*, not true stories about teenager girls becoming impregnated by eating a mango.[1107]

Obviously, the virgin birth vis-à-vis Krishna's mother represents a real, ancient Indian tradition, even if it is not strictly applicable to his specific nativity. In other words, at one point before Krishna was born, *Devaki would have been a virgin mother*, and the assumption that she remains so throughout the myth is thus understandable, particularly if we view the story as a typical anthropomorphization of natural forces, in this case specifically as concerns the sun (Krishna) and the dawn (Devaki). There could also be a parallel here with the story of Eve eating the fruit in the Garden of Eden, after which she suffers the fall from grace.

The fact that Devaki was also known by the epithet *kanya* is also suggestive. As Balfour states, "Kanya was a name of the mother of Krishna. She was a daughter of Yasuda Kanya, a maiden, a virgin, a girl … Kanya, the astronomical sign of Virgo."[1108]

In consideration of all these facts, as well as what we know about Buddha's conception in "purity" and the mythical virgin-mother motif in other cultures, it seems reasonable to place Devaki in the *parthenos* category.

The Indian virgin-mother motif makes itself startlingly clear in the *Bahvricha Upanishad*, a devotional to the Goddess in which appears the following:

> The Goddess was indeed one in the beginning. Alone she emitted the world-egg …
>
> Of Her was Brahma born; was Vishnu born …
>
> She, here, is the Power Supreme …
>
> She alone is Atman … She is the Science of Consciousness …
>
> She who is contemplated as "That which I am' or "I am He" … the Virgin, the Mother …

This text reveals the very ancient concept of the parthenogenetic creatrix of the cosmos, who needs no male to reproduce, bringing forth as a "virgin." Virgin and mother, alone she produces the "world-egg."

The goddess Devī is described in the *Chandi Mahatmayi*, *Devi Mahatmyam* or *Devīmāhātmyam* (sixth cent. AD/CE?) as the "virgin," "youthful virgin" and "mother."[1109] Both "Devi" and "Devaki" mean "divine." For the many reasons given above, and since Devaki is, in our opinion, not a historical figure but a mythical "incarnation" or anthropomorphization of the Indian Goddess, we would not be remiss in suggest-

1107 Hiltebeitel, 1.186.
1108 Balfour, 2.498.
1109 Dowson, 87.

ing that she too shared these epithets, including *kanya* or "virgin." This suggestion is likewise apt when it is recalled that Devaki was viewed as the "mother goddess."

Concerning Krishna, Bryant says, "As a pan-Indian deity, his worship takes on distinctive forms and unique flavors that today dominate entire regions all over the subcontinent."[1110]

In any event, the god Krishna is, like Christ, a product of a god and a "mortal woman."

Winter Solstice 'Birthday'

Earlier writers who asserted that Krishna was born at the winter solstice or on December 25 were confused over the name of the traditional birth month, Sravana, which generally represents July-August. However, the month of Shraavana and the "lunar mansion" Sravana have been confused, with the latter "belonging to" the constellation Makara in the Indian zodiac and Aquarius in the Western.[1111] Makara is the sign of Capricorn and the time of the winter solstice; hence, a "birth" in a lunar mansion symbolized by Makara may be mistaken as constituting "December 25," although in the current era the Indian winter solstice is celebrated on January 15.

Garbe asserted, "The celebration of Krishna's birthday … is an imitation of the Christian festival."[1112]

In the original edition of this book, I contended that Krishna was "born on December 25th," as suggested by a number of previous writers.[1113] For reasons given in my article "Was Krishna Born on December 25th?" and because Krishna is a solar hero and incarnation of the sun god Vishnu, who "rises" at the winter solstice ("Makara").

The "northern path of the sun," Uttarayana, is also the "presiding demigod" over the six months from the winter to summer solstices, although in Hindu practice this date has not been adjusted for precession. The passage at BG 8.24 refers to individuals who have died through the agency of or during the period of the gods Agni (fire), Jyotih (light), Ahah (daytime), Suklah (waxing moon/bright fortnight) and Uttarayanam (winter-summer months). Such individuals "attain the Ultimate Truth"[1114] or Brahma, achieving upon death enlightenment and liberation from reincarnation. The transliterated Sanskrit of BG 8.24 is:

agnir jyotir ahaḥ śuklaḥ ṣa-māsā uttarāyaṇam tatra prayātā gac-

1110 Bryant (2007), 3.

1111 "Nakshatra," en.wikipedia.org/wiki/Nakshatra

1112 Garbe (1914), 36.

1113 See, for example, Kersey Graves and Godfrey Higgins.

1114 BG 8.24, www.bhagavad-gita.org/Gita/verse-08-24.html.

chanti brahma brahma-vido janāḥ

This passage is highly astrotheological, as *uttarayana* is not only a time of light and life, it is the title of the god who presides over that solar period. In a sense, therefore, the demigod or god bearing the name or epithet *uttarayana* could be said to be "born" at the beginning of the period over which he presides (i.e., the winter solstice). The start of the winter solstice is celebrated with the festival of *makara sankrati*, which is commonly observed on January 14 in India at this time; a century ago *Encyclopedia Britannica* recorded the observation as taking place on January 12.[1115]

Regarding the two halves of the year, Fuller comments:

> The six solar months stretching from the winter to summer solstices, when the sun appears to move north and days lengthen, is the auspicious uttaryana. The other six months, when the sun moves south and days shorten, is the inauspicious dakshinayana. Moreover, because one human year equals one divine day, the uttarayana is the deities' daytime and the dakshinayana their night-time. The winter solstice is then sunrise, the spring equinox midday, the summer solstice sunset, and the autumn equinox midnight.[1116]

This binary division of the year is more important in the south than in the north of India, particularly in Tamil Nadu and Kerala.[1117] Vishnu's sleep is also part of a four-month period, during which demons are said to enter the world, as they do during the *dakshinayana* or half of the year from the summer to winter solstice. "Throughout northern India, Vishnu is said to fall asleep on the eleventh day of the bright fortnight of *ashadha* (June-July) and to wake up on the corresponding day in *karttika* (October-November)."[1118] The idea of Vishnu's sleep is ancient, although its rationale is rather obscure and numerous explanations have been advanced. Since this latter motif was emphasized in the north, while the southern Indians were more focused on the yearly motif, it appears that the attaching of Vishnu's sleep to the *dakshinayana* may have been a contrivance to make common ground between these different regions.

Concerning this subject, in a section called "The Repose of Vishnu," Col. James Tod remarks, "They term the summer solstice in the month of Asarh, 'the night of the gods,' because Vishnu (as the sun) reposes

1115 Chisholm, 13.493.
1116 Fuller, 110.
1117 Fuller, 110.
1118 Fuller, 109–11.

during the four rainy months on his serpent couch." [1119] Conversely, the "day of the gods" would be the period from the winter solstice to the summer solstice, the former serving as the start of the ancient Indian New Year as well.[1120]

Edward Balfour:

> *Kartik Ekadasi* is the 11th in some years, the 12th day of the light half of the month of Kartik or about the 8th November. On this day, Vishnu is supposed to rise from his four months' sleep and this has reference to the sun being at the winter solstice.[1121]

In *The Journal of Anthropological Research*, we learn that "Jones (1793:258) says that the sleep and rise of Vishnu were originally solar events related to the summer and winter solstices."[1122] The article notes, however, that in "Shanti Nagar they are not determined by the sun but by lunar days—the bright elevenths of Asharh and Karttik."

It has been contended, by Professor Hillebrandt for one, that the Visuvant should begin the year at the winter solstice (Sir William Ridgeway, 144). Bali, "king of the asuras," is "marked out" at the winter solstice, "but in a somewhat different manner from Vishnu." (Kelley, *Exploring Ancient Skies: A Survey of Ancient and Cultural Astronomy*. New York: Springer, 2011; 488). Pausha is near the winter solstice. The winter solstice is apparently one of Vishnu's three strides.[1123] The divine name or epithet *dyaus*, "Father Sky," whence comes "day," is equated with the winter solstice.[1124]

Uttaryana is also said to be the "day of the gods," while its counterpart is the "night of the gods."[1125] Interestingly, *uttarayana* is also taken to indicate "dawn," while its opposite *daksinayana* is the "gloaming."[1126] In this regard, then, *uttarayana* is the "sunrise," while *daksinayana* is the "sunset," and the vernal (*ciṣuvat*) and autumnal (*viṣuvat*) equinoxes represent "midday" and "midnight," respectively.[1127]

Makara refers to Capricorn, while *sankrati* is a transition. *Makara sankrati* is therefore the beginning or "birth" of the sun in Capricorn, which essentially is the same as "Christmas."

This winter-summer and summer-winter cycle is the same as that

1119 Tod (1920), 2.655.
1120 Tod (1920), 2.655.
1121 Balfour, 1.253.
1122 Journal of Anthropological Research (1964), 20.83.
1123 Chakraberty, *Racial History*, 284. [biblio]
1124 Gonda, 103.
1125 Raheja, 57.
1126 Beane, 188.
1127 Fuller, 110; Davis, R.H., 140.

represented by Osiris/Anubis and Jesus/John the Baptist. The sun in *uttarayana* is said to be progressing north towards the equator.[1128] Whether or not it is viewed as the "birthday" of the sun, as incarnated in Krishna or any other figure, it is clear that the winter-solstice transition or *uttaranaya sankrati* is an auspicious time of beginning, "waxing," renewal and "rebirth." Speaking of festivities held in winter, Eck says: "Not surprisingly, the Sun is especially honored during these winter months, when his warmth is welcomed. And these are good months for pilgrimage rounds."[1129]

Krishna Crucified?

In the original edition of the present volume, I included commentary about Krishna being "crucified" and "depicted on a cross with nail-holes in his feet, as well as having a heart emblem on his clothing." This perception comes from a debate in the eighteenth century concerning two identical images procured in India by Protestant missionary Rev. Dr. William Moor showing a crucified figure.[1130] Upon inquiry, Moor's pandit guessed that the figure was probably of the Indian god Wittoba, who, Moor relates, had a "pierced foot" in another image.[1131] Scholars have debated whether this image may be European, representing Jesus Christ, and later editions of Moor's work, such as that of Rev. Simpson, had this anecdote and the plate expunged.

The origin of Wittoba's wounded foot is accounted for in Indian mythology and is not a product of Christian influence. Moreover, Krishna's death under a tree from an arrow or sharp metal object through his foot is similar to Jesus's death on the "fatal tree." Krishna is also connected to Wittoba, who is yet another avatar of Vishnu.

The presence of figures in cruciform is known in India, Tibet and Nepal, especially as concerns the god Indra, according to the Catholic Jesuit missionary Father Huc. During the seventeenth century, Huc traveled extensively throughout Asia and wrote volumes about his travels, including the similarities between Catholicism and Buddhist religions. He also related that there were numerous gods in cruciform placed at crossroads. It is clear from this example and others that many gods, goddesses and other figures of pre-Christian antiquity were depicted in cruciform or on a cross, a motif only later adopted into the gospel story.

The orthodox depiction of Krishna's death has him shot in the foot by a hunter's arrow while under a tree, reminiscent of the death of Achil-

1128 Hegde, 97.

1129 Eck, 274.

1130 Moor, 419–20, citing plate 98 in his volume.

1131 Moor, 418, citing plate11, fig. 6.

les. But, as is typical in mythology, there are variant versions of his death. In *The Bible in India*, citing as his sources the *Bhagavad Gita* and Brahminical traditions, French scholar and Indianist Jacolliot tells of a version in which Krishna knows the time of his fated death and, parting from his disciples, goes to the Ganges for purification. He plunges into the sacred river, then kneels and prays, awaiting death, which is not long in coming. He had once exposed the crimes of a man named Angada who now seeks revenge. The assassin fires several arrows. For this he is condemned, like the Wandering Jew of Christian legend, to wander forever along the banks of the Ganges, subsisting on the rotting flesh of those who had died there. Having killed the divine avatar, Angada hung his body on the branches of a tree, leaving it for the circling vultures. But when a crowd gathered, following the disciple Arjuna, to take charge of the holy corpse, it was gone, miraculously replaced by a cloaking of great red flowers redolent of the sweetest perfume.

This scenario would certainly seem to count as a crucifixion, and not just figuratively. Criminals were not infrequently affixed to sturdy trees in lieu of carven beams. When this version of Krishna's death has the god-man impaled by many arrows, not just one, we have to think of the nails with which the victims of crucifixion were pinned to their gibbets. And of course, we are to understand the disappearance of the body and its replacement by fragrant flowers as tokens of ascension and renewed life. Moreover, this legend is evidently but a variant of the *orthodox* tale, constituting an apparently esoteric tradition recognizing Krishna's death as a crucifixion. Nor is Jacolliot the only comparative religionist to note the existence of this version of Krishna's passion.

It is not just tradition but also artifacts that have led to the conclusion that Krishna was crucified. Indeed, numerous images of crucified gods have been found in India, one of whom apparently is intended as Krishna, though one will look in vain for this information in mainstream resources such as encyclopedias.

Moreover, it appears that Krishna is not the first Indian god depicted as crucified. Prior to him was another incarnation of Vishnu, the avatar named Wittoba or Vithoba, who has often been identified with Krishna. Earlier copies of Moor's Hindu Pantheon features representations of Krishna (as Wittoba), with marks of holes in both feet, and in others, of holes in the hands. In Figures 4 and 5 of Plate 11 (in Moor's work), the figures have nail-holes in both feet. Plate 6 has a round hole in the side.

The Wittoba temples where these images came from are located at Terputty and Punderpoor. Terputty was, in Moor's time, under the control of the British, who had purchased the site. It may be asked why the

British would be so interested in an avatar purportedly so minor and unimportant as to warrant exclusion of his story from their reports. The avatar was, in fact, important enough to be widespread and to have names in a number of different dialects, names or titles that included Wittoba, Ballaji, Vinkatyeish, Terpati, Vinkratramna Govinda and Takhur. Concerning Ballaji, Higgins says, "The circumstance of Ballaji treading on the head of the serpent shows that he is, as the Brahmins say, an Avatar of Cristna."

Any evidence of crucified gods in India—asserted by some to be commonplace in sacred areas, but hidden by the priesthood—may today be scant. It is an intriguing coincidence that many of the scholars who unwillingly and against interest exposed this information were not only Christian but also British, and that the British took over pertinent places, possibly with the intent of destroying such evidence, among other motives. As Higgins—himself a Brit—says: "And when we perceive that the Hindoo Gods were supposed to be crucified, it will be impossible to resist a belief that the particulars of the crucifixion have been suppressed."

Nor does the mystery end there. In his comments concerning the various enigmatic images of an Indian god crucified, Rev. Lundy also acknowledges other striking assertions, regarding purported *Irish* crucifix images:

> Was Krishna ever crucified? Look at Fig. 61 and see. It is indeed an ancient Irish bronze relic, originally brought to the island from the East by some of the Phoenicians. It is unlike any Christian crucifix ever made. It has no nail marks in the hands or feet; there is no wood; no inscription; no crown of thorns, but the turreted coronet of the Ephesian Diana; no attendants; the ankles are tied together by a cord; and the dress about the loins is like Krishna's. It is simply a modification of Krishna as crucified. Henry O'Brien thinks it is meant for Buddha. But another most accomplished Oriental scholar says it is Krishna crucified: "One remarkable tradition avers the fact of Krishna dying on the fatal cross (a tree), to which he was pierced by the stroke of an arrow, and from the top of which he foretold the evils that were coming on the earth, which came to pass from thirty to forty years afterwards, when the age of crimes and miseries began; or about the same length of time as intervened between our Lord's crucifixion and the destruction of Jerusalem, an age of bitter calamities and crimes."

Another Indian sun god apparently frequently depicted as crucified is Indra, who as a solar hero could be considered interchangeable with Wittoba and Krishna. The crucifixion of Indra is likewise recorded in the monk Georgius's *Alphabetum Tibetanum*, p. 203, according to Higgins, who provides pertinent passages in the original Latin: "*Nam A effigies est ipsius Indrae crucifixi signa Telech in fronte manibus pedibuseque gerentis*."

Although written in the eighteenth century, this work is in Latin, which was commonly used by the better educated precisely in order to go over the heads of the masses and keep secrets from them. Father Georgius's book contained images of this *Tibetan* savior "as having been nailed to the cross. There are five wounds, representing the nail-holes and the piercing of the side. The antiquity of the story is beyond dispute." Titcomb also relates the crucifixion of Indra as found in Georgius: "The monk Georgius, in his *Tibetanum Alphabetum* (p. 203), has given plates of a crucified god worshipped at Nepal. These crucifixes were to be seen at the corners of roads and on eminences. He calls it the god Indra."

In *Asiatic Researches*, Col. Wilford, another pious Christian, verifies that the "heathen" Hindus venerated crosses in public places and at crossroads. The appearance of the crucified gods as roadside protectors is logical: If you were going to put up an image of a god as a protector, would you not make his arms as widespread as possible (i.e., in cruciform)? In fact, it would be surprising if such images did *not* exist.

Resurrection?

In the *Vishnu Purana*, Krishna's death is related thus:

> The divine Govinda then, having concentrated in himself that supreme spirit which is one with Vásudeva, was identified with all beings. Respecting the words of the Brahman, the imprecation of Durvásas, the illustrious Krishńa sat engaged in thought, resting his foot upon his knee. Then came there a hunter, named Jará, whose arrow was tipped with a blade made of the piece of iron of the club, which had not been reduced to powder; and beholding from a distance the foot of Krishńa, he mistook it for part of a deer, and shooting his arrow, lodged it in the sole. Approaching his mark, he saw the four-armed king, and, falling at his feet, repeatedly besought his forgiveness, exclaiming, "I have done this deed unwittingly, thinking I was aiming at a deer! Have pity upon me, who am consumed by my crime; for thou art able to consume me!" Bhagavat replied, "Fear not thou in the least. Go, hunter, through my favour, to heaven, the abode of the gods." As soon

> as he had thus spoken, a celestial car appeared, and the hunter, ascending it, forthwith proceeded to heaven. Then the illustrious Krishńa, having united himself with his own pure, spiritual, inexhaustible, inconceivable, unborn, undecaying, imperishable, and universal spirit, which is one with Vásudeva, abandoned his mortal body and the condition of the threefold qualities.[1132]

Although Krishna does not resurrect bodily, he is killed and then alive again, which is the point of any comparison using the term "resurrection." See also commentary by Lundy, who, puzzling over these detailed similarities, averred that the Krishna myth could not have been copied from Christianity but that it "must be an original product of the Hindu mind, working upon the old Patriarchal prophecies respecting the Christ, as they were contained in the old universal and primeval Revelation."[1133]

A common date for the "historical" Krishna believed in by millions of Hindu devotees is 3228 BCE.[1134] Devotees also believe Krishna lived to be 125 years old, an interesting figure, in consideration of a tradition that, after his death and resurrection, Christ lived in India to the ripe old age of 125 or so.

The Origin of Krishna Worship

Bryant gives the following literary evidences for Krishna from antiquity:

> The worship of Krishna as a divine figure can be traced back to well before the Common Era.... There is no obvious reference to Krishna in the *Rigveda*, the oldest Indic text, dated to circa 1500 BCE, although the name does appear a handful of times in the hymns (a few scholars have unconvincingly tried to connect these instances with him or with some proto-figure from whom he evolved). Most instances of the word *Krishna* in the *Rigveda*, however, are simply in its meaning as the adjective "black." It is in the late Vedic period, as represented by the *Chandogya Upanishad*, a philosophical text of around the sixth century BCE, that we find the first plausible—but still questionable—reference to the Puranic Krishna.
>
> Less questionable references, however, emerge subsequent to this point in time. In Yaska's *Nirukta*, an etymological dictionary of around the fifth century BCE, there is a reference to the

1132 Wilson, H.H., 612.

1133 Lundy, 161.

1134 See, for example, "SriKrishna—his life and teachings." archives.amritapuri.org/bharat/symbolism/srikrishna.php

> Shyamantaka jewel in the possession of Akrura, a motif from a well-known Krishna story. There is a brief reference to Krishna under his patronymic of Vasudeva in the famous Sanskrit grammar, the *Ashtadhyayi* of Panini, dated around the fourth century BCE, which is important because, given similar references in other texts of this period, it may indicate that the author considered Krishna a divine being. In the *Baudyana Dharma Sutra*, also of around the fourth century BCE, there is an invocation to Vishnu using twelve names including Keshava, Govinda and Damodara, which are names associated with Vishnu in the form of Krishna, thereby pointing to the latter's divine status in this very period. These names also reveal an awareness of several stories that are fully developed in later texts, as do, in the same period, a number of references in the *Arthashastra*, a Machiavellian political treatise. Along the same lines, in the *Mahanarayana Upanishad* of the *Taittriya Aranyaka*, around the third century BCE, a *gayatri mantra* associates Vasudeva with Narayana and Vishnu. Another significant source of references prior to the Common Era is Patanjali, the commentator on the famous grammar of Panini in the second century BCE. In his commentary (3.1.26), Patanjali mentions one of the most important episodes in Krishna's life, *Kamsavadha*, the killing of Kamsa, as represented in tales and theatrical performances, adding that the events were considered to have taken place long ago. Patanjali further makes a number of other clear references to Krishna and his associates as they are known in later texts.

In consideration of the importance afforded the Rigveda, which does indeed contain mention of a divine *krishna*, albeit "she" is a female, it may be possible that here we do find a germ, if small, of the later Krishna myth. Efforts in the past to isolate this germ have noted that the southern Indian black races had their own black god, Mayon. Although the "birthplace" of Krishna is represented as Mathura, in the northeast of the Subcontinent, it is possible the priesthood there derived inspiration from both the *krishna* in the RV and a number of deities known in India, such as Mayon.

Bryant also comments:

> Early Buddhist sources also provide evidence of the worship of Krishna prior to the Common Era. The *Niddesa*, one of the books of the Pali canon of the fourth century BCE, speaks somewhat derogatorily of those devoted to Vasudeva (Krishna) and Baladeva (Krishna's brother).... The Buddhist *Ghata Jata-*

> *ka* text also mentions characters from the Krishna story.... That both early Buddhist and Jain sources saw fit to appropriate these legends in some form or fashion points to their presence and significance on the religious landscape of this period.[1135]

We know from the Heliodorus column found at Besnagar, India, that as early as around 100 BCE, Krishna is worshipped as a divine figure. As Bryant comments:

> The inscription is particularly noteworthy because it reveals that a foreigner had been converted to the Krishna religion by this period—Heliodorus was a Greek.
>
> That the Krishna tradition was prominent enough to attract a powerful foreign envoy in the first century BCE might suggest that it had already developed deep roots by this time.[1136]
>
> After presenting a survey of the literature on the subject, Sunil Kumar Bhattacharya remarks:
>
> Although the Krishna legend goes back perhaps as far as the eighth century BC, the first epigraphic evidence is found in the second century BC. The earliest sculptures of Krishna, however, belong to the first century AD, in the Kusāṇa-Kshatrapa period at Mathura.[1137]

Others advocate an earlier date for Krishna. Radhakrishnan, asserts: "By the fourth century before Christ, the cult of Vasudeva was well established."[1138] It appears that the bulk of the composite, accreted Krishna myth was created after the sixth century BCE, when his traditional "birthplace" of Mathura became the capital of the Surasena "great realm."

Thundy also contends for a pre-Christian date for the Krishna myth: "He is celebrated as a warrior and religious teacher in the *Mahabharata* completed probably in the third century BC."[1139]

Some of these motifs, such as the Kalki avatar returning to earth on a white horse, make their appearance in writing relatively late, in this case the seventh century. Hence, it has been contended that this theme is copied from Christianity, rather than possibly the other way around. However, in Indian religion and mythology many very ancient ideas are recycled, as accretions to other concepts, including various deities, which continually take form and shape over a period of hundreds or thousands of years. This motif of a savior coming on a white horse is

1135 Bryant (2007), 5.
1136 Bryant (2007), 6.
1137 Bhattacharya, 27.
1138 Radhakrishnan, 29.
1139 Thundy (1993), 97.

non-Christian and evidently predates the Common Era.

The Rigveda

As concerns the date when some form of Krishna worship begins to appear in the historical record, analysis of the Rigveda indicates a divine *kṛṣṇa* figure ("the black" or "the dark") in germ (and opposite gender) sometime between 1700 and 1000 BCE, the conservative dating for the text's composition. Others argue for composition as early as 3000 BCE. One verse cited as a germ of Krishna is RV 8.96.13a:

ava drapso aṃśumatīmatiṣṭhadiyānaḥ kṛṣṇo daśabhiḥ sahasraiḥ

Translated by Griffith (at RV 8.85.13): "The Black Drop sank in Amsumati's bosom, advancing with ten thousand round about it," the "black drop" possibly referring to a Krishna germ.

In the *Rigveda* and *Samveda* we read of an *asura* king named "Krishnasur" or "black asura" who has been supposed in the past to represent *the* Krishna. This contention has been contested, however, because their "histories" diverge. But this is a problem only if one imagines that the Krishna of devotion is a "historical" figure. But it is always possible that, if Krishnasur himself is historical to some extent, the mythical Krishna character could be based in part on him. But Krishnasur is said to be a king among the Asuras—themselves mythical "power-seeking deities" who figure prominently in the Vedas; thus, Krishnasur is yet another mythical figure, one that could quite possibly have contributed to the Krishna character. Krishnasur appears at RV 8:96:15, just two verses after the *krishna* at RV 8.96.13, which further suggests a connection between the two.

Mainstream scholarship contends that these various *krishnas* are different from the "real" Krishna, whose worship currently is traceable textually only to around the fourth century BCE, if that. Yet, contrary to the fervently held beliefs of millions of devotees, academia accepts that the Krishna figure is a mythical compilation whose myth was accreted numerous times over a period of centuries to millennia. This type of long-term story weaving is common in religion and mythology.

It thus appears that Krishna was not a "real person" who may have lived at some point in history. Rather, he seems to be a mythical figure whose exploits and sayings were tree rings growing around a core of the various *krsnas* in the Rigveda and other early texts. The more concrete formation of the Krishna character occurred between the beginning and middle of the first millennium BCE. The *krsna* germ, however, may date earlier than that, as in India certain religious concepts appear to be traceable to at least 12,000 years ago in the southern part, where thrived the "Black God."

The term *krsna* or, as transliterated elsewhere, *kR^iShNA*, appears in one form or another in the Rigveda upwards of 50 times. The word "*arjuna*" and its various forms are utilized more than a dozen times in the Rigveda, translated as "white," "clear," "silver" and "gold," among others. The fact that *krisna*, meaning "black," and *arjuna*, meaning "white," appear together in early Indian literature might suggest a comparison to sets of chromosomes waiting to come together to give rise to the later mythology.

The Puranas

As his myth developed, Krishna was made dominant over other, older gods, including and especially the hero of the Vedas, Indra. Monier-Williams states:

> Krishna as a youth contested the sovereignty of Indra, and was victorious over that god, who descended from heaven to praise Krishna, and made him lord over the cattle [Hariv. 3787ff; 7456ff; VP.][1140]

This was evidently one of the most important roles for an Indian god, given the value ascribed to cattle in Indian culture. The cow in the RV is symbolic of the Dawn and the goddess of Speech.[1141]

The *Harivaṃśa Purana* evidently dates to around the first or second centuries BCE to the first century AD/CE (with some later interpolations), representing the "Lineage of Hari," an epithet of Vishnu. The Harivaṃśa is set in time to explain Krishna's birth and ascension prior to the *Mahabharata*.

Although hundreds of millions revere Krishna as a god, other Indians viewed him as "an impious wretch." Monier-Williams remarks: "Krishna is one of the nine black Vasu-devas; with Buddhists he is the chief of the black demons, who are the enemies of Buddha and the white demons.[1142] The question, then, is why Krishna gained dominance over the older Vedic gods—why the "dark" or monthly waxing of the moon? Was there a priesthood presiding over the dark fortnight of the moon, as there was with the sun and moon in so many places globally? Was this dark fortnight especially sacred to shepherds/cowherds? What is the nature-worshiping connection?

Krishna Grows as Scripture Grows

> Krishna appears as the leader of the Yadava tribe and the son of Devaki in the pre-Buddhist *Chandogya Upanishad.* He is a knower of the Brahman and a pupil of Ghora Angirasa

1140 Monier-Williams, 308.
1141 O'Flaherty, RV, 71.
1142 Monier-Williams, 308.

(III.17.6).[1143] By the time of the *Mahabharata* (fifth–eighth cent. BCE to fifth cent. AD/CE), the Krishna figure begins to appear in the epics. The *Mahabharata* is taken by many pious devotees to be a "historical" record of real people who lived at a certain point in remote Indian history. But there are many reasons to suppose this text significantly reflects mythology, specifically astral religion or astrotheology and much other wisdom. When viewed in this manner, both the poetic and scientific value of the *Mahabharata* increases; it need not have value only because it purportedly depicts "history." On the contrary, the brilliance in this text lies in its symbolism, its allegory and its mythical conveyance of exciting and important ideas and insights into life. This meaning, in fact, is only reduced when the text is taken to be historical.

The Bhagavad Gita or 'Song of God'

The *Bhagavad Gita* is the section of the *Mahabharata* in which many correspondences between Krishnaism and Christianity occur. It has been widely dated to somewhere between the second century BCE and the second century AD/CE (see below). Brockington's conclusion is that it is a first-century composition, possibly redacted in the second century. In any event, it is agreed that the text shows no evidence of having been influenced by Christianity and is largely if not entirely pre-Christian, since the Christian missionary effort in actuality did not occur until the second century for the most part. Jean W. Sedlar concludes that "even the latest date ordinarily accepted for the Gita—the second century AD—seems too early to justify any reasonable hypothesis of Christian influence upon it."[1144]

The consensus of mainstream academia is that the Greek ambassador Megasthenes (fl. 302–288 BCE), in writing of the Indian "Hercules," identified the god as Krishna. Against this assertion, Dahlquist elucidates many important differences between the two figures and argues for Megasthenes's "Hercules" as the god Indra. If Megasthenes *is* referring to Krishna, his account serves as one of the earliest confirmations of Krishna-worship in his fully anthropomorphized form. The fact that Megasthenes was said in antiquity by Arrian, Diodorus and Strabo to be describing the "Sourasenoi," who are undoubtedly the Surasenas or Shurasenas, tends to confirm that the Seleucid ambassador was indeed referring to Krishna in his depiction of the Indian "Herakles."[1145]

1143 Thundy (1993), 97.
1144 Sedlar, 188.
1145 See Bryant (2007), 5.

Bryant argues against the contention that the *Bhagavad Gita* was "somewhat enhanced in the colonial period" by pointing out that anyone making such revisions would be "expected to write a commentary on the *Gita* as one of the three main textual sources of scriptural authority."[1146] The composition of the *Bhagavad Gita*, for example, while attributed to Krishna Dwaipayana Vyasa, has been dated to various centuries, as early as the fifth to second centuries BCE and as late as several centuries into the Common Era.[1147] For example, one Indian scholar, G.S. Khair, argues for the Gita's composition during three different periods, from before the sixth to the third centuries BCE..[1148] As concerns the *Bhagavad Gita* being a later insertion into earlier layers in the *Mahabharata*, evidently composed in stages between the fifth century BCE and the fifth century AD/CE, Brockington's argument is sound that, after Krishna's stunning revelation of himself to Arjuna as the Supreme Being in the *Gita*, Arjuna is oddly casual with Lord Krishna in the rest of the Mahabharata,[1149] indicating the whole episode is an interpolation (and is non-historical, obviously). Brockington's further philological analysis, such as the focus on different divinities or the frequency of the word "Vishnu," likewise indicates the Gita to be an interpolation, written at a different time period by a different author.

Brockington concludes:

> The usual dating of the *Bhagavadgītā* to about the 2nd century BC seems to be based on the one hand on the recognition of its secondary status within the *Mahābhārata* and on the other hand on general assumptions about the early development of Vaisnavism. However, the linguistic and stylistic features of the *Bhagavadgītā* suggest a considerably later date, more like the 1st century AD.[1150]

Richard V. De Smart sees in the Gita a blend from nine traditions, including Brahmanism, Buddhism, Jainism, Shivaism, Upanishadic doctrines, the "Vasudeva-Krsna cult," Vaisnava and Yoga.[1151]

BG 10.13 reveals itself to have been written long after the original *Mahabharata*: "So the ancient seers spoke of you, as did the epic poet Vyasa and the bards."[1152] Clearly, the author of this verse knew about

1146 Bryant (2007), 4.
1147 See the work of John Brockington arguing for a date of composition during the first century AD/CE.
1148 Brockington, 268.
1149 Brockington, 270.
1150 Brockington, 157.
1151 Brockington, 270.
1152 Stoller Miller, 91.

the *Mahabharata*—the epic by Vyāsadeva—as a text separate from and predating the *Bhagavad Gita*. "Arjuna's" words also indicate the author himself is not Vyasadeva, traditional author of the MBh and BG. If Vyasa was the composer of the *Mahabharata* from beginning to end, including the BG, why would Arjuna speak of him as if he were in the past, as if he had already written the text in which Arjuna's "historical" actions and speech were supposedly recorded? In other words, this verse was clearly not spoken by a "historical" Arjuna; nor is it a product of Vyasadeva, since it speaks of him in the past. This passage, if not the entire BG, clearly constitutes an interpolation into the *Mahabharata*.

Moreover, the "ancient seers"—*rsayah* in the Sanskrit—are the rishis who composed the Vedas and Upanishads, revealing, possibly, that the BG writer perceived the *kṛṣṇa* in those texts to be suggestive of Lord Krishna. If this ancient writer perceives the "dark" of the Rigveda to be the god Krishna of the MBh and BG, then it may be logical for us to follow his lead.

Vishnu and Bhagavata Puranas

Like many other Indian texts,[1153] the *Vishnu Purana* appears to have been composed over several centuries, with dates ranging from the first century BCE to the tenth century AD/CE. The part of the *Vishnu Purana* that details Krishna's life is called the *Bhagavat Purana/Bhāgavata Purāṇa*, Śrí Bhágavata or Śrīmad Bhāgavatam, the extant version of which dates possibly to between the sixth and ninth to tenth centuries AD/CE but may reflect much older traditions.[1154]

The Phoenicians and Ireland

The story of Krishna as recorded in the ancient Indian legends and texts evidently penetrated the West on a number of occasions. One theory outside the mainstream holds that some form of Krishna worship made its way to Europe as early as 800 BCE, possibly brought by Phoenicians, whose connection to India is indicated by the elephant ivory trade through Phoenician cities as far back as several centuries BCE.[1155] This

1153 "The Puranas are a type of traditional Hindu texts that took form during the medieval period, often both informed by earlier material and undergoing later interpolations."

1154 Wilson (1840: xxi) accepted the composition of the BP by the grammarian Vopadeva, which he dated to the twelfth century.

1155 Handy, 160: "The hand carving of ivory for export from the Phoenician cities can be documented from the thirteenth to the seventh centuries BCE. These works appear originally to have been carved in local hippopotamus tusk ivory, until the animal became scarce and then extinct in the region; then the carvers extended their use of elephant tusk ivory imported from Africa, through Egypt, from India, through Mesopotamia, and perhaps from as close as inland Syria."

migration, too, could have occurred through the Phoenicians, who, it has been suggested, routinely traveled to the British Isles to buy tin.

As Anand states:

> Centuries before history was ever recorded we already find Asians engaged in free navigation and maritime trade in the Indian Ocean. According to some historians, the commerce between India and Babylon must have been carried on as early as 3000 BC. Apart from land routes, one of the most important trade routes joining India and the West was that which ran from India to the Red Sea up the Arabian coast. It linked India not only to the gold fields and wealthy incense country of southern Arabia, but to Egypt and Judea. From Judea, Indian goods found their way into the Mediterranean through the adjacent ports of Tyre and Sidon.
>
> There is also some archaeological evidence about maritime trade in the Mediterranean in a period which runs back into darkness. It is suggested by historians that Indians and Phoenicians probably traded on the shores of Arabia. During their heyday, Phoenicians were everywhere in the Mediterranean and founded several colonies around 1500 BC.[1156]

Alexander and the Greeks

Certain elements of Krishna worship and Indian culture were apparently injected into Western culture on several other occasions, including by Alexander the Great after the expansion of his empire and his sojourn in India. During the Hellenistic period that followed, the Greco-Indian kingdom on the western side of India and in Persia combined Greek and Indo-Aryan culture for centuries before the Common Era. A number of envoys and embassies from India to the Mediterranean followed the Roman "discovery" of the sailing route from the Red Sea to India during the reign of Augustus.

Apollonius of Tyana

Some say that Krishna's worship was reintroduced during the first century AD/CE by the Greek sage and miracle worker Apollonius of Tyana, who carried a fresh copy of the Krishna story in writing to the West, where it made its way to Alexandria, Egypt. Graham relates the tale:

> The argument runs thus: There was in ancient India a very great sage called Deva [Bodhisattva]. Among other things he wrote a mythological account of Krishna.... About 38 or 40 AD, Apollonius while traveling in the East found this story.... He considered it so important he translated it into his own language,

1156 Anand, 10.

> namely, Samaritan. In this he made several changes according to his own understanding and philosophy. On his return he brought it to Antioch, and there he died. Some thirty years later another Samaritan, Marcion, found it. He too made a copy with still more changes. This he brought to Rome about 130 AD, where he translated it into Greek and Latin.[1157]

In this possible Indian text allegedly reworked by Apollonius we might have the origins of Marcion's Gospel of the Lord, which he claimed was the Gospel of Paul.

In addition to the gospel story, the moralistic teachings purportedly introduced by Jesus were established long before by Krishna, among others. These similarities constitute the reason Christianity has failed, despite repeated efforts for centuries, to make much headway in India, as the Brahmans have recognized Christianity as a relatively recent imitation of their much older traditions, which they consider superior. As Higgins relates:

> The learned Jesuit Baldaeus observes that every part of the life of Cristna [Krishna] has a near resemblance to the history of Christ; and he goes on to show that the time when the miracles are supposed to have been performed was during the Dwapara-jug, which he admits to have ended 3,100 years before the Christian era. So that, as the Cantab says, *If there is meaning in words, the Christian missionary admits that the history of Christ was*

1157 Graham, 290. This Deva Bodhisattva may be the disciple of Nagarjuna Bodhisattva, these being two of the three founders of the "Three Shastra Sect." The son of the king, this Bodhisattva named Deva, lived on "Simhala" or "Ceylon," today's Sri Lanka, as discussed in the *Si-Yu-Ki : Buddhist Records of the Western World* (4) by the Chinese Buddhist monk and scholar Hiuen Tsiang or Xuanzang. (Beal, 1.188.) Xuanzang (c. 602–664) tells us that Deva Bodhisattva had a "supernatural appearance" (Beal, 1.189), while we also learn that he was the "20th lineal successor of the Dharma, [who] was killed by heretics." (Tanabe, 185) This individual appears to be the same Deva Bodhisattva who composed the "Treatise of the Great Zealous Disciple." (Yin-shun, 246.) He is also called Āryadeva. The Tibetan story concerning "Acharya" Aryadeva has him being "miraculously born of a lotus in the pleasure garden of the king of the Simhala island." (Tāranātha, 123) It is difficult to say if this person may have been involved in the composition of a Krishna "biography" or, rather, mythography, since Deva Bodhisattva was obviously a Buddhist, not a Krishna-worshipper. However, especially a few centuries before the Common Era, the cults of both godmen with their similar tales were thriving in India and were frequently confounded. Even their priests were interchangeable. In other words, there was no hard and fast line between them.

founded upon that of Crishnu [Krishna].[1158]

Reflecting the bigotry of the priestly caste, it is said in Bhagavata the Purana that "these works may not be accessible to women, Śúdras, and mixed castes."

Just like the writers of the gospels when they pretend to be "prophesying" events that have already happened, such as the destruction of the Jerusalem Temple in 70 AD/CE, authors of various Indian writings engage in *post factum* "prophecy," or after-the-fact "predictions."

Mithra of Persia

Mithra/Mitra is a very ancient god found both in Persia and India and predating the Christian savior by hundreds to thousands of years. In fact, the cult of Mithra was shortly before the Christian era "the most popular and widely spread 'Pagan' religion of the times," as Wheless says.

> Mithraism is one of the oldest religious systems on earth, as it dates from the dawn of history before the primitive Iranian race divided into sections which became Persian and Indian.... When in 65–63 BC, the conquering armies of Pompey were largely converted by its high precepts, they brought it with them into the Roman Empire. Mithraism spread with great rapidity throughout the Empire, and it was adopted, patronized and protected by a number of the Emperors up to the time of Constantine.[1159]

Ken Humphreys likewise summarizes the great popularity of Mithraism in the centuries before the Christian era:

> The cult of Mithras was actually of very ancient lineage, traceable in one form or another through at least two thousand years. In origin it was the primordial sun-worship—the father of all religion. Iconography showed Mithras, in Phrygian cap and cloak, riding his fiery chariot across the sky. But it was also an eastern religion, reaching the Roman world from India via Persia. Traditional hostility with Persia did not favour Rome adopting a religion of its enemies. This changed however in the 60s BC when Pompey's legions first entered Syria. Mithraism had so well established itself in the Commagene, Armenia and eastern Anatolia that whole dynasties of kings had called themselves "Mithridates" ("justice of Mithra").[1160]

Mithraism arose in the Western part of the Roman Empire well be-

1158 Higgins, I, 197.
1159 Wheless, FC, 20.
1160 Humphreys (2005), 109–110.

fore Christianity. Mithraic monuments and other artifacts abound all over Europe from an earlier period than those of Christianity. Indeed, Mithraism represented the greatest challenge to Christianity, which won out over its competitor cult.

Mithra has the following in common with the Christ character:

- Mithra was born of a virgin on December 25 in a cave, and his birth was attended by shepherds bearing gifts.
- He was considered a great traveling teacher and master.
- He had 12 companions or disciples.
- Mithra's followers were promised immortality.
- He performed miracles.
- As the "great bull of the Sun," Mithra sacrificed himself for world peace.[1161]
- He was buried in a tomb and after three days rose again.
- His resurrection was celebrated every year.
- He was called "the Good Shepherd" and identified with both the Lamb and the Lion.
- He was considered the "Way, the Truth and the Light," and the "Logos," "Redeemer," "Savior" and "Messiah."
- His sacred day was Sunday, the "Lord's Day," hundreds of years before the appearance of Christ.
- Mithra had his principal festival on what was later to become Easter.
- His religion had a eucharist or "Lord's Supper," at which Mithra said, "He who shall not eat of my body nor drink of my blood so that he may be one with me and I with him, shall not be saved."[1162]
- "His annual sacrifice is the Passover of the Magi, a symbolical atonement or pledge of moral and physical regeneration."[1163]

Furthermore, the Vatican itself is built upon the papacy of Mithra, and the Christian hierarchy is nearly identical to the Mithraic version it replaced. As Walker states:

> The cave of the Vatican belonged to Mithra until 376 AD, when a city prefect suppressed the cult of the rival Savior and seized the shrine in the name of Christ, on the very birthday of the pagan god, December 25.[1164]

Walker also says:

> Christians copied many details of the Mithraic mystery-re-

1161 O'Hara, 65.
1162 Lockhart, 65.
1163 Pike, 613.
1164 Walker, B. (1983), 155.

ligion, explaining the resemblance later with their favorite argument that the devil had anticipated the true faith by imitating it before Christ's birth.[1165]

Shmuel Golding states, in *The Book Your Church Doesn't Want You to Read*:

> Paul says, "They drank from that spiritual rock and that rock was Christ" (I Cor. 10:4). These are identical words to those found in the Mithraic scriptures, except that the name Mithra is used instead of Christ. The Vatican hill in Rome that is regarded as sacred to Peter, the Christian rock, was already sacred to Mithra. Many Mithraic remains have been found there. The merging of the worship of Attis into that of Mithra, then later into that of Jesus, was effected almost without interruption.[1166]

The legendary home of Paul, Tarsus, was a site of Mithra worship.

Of "Mithraism," the *Catholic Encyclopedia* states: "The fathers conducted the worship. The chief of the fathers, a sort of pope, who always lived at Rome, was called 'Pater Patrum' or 'Pater Patratus.' The members below the degree of pater called one another 'brother.'"[1167] The Mithraic pope was also known as Papa and Pontimus Maximus.

Virtually all of the elements of the Catholic ritual, from miter to wafer to altar to doxology, are directly taken from earlier Pagan mystery religions. As Taylor states, "'That Popery has borrowed its principal ceremonies and doctrines from the rituals of Paganism,' is a fact which the most learned and orthodox of the established church have most strenuously maintained and most convincingly demonstrated."

Prometheus of Greece

The Greek god Prometheus is said to have migrated from Egypt, but his drama traditionally took place in the Caucasus mountains. Prometheus shares a number of striking similarities with the Christ character:

- Prometheus descended from heaven as God incarnate to save mankind.
- He had an "especially professed" friend, "Petraeus" (Peter), the fisherman, who deserted him.[1168]
- He was crucified, suffered and rose from the dead.
- He was called the Logos or Word.

1165 Walker, B. (1983), 663.
1166 Leedom, 203.
1167 CE, 10.403.
1168 Doane, 193.

Quetzalcoatl of Mexico

Modern scientific orthodoxy allows neither for an early dating (sixth century BCE) of the Mexican god Quetzalcoatl nor for pre-Columbian contact between the "Old" and "New" Worlds, other than the presence of Vikings in Newfoundland. The evidence, however, reveals that the basic mythos discussed here was indeed in Mexico long before the Christian era there.[1169] Tradition holds that the ancient Phoenicians, expert navigators, knew about a "lost land" to the West; however, DNA studies so far provide no indication of Semitic presence in the Americas prior to Columbus, nor is there any concrete archaeological evidence for such a contention. The close and detailed correspondences between Christianity and Mesoamerican religion nevertheless seem inexplicable as coincidence; if they are not a reflection of pre-Columbian contact, they may indicate a tradition brought over with the Siberian immigrants across the Bering Strait more than 10,000 years ago.

However it got there, there can be no doubt as to the tremendous similarity between the Mexican religion and Catholicism. As Doane remarks:

> For ages before the landing of Columbus on its shores, the inhabitants of ancient Mexico worshiped a "Saviour"—as they called him—(*Quetzalcoatle*) who was *born of a pure virgin. A messenger from heaven announced to his mother that she should bear a son without connection with man.* Lord Kingsborough tells us that the annunciation of the *virgin Sochiquetzal*, mother of Quetzalcoatle—who was styled the "*Queen of Heaven*"—was the subject of a Mexican hieroglyph.[1170]

Quetzalcoatl was also designated the morning star, was tempted and fasted for 40 days, and was consumed in a eucharist using a proxy, named after Quetzalcoatl. As Walker says:

> This devoured Savior, closely watched by his ten or twelve guards, embodied the god Quetzalcoatl, who was born of a virgin, slain in atonement for primal sin, and whose Second Coming was confidently expected. He was often represented as a trinity

1169 The term "Christian era" is a misleading one, in that when it purportedly began, with the alleged birth of Christ around 1 AD/CE (or 4 BCE, etc.), the entire world did not suddenly become aware of this change or know about Jesus and Christian doctrine. In the Americas, "pre-Christian" refers to the era before Columbian contact in the fifteenth century. There simply is no evidence for Jews or Christians having influenced Mesoamerican or South American religion and mythology.

1170 Doane, 129.

> signified by three crosses, a large one between the smaller ones. Father Acosta naively said, "It is strange that the devil after his manner hath brought a Trinity into idolatry." His church found it all too familiar, and long kept his book as one of its secrets.[1171]

The Mexicans revered the cross and baptized their children in a ritual of regeneration and rebirth long before the Christian contact.[1172] One of the few existing Codices contains an image of the Mexican savior bending under the weight of a burdensome cross, in exactly the same manner in which Jesus is depicted. The Mexican crucifix depicted a man with nail holes in feet and hands, the Mexican Christ and redeemer who died for man's sins. In one crucifix image, this Savior was covered with suns.[1173] Furthermore, the Mexicans had monasteries and nunneries, and called their high priests *Papes*.[1174]

The Mexican savior and rituals were so disturbingly similar to the Christianity of the conquering Spaniards that Cortes was forced to use the standard, specious complaint that "the Devil had positively taught to the Mexicans the same things which God had taught to Christendom."[1175] The Spaniards destroyed as much of the evidence as was possible, burning books and defacing and wrecking temples, monuments and other artifacts.

Kingsborough says, "As in the tradition current in Yucatan of Bacab and his crucifixion … so in these Mexican paintings many analogies may be traced between the events to which they evidently relate and the history of the crucifixion of Christ as contained in the New Testament. The subject of them all is the same, being the death of Quetzalcoatle upon the cross, as an atonement for the sins of mankind. In the fourth page of the Borgian Manuscripts he seems to be crucified between two persons who are in the act of reviling him."[1176]

Serapis of Egypt

Another god whose story was very similar to that of Christ, the evidence for which was also largely destroyed, was the Egyptian deity Serapis or Sarapis, who was called the "Good Shepherd" and considered a healer. Walker says of Sarapis:

> Syncretic god worshipped as a supreme deity in Egypt to the end of the 4th century AD. The highly popular cult of Sarapis used

1171 Walker, B. (1983), 47.
1172 Higgins, II, 30–31.
1173 Doane, 200.
1174 Doane, 404.
1175 Carpenter, 25.
1176 Kingsborough, 6.166.

> many trappings that were later adopted by Christians: chants, lights, bells, vestments, processions, music. Sarapis represented a final transformation of the savior Osiris into a monotheistic figure, virtually identical to the Christian god.... This Ptolemaic god was a combination of Osiris and Apis.... As Christ was a sacrificial lamb, so Sarapis was a sacrificial bull as well as god in human form. He was annually sacrificed in atonement for the sins of Egypt.[1177]

The image of Serapis, which once stood tall in the Serapion/Serapeum at Alexandria, was adopted by the later Christians as the image of Jesus, and the cult of Serapis was considered that of the original Christians. As Albert Churchward states:

> The Catacombs of Rome are crowded with illustrations that were reproduced as Egypto-gnostic tenets, doctrines, and dogmas which had served to Persian, Greek, Roman, and Jew as evidence of the non-historic origins of Christianity. In the transition from the old Egyptian religion to the new Cult of Christianity there was no factor of profounder importance than the worship of Serapis. As the Emperor Hadrian relates, in his letter to Servianus, "Those who worship Serapis are likewise Christians: even those who style themselves the Bishops of Christ are devoted to Serapis."[1178]

Tammuz of Babylon

Tammuz and his Sumerian counterpart Dumuzi share many similarities to the story of Jesus Christ. Ezekiel 8:14–15: "Then he brought me to the door of the gate of the LORD's house which was toward the north; and, behold, there sat women weeping for Tammuz."

From *The Wycliffe Bible Commentary*, Electronic Database. Copyright (c) 1962 by Moody Press:

> Tammuz. This god can be traced back to the Sumerian Dumuzi, the god of the subterranean ocean and a shepherd deity, whose sister-consort, Inanna-Ishtar, descended into the lower world to bring him back to life. In his worship are similarities to that of Egyptian Osiris, the Canaanite Baal, and the Syrian Adonis. Gebal or Byblos, twenty-one miles north of Beirut, was the great seat of Adonis worship. The nightly death of the god, the god's dying before the touch of winter, or the vernal god's dying with the parched summer are variations on the theme of death and resurrection. Mourning for the god was followed by a

1177 Walker, B. (1983), 893.

1178 A. Churchward, 367.

celebration of resurrection.

Note the parallels.

- Similar to Jesus when he is paraded in a purple robe as "King of the Jews," the Sumerian son of God/dess Dumuzi is also depicted as "clothed in a magnificent garment."[1179]
- As is Christ to those who kill him, Dumuzi is delivered into the hands of "demons," after which he is bitterly wept over.[1180]
- As in the temptation of Jesus, Dumuzi is depicted as escaping from "his demons."[1181]
- As Jesus is identified with the serpent, so too is Dumuzi equated with the snake.[1182]

In the ninth to tenth century AD/CE, Arab Muslim writer Ibn Wahshīya recounted a legend about Tammuz found in Nabatean literature:

> I lit upon another Nabathaean book, in which the legend of Tammūz was narrated in full; how he summoned the king to worship the seven (planets) and the twelve (signs of the Zodiac), and how the king put him to death, and how he lived after being killed, so that he had to put him to death several times in a cruel manner, Tammūz coming to life again after each time, until at last he died; and behold, it was identical with the legend of St. George that is current among the Christians. At that time, Tammūz was still being lamented in July by the Sabians of Harran and Babylonia.[1183]

Over the past several decades, Dumuzi's resurrection has been disputed by mainstream scholars for lack of explicit attestation in the ancient texts.[1184]

Zoroaster/Zarathustra

Many people, believers and scholars alike, have believed that Zoroaster was a single, real person who spread the Persian religion around 660 BCE. However, Zoroastrianism is asserted to have existed 10,000 years ago, and there have been at least "seven Zoroasters … recorded by different historians."[1185] Thus, it is clear that Zoroaster is not a single person but another rendering of the ubiquitous mythos with a different

1179 "Inana's descent," 348–353.
1180 "Inana's descent," 354–358, 284–293.
1181 "Inana's descent," 376–383.
1182 "Inana's descent," 368–375.
1183 Christian Remembrancer, 41.262.
1184 See, for example, James, E.O., 8.
1185 Higgins, 591.

ethnicity and flavor. Zoroaster's name means "son of a star," a common mythical epithet, which Jacolliot states is the Persian version of the more ancient Indian "Zuryastara (who restored the worship of the sun) from which comes this name of Zoroaster, which is itself but a title assigned to a political and religious legislator." Zoroaster has the following in common with the Christ character:

- Zoroaster was born of a virgin and "immaculate conception by a ray of divine reason."[1186]
- He was baptized in a river.
- In his youth he astounded wise men with his wisdom.
- He was tempted in the wilderness by the devil.
- He began his ministry at age 30.
- Zoroaster baptized with water, fire and "holy wind."
- He cast out demons and restored sight to a blind man.
- He taught about heaven and hell, and revealed mysteries, including resurrection, judgment, salvation and the apocalypse.[1187]
- He had a sacred cup or grail.
- He was slain.
- His religion had a eucharist.
- He was the "Word made flesh."
- Zoroaster's followers expect a "second coming" in the virgin-born Saoshyant or Savior, who is to come in 2341 CE and to begin his ministry at age 30, ushering in a golden age.

That Zoroastrianism permeated the Middle East prior to the Christian era is well-known. As Mazdaism and Mithraism, it was a religion that went back centuries before the purported time of the "historical" Zoroaster. Its influence on Judaism and Christianity is unmistakable:

> When John the Baptist declared that he could baptize with water but that after him would come one who would baptize with fire and with Holy Ghost, he was uttering words which came directly from the heart of Zoroastrianism.[1188]

"Zoroaster" considered nomads to be evil and agriculturalists good, and viewed Persia, or Iran, to be the Holy Land. Like his Christian missionary counterparts, he believed that the devil, Angra Mainyu or Ahriman, "sowed false religions," which his followers later specified as Judaism, Christianity, Manichaeism, and Islam.[1189] And, like its offspring Yahwism, Zoroastrianism was monotheistic and forbade images or idols

1186 Graves, 45.
1187 Larson, 88.
1188 Larson, 89.
1189 Larson, 91.

of God, who was called in Zoroastrianism "Ormuzd" or "Ahura-Mazda." Thus, religious intolerance may also be traced to its doctrines. Larson relates the influence of Zoroastrianism on Christianity:

> Among the basic elements which the Synoptics obtained from Zoroastrianism we may mention the following: the intensely personal and vivid concepts of hell and heaven; the use of water for baptism and spiritual purification; the savior born of a true virgin-mother; the belief in demons who make human beings impure and who must be exorcised; the Messiah of moral justice; the universal judgment, based upon good and evil works; the personal immortality and the single life of every human soul; the apocalyptic vision and prophecy; and the final tribulation before the Parousia.... In addition, Paul, Revelation, and the Fourth Gospel drew heavily upon Zoroastrianism for elements which are absent from the Synoptics: e.g., the doctrine of absolute metaphysical dualism, the Logos concept, transformation into celestial spirits, the millennial kingdom, Armageddon, the final conflagration, the defeat of Satan, the renovation of the universe, and the celestial city to be lowered from the Supreme Heaven to the earth.[1190]

As Wheless states:

> All these divine and "revealed" doctrines of the Christian faith we have seen to be originally heathen Zoroastrian mythology, taken over first by the Jews, then boldly plagiarized by the ex-Pagan Christians.[1191]

Other Saviors and Sons of God

Many of the other sons of God, plus several "daughters of God" and goddesses such as Diana Soteira, share numerous aspects with the Christian savior, such as the following.

The Orphic religion is similar to Christianity. In *Jesus Christ: Sun of God,* David Fideler relates of the Greek hero/god Orpheus:

> Orphism promulgated the idea of eternal life, a concept of "original sin" and purification, the punishment of the wicked in the afterlife, and the allegorical interpretation of myth, which the early church fathers applied to the Christian scriptures. Orpheus was known as the Good Shepherd, and Jesus was frequently represented as Orpheus, playing music and surrounded by animals, a symbol of the Peaceable Kingdom or Golden Age, representing

1190 Larson, 105.

1191 Wheless, FC, 90.

the ever-present harmony of the Logos. Like Orpheus, Jesus descended to Hell as a savior of souls.[1192]

Indeed, as Werner Keller relates:

> In Berlin … there is a small amulet with a crucified person, the Seven Sisters and the moon which bears the inscription ORPHEUS BAKKIKOS. It has a surprisingly Christian appearance. The same can be said of a representation of the hanging Marsyas in the Capitoline Museum in Rome.[1193]

The list of "dying and rising gods," "resurrection deities" or "life-death-rebirth deities" includes:

> Adonis, Amun, Andjety, Antinous, Asclepius, Ataegine, Attis, Baal, Baiame, Baldr, Chinnamasta, Coatlicue, Cronus, Damu, Dionysus, Dumuzi, Eshmun, Euri, Geštinanna, Green Man, Gullveig, Heitsi-eibib, Heqet, Inanna, Ishtar, Isis, Izanagi, Jarilo, Jesus, Julunggul, Kaknu, Kali, Khepri, Krishna, Manannán mac Lir, Melqart, Moremi, Nut, Obatala, Odin, Opheus, Osiris, Persephone, Phoenix, Proserpina, Queen of Heaven, Quetzalcoatl, Ra, Shiva, Tammuz, Vayu, Veles, Wawalag, Xipe Totec, Zalmoxis, Zorya, Zywie.[1194]

Conclusion

It is evident that Jesus Christ is a mythical character based on these various ubiquitous godmen and universal saviors who were part of the ancient world for thousands of years prior to the Christian era. As Massey says:

> The same legend was repeated in many lands with a change of name, and at times of sex, for the sufferer, but none of the initiated in the esoteric wisdom ever looked upon the Kamite Iusa, a gnostic Horus, Jesus, Tammuz, Krishna, Buddha Witoba, or any other of the many saviours as historic in personality for the simple reason that they had been more truly taught.[1195]

The existence and identity of all these mysterious characters who are so identical in their persona and exploits, constituting the universal mythos, have been hidden from the masses as part of the Christ conspiracy.

1192 Fideler, 175.

1193 Keller, 392.

1194 Adapted from the Wikipedia articles "Dying god," "Life-death-rebirth goddesses" and "Life-death-rebirth gods."

1195 Massey, EBD, 51.

Astrology and the Bible

"And God said, 'Let there be lights in the firmament of the heavens to separate the day from the night; and let them be for signs and for seasons and for days and years.'"

—Genesis 1:14

"For everything there is a season, and a time for every matter under heaven: a time to be born, and a time to die; a time to plant, and a time to pluck up what is planted."

—Ecclesiastes 3:1–2

"Can you lead forth the Mazzaroth in their season, or can you guide the Bear with its children?"

—Job 38:33

"Mazzaroth [מזרה/mazzarah]: a) the 12 signs of the Zodiac and their 36 associated constellations."[1196]

—*Strong's Concordance of the Bible* (H4216)

"And he deposed the idolatrous priests whom the kings of Judah had ordained to burn incense in the high places at the cities of Judah and round about Jerusalem; those also who burned incense to Baal, to the sun, and the moon, and the constellations [/*mazzalah*], and all the host of the heavens."[1197]

—2 Kings 23:5

> "The Hebrews gave this name [*mazzalah*] to the *twelve signs of the Zodiac ... the circles of palaces*; these were imagined to be the lodging-places of the sun during the twelve months."

—*Gesenius's Hebrew and Chaldee Lexicon to the Old Testament Scriptures* (CCCCLXI)

The Christian religion was thus founded largely upon the numerous

1196 See, for example, *The New Strong's Concordance of the Bible* (397). Interestingly, the Hebrew word following מזרה/*mazzarah* (H4216), מזרח or *mizrach*, is defined by *Strong's* (H4217) as "place of the sunrise, east." Adding to the intrigue, the Latin of the Vulgate translates *mazzaroth* as *lucifer*, the lightbearer and morning star.

1197 As it does at Job 38:22, the Greek Septuagint renders the Hebrew here as μαζουρωθ or *mazouroth*, resembling *mazzaroth*/*mazzarah*, more than *mazzalah*. It is clear that the two words are interchangeable. Indeed, in *Treasury of Scripture Knowledge* (361), Rev. Dr. Reuben Archer ("R.A.") Torrey defines *Mazzaroth* as "the twelve signs" and adds: "Probably the same as *mazzaloth*. 2 Ki. 23.5." Concerning this verse and this word, Torrey also comments that "the Targumists and Rabbins often employ the words *tereysar mazzalaya*, to denote the signs of the zodiac." (Torrey, 272) Jerome's Vulgate renders this word מזלוה/*mazzalah* in Latin as *duodecim signis* or "twelve signs."

gods, goddesses, religions, sects, cults and mystery schools that thrived around the globe prior to the Christian era, even in the Hebrew world, where the Israelites worshipped numerous gods, including "the sun, the moon, and the stars and all the host of heaven." In order to determine the framework upon which the Christian conspirators[1198] hung their myths, in fact, we will need to turn to that ancient body of knowledge which in almost every culture has been considered sacred and which the priests have kept to themselves: the science of astrology.

The Christian masses, of course, are repeatedly taught to reject all forms of "astrology" or "star-gazing" as the "work of the Devil," and any number of biblical texts are held up to assert that astrology is an evil to be avoided at all costs. This animosity towards studying the heavenly bodies and their interrelationships is in reality propaganda designed to prevent people from finding out the truth about the Bible, which is that it is loaded with astrological imagery, as evidenced by the fact that the Hebrew gods were in large part celestial bodies. The Bible is, in actuality, basically an astrotheological text, a reflection of what has been occurring in the heavens for millennia, localized and historicized on Earth. This fact is further confirmed by numerous biblical passages concerning the influences of the heavenly bodies, but it also becomes clear through exegesis of the texts from an informed perspective.

The Catholic Church has feverishly discouraged star-gazing by its flock. The laity were so frightened by the Church's wrath toward astrology that sailors dared not even look up at the stars, a habit crucial to their occupation. And yet the Church itself has been a longtime practitioner of astrology! Many of the Church hierarchy have not only "looked to the stars" but have been regular, secret adepts of the same "magical arts" widely practiced by Pagans but publicly condemned by Christians,[1199] and it would be safe to assume that this practice continues to this day behind the scenes. Numerous churches and cathedrals, such as Notre Dame in Paris, have abundant astrological symbols, full zodiacs, etc. In the nineteenth century, the papal throne, St. Peter's chair, was cleaned, only to reveal upon it the 12 labors of Hercules,[1200] who, as we have seen, was a sun god. As Walker states:

1198 This mention of "Christ Conspirators" refers to the authors of the Gospels, who appear to have expected to retain control of the sharing of the symbolic allegory in the texts among initiates. A further "Christ Conspiracy" is the later activity of the orthodox dogmatists in the church who insisted the Gospel events occurred as described and suppressed alternative Gnostic interpretations.

1199 Wheless, FC, 164.

1200 Higgins, I, 691.

> Astrology survives in our own culture because Christianity embraced it with one hand, while condemning it as a devilish art with the other. Church fathers like Augustine, Jerome, Eusebius, Chrystostom, Lactantius, and Ambrose all anathematized astrology, and the great Council of Toledo prohibited it for all time. Nevertheless, six centuries later the consistory and the dates of popes' coronations were determined by the zodiac; aristocratic prelates employed their own personal astrologers; and signs of the zodiac appeared all over church furnishings, tiles, doorways, manuscripts, and baptismal fonts. The traditional Twelve Days of Christmas were celebrated by taking astrological omens each day for the corresponding months of the coming year.[1201]

Despite its outward vilification by the clergy, astrology has also been used by countless kings and heads of state privy to the astrological, as opposed to literal, nature of the Bible. Biblical literalists, by contrast, claim that everything in the Bible occurred literally and factually upon the earth, including the talking snake, Noah's ark, the parting of the Red Sea, the raising of the dead and numerous other incredible miracles restricted to the biblical peoples at that time in that part of the world. The miraculous and implausible exploits of other cultures, however, are to be tossed aside as unhistorical, mythological and downright ridiculous. As we have seen and will continue to see, these other cultures had stories identical to those found in the Bible. Applying the same standard Christian apologists use for competing faiths and their narratives, should we not also toss out the Judeo-Christian versions as "merely" mythological and allegorical at best, and diabolical at worst? There is no particular reason to regard the various biblical tales as any more factual than those of the Greek gods or the *Arabian Nights*. As allegory, however, they are seen to preserve an ancient wisdom that goes back well beyond the founding of the Hebrew nation, into the deepest mists of time.

Although many people think astrology is meaningless mumbo-jumbo, it is not merely casting horoscopes but is in fact a science, as "astrology" means the study of the celestial bodies (astronomy) and their terrestrial influences. The only difference between the well-respected astronomy and the vilified astrology is that astronomy charts the movements and constitution of the celestial bodies, while astrology attempts to determine their interrelationships and meaning. The sacred science of astrology began with astronomy, when humans noticed that they could determine some regularity in life by observing the skies and heavenly

1201 Walker, B. (1983), 287.

bodies, both nighttime and daytime. They could thus predict the seasons, including the times of planting and harvest, as well as the annual flooding of the Nile. They also noticed the sun's effects on plants, as well as the moon's waxing and waning and its effect on the tides. The knowledge of the heavens was also essential in seafaring, as stated, and a variety of ancient peoples were extraordinary seafarers for millennia. Thus, in reading the stars, humans could make sense of the universe and find lessons applicable to daily life. Higgins explains:

> Among all the ancient nations of the world, the opinion was universal that the planetary bodies were the disposers of the affairs of men. Christians who believe in Transubstantiation, and that their priests have an unlimited power to forgive sins, may affect to despise those who have held that opinion … but their contempt is not becoming, it is absurd.… It was thought that the future fortunes of every man might be known, from a proper consideration of the state of the planets at the moment of his birth.… This produced the utmost exertion of human ingenuity to discover the exact length of the periods of the planetary motions: that is, in other words, to perfect the science of astronomy. In the course of the proceedings it was discovered, or believed to be discovered, that the motions of the planets were liable to certain aberrations, which it was thought would bring on ruin to the whole system, at some future day.[1202]

As time went on, this science became increasingly complicated, as the infinite stars were factored in and as the heavens changed. Recognizing the interaction between the planetary bodies and their influence on Earth, the ancients began to give the heavens shape and form, persona and attitude. In order to pass along this detailed information, which was, and continues to be, so important to all aspects of life, the ancients personified the heavenly bodies and wove stories about their "exploits," giving them unique personalities and temperaments that reflected their particular movements and other qualities, such as color and size. These stories were passed down over the many millennia basically by a priesthood, because they were valued for their sacred astronomical, astrological and mathematical meaning. As Higgins says, "astrology was so connected with religion that it was impossible to separate them."[1203] These celestial movements and/or the revered stories about them were recorded in stone all over the world, in great monuments and

1202 Higgins, I, 207–8.
1203 Higgins, I, 559.

in city layouts. These monuments constitute much of our proof that the ancients possessed this amazingly intricate knowledge, but we can also find enormous evidence of it in the legends and writings of the ancients, including the Judeo-Christian Bible, which is rife with symbolism and allegory.

Those individuals who believe the Bible to be the "literal word of God" are not only unaware of its symbolism, they are also ignorant of the passages within the Bible itself which clearly reflect that at least certain aspects of the biblical tales are *allegory*. For example, at Ezekiel 23, the author tells a long story about two sisters, Oholah and Oholibah, and their "faithless harlotry" when "their breasts were pressed and their virgin bosoms handled." Just as we get to the good stuff, "Ezekiel" springs it on us that he is speaking ***allegorically*** about the cities of Samaria and Jerusalem, which are accused of having "played harlot in Egypt"; in other words, they worshipped other gods. It is rather evident that Ezekiel is enjoying this sexual allegory, as he goes into gleeful detail about the transgressions of the "sisters" and their "nakedness" and "bed of love." It is also evident that this type of allegorical speech is used more often in the Bible than its writers and proponents would wish to admit. As in the lusty Ezekiel tale, a number of other biblical places, nations and tribes are frequently referred to allegorically as "he" or "she," which makes it difficult to figure out whether the speaker is talking about a person, group, place or thing.

The Christian cheerleader "Paul" also knew that there was allegory in the Bible, as he so stated at Galatians 4:22–25, in reference to the story of Abraham having sons by two women. Though we are led in the Old Testament to take these women as real, historical characters, Paul sees a deeper significance.

> Now this is ***allegory***: these two women are two covenants. One is from Mount Sinai, bearing children for slavery; she is Hagar. Now Hagar is Mount Sinai in Arabia; she corresponds to the present Jerusalem, for she is in slavery with her children.

Thus, again, we discover that biblical characters are not actual persons but allegories for places. We also discover that certain places are allegories for other places: And "their dead bodies will lie in the street of the great city which is ***allegorically*** called Sodom and Egypt, where their Lord was crucified" (Rev. 11:8). Of course, this fact is hidden by some translators, who render the word "allegorically" as "spiritually."

Other early Christians also knew about the allegorical nature of the Bible, but their later counterparts began in earnest the profitable push for utter historicization, obliterating millennia of human study and knowledge, and propelling the Western world into an appalling Dark Age. St. Athanasius, bishop and patriarch of Alexandria, was not only aware of the allegorical nature of biblical texts, but he "admonishes us that 'Should we understand sacred writ according to the letter, we should fall into the most enormous blasphemies.'"[1204] In other words, *it is a sin to take the Bible literally!*

Christian father Origen, called the "most accomplished biblical scholar of the early church," admitted the allegorical and esoteric nature of the Bible: "The Scriptures were of little use to those who understood them literally, as they are written."[1205] St. Augustine, along with Origen, was forceful in his pronouncement of Genesis as allegory: "There is no way of preserving the literal sense of the first chapter of Genesis, without impiety, and attributing things to God unworthy of him."[1206]

Thus, it is understood that there is allegory and symbolism in the Bible. What is also understood is that, despite protestations to the contrary, the stars, sun and moon are described and utilized repeatedly within an allegorical or astrological context by biblical writers. In fact, in examining biblical texts closely, we further discover that various places and persons, portrayed as actual, historical entities, are in fact allegories for the heavens and planetary bodies. In reality, virtually all Hebrew place-names have astronomical meanings.[1207] So prevalent is this axiom "as above, so below," it is obvious that the "chosen" were as enchanted with the heavens as their adversaries and neighbors, such as the Chaldeans, master astrologers jealously reviled by their Hebrew counterparts. Contrary to popular belief, the reverence displayed by other peoples for "God's heavens" is also exhibited by the Israelites, whose very name, as we have seen, is astrotheological. Indeed, from the very beginning, the biblical people were encouraged to study the stars and signs in the heavens, as at Genesis 1:14, which basically describes the zodiac: "And God [Elohim] said, Let there be lights in the firmament of the heaven to divide the day from the night; and let them be for signs, and for seasons, and for days, and years."

Despite the negative comments and exhortations found in the Bible against astrology, star-gazing, soothsaying and divination, we discover various passages that clearly refer to these magical arts and their objects of reverence with favor. In fact, at several points the heavens are personified and appear as wondrous characters whose praises are sung by

---

1204 Pike, 266.
1205 Higgins, II, 270.
1206 The Literal Interpretation of Genesis 1:19–20, Chapt. 19 [AD 408]
1207 Higgins, I, 423; II, 136.

biblical characters, in precisely the same manner as their Pagan counterparts. In the Book of Job, we find unambiguous references to astrology. The book personifies the "morning stars"—the "sons of God"—and has them "joyfully crying out." In trying to make Job feel small and obey him, the Lord presents a list of his own divine attributes, including the ability to command the happy heavens:

> Can you bind the chains of the Pleiades, or loose the cords of Orion? Can you lead forth the Mazzaroth in their season, or can you guide the Bear with its children? Do you know the ordinances of the heavens? Can you establish their rule on the earth? (Job 38:31–33)

The "Mazzaroth" is, in fact, the Zodiac, as noted in Strong's Concordance of the Bible. Orion is a prominent player on the cosmic stage, as is the Bear. The Pleiades, or "Seven Sisters," have been since very ancient times elements of many mythologies and astrotheologies, including the Egyptian, Babylonian, Indian, Greek, Japanese, Australian and Mexican. The presentation of the seven sisters as "judges" is a common theme, and it was thought at times that they required sacrifice as propitiation. The Pleiades factor into Judaism more than is admitted, as some of the numerous "sevens" mentioned throughout the Bible refer to these "sisters," as Walker relates:

> [The Pleiades] were probably represented in pre-patriarchal Jerusalem by the holy Menorah (seven-branched candlestick) symbolizing the sevenfold Men-horae or Moon-priestesses, as shown by its female-genital decorations, lilies and almonds (Exodus 25:33).[1208]

After the patriarchy took over, it would seem, the menorah came to represent only the sun, moon and five visible planets, as will be seen.[1209]

Also in Job, a book replete with celestial imagery, the author portrays the Lord as he who "described a circle upon the face of the waters

---

1208 Walker, B. (1983), 804.

1209 Further evidence of Jewish astrology, astrolatry or astrotheology appears in Philo (*Moses* 2.102-3), in which he "interprets the seven-branched menorah at the time of the Temple as an astral symbol of heaven, planets (stars), the zodiac and the seasons. Philo in his allegorical explanation to Exodus (supp. II, *Questions and Answers on Exodus*, pp. 22, 125) proposes that the menorach as a whole symbolizes the heavens. The main stem represents the sun, the side branches symbolize the three months in every season, and the menorah lamps are lit night and day like stars. Josephus (*Ant.* 3.144–45, 182; *War* 5.217) maintains that the menorah symbolizes the seven planets." (Hachlili (2001), 188–9) Hachlili notes that these "seven planets" are "sun, moon, Mercury, Mars, Venus, Jupiter and Saturn, although the sun and moon are not planets."

at the boundary between light and darkness. The pillars of heaven tremble … his hand pierced the fleeing serpent." In mythology the heavens are depicted as an "abyss of waters," so this scripture is a reference to the zodiacal circle, "described" or drawn by God. The "boundary between light and darkness" is, naturally, the horizon, and the trembling "pillars of heaven" are the same held up by Samson, the "bright sun." In addition, "his hand piercing the fleeing serpent" could refer to the Egyptian god Set/Seth, the constellation of Serpens, or the sky itself; however, this last part could also be translated as the "crooked serpent" who does not flee but is *formed* by the Lord's hand, representing Scorpio. Of this mysterious and clearly astrological work attributed to Job, Anderson says, "the whole book is a complete description of the Masonic ceremonies or Egyptian Masonry, or trial of the dead by Osiris."[1210]

In Psalm 19, we hear about the heavens "telling the glory of God … there is no speech, nor are there words; their voice is not heard; yet their voice goes out through all the earth, and their words to the end of the world." To the uninitiated, this sounds strange—how can the heavens tell the "glory of God"? And how do their "voice" and "words" go out to the end of the world without speech or words? The word for "voice" in the Hebrew is properly translated as "line." This line or lines are the cosmic rays coming off the various planetary bodies, lines that were perceived by the ancients to penetrate the earth as well, a perception that made them urgent to establish the "kingdom of heaven on Earth" by emulating what was happening in the heavens. Anderson explains the importance of the lines or rays:

> Among the Eastern nations it was taught that all spiritual life first came from the sun, and its magnetic descent to the earth, becoming earth-bound, or dwelling in the earth, and after passing through a series of evolutions, and different births and changes from the mineral, vegetable, and animal kingdoms, ascending or descending the scale [like Jacob's angels], according to the good or evil magnetic rays at its births and its various probationary existences, at last purified and intellectually refined, and master of itself, the *pure* Ra, or *astral* body, at last was drawn back into the bosom of the father, sun, from whence it was first originated.[1211]

Thus, astrology, or astro*logos* in the Greek, has been considered the "word of God," as evidenced by the Bible's singing stars and heavens passing along their "voice" and "words" through the earth.

The Psalm continues: "In [the heavens] he has set a tent for the sun."

1210 Anderson, 113.
1211 Anderson, 20.

This "tent" or "tabernacle" represents a holy sanctuary or house of worship; thus, the heavens are truly the temple of the sun, as well as of the other celestial bodies. This heavenly temple was, however, continuously recreated all over the planet, as continues to this day, unbeknownst to the masses.

At Job 9, it is explicit that God is the Divine Architect of the Zodiac "who made the Bear and Orion, the Pleiades and the chambers of the south." And again at Amos 5:8: "He who made the Pleiades and Orion, and turns deep darkness into the morning and darkens the day into night." The Lord "builds his upper chambers in the heavens and founds vaults upon the earth" (Amos 9:6). And he is praised for his astrological creation: "Thou has made the moon to mark the seasons; the sun to know its time." Like the Lord himself, his creations such as the sun, moon and skies are considered righteous and eternal, as is reflected at Psalm 89:37 and at Daniel 12:3; thus, the heavenly bodies served as sacred symbols and representatives of God.

From these various biblical passages, it is obvious that the Lord is not only the architect of the heavens but is pleased with both his stellar creations and his ability to command them. That being the case, it is equally obvious that astrology is not evil, unless the Lord is evil, an idea widely subscribed to by the Gnostics, who made the assessment that anyone in charge of this chaotic and crude "lower" world must be a villain. But, if "God" is good, then "his" creation must be good, and the biblical writers make it clear that astrology and the zodiac are their Lord's creation.

That the stars, moon and sun were considered to have personality is also explicit from biblical texts. Origen opined, and was ridiculed by "heretics" and "heathens" for his opinion, that "all the stars and heavenly bodies are living, rational beings, having souls," and he quotes Isaiah 14:12 in proof of this, saying that the Lord has "given commandments to all the stars."[1212]

At Psalm 147:4, the stars have names, given to them by "the Lord." That biblical writers were aware of the constellations is also clear from Isaiah 13:10: "For the stars of the heavens and their constellations will not give their light." The fact that the Hebrews believed the sun and moon had personality and animation is further reflected at Isaiah 24:23: "Then the moon will be confounded, and the sun ashamed." The sun and moon are again anthropomorphized or personified at Psalm 148:3, when they are urged to praise the Lord.

The importance of the skies is repeatedly emphasized throughout

1212 Wheless, FC, 150–1.

the Old Testament, with the sun and moon even considered the "rulers" of the day and night, made out of the Lord's "steadfast love" (Ps. 136:9). In the Song of Solomon, an embarrassment to God-fearing Christians for its overt sexuality, "Solomon" uses celestial imagery to describe his beloved: "Who is this that looks forth like the dawn, fair as the moon, bright as the sun" (Song 6:10).

The sun and moon are also considered to be healing, as reflected at Isaiah 30:26, in which the light of the sun and moon increase "in the day when the Lord binds up the hurt of his people, and heals the wounds inflicted by his blow." (And this from a "loving" God!) Furthermore, the arts of medicine and astrology were inextricably linked, because medicines were frequently dispensed not only based upon symptoms but also on natal charts and other astrological castings; hence, "physicians" or "doctors" were also astrologers, as well as priests and prophets. As John M. Allegro says:

> To know the correct dosages in these cases required an appreciation of the susceptibility of the patient to the drug's effects, perhaps the most difficult calculation of all. Much depended on the recipient's "fate" allotted him at his birth, the factor that determined his individuality, his physical stature, the colour of his eyes, and so on. Only the astrologer could tell this, so the art of medicine was itself dependent for success on astrology and the considerable astronomical knowledge this presupposed.... The combined arts of medicine and astrology were known and practiced by the Sumerians and their Mesopotamian successors, as we know from their cuneiform records as well as the repute they enjoyed in this respect in the ancient world.... These traits of character and bodily constitution could be determined by astrological means, so the early doctors were also astrologers. [The early doctor] was also a prophet, a prognosticator. The arts of healing and religion were inseparable.[1213]

Biblical Sun- and Moon-Worshippers

Thus, we can see that astrology is not at all "evil," as acknowledged abundantly by biblical writers. In fact, as noted, the polytheistic Hebrews and Israelites worshipped a variety of Elohim, Baalim and Adonai, many of which were aspects of the sun, such as El Elyon, the Most High God. In addition, Amos 5:26 mentions the mysterious "Kaiwan," the "star-god" of the house of Israel. This star-god is El, the sun, or Saturn, the "central sun," whom, as stated, the Hebrews worshipped,

1213 Allegro, SMC, 31-5.

as reflected by their sabbath on Saturday. As also noted, Yahweh, or Iao, was likewise a sun god. Furthermore, we have already seen that Solomon, for one, worshipped in the manner of the pre-Yahwist cultures, revering Chemosh, the Moabite sun god, for example.

The Hebrews were also "moon-worshippers" in that many of their feasts and holidays revolved around the movements and phases of the moon. Such moon-worship is found repeatedly in the Old Testament (Ps. 81:3; 104:19; Isa. 66:23, Ez 46:3, Jmh 8:2), and to this day Jews celebrate holidays based on the lunar calendar. At Isaiah 47, these moon-worshippers are equated with astrologers (i.e., "those who divide the heavens, who gaze at the stars, who at the new moons predict what shall befall you").

The Jewish nighttime worship is also reflected in the Epistle to Diognetus, an early Christian writing which further demonstrates that astrology was important to Christians, as, while the author obviously does not like the way in which Jews are consulting the heavens, he does consider the "cycle of the seasons" to be "divinely appointed":

> [The Jews] scrutinize the moon and stars for the purpose of ritually commemorating months and days, and chop up the divinely appointed cycle of the seasons to suit their own fancies, pronouncing some to be times for feasting and others for mourning.

As we can see, the Hebrews/Israelites, like other peoples around the world, revered a number of aspects of the heavens, both the night sky and the day. Also clear from biblical texts is that the Hebrew people were constantly confused as to who "the Lord" really was and what he wanted from his chosen, as they are endlessly being bounced to and fro in their reverence for the heavens. In fact, as is written in the *Book of Jasher*, which is given scriptural authority at Joshua 10:13 and 2 Samuel 1:18 but which was suppressed in large part because of its obvious astrological imagery, Abraham's father Terah "had twelve gods of large size, made of wood and stone, after the twelve months of the year, and he served each one monthly" (Jash. 9:8).[1214] Abram himself is also represented as first worshipping the sun, until it set, and then the moon: "And Abram served the sun in that day and he prayed to it … and Abram served the moon and prayed to it all that night" (9:14–17). Abram eventually realizes that "these are not gods that made the earth and mankind but the servants of God."

This epiphany is no great thing, actually, as the intelligentsia of

1214 This information comes not from the ancient text cited glancingly in Joshua and 1 Samuel, but from a centuries-later midrashic work designed to supply the lack of the original. It is a fascinating compilation of traditional lore.

virtually all cultures viewed the planetary bodies as divine proxies or "limbs" of the Almighty Itself. Abraham then goes on to destroy his father's gods, yet the Hebrews did not give up their astrotheology, which was, in fact, what the Hebrews/ Israelites were constantly "whoring after." As noted, by the time of reformer King Josiah, the kings of Judah reportedly erred terribly when they established the worship of the heavens, even though their predecessors had been applauded for doing the same:

And he deposed the idolatrous priests whom the kings of Judah had ordained to burn incense in the high places at the cities of Judah and round about Jerusalem; those also who burned incense to Baal, to the sun, and the moon, and the constellations, and all the host of heavens. (2 Kings 23:5)

These kings of Judah were sun-worshippers, as is made clear at 2 Kings 23:11, when Josiah "removed the horses that the kings of Judah had dedicated to the sun."

> The earliest reference to the sun as a deity [in the Bible], though it is not mentioned there by name, appears in the second commandment: "You shall not make for yourself a sculptured image or any likeness of what is in the heavens above" (Exod. 20:4). Concrete references to the sun appear when the Children of Israel are warned against worshipping celestial deities: "And when you look up to the sky and behold the sun and the moon and the stars, the whole heavenly host, you must not be lured into bowing down to them or serving them" (Deut. 4:19). No doubt, the negative attitude of the Jewish scriptures to the sun reflects the ancient struggle of the new monotheistic religion against the pagan world, for which the sun god was one of the most popular deities. The biblical sources witness that this struggle was not easy and mention worship of the sun among the sins of the Children of Israel. Such criticism is mentioned concerning the Israelite kings (2 Kings 17:16; 21:3, 5; 23:4, 5; 2 Chr. 33:3, 5) and in the words of the prophets (Jer. 8:2; 19:13; Zeph. 1:5).[1215]

It is evident that there are a number of characters or factions in the Old Testament depicting themselves as "the Lord," with tension between the Psalmist's praise of the heavens as creations of the Almighty himself, and the line that worship of the heavens is considered idolatrous.

Ezekiel

Ezekiel provides an interesting testimonial to the practice of polytheism and astrology by the Hebrews/Jews as, in a "vision," Yahweh

1215 Poorthuis, 479.

conducts a tour of Israel's "abominations" that includes a trip into the Jerusalem temple's "inner court that faces north, where was the seat of the image of jealousy, which provokes to jealousy." The "image of jealousy," of course, is Yahweh, El Qanna, the jealous god; however, it seems that the "living God" was even jealous of his own image, apparently considering it an idol. Next Ezekiel is shown a hole in the north court wall, which he excavates to find a door:

> And [God] said to me, "Go in, and see the vile abominations that they are committing here." So I went in and saw; and there, portrayed upon the wall round about, were all kinds of creeping things, and loathsome beasts, and all the idols of the house of Israel. And before them stood seventy men of the elders of the house of Israel, with Jaazaniah the son of Shaphan standing among them. Each had his censer in his hand, and the smoke of the cloud of incense went up. Then he said to me, "Son of man, have you seen what the elders of the house of Israel are doing in the dark, every man in his room of pictures? For they say, 'The LORD does not see us, the LORD has forsaken the land.'" He said also to me, "You will see even greater abominations which they commit."

Thus we find the elders of Israel performing in the hidden chamber of the temple their secret, esoteric religion, which was basically astrological. This Shaphan, father of Jaazaniah, evidently and ironically was the scribe of Hilkiah, the Zadokite priest who purportedly "found" the law that caused Josiah to go berserk and destroy the other gods and high places. It should also be noted that El Qanna's inner court to the north was reserved only for the Zadokite priesthood, which became the Sadducees.

Ezekiel then goes on to describe the Hebrew women at the entrance of the temple's north gate who were weeping for Tammuz, the Syrian/Samaritan savior/fertility/sun god who annually died and was resurrected. Ezekiel is next shown "between the porch and the altar" of the "temple of the Lord" some 25 men, "with their backs to the temple of the Lord, and their faces toward the east, worshipping the sun to the east." Such were the "abominations" of the house of Israel, for which the jealous/zealous god commanded a group of Yahwist thugs to slaughter the Hebrews, smiting "old men outright, young men and maidens, little children and women," who were not worshipping properly (i.e., according to the Yahwist bias). Consequently, El Qanna, the jealous/zealous god, orders the extermination of Jews and Hebrews who were worshipping other Elohim, as their fathers had before them.

Despite "the Lord's" purported hatred of these "abominations," he then goes on to show Ezekiel the zodiacal circle, the celebrated "wheel within a wheel," about which so much tortured speculation has been offered, including the latest that the wheel represents a spaceship. Unfortunately for the X-philes, Ezekiel's allegories—and *he is commanded by the Lord to speak in allegory* (17:1–2; 24:3)—are a bit less mysterious, as the wheel is nothing more cryptic than the visible stars of the zodiac, with the four "cherubim," the man, ox, lion and eagle, representing the cardinal points and four elements: the constellation Aquarius (air), Taurus (earth), Leo (fire) and Scorpio (water). The four brightest stars near the ecliptic, Aldebaran in Taurus, Regulus in Leo, Antares in Scorpio and Fomalhaut near Aquarius, marked the cardinal points of the solstices and equinoxes around 4000 BCE, but have since precessed by a full season. Walker elucidates upon these creatures:

> Ezekiel's four-faced creature composed of eagle, lion, bull, and man, was piously interpreted as prophesying the four evangelists; but the original biblical description was copied from the fabulous composite beasts of Assyria, who represented the four seasons of the year.[1216]

Biblical Diviners and Astrologers

The Bible contains numerous references to esteemed biblical characters using the "arts of divination" to their and their Lord's benefit. Naturally, where characters are favored by biblical writers, these astrological and magical arts are perfectly good, but when used by those not favored, they are "evil." Regardless of this prejudice, there is no doubt that "good" biblical characters practiced the magical arts. In fact, in the earliest parts of the Bible, divination is praised as a way to commune with God or to *divine* the future (Gen. 30:27). Indeed, the word "divination" comes from the word "divine," which is a demonstration that divination was originally considered *godly* and not evil.

Divination does not fall out of favor until later books, eventually being considered as "sin" in the first book of Samuel, in which the Israelite king Saul uses a diviner to "divine for me by a spirit and bring up for me whomever I shall name to you." The diviner or medium, whom Saul is approaching in disguise, objects to his request, saying, "Surely you know what Saul has done, how he has cut off the mediums and the wizards from the land. Why then are you laying a snare for my life to bring about my death?" It is interesting that *this* Saul, like the Saul of the New Testament, is notorious for persecuting people of a different faith.

Moreover, when describing the men who joined David in his fight

1216 Walker, B. (1983), 401.

against Saul, biblical writers obfuscate the occupation of the men of the tribe of Issachar: "Of Issachar men who had understanding of the times, to know what Israel ought to do, two hundred chiefs, and all their kinsmen under their command" (1 Chr. 12:32). In reality, these "men who had understanding of the times" are astrologers, and quite a lot of them at that. It is obvious that, despite protestations to the contrary, the Israelites used astrologers to "know what Israel ought to do." Furthermore, from the repeated biblical exhortations against these magical arts, it is clear that large numbers of people in Israel and Judah were practicing astrology and divination, as indicated at Isaiah 3:2, for example, where "the Lord" takes away from Judah and Jerusalem "the judge and prophet, the diviner and elder." The "judges" in the Old Testament are also priests and, in fact, judicial astrologers.[1217]

Furthermore, although Abraham in Jasher is represented as turning away from the sun and moon, his title "of the Chaldeans" was a reference to his status as an astrologer, a tradition supported by Church historian Eusebius who claimed that Abraham "taught the science to the priests of Heliopolis or On."[1218]

Moses and the Tabernacle

For centuries, the character Moses has been held in high esteem, his every word studied and each move charted. Yet, few have understood the true nature of his "covenant with the Lord," as reflected by the esoteric or mystical meaning of Moses's tabernacle, which, in fact, is the "tent of the sun." Jewish historian Josephus, who was an initiate of several secret societies, elucidates upon Moses's tabernacle:

> And when [Moses] ordered twelve loaves to be set on the table, he denoted the year, as distinguished into so many months. By branching out the candlestick into seventy parts he secretly intimated the *Decani*, or seventy divisions of the planets; and as to the seven lamps upon the candlesticks, they referred to the course of the planets, of which that is the number.... Now the vestment of the high priest being made of linen, signified the earth; the blue denoted the sky, being like lightning in its pomegranates, and in the noise of the bells resembling thunder.... Each of the sardonyxes declares to us the sun and the moon; those, I mean, that were in the nature of buttons on the high priest's shoulders. And for the twelve stones, whether we understand by them the months, or whether we understand the like number of the signs of that circle which the Greeks call the Zodiac, we shall not be mistaken in their meaning.

1217 Anderson, 105.
1218 Higgins, I, 85, 593.

The 12 stones, traditionally thought to symbolize the tribes or "sons" of Jacob, are also attested by Philo of Alexandria as forming the breastplate or ephod of the high priest to represent the twelve signs of the zodiac, which Josephus firmly corroborates.[1219] Josephus is also explicit in relating other aspects of Jewish "history" as being astrological. Therefore, this astrological or astrotheological meaning of the Bible has been known a very long time. As Higgins says:

> [The] Mosaic account ... is allowed by all philosophers, as well as most of the early Jews and Christian fathers, to contain a mythos or allegory—by Philo, Josephus, Papias, Pantaenus, Irenaeus, Clemens Alex., Origen, the two Gregories of Nyssa and Nazianzen, Jerome, Ambrose.[1220]

Jacob and his Sons and Ladder

The "father" of these 12 constellations or tribes, Jacob, is "the supplanter" (*Iakovo*), which was a title for the adversary and twin of the sun, Set, or Seth, the night sky. Each of the 12 tribes had its own totem, god and religious accoutrements, brought "out of Egypt." As demonstrated by the biblical texts, these groups did not reside peacefully with each other but fought constantly among themselves and with outsiders over whose god was superior and whose rituals and symbols were divinely inspired and correct.

As to their zodiacal designations,[1221] a possible reconstruction is that

1219 Jackson, 151; A. Churchward, 348.

1220 Higgins, I, 34.

1221 Wiki, "Zodiac": "Knowledge of the Babylonian zodiac is also reflected in the Hebrew Bible. E. W. Bullinger interpreted the creatures appearing in the books of Ezekiel and Revelation as the middle signs of the four quarters of the Zodiac, with the Lion as Leo, the Bull is Taurus, the Man representing Aquarius and the Eagle standing in. Some authors have linked the twelve tribes of Israel with the twelve signs. Martin and others have argued that the arrangement of the tribes around the Tabernacle (reported in the Book of Numbers) corresponded to the order of the Zodiac, with Judah, Reuben, Ephraim and Dan representing the middle signs of Leo, Aquarius, Taurus and Scorpio, respectively. Such connections were taken up by Thomas Mann, who in his novel *Joseph and His Brothers*, attributes characteristics of a sign of the zodiac to each tribe in his rendition of the Blessing of Jacob." While it may be claimed that there is no evidence for the 12-division zodiac before the 12 tribes were founded, hence they could not have been established based on these divisions, the fact is that there is no evidence for the existence of the 12 Tribes before the sixth century, which happens to be the time when the 12-division zodiac began to flourish. Moreover, the sacred number 12 possessed significance much earlier than the sixth century, as evidenced by the duodecimal deities in Egyptian mythology, and the simple astronomical fact central to ancient calendars that the solar

Jacob's first-born, Reuben, is Aquarius, "the beginning of my strength … unstable as water." Simeon and Levi, "the brothers," are Gemini. Judah, the "lion's whelp," is Leo. Zebulun, who "shall be for an haven of ships," may correspond to Libra, "the ship sign, or arc, or ark."[1222] Issachar is a "strong ass, crouching between the sheepfold's burdens," possibly corresponding to the bull of Taurus, the "workhorse." Of Jacob's son Dan, Anderson relates:

> "Dan shall be the serpent by the way, an adder in the path, that biteth the horse heels, so that his rider shall fall backwards." This is … the scorpion, or serpent, and alludes to that constellation which is placed next to the centaur or armed horseman, or Sagittarius, which *falleth* backward into the winter solstice of [Capricorn].[1223]

Jacob's son Gad is a reversal of Dag, the fish god, possibly representing Pisces. It was said of Asher that he would have "rich food" or "fat bread;" thus, he would correspond to Virgo, the bread-giver or fall harvest. Naphtali is "a hind let loose," representing Capricorn, the goat. Joseph, who was fiercely attacked by archers, is Sagittarius. The son of Rachel the "Ewe," Benjamin, the "ravenous wolf" who "divides the spoil," would be Aries, who "comes in like a lion" and divides spring and winter. According to Anderson, the "fruitful bough" of Joseph representing his sons, Ephraim and Manasseh, could share the "portion divided between them" of the "double-sign" of Cancer. Joseph himself, is "an interpreter of dreams and a noted magician" with a magical "silver cup," by which he divines.

Jacob's ladder with the 72 angels ascending and descending (according to post-biblical lore) (according to post-biblical lore) represents the 72 decans, or portions of the zodiac of five degrees each. The same ladder story is found in Indian and Mithraic mythology, as Doane relates:

> Paintings representing a scene of this kind may be seen in works of art illustrative of *Indian Mythology*. Manrice speaks of one, in which he says:
>
> "The souls of men are represented as ascending and descending (on a ladder), according to the received opinion of the sidereal Metempsychosis."

---

year has about twelve lunar months. The point here is that, regardless of whether or not the tribes actually existed, they were perceived in antiquity to represent the 12 divisions of the zodiac.

1222 Anderson, 66.

1223 Anderson, 66.

And Count de Volney says:

In the cave of Mithra *was a ladder with seven steps*, representing the seven spheres of the planets by means of which *souls ascended and descended*. This is precisely the ladder of Jacob's vision.[1224]

In addition, the name "Jacob" is a title for a priest of the Goddess Isis,[1225] which is fitting, since she is the Queen of Heaven who rules over the night sky.

Joshua/Jesus, Son of Nun

Joshua, or *Jesus*, son of Nun (the "fish"), was regarded as the second great prophet after Moses, leading the Israelites to the promised land in Jericho, first encamping at Gilgal, or *Galilee*. Like Jacob, Joshua sets up twelve stones representing the tribes and the signs of the zodiac. The account of how, in Joshua's day, the sun stood still has spawned much tortured speculation. In reality, it occurred twice each year and still does, at the solstices, as the meaning of the word "solstice" is "sun stands still," the time when "the sun changes little in declination from one day to the next and appears to remain in one place north or south of the celestial equator."[1226] The sun also reportedly stood still at the death of Krishna, centuries earlier: "1575 years before Christ, after the death of Cristna (Boodh the son of Deirca), the sun stood still to hear the pious ejaculations of Arjoon."[1227] This solstice motif likewise appears in the mythologies of China and Mexico.[1228]

Of the Book of Joshua, Higgins relates:

> Sir William Drummond has shown that the names of most of the places in Joshua are astrological; and General Vallancey has shown that Jacob's prophecy is astrological also, and has a direct reference to the Constellations.[1229]

As to Joshua and various other aspects of the Old Testament, Higgins sums it up:

> The pretended genealogy of the tenth chapter of Genesis [from Noah on down] is attended with much difficulty. It reads like a genealogy: it is notoriously a chart of geography.... I have no doubt that the allotment of lands by Joshua was astronomical. It was exactly on the same principle as the nomes of Egypt, which every one knows were named astronomically, or rather,

1224 Doane, 45.
1225 Anderson, 66.
1226 Webster's.
1227 Higgins, I, 197.
1228 Doane, 91.
1229 Higgins, I, 370.

> perhaps, I should say, astrologically. The double meaning is clear … Most of the names … are found in the mystic work of Ezekiel.… [Genesis's tenth] chapter divides the world into 72 nations. Much ingenuity must have been used to make them agree with the exact number of dodecans into which the great circle was divided.[1230]

In this same regard, a Muslim convert from Judaism, Abd'allah Ebn Saba, elevated Joshua to a divine status, as did various Shi'ite Muslims concerning a number of their imams.[1231]

Daniel

In the famous scene where Daniel interprets the dreams of Cyrus and Nebuchadnezzar, it is implied that, while the others who attempted to do likewise were astrologers, soothsayers and the like, Daniel himself was not. On the contrary, Daniel, too, was an astrologer, and we also discover he is not a historical character, as Walker relates:

> Writers of the Old Testament disliked the Danites, whom they called serpents (Genesis 49:17). Nevertheless, they adopted Dan-El or Daniel, a Phoenician god of divination, and transformed him into a Hebrew prophet. His magic powers were like those of the Danites emanating from the Goddess Dana and her sacred serpents. He served as court astrologer and dream-interpreter for both the Persian king Cyrus, and the Babylonian king Nebuchadnezzar (Daniel 1:21, 2:1), indicating that "Daniel" was not a personal name but a title, like the Celtic one: "a person of the Goddess Dana."[1232]

Graham states:

> The story of Daniel was taken from a northern Syrian poem written before 1500 BC. The hero, Daniel by name, was a son of El or God—the source of the Hebrew El. He was a mighty judge and lawgiver, also a provider for his people. This poem about him became so widely known that many races used its hero as a model for their own.[1233]

As for his "visions," Larson says, "It is evident that the apocalyptic tribulations of Daniel and those described in the New Testament are appropriated from the literature of the Zoroastrians."[1234] Furthermore, although Daniel's "prophecies" are frequently called astoundingly accu-

---

1230 Higgins, I, 265.
1231 Sale, 125.
1232 Walker, B. (1983), 207.
1233 Graham, 256.
1234 Larson, 99.

rate, proving the Bible to be the inspired Word of God, they were actually written after the fact. In particular, the so-called prophecy at Daniel 9:24–27, referring to the "coming of an anointed one," has been piously interpreted as a prediction of Jesus's advent. But in the next paragraph, Daniel reveals whom he is really discussing: King Cyrus. Cyrus, in fact, is called the "Lord's Christ," as at Isaiah 45:1: "Thus says the Lord to his *Christ*, to Cyrus."

Even in antiquity the authenticity of the Book of Daniel was called into question. As Rev. Kampmeier states:

> The book of Daniel in the Old Testament expressly claims to have been written by a certain Daniel living at the time of the Babylonian Exile. It is well known now, that this book was written almost 400 years later during the time of the Maccabees. This was even proven to be so by the neo-Platonist Porphyry as early as the third century, for which reason his books were later burned by order of the Emperor Theodosius, in order that his criticism of the book of Daniel should not become generally known. Since the beginning of the last century, however, the authenticity of the book has been given up more and more, and no unprejudiced Bible scholar accepts it any longer.[1235]

Esther

In the story of the heroine Esther, her husband-to-be, King Ahasuerus, becomes enraged by the behavior of his current wife, Queen Vashti, so he takes council with "the wise men who knew the times—for this was the king's procedure toward all who were versed in law and judgment." These "wise men who knew the times" were astrologers, whom the king evidently considered "versed in law and judgment" and indispensable to the workings of his domain. This book is, however, not historical, as "Esther" is a remake of the Goddess and Queen of Heaven Ishtar, Asherah, Astarte, Astoreth or Isis, from whom comes "Easter." Of Esther, Walker relates:

> "Star," the Hebrew rendering of Ishtar or Astarte. The biblical book of Esther is a secularized Elamite myth of Ishtar (Esther) and her consort Marduk (Mordecai), who sacrificed to the god Hammon, or Amon (Haman). Yahweh was never mentioned, because the Jews of Elam worshipped Marduk, not Yahweh.... Even the Bible story admits that Esther-Ishtar was not the real name of the Elamite-Jewish queen. Her real name was Hadassah (Esther 2:7).[1236]

1235 Carus, 21.54.

1236 Walker, B. (1983), 286.

Walker continues:

> The story of Esther is an allegorical tale of the intercession of Ishtar, whom the Jews worshipped at the time, with the king who was supposed to be her consort, on behalf of the subject Jewish tribes. Interwoven with this theme is that of the ritual sacrifice.[1237]

The name Ishtar is Semitic and earlier was pronounced Eshtar.[1238]

Van der Toorn, et al., also say, "As a deity, Ishtar is not mentioned in the Bible. Commonly, the name *'estēr*, Esther, has been interpreted as derived from Ishtar."[1239] The connection between Esther and Asherah is noteworthy, in that the second set of Ten Commandments given to Moses sets as the first command from God that the Israelites should destroy the groves of Asherah (Exodus 34:13).

The Dial of Ahaz

In 2 Kings and in Isaiah, the reformer king Hezekiah on his death bed calls upon the Lord, who adds 15 years onto his life by making "the shadow cast by the declining sun on the dial of Ahaz turn back ten steps. So the sun turned back on the dial the ten steps by which it had declined." This story represents the correction of the calendar to align with the changing heavens. Higgins elucidates:

> The cycles would require correcting again after several revolutions, and we find Isaiah making the shadow go back ten degrees on the dial of Ahaz. This would mean nothing but a second correction of the Neros [600-year cycle], or a correction of some cycle of a planetary body, to make it agree with some other. In the annals of China, in fact of the Chinese Buddhists, in the reign of Emperor Yau (a very striking name, being the name of the God of the Jews), it is said that the sun was stopped ten days, that is, probably, ten degrees of Isaiah, a degree answering to a year, 360 degrees and 360 days.[1240]

Deborah

The great biblical prophet Deborah was also an astrologer, who, in order to defeat Sisera's armies, uses the stars: "From heaven fought the stars, from their courses they fought against Sisera" (Judg. 5:20). Naturally, like Daniel, Esther, et al., Deborah is a deity of an older age rendered human:

1237 Walker, B. (1983), 829.

1238 van der Toorn, 452.

1239 van der Toorn, 455.

1240 Higgins, I, 197.

The Son of God Is the Sun of God

"There is nothing new under the sun."

—Ecclesiastes 1:9

"Probably the most provocative issue related to the nature of sun worship in ancient Israel … is the specific claim that Yahweh was identified with the sun."

—Rev. Dr. J. Glen Taylor, *Yahweh and the Sun: Biblical and Archaeological Evidence for Sun Worship in Ancient Israel* (20)

"The sun as witness to a contract or oath was known in the Jewish community in the land of Israel from the Bible, which had a central role in synagogue ritual."[1241]

—Dr. Yaffa Englard, "Mosaics as Midrash: The Zodiacs of the Ancient Synagogues"

"The cult of Sol Invictus, the 'Invincible Sun,' became dominant in Rome and in other parts of the empire during the early part of the second century AD. And evidence abounds that Roman sun cults influenced Christian thought and liturgy."

—Dr. Samuele Bacchiocchi, *Signs of the Times* (8)

"The result of the Church's encounter with the sun-cults of antiquity was nothing less than the dethronement of Helios."

—Dr. Hugo Rahner, *Greek Myths and Christian Mystery* (93)

"The symbolism in which Christ's divinity was clothed after his death came from the Sun. In the contemporary Hellenistic world, both the Greek Sun god Helios and the Persian and Roman Sun god Mithras portrayed the celestial drama of resurrection through the risen Sun, reborn from death every dawn and every midwinter at the winter solstice. As Mithras was called the Sol Invictus, so Christ was to be the new invincible Sun, whose birth was timed (four centuries after he died) to the winter solstice in the image of the reborn Sun—as was the birth of Mithras. Christ's God was beyond Sun and Moon as the transcendent Creator of the natural world, but the Sun and Moon played a crucial role in the Christian imagination through the complementary figures of Christ and Mary."

—Dr. Jules Cashford, "Sun and Moon in Christianity," *The Moon* (164)

Over the ages, the ancients did not simply observe the movements of the celestial bodies but personified them and created stories about them that were recreated upon the earth. Out of this polytheistic, astrological

1241 Avery-Peck, 20.*

atmosphere came the "greatest story ever told." The gospel tale is in fact astrotheological and non-historical, recording the mythos found around the globe for eons. Thus the Christian religion, created and shored up by forgery, fraud and force, is in reality astrotheological and its founder is mythical. Christianity is based on many thousands of years of observation by the ancients of the movements and interrelationships of the celestial bodies and the earth. One of the favorites of these bodies, understandably, was the sun.

The sun has figured in the stories of every culture. In many places and eras, the sun was considered the most visible proxy of the divine and the most potent bestower of Spirit. It was regarded as the first entity in "the Void" and the progenitor of all life and matter. The sun also represented the Archetypal Man, as human beings were perceived as "solar entities." In addition to being a symbol of the spirit because it rises and sets, the sun was the "soul of the world," signifying immortality, as it is eternally resurrected in the spring after its annual "dying" in winter or its daily setting at dusk. The sun was also considered the purifier of the soul. Hence, from at least the Egyptian age down to the Gnostic Christians, the sun, along with the moon and other celestial bodies, was viewed as a "guide" into the afterlife. Gnostic Zoroastrians saw the sun as "the Archimagus, that noblest and most powerful agent of divine power, who 'steps forth as a Conqueror from the top of the terrible Alborj to rule over the world which he enlightens from the throne of Ormuzd.'"[1242] Long before the Christian era, the sun was known as the "Son of Ormuzd," the "Mediator," while his adversary, Ahriman, represented the darkness, which caused the fall of man.[1243]

The sun was considered the "Savior of the World," as its rising brought light, warmth and life to the planet, natural themes echoed in the Gospel depiction of Jesus Christ. It was revered for causing seeds to burst and thus giving its life for plants to grow; hence, it was seen to sacrifice itself in order to provide fertility and vegetation. The sun is the "tutelary genius of universal vegetation,"[1244] as well as the god of cultivation and the benefactor of humankind. When the sun "dies" in winter, so does the vegetation, to be "resurrected" in the spring. The first fruits, vine and grain were considered symbols of the sun's strength and were ritualistically offered to the divine luminary. The solar heroes and gods were said to be teachers as well, because agriculture, a science developed out of astronomy, freed mankind to pursue something other than

1242 Pike, 612.
1243 Pike, 613.
1244 Pike, 475.

food, such as other sciences and the arts.

The various personifications of the sun thus represent the "image of fecundity which perpetuates and rejuvenates the world's existence."[1245] In their fertility aspects, the sun was the phallus, or lingam, and the moon was the vulva, or yoni, making the sun and moon represent the male and female generative principles, the generators of all life on Earth.

In the mythos, the two pillars or columns of the Celestial Temple, the mysterious Jachin and Boaz, are the sun and moon.[1246] Of the relationship between the sun and moon, Hazelrigg adds: "The Sun may be likened to a wire through which the planetary messages are electrically transmitted, and of which the lunar moisture is the insulation."[1247]

In the ancient world, light was the subject of awe, and the sunlight's ability to make plants grow was considered magical and miraculous. So special is light that the writer of Ecclesiastes 11:7 waxes, "Light is sweet, and it is pleasant for the eyes to behold the sun." We know that it is *not* pleasant for the eyes to look directly at the sun; it is, however, pleasant for humanity to behold the sun as it rises in the morning, bringing light and life. Indeed, the sun itself is the "face of the divine" upon which it is impossible to look.

Thus the sun was very important to the ancients, so much so that around the world for millennia a wide variety of peoples have built solar temples, monuments and entire religions with priestesses and priests of the Sun, along with complex rituals and accoutrements, continued in the Christian practice of orienting church altars to the rising sun in the east. Within these religions is contained the ubiquitous mythos, a template or archetypical story that personifies the heavens and Earth, and rolls them into a drama about their interrelationship. Rather than being an entertaining but useless "fairytale," as myths are erroneously considered to be, the mythos is designed to pass along from generation to generation information vital to life on Earth, an essential survival tool so that can remember key facts. The knowledge, or gnosis, of the celestial mythos, was central to oral human culture and ritual, but this core practice, recognizing knowledge as the main source of social power, came under assault with the growth of military empires who sought to centralize religion.

The celestial mythos is complicated because the solar myth is intertwined with lunar, planetary, stellar and terrestrial myths. In addition, as various celestial characters rose and fell and many of them took on or

1245 Pike, 594.
1246 Pike, 776.
1247 Hazelrigg, 56.

lost functions as the focus switched from stars to moon to sun to other planets, and back again.

For example, Horus is the Sun God and is also the North Pole star, while his twin brother-cum-adversary, Set, represents not only darkness but also the South Pole. Furthermore, as time progresses and the skies change, as with the precession of the equinoxes and the movements of the sun annually through the zodiac and daily through its "houses," the attributes of the planetary bodies within the mythos also change. Moreover, the incorporation of the phases of the moon into the mythos adds to its complexity:

> The Moon, like the Sun, changed continually the track in which she crossed the Heavens, moving ever to and fro between the upper and lower limits of the Zodiac; and her different places, phases, and aspects there, and her relations with the Sun and the constellations, have been a fruitful source of mythological fables.[1248]

An example of the complexity of the mythos is provided by the story of the "Queen of Heaven," the goddess Isis, mother of Horus, who is not only the moon that reflects the sun, but the original creator, as well as the constellation of Virgo. As the moon, she is the "woman clothed with the sun," and as the Virgin, she is the sun's mother. Isis is also Stella Maris, the "Star of the Sea," as she regulates the tides, a fact known about the moon eons ago.

The sun and moon were deemed to be one being in some cultures or twins in others. Although most religions considered the sun to be "male," the sun was also regarded as female in many traditions, including in Alaska, Anatolia, Arabia, Australia, Canaan, England, Germany, India, Japan, North America and Siberia. The sun's feminine side was, suppressed by the patriarchy. As Walker says:

> The popular European tradition usually made the sun male and the moon female, chiefly to assert that "his" light was stronger, and that "she" shone only by reflected glory, symbolic of the position of women in patriarchal society. However, Oriental and pre-Christian systems frequently made the sun a Goddess.[1249]

When eclipses occurred, it was said that the moon and sun were uniting to create lesser gods. Thus, the pantheon kept growing.

When one factors into this complexity the fertility aspect of the gods and goddesses of the grape and grain, along with the sexual imagery found in all mythologies and religions, one can understand why it has been so difficult to sort it all out.

1248 Pike, 469.

1249 Walker, WDSSO, 353.

The Zodiac

The zodiac as we have it now evidently was refined by the Greeks between the fourth and first centuries before the Common Era. However, its earlier Babylonian rendition was in existence by at least the seventh century BCE, evolving from an earlier version called the "MUL. APIN catalogue," composed around 1000 BCE.[1250] and the Babylonian star catalogues.[1251] There are indications that earlier renderings could be found in Egypt and possibly on the Karanovo disc from Bulgaria, dating to some 4,800 years ago. The exact form of the zodiac is not relevant to whether or not the twelve tribes of Israel represent the signs, although in later times these assignments were made, as we find Jews significantly knowledgeable about the zodiac and astrology. It appears that the Egyptians may have possessed the motif of the sacred number of 12 divisions at least 4,800 years ago, as found in the stone circle at Nabta Playa.

These sources serve as rudimentary evidence for the earlier use of the zodiac and possibly also for knowledge of the equinoctial precession, which was apparently noticed by the world's keen sky-watching cultures during tens of thousands of years of observations, in view of the slowly changing use of constellations to mark the seasons.

As I state in *Jesus as the Sun throughout History*, the "bear with its children" (Job 38:22) refers to the constellation of Ursa Major and the three stars in its tail.[1252] This Mazzaroth scripture concerning the zodiac from Job 38:31 would have originated before Moses purportedly gathered the 12 tribes of Israel, allegedly in the thirteenth century.[1253]

1250 Dating to possibly 3,000 or more years ago, the MUL.APIN depicted a lunar path of 17 or 18 stations, "recognizable as the direct predecessor of the twelve-sign zodiac." These included the Babylonian equivalents of the twelve zodiac signs, as well as the Pleiades, Orion, Perseus, Auriga and Andromeda. ("Babylonian star catalogues.") As we can see, even at this early date astronomers had already documented major zodiacal details.

1251 The Babylonian star catalogues: "A few of the constellation names in use in modern astronomy can be traced to Babylonian sources via Greek astronomy. Among the most ancient constellations are those that marked the four cardinal points of the year in the Middle Bronze Age (i.e., Taurus 'The Bull,' from GU4. AN.NA 'The Steer of Heaven,' marking vernal equinox); Leo 'The Lion,' from UR.GU.LA 'The Lion,' marking summer solstice; Scorpius 'The Scorpion,' from GIR.TAB 'The Scorpion,' marking autumn equinox; Capricornus 'Goat-Horned,' from SUḪUR.MAŠ 'The Goat-Fish,' marking winter solstice ("Babylonian star catalogues.")

1252 McClintock, 381.

1253 Scientific analysis places the actual writing of much of the Old Testament

took place above.'"[1] The astrological imagery was the major difference between Gnosticism and Christianity, as well as one primary reason the Gnostics were suppressed and their texts destroyed or mutilated.

There are many concealed references to astrology in the canonical scriptures that are not as clear as those examined here. What is clear is that the Hebrews and Christians were no more "astrology-free" than any of their contemporaries or predecessors, although the latter, such as the Chaldeans and Babylonians, were far more skilled (and gnostic) in the astrological arts. Indeed, Karl Anderson, master navigator and author of *Astrology in the Old Testament*, calls the Bible "that greatest of all astrological works."[2]

Astrology is no more "evil" than are the sky and the heavenly bodies, which biblical writers claimed were divine emanations of the Grand Architect. The vilification of astrology is not merely a sign of ignorance but, by insisting that its adherents were either lacking in wisdom or led astray by the devil, of cultural bigotry, as astrology has been appreciated and utilized in countless cultures around the globe. The ancients were, in fact, constantly reenacting the movements of the heavens, a reenactment that was eventually literalized and carnalized as "The Greatest Story Ever Sold."

1 Graham, 354.
2 Anderson, 10.

The Zodiac

One of the Dead Sea Scrolls (4Q318), the "Qumran brontologion" or divination text, contains a list in Aramaic—the earliest yet found—of the twelve signs of the zodiac, the same as we have today, but different from the earlier Mesopotamian version.[1254] This text is dated from between the second century BCE. and the first century AD/CE.[1255] and indicates that "this zodiac calendar was based upon late Babylonian zodiac calendrical traditions."[1256]

Philo (**QE** 1.1) says, "For they call the Ram, the head of the zodiac, since in it the sun appears to produce the vernal equinox."[1257] (See also Josephus, *Ant.* 3.248)

Dr. Englard remarks:

> The zodiac with the sun at the center, accompanied by the moon, a star or stars, and around it the seasons of the years, thus symbolized the witnesses to the eternal covenant between God and his people, his messiah, and his priests, as expressed in the Bible and in Rabbinic literature. The formal array was adopted from the Hellenistic-Roman culture and might also have originated in the Ancient Near East.[1258]

As the mythos developed, it took the form of a play, with a cast of characters, including the 12 divisions of the sky called the signs or constellations of the zodiac. The symbols that typified these 12 celestial sections of 30° each were not based only on what the constellations actually look like but represent aspects of earthly life. Thus, the ancient peoples were able to incorporate these earthly aspects into the mythos and project them onto the all-important celestial screen.

These zodiacal designations have varied from place to place and era to era over the tens of thousands of years during which people have observed, the skies, and this for a number of reasons, including the changes in the skies brought on by the precession. For example, Scorpio is not

---

no earlier than the postexilic period (i.e., after the "Babylonian Captivity" in the sixth century). (See Finkelstein's *The Bible Unearthed.*)

1254 Wise, et al., 387. The word "brontologion" means "thunder oracle," reflecting an ancient tradition as found also in Babylon, whereby the thunder god was propitiated to reveal the future. (Wise, et al., 387; Harris, Rendel, 48)

1255 Jacobus, 365–6.

1256 Jacobus, "4Q318: A Jewish Zodiac Calendar at Qumran?" Abstract, www.escholar.manchester.ac.uk/
uk-ac-man-scw:128116

1257 Jacobus, 376.

1258 Avery-Peck, 20.

only the eagle but also the scorpion. It is difficult to determine absolutely all of their origins, but the current zodiacal symbols or totems are or may have been devised as follows, based on the formula made by inhabitants of the northern hemisphere:

- Aries is represented as the Ram/Lamb because March/April is the time of the year when lambs are born.
- Taurus is the Bull because April/May is the time for ploughing and tilling.
- Gemini is the Twins, so-called for Castor and Pollux, the twin stars in its constellation, as well as because May/June is the time of the "increase" or "doubling" of the sun, when it reaches its greatest strength.
- After the sun reaches its strength at the summer solstice and begins to diminish in Cancer (June/July), the stars are called the Crab, who "backslides."
- Leo is the Lion because, during the heat of July/August, the lions in Egypt would come out of the hot desert.
- Virgo, originally the Great Mother Earth, is the "Gleaning Virgin, who holds a sheath of wheat," symbolizing August/ September, the time of the harvest.
- Libra (September/October) is the Balance, reflecting the autumnal equinox, when the day and night are again even in length.
- Scorpio is the Scorpion because in the desert areas the fierce storms of October/November were called "scorpions" and because this time of the year is the "backbiter" of the sun as it begins to wane.
- Sagittarius is the "vindictive Archer" who side-wounds and weakens the sun during its approach in November/ December towards the winter solstice.
- In Capricorn, the weakened sun encounters the "filthy, ill-omened He-goat," who drags the solar hero down in December/January.
- Aquarius is the Water-Bearer because January/February is the time of winter rains.
- Pisces is represented by the Fishes because February/ March is the time when the thinning ice is broken and the fattened fish are plucked out.[1259]

The story of the skies was so important to the ancient agrarian societies that they were singularly focused on it and their lives in effect revolved around how the stars marked the seasons. As we have seen, however, the heavens were revered not only by so-called Pagans but also by biblical peoples, including the Israelites, whose very name and various Elohim were also stars and aspects of the solar-celestial mythos.

1259 Hazelrigg, 43.

In the Bible, the sun is worshipped in various forms by the Hebrews and "kings of Judah." It is also overtly personified and imbued with divine and ethical qualities, as in Deuteronomy: "But thy friends be like the sun as he rises in his might." Throughout the Old Testament important deeds are done "in the sight of this sun," "before the sun," or "under the sun," revealing the ages-old perception of the sun as God's proxy, judge or "eye." So significant was the solar orb that it was ever a grave concern that the sun would "go down on the prophets."

At Psalm 113:3, the chosen are instructed to praise the Lord from the "rising of the sun to its setting." Psalm 85:11 states, "Faithlessness will spring up from the ground, and righteousness will look down from the sky." Psalm 84:11 reads, "For *the Lord God is a sun* and shield." At Psalm 68:32, the faithful are instructed to "sing praises to Jah, to him who rides in the heavens, the ancient heavens … whose majesty is over Israel, and his power is in the skies," exactly as was said about the ubiquitous solar hero.

At Psalm 72:17 we read, "May his name endure for ever, his fame continue as long as the sun," and at Malachi 1:11: "For from the rising of sun to its setting my name is great among the nations." The Lord's name is not said to be great *after* the setting of the sun, during the night, because his "name" *is* the sun, which, as we have seen, Iao, Jah, and YHWH all mean. Thus the Hebrew esteem for the sun is evident. The story of the solar hero is also found in numerous places in the Old Testament, but these stories are masked by carnalization and historicization, giving us characters like Samson, Enoch, Moses, Elijah, Isaac, and Esau. Indeed, so important was the sun to the ancients, including the Israelites, that they created a "Sun Book," a "Helio Biblio," or "Holy Bible,"[1260] the original of which can be found in the myths encoded in stone and story around the ancient world millennia before the Judeo-Christian Bible was compiled.

The word "Bible" itself comes from the City of the Great Mother: Byblos in Phoenicia. As Walker relates, "'Bibles were named after her city because the earliest libraries were attached to her temple."[1261] As noted, the Judeo-Christian Bible was written by a number of hands, edited numerous times, and contains countless errors and inaccuracies. It is a rehash of ancient legends and myths, and is not, therefore, the "infallible Word of God." "Such," says Graham, "is the Bible's 'revealed truth'—other races' mythology, the basis of which is cosmology."[1262]

1260 Hotema, EBD.
1261 Walker, B. (1983), 127.
1262 Graham, 74.

The cosmology or celestial mythos has in reality been hidden from the masses for many centuries for the purposes of enriching and empowering the ruling elite. Its conspiring priest-kings have ruled empires in full knowledge of it since time immemorial and have "lorded" it over the heads of the "serfs."

Conversely, the existence of the motif of 12 tribes serves as further evidence that they were not devised until after the Babylonian Exile, since that is when the Jews would have been exposed to the all-important 12-division zodiac.

The Sun of God

Within the Sun Book or Holy Bible was incorporated by such priestcraft the most consolidated version of the celestial mythos ever assembled, the story of the "son of God." First, we have seen that "God" *is* the sun. Second, in Job 38 the stars are called "sons of God"; hence, one star would be a "son of God," as well as a "son of the Sun." Thus, *the son of God is the sun of God.*

As I state in "Jesus as the Sun throughout History," the exploration of Christ as a solar figure includes a study of ancient sun worship not only in the Pagan world but also in Israel, as exhibited by the solar nature of Jesus's purported Father, the Israelite god Yahweh. Demonstrating the copious substantiation for Israelite sun worship, especially as concerns the main Jewish god, in Yahweh and the Sun: Biblical and Archaeological Evidence for Sun Worship in Ancient Israel, the Rev. Dr. J. Glen Taylor, a theologian and professor of Old Testament and Biblical Proclamation at Wycliffe College, remarks:

> This book is a slightly revised version of my doctoral dissertation entitled "Solar Worship in the Biblical World" which was submitted to the Graduate School of Yale University in the Spring of 1989. As may be judged from the title of that work, I had at one time planned to cover more territory than sun worship in ancient Israel, but found the material pertaining to ancient Israel so vast that I never got beyond it.[1263]

It is no longer mysterious when the Psalmist (84:11) intones, "For the LORD God is a sun and a shield." Another Psalmist (27:1) declares, "The LORD is my light and my salvation." The Hebrew word for "sun" is שמש or *shemesh*, which is the popular ancient Semitic name for the sun god, as in the Mesopotamian Shamash.

Interestingly, two other Babylonian sun-god names, Ninurta and Nergal (2 Kings 17:30), correspond respectively to the morning/spring-

1263 Taylor, R., 7.

time sun and noon/summer solstice sun.[1264] Such a development of associating morning and spring, the vernal beginning, and noon and the summer, the maturing season, would indicate further a connection between the evening sun—as found in the Egyptian mythology, represented by Atum—and the autumnal equinox, as well as the night sun—represented by Osiris, for one—with the winter solstice. Indeed, depending on the star list, either Marduk or Ninurta/Ninib symbolizes the morning/spring sun, while Ninurta or Nergal represents the noon/summer sun and Nabu/Nebo the evening/fall sun or the night/winter sun.[1265] These motifs demonstrate once more the logicality and rationality of ancient astrotheological ideas. These gods also represent various planets: Marduk is Jupiter, Ninurta represents Mars, Nebo is Mercury and Nergal Saturn.[1266]

The solar mythos, in fact, with its natural recurring annual death and rebirth, explains why the narratives of the sons of God previously examined are so similar, with a godman who is crucified and resurrected, who does miracles and has 12 disciples, etc.: To wit, these stories were in actuality based on the movements of the sun through the heavens. In other words, Jesus Christ and the others upon whom he is predicated are personifications of the sun, telling the real natural story in human form, and the gospel fable is merely a repeat of a mythological formula revolving around the progress of the sun through the sky.

For example, many of the world's crucified godmen have their traditional birthdays on December 25 ("Christmas"). This date is set because the ancients recognized that (from a geocentric perspective in the northern hemisphere) the sun makes an annual descent southward until after midnight of December 21, the winter solstice, when it stops moving southerly for three days and then starts to move northward again. During this time, the ancients declared that "God's sun" had "died" for three days and was "born again" after midnight of December 24. Thus, these many different cultures celebrated with great joy the "sun of God's" birthday on December 25. The following are the main characteristics of the "sun of God":

- The sun "dies" for three days at the winter solstice, to be born again or resurrected on December 25.
- The sun of God is "born of a virgin," which refers to the new or "virgin" moon, the daily birth of the sun at dawn and the constellation of Virgo.
- The sun's "birth" is attended by the "bright Star," either Sirius/

1264 Leslie, 36.
1265 Jackson, S.M., 1.411; Thierens, 35.
1266 Thierens, 35.

Sothis or the planet Venus, and by the "Three Kings," representing the three stars in the belt of Orion.

- The sun at its zenith, or 12 noon, is in the house or heavenly temple of the "Most High." This could match how "he" begins "his Father's work" at "age" 12.
- The sun enters into each sign of the zodiac at 30°; hence, the "Sun of God" begins his ministry at "age" 30. As Hazelrigg states, "the Sun of the visible heavens has moved northward 30° and stands at the gate of Aquarius, the Water-bearer, or John the Baptist of the mystic planisphere, and here begins the work of ministry in Palestine."[1267]
- The sun is the "Carpenter" who builds his daily "houses" or 12 two-hour divisions.
- The sun's "followers" or "disciples" are the 12 signs of the zodiac, through which the sun must pass.
- The sun is "anointed" when its rays dip into the sea.[1268]
- The sun "changes water into wine" by creating rain, ripening the grape on the vine and fermenting the grape juice.
- The sun "walks on water," referring to its reflection.[1269]
- The sun "calms the sea"[1270] as he rests in the "boat of heaven."[1271] (Matt. 8:23–7)
- When the sun is annually and monthly re-born, he brings life to the "solar mummy," his previous self, raising it from the dead.
- The sun triumphantly "rides an ass and her foal" into the "City of Peace" when it enters the sign of Cancer, which contains two stars called "little asses," and reaches its fullness.[1272]
- The sun is the "Lion" when in Leo, the hottest time of the year, called the "throne of the Lord."
- The sun is "betrayed" by the constellation of the Scorpion, the backbiter, the time of the year when the solar hero loses his strength.
- The sun is "crucified" between the two thieves of Sagittarius and Capricorn.
- The sun is hung on a cross, which represents its passing through

---

1267 Hazelrigg, 163.

1268 Anderson, 206.

1269 Massey, HJMC, 21.

1270 The gospel pericope of Jesus controlling and calming the storm evidently comes from Psalm 107:25, 29: "For he commanded, and raised the stormy wind, which lifted up the waves of the sea … he made the storm be still, and the waves of the sea were hushed." The LORD also kicks up a storm in Jonah (1:4).

1271 Leedom, 27.

1272 Pike, 465.

the equinoxes, the vernal equinox being Easter.

- The sun darkens when it "dies": "The solar god as the sun of evening or of autumn was the suffering, dying sun, or the dead sun buried in the nether world."[1273]
- The sun does a "stutter-step" at the winter solstice, unsure whether to return to life or "resurrect," doubted by his "twin" Thomas.
- The sun is with us "always, to the close of the age" (Matt. 28:20), referring to the ages of the precession of the equinoxes.
- The sun is the "Light of the World," and "comes on clouds, and every eye shall see him."
- The sun rising in the morning is the "Savior of mankind."
- The sun wears a corona, "crown of thorns" or halo.
- The sun was called the "Son of the Sky (God)," "All-Seeing," the "Comforter," "Healer," "Savior," "Creator," "Preserver," "Ruler of the World," and "Giver of Daily Life."[1274]
- The sun is the Word or Logos of God, providing the rational framework for life.

The all-seeing sun, or "eye of God," was considered the judge of the living and dead who returned to Earth "on a white horse."[1275]

A. Churchward demonstrates the complex yet poetic celestial mythology of the Egyptians, developed around the core mythos long prior to the Christian era:

> The Sun was not considered human in its nature when the Solar force at dawn was imaged by the Lion-faced Atum, the flame of the furnace by the fiery serpent Uati, the Soul of its life by the Hawk, the Ram, or the Crocodile. Until Har-ur the elder Horus was depicted as the child in the place of the calf or lamb, fish, or shoot of papyrus plant, which now occurred in the Solar Cult, no human figure was personalized in the Mythology of Egypt.... Isis in this Cult takes the place of Hathor as the Mother-Moon, the reproducer of light in the underworld. The place of conjunction and of rebegettal by the Sun-god was in the underworld, when she became the woman clothed with the sun. At the end of lunation the old Moon died and became a corpse; it is at times portrayed as a mummy in the underworld and there it was revivified by the Sun-god, the Solar fecundation of the Moon representing the Mother, resulting in her bringing forth the child

1273 Massey, EBD, 50.
1274 Doane, 472, 478, 492, 562.
1275 Doane, 497–8.

of light, the "cripple deity," who was begotten in the dark.[1276]

Massey provides another sketch of the mythos as applied to Horus, who, like Baal, was the sun in the Age of Taurus:

> [The] infant Horus, who sank down into Hades as the suffering sun to die in the winter solstice and be transformed to rise again and return in all his glory and power in the equinox at Easter.[1277]

As documented extensively in my 2009 book *Christ in Egypt*, the story of Jesus is virtually identical in numerous important aspects to that of Horus, a solar myth. Higgins spells it out:

> The history of the sun … is the history of Jesus Christ. The sun is born on the 25th of December, the birthday of Jesus Christ. The first and greatest of the labours of Jesus Christ is his victory over the serpent, the evil principle, or the devil. In his first labor Hercules strangled the serpent, as did Cristna, Bacchus, etc. This is the sun triumphing over the powers of hell and darkness; and, as he increases, he prevails, till he is crucified in the heavens, or is decussated in the form of a cross (according to Justin Martyr) when he passes the equator at the vernal equinox.[1278]

At Malachi 4:2, YHWH says, "But for you who fear my name the sun of righteousness shall rise, with healing on its wings." Who is this? Malachi is the last book of the Old Testament, and this scripture is one of the last in that book, which leads directly into the story of Jesus, who was indeed called by the Church fathers the "sun of righteousness." Malachi's sun of righteousness rising with "healing on its wings" is, in reality, the saving light that ends the gloom of night, the daily resurrection of sunrise, and the birth of the sun of a new age, who was carnalized and historicized in Jesus Christ. As "*shamash*," which is the Hebrew word for sun and the name of the Babylonian sun god, Malachi's righteous sun is also Solomon's Moabite god Chemosh, which is the same as *shamash* in Hebrew, an ironic development considering Chemosh was later demonized by the Christians.

Jesus's solar attributes are also laid plain by the story of his followers waiting to go to his "tomb" until *sunrise*, when "he is risen." In John 2, Jesus says, "Destroy this temple, and in three days I will raise it up"; however, as John relates, "he spoke of the temple of his body," an admission of biblical allegory. In this statement Jesus describes his own *solar* resurrection, not that of the Jerusalem Temple, although the original "Temple of the Most High" is indeed the same Temple of the Sun

1276 A. Churchward, 226.

1277 Massey, EBD, 9.

1278 Higgins, II, 144.

that is Jesus's "body." In fact, Jesus is called the "son of the Most High God" (Luke 8:28; Mark 5:7) and a priest after the order of Melchizedek, who was the priest of the Most High, El Elyon, or Helios, the sun. At Acts 26:13, regarding his conversion, Paul says, "At midday, O king, I saw on the way a light from heaven, brighter than the sun, shining round me and those who journeyed with me," the light, of course, being Jesus. The words "at midday" represent the sun at its zenith, when it is doing its work in the Temple of the Most High, brighter than at any other time.

As expected, the early Christians were considered sun-worshippers, like their "Pagan" counterparts, although "sun-*worship*" is an inaccuracy, since the ancients did not "worship" the sun as the "one god" but revered it as one of the most potent symbols of the quality of divinity. For example, Krishna was considered not the sun itself but the *light* in the sun and moon,[1279] making him, like Jesus, brighter than the sun. Like their predecessor temples, many early Christian churches faced the east, or the place of the rising sun. In fact, as Doane relates, "Tertullian says that Christians were taken for worshipers of the Sun because they prayed towards the East, after the manner of those who adored the Sun."[1280] Tertullian's actual words from his Apology are as follows:

> Others, again, certainly with more information and greater verisimilitude, believe that the sun is our god. We shall be counted Persians perhaps, though we do not worship the orb of day painted on a piece of linen cloth, having himself everywhere in his own disk. The idea no doubt has originated from our being known to turn to the east in prayer. But you, many of you, also under pretense sometimes of worshipping the heavenly bodies, move your lips in the direction of the sunrise. In the same way, if we devote Sun-day to rejoicing, from a far different reason than Sun-worship, we have some resemblance to those of you who devote the day of Saturn to ease and luxury, though they too go far away from Jewish ways, of which indeed they are ignorant.

In his protestations and refutations of critics, Tertullian further ironically admits the true origins of the Christ story and of all other such godmen by stating, "*You say we worship the sun; so do you.*"[1281] Interestingly, a previously strident believer and defender of the faith, Tertullian later renounced Catholic Christianity to join the Montanist sect.[1282]

Christ was frequently identified as and/or with the sun by other early

1279 Doane, 284.

1280 Doane, 500–2.

1281 Wheless, 147.

1282 Wheless, 144.

orthodox Christian fathers, including St. Cyprian (d. 258), who "spoke of Christ as the true sun (*sol verus*)," and St. Ambrose (@ 339–397), Bishop of Milan, who said of Christ, "He is our new sun."[1283] Other Church fathers who identified Christ with, if not as, the sun include St. Gregory of Nazianzus (c. 330–c. 389), and St. Zeno of Verona (d. c. 375), who "calls Christ '*Sol noster, sol verus*.'" Moreover, this overt Christian sun-worship was not a short-lived aberration, as Christian proponents would portray it. Wheless relates that "Leo the Great in his day (440–461) says that it was the custom of many Christians to stand on the steps of the Church of St. Peter and pay homage to the Sun by obeisance and prayers."[1284]

As to such "insider" knowledge of the true meaning of Christianity, Doane remarks:

> Many Christian writers have seen that the history of their Lord and Saviour is simply the history of the Sun, but they either say nothing, or, like Dr. Parkhurst and the Rev. J. P. Lundy, claim that the Sun is a type of the true Sun of Righteousness.

This type of sophistry has been used frequently in religious debate to squeeze out of a tight corner. Yet the Christian conspirators cannot hide the fact that their "Lord's Day" is indeed *Sun-day*; hence, their Lord is the sun.

Even though this information has been well hidden, the early Christians were aware that Christ was the sun, as they were truly Gnostic and the solar myth was known all around them. When a member of at least one such Gnostic sect wished to become orthodox, he was compelled to renounce his "heresy" of equating Christ with the sun. Higgins relates the following of the influential and widespread Gnostic group called the Manichaeans:

> When a Manichaean came over to the orthodox he was required to curse his former friends in the following terms: "I curse Zarades [Zarathustra/Zoroaster] who, Manes said, had appeared as a God before his time among the Indians and Persians, and whom he calls the sun. I curse those who say *Christ is the sun*, and who make prayers to the sun, and to the moon, and to the stars, and pay attention to them as if they were really Gods, and who give them titles of most lucid Gods, and who do not pray to the true God, only towards the East, but who turn themselves round, following the motions of the sun with their innumerable supplications. I curse those persons who say that Zarades and

1283 www.christianism.com

1284 Wheless, 30.

> Budas [Buddha] and Christ and Manichaeus and the sun are all one and the same."[1285]

In his Second Apology, Justin Martyr acknowledges that certain Gnostics were "sun-worshippers" and says:

> Accordingly, Menander seems to me to have fallen into error when he said: "O sun! for thou, first of gods, ought to be worshipped, by whom it is that we are able to see the other gods." For the sun never could show me the true God; but that healthful Word, that is the Sun of the soul, by whom alone, when He arises in the depths of the soul, the eye of the soul itself is irradiated.

In order to obfuscate the origins of Christianity, Justin is attempting to distinguish between the sun of the Gnostics, which was the solar orb, and the "sun (*sol*) of the soul" in the "person" of Jesus Christ. In fact, the sun of the Gnostics and other "sun-worshippers" also represented the cosmic and cellular "sun" found in living things, including human beings, who, Gnostics taught, can become *illuminated*. Thus, both Gnostic and orthodox Christians were addressing the same "sun of the soul," but the orthodox insisted on putting a particular face and shape to it. One might also wonder how the *omnipresent* divine is separated out of its creation, such that it is "everywhere" but not in the sun, moon, stars, sky, earth and all of creation. To reiterate, the ancients were not just monotheistic, polytheistic and "atheistic"—as the Christians called, and were called by, their adversaries—but pantheistic, seeing the divine in everything, as is the definition of omnipresence.

It is clear that from early times Christ was correctly perceived by the Gnostic sects as the sun, a fact that the historicizing Christians were continuously compelled to combat, as in the anti-Manichaean oath specifically designed to refute such assertions. Yet, as Higgins states, "the Sun, Iao, and Jesus, were all taken for the same being by the ancients, and it will require more than the skill of the whole priesthood to disprove it."[1286]

Furthermore, the adoption (or, rather, creation) of Christianity was not much of a stretch for the Roman conspirators:

> In the early Christian era, Roman emperors were routinely identifying themselves with the sun god and all his symbols: cross, eagle, fire, gold, lion, and so on. Constantine I, whom conventional history hails as the first Christian emperor, was actually a worshipper of the sun god, whose image he placed on his coins,

---

1285 Higgins, I, 722.
1286 Higgins, I, 325.

dedicated to "the invincible sun, my guardian."[1287]

In fact, a 100-lire coin issued by the Vatican depicts a woman, symbolizing the Church, holding a cup in her right hand, which represents the "pagan sunburst wafer god."[1288] This "wafer" or host, used in Communion by the Catholic Church as a symbol for the body of Christ, is actually a very ancient symbol for the sun. The Catholic "monstrance" or "ostentorium," the device used to serve the "Lord's host," is also a sunburst, as admitted by Catholic authorities.[1289] Christian art, like that of Buddhism and Hinduism, makes extensive use of the halo or *sunburst* behind its godman, mother of God, and saints. As Massey says, "The halo of light which is usually shown surrounding the face of Jesus and Christian saints, is another concept taken from the sun god."

The solar nature of Jesus Christ is thus reflected in art, explaining why nobody knew what he looked like and why he was variously represented as a sun god, such as Apollo or Elias. As Biedermann says:

> In Christian iconography the sun, rising over and over again in the East, symbolizes immortality and resurrection. There are fourth-century mosaics showing Christ as a Helios-figure in a solar chariot surrounded by sunbeams, or surrounded by a solar nimbus. Since Christ is also triumphant over time (*chronocrator*), he is frequently associated with the sun (which measures out the length of each day) in Romanesque art.[1290]

The term "associated with" is a typical historicizing obfuscation, because Christ *is* the sun, which Christian artists have obviously known. The Apollo/Helios/Jesus image is often very light of complexion, with short blond hair, reflective not of an actual person but of the light and color of the sun. Other solar depictions include men with red hair, representative of the setting and summer sun, and black images symbolizing the orb in the dark underworld of night, which is the reason for the black bambinos and crucifixes in churches around the globe, not only of Jesus but also of Krishna and other solar heroes. As stated, these black crucifixes have led some to posit that Jesus was black (i.e., African); however, despite this compulsion to make Christ "all things to all people," these images depict the black or nighttime sun. In fact, they are part of the mythos, which holds that the solar orb and night sky are a dual-natured god, represented by "twins" battling for supremacy.

Let us now see further how the solar mythos was passed to us as

1287 Walker, WDSSO, 15.
1288 www.aloha.net/~mikesch/monstr.htm
1289 www.aloha.net/~mikesch/monstr.htm
1290 Biedermann, 330.

the Christian myth. To do so, we will also be following the sun's annual movements through the heavenly zodiac:

- According to legend, Jesus was born in a stable between a horse and a goat, symbols of Sagittarius and Capricorn.
- He was baptized in Aquarius, the Water-Bearer.
- He chose his first disciples, fishermen, in Pisces, the sign of the fishes.
- He became the Good Shepherd and the Lamb in Aries, the Ram.
- Jesus told the parables of the sowing and tilling of the fields in Taurus, the Bull.
- In Cancer, "the celestial Sea of Galilee,"[1291] he calmed the storm and waters, spoke of backsliders (the Crab), and rode the ass and foal in triumph into the City of Peace, Jerusalem.
- Jesus was the Lion in Leo.
- Virgo, the virgin holding the sheaf of wheat, symbolizes both Mary and the bread in the loaves and fish miracle.
- In Libra, Christ was the true vine in the Garden of Gethsemane, the "wine press," as this is the time of the grape harvest.
- Jesus was betrayed by Judas, the "backbiter," or Scorpio.
- In Sagittarius, Jesus was wounded in the side by the Centaur, or centurion.
- He was crucified at the winter solstice between the "two thieves" of Sagittarius and Capricorn, who sapped his strength.

Roberts elaborates the solar drama:

> [The] passage of the Sun, in its annual course through the constellations of the Zodiac; having his birth in the sign of the Goat, the Augean stable of the Greeks; his baptism in Aquarius, John the Baptist in the heavens; his triumph when he becomes the Lamb of God in Aries; his greatest exaltation on St. John's, the beloved disciple's, day, on the 21 of June, in the Sign of the Twins, the emblem of double power; his tribulation in the Garden of Gethsemane, in the sign of the rural Virgo; his betrayal in the sign of Scorpio, the malignant emblem of his approaching death in the stormy and adverse sign, Sagittarius, and his resurrection or renewed birth on the twentyfifth of December in the same sign of the celestial Goat.

Regarding the mysterious Garden of Gethsemane, Wells says, "'They went to a place which is called Gethsemane'. Nothing is known of such a place."[1292] In fact, the Garden exists in the

1291 Hazelrigg, 161.
1292 Wells, DJE, 136.

sky. In addition, Jesus in the "upper room" symbolizes the sun in the "upper signs," as the two equinoxes divide the solar orbit into two halves, also represented by the two genealogies of Jesus in the gospels.[1293]

Hazelrigg gives the astrological meaning of the annunciation of the divine one's birth:

> Directing our gaze to the right, we see rising on the eastern angle of the planisphere the constellation of the Virgin, the sixth sign of the Zodiac, or sixth month, reckoning from March (Aries). "And in the sixth month the angel Gabriel was sent from God … to a virgin espoused by a man whose name was Joseph, of the house of David; and the virgin's name was Mary."—Luke i. 26, 27.[1294]

He further explains the Passion as it appears in the mythos:

> In due order, the next quarter introduces the Passion—a term appositely chosen and applied—prefaced under Aries, the first sign of the fiery triplicity, which is the Vale of Gehenna.... Thence comes Calvary, conformably with the crossification of the Sun of Nature at the gate of Libra, with the zodiacal Virgin recumbent next to this point of supreme sacrifice.[1295]

The story of the sun is a daily, monthly, annual and precessional drama that takes place cyclically and over thousands of years. In order to change the mythos into the life of a man—in other words, to personify and historicize it—it was necessary to make the tale linear, resulting in discrepancies between the stories of the sun and that of the "historical" Jesus. For example, while the sun "dies" and is "reborn" or "resurrected" daily, monthly, annually and precessionally, as a "person" Jesus can only undergo such experiences once. In the early Christian period, when the story was still being formulated, yet another debate raged as to how long after beginning his ministry Christ was supposed to have suffered his passion, with a common portrayal that it occurred "in the 12th month after his baptism" (i.e., at the winter solstice), following his baptism in Aquarius, as acknowledged by Irenaeus, who wrote against the "heretics": "[T]hey affirm that He suffered in the twelfth month, so that He continued to preach for one year after His baptism." Irenaeus then insists that Christ "did not suffer in the twelfth month after his baptism, but was more than fifty years old when he died." Irenaeus's statements reveal not only Jesus's solar nature but also that by his time (c. 140–c. 200) the

1293 Hazelrigg, 120.
1294 Hazelrigg, 105.
1295 Hazelrigg, 165.

gospel story was not "set in stone" as it would have been had it happened in history. In fact, some of the writings of the early Christian fathers demonstrate that they are discussing a number of different individuals, which is to be expected, since the Christ character is a composite of many.

These various debates reflect the complexity of the mythos, as further illustrated by Massey:

> When it was discovered that the moon was a mirror to the solar light, the sun-god as Osiris was reborn monthly in or of the moon! Thus, the resurrection in three days became that of the luni-solar god.... The Christ who rose again in three days for the fulfillment of scripture must be the Christ according to that scripture which contained the mythos, and the fulfillment of scripture was the completion of astronomical cycles, whether lunar, solar, or Precessional.[1296]

The character of Jesus Christ was in fact created as the solar avatar or hero of the Age of Pisces, into which the sun was moving during the first centuries before the Christian era, an ill-omened time between ages of celestial "no man's land." Jesus as the Lamb of God was a remnant of the previous Age of Aries:

And as it approached the "gates of Spring," "the Lamb of God," or the Lamb of March gathered up "the sins of the world," or the sins of the Winter, and bore them away. And thus was realized, astronomically, not only "the Lamb of God taking away the sins of the world," but also the death and resurrection of the Son of God, or the sun-God, more properly.[1297]

Massey describes the changes of the ages:

> When Horus had fulfilled the period of 2155 years with the Easter Equinox in the Sign of Aries, the birthplace passed into the Sign of Pisces, when the Ever-Coming One, the Renewer as the Eternal Child who had been brought forth as a Lion in Leo, a Beetle in Cancer, as one of the Twins in Gemini, as a calf in the Sign of the Bull, and a Lamb in the Sign of the Ram, was destined to manifest as the Fish, in the Sign of the Fishes. The rebirth of Atum-Horus, or Jesus, as the Fish Iusaas, and the Bread of Nephthys, was astronomically dated to occur in Beth-Lechem—the House of Bread—about 255 BC, at the time the Easter Equinox entered the Sign of Pisces.

Massey also states that "Horus in Egypt had been a fish from time

---

1296 Massey, HJMC, 108–9.
1297 Graves, BS, 81.

immemorial, and when the equinox entered the sign of Pisces, Horus was portrayed as *Ichthys* with the fish sign over his head." He further says, "The Messiah who manifested in this sign was foreordained to come as Ichthys the fisherman, or, doctrinally, the fisher of men."[1298]

Thus Jesus is the Piscean fish god, who, at Luke 24:11–2, upon his resurrection is made to ask, "Do you have any fish?", establishing the choice of communion food of the new age. Hence the Catholic requirement to eat fish instead of meat on Fridays. In addition, the early Christians were called "*Pisciculi*"—"little fishes."[1299] As the solar hero of the Piscean Age, Jesus is also made to say, "I am with you always until the close of the age." It is now the close of the Age of Pisces, and the sun is moving into the Age of Aquarius, a "second coming" that signifies the changing of the guard.

Emperor Aurelian kicked the movement into high gear with his "one god, one empire, one emperor" campaign that elevated the sun above all others. From the evidence, it seems quite clear that his effort was co-opted by Christians, who, as Paine has pointed out, turned the sun god into a man—again, this time a Jewish one.

In consideration of the vast role the sun had played in ancient religion, mythology, and philosophy, its concealed use in the New Testament is indicative of a number of issues. First, the masses could hardly be expected to embrace a new version of the solar faith that *completely* suppressed the sun's glory. This is a major reason the important solar attributes, rituals and holidays, etc., we have examined were retained. Second, the purpose of the gospel writers was to raise the Jewish historical Jesus above the sun, giving him dominion over the sun in order to hide the origins of much Christian theology and mythology.

In the *Timaeus* (39b4f), Plato explains that "Helios receives its light from the Demiurge."[1300] Thus, the sun "becomes a mediator between the divine world and ours."[1301] This mediator status is, of course, reserved for Jesus in the New Testament, once again demonstrating Christ's solar role.

1298 Massey, HJMC, 20.
1299 Higgins, 568.
1300 Van den Berg, 147.
1301 Van den Berg, 147.

Bronze solar horse and car, Denmark c. 1000 BCE

Jesus as the Sun God in the solar chariot with white horses, Mosaic c. 240 CE, found under the altar at St. Peter's in Rome

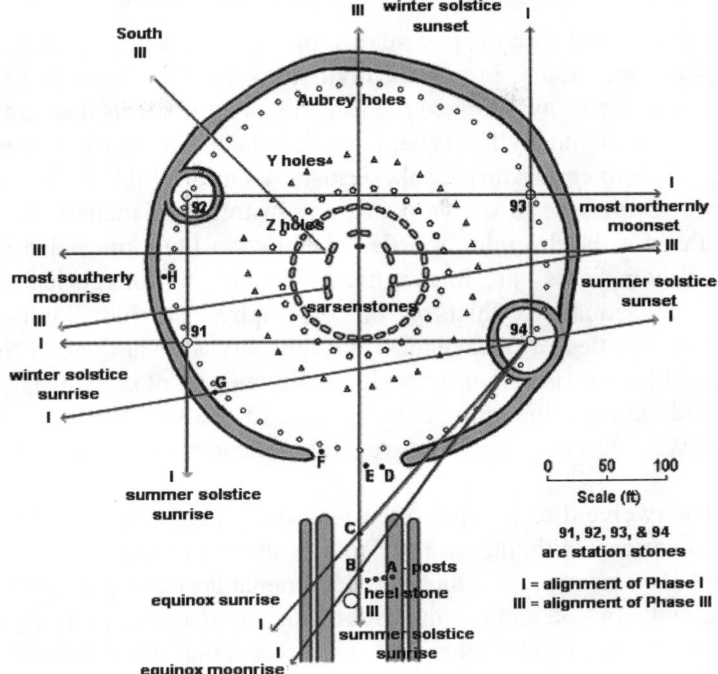
Stonehenge from above with apparent astronomical alignments.
III winter solstice sunset I
South III
Aubrey holes
Y holes
Z holes
sarsenstones
92
93
91
94
most northernly moonset
III
most southerly moonrise
H
summer solstice sunset
winter solstice sunrise
G
F
E D
C
B
A posts
heel stone
summer solstice sunrise
equinox sunrise
equinox moonrise
0 50 100
Scale (ft)
91, 92, 93, & 94 are station stones
I = alignment of Phase I
III = alignment of Phase III

The Disciples Are the Signs of the Zodiac

The son of God with the twelve disciples is not historical but an old astrological motif found in ancient mythology for thousands of years. Jesus and the twelve symbolized the sun and its movements through the heavens. But then the myth was carnalized, Judaized, and historicized in the gospel tale of Jesus Christ. Like Jesus, the famous biblical disciples are recorded nowhere in the works of any historian of their time. The only source for the disciples/apostles is Christian literature, where the stories of their "lives" are in fact highly apocryphal, allegorical and, therefore, inadequate as "history" or "biography." Of these fables regarding the apostles, Walker relates: "Guignebert says 'not one of them is true.... [T]here exists no information really worthy of credence about the life and works of the immediate Apostles of Jesus.'"[1302]

G.A. Wells has his own doubts regarding the gospel tradition of "the twelve":

> The twelve disciples are often regarded as guarantors of Jesus' historicity, although we are told nothing of most of them except their names, on which the documents do not even agree completely. In Mk. and Mt. the list of names is also very clumsily worked into the text. All this makes it obvious that the *number* is an older tradition than the *persons*; that the idea of the twelve derives not from twelve actual disciples, but from other sources.[1303]

And ben Yehoshua says:

> The first time that twelve apostles are mentioned is in the document known as the *Teaching of the Twelve Apostles* [Didache]. This document apparently originated as a sectarian Jewish document written in the first century CE, but it was adopted by Christians who altered it substantially and added Christian ideas to it. In the earliest versions it is clear that the "twelve apostles" are the twelve sons of Jacob representing the twelve tribes of Israel. The Christians later considered the "twelve apostles" to be allegorical disciples of Jesus.

In fact, Eusebius himself gives a clue to the cosmic origins of "the Twelve" when he says, "At that very time it was true of His apostles that *their speech went out to the whole earth, and their words to the ends of the world.*"[1304] This line comes from Psalm 19:4, which, refers to the starry constellations, whose "voice" penetrates the earth.

1302 Walker, B. (1983), 48.
1303 Wells, DJE, 122.
1304 Eusebius, 77.

In reality, the 12 patriarchs, 12 tribes of Israel and 12 disciples, come from the number of the astrological signs, the lunar months, reflecting the relation between the sun and moon. These astrotheological observations also gave rise to the 12 "houses" through which the sun passes each day and the 12 hours of day and night. Like the 12 Herculean tasks, and the 12 "generals" of Ahura-Mazda, Jesus's 12 "disciples" symbolize the zodiacal signs and do not depict any literal figures who played out a drama upon the earth circa 30 CE.

Hazelrigg sums up the gospel tale thus:

> [The] Romans … personified our sun, or centre of the solar system, as a living man, and the twelve signs of the zodiac as his twelve disciples; and the ingress of the sun through the different signs, as this man called Son of God, as going about doing his Father's work, or, rather, doing the will of the Father.[1305]

Higgins elucidates upon the zodiacal role of "the twelve" in the mythos:

> The number of the twelve apostles, which formed the retinue of Jesus during his mission, is that of the signs, and of the secondary genii, the tutelary gods of the Zodiacal signs which the sun passes through in his annual revolution. It is that of the twelve gods of the Romans, each of whom presided over a month. The Greeks, the Egyptians, the Persians, each had their *twelve* gods, as the Christian followers of Mithra had their *twelve* apostles. The chief of the twelve Genii of the annual revolution had the barque and the keys of time, the same as the chief of the secondary gods of the Romans or Janus, after whom St. Peter, Bar-Jona, with his barque and keys, is modelled.[1306]

Peter the Rock

The disciple, apostle and saint Peter, "the Rock" to whom so much of the Christian religion is entrusted, is easily revealed to be a mythological character and an old motif:

> Long before Christian times, the "hierophant," or chief high priest and main spokesman for the son of God on Earth, appears to have been called by the title "PETR," or "Peter," meaning "the rock." Providing the apparent origin of the name Christ is said to have assigned to his strangely named prime disciple, Peter.

This PETR was the rock of Vatican Hill upon which was built the Mithraic brotherhood. Walker relates the ultimate purpose of the insertion of the Peter character:

1305 Anderson, 18.
1306 Higgins, I, 781-2.

> The myth of St. Peter was the slender thread from which hung the whole weighty structure of the Roman papacy.... Unfortunately for papal credibility, the socalled Petrine passage was a forgery. It was deliberately inserted into the scripture about the 3rd century AD. as a political ploy, to uphold the primacy of the Roman see against rival churches in the east. Various Christian bishoprics were engaged in a power struggle in which the chief weapons were bribery, forgery, and intrigue, with elaborate fictions and hoaxes written into sacred books, and the ruthless competition between rival parties for the lucrative position of God's elite.... Most early churches put forth spurious claims to foundation by apostles, even though *the apostles themselves were no more than the mandatory "zodiacal twelve" attached to the figure of the sacred king.*[1307]

Jesus is said to give the keys of the kingdom to Peter, yet he then turns around and calls Peter "Satan," ironically implying that his church is to be built upon the "rock of Satan." Peter was thus the "gatekeeper" of heaven, likewise a role within the mythos. As Robertson relates: "there is to be noted the remarkable coincidence that in the Egyptian Book of the Dead, Petra is the name of the divine doorkeeper of heaven."[1308] Massey expands upon Peter's role and his counterpart in Egyptian mythology:

> Kabhsenuf the hawk-headed is the refresher of his brethren, and this office is assigned to Peter as feeder of the sheep. It was Peter who rushed into the water to meet Jesus, and in the *Ritual*—when the dead Osiris has risen and come forth ... *Kabhsenuf wets his limbs in the streams for them to guard Osiris.*[1309]

"Peter" is not only "the rock" but also "the cock," or penis, as the word is used as slang to this day. As Walker says, "The cock was also a symbol of Saint Peter, whose name also meant a phallus or male principle (*pater*) and a phallic pillar (*petra*). Therefore, the cock's image was often placed atop church towers."[1310] Higgins elucidates the phallic nature of Peter the rock:

> On this *stone*, which was the emblem of the male generative principle, the Linga, Jesus founded his church. This sacred stone is found throughout all the world. In India at every temple. The Jews had it in the stone of Jacob, which he anointed with oil.

1307 Walker, B. (1983), 787. (Emphasis added)
1308 Robertson, 133.
1309 Massey, HJMC, 144.
1310 Walker, WDSSO, 397.

> The Greeks, at Delphi, like Jacob, anointed it with oil. The black stone was in the Caaba, at Mecca, long before the time of Mohammed, and was preserved by him when he destroyed the Dove and the Images. He not only preserved it, but he caused it to be built into the corner of the sacred Caaba, where it is now kissed and adored by all Mohammedans who make the pilgrimage to Mecca.... Mr. Bryant says, "When the worship of the sun was almost universal, this was one name of that deity, even among the Greeks. They called him Petor, and Petros, and his temple was styled Petra." Where the temples had this name ... there was generally a sacred stone which was supposed to have descended from heaven.... Mr. Bryant observes, "Pator or Petor, was an Egyptian word; and Moses, speaking of Joseph and the dreams of Pharaoh, more than once makes use of it."[1311]

Furthermore, the veneration of the peter or lingam is reflective of the homoeroticism within the patriarchal cults. So fervent was this lingam-worship that the "cock" was considered the "Savior of the World":

> The cock was another totemic "peter" sometimes viewed as the god's alter ego. Vatican authorities preserved a bronze image of a cock with an oversize penis on a man's body, the pedestal inscribed "The Savior of the World." The cock was also a solar symbol.[1312]

Peter was a remake of the Roman god Janus; thus, he was associated with the month of January, "when the sun entered the sign of Aquarius, symbol of both the gate of the year and the Pearly Gate of Maria-Aphrodite."[1313] As Doane says:

> The Roman god Jonas, or Janus, with his keys, was changed into Peter, who was surnamed Bar-Jonas. Many years ago a statue of the god Janus, in bronze, being found in Rome, he was perched up in St. Peter's with his keys in his hand: the very identical god, in all his native ugliness. This statue sits as St. Peter, under the cupola of the church of St. Peter. It is looked upon with the most profound veneration: the toes are nearly kissed away by devotees.[1314]

Like the canonical gospels, the Christianized Peter tales were not in existence at the time of Justin Martyr (100–165), who, as Blavatsky relates,

> writing in the early part of the second century *in Rome*, where he fixed his abode, eager to get hold of the least proof in favor of the truth

1311 Higgins, I, 645.
1312 Walker, B. (1983), 79.
1313 Walker, B. (1983), 789.
1314 Doane, 399.

for which he suffered, seems *perfectly unconscious of [St. Paul's] existence!!* Neither does any other writer of any consequence mention him in connection with the Church of Rome, earlier than the days of Irenaeus, when the latter set himself to invent a new religion, drawn from the depth of his imagination.[1315]

Judas the Betrayer

Although he is one of the most vilified characters in all literature, Judas was actually a key figure in "God's Plan" for salvation through blood-atonement and was charged by Jesus to betray him, an assignment which he obeyed, thus proving himself to be the best of the disciples. However, the gospel tale of the betraying kiss of Judas makes no sense as history. If such a wannabe king of the Jews existed and was famed throughout the land, there would be no need for Judas's kiss to identify him. And we must ask why he needed to kiss Jesus at all—would not a simple finger pointing or handshake have sufficed? The kiss is not only homoerotic but serves as a literary device, as it was part of an ancient ritual played out on a regular basis.

Judas represents Scorpio, "the backbiter," the time of year when the sun's rays are weakening and the sun appears to be dying. Judas also serves as the last hour of the day, since the twelve disciples also symbolized the twelve hours of daylight.[1316] In the Horus myth, the role of the betrayer is played by Set or Typhon, who is portrayed as having red hair, the color of the sun-*set*. When the mythos was Judaized, the betrayer became Judas, who was depicted with red hair.

Judas, of course, is yet another ancient god given historical dress, as Judas is the same word as Judah. As Walker relates:

> Formerly, Judas was an ancestral god, father of the nation of Judah and of Jews (*Judaei*). As Jude, or Jeud, he was the "only-begotten son" of the Divine Father Isra-El. Judas was a dynastic name for priest-kings of Judea for a hundred years after Judas Maccabeus restored ancient sacrificial customs to the temple of Jerusalem in 165 BC. Thus the kingly name of Judas was commonly given victims sacrificed as surrogates for a reigning monarch.[1317]

Indeed, as Judas betrayed Jesus, so did Judah betray his brother Joseph. It seems that the name Judas was used to put the onus of Jesus's death on the Jews and to cast aspersions on them for refusing to believe the newly created tale, thus betraying their own "brethren" who

1315 Blavatsky, IU, II, 24fn.

1316 Walker, B. (1983), 483.

1317 Walker, B. (1983), 481.

were promulgating it, some of whom were Jews and others Samaritan Israelites. Joseph also represented the northern kingdom of Israel. Accordingly, the Old Testament Joseph story depicted the betrayal of the northern kingdom by the southern, as does the gospel tale. This type of personification of a nation or people as a character in a drama is common in mythmaking and continues on into the New Testament. Another example appears in the "Fragments of Papias," an early Church father who wrote an exegesis on the *Logia Iesou*, or Sayings/Oracles of Jesus, in which Papias gives an account of Judas's death, which also contradicts the gospel story:

> Judas walked about in this world a sad example of impiety; for his body having swollen to such an extent that he could not pass where a chariot could pass easily, he was crushed by the chariot, so that his bowels gushed out.

This tale is not historical but allegorical, representing the "bloated" Judah/Judea being crushed by the "chariot" of Rome, which dispelled its inhabitants outward. Furthermore, the gospel accounts of Judas's death are contradictory and allegorical, explainable only in terms of him being an ancient character within the mythos.

Judas has also been identified with the moon, which demonstrates once again the complexity of the mythos. At one point, the stellar cult was dominant, then the lunar cult, then the solar cult, and so on. The lunar cult was generally matriarchal, and the solar patriarchal. Thus, we have a battle between not only the sun and the moon but also the male and the female. As to Judas's lunar nature, Massey says:

> The French retain a tradition that the man in the moon is Judas Iscariot, who was transported there for his treason to the Light of the World. But that story is pre-Christian, and was told at least some 6,000 years ago of Osiris and the Egyptian Judas, Sut, who was born twin with him of one mother, and who betrayed him, at the Last Supper, into the hands of the 72 Sami, or conspirators, who put him to death. Although the Mythos became solar, it was originally lunar, Osiris and Sut having been twin brothers in the moon.[1318]

Matthew the Scribe

Regarding the apostle Matthew, to whom was attributed the recording of the "Oracles of the Lord," Massey describes his counterpart within the Egyptian version of the mythos of the Lord Horus:

> TahtMatiu was the scribe of the gods, and in Christian art Matthew is depicted as the scribe of the gods, with an angel stand-

1318 Massey, Lectures on the Moon.

> ing near him, to dictate the gospel.... Tradition makes Matthew to have been the *eighth* of the apostles; and the eighth (Esmen) is a title of TahtMatiu. Moreover, it is Matthias, upon whom the lot fell, who was chosen to fill the place of the Typhonian traitor Judas. So was it in the mythos when Matiu (Taht) succeeded Sut [Set], and occupied his place after the betrayal of Osiris.... It is to the Gnostics that we must turn for the missing link between the oral and the written word; between the Egyptian *Ritual* and the canonical gospels; between the Matthew who wrote the Hebrew or Aramaic gospel of the sayings, and TahtMatiu, who wrote the *Ritual*, the Hermetic, which means *inspired* writings, that are said to have been inscribed in hieroglyphics by the very finger of *Mati* himself.[1319]

Thomas the Twin

The disciple Thomas appears in the canonical gospels, mostly in John. He is a highly influential character, chosen to verify Christ's resurrection by touching him. Of this incident, Walker states:

> Later, an unknown Gospel writer inserted the story of doubting Thomas, who insisted on touching Jesus. This was to combat the heretical idea that there was no resurrection in the flesh, and also to subordinate Jerusalem's municipal god Tammuz (Thomas) to the new savior. Actually, the most likely source of primary Christian mythology was the Tammuz cult in Jerusalem. Like Tammuz, Jesus was the Bridegroom of the Daughter of Zion.[1320]

The Syrian and Jerusalemite god Thomas/Tammuz was given the role of the "genius" of the time when the sun is at its weakest, during the winter solstice. As Carpenter states, "the Church dedicates the very day of the winter solstice (when any one may very naturally doubt the rebirth of the Sun) to St. Thomas, who doubted the truth of the Resurrection!"[1321] Indeed, the hierarchy of Jerusalem when Tammuz was worshipped there was composed of, as we have seen from Ezekiel, the elders "behind the hidden door," constituting the Zadokite/Sadducean priesthood, who, in fact, did not believe in the resurrection of the flesh. Tammuz's name is still retained in the Hebrew month of Tammuz.

Thomas is called Didymus, a name that "comes from the Greek word Didymos, the Greek equivalent of the Roman Gemini, the zodiacal twins."[1322] "Thomas" itself also means "twin" in Aramaic/Syriac. Hence

1319 Massey, HJMC, 157–8.
1320 Walker, B. (1983), 467–8.
1321 Carpenter, 51.
1322 Graham, 318.

Didymus Thomas is a redundancy that is not the name of any disciple but a rehash of the ancient story of the twin god. As Walker says, "Judas and Jesus seem to have been traditional names taken by victims in whom the god Tammuz was incarnate,"[1323] referring to the sacred king ritual enacted in Judea, as well as many other places.

It is said that "Thomas" preached to the Parthians and Persians, but the original point was that these groups were followers of Tammuz (or Dumuzi, the Sumerian version of his name). Although it was alleged that Thomas's tomb was in Edessa, tradition also claims that he died near Madras, India, where *two* of his tombs are still shown. This tale reportedly comes from the fact that when Portuguese Christian missionaries arrived in southern India they found a sect who worshipped a god named "Thomas" and whose religion was nearly identical to Christianity. So disturbed were the Christian missionaries that they created elaborate stories to explain the presence of the "St. Thomas Christians," claiming that the apostles Thomas and/or Bartholomew had at some point traveled to India, preached and died there.

The one aspect that truly perplexed the Christians, however, was that Christ was not the object of adoration in this sect. It was thus determined that this strange sect was heretical yet Christian, even though Christ was not its god. The reality is that these Indian "Christians" were worshipping Tamus or Tammuz, the sacrificed savior-god long prior to the Christian era.[1324] This Indian Tamus/Thomas sect evidently had a gospel written in ancient Chaldee, or proto-Hebrew. In fact, these "St. Thomas Christians" were Indian Nazarene-Carmelites,[1325] as were the Nazarenes of St. John, or Mandaeans. Of the Nazarenes, Higgins further asserts:

> [These] Mandaites or *Nazareens* or Disciples of St. John, are found in central India, and they are certainly not disciples of the Western Jesus of Nazareth.... all Gnosticism came originally from India ... the Mandaites or Nazareens are no other than the sect of Gnostics, and the extreme East the place of their birth.1326

There are also traces of Tammuz/Thomas worship in China, where he was apparently considered to be an incarnation of Buddha.[1327]

1323 Walker, B. (1983), 995.
1324 Higgins, I, 663–4.
1325 Higgins, I, 808.
1326 HIggins, I, 657–8.
1327 Higgins, I, 755.

Paul the Apostle

In the gospel tale, as extended in Acts, Paul is not one of "the twelve" but the most influential convert after Jesus's death. Paul acted as a missionary and pastor and had "an unshakable determination to collect money from his largely Gentile churches and to deliver the collection himself to the Jewish Christian Church in Jerusalem."[1328]

Paul claims in Acts, "My manner of life from my youth, spent from the beginning among my own nation and at Jerusalem, is *known by all the Jews*." But, like Jesus and the twelve, he does not appear in any historical record, although some of the events in his life must have been fairly significant—if they happened. But there is no mention in Josephus or anyone else of the "two hundred soldiers with seventy horsemen and two hundred spearmen" who allegedly went "as far as Caesarea" to bring Paul before the governor Felix. As Graham relates, the historian Seneca was "the brother of Gallio, proconsul of Achaia at precisely the time Paul is said to have preached there. While he wrote of many lesser things, no mention is made of Paul or the wonder-working Christ."[1329] Paul's life story has the same air of mythology as many great "men," changing to suit the teller. For instance, in the New Testament, there are three different accounts of his conversion (Acts 9:7; 22:9; 26:13ff).

Like so many other biblical characters, Paul is fictitious. In fact, it has been claimed that "historical" details later added to the gospel version of the mythos were taken from the life of Apollonius of Tyana. In this theory, Apollonius was also called "Apollos," or "Paulus" in Latin. Many elements of Paul's life agree with those of Apollonius, including the route of his journeys, which is almost identical to that of Apollonius according to Philostratus's account of his life. The fact that Paul was from a predominantly Greek town, Tarsus, and resembled a Greek more than anything else lends credence to this claim, as, according to Philostratus, the Greek Apollonius spent part of his youth in Tarsus. Like those of Paul, Apollonius's journeys originated in Antioch. Apollonius is also recorded as having traveled to India with his faithful disciple Damis (Demas) and visited the Brahmans. While on this journey, Philostratus reports, Apollonius "acquired from the Arabians a knowledge of the language of animals," an interesting story considering that Paul alleges in Galatians that he made a three-year visit to Arabia, during which time legend holds he learned various mysteries. Paul's purported visit to "Arabia," or the east, also corresponds with the claim that Apollonius went to the east, where he gathered various books, including

1328 Funk & Wagnall's.

1329 Graham, 292.

those containing the story of Krishna.

Apollonius returned home from India, as Waite relates, "by going south to the sea, thence by vessel, up the Euphrates to Babylon, then, by way of Antioch, to Cyprus and Paphos."[1330] The journey from Antioch to Cyprus exactly parallels Paul's in Acts. Apollonius then went to Ephesus, where the people flocked to him and where he did miracles, as he did afterwards in Athens, the same route taken by Paul, although purportedly in the opposite direction. Like Paul, Apollonius next went to Corinth, where he had a disciple named Lycian, or Luke. After traveling around Greece, he then proceeded to Rome, where he was accused of treason, then went to Spain and Africa, finally returning to Italy and Sicily.

After traveling to Alexandria and down into Nubia, to an ancient Gymnosophic/Buddhist/Brahmanical community, Apollonius returned to Italy, Greece and on to the Hellespont, where he challenged wandering Egyptians and Chaldeans who were defrauding the people in a typical priestly manner. In passing through this area, Apollonius could have stopped at Samothrace, the island home of the exalted mysteries and one of the potent seats of the pre-Christian Iasios/Jesus cult, a journey also taken by Paul. Like Paul, Apollonius was summoned to Rome and put in prison, from which he escaped. Many other miracles were attributed to him, including an appearance in his hometown of Tyana after his death.

It was said that Apollonius was not fond of Judea and that he preached mostly to the Gentiles, just like Paul, according to the biblical tale.

Furthermore, a number of the "historical" details in the New Testament parallel Josephus's histories, including elements of the life of Paul:

> Both Josephus and Paul made a disastrous sea voyage on their way to Rome. Both crews swam to safety after their ship was abandoned to the storm, which drove them into the Adria. Both crews boarded a second ship which took them to Rome, their destination. The purpose of the sea voyage, in both stories, was to deliver the priestly prisoners (Paul in the New Testament and an unnamed priest in Josephus) in bonds, to Rome to be tried before Caesar. In both stories the prisoners have been previously tried in Jerusalem by the procurator Felix.[1331]

Like Jesus, Paul is a patchwork of characters. It has been argued that he is also a rehash of the Greek hero Orpheus, who, with his companion *Timothy*, traveled around the same area as later reported of Paul,

1330 Waite, 105.
1331 Holley, 40.

preaching in the name of Dionysus (i.e., "IHS," "IES," "JES," "Iasios," "Iesios," "Jason," "Jesus," or other variants), the Savior of the Samothracian mysteries and pre-Christian Jesus cult.

The Orphic rites were very similar to the successor Christian rites. One example of an Orphic scripture includes, "All things were made by One godhead in three names, and that this god is all things"[1332]; thus Orpheus is a pre-Christian advocate of the Trinity, as well as pantheism. Walker elucidates upon the Orphic mystery cult and its similarity to Christianity, as well as to Buddhism:

> Orphism was a kind of western Buddhism, with escape from the karmic wheel effected by ascetic contemplation, spiritual journeys of the astral-projection type, and elaborate revelations. "Orphism was steeped in sacramentalism, which flooded the later Mysteries and flowed into Christianity. Salvation was by sacrament, by initiatory rites, and by an esoteric doctrine.... Orphism was the most potent solvent ever introduced into Greek religious life ... [T]he Orphics sowed the seeds of distrust toward the national and hereditary principle in religion, and made the salvation of the individual soul of first importance. In this way Orphism had enormous influence upon the subsequent history of religion." ... Orphism became one of the most serious rivals of Christianity in the first few centuries AD, until the church devised ways to identify the Orphic savior with Christ.... The Orphic Gospel was preached throughout the Mediterranean world for at least twelve centuries. It contributed much to Christian ideology.... The Orphic revelation was virtually indistinguishable from the Christian one.[1333]

Thus Orphism was what could be called a "salvation cult," at the head of which was the savior, "IES." Orpheus has also been identified with Krishna[1334] and with Horus, or Orus, as "Orpheus" could be translated as "voice of Or," "Or," appropriately, meaning "light" in Hebrew.

Furthermore, it was said of Apollonius that he had been given his master Pythagoras's travel journals, which allowed him to gain access to the secret brotherhoods of the east. Upon his return, he follows virtually the same route as Orpheus and Paul, including passing through Samothrace several times. It would seem, therefore, that Apollonius was deliberately attempting to reproduce Orpheus's mythical teaching route.

1332 Doane, 375.
1333 Walker, B. (1983), 745–8.
1334 Higgins, 589.

John the Baptist/Baptizer

John the Baptist (or Baptizer) is a remake of Horus's baptizer, Anup, both of whom lost their heads, among other similarities. There are varied astrotheological interpretations of John/Anup the Baptist/Baptizer, as is to be expected, since the mythos was everchanging and evolving. John the Baptist was the sign of Aquarius, into which the sun moves and is "baptized" after advancing to the "age" of 30°. As Walker relates:

Medieval monks tried to Christianize the zodiac as they Christianized everything else, by renaming it the *Corona seu Circulus Sanctorum Apostolorum*: the Crown of the Circle of the Holy Apostles. They placed John the Baptist at the position of Aquarius, to finish off the circle.[1335]

The Baptist's identity is also presented in astral terms by Goodman:

> [The] greatest denouement awaits the investigator who makes use of the Julian calendar in the Roman Catholic calendar of Saints in connection with the large zodiac. He will find that the death of John the Baptist is fixed on August 29th. On that day, a specially bright star, representing the head of the constellation Aquarius, rises whilst the rest of his body is below the horizon, at exactly the same time as the sun sets in Leo (the kingly sign representing Herod). Thus the latter *beheads* John, because John is associated with Aquarius, and *the horizon cuts off the head of Aquarius!*[1336]

Eastern texts depict solar radiation as the "perpetual beheading of the sun."

As to the role of the Baptist in the Egyptian version of the mythos, Massey says:

> Anup was the crier of the way and guide through the wilderness of An, the black land. John's is the voice of one crying in the wilderness.... John was decapitated by the monster Herod, and Anup is portrayed as headless in the planisphere just over the Waterman.... The headless Anup is a type of demarcation: a sign of the division of the solstice. The river of the division is the Iaru-tana [Eridanus] or Jordan.... This can be seen in the planisphere, with the beheaded Anup as the original John.[1337]

Massey further elaborates:

In the Zodiac of Denderah we see the figure of Anup portrayed with his head cut off; and I doubt not that the decapitated Aan or

1335 Walker, WDSSO, 286.
1336 Jackson, 185.
1337 Massey, HJMC, 119.

Anup is the prototype of the Gospel John who was above the river of the Waterman, the Greek Eridanus, Egyptian Iarutana, the Hebrew Jordan.[1338]

The biblical story of John's birth is also an aspect of the mythos: Anna, the mother of John, became supernaturally pregnant in her old age and gave birth at the summer solstice, six months before Mary gave birth to Jesus. As Massey says, "The fact of John and Jesus being born six months apart shows a solar phase of the mythos."[1339] Furthermore, the double-headed Roman god Janus's mother was also known as Anna, and John the Baptist and Jesus would thus be the same double-headed god (i.e., "Jan-Essa"), also an Indian savior name.

Higgins explains that John "the Forerunner" represents the six-month cycle from the winter solstice to the summer, decoding the mysterious passage at John 3:30:

> Jesus came to his exaltation or glory on the 25th of March, the Vernal equinox. At that moment his cousin John was at the Autumnal equinox: as Jesus ascended John descended. John makes the Baptist say, chapter iii, ver. 30, *He must increase, but I must decrease....* How can any one doubt that what was admitted by the fathers was true—that Christians had an *esoteric* and an *exoteric* religion?[1340]

In other words, the fathers knew—have continued to know—what it is they truly represent, yet they have conspired to deceive the people. Hazelrigg elaborates upon the passage, also demonstrating the complexity of the mythos:

> The Baptism came at the thirtieth year, or after the Sun's passage through the thirty degrees of Capricorn and coincident with his entry into Aquarius, the Water Bearer, who is John the Baptist. The assertion of John (iii. 30) that "He (the infant Jesus) must increase, but I must decrease," corresponds with the fact that John's nativity was June 24th, when the Sun has reached its highest altitude and its declination begins to decrease; that of Jesus was December 25th, when the Sun accomplishes that first degree of its ascending arc, and is thence led up into the wilderness (winter).[1341]

And Higgins relates:

> [The] Baptist was Elias, that is, in plain Greek, the sun—

1338 Massey, Lectures on the Moon.
1339 Massey, HJMC, 123.
1340 Higgins, I, 647.
1341 Hazelrigg, 119–20.

'HlioV [Helios].... Now John the Baptist or the Prophet, Regenerator by means of water, who was also a revived Elias, was the immediate forerunner of Jesus—in almost every respect an exact copy of Bala-rama, the forerunner of Cristna. And John the Baptist, or Saviour of men by means of water, was the Oannes or Avatar of Pisces.[1342]

The carnalized and Judaized John the Baptist was a "Nazarene" or Nazarite, which is to say that he was a member of a "brotherhood of the sun." As Hazelrigg says, "He was a Nazarite; and it is a curious and striking circumstance that the fountain of Aenon, where he baptized, was sacred to the sun."[1343]

Andrew

Purportedly a fisherman from Bethesda, the apostle Andrew was said to have been crucified at Patras, Greece, in an apparent Paschal sacrifice: "the springtime sacrifice of Jesus was emulated by other heroes, such as Andrew, Philip, or Peter."[1344]

"Andrew" was in reality a local god of Patras, in all probability ritually sacrificed as a sacred king on a periodic basis. Concerning Andrew, Walker states:

> From Greek *andros*, "man" or "virility," a title of the solar god of Patras, in Achaea, where the apostle Andrew was supposed to have been crucified after founding the Byzantine papacy. St. Andrew's legend was invented to counter Rome's claim to primacy through its own legend of St. Peter.... Patras, the site of Andrew's alleged martyrdom, was an old shrine of the phallic-solar father-god variously called Pater, Petra, or Peter, whose name has the same basic meaning as Andrew.[1345]

Hazelrigg elaborates on Andrew's astrological nature:

The Sun as St. Andrew is the genius who presides over the autumn quarter that begins with the solar "crossification" into Libra; hence Paul's reference to his crucifixion in Romans, vi. 6. This is why St. Andrew is ever depicted as an old man holding at his back a saltier cross, indicative of this orbital angle in the Sun's passage over the equator.[1346]

In the Egyptian version of the mythos Andrew is equivalent to Hapi or Shu, one of the brothers of Horus.

1342 Higgins, I, 655–6.
1343 Higgins, II, 66.
1344 Walker, WDSSO, 153.
1345 Walker, B. (1983), 32.
1346 Hazelrigg, 24–5.

Philip

The apostle Philip was said to be born in Bethesda As a follower of John the Baptist, Philip would have been a Mandaean/Nazarene. He was present at the feeding of the multitudes; thus, a "common symbol for Philip is a loaf, reflecting the story of the loaves and fishes."[1347] Astrologers have speculated that Philip represents the constellation of Virgo, the goddess of the grain, although he was associated with Libra, which is also a time of harvest.

Bartholomew

Bartholomew was supposed to be a native of Galilee, and legend said that he went to India, Armenia, Mesopotamia, Ethiopia and Persia. Like the other disciples, however, Bartholomew is a mythical character, no doubt found in the aforementioned places. As Walker relates:

> Pseudo-saint based on a sacred king's title: Bar-Tholomeus, "son of Ptolemy." He was inserted into the Gospels as an apostle, but hagiographers gave him a different origin. He was called a son of "Prince Ptolemeus," crucified in Armenia, and flayed like the satyr Marsyas.... An alternative history made Bartholomew a missionary to India, where he overthrew the idols of the oddly non-Indian deities Astarte and Baal-Berith. With many miracles, Bartholomew converted the king of that country to Christianity, but the king's brother was unaccountably permitted to crucify, flay, and behead the saint afterward.[1348]

James the Brother

James, "brother of Jesus" and "brother of the Lord," is equivalent in the Egyptian version of the mythos to Amset, brother of Osiris and brother of the Lord.[1349] As Massey says:

> James is also identified with the carpenter in the gospels.... *This is the character of Amset ... the carpenter*. Amset as devourer of impurity denotes the great purifier, and James has the traditional reputation of having been a great purifier.[1350]

James is also the same word as Jacob, the supplanter, the title of Set, as in Am-*set*, the "brother" of Horus.

James the Greater and John the Evangelist, the Sons of Thunder

The brothers James and John are called "Boanerges," the "sons of

1347 Funk & Wagnall's.
1348 Walker, B. (1983), 92.
1349 Massey, HJMC, viii.
1350 Massey, HJMC, 147.

Thunder," a mythical designation. As Price remarks, "In other words, the sons of Zeus, namely Castor and Pollux."[1351] The lightning and thunderbolts of Lord Zeus were called "Brontes" and "Arges," a role held by the brothers in Luke: "And when his disciples James and John saw this, they said, Lord, wilt thou that we command fire to come down from heaven, and consume them?"

John, the beloved of Christ, also is a rehash of Arjuna, the beloved disciple of Krishna: "In the Tibetan language John is called Argiun. This is Arjoon, (*Ar-John,*) the coadjutor of Cristna."[1352] In addition, as Arjuna was the cousin of Krishna, so was John the cousin of Christ.[1353]

Mark

Although some people think Mark was one of Jesus's original 12 disciples, the gospels do not list him in their ranks. His main role, according to tradition, was to serve as Peter's scribe. As one of the four evangelists, Mark represents one of the cardinal points of the zodiac, as described by Irenaeus. The evangelists are extensively depicted in Christian art as symbolized by the four creatures of the apocalypse: the man, ox, lion and eagle, which, again, stand for the four cardinal points of the zodiac, or Aquarius, Taurus, Leo and Scorpio. In this cardinal designation Mark is linked to the summer, symbolized by Leo the lion.

Luke

Luke also is not one of "the twelve" but attached himself to Paul. He was a "physician," that is, a *Therapeut*, as were all the "doctors" of the Church. Luke was said to have traveled to Greece, Macedonia, Jerusalem and Rome as a companion of Paul, yet "scholars doubt the strong connection between Luke and Paul." As ben Yehoshua says:

> We must also doubt the story of Luke "the good healer" who was supposed to be a friend of Paul. The original Greek for "Luke" is "Lykos" which was another name for Apollo, the god of healing.

Thus, Luke is yet another tutelary god whose name was used in order to include the people and priesthood of a particular culture in the "universal" (i.e., Catholic, church).

Thaddeus/Jude and Simon the Zealot/Canaanite

Thaddeus is also called "Jude son of James" and sometimes Leb-

1351 Price, R. (2006), 78.
1352 Higgins, I, 658.
1353 Higgins, II, 137.

baeus, although these associations are made simply because the gospel lists of the disciples contradict each other. Jude and Simon share a feast day on October 28. Simon preached in Egypt and was joined by Jude in Persia. The stories say Simon either suffered martyrdom by being sawed in half or died peacefully at Edessa, a discrepancy that demonstrates his non-historical nature. Christian tradition associates Jude with Aquarius and Simon with Capricorn.

However, the zodiacal designations of the apostles vary from source to source as they are associated with different signs, and Judas the Betrayer, of course, was not included in Christian iconography but was replaced in the story by Matthias and in the zodiac by Jude/Judas Thaddeus, who evidently also at one point symbolized Scorpio. This confusion reveals the state of affairs when the different factions of the unifying brotherhood were being incorporated and doctrine was being violently debated. Of course, *exo*terically the zodiacal connection of these biblical characters was eventually severed, yet it continued *eso*terically, variants and all. Regardless of how they were designated, the apostles and other disciples named herein were not real people. As Wheless says:

> [T]he Holy Twelve had no existence in the flesh, but their "cue" being taken from Old Testament legends, they were mere names—*dramatis personae*—masks of the play—of "tradition," such as Shakespeare and all playwrights and fiction-writers create for the actors of their plays and works of admitted fiction.[1354]

Indeed, they were part of the ubiquitous mythos and ritual enacted in many cultures long prior to the Christian era, constituting what later became the gospel story.

1354 Wheless, 127.

St. Peter's Square at the Vatican with an Egyptian obelisk at the center serving as a sundial, marking the summer and winter solstices as well as the spring and fall equinoxes

The Gospel Story

In addition to the "lives" of Christ and the twelve, virtually the entire gospel story can be traced to older mythologies as part of the ancient mythos revolving around the celestial bodies and movements. Many of these elements have already been discussed, and a thorough exploration would require another volume, but we can examine a number of such aspects of the Christian tale and doctrine in greater detail, beginning with the creation of the universe and the all-important Fall that requires the saving grace of Jesus.

Genesis

It has long been known that the story of cosmic origins as found in the Judeo-Christian Bible is based on more ancient versions, especially those of Egypt and Babylon. Similar tales can also be found in China, Japan, India, Scandinavia, and the British and Irish isles, to name a few. Obviously, then, no one culture has a lock on "God" or creation—a fact that cannot be emphasized enough. Nor has the biblical story ever been adequate to explain truly the origins of the cosmos; in fact, it is merely a mythologized, simplified explanation filtered through and for finite minds. Of the biblical Genesis, Walker says,

> However absurd, these myths still maintain a hold on vast numbers of people deliberately kept in ignorance by an obsolete fundamentalism. Even educated adults sometimes insist that an omni-

scient god created the world for a purpose of his own.[1355]

Adam, Eve and the Garden of Eden

Like other major biblical characters and tales, the fable of Adam, Eve and the Garden of Eden is based on much older versions found in numerous cultures around the globe. The Hindu version of the first couple was of Adima and Heva, hundreds if not thousands of years before the Hebraic version, as Hindus informed Christian missionaries centuries ago.[1356] Jackson relates that these myths "seemed to have originated in Africa, but they were told all over the world in ancient times."[1357] We will not find any historical Adam and Eve in Mesopotamia or anywhere else.

In the Sumerian and Babylonian versions of the Garden of Eden myth, from which the Hebrew one is also derived, the original couple were created equal in stature by the great Goddess. When the patriarchy took over the story, it changed it to make women not only inferior but also guilty of the downfall of all mankind. Of this demotion, Stone says:

> Woman, as sagacious advisor or wise counselor, human interpreter of the divine will of the Goddess, was no longer to be respected, but to be hated, feared or at best doubted or ignored.... Women were to be regarded as mindless, carnal creatures, both attitudes justified and "proved" by the Paradise myth.... Statements carefully designed to suppress the earlier social structure continually presented the myth of Adam and Eve as divine proof that man must hold the ultimate authority.[1358]

Far from being literal history, the Garden of Eden/Paradise story takes place in the heavens. Hazelrigg points out that the tale as taken literally by the "devoted biblicist" is a demeaning portrayal of "God," as it declares that "God" is vengeful towards his own flawed progeny,

> the gullible pair whom He had created "in His image" seemingly for the sole purpose that He might send a serpent of iniquity to tempt the weakness and depravity so inadvertently implanted in their godly-begotten natures. A monstrous doctrine, indeed, that can picture a God so sinister in purpose as to betray the innocence of His own offspring![1359]

Yet, common sense has failed to prevail, as numerous theories have

---

1355 Walker, B. (1983), 186.

1356 For further discussion see, *Suns of God*, p. 212, *The Bible in India*, Jacolliot, 1870

1357 John G. Jackson, Was Jesus Christ A Negro?: And The African Origin of the Myths & Legends of the Garden of Eden, 1933

1358 Stone, 221-5.

1359 Hazelrigg, 33.

sprung up as to the "true" location of the Garden of Eden.

Walker further states:

Seventeen hundred years ago, Origen wrote of the Garden of Eden myth: "No one would be so foolish as to take this allegory as a description of actual fact." But Origen was excommunicated, and countless millions have been precisely that foolish.[1360]

The list of numerous "Adam and Eve" couples or first man-first woman myths from around the world includes the following: Abrahamic, Australian Aborginal, Chinese, Cowichan, Greek, Hindu, Hotcak, Kikuyu, Lakota, Norse, Pachacama, Inca, Polynesian, Marikoriko, Tiki, Philippine, Shintoist.[1361]

Adam

Adam is not a historical character, as the word "Adam" simply means "man" and was originally not a person's name. Adam is Atum or Amen in Egypt, the archetypal man and son of Ptah the Father.[1362] In the Chaldean scriptures, from which the Israelite writings were in large part plagiarized, he is called "Adami," and in the Babylonian he is "Adamu" or "Adapa."[1363] As in the Hebrew version, the Sumero-Babylonian Adamu was prevented by the gods from eating the fruit of immortality, so that he would not "be as a god." Adam is also "adamah," which means "bloody clay," referring to menstrual blood.[1364] Walker explains that "the biblical story of God's creation of Adam out of clay was plagiarized from ancient texts with the patriarchs' usual sex-change of the deity," who was the Sumero-Babylonian "Potter" goddess Aruru.[1365]

Eve

The biblical Eve is also not a literal figure who either caused the downfall of mankind or gave birth to it, although geneticists have posited a "Genetic Eve," a mitochondrial progenitor of all humanity, living in Africa over 150,000 years ago. Rather, Eve is the archetypal female and goddess found around the globe.

The biblical title of Eve, "Mother of All Living," was a translation of Kali Ma's title *Jaganmata.* She was also known in India as Jiva or Ieva, the Creatress of all manifested forms.[1366]

As stated, earlier mythologies placed the created woman on the

1360 Walker, B. (1983), 292.
1361 "First man or woman," en.wikipedia.org/wiki/First_man_or_woman
1362 A. Churchward, 315.
1363 S. Langdon, "Expository Times" Vol. 43 (1931-32) P. 45
1364 Walker, WDSSO, 337.
1365 Walker, B. (1983), 815.
1366 Walker, B. (1983), 108.

same par with the man, rather than as a mere "rib." In some of these ancient tales, Eve was superior to Adam and even to God, as his "stern mother."[1367] According to one myth, before God made Eve he created Lilith as Adam's equal, but she proved to be too troublesome for the patriarchy, as she did not want to submit to Adam's sexual advances and demanded her own house. The liberated Lilith thus had to be killed off by both God and biblical scribes. One may suspect there was more to the story, as Walker explains: "Hebraic tradition said Adam was married to Lilith because he grew tired of coupling with beasts, a common custom of Middle-Eastern herdsmen, though the Old Testament declared it a sin."[1368]

Eve is one with Isis-Meri and, therefore, the Virgin Mary and the constellation of Virgo, as well as the moon.[1369] In the original astrotheological tale, as Virgo rises she is followed or "bitten on the heel by Serpens, who, with Scorpio, rises immediately behind her."[1370] This astronomical observation is behind the passage at Revelation 12:14: "But the woman was given the two wings of the great eagle that she might fly from the serpent into the wilderness." Scorpio is not only represented by the scorpion but by the eagle as well.

The Serpent

The serpent symbol is found around the world and represents divine wisdom, as is confirmed by Jesus, when he is made to say, "Be ye wise as serpents." The serpent was the "phallic consort" of the Goddess, and serpents were found under her temples, apparently used to induce prophetic and hallucinatory trances by their venom. The Egyptian queen Cleopatra may have died during such a ritual with an asp, according to an apocryphal story. These female priestesses were called "pythonesses" and, as receivers of prophecy and divine revelation, were reviled by Ezekiel for gaining knowledge "out of their own heads," as if their manner of revelation were different from his own.

The serpent's shedding of skin and constant renewal made it a symbol of eternity and immortality, and thus of divinity and many gods. In fact, the title of "serpent" formerly conveyed sacerdotal duties, as opposed to being an aspersion. As Pike relates:

> In the Mysteries of the bull-horned Bacchus, the officers held serpents in their hands, raised them above their heads, and cried aloud "Eva!" the generic oriental name of the serpent, and the par-

1367 Walker, B. (1983), 291.
1368 Walker, B. (1983), 541.
1369 Hazelrigg, 35.
1370 Pike, 497.

ticular name of the constellation in which the Persians place Eve and the serpent.[1371]

This description reveals the origins of the New Testament exhortation to "take up serpents," and those who participate in such rituals are continuing an ancient tradition that dates back at least 4,000 years. Although the serpent is portrayed as evil in the Judeo-Christian ideology, it was not always considered so by the Hebrews. As Walker relates:

Early Hebrews adopted the serpent-god all their contemporaries revered, and the Jewish priestly clan of Levites were "sons of the Great Serpent," i.e., of Leviathan, "the wriggly one."[1372]

The Hebrew veneration for the serpent-god is clear from Numbers 21:9: "Moses made a serpent of brass, and put it upon a pole, and it came to pass that if a serpent had bitten any man, when he beheld the serpent of brass he lived." Of this interesting fetish, which is also the caduceus of Aesclepius, the Greek god of healing, Stone says, "And in Jerusalem itself was the serpent of bronze, said to date back to the time of Moses and treasured as a sacred idol in the temple there until about 700 BC."[1373]

Moses's serpent cult fell out of favor during the reign of Hezekiah, king of Judah, who "removed the high places, and broke the pillars, and cut down the Asherah. And he broke in pieces the bronze serpent that Moses had made, for until those days the people of Israel had burned incense to it; it was called Nehushtan" (2 Kings 18:4). Moreover, Walker relates:

> The biblical Nehushtan was a deliberate masculinization of a similar oracular she-serpent, Nehushtah, Goddess of Kadesh (meaning "Holy"), a shrine like that of the Pythonesses. Israelites apparently violated the sanctuary and raped its priestesses, but "Moses and Yahweh had to placate the angry serpent goddess of Kadesh, now deposed, by erecting her brazen image.... Mythologically, the serpent is always a female divinity."[1374]

In addition, in the Bible the serpent, vilified "in the beginning," then venerated, then vilified again, is once more venerated as it is later associated with Christ, as a "type of" him: "And as Moses lifted up the serpent in the wilderness, even so must the Son of Man be lifted up" (John. 3:14). Indeed, the serpent was considered the savior of mankind for its role in bringing wisdom.

The serpent is, naturally, a celestial symbol, representing both the

---

1371 Pike, 494.
1372 Walker, B. (1983), 905.
1373 Stone, 209.
1374 Walker, WDSSO, 387.

constellation of Serpens and the entire heavens, with the sun as one eye and the moon as the other. The serpent was the "Prince of Darkness," the ruler of the night sky, and its vilification is also a rejection of the stellar cult in favor of the solar.

The Original Fall/Sin

The "original fall" or "sin" has been interpreted by literalists as meaning both the transgression of Adam and Eve in disobeying God and getting kicked out of Eden, and the manner in which humans procreate (i.e., sex). It has been admitted by Christians that the concept of the original fall/sin of man and his expulsion from the Garden of Eden is integral to the need for a savior in the Christian religion. For example, "reformed" ex-Father Peter Martyr said:

> Were this Article [of faith] to be taken away, there would be no original sin; the promise of Christ would become void, and all the vital force of our religion would be destroyed.[1375]

This fervent belief is a main reason why Christian proponents are so vehemently opposed to the theory of evolution, as it demonstrates the lack of an original fall or sin that requires a savior. Regarding the theory of evolution and its effect on Christianity, Walker relates:

> The American Episcopal Church said: "If this hypothesis be true, then is the Bible an unbearable fiction … then have Christians for nearly two thousand years been duped by a monstrous lie."[1376]

Indeed, Jackson expresses his disgust at "that damnable doctrine of original sin, which slanders nature and insults all mankind."[1377] And Higgins remarked, in the early 1800's:

> Perhaps we do not find in history any doctrine which has been more pernicious than that of Original Sin. It is now demoralizing Britain. It caused all the human sacrifices in ancient times.[1378]

Like so many aspects of Christianity, the notion of original sin was unoriginal: "The *Indians* are not strangers to the doctrine of *original sin*. It is their invariable belief that *man is a fallen being*; admitted by them from time immemorial."[1379]

Rather than representing the sinful nature of man, however, the "fall" never happened, as Gerald Massey affirms:

> The fall is absolutely non-historical, and the first bit of stand-

1375 Wheless, 72.
1376 Walker, B. (1983), 292.
1377 Jackson, 123.
1378 Higgins, I, 255, 511.
1379 Doane, 189.

ing-ground for an actual Christ the Redeemer is missing in the very beginning, consequently anyone who set up, or was set up for, an historical Savior, from a non-historical fall, could only be an historical impostor.[1380]

The Garden of Eden tale is not literal but allegorical, occurring in the heavens, as the Fall actually takes place when the sun passes through the autumnal equinox, in the sign of the Virgin (Eve). As the sun crosses into Libra, "he" descends or *falls* into "the winter quarter or 'fall' of the year—a title most consistent with the phenomenon itself," as Hazelrigg says. Hazelrigg further outlines the "deep astrology" of the celestial Garden of Eden drama:

> The serpent of iniquity, who plays the part of the Tempter, must therefore be viewed in an astronomical rather than an ethical or moral character, which, for purposes of allegory, has not been made an enviable one. He is the villain of the drama, and rather an elongated one at that, for, as found described on the planisphere "his tail drew after him a third part of the stars of heaven" (Rev. xii, 4), or from Cancer to Libra, which are four constellations, a third of the twelve. Going before, he leads the woman towards the setting point in the west, therefore his office is to "seduce" (Latin *seducere*, to lead on or go before), while the enamored Adam follows in true conjugal spirit towards the horizon, driven forth by the Power that causes the revolution of the heavens which carries them out of the Garden. At the moment of expulsion, or as the figures of Adam (Bootes) and Eve [Virgo] are sinking from sight below the western line, the constellation Perseus appears in the east, grim in armor and helmet, a being of vengeance holding aloft a flaming sword.[1381]

Regarding the Garden of Eden tale, Graham spells it out:

> The world was not created by this God in six days or a million. There was no Garden of Eden or talking snake. There was no first man, Adam, or woman, Eve. They did not commit a moral sin and so we are not under condemnation for it. They did not fall from grace and so there is no need for redemption.[1382]

Thus, Christianity's foundation is false, mythical and unoriginal, as is the gospel story itself.

The Virgin Mother of the Divine Redeemer

The virgin mother and her divine child are a ubiquitous motif in the

1380 Massey, HJMC, 185.
1381 Hazelrigg, 35–36.
1382 Graham, 234–5.

ancient world, long before the Christian era. In the solar myth, the "sun of God" was considered to be born of the new, or virgin, moon. The Virgin birth aspect also comes from the observation that in earlier ages (5000 BCE) the constellation of Virgo rose before dawn on the solstice:

> At the moment of the Winter Solstice, the Virgin rose heliacally (*with* the Sun), having the Sun (Horus) in her bosom.... Virgo was Isis; and her representation, carrying a child (Horus) in her arms, exhibited in her temple, was accompanied by this inscription: "I AM ALL THAT IS, THAT WAS, AND THAT SHALL BE; and the fruit which I brought forth is the Sun."[1383]

Bethlehem

As the early Christian doctor Jerome admitted, the "little town of Bethlehem" was a sacred grove devoted to the Syrian solar-fertility-savior god Adonis (Tammuz), who was born hundreds of years before the Christian era in the same cave later held to be the birthplace of Jesus. Like Jesus, Adonis was born on December 25[1384] of the Virgin Myrrha, who was:

> a temple-woman or hierodule, identified with Mary by early Christians, who called Jesus's mother Myrrh of the Sea.... Syrian Adonis died at Easter time. . . Adonis died and rose again in periodic cycles, like all gods of vegetation and fertility. He was also identified with the sun that died and rose again in heaven.[1385]

Adonis/Tammuz was a favorite Semitic and Hebrew god, and each year during his passion in Jerusalem, women "wailed for the dead savior Tammuz in the temple of Jerusalem, where Ishtar was worshipped as Mari, Queen of Heaven (Ezek. 8:14)."[1386] At this time, Adonis/Tammuz wore a "crown of thorns" made of myrrh. Walker relates of Tammuz:

> The *Christos* or sacred king annually sacrificed in the temple at Jerusalem ... the Romans called Tammuz the chief god of the Jews.... A month of the Jewish calendar is still named after Tammuz ... Tammuz was imported from Babylon by the Jews, but he was even older than Babylon. He began as the Sumerian savior-god Dumuzi, or Damu, "only-begotten Son," or "Son of the Blood." He fertilized the earth with his blood at the time of his death, and was called Healer, Savior, Heavenly Shepherd. He tended the flocks of stars, which were considered souls of the dead in heaven. Each year on the Day of Atonement he was sacrificed in the form of a lamb....

1383 Pike, 455.
1384 Doane, 364.
1385 Walker, B. (1983), 10.
1386 Walker, B. (1983), 1026.

Though Tammuz occupied the central position in the sacred drama at Jerusalem, the New Testament transformed him into a mere apostle of the new dying god, under the Greek form of his name, Thomas.[1387]

As a fertility god, Adonis/Tammuz was representative of "the spirit of the corn," and "Bethlehem" means, the "House of Bread," "House of Corn," or "house of bread-corn, grain or wheat."[1388] This motif is passed down in the Christian myth when Jesus, like his predecessor Horus, says, "I am the bread of life" (John 6:48). Like so many other places in Israel, Bethlehem was first situated in the mythos and then given location on Earth.

Nazareth

The town of Nazareth did not appear on Earth until after the gospel tale was known. As Holley says, "There is no such place as Nazareth in the Old Testament or in Josephus' works, or on early maps of the Holy Land. The name was apparently a later Christian invention." In fact, the town now designated as Nazareth is near Mt. Carmel, indicating it was the Carmelites who created it.

Jesus, therefore, was not from Nazareth, which did not exist at the time of his purported advent. The real purpose for putting him there was to make of him a Nazarene or Nazarite, as he was, like the most famous Nazarite, Samson, a solar myth. The title comes from the Egyptian word "*natzr*," which refers to "the plant, the shoot, the natzar … the true vine," as is used in Isaiah 11:1, the branch of Jesse, in Hebrew 'weneser visay,' seen by Christians as among the most important prophecies of Jesus of Nazareth. Nazarite is also an epithet for the sun, which gives life to the grape vine.[1389] Nazarite is also translated as "prince," as in "prince of peace." The Nazarites/Nazarenes were ascetics who were not to shave their heads or beards unless for ritualistic purpose, because their hair was a symbol of holiness and strength, representing the sun's "hair" or rays, which is why the solar hero Samson becomes weak when the woman Delilah cuts his hair. When the hair was long, the Nazarite would have nothing to do with the grape, vine or wine, but when the Nazarite was shorn in a ritual, he would then drink wine. This story reflects the time of the year when the grapes ripen and wine is made, as the sun's rays weaken.

Thus, we see that Nazareth is not the birthplace of Jesus but represents yet another aspect of the solar mythos. As Massey states, "The

1387 Walker, B. (1983), 970–1.

1388 Massey, HJMC, 27.

1389 Massey, GHC.

actual birthplace of the carnalized Christ was NEITHER BETHLEHEM NOR NAZARETH, BUT ROME!"[1390]

The Manger and Cave, Birthplace of Many Gods

In Christian tradition, Jesus was said to be born variously in a manger, stable and/or cave, like many earlier gods. Like Jesus, the Greek god Hermes was also wrapped in swaddling clothing and placed in a manger, as was Dionysus.[1391]

The cave/manger motif is part of the mythos, representing both the winter and the setting of the sun, when it appears to go underground or into the underworld, which is the womb of both the heavens and earth. Walker says, "The cave was universally identified with the womb of Mother Earth, the logical place for symbolic birth and regeneration."

The confusing stories regarding the solar babe being born in a cave, manger *and/or* stable reflect the changing of the heavens, specifically the precession of the equinoxes. The Greeks called the constellation of Capricorn the stable of ugeas, from the twelve labors of Hercules, marking the location of the sun at the winter solstice, because the Sun's brightness, the meaning of Augeas, appears to rest, or "stable" during the winter solstice. As Massey states:

> [T]he cave and the stable are two types of the birthplace at the solstice.[1392]

Herod and the Slaughter of the Innocents

The "slaughter of the infants" is yet another part of the standard mythos, an element of the typical sacred-king tradition found in many mythologies, whereby the reigning monarch tries to prevent the fulfillment of a prophecy that a newborn king will overthrow him. As Walker says, "Innocents were slaughtered in the myths of Sargon, Nimrod, Moses, Jason, Krishna and Mordred as well as in that of Jesus."[1393] They are also slain in the stories of Oedipus, Perseus, Romulus and Remus, and Zeus.

The Three Wise Men and the Star in the East

A favorite of children everywhere, the story of the three wise men or magi and the star in the east attending the birth of Jesus is also found in other mythologies. The three wise men or kings are the three stars in Orion's belt "whose rising announced the coming of Sothis, the Star of Horus/Osiris: that is, Sirius, the brightest star in the sky, whose coming

1390 Massey, HJMC, 28.
1391 Jackson, 206.
1392 Massey, HJMC, 41.
1393 Walker, B. (1983), 435.

heralded the annual flood of the Nile."[1394] In addition, it would be very appropriate for the three kings worshipping the babe to be considered magi, since magi were sun-worshippers. Furthermore, the gifts of the wise men to the Divine Child are also a standard part of the mythos. As Higgins remarks, "It is a striking circumstance that the gifts brought by the Magi, gold, frankincense and myrrh, were what were always offered by the Arabian Magi to the sun."[1395]

By specifically naming these three "magi," it would seem that the Christian creators intended to supersede Mithraism, having Zoroastrian/Mithraic holy men bend their knee to the new Jewish Lord and Savior. The fact of this motif appearing in other pre-Christian religions may indicate a priestly formula of passing the baton, so to speak.

Of the famous star Walker says, "Ancient Hebrews called the same star Ephraim, or the Star of Jacob. In Syrian, Arabian and Persian astrology it was Messaeil—the Messiah."[1396] Massey elaborates:

> [The] Star in the East will afford undeniable data for showing the mythical and celestial origin of the gospel history. When the divine child is born, the wise men or magi declare that they have seen his star in the east.... The three kings or three solar representatives are as ancient as the male triad that was first typified when the three regions were established as heaven, earth, and netherworld, from which the triad bring their gifts.... When the birthplace was in the sign of the Bull [@6,500–4,400 BP], the Star in the East that arose to announce the birth of the babe was Orion, which is therefore called the star of Horus. *That was once the star of the three kings;* for the *"three kings"* is still a name of three stars in Orion's belt.

The star in the east has also been associated with the planet Venus, as the "morning star," heralding the arrival of the "sun of God," who is also called the "morning star," a title linked to Jesus Christ in 2 Peter 1:19 , Revelation 2:28 and Revelation 22:16. This appearance was not a single historical occurrence but a recurring celestial observation that long preceded the Christian era. Furthermore, as Higgins says, "Every Amid or *Desire of all nations* had a star to announce his birth."[1397] The births of Abraham and Moses, among so many others, were also attended by stars.[1398] As Doane says, "The fact that the writer of this story

1394 Walker, WDSSO, 75.
1395 Higgins, II, 96.
1396 Walker, B. (1983), 749.
1397 Higgins, II, 95.
1398 Higgins, I, 560.

speaks not of *a star* but of *his star*, shows that it was the popular belief of the people among whom he lived, that each and every person was born under a star, and that this one which had been seen was *his star*."[1399]

Jesus at Ages 12 and 30

Like Jesus, Horus has no history between the ages of 12 and 30, "and the mythos alone will account for the chasm which is wide and deep enough to engulf a supposed history of 18 years."[1400]

Jesus/Horus in the Temple in fact represents the sun of God at midday, 12 noon, its highest point, thus being the "Temple of the Most High." The story of Jesus being baptized and beginning his ministry at age 30 recalls the identical tale of Horus, representing the sun moving into a new constellation at 30°. Jesus is alternatively depicted as beginning his ministry at 28 years, which represents the 28-day cycle of the moon, or the month, as reckoned by the Egyptians.

The Dove at the River Jordan

When Jesus is baptized in the Jordan River by John the Baptist a dove appears to signal that he is the Son of God. This story resembles the anointing of Osiris by Anubis. The River Eridanus, a name remarkably similar to Jordan, was equated by ancient astronomers with the Nile, and the dove represents the goddess Hathor, who brings Horus forth as an adult in a ceremony symbolizing rebirth. Higgins says:

> When Jesus was baptized by that very mysterious character [Joannes] in the Jordanus, the holy Spirit descended on to him in the form of a dove, and a fire was lighted in the river. Now I cannot help suspecting that a mystic union was meant to be represented here between the two principles—in fact the reunion of the sects of the Linga and the Ioni or Dove—which we yet find in Jesus and his mother in the Romish religion.[1401]

The Forty Days and Temptation in the Wilderness

Many savior gods, including Buddha, Horus, Manu, Quetzalcoatl and Zoroaster, were tempted in the wilderness as a standard part of the mythos. The Jesus-Satan temptation myth evolved from the tale about the Egyptian "twins" Horus-Set, representing the struggle between light and dark, day and night, and winter and summer. Churchward explains these elements of the mythos:

> The Gospel story of the Devil taking Jesus up into an exceeding high mountain from which all the kingdoms of the world and the glory of them could be seen, and of the contention on the summit is

1399 Doane, 140.
1400 Massey, HJMC, 58.
1401 Higgins, I, 648.

originally a legend of the Astronomical Cult, which has been converted into history in the Gospels. In the Ritual … the struggle is described as taking place upon the mount, i.e., "the mountain in the midst of the Earth, or the mountain of Amenta which reaches up to the sky," and which in the Solar Cult stood at the point of the equinox, where the conflict was continued and the twins were reconciled year after year. The equinox was figured at the summit of the mount on the ecliptic and the scene of strife was finally configurated as a fixture in the constellation of the Gemini, the sign of the twin-brothers, who for ever fought and wrestled "up and down the garden," first one, then the other, being uppermost during the two halves of the year, or of night and day.… This contention in the wilderness was one of the great battles of Set and Horus.… Forty days was the length of time in Egypt that was reckoned for the grain in the earth before it sprouted visibly from the ground. It was a time of scarcity and fasting in Egypt, the season of Lent.… The fasting of Jesus in the desert represents the absence of food that is caused by Set in the wilderness during the forty days' burial for the corn, and Satan asking Jesus to turn the stones into bread is a play on the symbol of Set, which in one representation was rendered as "a stone." The contest of the personal Christ with a personal Satan in the New Testament is no more historical fact than the contest between the seed of the woman and the serpent of evil in the Old. Both are mythical and both are Egyptian Mysteries.[1402]

This battle between Set and Horus was also re-enacted upon the earth, as the stellar, lunar and solar cult priests and their followers have fought among themselves for millennia.

This particular part of the mythos was rejected by early Christian fathers as being "fabulous," but, like many other elements of the solar myth, it was later added in order to make the godman more competitive, "to show that Christ Jesus was proof against all temptations, that *he* too, as well as *Buddha* and others, could resist the powers of the prince of evil."[1403]

The Wedding Feast at Cana/Turning Water into Wine

In the gospels, Jesus changes water into wine during the wedding at Cana as proof of his divinity. Once again, this tale is found in other mythologies and is part of the solar mythos. Long before the Christian era, Dionysus/Bacchus was said to turn water into wine, as related by A.J. Mattill, Jr.:

1402 A. Churchward, 387–9.
1403 Doane, 175.

This story is really the Christian counterpart to the pagan legends of Dionysus, the Greek god of wine, who at his annual festival in his temple of Elis filled three empty kettles with wine—no water needed! And on the fifth of January wine instead of water gushed from his temple at Andros. If we believe Jesus' miracle, why should we not believe Dionysus's?[1404]

As Walker says:

> The story of his miracle at Cana was directly modeled on a Dionysian rite of sacred marriage celebrated at Sidon; even the Gospels' wording was copied from the festival of the older god.[1405]

In pre-Christian times, priests would turn water into wine to fool the gullible masses into believing they had miraculous powers. At Corinth, where "Paul" purportedly taught, there existed a water-to-wine device into which water was poured and then diverted by priests, who, hiding inside the covered parts of the sluice, would pour wine out the other end. Another such device was used at Alexandria.

As we have seen, the sun was considered to change water into wine when, following the rains, the grapes would ripen on the vine and ferment in the heat after picking.

Mary Magdalene

In the New Testament, Mary Magdalene has a pivotal role as, despite her alleged unworthiness, and later denigration as prostitute, Magdalene holds the honor of anointing the new king, Jesus, with oil, an act that makes him the Christ, implicitly making her a priestess. It is also Mary Magdalene, and not his male apostles, to whom Jesus first allegedly appears after the miracle of his resurrection. In the early Gnostic-Christian gospels Mary Magdalene is the most beloved disciple of Jesus. Some traditions asserted that Jesus and Mary were lovers who created a bloodline, to which a number of groups have laid claim. Nevertheless, like Jesus and the twelve, Magdalene is not a historical character but an element of the typical solar myth/sacred king drama: the sacred harlot. As such, she was highly revered, which explains why she is given top honors in the gospel story. As Walker states:

> Thus, it seems Mary the Whore was only another form of Mary the Virgin, otherwise the Triple Goddess Mari-Anna-Ishtar, the Great Whore of Babylon who was worshipped along with her savior-son in the Jerusalem temple. The *Gospel of Mary* said all three Marys of the canonical books were one and the same....

1404 Leedom, 125.

1405 Walker, B. (1983), 464.

> The seven "devils" exorcised from Mary Magdalene seem to have been the seven Maskim, or Anunnaki, Sumero-Akkadian spirits of the seven nether spheres, born of the Goddess Mari.... The Gospels say no men attended Jesus's tomb, but only Mary Magdalene and her women. Only women announced Jesus's resurrection. This was because men were barred from the central mysteries of the Goddess. Priestesses announced the successful conclusion of the rites, and the Savior's resurrection. The Bible says the male apostles knew nothing of Jesus's resurrection, and had to take the women's word for it (Luke 24:10–11). The apostles were ignorant of the sacred tradition and didn't even realize a resurrection was expected: "They knew not the scripture, that he must rise again from the dead" (John 20:9).[1406]

Walker also relates:

> Mary alone was the first to observe and report the alleged miracle. In just such a manner, pagan priestesses had been announcing the resurrection of savior gods like Orpheus, Dionysus, Attis, and Osiris every year for centuries.... Mary Magdalene was described as a harlot; but in those times, harlots and priestesses were often one and the same. A sacred harlot in the Gilgamesh epic was connected with a victim-hero in a similar way: "The harlot who anointed you with fragrant ointment laments for you now." ... Under Christianity, priests soon took over all the rituals that had been conducted by women, declaring that women had no right to lead any religious ceremony whatever.[1407]

Of course, this exclusion and degradation of women is in direct defiance of Jesus's rebuke of Judas, in which Jesus is made to say that the woman who anointed him would be remembered in all the nations. And she should be remembered for good reason, for "the Christian derivate of Mari-Ishtar is Mary Magdalene, the sacred harlot who said harlots are 'compassionate of all the race of mankind.'"[1408]

Walker says of the various Marian legends:

> Much Christian myth-making went into the later history of Mary Magdalene. She was said to have lived for a while with the virgin Mary at Ephesus. This story probably was invented to account for the name Maria associated with the Ephesian Goddess. Afterward, Mary Magdalene went to Marseilles, another town named after the ancient sea-mother Mari. Her cult centered

1406 Walker, B. (1983), 614.
1407 Walker, WDSSO, 88–9.
1408 Walker, B. (1983), 496.

there. Bones were found at Vézelay and declared to be hers. Her dwelling was a cave formerly sacred to the pagans, at St. Baume (Holy Tree).[1409]

The Five Loaves, Two Fishes, Twelve Baskets

In the gospel tale, Jesus feeds firstly the 5,000 men and their families with five loaves and two fishes, and then 4000. This alleged miracle appears six times in the Gospels. The two fishes symbolize both the sun and moon and the zodiacal sign of Pisces. The five loaves represent the five smaller planets, and the opposing zodiac sign of Virgo, whose main star Spica represents a spike of wheat. The story is like the five loaves requested of the priests by David at 1 Samuel 21:3. Later in the gospel myth, the number of the loaves is seven, representing the seven "planets" used to name the days of the week. "Jesus," the sun, "breaks up" the multiplied loaves with 12 "baskets" or constellations, symbolizing the twelve signs of the zodiac and the creation of the countless stars and the placement in the heavens. The shift of the equinoxes at the time of Christ into the constellations of the loaves and fishes, Virgo and Pisces, marks Jesus Christ as the imagined avatar of the new age of Pisces. The Gnostic theme from ancient astronomer-priests here is that understanding the visible cosmos is the basis to create universal abundance.

Furthermore, as the sun was considered the "fisher," so was the Greek version of the Great Mother, Demeter, called "Mistress of Earth and Sea, multiplier of loaves and fishes."[1410] Bread and fish are pre-Christian communion foods eaten at sacred feasts, often following the resurrection of their god, as part of an initiation into ancient mystical knowledge.

Regarding this pericope, Price remarks:

> The basis for the miraculous feeding stories in Mark's gospel is the story of Elisha multiplying twenty barley loaves for a hundred men in 2 Kings 4:42–44.[1411]

The Devils and the Swine

The story of Jesus exorcising the Gadarene/Gerasene Demoniac is also Egyptian in origin. As Massey states:

> The devils entreat Jesus not to bid them depart into the abyss, but as a herd of swine were feeding on the mountain they ask permission to enter into these. "*And he gave them leave.*" Then the devils came out of the man and entered the swine, which ran down into the lake—exactly as it is in the Egyptian scenes of the judgment, where condemned souls are ordered back into

1409 Walker, B. (1983), 615.
1410 Walker, WDSSO, 105.
1411 Price, R. (2006), 85.

> the abyss, and they make the return passage down to the lake of primordial matter by taking the shape of the swine.[1412]

The research of Dr. Dennis MacDonald comparing this pericope with a scene from the *Odyssey* (9:101–565) is also useful in noting a non-Israelite origin of this story, which could still likewise stem from Egyptian mythology: "The demoniac is based on Polyphemus the Cyclops, while the pigs come from Circe's transformation of Odysseus' soldiers into swine."[1413]

Sword-Wielding Prince of Peace

The statement that Jesus, the "Prince of Peace," comes to bring a sword (Matt. 10:34) has disturbed Christian ethicists for centuries. Indeed, the sword business has led to an atrocious amount of human suffering, as wild-eyed Christian fanatics descended upon the world, slaughtering millions under the banner of the "Prince of Peace." This contradiction also can be explained only within the solar mythos. When the sun is being swallowed by the darkness, he must fight with the sword until he arrives the next day to bring peace.

The Transfiguration on the Mount

Jesus is "transfigured" on a mountain in front of his disciples, Peter, James and John. The transfiguration is also a part of the sun mythos, as several other savior-gods were likewise transfigured on mountaintops. Massey explains the mythical meaning of the transfiguration:

> The scene on the Mount of Transfiguration is obviously derived from the ascent of Osiris into the mount of the moon. The sixth day was celebrated as that of the change and transformation of the solar god into the lunar orb, when he re-entered on that day as the regenerator of its light. With this we may compare the statement made by Matthew, that "after six days Jesus" went "up into a high mountain apart; and he was transfigured," "and his face did shine as the sun, and his garments became white as the light."[1414]

Regarding this pericope, Price notes:

> "And six days later" must be understood as a pointer to Exod. 24:12–16. God calls Moses up the mountainside, Moses takes Joshua (Greek: Jesus) with him, the glory cloud covers the mountain for six days, and on the seventh day the divine voice calls Moses from the depth of the cloud. Mark has apparently foreshortened the process. The glowing apparition of Jesus is obviously derived from

1412 Massey, HJMC, 63.
1413 Price, R. (2006), 81.
1414 Massey, HJMC, 78.

that of Moses in Exod. 34:29, as well as perhaps from Mal. 3:2.[1415]

The Ass

The riding of the ass into "Jerusalem," "City of Peace," or the "Holy City," occurs in Egyptian mythology at least two thousand years prior to the Christian era. The ass is the totem animal of Set, who rides it into the city in triumph. Massey explains the astrological meaning of this episode:

> Neither god nor man can actually ride on the ass and her foal at the same time. Such a proceeding must be figurative; one that could not be humanly fulfilled in fact. We have seen how it was fulfilled in the mythos and rendered in the planisphere. The ass and its colt are described in the Book of Genesis as belonging to the Shiloh [king] who binds them to the vine.... The vine to which the ass and foal were tethered is portrayed in the decans of Virgo, the ass and colt being stationed in those of Leo; the two asses in the sign of Cancer.[1416]

Set, Horus's "twin," is sometimes represented as an ass-headed god, crucified and wounded in the side. Walker elaborates on the twin-god myth:

> Thus, Set and Horus were remnants of a primitive sacred-king cult, which the Jews adopted. The story of the rival gods appeared in the Bible as Seth's supplanting of the sacrificed shepherd Abel, evidently the same "Good Shepherd" as Osiris-Horus (Genesis 4:25). Their rivalry was resolved in Egypt by having the pharaoh unite both gods in himself.... Similarly, the Jewish God uniting both Father and Son was sometimes an ass-headed man crucified on a tree. This was one of the earliest representations of the Messiah's crucifixion. Some said Christ was the same as the Jewish ass-god Iao, identified with Set.[1417]

And Massey further elucidates:

> In the pictures of the underworld, the ass-headed god is portrayed as bearer of the sun.... In the Greek shape of the mythos, Hephaistos ascends to the heavens, or to heaven, at the instigation of Dionysus, and is depicted as returning thither riding on an ass.... The wine-god intoxicated him and led him heavenwards; in which condition we have the Hebrew Shiloh, who was to come binding his ass to the vine, with his eyes red with wine; his garments being drenched in the blood of the grape, and he as obvi-

1415 Price, R. (2006), 90.
1416 Massey, HJMC, 121.
1417 Walker, B. (1983), 68.

ously drunk as Hephaistos.[1418]

Sut/Set was also the biblical Seth, son of Adam, or Atum, the primordial being. Like the Egyptian Set, the biblical Seth is the "enemy of the Egyptian gods." He is also the progenitor of the Hebrew people. In fact, Massey relates that the Jews were "Suttites" or Sethians "from the very beginning, and Sut was worshipped by the Christians in Rome."[1419] Set was thus revered in ancient Palestine, which is in fact named after him, "Pales" being his Roman name. Regarding this ass-headed twin, Doresse explains:

> It is upon certain monuments of Egypt that we find the most ancient proofs of the attribution of a donkey's head to a god, who was to become progressively identified with the god of the Jews. This originated from the Asiatic god Sutekh, whom the Egyptians assimilated to one of their own greatest gods: Seth, the adversary of Osiris. They represent Seth also, after the period of the Persian invasions, with a human body and an ass's head. Afterwards, this god Seth was definitely regarded by the Egyptians ... as the father of the legendary heroes Hierosolymus and Judaeus—that is, as the ancestor of the Jews![1420]

As concerns the pericope of Jesus instructing his disciples to steal the ass and the colt, Price notes, "This story derives from 1 Sam. 9."[1421]

The Jews as Vipers and Children of the Devil

The insult by Jesus of Jews as a "brood of vipers" Matthew 3, 12, 23) and the "children of the devil" (John 8:44) is one of the ugly sticking points of the gospel fable that have caused a great deal of trouble on this planet. Allegedly "good Christians" have used these aspersions to justify their hatred and violence towards Jews, all the while worshipping some of them. But this Gospel story has no historical basis, with "the Jews" in the Gospel better understood as representing "mythological devils, vipers, and other Typhonian types." In the Egyptian story, Set, the enemy of Horus, commands the Apophis or deadly viper, as well as "the strangling snakes" and various demons and devils. The story is also reflective of the fact that the Jews were followers of Set, the serpent of the night sky.

The Last Supper/Eucharist

The Eucharist, or the sharing of the god's blood and body, has been a sacred ritual within many ancient mystery religions, and the line ascribed

1418 Massey, HJMC, 123–7.
1419 Massey, HJMC, 123–7.
1420 Doresse, 42.
1421 Price, R. (2006), 97.

to Jesus, "This is my blood you drink, this is my body you eat,"[1422] is a standard part of the theophagic (god-eating) ritual. While this cannibalistic rite is now allegorical, using bread and wine, in the past participants actually ate and drank flesh and blood, using a sacrificed human or animal, as the consuming of the flesh has been thought magically to bestow the capacities of the victim upon the eater.

The Christian form of the Eucharist is closely similar to the ritual practiced as part of the Eleusinian Mysteries, in detail, as Christians grudgingly admitted from the beginning. The Eleusinian Eucharist honored both Ceres, goddess of wheat, and Bacchus/Dionysus, god of the vine.

Both Tibetan Buddhists and, on the other side of the globe, pre-Columbian Mexicans, held many points in common with Roman Catholicism without having borrowed them. As Higgins relates:

> Father Grebillion observes also with astonishment that the Lamas have the use of holy water, singing in the church service, prayers for the dead, mitres worn by the bishops; and that the Dalai Lama holds the same rank among his Lamas that the Pope does in the Church of Rome: and Father Grueger goes farther; he says, that their religion agrees, in every essential point, with the Roman religion, without ever having had any connection with Europeans: for, says he, they celebrate a sacrifice with bread and wine; they give extreme unction; they bless marriages; pray for the sick; make processions; honour the relics of their saints, or rather their idols; they have monasteries and convents of young women; they sing in their temples like Christian Monks; they observe several fasts, in the course of the year, and mortify their bodies, particularly with the discipline, or whips: they consecrate their bishops, and send missionaries, who live in extreme poverty, travelling even barefoot to China.[1423]

Thirty Pieces of Silver and Potter's Field

According to the Gospel of Matthew, when Judas betrays Jesus for 30 pieces of silver, he is wracked with guilt and hangs himself, after which the priests who originally paid him off spend his (returned) blood-money to purchase the "Field of Blood," or the potter's field. However, in Acts Judas is represented as having his guts explode in the field, thus its bloody name. Obviously, these accounts are not history; indeed, they are found in older mythologies. Walker relates an earlier version from which the biblical tale was molded:

> The Sumero-Babylonian Goddess Aruru the Great was the

1422 This wording comes from Jesus Christ Superstar.
1423 Higgins, I, 232.

> original Potter who created human beings out of clay.... The Goddess was worshipped as a Potter in the Jewish temple, where she received "thirty pieces of silver" as the price of a sacrificial victim (Zechariah 11:13). She owned the Field of Blood, Alcedema, where clay was moistened with the blood of victims so bought. Judas, who allegedly sold Jesus for this same price, was himself another victim of the Potter. In the Potter's Field he was either hanged (Matthew 27:5) or disemboweled (Acts 1:18), suggesting that the Potter was none other than the Goddess who both created and destroyed.[1424]

In the luni-solar mythos, the 30 pieces of silver represent the 30 days of lunation.

Peter's Denial and the Cock Crowing

While foretelling his betrayal, Christ claims that Peter, his "rock," will deny him three times before the cock crows. This element is found in other myths and earlier traditions. As Walker states:

> It is said in the *Zohar* that a cock crowing three times is an omen of death.... The Gospel story of Peter's denial of Christ, three times before cockcrow, was related to older legends associating the crowing with the death and resurrection of the solar Savior.[1425]

"St. Peter," despite his denial of Christ, is considered the gatekeeper of heaven. The story is not historical but astronomical in origin, with Peter and the cock being one and representing the announcement of the morning sun, whom Peter "the gatekeeper/cock" finally allows to pass after denying him. As Walker relates:

> The resurrected god couldn't enter into his kingdom until dawn. The angel of annunciation appeared as a cock, "to announce the coming of the Sun," as Pausanias said. At cockcrow, the Savior arose as Light of the World to disperse the demons of night. But if he tried to enter into his kingdom earlier, disrupting the cycles of night and day, the Gatekeeper would deny him. The ritualistic denial took place also in the fertility cults of Canaan, where the dying god Mot was denied by a priest representing the Heavenly Father. This story made difficulties for Christian theologians, when the pagans inquired why Jesus should found his church on a disciple who denied him instead of a more loyal one.[1426]

1424 Walker, B. (1983), 815.
1425 Walker, WDSSO, 397.
1426 Walker, B. (1983), 79.

As the cock who announces the risen savior, Peter is associated with the sign of Aries, following the spring equinox when the sun overcomes the night and starts its journey to fullness.

The Sacrifice of the Sacred King

The gospel story is basically a remake of the ubiquitous ancient myth of the sacred king drama and sacrifice. This myth and its ritual were common around the Mediterranean both at the purported time of Jesus and long prior (e.g., in Greece, Italy, Asia Minor, the Levant and Egypt). The story was originally allegory, with the characters representing the celestial bodies and natural forces, but it became degraded as it was enacted upon Earth, with the solar hero who gives his life to the world represented by an actual flesh-and-blood sacrifice.

The sacred king drama is a scapegoating ritual in which the evils of the people are placed upon the head of a person or animal, such as a goat, often by jeering at him as he is paraded through the streets. Dujardin describes the scapegoat ritual: "The sins of the community are magically reassembled in the person of the god, in slaying the god one is rid of the sins, and the god returns to life freed from the sins."[1427]

Dujardin further relates the typical "scapegod" drama, which involved either an actual king or a proxy, criminal or otherwise:

> The god is anointed king and high-priest. He is conducted in a procession, clothed in the mantle of purple, wearing a crown, and with a sceptre in his hand. He is adored, then stripped of his insignia, next of his garments, and scourged, the scourging being a feature of all the analogous rites. He is killed and the blood sprinkled on the heads of the faithful. Then he is affixed to the cross. The women lament the death of their god.... This happened at the third hour—namely, at nine o'clock in the morning. At sunset the god is taken down from the cross and buried, and a stone is rolled over the sepulchre.... Many of the sacrifices of the gods took place in the springtime, such as the death and resurrection of Attis, and conform to the gospel tradition which places the Passion of Jesus at the time of the Jewish Passover.[1428]

During the sacrifice, the sacred king's legs may be broken, but the highest sacrifice—that for sin-atonement—calls for a blemish-free victim; thus, it is written that Jesus was spared this mutilation, so that "scripture might be fulfilled." At times, the victim was slain by having his heart pierced by a sacred lance; at others, he was wounded by the spear and left to die in the sun. Often it was necessary for the victim

1427 Dujardin, 8–9.

1428 Dujardin, 56.

to be willing if reluctant, like Jesus. Sometimes the victims, who could also be unwilling prisoners of war, were given a stupefying drug such as datura or opium, the "vinegar with gall" or "wine with spices" given to Jesus.

This drama also served as a fertility rite, and the god-king was considered a vegetation deity. After his sacrifice, his blood and flesh were to be shared, sometimes in a cannibalistic eucharist and usually by being spread upon the crop fields so that they would produce abundance. In some places such ritual sacrifice was done annually or more often. Thus, it has never been a one-time occurrence in history, 2,000 years ago, but has taken place thousands of times over many millennia. As Massey says:

> The legend of the voluntary victim who in a passion of divinest pity became incarnate, and was clothed in human form and feature for the salvation of the world, did not originate in a belief that God had manifested once for all as an historic personage. It has its roots in the remotest past.[1429]

The sacred king drama had already taken place in the Levant for thousands of years prior to the Christian era. As Frazer relates:

> Among the Semites of Western Asia the king, in a time of national danger, sometimes gave his own son to die as a sacrifice for the people. Thus Philo of Byblus, in his work on the Jews, says: "It was an ancient custom in a crisis of great danger that the ruler of a city or nation should give his beloved son to die for the whole people, as a ransom offered to the avenging demons; and the children thus offered were slain with mystic rites. So Cronus, whom the Phoenicians call Israel, being king of the land and having an only-begotten son called Jeoud (for in the Phoenician tongue Jeoud signifies 'only-begotten'), dressed him in royal robes and sacrificed him upon an altar in a time of war, when the country was in great danger from the enemy."[1430]

Robertson elucidates on Jewish sacrifice:

> [Hanged] men in ancient Jewry were sacrifices to the Sun-god or Rain-god. It may be taken as historically certain that human sacrifice in this aspect was a recognized part of Hebrew religion until the Exile.... Hanging is not to be construed in the narrow sense of death by strangulation. The normal method of "crucifixion" was hanging by the wrists.[1431]

1429 Massey, EBD, 51.
1430 Frazer, 340–1.
1431 Robertson, 36.

In the gospels, while plotting Jesus's death, high priest Caiaphas ("rock" or "oppressor") says to his colleagues, "it is expedient … that one man should die for the people, and that the whole nation should not perish," a reference to the ritual of scapegoating that demonstrates Christ's was an expiatory and not a punitive sacrifice.

The Passion

The scapegoat ritual is also the "Passion" of the sacred king. The Passion of Jesus is well-known because it has been acted in plays or on the streets in many nations each year for centuries. The simple fact is that the Passion was also acted out in the same manner long prior to the purported advent of the Christ character, as there have been "Passions" of a number of savior-gods and goddesses. As Dujardin relates:

> Other scholars have been impressed by the resemblance between the Passion of Jesus as told in the gospels and the ceremonies of the popular fetes, such as the Sacaea in Babylon, the festival of Kronos in Greece, and the Saturnalia in Italy.... If the stories of the Passions of Dionysus, Attis, Osiris and Demeter are the transpositions of cult dramas, and not actual events, it can hardly be otherwise with the Passion of Jesus.

The following passion is not the story of Jesus but that of Baal or Bel, clay tablets discovered in Nineveh, Assyria, 2,700 years ago known as "Marduk's Ordeal" with four fragments in the British Museum's collections:

- Baal is taken prisoner.
- He is tried in a hall of justice.
- He is tormented and mocked by a rabble.
- He is led away to the mount.
- Baal is taken with two other prisoners, one of whom is released.
- After he is sacrificed on the mount, the rabble goes on a rampage.
- His clothes are taken.
- Baal disappears into a tomb.
- He is sought after by weeping women.
- He is resurrected, appearing to his followers after the stone is rolled away from the tomb.[1432]

In addition, it is obvious that a number of the specifics of the Christian passion are lifted from the book of Psalm (22, 69:21), which in turn

1432 H. Zimmern, *"Babylonische Vorstufen der vorderasiatischen Mysterienreligionen"* ZDMG vol. 76, 36–54, 1922. Stephen Langdon, "*The Babylonian Epic of Creation*," page 50, 1923. Tikva Frymer-Kensky, "*The Tribulations of Marduk*," Journal of the American Oriental Society, vol. 103: 1983, pp. 131-41.

is based on older traditions, as Psalms in fact represents a reworking of Canaanite/Egyptian sayings.

The Passion as related in the gospels is easily recognized as a play through a number of clues. For example, Jesus is made to pray three times while his disciples are asleep, so that no one is there to hear or see the scene, yet it is recorded. Robertson explains: "On the stage, however, there is no difficulty at all since the prayer would be heard by the audience, like a soliloquy."[1433] Another clue is the compression in time of the events, as well as their dramatic tone. The whole gospel story purports to take place over a period of a few weeks, and the entire "life of Jesus" represents about 50 hours total. Furthermore, Robertson states:

> The fact that the whole judicial process took place in the middle of the night shows its unhistorical character. The exigencies of drama are responsible for hunting up "false witnesses" throughout Jerusalem in the dead of night.... The Crucifixion and Resurrection scenes, even the final appearance in Galilee, are set forth in Matthew as they would be represented on a stage. The gospel ends abruptly with the words of the risen Lord. Where the play ends, the narrative ends.[1434]

"Let His Blood Be Upon Us and Our Children"

The blood of the scapegoat was sprinkled upon the congregation or audience of the play, who would cry, "Let his blood be upon us and our children," a standard ritual line that was designed to ensure future fertility and the continuation of life. This ritual is reflected at Exodus 24:8, when Moses throws the oxen blood on the people to seal the Lord's covenant with them, showing that later anti-Semitic use of this verse involves only a superficial reading. The blood motif was subsequently passed down in the Christian doctrine of being "washed in the blood of the Lamb of God." It is also displayed in the Epistle to the Hebrews, where the priests have even developed a "technology" to emulate the sprinkling of the blood.

Golgotha, "Place of the Skulls"

The site where Jesus is crucified is called Golgotha or Calvary, which is the Latin for "place of bare skulls." According to Doane, the word Golgotha does not appear in Jewish literature, nor is there any evidence of such a place near Jerusalem. As Dujardin states:

> As in the case of Nazareth, no trace of [Golgotha] is to be found prior to the gospels. This is inexplicable, for the story plac-

1433 Robertson, 49.
1434 Robertson, 50–1.

> es Golgotha at the gates of Jerusalem.... These considerations suggest that the Golgotha which was the actual place of the sacrifice must have been situated elsewhere. Golgotha, Goulgoleth in Hebrew, was both a common and proper name, and one may infer that Jesus was crucified on one of the numerous hills in Palestine described as a goulgoleth. It would also appear that Goulgoleth was an expletive form of Golgola ... and that Golgola is the same as Gilgal. Now, Gilgal is both a common name signifying a circle (applicable to the ancient megalithic circles that we call cromlechs—namely, the sacred or high places of Canaan) and also a proper name of several cities. If Jesus was sacrificed on a gilgal—namely, an ancient cromlech—we are face to face with the most ancient of Palestinian cults.... The Bible, in fact, narrates that a certain place called Gilgal was the principal centre of the patriarch Iehoshoua—namely, Jesus-Joshua.... Jesus-Joshua the ancient patriarch, who appears to have been a Palestinian god.... At all events the fact remains that Golgotha of the gospels is a gilgal, that a gilgal is a sacred circle in Palestine, and that it was in a gilgal that the old Jesus-Joshua had his headquarters—namely, a sanctuary.[1435]

Indeed, in the Old Testament, there are only three cases of crucifixion, all of which are kings, seven in total, sacrificed by Joshua at the "high places" of Gilgal, Ai and Makkeda. These sacred kings are sacrificed not *by* Joshua/Jesus but in his name.

In addition, the Mexican savior-god and solar myth, Quetzalcoatl, was also crucified at the "place of the skull," a tale told long before contact with Christians. It should also be noted that there were "calvaries" (i.e., sacred mounts where a cross was erected), in numerous places prior to the Christian era. These mounts were usurped by Christians, and the crosses reinterpreted.

The Crucifixion

As we have seen, a number of savior-gods and goddesses have been executed or crucified in atonement for "sins" and/or as a fertility rite. As part of the standard sacred king drama, the crucifixion of the "King of Kings" is in no way historical, except that it happened thousands of times around the globe in ritual. In the ancient world, there were two basic types of crucifixion: the punitive type designed to punish, and the expiatory designed to achieve forgiveness for sin. Although evemerists have tried to find in Jesus a "historical" criminal who was punitively executed, the fact is that his crucifixion is allegorical, not factual, and

1435 Dujardin, 58–9.

expiatory, not punitive.

The typical sacrificial victim was killed before being placed on the cross, tree or stake, but in the expiatory sacred king drama, which was more important and ritualistic than the average sacrifice, the victim remained alive as part of the play, so he could utter mournful words and garner pity from the audience.

In addition, Jesus would have been crucified at the holy time of Passover only if he were an expiatory sacrifice. As Graham says:

> Now is it not strange that the crucifixion should take place during the Passover? Among the Jews this was a most sacred occasion. For them to crucify anyone at this time, they would have to break at least seven of their religious laws.[1436]

Dujardin sums it up:

The crucifixion was a reality, but it was not a judicial execution; it was a sacrifice. And there was not simply one historic sacrifice, but innumerable crucifixions of the god Jesus in Palestine.[1437]

Although the ritual was reduced to a human drama, it remains ultimately symbolic:

> The Christian doctrine of the crucifixion with the victim raised aloft as the sin-offering for all the world is but a metaphrastic [changed from one form to another] rendering of the primitive meaning, a shadow of the original.[1438]

That "original" crucifixion is properly the "crossification" of the sun through the equinoxes, a reason why there are differing accounts of the crucifixion in the New Testament. In the Synoptic version Jesus's mother is not among the women watching. This omission reflects that the cross, actually represents the precession of the sun at the vernal equinox, from the constellation of Aries into Pisces. The crossification/crucifixion of the autumnal equinox, however, symbolizes the constellation of Virgo; symbol of the Virgin Mary; hence, the Virgin Mary is present in John's Gospel.

There are also two dates of crucifixion, likewise explainable only within the mythos: "The 14th of the month would be the lunar reckoning of Anup=John, and the 15th, that of Taht-Mati=Matthew in the two forms of the Egyptian Mythos.... Both cannot be historically correct, but they *are* both astronomically true."[1439]

1436 Graham, 345.
1437 Dujardin, 57.
1438 A. Churchward, 364.
1439 Massey, GHC, 32.

The Three Marys at the Crucifixion

In John's version of the crucifixion story, not only the Virgin Mary but also the other two gospel Marys are present. In the Egyptian version of the mythos, the three Meris appear at the death of Horus. Of the Jesus tale, Walker relates: "The three Marys at the crucifixion bore the same title as pagan death priestesses, *myrrhophores*, bearers of myrrh."[1440] The three Marys/Meris are the Moerae or fates:

> Three incarnations of Mari, or Mary, stood at the foot of Jesus's cross, like the Moerae of Greece. One was his virgin mother. The second was his "dearly beloved." ... The third Mary must have represented the Crone (the fatal Moera), so the tableau resembled that of the three Norns at the foot of Odin's sacrificial tree. The Fates were present at the sacrifices decreed by Heavenly Fathers, whose victims hung on trees or pillars "between heaven and earth."[1441]

The Spear of Longinus

Longinus was the name of the Roman soldier who stuck Jesus in the side with a spear. Legend held that Longinus was blind and was subsequently cured by Jesus's blood. Again, this is not a historical event but part of the mythos and sacred king ritual, as Walker relates:

> The true prototype of the legend seems to have been the blind god Hod, who slew the Norse savior Balder with the thrust of a spear of mistletoe.... March 15, the "Ides of March" when most pagan saviors died, was the day devoted to Hod by the heathens, and later Christianized as the feast day of the Blessed Longinus.[1442]

Walker also states:

> Up to Hadrian's time, victims offered to Zeus at Salamis were anointed with sacred ointments—thus becoming "Anointed Ones" or "Christs"—then hung up and stabbed through the side with a spear.[1443]

In addition, the Scandinavian god Odin, and the god Marsyas of Mindanao in the Philippines were hung on a "fatal tree" and stabbed with a spear.[1444] The Hindu god Vishnu (Bal-ii) was crucified with spear in his side, bearing the epithet "side-wounded."[1445] The gods Wittoba

1440 Walker, WDSSO, 467.
1441 Walker, B. (1983), 469.
1442 Walker, B. (1983), 549.
1443 Walker, B. (1983), 469.
1444 Frazer, 410–12.
1445 Higgins, I, 572, 670.

and Adonis were also crucified and "side-wounded" saviors.[1446]

Although a myth, many "authentic" "spears of Longinus" have been "found" in the Christian world. Indeed, according to modern legends, Hitler spent a great deal of time, money and energy to track down the "true" spear, believing that it, like so many other "sacred" objects, held occult powers.

The side-wounding in the mythos reflects the position of the sun near Sagittarius, the archer.[1447]

My God, My God, Why Hast Thou Forsaken Me?

The pitiful and mournful words uttered by Jesus as he hung on the cross were another standard part of the mythos and ritual, found in older traditions such as the sacrifice of Aleyin by his Virgin Mother Anath, "twin of the Goddess Mari as Lady of Birth and Death, worshipped by Canaanites, Amorites, Syrians, Egyptians, and Hebrews."[1448] As Walker further relates:

In the typical sacred-king style, Mot-Aleyin was the son of the Virgin Anath and also the bridegroom of his own mother. Like Jesus too, he was the Lamb of God. He said, "I am Aleyin, son of Baal (the Lord). Make ready, then, the sacrifice. I am the lamb which is made ready with pure wheat to be sacrificed in expiation."

After Aleyin's death, Anath resurrected him and sacrificed Mot in turn. She told Mot that he was forsaken by his heavenly father El, the same god who "forsook" Jesus on the cross. The words attributed to Jesus, "My El, my El, why hast thou forsaken me?" (Mark 15:34), apparently were copied from the ancient liturgical formula, which became part of the Passover ritual at Jerusalem.[1449]

The Rending of the Curtain of the Temple

When Jesus dies, he cries out with a loud voice and "yields up his spirit," after which, Matthew relates, "the curtain of the temple was torn in two, from top to bottom; and the earth shook, and the rocks were split; the tombs also were opened, and many bodies of the saints who had fallen asleep were raised, and coming out of the tombs after his resurrection they went into the holy city and appeared to many."

Obviously, this event did not happen literally and historically. Such a tremendous occurrence would hardly have escaped the notice of historians and scientists of the day, yet not a word is recorded of it anywhere. The same tale is told of a number of other sun gods and is only

1446 Doane, 185, 218.
1447 Anderson, 60.
1448 Walker, B. (1983), 29.
1449 Walker, B. (1983), 30–1.

explainable within the mythos. In the Egyptian version, Horus rends the curtain or veil of the tabernacle or temple, which means that in his resurrection, he removes the mummified remains of his old self as Osiris. This scene represents the new sun being born or resurrected from the old, dead one. The refreshed spirit pierces the veil, with a loud cry of his resurrection and with the quaking of Amenta, "the earth of eternity." As Massey states:

> The [gospel] scene has now been changed from Amenta [land of the dead] to the earth of Seb [Joseph] by those who made "historic" mockery of the Egyptian Ritual, and sank the meaning out of sight where it has been so long submerged.[1450]

The Darkening of the Sun at the Crucifixion

The earth-shattering event of the sun darkening at Christ's crucifixion is also not historical; hence, it appears in no other writing of the day, a detail bothersome to believers and evemerists alike. As Hazelrigg relates:

> Thus, C. Plinius Secund, the elder, and Seneca, both worthy philosophers, wrote in the first century of our Era, dealing exhaustively in accounts of seismic phenomena, but nowhere do they mention the miraculous darkness which is said to have overspread the earth at the crucifixion; neither do they make mention anywhere in their voluminous texts of a man Jesus.[1451]

Like the other contradictory and impossible events of the biblical narrative, this event makes sense only in terms of the mythos. The same mythical darkening of the sun occurred at the deaths of Heracles/Hercules, Krishna, Prometheus, Buddha and Osiris.[1452] The phenomena upon the death of Buddha are actually more impressive than those accompanying Christ's death, as not only did darkness prevail, but "a thousand appalling meteors fell."[1453] This darkening is only natural, in that when the sun is "crucified," it goes out.

The Resurrection

Discussing the Gymnosophs, Chaldeans and Magi or "Magians," in his *Lives of Eminent Philosophers* (1.9) Diogenes Laertius (fl. c. third cent. AD/CE) relates that, per the Greek historian Theopompus (b. c. 380 BCE), "according to the Magi, men will have a resurrection and be immortal."[1454] The Greek word translated here as "to have a resurrection,"

1450 Massey, EBD, 79.
1451 Hazelrigg, 178.
1452 Walker, B. (1983), 393.
1453 Doane, 207.
1454 Laertius/Yonge, 8.

rendered elsewhere as "live in a future life," is ἀναβιώσεσθαι or *anabiosesthai*, which means "return to life" or "call back to life."[1455] Diogenes further confirms that this discussion of resurrection is confirmed by another writer of the fourth century BCE, Eudemus of Rhodes.

As Origen (*Against Celsus* 3.33) points out, Celsus was skeptical of the Jesus tale because he was well-read in Greek "histories" (e.g., the stories of myth and legend), with their parables of resurrection including that of Cleomedes of Astypalaea, who, like Osiris and Noah, "entered into an ark," from which he was eventually released.[1456] Pausanias (4.9/6.9.7–8) relates the belief that in 495 BCE. Cleomedes of Astypalaea entered into an ark, chest, box or "tomb," which upon opening was found to be empty. He was then given divine honors and venerated as a god.[1457]

In his description of Alexander of Abonutichus as an "Oracle-Monger" (24), Lucian (second century AD/CE) remarks:

> He had begun sending emissaries abroad to make the shrine [oracle] known in foreign lands; his prophecies, discovery of runaways, conviction of thieves and robbers, revelation of hidden treasure, cures of the sick, restoration of the dead to life—all these were to be advertised.[1458]

From Herodotus (4.95), we read the account of the Thracians who mourned Zalmoxis "as one dead." Zalmoxis, meanwhile, "abode in a secret chamber three full years, after which he came forth from his concealment, and showed himself once more to his countrymen, who were thus brought to believe in the truth of what he had taught them."[1459]

Quoting Antigonus, Lucian (26) says, "I know a man who came to life more than twenty days after his burial, having attended the fellow both before his death and after he came to life."[1460]

Lucian (13) also talks about "calling mouldy corpses to life."

As we have seen, numerous gods, goddesses and other figures of antiquity have been depicted as having been resurrected, in the case of astral mythology an ongoing, unhistorical event representing various forces and bodies in nature and the cosmos, largely revolving around the sun. As Dujardin relates:

> The word "resurrection" means today the return from death to

1455 Pocket Oxford Classical Greek Dictionary, 22.
1456 Roberts, A. (1885), 4.477.
1457 Pausanias/Shilleto, 1.378.
1458 Lucian/Fowler, 2.223.
1459 Herodotus/Rawlinson, 3.86.
1460 Lucian/Harmon, 3.361.

> life, but the resurrection of gods never takes the form of a simple return to life after the manner of Lazarus. In primitive religions resurrection expresses a re-commencement analogous to that of Nature in spring, and it is usually concerned with the renewal of vegetation and of the species. But it is not only a re-commencement, it is also a renovation. In the sacrifice of Elimination the god comes to life again rejuvenated. Thus, the resurrection is the completion—or rather, the object—of the sacrifice; the god is put to death in order that he may return to life again regenerated.... Dionysus and Osiris are reborn, renovated and also glorified; dead to life terrestrial, they revive to life divine.... The god dies and comes to life again only in order that through him the human society may renew itself.[1461]
>
> If the resurrection of Jesus cannot be believed except by assenting to the fantastic descriptions included in the Gospels, then Christianity is doomed. For that view of resurrection is not believable, and if that is all there is, then Christianity, which depends upon the truth and authenticity of Jesus' resurrection, also is not believable.[1462]

Because of the past centuries of work in the field of comparative religion and mythology, a furious debate has taken place over the last several decades as to the nature of the resurrection of deities and figures in other cultures, many of them pre-Christian. It has been widely accepted for decades to centuries that there were indeed other figures in pre-Christian religions who had been believed resurrected, thus rendering Christ's resurrection a comparatively late and commonplace occurrence. But the uncomfortable implications of these facts have caused apologists to attempt to split hairs in order to deny the similarity between the Christian and non-Christian resurrections. For example, it is claimed that the blatantly obvious parallel between Jesus and the Egyptian god Osiris, who is depicted continuously throughout Egyptian literature as having been resurrected, is not relevant, because Osiris was not resurrected into this world but remained in the afterlife. This contention is erroneous, however, as the Osiris myth most certainly does tell of a post-resurrection presence on Earth.

These attempts to deny the continuity between Christianity and earlier mythology have been unsuccessful. The older stories are indeed

1461 Dujardin, 70–1.

1462 Spong, 238. Spong follows this logical assessment with a testament of faith that attempts to appeal to some mystical sense of resurrection that transcends the "literal narratives." This distinction appears to be sophistic.

quite similar to that of Christ. Besides, the resurrection motif is found even in the Bible itself, applied to human beings who most assuredly were claimed to have been resurrected from the dead, back to life on this earth (1 Kings 17:17–24; 2 Kings 4:32–37; 2 Kings 13:21). In any event, despite the impression given to the masses, the fact is that the motif of resurrection from the dead existed long before Christ's alleged advent. In his biography of the Greco-Syrian godman Apollonius of Tyana (4.45), Philostratus (fl. 200 CE) relates the story of the sage raising a girl from the dead by touching her and whispering a secret spell, after which she went home, "just as Alcestis did when she was brought back to life by Hercules."[1463] Here we see two separate accounts of godmen raising people from the dead.

The Ascension on the Mount of Olives

Many gods and goddesses around the world ascend to heaven in one way or another, such as the Sumerian god Etana, a "shepherd who ascended to heaven."[1464] There were also pre-Christian figures such as the biblical prophet Elijah, said to have been taken up to heaven in a fiery chariot, an obvious symbol for the noontide ascension of the sun to its zenith, the high point at the meridian.

Prior to Christianity, the Mount of Olives was used as a sacrificial site for the Red Heifer rite of the Hebrews,[1465] who in turn took this rite from Egypt. As Churchward relates:

> Jesus rises in the Mount of Olives, but not on the Mount that was localized to the east of Jerusalem. The Mount of Olives as Egyptian was the mountain of Amenta. It is termed "Mount Bakhu," "the mount of the olive-tree," where the green dawn was represented by this tree instead of by the Sycamore. Mount Bakhu, the mount of the olive-tree, was the way of ascent for the risen Saviour as he issued forth from Amenta to the land of the spirits in heaven.[1466]

Massey elucidates: "And from the mount called Olivet, Jesus vanished into heaven—Olivet being a typical Mount of the equinox from which the solar god ascended."[1467]

The ascension is significant, as without it much of the purpose for the Christian religion crumbles. Yet, as Graham remarks:

> The ascension of Christ is a very important part of Christian

1463 Philostratus/Conybeare, 1.459.
1464 Wright, J., 45, citing the *Sumerian King List.*
1465 Robertson, 37.
1466 A. Churchward, 376.
1467 Massey, HJMC, 78.

> doctrine; it implies immortality, triumph over death, a heaven world beyond, and a possible Second Coming. Why then did Matthew and John ignore it? Luke mentions it only in one little verse of nineteen words, a sort of postscript not found in some manuscripts. And someone added to Mark a mere reference to it with the telltale little sign ¶.[1468]

Like so many other biblical tales, the accounts of the ascension are contradictory, with Luke placing it three days after and Acts 40 days after the resurrection. These discrepancies are explainable not as history but within the celestial mythos, representing the lunar resurrection at the autumnal equinox and the solar at the vernal equinox.

Many other elements, such as the flight into Egypt,[1469] the woman at the well, the pool of Bethesda, the cursing of the fig tree, the reapers of the harvest, Salome and the "Dance of the Seven Veils," the two sisters Mary and Martha, Marys as mother of Jesus, the palms in Jerusalem, the purple robe, and the seven fishers in the boat are also found in other mythologies. The pool of Bethesda, for example, represents one of the mysteries of the secret societies and mystery schools.

Conclusion

It has been calculated that aside from the 40 days in the wilderness, and his supposed appearance as a boy in the temple, everything related in the New Testament about what Jesus said and did could have taken place within a period of three weeks. The gospel story, then, hardly constitutes a "biography" of any historical value about the life of one of the world's purported great movers and shakers. What it does record is a "history" of the development of religious ideas and how they are usurped and passed along from one culture to another. The gospel is also reflective of a concerted effort to unify the Roman world under one state religion, drawing upon the multitudes of sects and cults that existed at the time. Most of all, however, the story records the movements of planetary bodies and the forces of nature in a mythos that, when restored to its original, non-carnalized, non-historicized grandeur, portrays the cosmos in a manner not only illuminating but also entertaining.

1468 Graham, 359–60.

1469 See, for example, my book *Suns of God*. As one example, Humphreys asserts: "The 'Flight to Egypt' in Matthew, was probably written into the story by the Church of Alexandria—it appears in none of the other gospels and contradicts the return to Nazareth."

The Annunciation, Conception, Birth, and Adoration of the Child.

"In this picture we have the Annunciation, the Conception, the Birth, and the Adoration, as described in the First and Second Chapters of Luke's Gospel; and as we have historical assurance that the chapters in Matthew's Gospel which contain the Miraculous Birth of Jesus are an after addition not in the earliest manuscripts, it seems probable that these two poetical chapters in Luke may also be unhistorical, and be borrowed from the Egyptian accounts of the miraculous birth of their kings."

—Dr. Samuel C. Sharpe, *Egyptian Mythology and Egyptian Christianity* (p. 19)

"The appearance of the three stars in a line with Sirius occurred in the night sky over Egypt thousands of years ago, pointing to the horizon as the new sun was born at the winter solstice. Thus, it could be asserted that the three kings trailing the bright star announced the birth of the savior at the winter solstice in Egypt, ages prior to the same event purportedly taking place in Judea."

—StellarHousePublishing.com/star-east-three-kings.html

Other Elements and Symbols of the Christian Myth

In addition to the multitude already examined, there are many other aspects of the Bible and the Judeo-Christian tradition that derive from other, older cultures and mythologies. To outline them all would require another volume, which would include such concepts as Ash Wednesday, the Assumption of the Virgin, Gog and Magog, Son of Man, Immanuel and the Stations of the Cross, among others. Some of the more important symbols in the Christian myth are as follows.

The Alpha and Omega

In the gospel tale, Jesus is purported to be the "Alpha and Omega, the beginning and end," but these sentiments were plagiarized from older sources, including the Goddess Isis, in whose temple at Sais, Egypt, it was carved, "I am all that has been, that is, and that will be." As Walker says, "Alpha and omega, the first and last letters of the alphabet, were frequently applied to the Goddess who united in birth and death."[1470] The precession theme of Jesus Christ as the avatar of the New Age of Pisces also reflects this theme of the end of the previous Age of Aries and the beginning of the Age of Pisces.

Angels and Devils

The concepts of angels and devils in no way originated with Judaism or Christianity but are found in many other cultures around the globe. The Jews, in fact, took the names of some of their angels from the Persians.[1471]

Although Judaism and Christianity have portrayed them exclusively as male, a trend largely ignored by angel enthusiasts today, angels were originally considered female in several cultures, such as the Indian and Persian. Indeed, the seven archangels of Christianity are masculine remakes of the Seven Hathors of Egypt, which were female.[1472]

As part of the mythos, the good and bad angels (devils or demons) actually represent the *angles* or aspects of the zodiac, whose influences were determined to be either benevolent or malevolent. Often the concepts were inverted in Christianity, with daimons (Greek) and devas (India) imagined as good rather than evil entities.

Antichrist

The term "Antichrist" has been applied to numerous rulers and dissidents over the centuries. Because of the hideous and evil abuses of the Catholic Church for centuries, a number of popes were deemed "Anti-

1470 Walker, B. (1983), 195.
1471 Higgins, II, 88.
1472 Walker, B. (1983), 232-3.

christs," including Clement VII. Anyone who claims that Jesus Christ never existed could also be called "Antichrist," based on the statements in the letters from John. Eminent philosopher Friedrich Nietzsche was proud to claim, the title of Antichrist, because he viewed "Christ" as an icon of oppression and resentment. Although many people have been persecuted for denying Jesus Christ, Christ himself is made to say, "And every one who speaks a word against the Son of man will be forgiven" (Luke 12:10).

It is clear from biblical writings that during the early years of the Christian era, numerous "Christs" or messianic individuals were running about the Roman world, jockeying for position. These were such a threat to the "true" Christ's representatives that they felt the need to dispense with the competition by forging the Epistles of John sometime during the second century: "Children, it is the last hour; and as you have heard that antichrist is coming, so now many antichrists have come" (1 John 2:18).

Walker suggests the astral meaning of antichrist: "The Christian equivalent of the Chaldean Aciel, lord of the nether world, counterbalancing the solar god of heaven."[1473] In other words, it was the night sky.

Armageddon

In the earlier Persian version of the mythos, the devil Ahriman was to bring his legions against the holy nation, which in this case was Persia, or Iran, where Armageddon was to be fought. Thus, Armageddon is yet another ages-old concept that did not originate with Judaism, Christianity or the Bible.

Baptism

Baptism is quite common around the world, long predating the Christian era, as is evidenced by the fact that it was already in practice when Jesus encountered John the Baptist. As Massey says, "Baptismal regeneration, transfiguration, transubstantiation, the resurrection and ascension, were all Egyptian mysteries."[1474]

Baptism was done by the sprinkling of water or by immersion. It was also by "holy wind/spirit" and by fire, the latter quite popular in many parts of the world. It is especially associated with Persian Zoroastrianism. In the baptism by fire, the participant, willing or otherwise, is generally passed through the fire unharmed. Baptism by fire was still practiced as late as the last century in India and Scotland.[1475]

1473 Walker, B. (1983), 40.
1474 Massey, EBD, 80.
1475 Doane, 824.

Christmas

Many people today are aware that Christmas, December 25, is dated from the winter solstice and not the actual birthdate of the Jewish savior-god, yet writers continue to look for some other birthdate, because this must be one of the numerous significant "historical" facts somehow overlooked by the gospel writers. Over the centuries, a number of birthdates had been put forth until the Western church decided to incorporate the December 25 element of the typical sun god mythos, in large part to usurp the followers of Mithra who was born on that date, marking the rebirth of the sun three days after its symbolic death at the winter solstice, a pattern that gave rise to the Easter myth, with great importance for agrarian societies in their reliance on the seasons.

Many have noticed the December birthdate does not match the alleged circumstances of the birth, which could not have taken place in the winter, with "shepherds tending their flock in the fields," etc. A date earlier adopted in Christianity and still maintained by the Eastern Orthodox church is January 6, which, however, clashes just as badly with the biblical tale, since it is also in winter. Ben Yehoshua relates the origins of the January 6 date: "Originally the eastern Christians believed that [Jesus] was born on 6 January.... Osiris-Aion was said to be born of the virgin Isis on the 6 January and this explains this date for Christmas."

The early Western Church fathers assigned two birthdays to Jesus: One at Christmas (winter solstice) and the other at Easter (vernal equinox),[1476] which is to be expected, since these dates are not historical but are reflective of the various stages of the sun. The dual birthdate is found in Egyptian mythology as well, as Horus was said to have been born as a babe on December 25 as discussed by Macrobius in the *Saturnalia* and by Plutarch in *On Isis and Osiris*. The birth of Horus at the solstice is the only possible date, given his close association with the rising sun, which is metaphorically born at that time each year. Sir Norman Lockyer[1477] explains that many temples in Egypt dedicated to Horus are oriented to the position of the sunrise on the winter solstice to commemorate the birth of Horus, later reborn as a man on the vernal or spring equinox. March 25 is the date traditionally held as the resurrection of the Savior Adonis, as well as of Christ, as related by Byzantine writer Cedrenus:

> The first day of the month ... corresponds to the 25th of March ... On that day Gabriel saluted Mary, in order to make her conceive the Saviour.... On that very same day, our God Saviour (Christ Je-

1476 Massey, HJMC, 39.

1477 Lockyer, *The Dawn of Astronomy: A Study of the Temple Worship and Mythology of the Ancient Egyptians* (1894)

sus), after the termination of his career, arose from the dead; that is, what our forefathers called the Pass-over, or the passage of the Lord.[1478]

The "babe" aspect reflects the "smallness" of the sun in December (northern hemisphere), while the "man" born again or resurrected in spring signifies the sun passing over (Passover or "Crossification") the celestial equator, when the day and night are briefly equalized, and the day then begins to become longer than the night. Thus, it was said that the solar hero had two birthdays and two mothers.

Mangasarian concludes:

> The selection of the twentyfifth of December as [Jesus's] birthday is not only an arbitrary one, but that date, having been from time immemorial dedicated to the Sun, the inference is that the Son of God and the Sun of heaven enjoying the same birthday, were at one time identical beings. The fact that Jesus' death was accompanied with the darkening of the Sun, and that the date of his resurrection is also associated with the position of the Sun at the time of the vernal equinox, is a further intimation that we have in the story of the birth, death, and resurrection of Jesus, an ancient and nearly universal Sunmyth, instead of verifiable historical events.

The Cross and Crucifix

The cross and crucifix are very ancient symbols found around the world long prior to the supposed advent of the Christian savior. In the gospel story Jesus tells his disciples to "take up the cross" and follow him. Obviously, the cross already existed and was a well-known symbol, so that Jesus did not even have to explain this strange statement about an object that, we are led to believe, only gained significance after Jesus died on it. The pre-Christian reverence for the cross and the crucifix (e.g., the cross with a man on it), is admitted by the "holy Father" Minucius Felix (211):

> As for the adoration of the cross which you (Pagans) object against us (Christians) … that we neither adore crosses nor desire them; you it is, ye Pagans … who are the most likely people to adore wooden crosses … for what else are your ensigns, flags, and standards, but crosses gilt and beautiful. Your victorious trophies not only represent a simple cross, but a cross with a man on it.[1479]

The early Christians were actually repulsed by the image of a man

1478 Doane, 226.

1479 Doane, 197.

hanging on the cross, which was not adopted by the Christian church until the seventh century. In fact, the crucifix with a man on it had been imported to Rome from India ages before the Christian era. Indeed, as Walker states, "Early Christians even repudiated the cross because it was pagan.... Early images of Jesus represented him not on a cross, but in the guise of the Osirian or Hermetic 'Good Shepherd,' carrying a lamb."[1480] As Taylor recounts:

> On a Phoenician medal found in the ruins of Citium, and engraved in Dr. Clarke's *Travels*, and proved by him to be Phoenician, are inscribed not only the cross, but the rosary, or string of beads, attached to it, together with the identical *Lamb of God, which taketh away the sins of the world.*

The cross was also revered by the ancient people called the Pygmies. As A. Churchward relates:

> This primary Sign or Symbol, fashioned in the beginning by the African Pygmies to represent "The One Great Spirit," has been carried on by the various cults during human evolution, down to the present-day Cross of the Christian Doctrines; it has always represented the *One Great One*.[1481]

Churchward thus reveals that the Pygmies were very early monotheists, evidently thousands of years before the Judeo-Christian era. He also reveals the true meaning of the cross: "Fundamentally the Cross was astronomical. A Cross with equal arms denotes the time of equal day and night, and is a figure of the equinox."[1482] And, as Derek Partridge says, "What a cross with a circle in it ... truly represents is the sun waning or dying on the zodiac, and not a man."[1483] For more about the Pygmies read, "Pygmy Kitabu" (1973) by anthropologist Dr. Jean-Pierre Hallet, who spent 30 years living with the Pygmies and relates numerous detailed legends of the Pygmy people of the Ituri Forest in the Congo, including their origin and savior myths.

The cross is the celestial emblem of the sun but it also serves as a phallic symbol. As Carpenter relates, "The well-known T-shaped cross was in use in pagan lands long before Christianity, as a representation of the male member."[1484] Walker says, "The cross was also a male symbol of the phallic Tree of Life."[1485]

1480 Walker, B. (1983), 188.

1481 A. Churchward, 9.

1482 A. Churchward, 363.

1483 "The Naked Truth."

1484 Carpenter, 183.

1485 Walker, B. (1983), 188.

Of the Pagan origins of Christianity and the cross, Higgins concludes:

> Mr. Ledwick has observed that the presence of Heathen devices and crosses on the same coin are not unusual, as Christians in those early times were for the most part Semi pagans. This is diametrically opposed to all the doctrines of the Protestants about the early purity of the religion of Christ, and its subsequent corruption by the Romists.... In fact it is mere nonsense, for there can be no doubt that the cross was one of the most common of the Gentile symbols, and was adopted by the Christians *like all their other rites and ceremonies* from the Gentiles.[1486]

Easter

Summing up "Easter," historian Dr. Stephen Benko comments: "Our Good Friday and Easter celebrations are held at the same time in the spring when pagan mourners lamented the death of Attis and rejoiced at his resurrection."[1487]

Easter celebrations date back into remotest antiquity and are found around the world, as the blossoming of spring was a central concern of the ancients, who revered this life-renewing time of the year, when winter had passed and the sun was "born again," as the day became longer than night. Easter, is timed at the Passover, and Jesus represents the Passover Lamb ritually sacrificed every year by a number of cultures, including the Egyptians, possibly as early as 4,000 years ago and continuing to this day in some places. As ben Yehoshua relates:

> The occurrence of Passover at the same time of year as the pagan "Easter" festivals is not coincidental. Many of the Pessach customs were designed as Jewish alternatives to pagan customs. The pagans believed that when their nature god (such as Tammuz, Osiris or Attis) died and was resurrected, his life went into the plants used by man as food. The matza made from the spring harvest was his new body and the wine from the grapes was his new blood. In Judaism, matza was not used to represent the body of a god but the poor man's bread which the Jews ate before leaving Egypt.... When the early Christians noticed the similarities between Pessach customs and pagan customs, *they came full circle* and converted the Pessach customs *back* to their old pagan interpretations. The Seder became the last supper of Jesus, similar to the last supper of Osiris commemorated at the Vernal Equinox. The matza and wine once again became the body and

1486 Higgins, I, 219.
1487 Benko, 164.

blood of a false god, this time Jesus. Easter eggs are again eaten to commemorate the resurrection of a "god" and also the "rebirth" obtained by accepting his sacrifice on the cross.[1488]

Easter is "Pessach" in Hebrew, "Pascha" in Greek and "Pachons" in Latin, and "Pa-Khunsu" in Egypt, Khunsu being a name for Horus. As Massey says, "The festival of Khunsu, or his birthday, at the vernal equinox, was at one time celebrated on the twenty-fifth day of the month named after him, *Pa-Khunsu*."[1489] As Jackson states:

> The Easter ceremonies still performed in Greek and Roman Catholic churches in Europe are so similar to the ancient rites of the Adonic cult that Sir J.G. Frazer has concluded that these churches actually derived these rites from the ancient worshippers of Adonis.[1490]

And Walker relates:

> Christians ever afterward kept Easter Sunday with carnival processions derived from the mysteries of Attis. Like Christ, Attis arose when "the sun makes the day for the first time longer than the night." ... But the spring Holy Week was not really Christian. Its origin was a universal Indo-European tradition of extreme antiquity, probably traceable to the Holi festivals of India which celebrated the rebirth of spring with joyous orgies.[1491]

The Easter celebration was also found in Mexico, to the astonishment of the invading Catholics:

> According to the Franciscan monk Sahagun, our best authority on the Aztec religion, the sacrifice of the human god fell at Easter or a few days later, so that, if he is right, it would correspond in date as well as in character to the Christian festival of the death and resurrection of the Redeemer.... Women came forth with children in their arms and presented them to him, saluting him as a god. For "he passed for our Lord God; the people acknowledged him as the Lord."[1492]

In Anglo-Saxon, Easter or Eostre is goddess of the dawn, corresponding to Ishtar, Astarte, Astoreth and Isis. The word "Easter" shares the same root with "east" and "eastern," the direction of the rising sun.

Furthermore, the fact that there is no set date for Easter is only explainable within the mythos of the sun and moon and not as the histori-

---

1488 ben Yehoshua (emphasis added).
1489 Massey, HJMC, 35.
1490 Jackson, 58.
1491 Walker, B. (1983), 78–9.
1492 Frazer, 681.

cal death and resurrection of a savior-god. As Jackson relates:

> Everyone knows that Easter is a roving date in the calendar, since it is the first Sunday after the first full moon after the Vernal Equinox (the beginning of Spring). Easter, therefore, cannot be the date of the death of any historical personage. Two dates are given in the New Testament for the time of crucifixion, namely: the 14th and 15th of the month of Nisan. Why this discrepancy?
>
> The true explanation was given by Gerald Massey:
>
> > "The Synoptics say that Jesus was crucified on the 15th of the month of Nisan. John affirms that it was on the 14th of the month. This serious rift runs through the very foundation! … The crucifixion (or Crossing) was, and still is, determined by the full moon of Easter. This, in the lunar reckoning, would be on the 14th in a month of twenty-eight days; in the solar month of thirty days it was reckoned to occur on the 15th of the month. Both unite, and the rift closes in proving the Crucifixion to have been astronomical, just as it was in Egypt, where the two dates can be identified."[1493]

The date of Easter, when the godman was purportedly crucified and resurrected, was debated for centuries. One "distinguished churchman," as Eusebius calls him, Anatolius, reveals the meaning of Easter and of Christ, as well as the fact that astrology was a known and respected science used in Christianity, when he says:

> On this day [March 22] the sun is found not only to have reached the first sign of the Zodiac, but to be already passing through the fourth day within it. This sign is generally known as the first of the twelve, the equinoctial sign, the beginning of months, head of the cycle, and start of the planetary course.… Aristobolus adds that it is necessary at the Passover Festival that not only the sun but the moon as well should be passing through an equinoctial sign. There are two of these signs, one in spring, one in autumn, diametrically opposed to each other.[1494]

Heaven and Hell

The concepts of heaven and hell were not introduced by the Judeo-Christian tradition but existed for millennia in other cultures, such as in Persia and India. The Tibetans depict several levels of heaven and hell, which is a temporary state of mind, rather than enduring torture. The afterlife was also a common theme in the Egyptian theology, which tended to be more upbeat and less focused on the torments of hell. As

1493 Jackson, 197–8.
1494 Eusebius, 252-3.

Massey relates:

> The prototypes of hell and purgatory and the earthly paradise are all to be found in the Egyptian Amenta.... The Egyptian hell was not a place of everlasting pain, but of extinction of those who were wicked irretrievably. It must be admitted, to the honour and glory of the Christian deity, that a god of eternal torment is an ideal distinctly Christian, to which the Egyptians never did attain. Theirs was the all-parental god, Father and Mother in one whose heart was thought to bleed in every wound of suffering humanity, and whose son was represented in the character of the Comforter.[1495]

The word "Hell" is also derived from the European goddess Hel, whose womb was a place of immortality. The Christians demonized this womb and made it a place of eternal damnation, and, since volcanoes were considered entrances into the womb of Mother Earth, it became a fiery hell. The original Pagan hell had no fixed locality and was often situated in the same place as heaven.

The nature of hell has thus varied with the culture and era. Some cultures thought hell was the harsh winter; thus, it was located near the South Pole, the "bottomless pit," from which winter was thought to come. This version of hell is reflected in the Christian scriptures: Matthew and Jude both speak of a hell of darkness, while Matthew also refers to a hell of light/fire. Matthew also speaks of a hell where the body and soul are annihilated, and one where the soul is punished for eternity. In the Bible in general, hell is depicted as being limited yet endless; it is upper *and* lower. Hell is also biblically portrayed as a lake of fire and brimstone, yet a bottomless pit, etc.

The descent into hell by the savior is a common occurrence within many mythologies, found in the stories of Adonis, Bacchus, Balder, Hercules, Horus, Jesus, Krishna, Mercury, Osiris, Quetzalcoatl and Zoroaster.[1496] This part of the mythos represents the sun entering into the womb of darkness, nightly and seasonally. The sun, of course, is the only expert on hell who has returned to tell about it; hence, it is the sun who is the immortal authority on the afterlife. Graves interprets the meaning of hell within the mythos in terms of the sun:

> The word astronomers use to indicate the sun in its high point of ascension is perihelion [the date each year when the earth is closest to the sun]. Now you may notice there is a Hell in this word (peri-*hel*-ion); at least it can be traced to Hell, or Hell

1495 Massey, EBD, 107–9.
1496 Doane, 214–5.

> to it. *Hel*ion, the last part of this word was pronounced by the Greeks *Elios*, and is synonymous with Acheron, which is generally translated Hell. So that we have "peri," which means around, about, and "helion," *Hell*—that is, the sun roundabout Hell.[1497]

Basically, the concepts of eternal heaven and hell have been utilized to suit the needs of the manipulating priests, who sell their wares by means of greed for heaven and fear of hell. As Doane says:

> *Heaven* was born of the sky, and nurtured by cunning priests, who made man a coward and a slave. *Hell* was built by priests, and nurtured by the fears and servile fancies of man during the ages when dungeons of torture were a recognized part of every government, and when God was supposed to be an infinite tyrant, with infinite resources of vengeance.[1498]

The Holy Ghost

In many cultures, the Holy Ghost was considered female, as Sophia, Sapientia, or Hokmah—Wisdom—"but the patriarchy masculinized it."[1499] As Christ was the sun, the Holy Ghost was the moon, which was often considered female.[1500] Although the Holy Ghost is a cherished concept, representing God's very spirit and goodness, Wheless remarks:

> The "Holy Ghost" itself, it is claimed by the Bible and the Church, inspired and decreed by positive command all the bloody murders and tortures by the priests from Moses to the last one committed; and the spirit of them lives and is but hibernating to-day. The Holy God of Israel, whose name is Merciful, thus decreed on Sinai: "He that sacrificeth to any gods [elohim], save unto Yahweh only, he shall be utterly destroyed" (Ex. xxii, 20).[1501]

The Holy Grail

The cup or chalice used by Christ in the biblical tale to convey "his blood" was, like so many other "relics," considered to possess magical powers of the highest kind. Thus the "Holy Grail" became the object of much attention and many bloody "quests" for those seeking such powers. Of course, there was no "real" Grail, but this fact did not stop anyone from either looking for it or claiming they already possessed it. Of the frenzy surrounding the Holy Grail, Walker says:

> If the Grail was nothing more than the cup of Christ's blood,

1497 Graves, BS, 78–9.
1498 Doane, 391.
1499 Walker, WDSSO, 219.
1500 Walker, WDSSO, 287.
1501 Wheless, *IISGW*

> then there was no reason for the great Quest at all. The cup of Christ's blood was readily available to all, in every chapel; and even though it was called a holy sacrament, its discovery somehow lacked thrills. As matters turn out, to Christianize the Grail was to neutralize the magnetism of its secret nature.[1502]

Naturally, the Grail myth existed prior to the Christian era. As Walker also relates:

> The real origins of the Holy Grail were not Christian but pagan. The Grail was first Christianized in Spain from a sacred tradition of the Moors. Like the Celts' holy Cauldron of Regeneration, which it resembled, the blood-filled vessel was a womb symbol meaning rebirth in the Oriental or Gnostic sense of reincarnation. Its connotation was feminine, not masculine.[1503]

The temple where the Grail was kept was in actuality not localized on Earth but in the heavens, surrounded by the 72 "chapels" or decans of the zodiac. Graham gives the "deep astrological" meaning of the Grail:

> The first decanate of Leo is the Crater, or Cup, the solar crucible; the second is Centaurus, the soldier on horseback. It was of this Cup the Sun of God drank, and it was this soldier that bound him and led him away to be crucified on Golgotha, Egypt, Earth.[1504]

The Holy Land

Rather than being a designation of a particular place on Earth, the "Holy Land" is the direction of east, "the place of coming forth," where the sun god Horus appears.[1505]

Ichthys, the Fish

As we have seen, Jesus is the solar avatar of the Age of Pisces, the Fishes. Dujardin relates the origin of the Fish and its identification with Jesus:

> This title [Ichthus, the Fish] was a survival of the primitive cults of the time when the gods had the form of animals.... The following facts are significant: (1) Jesus is actually called the Fish, Ichthus. (2) He is represented in the form of a fish in the Catacombs. (3) Tertullian calls him "our fish." (4) Heretical sects worshipped him as "the serpent," into which animal Jahvehism transformed the primitive fish-god.... (5) The cult of the fish is attested by the story of the loaves and fishes in the Gospels....

1502 Walker, B. (1983), 354.
1503 Walker, B. (1983), 354.
1504 Graham, 354–5.
1505 A. Churchward, 290.

> The patriarch Joshua, who was plainly an ancient god of Palestine and bore the same name as the god of Christianity, is called the son of Nun, which signifies "son of the fish."[1506]

Augustine said of Jesus, "he is a fish of the living water."[1507]

The Lamb of God

As we have seen, a number of godmen around the world have been considered the "Lamb of God." This ubiquitous designation is not reflective of hordes of historical saviors but is another aspect of the mythos, dealing with the sun in the Age of Aries. During the Age of Taurus, the Bull motif was ever-present, while in the age of Aries it was the Lamb: "Afterward the Ram or Lamb became an object of adoration, when, in his turn, he opened the equinox, to deliver the world from the wintry reign of darkness and evil."[1508]

When the sun was in Taurus, the bull was sacrificed, and in Aries, it was the lamb or ram. Christianity was created as the sun moved into Pisces, hence the fish symbol and the fisherman motif. Yet the old title of "Lamb of God" remained attached to Christ, and at Easter orthodox Christians still slaughter lambs, in holding with the ancient Pagan rituals. The slaughter of fish, apparently, is not bloody enough for blood-atonement purposes. Since the symbol of the coming Age of Aquarius is a "man carrying a pitcher of water" (Luke 22:10), we certainly should hope religionists will not begin to sacrifice bottled water deliverers or waiters.

The Logia (Sayings), Sermon on the Mount, Beatitudes and Parables

Over the millennia much has been made of the "Sayings" or Logia of Jesus, also known as the "Sayings of the Savior," "Sayings of the Sage" ("Logoi Sophon"), the "Gnomologue," the "Oracles of Jesus/the Savior," the "Hebrew Oracles," the "Oracles of Matthew," which are one of the two main subdivisions of the gospels, the other being the narrative. The sayings or logia constituted one of the many shared texts used separately by the evangelists in the creation of the gospels. This logia collection was eventually publicized as the "Gospel of Q," or just plain "Q," for *Quelle* in German, meaning "source." Q scholars have distinguished three successive strata of the sayings, Q^1, Q^2 and Q^3. In other words, the original Q collection was twice expanded with more explicitly Christian sayings. Dismissing virtually the entire gospel story as mythical, Q scholarship attempts to find the "real" Jesus in a handful

1506 Dujardin, 53–4.
1507 Higgins, I, 636.
1508 Pike, 448.

of sayings from Q^1. It should be noted that the initial logia, constituting Q^1, do not have any Jewish affiliation except the word "Solomon," and that Q^2 and Q^3 only mention the Pharisees and not Sadducees.

In finding a "historical Jesus" in Q^1, historicizers are thus left with a "man" who "was first remembered as a Cynic sage and only later imagined as a prophet who uttered apocalyptic warnings."[1509] However, in reducing Jesus to a handful of logia we are left with nearly verbatim sayings from manuscripts preceding the Christian era, demonstrating that this Q Jesus already existed, non-historically and mystically, for centuries if not millennia. In other words, the *Logia Iesou*, as they are called in Greek, are not, as has been supposed, the "genuine" sayings of the "historical" Jesus but represent orally transmitted traditions common in the various brotherhoods and mystery schools long before Christianity was created.

Various gospel texts are in fact repetitions of the sayings of Horus, as the Word, or Iu-em-hept, 3,000 years before the Christian version.[1510] As Massey states:

> The "sayings" were common property in the mysteries ages before they were ever written down.... The "logia" in the twenty-fifth chapter of Matthew reproduce not only the sayings, but also the scenery of the Last Judgment in the Great Hall of Justice, represented in the [Egyptian] Book of the Dead.[1511]

Just as the gospel writers and church fathers claimed the logia or "oracles" were recorded by Matthew, so were the sayings of Osiris recorded by the scribe Taht-*Matiu*. In addition, the logia are those of Dionysus, serving as part of "the mysteries" found at Samothrace, for one.

Some of the sayings constitute the famous "Sermon on the Mount," also not original with Christ. Horus also delivered a Sermon on the Mount, and there is within the Egyptian Hermetic or Trismesgistic tradition a discourse called "The Secret Sermon on the Mount."[1512] The Egyptian Sermon sayings also found their way into the Old Testament. As Robertson says, "As for the Sermon on the Mount, of which so much is made, it is no more than a patchwork of utterances found in the Old Testament."[1513] Carpenter elaborates:

> The "Sermon on the Mount" which, with the "Lord's Prayer"

1509 Mack, 47.
1510 Massey, HJMC, 151.
1511 Massey, HJMC, 152-3. The sayings composing the Olivet Discourse in Matthew 25 do not form part of Q but instead depend on material original to Mark.
1512 Mead, DJL.
1513 Robertson, 64.

embedded in it, forms the great and accepted repository of "Christian" teaching and piety, is well known to be a collection of sayings from pre-Christian writings, including the Psalms, Isaiah, Ecclesiasticus, the *Secrets of Enoch*, the *Shemoneh Esrei* (a book of Hebrew prayers), and others.[1514]

Potter adds:

> Among the words of Jesus, you will recognize that much of the "Sermon on the Mount," especially the fifth chapter of Matthew, also the thirteenth of Mark and its parallels in the other gospels, sometimes called "The Little Apocalypse," seem almost verbatim quotations from the Books of Enoch, the Book of Jubilees, and the Testament of the Twelve Patriarchs.[1515]

A number of the elements or beatitudes of the Sermon are found in the doctrines of the pre-Christian Nazarenes, such as "Blessed are the poor in spirit, for theirs is the kingdom of heaven." As Massey states:

And these, for example, are amongst the "sayings" in the Book of the Nazarenes. "Blessed are the peacemakers, the just, and 'faithful.'" "Feed the hungry; give drink to the thirsty; clothe the naked." "When thou makes a gift, seek no witness whereof, to mar thy bounty. Let thy right hand be ignorant of the gifts of the left." Such were common to all the Gnostic Scriptures, going back to the Egyptian.

The sayings of the Lord were pre-historic, as the sayings of David (who was an earlier Christ), the sayings of Horus the Lord, of Elija the Lord, of Mana the Lord, of Christ the Lord, as the divine directions conveyed by the ancient teachings. As the "Sayings of the Lord" they were collected in Aramaic to become the *nuclei* of the earliest Christian gospel according to Matthew. So says Papias. At a later date they were put forth as the original revelation of a personal teacher, and were made the foundation of the historical fiction concocted in the four gospels that were canonized at last.

No matter who the plagiarist may be, the teaching now held to be divine was drawn from older human sources, and palmed off under false pretenses.... Nothing new remained to be inculcated by the Gospel of the new teacher, who is merely made to repeat the old sayings with a pretentious air of supernatural authority; the result being that the true sayings of old are, of necessity, conveyed to later times in a delusive manner.... The most important proclamations assigned to Jesus turned out to be false. The kingdom of God was not at hand; the world was not nearing its end; the catastrophe foretold never occurred; the

1514 Carpenter, 213.

1515 Potter, 169–70.

second coming was no more actual than the first; the lost sheep of Israel are not yet saved.[1516]

Many of the concepts contained in the logia/sayings, which are held up by Christian defenders as the core of Jesus's teachings and a reflection of his goodness and compassion, can also be found in the Vedas as spoken by the compassionate Krishna and in the Dhammapada attributed to the equally compassionate Buddha, as well as in the Tao Te Ching of the Chinese sage Lao Tzu (sixth century BCE).[1517]

Likewise, a number of Jesus's parables were derived from Buddhism and from the very ancient Indian sect of Jainism, such as those of the prodigal son and the sower.[1518] As Larson says, "We must thus summarize the basic teachings of Jesus, none of which were original to Him."[1519]

The Lord's Prayer

As concerns the supposed originality of the "Lord's Prayer," which is presented as having come clear out of the blue from the very mouth of the Lord Himself, Wheless says it best:

> Like the whole "Sermon on the Mount," the Prayer is a composite of ancient sayings of the Scripture strung together to form it, as the marginal crossreferences show throughout.

We might add that the "Scripture" referred to by Wheless is not only from the Old Testament but is part of the ancient mythos/ritual: "the Lord's Prayer was a collection of sayings from the Talmud, many derived from earlier Egyptian prayers to Osiris."[1520] Walker also relates that the Lord's Prayer was once the Lady's Prayer: "The plea for daily bread incorporated into the Lord's Prayer must have been a plea to the Goddess in earlier times, for she was always the giver of bread, the Grain Mother."[1521]

The Logos or Word

Jesus is called the "Word" or, "Logos," which, although it appears mysterious and mystical to the uninitiated, is actually commonplace in Greek parlance, as it has many meanings, including "word," "speech," "rumor" and "reason." The logos is in actuality a primitive concept, reflecting the way in which God created the world (i.e., through speech). The Logos concept is not new with Christianity but is applied to a num-

1516 Massey, GHC, 4–11.
1517 Steele, "Was Jesus a Taoist?"
1518 Larson, 349.
1519 Larson, 411.
1520 Walker, B. (1983), 469.
1521 Walker, WDSSO, 482.

ber of older deities in mythologies from the Mediterranean to China. Pike relates:

> The Word is also found in the Phoenician Creed. As in all those of Asia, a Word of God, written in starry characters, by the planetary Divinities, and communicated by the Demi-Gods, as a profound mystery, to the higher classes of the human race, to be communicated by them to mankind, created the world.[1522]

Of the Logos-Jesus concept in the Gospel of John, Wheless says:

> [There] can be no more positive and convincing proof that the Christ was and is a Pagan Myth—the old Greek "Logos" of Heraclitus and the Philosophers revamped by the Greek priest who wrote the first chapter of the "Gospel according to St. John" and worked up into the "Incarnate Son" of the old Hebrew God for Christian consumption as the most sacred Article of the Christian Faith and Theology.... Thus confessedly [in the *Catholic Encyclopedia*] is the Divine Revelation of the "Word made flesh" a Pagan-Jewish Myth, and the very Pagan Demiurge is the Christian Christ—"Very God"—and the "Second Person of the Blessed Trinity."[1523]

Lucifer

Isaiah 14:12–15 contains much astrotheological thought: The "day star" or *heylel* attempts to "ascend to heaven" and "raise my throne above the stars of God," to "ascend above the heights of the clouds" and "make myself like the Most High," at which point he is "brought down to Sheol, to the depths of the Pit." Here the phrase "Most High" is *Elyown*. The Hebrew word הילל or *heylel* is defined (*Strong's* H1966) as "Lucifer='light-bearer'; 1) shining one, morning star, Lucifer; a) of the king of Babylon and Satan." *Heylel* is rendered in the Greek LXX as ὁ ἑωσφόρος or Heosphoros, the name of the Greek god of "dawn bearing." Although *Strong's* does not define it as such, this term "morning star" is taken to refer to the planet Venus, but it also could be the other "day star," the sun, with whom Lucifer the "light bearer" was likewise identified.

The full title at Isaiah 14:12 is "Heylel ben Shachar," the "morning star, son of the dawn," whereas Shachar is the name of an Ugaritic god, the son of El.[1524] As Drs. Adela Yarbro Collins and John J. Collins comment: "That which comes forth at, or from, Dawn is the sun, the primary

---

1522 Pike, 268.
1523 Wheless, 155–6.
1524 Collins, 18

image for the deity in the Egyptian tradition."[1525] Therefore, Lucifer is the sun.

Concerning Isaiah 14:12–15, Botterweck remarks "this poem is likely based on a Canaanite myth recounting the rebellion of the deities Shahar and Shalim, manifestations of the Day Star Ashtar, against *'ēl 'elyôn* in an unsuccessful attempt to dethrone him. Thus, we have a respected Christian authority admitting that at least some of the Bible represents Canaanite mythology, rather than a record of what God revealed directly to the Israelites. How much more of the Bible is constituted by the *mythology* of the peoples of the region?

Although much is made of Lucifer, the "fallen angel," his name only appears translated as such in one verse in the King James Bible, at Isaiah 14:12, where he is called "son of the morning." "Lucifer" is also translated as "Day Star, son of Dawn." This passage describes the day star's "fall from heaven" after he attempts to "ascend to heaven; above the stars of God" to set his throne. From this single passage, an enormous tale has taken shape, with all sorts of speculation as to who Lucifer "really" was, including everything from the leader of the devils to that of evil aliens.

Despite all the political intrigue, Lucifer simply means "Light Bearer," and he was in earliest times a sun god, which is why he is called "Day Star, son of morning/dawn." The sun god Lucifer is "cast out of heaven" by the other angels, or stars, as night descends. This god/angel Lucifer is pre-Hebraic, found in Canaan, Egypt and Mesopotamia, and was not originally considered evil. Like the many gods of other cultures, Lucifer was vilified by the Christians so they could raise their own god above him. Ironically, since both are the day or morning star, Jesus and Lucifer are in fact one and the same.

The Lucifer myth can also be found in the Greek story of the "son of the sun," Phaeton, who was cast out of heaven by his Father after committing the crime of hubris. The story of Vulcan, the Roman solar god, is similar to the Lucifer myth, as he, too, is cast out of heaven by the gods as darkness descends.

Melchizedek

The mysterious king of Salem, Melchizedek, is mentioned in the Old Testament as the priest of the Most High God (El Elyon) who blessed Abraham. In the Epistle to the Hebrews, Jesus is named as a priest "after the order of Melchizedek," a passage serving to establish the Order of Melchizedek as the ultimate authority, beyond Abraham and Jesus. In fact, the Christian Gnostics considered Melchizedek a savior-god

1525 Collins, 18

higher than Jesus: "Melchizedek was the savior for angels, while Christ was only the savior for men."[1526]

Like that of so many other biblical characters, the identity of Melchizedek can be found in the pre-Yahwist cultures of the Levant. As Walker states, "Jeru-Salem was 'the House of Peace,' or of the god Salem, whose earlier city was ruled by Melchizedek (Genesis 14), the 'King of Light' called Molech in Phoenicia."[1527] Molech is the sun and fire god, originally from Persia and India, and worshipped by the Canaanites.[1528] The Molech/Melek cult also flourished in Paul's purported hometown of Tarsus, as Heracles-Melkart.[1529] and other Israelites worshipped Moloch/Molech/Melek/Milcom/Melchom:

> *Moloch* was a god of the Ammonites, also worshiped among the Israelites. Solomon built a temple to him, on the Mount of Olives, *and human sacrifices were offered to him*.[1530]

Sacrifice to Moloch/Molech was by burning, and when the "sons of Judah" thus incinerated their children (Jer. 7:31), drums were beaten and instruments were played to drown out the screams.

Though vilified by the Yahwists, as Walker says, "For a while, Molech was identified with Yahweh.... Levite priests eventually distinguished Yahweh from Molech and forbade the latter's worship (Lev. 18:21)."[1531]

The baptism of Molech was likewise by fire, which is why Christ, as high priest of the Order of Melchizedek, was said to baptize by fire (Matt 3:11). It is this baptism by fire, as well as immolation by fire, as in burnt offerings, that distinguishes the Order of Melchizedek; hence, when mention of the Order is made in the Bible, it serves as a reference to these rites, the practitioners of which are considered the "true" priesthood.

The Nativity

The birth celebration or nativity of the great savior existed as a ritual long prior to the Christian era. As Frazer says:

> The ritual of the nativity, as it appears to have been celebrated in Syria and Egypt, was remarkable. The celebrants retired into certain inner shrines, from which at midnight they issued a loud cry, "The Virgin has brought forth! The light is waxing!" The

1526 Walker, B. (1983), 631.
1527 Walker, B. (1983), 885.
1528 Higgins, I, 82.
1529 Walker, B. (1983), 1003.
1530 Doane, 108 fn.
1531 Walker, B. (1983), 1003.

> Egyptians even represented the new-born sun by the image of an infant which on his birthday, the winter solstice, they brought forth and exhibited to his worshippers.[1532]

Hazelrigg explains the meaning within the mythos of the nativity and the rest of the sacred king drama:

> The Nativity, the Betrayal, the Crucifixion, and the Resurrection are but quarterly stages in the mystic journey, expressed as a geometrical ratio in natural physics—ever the same whether applied to the four quarters of the day, the four lunar phases, the four cardinal points or seasons in the solar revolution.[1533]

The Sabbath

The Sabbath predates the Jewish religion and is found in the Middle East and India, where it signified the seventh-day rest of the Hindu Mother-Goddess Durga.[1534] Ignorant of its origins, the various Christian sects have been squabbling for centuries as to when the Sabbath should be observed, as ordained by the Jewish god Yahweh. The "purists," such as Seventh Day Adventists, believe that the Sabbath is to be observed on Saturday, rather than the "Pagan" day of Sunday adopted by the "corrupt" Catholic Church; however, Saturday is also a "Pagan" day, named for "Saturn." As Doane relates:

> The planet *Saturn* very early became the chief deity of Semitic religion. Moses consecrated the number seven to him.... "The *Seventh* day was sacred to *Saturn* throughout the east." ... "Saturn's day was made sacred to God, and the planet is now called *cochab shabbath*, 'The Sabbath Star.' The sanctification of the Sabbath is clearly connected with the word Shabua or Sheba, i.e., *seven*."[1535]

The Second Coming/Day of Judgment

Although billions of Christian believers over the centuries have been waiting endlessly for the Second Coming of Jesus, the "second coming" has been expected of numerous savior-gods, including Krishna, Buddha, Bacchus, Quetzalcoatl and others around the world. The same can be said of the end of the world, the millennium and the Day of Judgment. Of the Day of Judgment, Doane relates: "Prof. Carpenter, referring to the Egyptian Bible—which is by far the most ancient of all holy books—says: 'In the "Book of Dead," there are used the very phrases we find in the New Testament, *in connection with the day of*

1532 Frazer, 416.
1533 Hazelrigg, 16.
1534 Walker, WDSSO, 191.
1535 Doane, 393 fn.

judgment.'"[1536] The "Second Coming," in fact, is the return of the sun in a new precessional age. In his First Coming Jesus Christ was imagined as avatar of the zodiac age of Pisces, while the authors of the Gospels imagined the Second Coming of Jesus Christ as the dawn of the age of Aquarius.

The Seventy/Seventy-Two

The number of disciples is represented variously in the gospels, from 12 to 70 to 72. This numerical trio can be explained by the mythos and not as history. To begin with, "72" was often rounded off to 70, so the two numbers are interchangeable. Tradition holds that there are 72 names of God,[1537] which is appropriate, since 72 is yet another sacred number, the reason there are also 72 nations in the tenth chapter of Genesis. Like Jesus, Confucius (sixth century BCE) had 72 initiated disciples.[1538] Furthermore, the 72 are the same accomplices of Set who plotted the death of Osiris.

The 72 actually represent the decans or dodecani, divisions of the zodiacal circle into 5° each, also considered constellations. It takes 72 (71.62) years for the precession of the equinoxes to move one degree, possibly explaining the ambiguity between 70 and 72. The story of Jacob's Ladder with 72 ascending and descending angels is actually a reflection of the zodiac and the angles of the decans. Furthermore, the magical pentagram or pentacle is made from the division of the decans. Regarding the pentacle, the number 72 and the legendary 72 translators of the Hebrew Bible into Greek, Walker says:

> To draw a pentacle, one divides a circle into five arcs of seventy-two degrees each. Seventy-two is the prime magic number.... So magical was 72 that one of the most durable myths about the origin of the Bible called it the Book of the Seventy (Septuagint), claiming that it had been translated from Hebrew to Greek in the third century BC by seventy-two scholars simultaneously, and that each version was precisely the same as all seventy-one others. This silly story was an article of Christian faith throughout the Middle Ages.[1539]

In Gnostic texts, the chariot of Ezekiel is the wheel of the zodiac with the 72 dodecans, representing the "chariot of the Sun." Doresse relates the Gnostic interpretation: "The chariot, we are told, has been taken for a model by the seventy-two gods who govern the seventy-two

1536 Doane, 245.
1537 Higgins, I, 780.
1538 Higgins, I, 789.
1539 Walker, WDSSO, 73.

languages of the peoples."[1540]

Transubstantiation

The doctrine of transubstantiation, found at 1 Corinthians 10–12, represents the miraculous transformation of bread and wine into the body and blood of Christ in the ritual of the eucharist. However, this sort of magical ritual was practiced around the world in a variety of forms eons before the Christian era and is, therefore, in no way original to Christianity:

> [The] ancient Mexicans, even before the arrival of Christianity, were fully acquainted with the doctrine of transubstantiation and acted upon it in the solemn rites of their religion. They believed that by consecrating bread their priests could turn it into the very body of their god, so that all who thereupon partook of the consecrated bread entered into a mystic communion with the deity by receiving a portion of his divine substance into themselves. The doctrine of transubstantiation, or the magical conversion of bread into flesh, was also familiar to the Aryans of ancient India long before the spread and even the rise of Christianity.[1541]

This practice has been considered barbaric and savage by non-Catholic Christians and other religionists, not to mention ludicrous by non-religionists. The pre-Christian ancients knew that the transubstantiation was allegorical, not actual: "'When we call corn Ceres and wine Bacchus,' says Cicero, 'we use a common figure of speech; but do you imagine that anybody is so insane as to believe that the thing he feeds upon is a god?'"[1542]

The Trinity

The Trinity or triune deity is yet another aspect of the ubiquitous mythos, found in countless other cultures long prior to the Christian era. Obviously, then, the concept did not originate with Jesus; in fact, it was not formally adopted into Christianity until the Council of Nicea in 325. Like so many aspects of Christianity, The trinity was originally found in the Egyptian religion. As Albert Churchward says:

> Such mysteries as the Trinity, the Incarnation, and the Virgin Birth, the Transfiguration on the Mount, the Passion, Death, Burial, Resurrection and Ascension, Transubstantiation and Baptismal Regeneration, were all extant in the mysteries of Amenta

---

1540 Doresse, 166.
1541 Frazer, 568.
1542 Frazer, 578.

with Horus or Iu-em-Hotep as the Egyptian Jesus.[1543]

Jacolliot argues that the Trinity is also of Indian origin: "The Trinity in Unity, rejected by Moses, became afterwards the foundation of Christian theology, which incontestably acquired it from India."

Over the millennia, the Trinity took different forms: all-female, all-male and mixed. The earliest trinities in many places were all-female. As Walker relates:

> From the earliest ages, the concept of the Great Goddess was a trinity and the model for all subsequent trinities, female, male or mixed.... Even though Brahmans evolved a male trinity of Brahma, Vishnu, and Shiva to play these parts [of Creator, Preserver and Destroyer], Tantric scriptures insisted that the Triple Goddess had created these gods in the first place.... The Middle East had many trinities, most originally female. As time went on, one or two members of the triad turned male. The usual pattern was FatherMotherSon, the Son figure envisioned as a Savior.... Among Arabian Christians there was apparently a holy trinity of God, Mary, and Jesus, worshipped as an interchangeable replacement for the Egyptian trinity of Osiris, Isis, and Horus.[1544]

In the solar mythos, the Trinity also represents the sun in three stages: Newborn (dawn), mature (full-grown at 12 noon), and "old and dying, at the end of the day (going back to the Father)."[1545]

The Trinity is even found in Peru, a fact that prompted the perturbed Rev. Father Acosta to remark:

> It is strange that the devil after his manner has brought a Trinity into idolatry, for the three images of the sun called Apomti, Churunti, and Intiquaoqui, signify Father and Lord Sun, the Son Sun, and the Brother Sun.

In reality, these infamous "devil" comments are reflective of sheer cultural and racial bigotry, not to mention the appalling ignorance and stupidity of those supposedly entrusted by the "omniscient and omnipotent Lord God" with the instruction of the entire human race.

Thus we discover that the most important tenets, doctrines and other elements of the gospel story and Christian religion are unoriginal and mythological. Indeed, the onion of the "historical Jesus" has been peeled, and there remains no core to be found, only the pre-Christian mythos and ritual.

1543 A. Churchward, 393.
1544 Walker, B. (1983), 1018.
1545 Leedom, 200.

The Patriarchs and Saints Are the Gods of Other Cultures

Christianity was built upon a long line of myths from a multitude of nations and basically represents the universal astrological mythos and ritual. Crucial in its creation was a typical mythmaking device that when an invading culture takes over its predecessors, it often vilifies the preceding gods and goddesses or demotes them to lesser gods, patriarchs, prophets, kings, heroes and/or saints. Such mythmaking is found throughout the Old Testament: the "prophets" Daniel, Esther and Deborah began as ancient gods of other cultures. Prior to the vilification of the Baals of Canaan, Yahweh himself was a Baal. In fact, the Old Testament actually records the epics of Canaanite gods, as the 1975 discovery of 20,000 clay tablets nearly 4,500 years old in the ruins of the large city of Ebla (at Tell Mardikh in northwestern Syria) revealed. Of Ebla, John Fulton says, "It existed 1,000 years before David and Solomon and was destroyed by the Akkadians in around 1600 BC."[1546]

The language of these tablets is old Canaanite, very similar to biblical Hebrew, written in the Sumerian cuneiform script. These tablets contain hundreds of place names, a number of which are found in the Old Testament, including "Urusalima" (i.e., Jerusalem). They also contain the names of Hebrew "patriarchs" who, according to the Bible, would not exist for hundreds to over a thousand years later, such as "Ab-ra-mu (Abraham), E-sa-um (Esau), Ish-ma-ilu (Ishmael), even Is-ra-ilu (Israel), and from later periods, names like Da-'u'dum (David) and Sa-'u-lum (Saul)."[1547] The tablets also contain the Canaanite creation and flood myths from which the very similar biblical versions were obviously plagiarized. In reality, the Israelites were mainly Canaanites, passing along the myths of their ancestors, which were corrupted over the centuries.

Dujardin outlines the process by which "Baals" or "foreign" gods were changed into Hebrew patriarchs, kings, prophets and heroes:

1. The ancient divinities of Palestine are transformed by the Bible into historical characters and turned into servants of Jahveh.

2. Their sanctuaries are turned into sanctuaries raised by them to Jahveh, or into tombs where they are buried, or into monuments of their exploits. Sometimes, however, their names, or those of the animals that they had been originally, were given to a place, and were no longer used except to denote it.

3. The names of the clans, derived from these divinities and from the names of animals that they had originally been, became the names of persons, and were introduced into the interminable genealogies invented

1546 "A New Chronology—Synopsis of David Rohl's book A Test of Time"
1547 http://marlowe.wimsey.com/~rshand/streams/thera/canaan.html

to glorify great families of the Jewish state. All this was by way of assimilation.

4. Proscription was effected by devoting to abomination all the cults that offered resistance.

5. Also, by making impure such animals as had originally been ancient gods, by forbidding the eating of them, or by putting a curse on them.

6. And by transforming some of the rites and myths of these cults into historical legends.[1548]

In this manner, ancient gods of other nations were mutated into not only biblical individuals but also tribes and nations.

Noah and the Flood

The fable of Noah purports to be the true story of the progenitor of the human race; however, like so many other biblical characters, Noah is a myth, found earlier in India, Egypt, Babylon, Sumer and other places. The fact is that there have been floods and deluge stories in many different parts of the world, including but not limited to the Middle East. As Churchward says:

> There was never any *one Great Deluge* as in the Biblical rendering.... at least ten Great Deluges have taken place at each glacial epoch, when the snow and ice have melted.... There was also a great inundation once a year—when the Nile came down in flood. There is a portrayal on the monuments where Num is in his boat or Ark waiting for this flood.[1549]

Regarding the ubiquitous flood myth, Walker says:

> The biblical flood story, the "deluge," was a late offshoot of a cycle of flood myths known everywhere in the ancient world. Thousands of years before the Bible was written, an ark was built by the Sumerian Ziusudra. In Akkad, the flood hero's name was Atrakhasis. In Babylon, he was UtaNapishtim, the only mortal to become immortal. In Greece he was Deucalion, who repopulated the earth after the waters subsided [and after the ark landed on Mt. Parnassos].... In Armenia, the hero was Xisuthros—a corruption of Sumerian Ziusudra—whose ark landed on Mount Ararat. According to the original Chaldean account, the flood hero was told by his god, "Build a vessel and finish it. By a deluge I will destroy substance and life. Cause thou to go up into the vessel the substance of all that has life."[1550]

Xisuthros or Ziusudra was considered the "10th king," while Noah

---

1548 Dujardin, 82-3.

1549 A. Churchward, 353.

1550 Walker, B. (1983), 315.

was the "10th patriarch." Noah's "history" can also be found in India, where there is a "tomb of Nuh" near the river Gagra in the district of Oude or Oudh, which may be related to Judea and Judah. The "ark-preserved" Indian Noah was also called "Menu." Noah is also called "Nnu" and "Naue," as in "Joshua son of Nun/Jesus son of Naue," meaning not only fish but also water, as in the waters of heaven.

Noah's famous "ark," which misguided souls have sought upon the earth, is a motif found in other myths. As Doane relates, "The image of Osiris of Egypt was by the priests shut up in a sacred ark on the 17th of Athyr [Nov. 13], the very day and month on which Noah is said to have entered his ark."[1551] Noah is, in fact, another solar myth, and the ark represents the sun entering into the "moon-ark," the Egyptian "*argha*," which is the crescent or arc-shaped lunette or lower quarter of the moon. This "*argha* of Noah" is the same as Jason's "Argonaut" and "*arghanatha*" in Sanskrit.[1552] Noah's ark and its eight "sailors" are equivalent to the heavens, earth and the seven "planets" (i.e., those represented by the days of the week). As to the "real" Noah's ark, it should be noted that it was a custom, in Scotland for one, to create stone "ships" on mounts in emulation of the mythos, and many of these "arks" are still to be found.

Like Noah, the Sumerian Ziusudra had three sons, including one named "Japetosthes," essentially the same as Noah's son Japheth, also related to Pra-japati[1553] or Jvapeti, son of the Indian Menu, whose other sons possessed virtually the same names as those of Noah (i.e., Shem and Ham). As Hazelrigg says, "These parallel the Hindu version of the same myth, wherein *Menu Satyvrah* figures as Noah, and *Sherma*, *Charma*, and *Jvapeti* are easily identified with the offspring."[1554]

In the Bible, Noah's sons are depicted as the "fathers" of various nations and races: Shem is the progenitor of the Semites; Japheth, the Aryans; and Ham, the "Hamites," or Africans. The story was turned into racist propaganda, as the Semites are considered the best and Japhethites suitable enough to "dwell in the tents of the Semites," while the Hamites were to serve as slaves to the other two, as a punishment for Ham ridiculing the drunken, naked Noah. Not only is such a punishment absurdly harsh, but Noah is not a historical character; thus, a fable has served to justify slavery.

The sons of Noah, of course, are also not historical, as Shem "was

1551 Doane, 20 fn.
1552 Higgins, II, 15.
1553 Doane, 22-23fn.
1554 Hazelrigg, 49.

actually a title of Egyptian priests of Ra."[1555] The three sons of Noah, in fact, represent the three divisions of the heavens into 120° each.[1556] As characters in the celestial mythos, Noah corresponds to the sun and Shem to the moon, appropriate since the Semitic Jews were moon-worshippers.

Abraham and Sarah

Although Abraham is held up as the patriarch of the Hebrews and Arabs, the original Abraham and Sarah were the same as the Indian god Brahma and goddess Sarasvati, the "Queen of Heaven." The story of Abraham's migration reflects a Brahmanical tribe leaving India at the end of the Age of Taurus. This identification of Abraham and Sarah as Indian gods did not escape the notice of the Jesuit missionaries in India; indeed, it was they who first pointed it out.[1557] Concerning the patriarch and his wife, Walker states:

> This name meaning "Father Brahm" seems to have been a Semitic version of India's patriarchal god Brahma; he was also the Islamic Abrama, founder of Mecca. But Islamic legends say Abraham was a late intruder into the shrine of the Kaaba. He bought it from priestesses of its original Goddess. Sarah, "the Queen," was one of the Goddess's titles, which became a name of Abraham's biblical "wife." ... In the tale of Isaac's near-killing, Abraham assumed the role of sacrificial priest in the druidic style, to wash Jehovah's sacred trees with the Blood of the Son: an ancient custom, of which the sacrifice of Jesus was only a late variant.[1558]

Brahma and Sarasvati were apparently also turned into the Indian patriarch Adjigarta and his wife Parvati. Like Abram/Abraham, in the Indian version Adjigarta beseeches the Lord for an heir and eventually takes a young red goat to sacrifice on the mountain, where the Lord speaks to him. As in the biblical tale, a stranger approaches Parvati, who gives him refreshments, and tells her that she will bring forth a son named Viashagagana (Isaac), "the reward of Alms." When the child is 12, the Lord commands Adjigarta to sacrifice him, which the father faithfully begins to do, until the Lord stops him and blesses him as the progenitor of a virgin who will be divinely impregnated. Of the near-sacrifice by Abraham, Graham says, "This too is an old story and like so many others in the Bible, originated in India. Siva, like Abraham, was about to

1555 Walker, B. (1983), 902.
1556 Hazelrigg, 48.
1557 Higgins, I, 387.
1558 Walker, B. (1983), 5.

sacrifice his son on a funeral pyre, but his God, repenting, miraculously provided a rhinoceros instead."[1559]

Abraham also seems to have been related to the Persian evil god, Ahriman, whose name was originally Abriman. Furthermore, Graham states, "The Babylonians also had their Abraham, only they spelt it Abarama. He was a farmer and mythological contemporary with Abraham."[1560]

Hazelrigg relates that Abraham is also identified with the planet Saturn:

> "The Semitic name, Abraham," says Dr. Wilder, "appears to be made from the two words *Ab* and *Ram*, thus signifying 'The Father on High.' This, in astral theology, is a designation of the planet Saturn, or Kronos, and of the divinity bearing those names." … "Where, then, shall we find the difference between the patriarch Abraham and the god Saturn? Saturn was the son of Terra, and Abraham was the son of Terah." … "Our Father which art in heaven" was a direct prayer to this paternal principle, and for this reason Christ (Sun) is expressly denominated as the Son of Abraham, or *Son of the Father*, because the Sun is the center of a system about which Saturn describes an encompassing circle.[1561]

Regarding details of the Abramic story, Walker says:

> The biblical mother-shrine Mamre at Hebron included a sacred oak in a female-symbolic grove. Old Testament scribes pretended it was the home of Abraham, although even in the fourth century AD. it was still a pagan site, dedicated to the worship of "idols."[1562]

Furthermore, Abram's "Ur of the Chaldees" apparently does not originally refer to the Ur in Mesopotamia and to the Middle Eastern Chaldean culture but to an earlier location in India, where Higgins, for one, found the proto-Hebraic Chaldee language.

Regarding Sarah, Walker relates that the "original name of Israel meant 'the tribe of Sarah.' Her name was formerly Sara'i, The Queen, a name of the Great Goddess in Nabataean inscriptions. Priests changed her name to Sarah in the sixth century BC."[1563] These stories serve not as chronicles of individuals but of gods and tribes, so that, as Walker

---

1559 Graham, 125.
1560 Graham, 111.
1561 Hazelrigg, 14–15.
1562 Walker, B. (1983), 468.
1563 Walker, WDSSO, 331.

further relates, "Sarah was the maternal goddess of the 'Abraham' tribe that formed an alliance with Egypt in the 3rd millennium BC."[1564] Hence the story of Abraham and Sarah in Egypt.

Moses, the Exodus, the Ten Commandments

The legend of Moses, rather than being that of a historical Hebrew lawgiver, is found from the Mediterranean to India, with the character having different names and races, depending on the locale: "Manou" is the Indian legislator. "Nemo the lawgiver," who brought down the tablets from the Mountain of God, hails from Babylon. "Mises" is found in Syria, where he was pulled out of a basket floating in a river. Mises also had tablets of stone upon which laws were written, and a rod with which he did miracles, including parting waters and leading his army across the sea.[1565] In addition, "Manes the lawgiver" took the stage in Egypt, and "Minos" was the Cretan reformer.

Jacolliot traces the original Moses to the Indian Manou: "This name of Manou, or Manes … is not a substantive, applying to an individual man; its Sanscrit signification is *the man, par excellence*, the legislator. It is a title aspired to by all the leaders of men in antiquity."

Like Moses, Karna was placed by his mother in a reed boat and set adrift in a river to be discovered by another woman. The Akkadian Sargon also was placed in a reed basket and set adrift to save his life. In fact, "The name Moses is Egyptian and comes from *mo*, the Egyptian word for water, and *uses*, meaning saved from water, in this case, primordial."[1566] Thus, this title Moses could be applied to any of these various heroes saved from the water.

Walker elaborates on the Moses myth:

> The Moses tale was originally that of an Egyptian hero, Ra-Harakhti, the reborn sun god of Canopus, whose life story was copied by biblical scholars. The same story was told of the sun hero fathered by Apollo on the virgin Creusa; of Sargon, king of Akkad in 2242 BC; and of the mythological twin founders of Rome, among many other baby heroes set adrift in rush baskets. It was a common theme.[1567]

Furthermore, Moses's rod is a magical astrology stick used by a number of other mythical characters. Of Moses's miraculous exploits, Walker also relates:

Moses's flowering rod, river of blood, and tablets of the law

1564 Walker, B. (1983), 890.
1565 Graham, 147.
1566 Graham, 146.
1567 Walker, WDSSO, 441.

were all symbols of the ancient Goddess. His miracle of drawing water from a rock was first performed by Mother Rhea after she gave birth to Zeus, and by Atalanta with the help of Artemis. His miracle of drying up the waters to travel dry-shod was earlier performed by Isis, or Hathor, on her way to Byblos.[1568]

And Higgins states:

> In Bacchus we evidently have Moses. Herodotus says [Bacchus] was an Egyptian.... The Orphic verses relate that he was preserved from the waters, in a little box or chest, that he was called *Misem* in commemoration of the event; that he was instructed in all the secrets of the Gods; and that he had a rod, which he changed into a serpent at his pleasure; that he passed through the Red Sea dry-shod, *as Hercules subsequently did* ... and that when he went to India, he and his army enjoyed the light of the Sun during the night: moreover, it is said, that he touched with his magic rod the waters of the great rivers Orontes and Hydaspes; upon which those waters flowed back and left him a free passage. It is even said that he arrested the course of the sun and moon. He wrote his laws on two tablets of stone. He was anciently represented with horns or rays on his head.[1569]

It has also been demonstrated that the exodus from Egypt as reported in the Bible could not have happened in history. Of this implausible story, Mead says:

> Bishop Colenso's ... mathematical arguments that an army of 600,000 men could not very well have been mobilized in a single night, that three millions of people with their flocks and herds could not very well have drawn water from a single well, and hundreds of other equally ludicrous inaccuracies of a similar nature, were popular points which even the most unlearned could appreciate, and therefore especially roused the ire of apologists and conservatives.[1570]

The apologists and conservatives, however, have little choice in the matter, as there is no evidence of the Exodus and wandering in the desert being historical:

> But even scholars who believe they really happened admit that there's no proof whatsoever that the Exodus took place. No record of this monumental event appears in Egyptian chronicles of the time, and Israeli archaeologists combing the Sinai during intense

1568 Walker, B. (1983), 96.
1569 Higgins, II, 19.
1570 Mead, DJL.

searches from 1967 to 1982—years when Israel occupied the peninsula—didn't find a single piece of evidence backing the Israelites' supposed 40-year sojourn in the desert.

> The story involves so many miracles—plagues, the parting of the Red Sea, manna from heaven, the giving of the Ten Commandments—that some critics feel the whole story has the flavor of pure myth. A massive exodus that led to the drowning of Pharaoh's army, says Father Anthony Axe, Bible lecturer at Jerusalem's Ecole Biblique, would have reverberated politically and economically through the entire region. And considering that artifacts from as far back as the late Stone Age have turned up in the Sinai, it is perplexing that no evidence of the Israelites' passage has been found. William Dever, a University of Arizona archaeologist, flatly calls Moses a mythical figure. Some scholars even insist the story was a political fabrication, invented to unite the disparate tribes living in Canaan through a falsified heroic past.[1571]

Potter sums up the mythicist argument regarding Moses:

> The reasons for doubting his existence include, among others, (1) the parallels between the Moses stories and older ones like that of Sargon, (2) the absence of any Egyptian account of such a great event as the Pentateuch asserts the Exodus to have been, (3) the attributing to Moses of so many laws that are known to have originated much later, (4) the correlative fact that great codes never suddenly appear full-born but are slowly evolved, (5) the difficulties of fitting the slavery, the Exodus, and the conquest of Canaan into the known chronology of Egypt and Palestine, and (6) the extreme probability that some of the twelve tribes were never in Egypt at all.[1572]

As Churchward states, "Only one mention of the people of Israel occurs by name on all the monuments of Egypt.... There is no possibility of identifying this with the Biblical Israelites."[1573] He continues:

> Israel in Egypt is not an ethnical entity—the story represents the children of Ra in the Lower Egypt of Amenta, built or founded by Ptah, and entirely mythical.... The Books of Genesis, Exodus, and Joshua are not intentional forgeries; the subject-matter was already extant in the Egyptian Mysteries, and an exoteric version of the ancient wisdom has been rendered in the form of historic

1571 *Time*, 12/18/95.
1572 Potter, 27–8.
1573 A. Churchward, 292.

> narrative and ethnically applied to the Jews.... The chief teachers have always insisted on the allegorical nature of the Pentateuch. Thus it is seen that "Biblical History" has been mainly derived from misappropriated and misinterpreted wisdom of Egypt contained in their mythological and eschatological representation as witnessed by the "Ritual of Ancient Egypt."[1574]

The Exodus is indeed no historical event but embodies a motif found in other myths. As Pike says, "And when Bacchus and his army had long marched in burning deserts, they were led by a Lamb or Ram into beautiful meadows, and to the Springs that watered the Temple of Jupiter Ammon."[1575] And Churchward relates, "Traditions of the Exodus are found in various parts of the world and amongst people of different states of evolution, and these traditions can be explained by the Kamite [Egyptian] rendering only."[1576] Indeed, as Massey states, "'*Coming out of Egypt*' is a Kamite expression for ascending from the lower to the upper heavens."[1577] Churchward further outlines the real meaning of the Exodus:

> The Exodus or "Coming out of Egypt" first celebrated by the festival of Passover or the transit at the vernal equinox, occurred in the heavens before it was made historical as the migration of the Jews. The 600,000 men who came up out of Egypt as Hebrew warriors in the Book of Exodus are 600,000 inhabitants of Israel in the heavens according to Jewish Kabalah, and the same scenes, events, and personages that appear as mundane in the Pentateuch are celestial in the Book of Enoch.[1578]

Churchward continues, explaining the notorious "plagues."

> If we wish to show that the Jews' version was a fable, we can obtain the proofs in Egypt, and nowhere else. The sufferings of the Chosen People in Egypt, and their miraculous exodus out of it, belong to the celestial allegory.... The allegory of the Solar drama was performed in the mysteries of the divine nether-world, and had been performed by symbolical representations ages before it was converted into a history of the Jews by the literalizers of the Ancient Symbolism. The tale of the ten plagues of Egypt contains an esoteric version of the tortures inflicted on the guilty in the ten hells of the

1574 A. Churchward, 294–5.
1575 Pike, 466.
1576 A. Churchward, 322.
1577 Massey, HJMC, 28.
1578 A. Churchward, 300.

underworld.[1579]

The exodus out of Egypt refers to that out of Amenta, which "is described in the Ritual as consisting of two parts called 'Egypt and the desert land or wilderness.'"[1580] Of the ritualistic wandering in the wilderness, Churchward says:

> The Struggle of Set and Horus in the desert lasted forty days, as commemorated in the forty days of the Egyptian Lent, during which time Set, as the power of drought and sterility, made war on Horus in the water and the buried germinating grain.... These forty days have been extended into forty years, and confessedly so by the Jews.[1581]

In addition, the miraculous "parting of the Red Sea" has forever mystified the naive and credulous masses and scholars alike, who have put forth all sorts of tortured speculation to explain it. The parting and destruction of the hosts of Pharaoh at the Red Sea is not recorded by any known historian, not surprisingly, since it is not historical but rather a mytheme found in other cultures, including Ceylon/Sri Lanka. This motif is also found in the Hawaiian and Hottentot versions of the Moses myth, prior to contact with outside cultures.[1582] The crossing of the Red Sea is astronomical, expressly stated by Josephus to have occurred at the autumnal equinox,[1583] indicating its origin within the astro-mythos.

Moreover, the famed Ten Commandments are simply a repetition of the Babylonian Code of Hammurabi and the Hindu Vedas, among others. As Churchward says:

> The "Law of Moses" were the old Egyptian Laws ... this the stele or "Code of Hammurabi" conclusively proves. Moses lived 1,000 years after this stone was engraved.[1584]

Walker relates that the

stone tablets of law supposedly given to Moses were copied from the Canaanite god Baal-Berith, "God of the Covenant." Their Ten Commandments were similar to the commandments of the Buddhist Decalogue. In the ancient world, laws generally came from a deity on a mountaintop. Zoroaster received the tablets of law from Ahura Mazda on a mountaintop.[1585]

1579 A. Churchward, 324–5.
1580 A. Churchward, 325.
1581 A. Churchward, 325.
1582 A. Churchward, 323.
1583 Anderson, 106.
1584 A. Churchward, 304.
1585 Walker, B. (1983), 677.

Doane sums it up when he says, "Almost all the acts of Moses correspond to those of the Sun-gods."[1586] However, the Moses story is also reflective of the stellar cult, once again demonstrating the dual-natured "twin" Horus-Set myth and the battle for supremacy between the day and night skies, as well as among the solar, stellar and lunar cults. Churchward relates:

> The Jews strictly are of the Tribe, or Totemic Clan of Judah. The Israelites were not Jews, although some Jews may be Israelites. Moses and his followers have been termed Israelites, but there is no evidence that the "Israelites" were ever in Egypt except once when they made a raid, and were driven back with great slaughter. The Israelites, a mythological name, were a number of Totemic Tribes who originally left Egypt and went to the East during the Stellar Cult.[1587]

Joshua

As noted, early Christian father Tertullian made the ridiculous claim that "the Lord" had "rehearsed his subsequent incarnation" as Jesus by becoming characters recorded in the Old Testament. The major character about which Tertullian and the other fathers write is the prophet and warrior Joshua, son of Nun, also translated as Jesus, son of Naue, who allegedly led the Israelites into the "promised land" and destroyed the city of Jericho, among other such pillage and slaughter. Of Joshua's purported adventures, *Time* reports:

> Historians generally agree that Joshua's conquest would have taken place in the 13th century BC. But British researcher Kathleen Kenyon, who excavated at Jericho for six years, found no evidence of destruction at that time. Indeed, says Dead Sea Scrolls curator emeritus Broshi, "the city was deserted from the beginning of the 15th century until the 11th century BC." So was Ai, say Broshi and others. And so, according to archaeological surveys, was most of the land surrounding the cities. Says Broshi: "The central hill regions of Judea and Samaria were practically uninhabited. The Israelites didn't have to kill and burn to settle."[1588]

In reality, the patriarch Joshua was based on Horus as "Iusa," and the Joshua story represents the Horus cult in the Levant, when the stellar cult of the "sons of Seth" yielded to the solar. Joshua is not only Horus himself but also his "brother," the Egyptian god "Shu," or "Shu-si-Ra," the "auxiliary" or son of Ra and "Uplifter of the Heavens," and Joshua

1586 Doane, 51.
1587 A. Churchward, 291.
1588 Time, 12/18/95.

was said to be the "preserver" or "deliverer" sun in Aries.[1589] As Churchward says of Shu:

> He is the helper of Horus as the Solar God upon the horizon where the great battle is fought against the Apap of darkness.... This has been rendered in the Hebrew as "Joshua helping to fight the battle of the Lord." ... Shu was chief of the sustaining powers of the firmament, who were known in one phase as the seven giants. He then became the elevator of the Heavens that was imaged as the Cow of Nut. Lastly, he was the sustaining power with Atum-Horus in the Double Equinox.[1590]

In Canaan, Joshua was Baal Jehoshua, the "Lord of Salvation," but when his cult had been suppressed by the Levites/Yahwists, he was demoted to a Hebrew patriarch and hero of the northern kingdom. However, his worship was continued "underground" atop Mt. Carmel, site of a pre-Christian temple of the Lord Jesus, Baal Jeshouah.[1591]

Indeed, the Joshua cult was situated in basically the same area where the Christ drama allegedly took place, with Joshua mutating into Jesus.[1592] In fact, the cult of the solar hero Joshua performed the sacred king drama at Gilgal, which in Greek is Galilee (Jos. 12:23), so "Jesus of Galilee" could read "Joshua of Gilgal," and vice versa. Like Jesus, Moses, Horus, Perseus and others, Joshua was a "fatherless hero born of 'waters' (Maria)."[1593]

Furthermore, at 1 Corinthians 10:4 Paul claims that Christ "the Rock" followed the Hebrews at the time of their exodus out of Egypt, as did Joshua, according to the biblical myth. As Dujardin says, "The history of the ancient religion of Jesus goes back to the Stone Age and is prior to the settlement of the Canaanite tribes of Palestine."[1594] Robertson states:

> The hypothesis that Joshua is the original Jesus—the origin of the myths which blended in a composite pattern mistaken for real history—solves many problems.... The association of Joshua with conceptions of Logos, Son of God, and Messiah is present in the Pentateuch.[1595]

The association of Jesus with Joshua was admitted by early Chris-

---

1589 Higgins, I, 325.
1590 A. Churchward, 260–2.
1591 Higgins, I, 329.
1592 Dujardin.
1593 Walker, B. (1983), 676.
1594 Dujardin, 82.
1595 Robertson, 21-2.

tian fathers, particularly when they were trying to give scriptural authority to Jesus's alleged advent because the story was being challenged. In his Second Apology, Justin Martyr not only acknowledges but insists upon the Jesus-Joshua identification:

> JOSHUA WAS A FIGURE OF CHRIST.... Jesus (Joshua), as I have now frequently remarked ... when he was sent to spy out the land of Canaan, was named by Moses Jesus (Joshua). Why he did this you neither ask, nor are at a loss about it, nor make strict inquiries. Therefore Christ has escaped your notice; and though you read, you understand not; and even now, though you hear that Jesus is our Christ, you consider not that the name was bestowed on Him not purposelessly nor by chance.... But since not only was his name altered, but he was also appointed successor to Moses, being the only one of his contemporaries who came out from Egypt, he led the surviving people into the Holy Land; and as he, not Moses, led the people into the Holy Land, and as he distributed it by lot to those who entered along with him, so also Jesus the Christ will turn again the dispersion of the people, and will distribute the good land to each one, though not in the same manner.... For I have proved that it was Jesus who appeared to and conversed with Moses, and Abraham, and all the other patriarchs without exception, ministering to the will of the Father; who also, I say, came to be born man by the Virgin Mary and lives for ever.

Justin also appeals to the passage in the book of Zechariah in which Joshua,[1596] like Jesus, contends with the devil, comparing it with the "mystery of Christ," thus again virtually equating the Canaanite Baal/ Hebrew "prophet" with the Christian savior.

David

The great King David, from whose lineage Jesus, the "King of the Jews," was purported to have come, has been much exalted over the centuries. However, even though according to the biblical tale David was well-known and "all the kings of the earth sought the presence of Solomon" (2 Chronicles 9:23), there is no record of David in non-Hebraic sources, such as the histories of Herodotus and Hesiod. Nor are there any archaeological finds to bear out his existence, despite recent claims that a plaque was found bearing the words "house of David," because not only is the plaque's language oblique but Bible proponents, among others, have been known to salt sites and fabricate artifacts. As Roberta

1596 This Joshua, a candidate for High Priest, is not supposed to be Moses's successor Joshua, even if Justin identified the two.

Harris says in *The World of the Bible*, "Some of the best known Bible stories centre on King David, yet neither history nor archaeology can substantiate any of them."[1597]

Like so many other major characters in the Bible, David is non-historical. Massey evinced that David, "the eighth son of Jesse, whose thirty captains were changed, in keeping with the thirty days of the month, was the Hebrew form of the Kamite moon-god Taht-Esmun, the eighth, one of whose titles is '*the begetter of Osiris*, who was so called because the solar régime was subsequent to the lunar dynasty."[1598] In other words, Osiris/Jesus descends from Taht-Esmun/David, "as it is written."

Even the well-loved biblical Psalms attributed to David are not original but are Canaanite/Egyptian. As Massey says:

> The Psalms of David contain a substratum of the *Muthoi*, parables and dark sayings of old, which belonged to the hermeneutical Books of Taht, the Kamite Psalmist, and scribe of the gods. Those who were not in possession of the gnosis searched these writings for prophecy—after the fashion of Justin—upon which to establish the history.[1599]

These "dark sayings" and events were applied to Jesus, and their presence in the Psalms has been loudly touted as prophecy regarding "the Savior." In fact, many of the Psalms are paeans (song or hymn of praise) to the sun, which is how they are applicable to the solar myth Jesus. As Massey also says:

> Such sayings do not relate to prophecies that could be fulfilled in any future human history. The transactions and utterances in the psalm are personal to the speaker there and then, and not to any future sufferer. They may be repeated, but the repetition cannot constitute history any more than it fulfills prophecy. The repetition of the words in character points to the reapplication of the mythos in a narrative assumed to be historical.[1600]

Indeed, the fact that these sayings are repeated verbatim in the New Testament demonstrates that they were copied from older texts, rather than having been spoken by a historical character, unless he was merely an unoriginal scriptural parrot. If so, he would have been an Egyptian parrot. In this regard, Potter reproduces the fourteenth-century Egyptian monotheist Akhenaten's "Hymn to Aten" and states:

The reader who is familiar with the Psalms of David will have

1597 Harris, 72.
1598 Massey, HJMC, 105–6.
1599 Massey, HJMC, 111-3.
1600 Massey, HJMC, 113.

noted the many parallelisms between this hymn and the 104th Psalm, similarities in language and especially thought. The composition of the Hebrew Psalm is assigned by scholars to the Greek Period of Hebrew History, 332–168 BC; hence, the Egyptian hymn is at least a thousand years earlier. Even if David wrote the Psalm, as tradition has it, the Egyptian composition is over three centuries older. If anyone is guilty of plagiarism, it was not Akhenaten.[1601]

Of David and his psalm-singing, Gaster says:

> [In] a prominent position in the synagogue at Dura-Europus there is a fresco depicting an Orpheus-like figure by some identified as David ... a representation of the same scene occurs in a Jewish catacomb at Rome; and ... in various manuscripts of the Psalter David is indeed portrayed as Orpheus.[1602]

As a mythical character, therefore, David cannot be the progenitor of a historical Jesus.

Joseph, Father of Jesus

Jesus's lineage thus cannot be traced through his "earthly" father, Joseph, since Joseph was said to be a descendant of the mythical David. Naturally, Joseph also has his counterpart in older mythologies; for example, in the Egyptian version of the mythos, Seb is the earthly father of Horus. As Massey says:

> Seb is the god of earth, god the father on earth, therefore the especial father of the sun-god in the earth.... Thus Seb is the father of Osiris or Horus on earth. "My father is Seb ... my bread on earth (is) that of Seb." In the same way, house and food for the Christ are found by Joseph.... Seb and Meri (Nu) for earth and heaven would afford two mythic originals for Joseph and Mary as parents of the divine child. . . *Aseb* is the name of a typical seat or throne of rule, in accordance with the Hebrew *Iosheb*, to sit, to be enthroned.[1603]

Joseph is called "son of Heli," Heli or Helios meaning the sun. The name Joseph was also a title of a Hebrew priest. As Walker states:

> The priestly name of Joseph may have been bestowed upon Jewish counterparts of the priests known in Egypt as "fathers of the god." The function of such holy men was to beget, on the temple maidens [*almahs*], children who would be *sacer*: firstborn "sons of God" dedicated to the service of the deity.... The mythic proliferation of Marys and Josephs indicates that these were not

1601 Potter, 18–19.
1602 Gaster, 123.
1603 Massey, HJMC, 51-2.

> personal names but characters in the drama: The chosen husband who was yet not a husband; the father-of-God who was yet not a father; the virgin-mother-Goddess-priestess-queen who was also a *kadesha* or "Bride of God." … It can be shown that Joseph was indeed a divine name in Israel. The Egyptian form was Djoser or Tcheser.[1604]

Hazelrigg further demonstrates the antiquity of "Joseph," its existence in other cultures and its deep astrological meaning:

> And what of this espousal to Joseph, who was the Ioseppe of the Phoenicians, and Ananda of the Hindus, the Zeus—husband of Leto and the parent of Apollo—of the cosmogonic apologue? According to the Gospels: "Joseph went up to Nazareth, which is in Galilee, and came into the City of David, called Bethlehem, because he was of that tribe, to be inscribed with Mary his wife, who was with child." And here, in the City of David, or the celestial expanse, called Bethlehem, the sixth constellation, Virgo, the harvest mansion, do we discover Joseph (the constellation of Boötes, Ioseppe) and his wife Mary with the child. Here is personified a constellation whose very name (Io-seppe, the manger of Io, or the Moon) typifies the humble place of accouchement of all the Virgin Mothers, and, as related to Virgo, the genesis of all Messianic tradition.[1605]

In fact, the Greek name for the constellation of Boötes, or Adam, is Iosef or Joseph.[1606]

Mary, Mother of Jesus

The Virgin Mother motif is found around the globe, long before the Christian era, as was the name of the Goddess as "Meri," "Mari" or "Mary," representing the sea (Mer/Mar), which was governed by the Queen of Heaven, the moon. The Egyptian goddess Isis, for instance, was also called "MataMeri" ("Mother Mary") or just "Mari." As Walker says, "Mari" was the "basic name of the Goddess known to the Chaldeans as Marratu, to the Jews as Marah, to the Persians as Mariham, to the Christians as Mary.… Semites worshipped an androgynous combination of Goddess and God called MariEl (MaryGod), corresponding to the Egyptian MeriRa, which combined the feminine principle of water with the masculine principle of the sun."[1607] Walker also relates that

1604 Walker, B. (1983), 480.
1605 Hazelrigg, 108.
1606 Anderson, 126.
1607 Walker, B. (1983), 584.

"Mari" was a name for the sun goddess in Buddhism.[1608]

Like Mary, Isis was called "Queen of Heaven," "Our Lady," "Star of the Sea" and "Mother of God." The worship of Isis was spread throughout the Greco-Roman world, from Egypt to Britain, and was very popular in Rome during the first centuries before and after the beginning of the Christian era. In addition, Isis was the same as Ishtar, who was also called Mari and was worshipped in the Hebrew temple:

> Ishtar's priestesses apparently performed some version of the rite each year in the temple of Jerusalem, where the virgin form of the Goddess was called Mari, Mari-Anna, or Miriam, and her holy women annually wailed for the sacrificial death of Tammuz.[1609]

It should also be noted that "the Savior" was at times considered female; in other words, there have been female saviors as well. In fact, the words Isis and Jesus come from the same root, meaning "salvation" or "savior." It is for this reason that Jesus is depicted in Revelation as having "paps." These multiple "paps" or breasts reflect the "Mother of All Living," who was also the "Great Sow" with many teats.

The Goddess is also the Great Earth Mother, who was worshipped for millennia around the world. As Carpenter states:

> There is ample evidence that one of the very earliest objects of human worship was the Earth itself, conceived of as the fertile Mother of all things. Gaia or Gê (the earth) had temples and altars in almost all the cities of Greece. Rhea or Cybele, sprung from the Earth, was "mother of all the gods." Demeter was honored far and wide as the gracious patroness of the crops and vegetation. Ceres, of course, the same. Maia in the Indian mythology and Isis in the Egyptian are forms of Nature and the Earth-spirit, represented as female; and so forth. The Earth, in these ancient cults, was the mystic source of all life, and to it, as a propitiation, life of all kinds was sacrificed.... It was, in a way, the most natural, as it seems to have been the earliest and most spontaneous of cults—the worship of the Earth-mother, the all-producing eternal source of life, and on account of her never-failing ever-renewed fertility conceived of as an immortal Virgin.[1610]

When the Father Sky cult usurped that of Mother Earth, the Goddess was demoted in a variety of ways, including eventually being made into "Saint Mary." Walker also says, "Biblical writers were implacably op-

---

1608 Walker, WDSSO, 222.
1609 Walker, B. (1983), 453.
1610 Carpenter, 157.

posed to any manifestation of the Goddess."[1611] So completely was she purged that there is no word for "Goddess" in biblical Hebrew.

The Saints

Like Mary, many other Christian "saints" are not historical personages but are, in fact, the gods of other cultures, usurped and demoted in order to unify the Roman Empire. Of this saint-making Walker says, "The canon of saints was the Christian technique for preserving the pagan polytheism that people wanted, while pretending to worship only one God."[1612] The *Catholic Encyclopedia* itself admits,

It has indeed been said that the 'Saints are the successors to the Gods.' Instances have been cited of pagan feasts becoming Christian; of pagan temples consecrated to the worship of the true God; of statues of pagan Gods baptized and transformed into Christian Saints.[1613]

In the saint-making process, Christians took goddesses and gods such as Artemis (St. Artemidos/Ursula) and Dionysus (St. Denis), modified their names, and gave them great "historical" exploits. In addition, the Pagan temples or "tombs" of gods were converted into Christian churches. For example, the "tomb of Dionysus/Bacchus" was transformed into the church of St. Baccus.[1614] Higgins quotes Bochart on the adoration of saints:

They have transferred to their saints all the equipage of the Pagan Gods: to St. Wolfgang the hatchet, or hook of Saturn; to Moses the horns of Jupiter Hammon; to St. Peter the keys of Janus. In brief, they have chased away all the Gods out of the Pantheon at Rome, to place in their rooms all the Saints, whose images they worship with like devotion as those of the Pagan Gods sometimes were. They dress them up in apparel, they crown them with garlands of flowers, they carry them in procession, they bow before them, they address their prayers to them, they make them descend from heaven, they attribute to them miraculous virtues.[1615]

All these phony saints were highly profitable, of course, as fake relics such as their hair, fingers and other bones and body parts proliferated. As Walker states:

> The church that slaughtered the heathen for worshipping false gods was itself guilty of worshipping false saints—which, sometimes, were even the same deities as those of the heathen....

1611 Walker, WDSSO, 197.
1612 Walker, WDSSO, 172.
1613 Wheless, IIGW.
1614 Higgins, II, 74.
1615 Higgins, II, 81.

The church never lost sight of practical common sense on one point, however; saints were leading sources of its income, thanks to the mandatory pilgrimage system, donations, and tithes.... The multitudes of phony or commercial saints are treated by modern Catholic scholars with a rather amused tolerance, as if the saint-makers' fantasies held something of the same charm as tales invented by bright children. It is rarely admitted that these fantasies were not intended to charm but rather to defraud. The saints were made up to earn money for the church, and many of the made-up saints are still doing so, for the church refrains from publicizing their spurious origins lest such publicity might disappoint the faithful—which, translated, means the donations might cease.[1616]

St. Josaphat

In one of the more obvious Christian deceptions, in order to convert followers of "Lord Buddha" the Church canonized him as "St. Josaphat," which represented a Christian corruption of the Buddhistic title, "Bodhisat." As Wheless says:

[The] holy Saint Josaphat, under which name and due to an odd slip of inerrant inspiration, the great Lord Buddha, "The Light of Asia," was duly certified a Saint in the Roman Martyrology.[1617]

Walker elaborates:

Medieval saint-makers adapted the story of Buddha's early life to their own fictions, calling the father of St. Josaphat "an Indian king" who kept the young saint confined to prevent him from becoming a Christian. He was converted anyway, and produced the usual assortment of miracles, some of them copied from incidents in the life story of Buddha. St. Josaphat enjoyed great popularity in the Middle Ages, an ironical development in a Europe that abhorred Buddhism as the work of the devil.[1618]

St. Christopher

The beloved St. Christopher is another "Christian saint" who is a remake of an ancient god. As Massey states:

The well-known story of Christopher shows that he was a survival of Apheru, a name of Sut-Anup. It is related that he overtook the child-Christ at the side of the river Jordan, and, lifting him on his back, carried him across the waters. But all the while the won-

1616 Walker, B. (1983), 882

1617 Wheless, FC.

1618 Walker, WEMS.

drous child grew, and grew, and grew, as they went, and when they reached the other side the child had grown into the god. The genesis of this is the passage of the annual sun across the waters, which reaches the other side as the full-grown divinity.[1619]

The Christopher legend appeared in the Krishna myth as well.

As has been demonstrated, many of the great biblical heroes have been the "Baals" or gods of other cultures remade, as have been the Christian saints. This religion-making business utilized every bit of "technology" it could muster, building upon centuries of such behavior and bringing it to perfection.

The Meaning of Revelation

"A number of the books of the New Testament were disputed already in early Christianity, among the Christian scholars of the second to the fourth centuries, who were arguing over which books should be included in Scripture.

> "The most famous instance is the book of Revelation. A third-century Christian scholar of Alexandria, Egypt, named Dionysius, argued that the book was not actually written by Jesus's disciple John, the son of Zebedee. Dionysius's argument was compelling and continues to be compelling to scholars today. He maintained that the writing style of the book is so different from that of the Gospel of John that they could not have been written by the same person (modern scholars differ from Dionysius only in thinking that the Gospel too was probably not written by John). Dionysius thought there must have been two authors of the same name who later came to be confused as the same person. But it is interesting that Dionysius, according to the church father Eusebius, had a number of predecessors who had argued that Revelation was written not by a different man named John, but by a heretic named Cerinthus, who forged the account to promote his false teaching that there would be a literal future paradise of a thousand years here on Earth."

—Dr. Bart D. Ehrman, *Forged: Writing in the Name of God* (21)

Another biblical "code" in need of decipherment is the Book of Revelation, which has mystified and fascinated people for centuries with its bizarre imagery and purported prophecy. This fascination has led to endless speculation and interpretation of its "prophecy" by biblical literalists, who, being unable to do anything else with it, usually interpret Revelation allegorically. Needless to say, despite centuries of

1619 Massey, HJMC, 135.

attempts to decode the text and to associate its players with a variety of world leaders, nations and organizations, Revelation remains a mystery, because it is, in fact, not prophecy, and its drama does not take place on Earth.

As to the question of who actually wrote Revelation, the *Encyclopedia Biblica* says, "The author of Revelation calls himself John the Apostle. As he was *not* John the Apostle, who died perhaps in Palestine about 66, he was a forger."[1620] We would add that "died *perhaps*" is also accurate, in that John "lived not at all." Nor is the book unique, as it is purported to be. As Walker says:

> The Bible's *Book of Revelation* purports to be a doomsday-vision experienced by St. John the Divine, but it is in fact a collection of images and phrases from many sources. Literature of this kind was plentiful in the first few centuries AD.[1621]

In fact, many apocalypses were written prior to and during the Christian era, as the apocalypse was a genre of writing.

Even Eusebius calls Revelation "spurious" and further relates the words of Dionysius (c. 200–265), saint and head of the Alexandrian school after Origen:

> Some of our predecessors rejected the book and pulled it entirely to pieces, criticizing it chapter by chapter, pronouncing it unintelligible and illogical, and the title false. They say it is not John's and is not a revelation at all, since it is heavily veiled by its thick curtain of incomprehensibility: so far from being one of the apostles, the author of the book was not even one of the saints, or a member of the Church, but Cerinthus, the founder of the sect called Cerinthian after him.[1622]

This debate over Revelation is a recurring theme in the early Christian writings, in which a number of fathers and doctors at one point or another expressed their doubts as to the authenticity of not only Revelation but also virtually every text in the canon. This skepticism is all the more peculiar considering it was claimed that the apostolic lineage was continuous and "unbroken," and that there were allegedly established churches all along whose authorities surely would have known for a fact whether or not any apostle had written biblical texts. It also reveals the tremendous amount of duplicity engaged in by clergy and Biblicists who continue to assure the credulous populace that the books of the Bible were in fact written by those whose names are attached to them, know-

1620 Wheless.
1621 Walker, B. (1983), 856.
1622 Eusebius, 240.

ing full well that this assertion is false.

The Book of Revelation was rejected by a number of churches, particularly the eastern ones, because they knew it was a spurious manuscript compiled from much older texts. As Pike says, "The Apocalypse or Revelations, by whomever written, belongs to the Orient and to extreme antiquity. It reproduces what is far older than itself."[1623] Higgins concurs:

> That the work called the Apocalypse of St. John … is of *very great antiquity* is clearly proved by the fact that it makes the year only 360 days long—the same length that it is made in the third book of Genesis.[1624]

Based on its astrological imagery, Massey evinced that Revelation, rather than having been written by any apostle called John during the first century CE, was an ancient text dating to 4,000 years ago and relating the Mithraic legend of one of the early Zoroasters. The text has also been attributed pseudepigraphically to Horus's scribe, Aan, whose name has been passed down as "John." Jacolliot claimed that the Apocalypse/Revelation material was gleaned from the story of Krishna/Christna, an opinion concurred with by Hotema, who averred that the book was a text of Hindu mysteries given to Apollonius. In fact, the words "Jesus" and "Christ," and the phrase "Jesus Christ" in particular, are used sparingly in Revelation, revealing that they were interpolated (long) after the book was written, as were the Judaizing elements. Indeed, it is admitted by Christians that the book was worked on by a number of hands, including those of Andrew, Bishop of Caesarea, who wrote parts of Revelation in the sixth–seventh centuries CE.[1625]

Despite all the brouhaha surrounding it, Revelation is not a "book of prophecy." Hotema reveals the real meaning behind the book:

> It is expressed in terms of creative phenomena; its hero is not Jesus but the Sun of the Universe, its heroine is the Moon; and all its other characters are Planets, Stars and Constellations; while its stagesetting comprises the Sky, the Earth, the Rivers and the Sea.[1626]

In fact, Revelation records the mythos of the precession of the equinoxes, or the "Great Year," and was apparently originally written to usher in the Age of Aries, which began around 4,400 years ago. As Churchward says:

1623 Pike, 272.
1624 Higgins, I, 577.
1625 britannica.com/biography/Andrew-of-Caesarea
1626 "Intro," Massey's EBD.

The drama appears as tremendous in the Book of Revelation, because the period ending is on the scale of one Great Year. It *is not the ending of the world, but of a great year of the world.*[1627]

Churchward continues:

> The book is and always has been inexplicable, because it was based upon the symbolism of the Egyptian Astronomical Mythology without the gnosis, or "meaning which hath wisdom" that is absolutely necessary for an explanation of its subject-matter; and because the debris of the ancient wisdom has been turned to account as data for pre-Christian prophecy that was supposed to have its fulfillment in Christian history.[1628]

Sacred Numerology

The Book of Revelation is in fact an encapsulation of the ancient astrological mythos and religion, a part of which is sacred numerology. Indeed, several sacred numbers repeatedly make their appearance in Revelation, such as three, seven, 12, 24, etc. The "seven stars" or "spirits" are the seven "planets" that make up the days of the week and the Seven Sisters, which were variously the pole-stars or the Pleiades. These Seven Sisters corresponded to the Seven Hathors of the Egyptians, who were the "'seven beings who make decrees,' whom the dead would meet on their journey through the seven spheres of the afterlife."[1629] The Seven Hathors were also considered the seven gates, as mentioned in Revelation, representing both the night hours and the "seven months of summer." The seven "torches of fire" or seven-branch lampstand symbolize the sun in the middle, with the moon and five inner planets as satellites, corresponding to the days of the week. Concerning Jesus as the lamb with the seven horns and eyes, Wells says:

> Revelation's figuring the heavenly Jesus as a lamb with seven horns and seven eyes "which are the spirits of God sent forth into all the earth" (5:6) is a manifold reworking of old traditions. Horns are a sign of power (Deuteronomy 33:17) and in Daniel designated kingly power. The seven eyes which inform the lamb of what is happening all over the earth seem to be residues from ancient astrological lore … according to which God's eyes are the sun, the moon, and the five planets.[1630]

The Great City in Revelation is the city of the Gods, located in the heavens, with the 12 gates of the zodiac. The "tree of life" in the city that

---

1627 A. Churchward, 313.
1628 A. Churchward, 366.
1629 Walker, WDSSO, 76.
1630 Wells, WWJ, 179.

bears "twelve kinds of fruit" is also the zodiac, growing on both sides of the river of life, the Milky Way.

In addition, the 24 elders in white garments around the throne are the 24 hours of the day "around" the sun. The four angels "standing at the four corners of the earth" are the four cardinal points or *angles* of 90 degrees each. The 144,000 elect are the 360 degrees of the zodiacal circle multiplied by the four minutes it takes for the sun to move one degree, times a factor of 100.[1631]

The Four "Living Creatures"

Much has been made of the four mysterious creatures or cherubim found in Ezekiel and Revelation:

> And round the throne, on each side of the throne, are four living creatures, full of eyes front and behind: And the first animal was like a lion and the second animal was like a calf and the third animal had the face of a man and the fourth animal was like a flying eagle.

As in Ezekiel, these four animals represent the four cardinal points of the zodiac, marked by the four 'Royal Stars,' Aldebaran in Taurus the Bull, Regulus in Leo the Lion, Antares in Scorpio (formerly the Eagle), and Fomalhaut in Aquarius the man. The throne is the sun, and the multitudinous "eyes front and behind" are the infinite stars. The three pairs of wings of each beast represent the three signs of each of the four zodiacal quadrants. These "living creatures" were also found in Egypt. As Walker says, "Spirits of the four points of the year were sometimes called Sons of Horus."[1632]

Jackson suggests that the four beasts also represent Noah and his three sons (i.e., the various races). In this scenario, the lion is the lion of Judah, or Shem, "father" of the Semites; the bull symbolizes the Hamites of Egypt; the eagle is Japheth, progenitor of the Aryans; and the man is Noah, who is of the "Adamic" or "Atlantean" race.[1633]

The Four Horsemen

Concerning the frightening "four horsemen" endlessly interpreted and expected for almost two millennia, Jackson says:

> In the Apocalypse we read about the four beasts, and the four horsemen; the beasts were the zodiacal constellations and the horsemen were the planets....
>
> 1. The first horseman was a conqueror armed with a bow, wearing

1631 Anderson, 85.

1632 Walker, B. (1983), 900.

1633 Jackson, 187.

a crown, and riding a white horse. This was the planet Venus.

2. The second horse was red, ridden by a warrior with a sword. This was the planet Mars.

3. The third horse was black with the rider holding aloft a pair of balances. This was the planet Saturn.

4. The fourth horse was of pale-green or blue-green color, and his rider was death. This was the planet Mercury.[1634]

Thus, the four horsemen symbolizing plague, famine, war and death, awaited for so many centuries, have been here all along, just like Jesus, the *sun* of God.

The Woman Clothed with the Sun

The "woman clothed with the sun" is both the moon, which reflects or "wears" the sun, and the constellation of Virgo the Virgin, who has the moon under her feet and the stars above her head. As Graves explains:

> St. John's marvelous figure of "a woman clothed with the sun, the moon under her feet and a crown of twelve stars upon her head" (Rev. xii), is easily understood when viewed through an astronomical mirror. More appropriately may the astronomical virgin woman be said to be clothed with the sun, than could be said of any other of the twelve signs of the zodiac, judging from her situation among the signs and her relative position to the sun. There she stands, right in the focus of the sun's rays in August, the hottest month of the year, and thus is clothed with the sun more brilliantly than that of any other sign. Of course the moon is under her feet, while the twelve months of the year, or the twelve signs of the zodiac form her crown of twelve stars.[1635]

This motif is found in Persia, India and Egypt, among other places. In fact, the Berlin museum has an engraving of the Goddess (possibly Ishtar) in nearly the same posture, clothed with the sun, with the moon and stars above and the twelve signs of the zodiac surrounding her.[1636] At the Temple of Isis at Denderah was an image of a woman

seated at the center of a blazing sun crowned by twelve stars and with her feet resting on the moon. The woman was the symbol of Mother Nature; the sun represented creative strength; the twelve stars stood for the twelve signs of the Zodiac, and the Moon signified Matter and its domination by Spirit.[1637]

1634 Jackson, 149–50.
1635 Graves, BS, 74–5.
1636 Wells, WWJ, 181-2.
1637 Jackson, 137.

Walker relates the eastern custom regarding the woman:

> According to Tantric tradition, the Goddess concealed herself behind the sun's brightness; it was "the mayik vesture of Her who is clothed with the sun." This image reappeared in the New Testament as "the woman clothed with the sun." (Revelation 12:1).[1638]

The Seven Seals

Regarding the mysterious "seven seals" opened by "the Lamb" (i.e., the sun in Aries), Graham says:

> This part of the revelation is not from God but from Ezekiel, who got it from the Babylonians, the Assyrians and the Sumerians. The seven seals are identical with the seven decrees of Ishtar and Innana.[1639]

These "seven decrees" are the same as those of the Seven Hathors mentioned above, which are also the seven gates through which the Prince of Light must pass, representing hours of the night and months of the year.

The "Sweet" Scrolls

Both Ezekiel and the Revelator are given "sweet scrolls" to eat prior to their visions. These scrolls evidently represent magical practices. As Walker relates:

> Eating instead of reading a piece of magical literature was a common Oriental method of absorbing the virtue of magic words even when one is unable to read. In Tibet, Madagascar, China, and Japan it was customary to cure diseases by writing the curative charm on paper and eating the paper, or its ashes.... The same notion was often found in the west. The modern pharmacist's Rx began as a curative symbol of Saturn, written on paper and eaten by the patient.[1640]

It has also been suggested that these scrolls represented hallucinogenic drugs, which were commonly used in mystery schools and secret societies.

The Dragon and the Beast

The frightening Dragon and Beast of Revelation have intrigued people for centuries and occasioned much speculation as to their identities.

1638 Walker, WDSSO, 39.
1639 Graham, 366.
1640 Walker, B. (1983), 1033.

The favorite interpretation of the Beast has been the Catholic Church itself, particularly when it was murdering people by the millions. Again, the Book of Revelation is not prophetic, so this "Beast" is not applicable to any earthly kingdoms, organizations, "Antichrists" or peoples, etc. Graves gives the astrological meaning of the Dragon and Beast:

> St. John (Rev. 12) speaks of the Dragon having power to hurt the five months, and astronomically speaking, he does hurt the vegetable productions of the five principal prolific months of the year, with a vengeance. And St. John's monster, with the seven heads and ten horns, may find a solution in astronomy, or astro-theology, by assuming the seven heads to be the seven Summer months (as some nations divided the year in this way), and duplicating the five Winter months for the horns. And then, the story of the Dragon "pursuing the woman to destroy her male child," finds an easy explanation here. Turn to your almanacs, and you will notice that the Dragon or Scorpion is in pursuit of the woman, Virgin, sure enough, being the next sign in order in the zodiac; or direct your eyes to the heavens on a cloudless night, you will observe that just after the old maid (a virgin with a child in her arms, as the Persians show her) rises above the horizon in the East, up comes the old Scorpion called a serpent among the Persians; a Dragon in Phoenicia; Draco among the Romans, which is the Latin for Dragon.... The great Dragon, according to astronomical diagrams, is actually after the woman (Virgin) and her child, and was for thousands of years BC, and until modern astronomers caught him, and cast him into a bottomless pit, and substituted the eagle in his place.[1641]

Furthermore, Egyptian images of the Dragon were painted red; hence, "the great red Dragon."

The Mark of the Beast—666

The much ballyhooed number, 666, mentioned in Revelation as the "mark of the Beast," was in fact held sacred in the goddess-worshipping cultures as representative of female genitalia. When the Goddess was vilified by the patriarchy, she became the "Beast" and her sacred number the "mark." The number 666 was not held to be evil or a bad omen in Judaism, as is evidenced by the biblical story of Solomon possessing 666 talents of gold. In fact, it is a sacred number. As Higgins says:

> The Hexad or number *six* is considered by the Pythagoreans a perfect and sacred number; among many other reasons, because

1641 Graves, BS, 72-3.

> it divides the universe into equal parts. It is called Venus or the mother. It is also perfect, because it is the only number under X, ten, which is whole and equal in its parts. In Hebrew Vau is *six*. Is *vau* mother Eva or Eve?[1642]

In addition, Anderson points out that "666" also corresponds to the sun rising at 6:00 a.m., reaching its height six hours later, and setting at 6:00 p.m.[1643]

As "history" or "prophecy," the Book of Revelation is not only incomprehensible but destructive, not merely boggling the mind but causing people to see "Beasts" and "Antichrists" everywhere, thus creating prejudice and bigotry, and serving as a blueprint for Armageddon and the "*End Times*." Understood as astrology, or astrotheology, however, Revelation is powerful and informative, as it represents a condensed narration of the universal mythos and ritual, found throughout the Bible and revealed to be behind the Christ conspiracy. Its true meaning, of course, has been lost to the masses, as they have been told that astrology is "evil," a deliberate device to prevent them from studying it, because, with such astrological knowledge, they would understand clues such as Revelation 22:16, where the true nature of Jesus is clearly identified as the "morning star" (i.e., the sun), which is the real "revelation."

The Mysteries

It may be reasonably asked why, if the mythos and ritual are found around the world and thus in cultures not subjected to the censorship of the Catholic Church and Christian hierarchy, they are unknown. As noted, the mythos and ritual form part of "the mysteries" of secret societies, brotherhoods, priesthoods and mystery schools. As such, they were not to be revealed but dangled over the heads of the uninitiated. Of these secret societies, Allegro says:

> The whole point of a mystery cult was that few people knew its secret doctrines. So far as possible, the initiates did not commit their special knowledge to writing. Normally the secrets of the sect were transmitted orally, novices being required to learn direct from their mentors by heart, and placed under the most violent oaths never to disclose the details even under torture. When such special instruction was committed to writing, care would be taken that it should be read only by the members of the sect. This could be done by using a special code or cypher, as is the case with certain of the Dead Sea Scrolls. However, discovery

1642 Higgins, I, 221.
1643 Anderson, 137.

> of such obviously coded material on a person would render him suspect to the authorities. Another way of passing information was to conceal the message, incantations or special names within a document ostensibly concerning another subject.[1644]

In reality, the Christian religion was a revelation of these mysteries, which had existed for millennia. Indeed, "Paul" himself attested that his preaching of Jesus Christ served to reveal "the mystery which was kept secret for long ages but is now disclosed and through the prophetic writings is made known to all nations" (Rom. 16:25–26). In fact, it was because of the criminal revelation of this secret that the Christians were persecuted.

As the author of *The Other Jesus* says:

> Much is made of the fact that Christians were supposed to have been severely persecuted just for "worshipping Jesus," (and for no other reason) by the Romans during the first centuries AD. Although the degree to which Christians were actually persecuted by pagans has been wildly exaggerated, the truth is, early Christians did indeed seem to have evoked considerably more than their share of scorn and antagonism from pagan authorities. This is somewhat baffling because, as has often been pointed out, the official policy of the Roman Empire, both in principle and in practice, was one of permitting near total religious freedom. This extended even to the point of allowing many practices that even modern western nations would never permit in the name of religious freedom. But once you recognize that claiming you were about to "reveal the secrets of the Son of God Jesus" to the uninitiated public was a death penalty offense forbidden under the laws prohibiting people from "profaning" or "betraying the mysteries," you begin to at least partially understand why the pagan legal officials might have tended to take for granted that it was their duty to suppress "Christian" preachers. To them, certain aspects of Christian preaching represented blatant criminal activities. In the mind of the pagans, such sanctions against Christians were reasonable punishments for very definite, obvious and specific violations of the law, not unwarranted "persecutions" of people who were innocently worshipping God in their own way.

1644 Allegro, SMC, 42.

Essenes, Zealots and Zadokites

It has been established that the Christian religion is astrotheological, reflecting the mythos and ritual found ubiquitously long prior to the Christian era. The question remains as to how the Christian myth was created and by whom. In looking for the originators of Christianity, many people have pointed to the Essenes, the third Jewish sect besides the Pharisees and Sadducees in Jerusalem. Of course, because they cannot accept the non-historicity of virtually the entire gospel story and the Christian founder, such evemerists usually make the claim that beneath the countless layers of Pagan mythological lacquer there is yet a great master named Jesus who traveled around Palestine, ostensibly as a teacher of mysteries. The absolute dearth of evidence for such a master and his movement has perplexed researchers to no end, since, according to the gospel tales, not only had Jesus done wondrous works but so had his apostles, gaining fame near and far, and Christian churches with established hierarchies had popped up all over the Mediterranean during the first few decades after "the savior's" death. In their quest for such a leader and his organization, all that these seekers have been able to find is mention of the brotherhood of Essenes. Thus, because so little of the "history" presented in the New Testament appears in the historical or archaeological record, historicizing scholars have insisted that the Christians were the Essenes and that Christ must have been an Essene master and "teacher of righteousness" who, like John the Baptist, another purported Essene, went out preaching, baptizing and spreading the word of the Essene doctrine.

Like the mythicists' arguments, the Essene theory of Christian origins is repugnant to fundamentalists, because it posits the pre-existence of the Church, which would mean that Jesus was not its founder. The Church, according to such Christians, was not already established at the time of Christ's alleged advent but, under Christ's supernatural inspiration, miraculously caught fire and was empowered beyond all expectations, to spring up out of nowhere into a full-fledged movement, with extraordinary influence and, apparently, a good deal of wealth. In swallowing this yarn, then, we are supposed to accept that, within a number of years of Jesus's purported death, a ragtag band of illiterate fishermen and semiliterate peasants questionable in their faith in Jesus was able to establish a full-blown church, with bishops, deacons, parishes and rituals. All this they supposedly did, despite the fact that Jesus had said the end of the world was "close at hand."

The Myth of Primitive Christianity

In spite of this fervent belief, there remains no evidence for such a miraculous genesis, so scholars have been compelled to turn to the white-robed Essenes as the wellspring of Christianity. Within this theory, early Christianity was "pure" and "untainted" by corruption, which came only after it was institutionalized as the Catholic Church. Massey describes the "primitive Christianity" myth:

> Another popular delusion most ignorantly cherished is, that there was a golden age of *primitive Christianity*, which *followed* the preaching of the Founder and the practice of his apostles; and that there was a falling away from this paradisiacal state of primordial perfection when the Catholic Church in Rome lapsed into idolatry, Paganised and perverted the original religion.... Such is the pious opinion of those orthodox Protestants who are always clamouring to *get back beyond* the Roman Church to that ideal of primitive perfection supposed to be found in the simple teachings of Jesus, and the lives of his personal followers.... But when we do penetrate far enough into the past to see somewhat clearly through and beyond the cloud of dust that was the cause of a great obscuration in the first two centuries of our era, we find that there was no such new beginning, that the earliest days of the purest Christianity were prehistoric.[1645]

There is little foundation for the assumption of a peaceful, ideal beginning, because from its inception "pure" Christianity was full of bickering and power struggles, as reflected in the Epistles and Acts. In fact, the Church started out in a contentious manner and continued in this way for centuries, as is evidenced by the endless forged texts and bloody battles over doctrine.

In reality, the so-called pure Christianity would have been abhorrent to the followers of a simple morality such as the Essenes. For example, in addition to the squabbling, threats and apparent murders of converts such as in Acts, where Peter is depicted as having caused the deaths of a husband and wife over money, this "pure" Christianity included the exhortation of slaves to remain slaves, such as at 1 Timothy 6:1, which says, "Let all who are under the yoke of slavery regard their masters as worthy of all honor, so that the name of God and the teaching may not be defamed." (Obviously God's name is more important than living, breathing and suffering human beings, whose wretched state in itself should be a stain on God's good name in the first place.) Again, Colossians 3:22 says, "Slaves, obey in everything those who are your earthly masters"; and Titus 2:9 exhorts Christian leaders to "bid slaves to be submissive to their masters and to give satisfaction in every respect."

1645 Massey, GHC.

As noted, early Christians, in fact, were both slaves and slave owners. As Pagels says, "Many Christians were themselves slave owners and took slavery for granted as unthinkingly as their pagan neighbors."[1646] In other words, no egalitarian Christianity existed, and Christians were discouraged from inciting slaves to demand their freedom. As for the Essenes, "There is not a single slave among them," says Philo.

Thus, the "freedom-loving" Paul exhorts the Christians to submit to authority, not to rebel, as presumably his purported master would do and supposedly did do, according to the gospel story. Paul even claims that those same authorities who allegedly destroyed Jesus should be both obeyed "in everything" and basically equated with God Himself:

> Let every person be subject to the governing authorities. For there is no authority except from God, and those that exist have been instituted by God. Therefore he who resists the authorities resists what God has appointed, and those who resist will incur judgment.... For the same reason you also pay taxes, for the authorities are ministers of God, attending to this very thing. Pay all of them their dues, taxes to whom taxes are due, revenue to whom revenue is due, respect to whom respect is due, honor to whom honor is due. (Rom. 13)

Furthermore, the author of 1 Peter entreats:

> Be subject for the Lord's sake to every human institution, whether it be to the emperor as supreme, or to governors as sent by him to punish those who do wrong and to praise those who do right.... Fear God. Honor the emperor.

So much for the rebellious Jesus and his movement. No Essene would be preaching such things, but we can pretty much guess who would.

As to the real state of "pure" Christianity and its adherents, Fox relates:

> "In private houses nowadays," claimed the pagan Celsus, c. 170, "we see wool workers, cobblers, laundry workers and the most illiterate rustics who get hold of children and silly women in private and give out the most astonishing statements, saying that they must not listen to their father or schoolteachers, but must obey them. They alone know the right way to live, and if the children believe them, they will be happy. They whisper that they should leave their teachers and go down into the shops with their playmates in order to learn to be perfect."[1647]

1646 Pagels, AES, 52.
1647 Fox, 300.

Most of the early Christians were of the lower, uneducated classes, a fact that was a thorn in the side of Christian proselytizers, who were always very interested in gaining converts of high social status, by bribes of one sort or another. In the early Christian book the *Octavius* by Minucius, the protagonist "complained that Christians assemble the 'lowest dregs of society' and 'credulous women, an easy prey because of the instability of their sex.'"[1648] And, as Origen stated, most of the "lowest dregs" and poor had "very bad characters."

As Keeler says, "It sounds strange to hear persons in these days express a desire for a 'return to primitive Christianity, when all was peace and love.' There never was such a time."

The Essenes

Not only was there no "primitive" Christianity of love and peace that can be traced to the Essenes, but many of Jesus's own teachings were in contradiction to (or non-existent in) Essene philosophy. And Jesus's character and a number of his actions were contrary to the notion of him being an Essene master-healer. For example:

> A poor Canaanitish woman comes to him from a long distance and beseeches him to cure her daughter who is grievously obsessed. "Have mercy on me, O Lord," she pleads. But he answered her not a word. The disciples, brutes as they were, if the scene were real, besought him to send her away because she cried after them. Jesus answered, and said: "I was only sent to the lost sheep of the House of Israel." She worships him, he calls her one of the dogs.[1649] (Mt. 15:21–27)

In this passage, Jesus is not only uncompassionate, he is frankly rude, sexist and racist. Jesus is thus not the "gentle and loving son of God." Regarding Jesus's unmerited reputation as "Prince of Peace," Baigent and Leigh ask:

> Was Jesus indeed the meek lamblike saviour of subsequent Christian tradition? Was he indeed wholly non-violent? Why, then, did he embark on violent actions, such as overturning the tables of the money-changers in the Temple? … Why, before his vigil in Gethsemane, did he instruct his followers to equip themselves with swords? Why, shortly thereafter, did Peter actually draw a sword and lop off the ear of a minion in the High Priest's entourage?[1650]

The zealous Jesus's rash and brusque behavior is, in fact, contrary to the restraint and discipline of the peaceful Essenes.

1648 Fox, 300.
1649 Massey, GHC, 5.
1650 Baigent & Leigh, xvi.

In addition, the Essenes were not followers of the Hebrew Bible, or its prophets; nor did they subscribe to the concept of the original fall that required a savior. They did not believe in corporeal resurrection or a carnalized messiah. It was possibly they, among innumerable others, who were being addressed in the Second Letter of John: "For many deceivers have gone out into the world, *men who will not acknowledge the coming of Jesus Christ in the flesh.*" (2 John 1:7) The real Essenes, as described by Josephus, abhorred falsehood, and, unlike the Christian fathers, would not have mindlessly believed what is unbelievable. Moreover, the Essenes were teetotalers and ate to live, whereas the supposedly Essene Jesus appears to be a drunkard and glutton in comparison.

The forger of 1 Timothy makes a scathing attack on individuals who sound very much like the Palestinian Essenes:

> Now the Spirit expressly says that in later times some will depart from the faith by giving heed to deceitful spirits and doctrines of demons, through the pretensions of liars whose consciences are seared, who forbid marriage and enjoin abstinence from foods which God created to be received with thanksgiving.

In assailing those who prohibit marriage and preach what is apparently vegetarianism, "Paul" is referring to the Buddhistic, monastic fraternity that proliferated around the known world and included the Essenes.

Moreover, the Essenes studied the writings of the ancients and, being widespread around Palestine, certainly would have known its geography and topography. However, as noted, the New Testament writers do not, making numerous mistakes in their geographical descriptions.

Yet, despite all these disparities, many people still wish to label the Essenes as the earliest Christians, because, according to the Christian tale, the church grew far more rapidly than was possible, with its hierarchy and organization shooting up all around the Mediterranean within a few years and decades, implying a lengthy period of institutionalization. The New Testament churches would have been but recent franchises of a long-standing business. No doubt certain aspects of the New Testament were modeled after the white-robed monkishness of the Essenes, who were eventually swallowed up by the newly created religion, as well as by Judaism and any number of cults. However, the Jewish aspects of the Christ character are mainly Pharisaic, not Essenic. As Massey asserts:

> In proving that Joshua or Jesus was an Essene, there would be no more rest here than anywhere else for the sole of your foot upon the ground of historic fact. You could not make him to be the Founder of the Essene, Nazarite or Gnostic Brother-

> hoods, and communities of the genuine primitive Christians that were extant in various countries a very long while before the Era called Christian.... Philo-Judaeus ... was one of the Essenes—but does not seem to have met with the Gospel Jesus amongst them, or heard of him.[1651]

Furthermore, Josephus was himself an Essene a few decades after the purported advent of the great Essene master who allegedly made such a splash, yet this historian never heard of the "historical" Jesus. In other words, the Essenes themselves never recorded the gospel Jesus as one of their own; nor did they create him. Nor did Josephus once mention the numerous Christian churches and well-established hierarchies that had purportedly sprung up all over the place.

Qumran and the Dead Sea Scrolls

The idea of a monolithic Essene community from which Christianity issued was nonetheless given fuel with the discovery in 1947 of the caches of scrolls in caves near the ruined site of Qumran along the Dead Sea in present-day Palestine. However, there is yet another debate as to whether or not Qumran was indeed an Essene community. In fact, Josephus and Philo reported that the Essenes had no centralized location but dwelled in many cities and villages in Judea. Pliny asserted that some Essenes did reside by the Dead Sea, but their settlement was near En Gedi, dozens of kilometers south of Qumran. Also, Pliny stated that there was not a woman among the Essenes, whereas at Qumran the graves of women and children were found.

In reality, the archaeological finds indicate Qumran was *not* an Essene community but a waystation for travelers and merchants crossing the Dead Sea. In *Who Wrote the Dead Sea Scrolls?* Norman Golb evinced that Qumran was a fortress, not a monastery, as the site contains a large tower and a forge for weapons, both of which would be appropriate for the Jewish sect of the Zealots but not the Essenes. In addition, Golb posited that the scrolls were not written by any Essene scribes but constituted a collection from libraries in Jerusalem secreted in caves throughout eastern Palestine by Jews fleeing the Roman armies during the First Revolt of 70 CE. Of the theory that the scrolls represented only an Essene library, Golb says,

> The necessary implication of the Qumran-Essene theory was that while several hundred works of the four-thousand-strong Essene movement had escaped destruction, virtually no shred of manuscript stemming from the first century ad. population of Judaea as a whole—numbering at least two million individuals at the beginning of the First Re-

1651 Massey, GHC, 6–7.

volt—had been spared.[1652]

The Dead Sea collection is in fact eclectic, representing more than one sect or priesthood, competitors, in actuality. Although the scrolls are thus not connected to "the" Essenes as such, they represent "inter-testamental literature" and are extremely important in the quest for the origins of Christianity. Indeed, the absence of any early Christian writings or references to Jesus and his movement in this eclectic collection, some of which was no doubt from Jerusalem, serves as testimony that Christianity did not in fact yet exist when the scrolls were deposited, up to 40 and possibly more years after the purported death of Jesus. As Dr. Alan Snow states, "Some modern Biblical scholars and archaeologists believe that these scrolls could have been hidden in the caves as late as the Jewish revolt of 132–135 AD."[1653]

As to the contents of the scrolls, not only is no version of the term "Essene" found in them, but they actually contain non-Essenic and anti-Essenic ideas, as well as Hellenizing elements that could have been produced only by Hellenized "Jews" (i.e., Israelites) "zealous for the law" but also interpreting the law to allow "foreign" influence, in this case Greek. The fervent tone and warriorstance of some of the scrolls also belie any Essene origin and further indicate an attribution to the Zealots, who were, per Josephus, the "fourth sect of Jewish philosophy, [of whom] Judas the Galilean was the author," the term Galilean itself being used to denote a Zealot. The association with the Zealots is also confirmed by the presence of the scroll "Song for the Holocaust of the Sabbath" at both the caves near Qumran and the Zealot fortress of Masada. As Snow also says, "The authors of the Dead Sea Scrolls were Zealots and believed in the God-ordained destiny of the people of Israel."[1654]

The Zealots

From their contents, it is thus evident that a number of the more important original scrolls were written and deposited by "Zealots for the Law." As such, the authors were reflecting their history as representatives of the zealousness that emanated from their deity himself, who was not only a *jealous* but also a *zealous* god. In fact, although they are perceived as a separate sect, the "Zealots" constituted anyone who was, like their god, "zealous for the law," such as the various prophets, patriarchs, kings and assorted other heroes. Such zealousness did not end with the Old Testament, however, as "the" Zealots were overtly acknowledged in the New Testament, with the disciple "Simon the Canaanean," also

1652 Golb, 58.
1653 Leedom, 63–4.
1654 Leedom, 63–4.

called the "Zealot," and with the fiery gospel Judas, who resembles the zealous Judas mentioned by Josephus. As noted, however, Judas was the name of the ancestral savior-god of Judah, as well as of a number of Judaic kings and their sacrificial proxies, many of whom could be termed "Zealots." In any case, as is clear from his fanatical behavior and megalomania, Jesus himself is described as a Zealot and in fact was called "Jesus the Galilean" (Matt. 26:69). As Waite says:

> Not only was Jesus surrounded by Zealots, but he was himself a Zealot. It was in execution of a Jewish law, called "the law of the Zealots," that, with a whip made of small cords, he scourged the money-changers and drove them from the temple.[1655]

Peter was also called a Galilean, and his behavior in slicing off the servant's ear is certainly zealous. Paul is also obviously "zealous for the law," as seen.

According to Origen, "the" Zealots were a branch that broke off from the Essenes, which would explain the confusion between the two sects, both of which were also said to be offshoots of the Hasidic/Levitical priesthood, which was itself zealous, representing the Zealous God. Of this confusion between sects, Baigent and Leigh related that, in their search for the "historical" Jesus, they found themselves

> confronted by an apparently bewildering spectrum of Judaic cults, sects, and sub-sects, of political and religious organisations and institutions, which seemed sometimes to be militantly at odds with one another, sometimes to overlap. It became quickly apparent to us that the labels used to differentiate between the groups—Pharisees, Sadducees, Essenes, Zealots, Nazorenes—were neither accurate nor useful.[1656]

The zealous followers of Judas the Galilean were called *Sicarii* (hence *'Iscariot')*, named for the daggers they carried and plunged into the bosom of victims. Obviously, though they may have come from the same seed, the Zealots were not Essenes, as, in fact, the Essenes abhorred such violent zeal. However, other brotherhoods not only made use of such Zealots, they actually trained and funded them. "The" Zealots were, in general, lower-level initiates into secret societies, while the highest level were the sacerdotal class of Magi.[1657] If the higher level initiates wanted something done, the Zealots were the foot soldiers to send out.

Galilee and Samaria

Galilee plays an important role in the Christian drama, as it was at

---

1655 Waite, 517.
1656 Baigent & Leigh, xv.
1657 Jackson, 143.

Capernaum, in Galilee that Christ was said to have "come down" and spent part of his time. Although at one point a part of Israel/ Samaria, Galilee was multinational, with a largely Syrian influence, and by the first century BCE was mostly Gentile. Galilee was also known to be a stronghold of the zealous Jewish priesthood, the Sadducees. As Lockhart relates:

> [The] early "Penitents of Israel," composed of the purist Sadducees from the Temple in Jerusalem, left Judea and made their headquarters in the land of Damascus. Many sectaries founded settlements in the northern districts, and these "Elect of Israel" of the latter days interacted with like-minded spirits among the groups devoted to the old Nazarite way of life.[1658]

Galilee was thus a site for Sadducees displaced from the temple of Jerusalem, going back to the split between the kingdoms of Judah and Israel, when the Sadducees were called "sons of Zadok." Some of the Sadducees, however, remained in Jerusalem, where they held the high priesthood for centuries until they were driven out of the Sanhedrin by the Pharisees in the first centuries before and after the beginning of the Common Era.

As noted, the definition of and division between the various sects and priesthoods were not hard and fast. These groups' agendas or "interpretations of the law," in fact, depended on where they were located. Although they are deemed "purists" and "conservatives," the Sadducees were, in reality, Hellenizing Jews, and those who initially "repaired to" the northern kingdom of Israel became distinct from their counterparts in Jerusalem. The Israelite Sadducees apparently served as the "Jewish" priesthood not only in "Damascus," or Galilee, but also in Samaria, which is identified with Damascus at Isaiah 10:9: "Is not Samaria like Damascus?" Indeed, in Samaria, or Ephraim, there were several important Israelite sacred sites, such as Shiloh, Shechem, Beth-El and Mt. Gerizim, operated by the northern Levitical priesthood, which included Zadokites/Sadducees who left Judah on various occasions.

Like so many "sons of Israel," Israel/Ephraim/Samaria was accused by the Judeans of "whoring after other gods" and was purportedly punished for worshipping the "Harlot," or Goddess, and "Baal," the "golden calf" of Horus/Moloch (i.e., the sun). Lockhart describes the religion of the northern kingdom:

> The Israelite religion of northern Palestine so dear to the Nazarenes seems to have absorbed much of the worship of the Syrians and Phoenicians. This older faith carried folklore and ideas and us-

1658 Lockhart, D., 53.

ages foreign to its southern neighbour, and the pre-Christian Nazarenes of the north are shown by Epiphanius to have had an affinity with the gnostically inclined Samaritans, and the Samaritans with the Essenes.[1659]

Thus the northern Israelite religion, although ostensibly Yahwistic, was also "Pagan," following the old polytheism "of the fathers" and having greater correspondence to Gnosticism and Christianity than the Judean religion.

In addition, the biblical story concerning the split between the kingdoms is related by members of the Jerusalem or Judean priesthood in the "books of the prophets," which were rejected by the Israelites/Samaritans, who accepted only the Pentateuch, also known as the Torah or "Book of the Law."

According to these Judean books of the prophets, two centuries after the kingdom divided the entire Israelite population of Samaria was removed by the Assyrians and replaced with Persians or "Cutheans," who are portrayed by the Jews as the diabolical Samaritans. However, the Samaritans claimed they themselves were the original Israelites and true keepers of the law, and, like the Judeans, they maintained the right to interpret the Torah in their own favor. Lockhart describes the Samaritans and their side of the story:

> [The] Samaritans were a mixed population of Israelites and descendants of Assyrian colonists, and although professing a form of Judaism, slowly broke religious ties with both Galilee and Judea over the centuries. This break with Judaism also meant a break with the Temple cult at Jerusalem, and resulted in the Samaritans' building an independent temple on Mount Gerizim at the time of Alexander.... Viewing themselves as of a single, homogenous race, they claimed that they were actually the descendants of the Ten Tribes, utterly denying that the latter were ever deported *en masse* to Assyria as the Old Testament relates.[1660]

It seems that the "lost tribes" story was created by the Judeans to explain why the northern kingdom inhabitants, although "Jews," had a very different interpretation of Mosaic Law and worshipped after the manner of the original "Pagan" inhabitants. The story of the Israelite population being replaced also provided an excuse for the Jews to enslave the inhabitants of the northern kingdom, which, according to the scriptures, they did.

Furthermore, while the Jews considered the Samaritans to be "dogs,"

1659 Lockhart, D., 62.
1660 Lockhart, D., 205.

the feeling was mutual, and the Samaritans would claim their own right to serve as rulers over Israel, using the passage at Genesis 49:10: "The scepter shall not depart from Judah, nor the ruler's staff from between his feet, until *Shiloh* comes, and to him shall be the obedience of the peoples." Shiloh, as noted, is a northern kingdom sacred site, but the word also refers to the Messiah. In fact, the Samaritan Israelites were expecting their own Messiah, who in Greek was called "Dositheus," or "Gift of God." In addition, the early Christian texts the Clementine *Recognitions* states that:

> Dositheus was the founder of the sect of the Sadducees, which means probably nothing more historically than that Dositheus, as was to be expected of a Samaritan, rejected all the subsequently canonical books, and held to the Pentateuch alone.[1661]

Thus, the Clementine *Recognitions* associate the Sadducees with the Samaritans, as does the Pharisaic Talmud. Indeed, after their expulsion from the Sanhedrin, the remaining Judean Sadducees joined the Samaritans against the Judean Pharisaic priesthood.

The Zadokites/Sadducees

The rivalry between the priesthoods of Israel and Judah continued for centuries, extending into Galilee. At the end of the second century BCE, Galilee was violently subjugated by the Judeans: "Conquered by Aristobolus I in 104–103 BCE, Galilee was forcibly converted to Judaism, even to the extent of its population's having to undergo compulsory circumcision."[1662] Needless to say, like their Samaritan neighbors, the Galileans were not fond of the Judeans. In fact, Galilee was apparently a symbol of Judean oppression, which is evidently why Jesus was made to "come down" at Capernaum. After this invasion and forcible conversion, the ranks of the Herodian outpost Qumran supposedly swelled, evidently with Samaritans and Galileans, or Zealots "from Damascus," who also were the Sadducees, or "sons of Zadok" (i.e., "the priests who keep the covenant"), as the Zealots of the scrolls identified themselves. Indeed, Solomon Schechter, the discoverer of the Cairo edition of one important scroll also found at the Dead Sea—the "Zadokite Document," also known as the "Damascus Rule" or "Damascus Covenant"—considered the Dead Sea Zadokites an "offshoot" of the Sadducean sect, "possibly the Dositheans schism,"[1663] thereby also equating this Sadducean offshoot with the Samaritans.

According to Josephus, the Sadducees/Zadokites rejected the Pharisa-

1661 Mead, *DJL*, 361–362.
1662 Lockhart, 53.
1663 Golb, 83.

ic traditions not contained in "the law," which ostensibly meant that they spurned everything but the Pentateuch, again identifying the Sadducees with the Samaritan priesthood. However, the Sadducees/Zadokites were not only Samaritans but also Levites, such that they did at least interpret the teachings of the prophets, in their favor, of course. In this manner, the Zadokites of the scrolls appear to interpret the prophets to favor Israel/Ephraim/Samaria over the "wicked priests of Jerusalem," as in the commentary on Nahum: "when (eventually) the glory of Judah suffers dishonor, those in Ephraim who have hitherto been duped will flee from the midst of those men's congregations and, renouncing them that led them astray, attach themselves (once more) to (the true) Israel."[1664]

In addition, one Zadokite commentator virtually identifies himself as Syrian/Samaritan when he interprets Habakkuk 2:17, which refers to "the violence done to Lebanon," as "'Lebanon' stands here for the Communal Council." Concerning this statement, the author of *The Dead Sea Scriptures*, Theodore Gaster, notes, "The name Lebanon means 'white' (referring to the white cliffs). The point of the interpretation lies in the fact that the members of the Brotherhood wore white—as do the modern Samaritans and Mandaeans."[1665]

The author of the Zadokite Document reveals his own Samaritan affiliation when he says, "Nevertheless, in all of their generations He has ever raised up for Himself duly designated men.... And to these has He ever revealed His holy spirit at the hands of His anointed [Christ] and has ever disclosed the truth." Gaster calls these designated men "the anointed priests, custodians and teachers of the Law, which is here called 'the Truth,' as regularly among the Samaritans and Mandaeans."[1666] In fact, the Mandaeans were a Syrian pre-Christian brotherhood, one of the originators of Gnosticism whose high priests were called "Nasoreans" (i.e., Nazarenes/Nazarites). This passage also sounds Christian, obviously, and in fact represents a seed of the Gnostic-Christianity that would emanate out of Samaria/Galilee/Syria.

Furthermore, the author of the Zadokite Document refers to the split between the kingdoms and cites Amos 5:26, wherein "the Lord" says to Israel, "I will exile Sikkuth your king and Kiyyun your image, the star of your God … beyond Damascus." The Hebrew also translates, "You have borne the *tabernacle* of *Moloch* and Chiun your images, the star of your Elohim … beyond Damascus." The tabernacle of Moloch/Molech is also that of Saturn/El, the old Hebrew god, as is the star-god Kiyyun/

1664 Gaster, 316.
1665 Gaster, 346.
1666 Gaster, 108.

Chiun/ Kaiwan, a name "used to symbolize Israelite apostasy" (i.e., by Judeans against the northern kingdom). Of course, the goal of the Judean Amos's diatribe was to destroy Israel's high places and sanctuaries so its inhabitants would be forced to be involved in the centralized religion in Jerusalem. In addition, the objects of Amos's ire "hide themselves on the top of Carmel," which was a northern brotherhood stronghold or "monastery."

However, as Vermes says, "the Damascus Rule transforms this threat into a promise of salvation,"[1667] and the Zadokite author favorably interprets these passages by claiming that "Sikkuth your king" refers to the "Books of the Law" and "Kiyyun your image" to "the books of the prophets whose words the House of Israel has despised" (i.e., the post-Pentateuchal texts written by Judeans). The "star of your God" the Zadokite renders as "every such interpreter of the Law as indeed repairs to 'Damascus,' even as it is written: 'There shall step forth a star out of Jacob, and a scepter shall rise out of Israel.'"[1668] The Zadokite author further claims that they will be judged who "rejected the Covenant of God and the pledge which they swore in 'the land of Damascus'—that is, *the new covenant*." Thus these Zadokites/Sadducees were Syrian/Israelite/Samaritan/Carmelite worshippers of El/Molech who considered themselves the inheritors of the New Covenant and who emphasized that it was out of Israel, not Judah, that the "scepter" or, as they called him, the "Prince of the entire congregation" would come.

The story of Israel's "betrayal" with the shrine of Molech is important not only to the Zadokites but also to the zealous Christian disciple Stephen, who, at Acts 7, allegedly, repeats the episode in an allegorical recitation that in actuality represents the Hebrews' constant switching back and forth between the worship of the day and night skies. Stephen finishes off his speech with a mention of the "Righteous One, whom you have now betrayed and murdered," purportedly referring to Jesus. This title "Righteous," also applied to Abraham and the disciple James, could be translated as "Zadok," as the meaning of that name is "just" or "righteous." In fact, according to the genealogy in Matthew, Jesus himself is a "son of Zadok."

The Maccabean Revolt

Indeed, there was a "son of Zadok" named *Jesus* purportedly persecuted by "the Jews," during the Maccabean Revolt of 167 BCE, long prior to the alleged advent of the gospel Jesus. At that time, the Jerusalem Zadokite priestly family was deposed when the traditionalist Hasmoneans

1667 Vermes, 82.

1668 Gaster, 76.

sought to overthrow the Syrian leader Antiochus, who had captured the Jerusalem temple and, "determined to hellenize Judaea completely, forbade under penalty of death the observance of the sabbath and the practice of the rite of circumcision. In the temple he had a pagan altar, probably in honour of Zeus."[1669]

The Hellenizing charge under Antiochus was led by the "modernist" Zadokite Jesus, a "sage from Jerusalem," and was opposed by the Hasmonean/Maccabean Mattathias and his sons, one of whom was named *Judas*. This story served as a prototype for the gospel drama, with a Jesus who attempted to abrogate the Jewish religion by introducing a "foreign" influence and who was stopped by a Judas in league with traditionalists. This story and the gospel tale, in fact, retell the tale of ongoing rivalry between Israel and Judah. Furthermore, after the dethronement by the Maccabees, many of the remaining Jerusalem Zadokites scattered, some into Syria, Galilee and Samaria and others into Egypt, where the Zadokite high priest Onias IV, "in direct breach of biblical law erected a Jewish temple in Leontopolis with the blessing of King Ptolemy Philometor (182–146 BC),"[1670] an act that evidently scandalized the Palestinian priesthood and widened the rift.

The story of the Maccabean Revolt features a Jesus who can be considered the "teacher of righteousness" found in the Zadokite scrolls. However, the term "teacher of righteousness" is a title that could be applied to a number of individuals, past, present and future. "Teacher of righteousness" could also be translated the "teacher of Zadok," or "Zedek," and, conversely, the "sons of Zadok" could be called the "sons of righteousness."

The Order of Melchizedek

As noted, the "sons of Zadok" were the high priests, the only ones allowed to go to the north part of the temple to offer burnt offerings. The offering by burning is a mark of the cult of Molech, which, as we have seen, is being vindicated in the Zadokite Document. The cult of Molech has been demonstrated to be the same as the order of Melchizedek, whose name "king of Righteousness" could also be written "king of Zadok." As expected, Melchizedek takes an important role in the Zadokite literature. In one of the scrolls (11Q Melch), Melchizedek is depicted as the "savior-king who will bring peace and salvation to the faithful and condign punishment to the wicked and who will also mediate divine forgiveness for the former on the Final Day of Atonement."[1671] "And

1669 Wells, WWJ, 161.
1670 Vermes, 22.
1671 Gaster, 390.

Melchizedek will avenge the vengeance of the judgements of God … your *Elohim* reigns.… And your *Elohim* is Melchizedek."[1672]

The Zadokite brotherhood thus considered Melchizedek, or "righteous Molech," to be *their* El or god. Molech is the voracious deity to whom the Israelites sacrificed their children by burning, while beating drums and playing instruments to drown out the screams. That the Zadokites were worshippers of the Elohim and Adonai is also demonstrated when the Zadokite author says, "No one is to take the oath by EL—or by AD—," abbreviations utilized out of respect for the divinit(ies). As we have also seen, Molech, El and the various Elohim/Adonai represent aspects of the sun, and the esoteric sun-worshipping of the Zadokites/ Sadducees of the scrolls is further evidenced by the fact that they used a *solar* calendar, as opposed to the Judean lunar calendar. It should also be recalled that horoscopes were found at the Dead Sea, further demonstrating that the composers were esoteric adherents of the old religion. Also, the synagogues of Galilee/northern Israel, whence evidently came at least some of these Zadokites, commonly had zodiacs in mosaics on their floors.

Moreover, in the Dead Sea Scroll, "Invitation to Grace after Meals," the psalmist sings, "Although the Most High, forsooth, is Jacob's special Lord, yet does His majesty reach out over all that He has made." The special "Lord" is Adonai; the "Most High" is Elyon or Helios, the sun; and Jacob the Supplanter is Set, the night sky. This passage, then, could read, "Although the sun is the lord over the night sky." In addition, in the "Morning Hymn" the psalmist gushes, "Before Him goes a splendor; behind Him a surge of many waters." These verses refer to the sun as it rises in the morning, demonstrating the reverence the writer holds for the divine luminary.

Naturally, the Zadokite scroll writers also used the Tetragrammaton, YHWH/IEUE, although sparingly, compared to the evidently Pharisaic compositions found at the Dead Sea. The Tetragrammaton was used because it was believed that anything with the sacred name on it must not be destroyed; yet, the scrolls were ultimately shredded. Furthermore, as a typical priesthood attempting to dominate the world and procure total control over the people, the Zadokites were well trained to give an appearance of "monotheism" so they could claim to be "the Elect" and to hold the keys to the "one Jealous/Zealous God," the war god used to incite their soldier-Zealots. But, again, per Ezekiel, there was that "secret room behind the hole in the wall," which so angered the Jealous God and where the elders were no doubt engaged in the mysteries of "Righteous Molech," or Melchizedek.

1672 Vermes, 301.

The Zadokite Elect's predictions or intentions appear in another Dead Sea Melchizedek text, "The Last Jubilee," which reveals:

> The future king of Righteousness—that is, Melchizedek *redivivus*—will execute upon them God's avenging judgments, and at the same time deliver the [righteous] from the hands of Belial and all those spirits of his ilk.[1673]

In this paragraph we find another connection between the Dead Sea Scrolls and the New Testament (Hebrews 7), in which Jesus is made a "priest after the order of Melchizedek." The word "redivivus," meaning reborn, comes from a Latin term meaning "second-hand" as in "building materials," which sounds very much like the "cornerstone the builders rejected" (i.e., Jesus, as he is called in the gospel story). Hence, Jesus is "Melchizedek redivivus." This scroll does not serve as an astoundingly accurate "prediction," however, but as a *blueprint* for the creation of the ultimate godman.

Furthermore, the sons of Zadok, like Melchizedek, the priest forever, were the "priests whom God has chosen to keep His covenant firm for ever."[1674] This covenant was "now consummated" with "the church of the members of this Community," as was said in the scroll titled "The Messianic Kingdom."[1675] Regarding the word "church" in this text, Gaster says, "It is interesting to find in the Hebrew the same word (*knst*), the Syriac cognate of which was later adopted by the Christians to designate their own communion."[1676] Thus, we have yet another element connecting the Zadokites, Syria/Samaria and Christianity.

Joshua

The mention of Joshua in the scrolls provides another piece of the puzzle, since Joshua was a northern kingdom hero. In fact, he was the Carmelite/Israelite tribal sun god and savior, who served as a "type of Jesus" used in the creation of Christianity.

In discussing one of the "messianic expectation scrolls," regarding the "five Scriptural passages attesting the advent of the Future Prophet and the Anointed King and the final discomfiture of the impious," Gaster relates:

> The fifth is an interpretation of a verse from the Book of Joshua. An interesting feature of this document (not noticed by the original editor) is that precisely the same passages of the Pentateuch are used by the Samaritans as the stock testimonial to the

1673 Gaster, 435.
1674 Gaster, 97.
1675 Gaster, 443.
1676 Gaster, 470.

> coming of the Taheb, or future "Restorer". They evidently constituted a standard set of such quotations, of the type that scholars have long supposed to have been in the hands of New Testament writers when they cited passages from the Hebrew Bible supposedly confirmed by incidents in the life and career of Jesus.[1677]

These statements themselves constitute a virtual acknowledgement that the scroll author is a Samaritan and that Jesus was a remake of Joshua by Samaritans. Furthermore, since the scrolls evidently for the most part were not written at Qumran but gathered from elsewhere, possibly over a period of two centuries, it is feasible that some of these Samaritan Zadokites emanated out of the ancient monastery at Mt. Carmel, site of a Temple of Jupiter or Iao (Pater) that also served as a temple of Melchizedek and of Joshua.[1678] It was the apostate Israelites hiding on top of Carmel who so vexed Amos.

Their reverence for the sun and for solar gods and heroes, their solar calendar, overt astrological texts and zodiacs in their synagogues, as well as their white robes, all reveal that the Zadokites/Sadducees were remnants of the ancient priesthood of the sun. Furthermore, Gaster relates that the Dead Sea "sectarians" were expecting the end of the "Great Year."

> The [writers of the scrolls] were swept ... by other winds. One of these was a widespread and well-attested contemporary belief that the great cycle of the ages was about to complete its revolution.... When major upheavals occurred, it was promptly supposed that the cycle was nearing its end, that the Great Year was at hand, and that the cosmos was about to revert to chaos.... Then the cycle would begin again; a new world would be brought to birth.[1679]

The term "Great Year" usually refers to the precession of the equinoxes, of which the age then ending was Aries. According to Josephus, the phrase "Great Year" was also used to describe the 600-year "Phoenix" cycle,[1680] which was called by others "Neros." In accordance with the age-old practice of imagining heaven on Earth (i.e., reproducing below what was above), the priest-astrologers worldwide were no doubt intent on creating any number of new solar incarnations for the end of both "Great Years," an auspicious and unstable time indeed. The race was on, and whoever arrived first would get the "Phoenix" as well as

1677 Gaster, 393.
1678 Higgins, I, 329.
1679 Gaster, 8.
1680 Josephus, Antiquities, I, iii, 9.

dominate the Age of Pisces. The "Jews" basically won, but, as the Zadokites said, "And when the present era is completed, there will be no more express affiliation with the house of Judah; every man will 'mount guard' for himself."[1681] Which is to say that there would be no more overt Jews; rather, they would be priests of the "new covenant," or "new testament," as it would later be called.

The Zadokites and Christianity

It is evident that the Zadokites/Sadducees were attempting to produce a "future king of righteousness" to restore to them their traditional priestly role, a new Joshua/Jesus of the type of both the Old Testament and the Maccabean Revolt. Furthermore, the Zadokite Document says, the "scepter of Israel," also the "Prince of the entire Congregation," will destroy the "sons of Seth" (as at Num. 24:17). These "sons of Seth" were evidently the black-robed Pharisees, as mainly luni-stellar cult people, while the white-robed Sadducees were mainly solar cultists. These priesthoods and factions vying for supremacy thus reflect the same struggle between light and dark that goes on daily and nightly, as well as annually and precessionally. Thus, the solar cultist Zadokite covenanters called themselves a church and were expecting "Melchizedek redivivus" out of Israel/Samaria/Galilee who would destroy the "wicked priests of Jerusalem." In this way, the new Joshua or Jesus was to overthrow the Pharisees, as was imagined in the New Testament.

In their writings, the Zadokites are certain of the coming Messianic Age and the advent of a "wondrous child" who would be precocious at the age of two or three and dazzle his elders, the same traditionally said of Jesus. As Gaster says of the treatise he calls "The Wondrous Child":

> It is a prediction (one scholar has called it a horoscope) of the birth of a Wondrous Child, characterized as "the chosen of God" and of events which will ensue thereafter. The child will bear (like Krishna and Buddha) special marks on his body, and will be distinguished by precocious wisdom and intelligence. He will be able to prove the secrets of all living creatures, and no schemes against him will succeed.[1682]

Along with these several correspondences between the Zadokites and Christianity are many others. As Golb says, "Scholars of the New Testament have demonstrated abundant parallels between ideas it contains and those found in the scrolls."[1683]

The Christian origins can be seen further in the Zadokite Document:

1681 Gaster, 71.
1682 Gaster, 394.
1683 Golb, 335.

"And God will accept their atonement, and because they took refuge in His holy name they shall indeed see salvation at His hand."[1684] This very Christian sentence is not an interpolation but reflects one school of thought that shaped Christianity, representing one zealous "Jewish" branch of the ubiquitous pre-Christian salvation cult.

The connection between the Zadokites and Christianity is also evidenced by a variety of concepts and terms, such as the "Holy Spirit," "Salvation," "sons of Light" and "the Elect," a term also used by the Mandaeans/Nazarenes. There is likewise a link between the Mandaeans' Book of John the Baptist and the Genesis Apocryphon found at the Dead Sea.

Furthermore, the author of the Zadokite Manual of Discipline refers to the "deliberative council of the community" in which "there shall be twelve laymen and three priests schooled to perfection in all that has been revealed of the entire Law." Of this council and community, Gaster comments:

> No less interesting, and perhaps more exciting, than [the Dead Sea Scrolls'] connection with the Essenes are the many parallels which these texts afford with the organization of the primitive Christian Church. The community calls itself by the same name (*'edah*) as was used by the early Christians of Palestine to designate its legislative assembly as was used by that community to denote the council of the Church. There are twelve "men of holiness" who act as general guides of the community—a remarkable correspondence with the Twelve Disciples. These men have three superiors, answering to the designation of John, Peter and James as the three pillars of the Church.[1685]

Regarding this deliberative council composed of "presbyters," the Zadokite writer continues:

> Any knowledge which the expositor of the law may possess but which may have to remain arcane to the ordinary layman, he shall not keep hidden from them; for in their case there need be no fear that it might induce apostasy.

Here is an admission of the existence of the mysteries, i.e., the mythos and ritual "behind the hidden door." It is also a confession of the conspiracy to keep such mysteries secret from the masses and of their possible effect on them, i.e., that the people would fall away from the faith if they knew such secrets.

The Zadokite author further says of the council:

1684 Gaster, 79.

1685 Gaster, 39.

> When these men exist in Israel, these are the provisions whereby they are to be kept apart from any consort with froward men, to the end that they may indeed "go into the wilderness to prepare the way," i.e., do what Scripture enjoins when it says, "Prepare in the wilderness the way ... make straight in the desert a highway for our God" [Isa. 40:3].[1686]

As Gaster says, "The same quotation is used in the same sense by John the Baptist; Mat. 3:3; John 1:23," thus illustrating yet another important link between the Zadokites and Christianity.

Regarding the role of the "specially holy men," the Zadokite sage also states:

> Until the coming of the Prophet and of both the priestly and the lay Messiah, these men are not to depart from the clear intent of the Law to walk in any way in the stubbornness of their own hearts.

Gaster notes, "That is, the prophet foretold in Deut. 18:18, 'I will raise them up a prophet from among their brethren, like unto thee [Moses]; and I will put My words in his mouth, and he shall speak unto them all that I shall command him.'"[1687] The prophet who is supposedly predicted at Deuteronomy 18 is in fact Joshua—that is, *Jesus*, who is to act as a "mouthpiece of God." The priestly and lay Messiahs are, of course, *Christs*. The obvious conclusion is that when all else failed, i.e., when no such divine instruments were forthcoming, the conspirators rolled these exalted personages into one fictionalized character, i.e., Jesus the Christ.

Moreover, Gaster explains that the Manual of Discipline and Zadokite Document are similar to the Christian texts called the Didache, the Didascalia Apostolorum, and the Apostolic Constitutions of the early Church organization.[1688] The scrolls also contained Jewish apocrypha and pseudepigrapha, as well as texts with a Zoroastrian/Hellenistic Gnostic tinge, such as the "Memoirs of Patriarchs," the Psalms and the "Litany of the Angels," indicating that these Zadokites were of the same brotherhood at Antioch, whence came Gnosticism and where "Christians" were first so called. The Book of Enoch was found at the Dead Sea, as were scrolls containing quotations identical to one in the Epistle of Barnabas and one in the works of Justin Martyr, thus proving the connection between the Christians and the Zadokites.[1689]

It was not the Essenes who constituted the "Jewish" brotherhood

1686 Gaster, 61.
1687 Gaster, 63.
1688 Gaster, 40.
1689 Baigent & Leigh, 65.

from which Christianity issued but the Syro-Samaritan Gnostic "sons of Zadok," the authors of various Dead Sea Scrolls who were determined to restore their priesthood to its proper place as spiritual leaders of Israel and of all mankind, and who occupied some of the most important places depicted in the New Testament: Jerusalem, Galilee and Antioch. The Zadokites/Sadducees were the Palestinian contributors to the Christ conspiracy, constituting a sect that "held by the way" of Abraham and Melchizedek, and that, while exoterically representing the "One God," nevertheless esoterically worshipped and propitiated after the manner of the old solar cult and polytheistic, astrotheological religion. As members of the white-robed brotherhood, these Zadokites were in opposition to the black-robed "sons of Seth" who also claimed to represent the Jealous/Zealous God.

In their many internecine battles, the Zadokites were deposed in Jerusalem by the Hasids/Hasmoneans/Pharisees, and driven to Syria/Samaria and Egypt. With the destruction of Palestine, another wave of both Jewish and Samaritan refugees entered into the "foreign" brotherhood branches, especially that of Alexandria, one of the most important cities in the ancient world.

Alexandria: Crucible of Christianity

> "It should be remembered that in Alexandria, paganism, Judaism and Christianity never evolved in isolation. All of these forms of religion (evolved) magical practices that seduced both the humble members of the population and the most well-off classes. It was in Alexandria where new religious constructions were made to propose solutions to the problem of man, of God's world. Cults of Isis, mysteries of Mithra, and early Christianity bear witness to this."

—Egyptologist Dr. David Fabre, "Earliest Reference Describes Christ as 'Magician'"

> "A proper history for this period must therefore describe how pagans created in the second century both the theology for Jesus Christ—out of the Christology of Philo—and, out of the existing pagan, state structures, the organization of the Christian Churches."

—John Bartram, "Chrestians and the Lost History of Classical Antiquity"

> "The 'spiritual' home of chrestic archaeology—the chrestic movement—is clearly Alexandria and most likely the Royal Library there. Yet it is found across the Hellenistic world, most

particularly within the Persian orbit, from those small kingdoms contested with Rome, to Parthia and Greco-India."

—John Bartram, "The Vacuum of Evidence for Pre-4th Century Christianity"

"There are records from Alexandria that indicate the arrival of a steady stream of Buddhist monks and philosophers. They would surely have contributed to the philosophical speculations and syncretism for which the city was noted.

"In particular, it seems the original Therapeutae were sent by Asoka on an embassy to Pharaoh Ptolemy II in 250 BC."

—Ken Humphreys, *Jesus Never Existed* (102)

The confusion regarding the Essenes and early Christianity is understandable, because there was in fact a well-established organization, or "church," long prior to the Christian era, as has been demonstrated repeatedly with references to the numerous brotherhoods, priesthoods, sects and cults around the globe but also concentrated in the area in which the Christian drama is alleged to have taken place, i.e., Syria, Galilee, Samaria and Judea. In reality, as we have seen, like its savior and doctrine, Christianity's hierarchy was based on a variety of "Pagan" predecessors, such as the Mithraic and Brahmanical priesthoods, as well as on the Hellenistic-Jewish Zadokite/Sadducean model outlined in the Dead Sea Scrolls.

Although Christians have pretended such brotherhoods and organizations never existed, they are revealed throughout the New Testament, in which the nascent Christian church is already presented as having, in the words of Taylor,

> the full ripe arrogance of an already established hierarchy; bishops disputing for their prerogatives, and throne-enseated prelates demanding and receiving more than the honours of temporal sovereignty, from their cringing vassals, and denouncing worse than inflictions of temporal punishment against the heretics who should presume to resist their decrees, or dispute their authority.[1690]

Obviously, such an established institution could not have appeared overnight out of nowhere but was, in fact, pre-Christian. Concerning this pre-existing organization, Massey says:

> The existence of primitive and pre-historic Christians is acknowledged in the Gospel according to Mark when John says, "Master, we saw one casting out devils in thy name, and he followeth not us." … According to the account in Matthew, before ever a disciple had gone forth or could have begun to preach

1690 Taylor, R., 84.

> historic Christianity, there was a widespread secret organization ready to receive and bound to succour those who were sent out in every city of Israel. Who, then are these? They are called "The Worthy." That is, as with the Essenes, those who have stood the tests, proved faithful, and been found worthy. According to the canonical account these were the pre-historic Christians, whether called Essenes or Nazarenes; the worthy, the faithful, or the Brethren of the Lord.[1691]

In a somewhat similar vein, Doherty states:

> Within a handful of years of Jesus' supposed death, we find Christian communities all over the eastern Mediterranean, their founders unknown.... Paul could not possibly account for all the Christian centres across the Empire; many were in existence before he got there.... A form of Christian faith later declared heretical, Gnosticism, clearly preceded the establishment of orthodox beliefs and churches in whole areas like northern Syria and Egypt. Indeed, the sheer variety of Christian expression and competitiveness in the first century, as revealed in documents both inside the New Testament and out, is inexplicable if it all proceeded from a single missionary movement beginning from a single source.... Paul meets rivals at every turn who are interfering with his work, whose views he is trying to combat. The "false apostles" he rails against in 2 Corinthians 10 and 11 are "proclaiming another Jesus" and they are certainly not from Peter's group. Where do they all come from and where do they get their ideas? The answer seems inevitable: Christianity was born in a thousand places, in the broad fertile soil of Hellenistic Judaism. It sprang up in many independent communities and sects, expressing itself in a great variety of doctrines.[1692]

This "other" Jesus being proclaimed by a rival group was in fact the ubiquitous, non-historical Savior of the numerous cults and religions of the pre-Christian brotherhood network, and his name was a secret spell used, among other things, to "cast out devils."

The existence of "Christian" churches before "Jesus of Nazareth" is also attested by the author of the Epistle to the Philippians attributed to early Church father "Polycarp" (c. 69–155 BCE), in which he says of Christ, "he glories in you in all the churches *who then only knew God; for we did not then know him.*"[1693]

1691 Massey, GHC, 10.

1692 "The Jesus Puzzle," Net.

1693 The Lost Books of the Bible, 196.

The Therapeuts

As we have seen, the Zadokites/Sadducees of the scrolls constituted a major part of the eventual Christian edifice. However, as also demonstrated, there were numerous other religions, sects and brotherhoods, including and especially the Gnostics, whose earliest efforts to create a new religion were in fact non-historicizing and non-Judaizing, such that Christianity was not born solely of Judaism by any means. It was, in actuality, the creation of the Pagan priesthood, with a Jewish overlay.

In addition, the term "Essene" was used not only for the Palestinian sect, but, as Josephus says, there was "*another order* of Essenes," and Walker relates that at "the Ephesian temple of Artemis, the *melissae* were accompanied by eunuch priests known as *essenes*, meaning 'drones.'"[1694] In reality, there were several groups of "Essenes."

These pre-historic Christians were called by Philo not only Essenes but also Eclectics, Ascetics and Therapeuts, who were indeed members of a brotherhood that already had parishes, churches, bishops, priests and deacons long before the Christian era. Headquartered at Alexandria, this Therapeutan society also observed the same festivals as those of the "later" Christianity, and, like Christianity, pretended to have apostolic founders. Also like the historic Christians, these pre-historic "Christians" used scriptures they claimed were divinely inspired and had colonies at the same places claimed by the historic Christians, i.e., Rome, Corinth, Galatia, Ephesus, Philippi, Colosse and Thessalonica, as found in the Pauline epistles—all before the alleged advent of Jesus Christ.[1695]

Like "Essene," the Greek word "Therapeut" means "healer" or "physician," as in "physician of the soul." The Therapeuts were, in fact, salvation cultists, but their savior was the "light of the world that every eye can see," because, also like the Essenes and so many others, they were "sun-worshippers." They were therefore no strangers to the ubiquitous solar myth, which existed in virtually every culture of the day in myriad forms and which previously had been historicized a number of times in the Old Testament. As Philo stated regarding the Therapeuts:

> They turn to the east, and, as soon as they espy the sun rising, they stretch aloft their hands to heaven and start praying for a fair day, and for truth and clear judgement in their vision.[1696]

Like virtually the entire Mediterranean world, the Therapeuts also esteemed the Great Goddess, Isis/Mari, Herself a healer and savior. As Allegro relates: "The Therapeutae ... claimed Isis among their patrons.

1694 Walker, WDSSO, 414.
1695 Taylor, R. 70–76.
1696 Allegro, DSSCM, 111.

She was reckoned to cure the sick and to bring the dead to life, and she bore the title 'Mother of God.'"[1697]

Thus, the Therapeuts were basically "Pagan" "polytheists" and syncretizing Gnostics attempting to unify the solar, lunar and stellar cults. Doane says of this widespread and well-established brotherhood:

> For many centuries before the time of Christ Jesus there lived a sect of religious monks known as *Essenes*, or *Therapeuts*; *these entirely disappeared from history shortly after the time assigned for the crucifixion of Jesus*. There were thousands of them, and their *monasteries* were to be counted by the score. Many have asked the question, "What became of them?"[1698]

In short, they became the Christians, as it was they who created Christianity.

The Gospels in Egypt

If the Church's organization was well in place prior to the Christian era, so was the pre-existence of the entire gospel story, in bits and pieces around the "known world," eventually put together by the Therapeuts at Alexandria. That the original gospels and epistles were in the possession of the Therapeuts is attested to by Church historian Eusebius. In his admission, Eusebius first relates what Philo said of the Therapeuts:

> They possess also short works by early writers, the founders of their sect, who left many specimens of the *allegorical* method, which they take as their models, following the system on which their predecessors worked.[1699]

As noted, the Therapeuts were also the Gnostics, as is evidenced by the acknowledgment that their "short works" were *allegorical* rather than literal. The change from Gnostic to Orthodox Christianity, in fact, constituted the switch from knowledge of the allegory to blind faith in the literal. Eusebius goes on to say:

> It seems likely that Philo wrote this after listening to their exposition of the Holy Scriptures, and it is very probable that what he calls short works by their early writers were the gospels, the apostolic writings, and in all probability passages interpreting the old prophets, such as are contained in the Epistle to the Hebrews and several others of Paul's epistles.

Of the Therapeutan Church, Eusebius remarks, "These statements of Philo seem to me to refer plainly and unquestionably to members of

1697 Allegro, DSSCM, 157–8.
1698 Doane, 419.
1699 Eusebius, 52.

our Church." Eusebius's assertions are more than just peculiar when one considers he was *the* church historian who was purporting to be recording a continuous apostolic lineage, such that, had it really existed, these important aspects of the history of the Christian religion surely would have been widely known by virtually everyone indoctrinated into it.

Concerning Eusebius's admissions, Taylor states:

> Eusebius has attested, that the Therapeutan monks were Christians, many ages before the period assigned to the birth of Christ; and that the Diegesis and Gnomologue, from which the Evangelists compiled their gospels, were writings which had for ages constituted the sacred scriptures of those Egyptian visionaries.[1700]

These pre-Christian gospels and epistles were those of the Gnostics, especially of Marcion, creator of the first New Testament, who was an "anti-Jewish" *Samaritan* member of the Therapeutan brotherhood, which constituted, Eusebius admits, the early Christians. Marcion's texts originated at Antioch, which represented the birthplace or cradle of Christianity. However, it was at Alexandria, the crucible of Christianity, where many key ingredients were combined, including the Indian/Egyptian narratives and mysteries, and where the allegorical and astrotheological characters eventually began to be carnalized and Judaized.

This Therapeut origin of the autographs or original "gospel" texts would seem to contradict the fact that Jesus and his church were not Essenic, since the Essenes are frequently identified with the Therapeuts. However, there are important distinctions between the monkish sect of Palestine and the mystery school at Alexandria. As Philo stated, the Essenic communities in Palestine and Arabia "did not soar to such a lofty height of philosophic and mystic endeavour as the members of the community near Alexandria."[1701] The Essenes of Palestine were much simpler and more contemplative than the worldly Therapeuts, who were profoundly engaged in the mystery religions, initiations and rituals. While both were called "healers," these were two different sects, although they were connected, as is the case with numerous brotherhoods and secret societies. The Therapeuts were, in fact, a major part of the brotherhood network that stretched from Egypt to China and up into Europe. Indeed, many of the aspects in the gospels attributed to "the" Essenes, such as prayer, fasting, celibacy, baptism, contemplation, cleanliness, healing, etc., were in reality practices common to the monastic communities around the world for millennia.

1700 Taylor, R., 131.
1701 Taylor, R.

Regarding the confusion between the Essenes and Therapeuts, Waite says:

> By most writers the Essenes of Palestine and the Therapeuts of Egypt have been confusedly treated as the same people; or if not the same, it has been supposed that one was a branch or colony of the other. Later scholarship has shown, however, that neither of these theories is correct.[1702]

Eusebius also makes the distinction between the Therapeuts and Essenes when he relates a passage from Hegesippus stating that the Therapeuts were basically Christians but the Essenes were of the "various Groups of the Circumcision, among the Children of Israel, all hostile to the tribe of Judah and the Christ."[1703] Obviously, then, these Church fathers are acknowledging not only that the Therapeuts were the Christians and that the Essenes were not, but also that the Essenes were actually at odds with the Therapeuts.

Naturally, neither the Therapeuts nor the Essenes could be identified in the gospels, since that would serve to reveal the pre-existence of their Christian-like fraternities. Nevertheless, the Therapeutan ideology left its mark on the New Testament. In addition to the white-robed monkishness already discussed, the statements about the mysteries and the "kingdom of heaven" are references to initiation into the Therapeutan mystery school and doctrine. The Therapeutan network also included the Palestinian Nazarenes, which is why they are mentioned and why Jesus was claimed to be one of them, although the meaning was obfuscated to "Jesus of Nazareth" so that, again, the pre-existence of the brotherhood would not be known. As Wells says:

> In Acts 24:5 the hostile Jews describe Paul as a "ringleader of the sect of the Nazarenes"—which does not here mean "people from Nazareth" but "Christians." In the Talmud too the term is used as a Jewish term of abuse for Christians.... It is thus possible to hold that the adjective "Nazarene" originally designated a strict pre-Christian sect out of which Jesus and the Church emerged."[1704]

These Nazarenes were also Mandaeans and Gnostics; thus, they were Syrians and Samaritans, enemies of the Judeans. Furthermore, in addition to being a Nazarene, Paul calls himself a deacon, which was already a low-level office of the Therapeutan brotherhood. The evangelist Luke was also made to be a physician, or *Therapeut*. In the gospel

1702 Waite, 500.
1703 Eusebius, 129.
1704 Wells, DJE, 146.

story, Jesus is also depicted in the temple as making fools of the elders and *doctors*, i.e., Therapeuts. The early Christians called the Lord himself a "devoted physician," or Therapeut. Christian father Epiphanius confirms the association between Christianity and the Therapeutan brotherhood when he says, "Jesus, in the Hebrew, signifies a healer or physician. However that may be, this is the name by which they were known before they were called Christians."[1705] He is in fact referring to the "Jesseans" or "Essenes," i.e., "Therapeuts."

Furthermore, as noted, priests were considered "physicians of the soul," and the early Church hierarchy included "doctors," i.e., Therapeuts, who were also wandering drug-peddlers. In fact, the professions of medicine and divinity were inseparable, and those doctors or healers who received their degrees from the University of Alexandria were viewed as true apostles, while those who did not were deemed false. Of these priest-physicians, Higgins says:

> The Essenians were called physicians of the soul or Therapeutae; being resident of both Judaea and Egypt, they probably spoke or had their sacred books in Chaldee. They were Pythagoreans, as is proved by all their forms, ceremonies, and doctrines, and they called themselves sons of Jesse.... If the Pythagoreans or Coenobitae, as they were called by Jamblicus, were Buddhists, the Essenians were Buddhists. The Essenians ... lived in Egypt on the lake of Parembole or Maria, in *monasteries*. These are the very places in which we formerly found the Gymnosophists or Samaeans or Buddhist priests to have lived, which Gymnosophists are placed also by Ptolemy in North-eastern India.[1706]

And Doane states that "Dean Milman was convinced that the Therapeuts sprung from the 'contemplative and indolent fraternities' of India."[1707] Higgins continues:

> If the opinion be well founded, that their Scriptures were the originals of the Gospel histories, then it will follow almost certainly, that they must have been the same as the Samaneans or Gymnosophists of Porphyry and Clemen Alexandrinus, and their books, which they were bound by such solemn oaths to keep secret, must have been the Vedas of India; or some Indian books containing the mythoses of Moses and Jesus Christ.[1708]

Of the gospel account, Taylor states that "the travelling Egyptian

1705 Waite, 510.
1706 Higgins, I, 747.
1707 Doane, 423 fn.
1708 Higgins, II, 43.

Therapeuts brought the whole story from India to their monasteries in Egypt, where, sometime after the commencement of the Roman monarchy, it was transmuted in Christianity."[1709] These books were from either the northeast of India or the coast of Malabar, or both, and were evidently first taken to Antioch and then to Egypt, by Apollonius, Marcion and/ or others.

Like their eastern counterparts, the Therapeutan brotherhood had a savior-god and the attendant sayings and mysteries long before the Christian era. The Therapeuts were also followers of Serapis, "the peculiar god of the Christians," who had been created specifically to roll into one the various savior cults, thus providing the doctors with practice for their greatest creation. This savior-god of the brotherhood network extending from Britain to India was variously named IE, IES, Ieud, Judas, Joshua, Jason, Iesous, Iesios, Iasios, or other variants, which, again, represented a *secret spell*. Walker relates that "Iasus signified a healer or *Therapeuta*, as the Greeks called the Essenes, whose cult groups always included a man with the title of *Christos*."[1710] Here again is the pre-existence of the words "Jesus" and "Christ" that Eusebius was forced to admit in the face of charges that Christ was a fictional character.

The Alexandrian Jews

In the centuries before the Christian era, many Jews and other Israelites had migrated to Egypt, and by the third century BCE, there was already a large Jewish community at Alexandria. As confirmed by Apion, the Alexandrian Jews were "from Syria," i.e., they were Antiochans, Galileans, Samaritans and Zadokites/ Sadducees, the latter of whom, as Levites, transcended nationality and developed affiliation with the nation in which they lived. However, Josephus claimed that the "Alexandrian Jews" disputed with the Samaritans in Egypt over whose temple was "according to the law," the one at Jerusalem or that at Mt. Gerizim. According to Josephus, who was a Jew and, therefore, not a Samaritan, the case was pleaded before Ptolemy (63–47 BCE), who decreed the Jews the winners and had the Samaritan representatives executed. While "the Jews," or Judeans, thus may have been powerful within Alexandrian Judaism, they were not so within the Alexandrian mystery school, since, as noted, the "Jewish" Therapeuts were in large part Nazarenes and Samaritans, both of whom were enemies of the Judeans.

In the second century CE, after the destructions of both 70 and 135, increasing numbers of zealous Jews, Samaritans and other Israelites mi-

---

1709 Taylor, R.

1710 Walker, B. (1983), 464.

grated to Alexandria and joined the mystery schools, jockeying for position not only with each other but also with the non-Judaizing Gnostics, becoming ever more influential on the Gnostic effort. At that time, the salvationist literature started to become Judaized and Hebraicized, with the infiltration of the Yahwists and Joshua cultists, including, especially, the Zadokites or Sadducees. In fact, the Zadokite-Therapeut connection is apparently confirmed by the use of the specialized "pentecontad calendar" by both groups.[1711] The Zadokite-Therapeutan "Jews" were in fact Hellenistic, as opposed to traditionalist. However, within the Alexandrian school also were Judeans, with the result that the "Jewish" factions continued their centuries-long internecine squabbling. Yet, at this point, it was either do or die, because, according to Josephus, many of the Judeans had been wiped out, requiring various compromises from those within the Alexandrian school that shaped the gospel story. In this way, their combined efforts eventually produced the savior cult to top them all.

Why Make the Solar Myth into a Jewish Man?

The question is not *whether* Jesus and his religion were created but *why*: Why was the ubiquitous solar myth turned into a Jewish man? As reflected in the Bible, the Israelites, particularly the tribes of Judah and Levi, considered themselves the chosen people of God and the spiritual leaders of mankind (Deut. 7:6). They were a "priestly nation" who had determined that other nations should serve Israel or utterly perish (Isa. 60:10–12). The Israelites claimed that they had the right to kill the males of the enemy nations, "but the women and the little ones, the cattle, and everything else … you shall take as booty for yourselves" (Deut. 20:13–14). In fact, in the Old Testament the god of Israel repeatedly commanded his people to exterminate other cultures and to commit genocide. The Israelites also insisted that they had the right to lend money with interest to the "foreigners," but were not to do so with their "brethren" (Deut. 23:19–20). As Larson says, "The Chosen People were to bind themselves together by bonds of mutual solidarity, but all others they might deceive and exploit at will."[1712]

This supremacist mentality continued into the Christian era and can be found in the intertestamental literature, which includes the apocryphal and pseudepigraphical Jewish texts, as well as the Dead Sea Scrolls, one of which, the War Scroll, evidently a Judean text, calls for the destruction of the "Kittim," or "sons of Japheth," i.e., the Aryans, in

1711 Vermes, 48.
1712 Larson, 199.

this case the Romans. As another example, in the Jewish apocryphon 4 Esdras, written after the destruction of 70 CE, the fanatical author bitterly complains to the Lord:

> [As] for the rest of the nations which are sprung from Adam, you have said that they are nothing and are like spittle.... And now, Lord, behold, these nations ... rule over us and devour us. But we, your people, whom you called your first-born, only-begotten, chosen, and beloved, are delivered into their hands. If it was for our sakes that the world was created, why do we not possess it as our inheritance?[1713]

Larson elaborates upon the grandiosity of the Jews:

> The Jews considered themselves the chosen of Yahweh and attributed to Him their every victory, defeat, or chastisement.... No other people has ever been so conscious of ultimate primacy through supernatural intervention. This has given them cohesion and courage to persevere in the face of persecution and decimation. The conviction that every Jew will one day share in his divine destiny as a member of the world's ruling race has made him proud and has enabled him to survive unassimilated among the nations of the earth.... It was indeed a Judaeo-centric world.[1714]

According to scripture, the Gentiles would embrace the Jewish religion, and the Jewish empire would extend to all ends of the earth. Included in the promised inheritance was a deliverer or messiah to bring about "the kingdom." This messiah would be either a temporal, human leader who with his armies would overthrow the enemies of Israel, or a supernatural being who would do likewise, establishing an "everlasting" Jewish kingdom as well. In this struggle, in fact, God himself would appear: "Moreover, in line with what the prophet Zechariah had foretold (14.3–5), it was held that the Lord Himself would come with His heavenly legions and fight on behalf of his people."[1715] Furthermore, the passage in Zechariah describes the Lord appearing on the Mount of Olives, obviously used as a blueprint in the creation of Christianity.

The Jewish imperialism would thus come as the awaited deliverer destroyed the enemies and gave their booty to Israel. As Larson says, "This Messiah shall bring judgment upon the Gentiles and they shall become the slaves of Judah."[1716] In order for the messiah to be considered genuine, he had to incorporate various characteristics described in the

1713 Larson, 199–200.
1714 Larson, 195–197.
1715 Gaster, 386.
1716 Larson, 221.

Old Testament, such as being of the seed of Abraham, the tribe of Judah, and the house of David. He was to be born in Bethlehem of a virgin or young maiden and would be called "Mighty God, Everlasting Father, Prince of Peace."

At the time of destruction of the temple in 70, the Jewish world had been in turmoil for centuries. In 332 BCE, Alexander the Great conquered Palestine, and after his death Israel came under the rule of the Greek Ptolemies of Egypt. In 175 BCE, Antiochus of Syria invaded Jerusalem and set up an altar to Zeus and other "foreign gods." Around 88 BCE, Judean king Alexander Jannaeus allegedly crucified 800 Pharisees and had the throats of their wives and children cut in front of them, while Jannaeus himself drank and lay around with concubines. During the Judean Civil War between Pharisees and Sadducees during Jannaeus's rule, tens of thousands on both sides were killed. Next, the Romans moved into Palestine under Pompey around 63 BCE, an invasion that crushed the Jewish nation and increased messianic fever, resulting in the appearance of swarms of alleged messiahs and christs. As Larson says, "The land was a boiling cauldron of Messianic expectation, and many were daily awaiting the Son of Man arriving upon the clouds and surrounded by myriads of angels, coming to establish the 'everlasting kingdom.'"[1717] Of this era, Higgins relates:

> About sixty years before Christ the Roman empire had been alarmed by prodigies, and also by ancient prophecies, announcing that an emanation of the Deity was going to be born about that time, and that a renovation of the world was going to take place.... Josephus says, "That which chiefly excited them (the Jews) to war was an *ambiguous prophecy*, which was also found in the *sacred books that at that time someone*, within their *country, should arise*, that should obtain *the empire* of the *whole world*."[1718]

This messianic frenzy increased throughout the Roman occupation and was most intense during and after the purported advent of Christ. It is impossible to believe that, in such a desperate and fanatical environment, if Christ had been real, had done the miracles ascribed to him and—most importantly—*had satisfied all the scriptural requirements of the messiah*, the Jews would not have jumped with joy at his supernatural advent but would actually reject him and cause him to be killed. But the Jews did not accept him, as messiah after messiah rose up thereafter, as if Christ had never existed at all.... As Jacolliot remarks:

One fact has always astonished me. Through all the sacred books

1717 Larson, 204.
1718 Higgins, I, 187–9.

of primitive times of Egypt and the East, the old tradition of the Messiah had passed into the Hebrew law. How is it … that the Jews refused to recognize this Redeemer whom they expected so impatiently—and whom, even today, they still expect?[1719]

The Jews were literally dying for a supernatural deliverer and—lo and behold—an astounding, divine incarnation came along, with all the scriptural requirements of the messiah and the requisite miracles to demonstrate that he had the full power of God behind him, yet the Jews (and all historians of the day) completely ignored him—nay, they put him to death! In fact, *the world that followed Christ's alleged advent would have been impossible had he really existed at that time.*

Of course, in order to be saved by a deliverer, one has to have enemies, and the zealous Jews had created them everywhere by being extremely sectarian, arrogant and bigoted. The Jews as a whole were the only group exempt from a Roman law that compelled all subjects to conform to some degree to the state religion and political system, and their extreme sectarianism made them an annoyance to the empire. As Larson says:

> Philostratus, agreeing with classical writers generally, declares that "the Jews have long been in revolt not only against the Romans but against humanity"; and that they are "a race … apart and irreconcilable." This separation stemmed from, and then intensified, the Jewish faith. At least half a dozen times in three thousand years, their annihilation has been decreed.… It was experiences such as these which enabled the Hebrew genius to create a savior-cult which could defeat all others.[1720]

Yet the Jews were losing badly in their battle to maintain their separation, as they were being swallowed up by the Greek and Roman cultures, with their numerous cults and religions. In addition, many Jews disdained the oppressive Mosaic Law. These factors forced the priesthood to resort to its time-honored method of financing Zealots to re-establish its centralized religion. Larson describes the social climate in Palestine during this time:

> Palestine was filled with robbers, and no man's life was secure. Any wild-eyed seditionists could procure a following through extravagant promises. The activities of the Zealots were supplemented by those of the Sicarii, a secret society of assassins who mingled with the multitude in the crowded streets especially during feast and holy days, and struck down their victims with daggers.… Roman indignation was aroused since the Jews alone

1719 Jacolliot, 300.

1720 Larson, 195.

were rebellious.[1721]

In order to accomplish their ends, Jewish groups such as the Levitical priesthood, which had split into two main competing sects, the Sadducees and Pharisees, financed and organized military operations. Some of these operations may have emanated from the fortress at Qumran, financed by the Zadokites/Sadducees, whose wealthy compatriots had a stronghold at Alexandria. During this time, several violent, zealous "messiahs" such as Judas, Theudas, the Egyptian burst forth and attacked each other, Romans and wealthy Jews, until they were put down, with the resulting loss of much Jewish blood. After the First Revolt, famine struck, and mothers allegedly ate their children, even though the Romans had attempted to prevent these abysmal circumstances: "Again and again Titus offered generous terms for capitulation, which were scornfully rejected by men hourly awaiting the apocalyptic Messiah."[1722] Emperor Titus finally burned the temple and destroyed the city, during which time, Josephus claims, over a million Jews were killed or died from starvation, and hundreds of thousands more were enslaved. The two centuries around the beginning of the Common Era were, therefore, an utter disaster for the Jews. As Graham says:

> From about 100 BC to 100 AD, the orthodox Jewish priesthood suffered an eclipse. The promises of their scriptures had failed them—Jerusalem was destroyed and Israel was dispersed. Thereafter many Jews fled to Egypt, Rome and Greece, and those among them who might have become priests joined the schools of the Mysteries, among them that of the Gnostics.[1723]

Jerusalem was razed again under Hadrian in 135 CE after a revolt led by the Zealot Simeon Bar Cochba, who was appointed as the "star of Jacob" predicted in Numbers 24:17 and reiterated in the Zadokite Document found at the Dead Sea. But, say Baigent and Leigh, "Unlike the revolt of AD 66, Simeon's insurrection, commencing in AD 132, was no ill-organized conflagration resulting, so to speak, from spontaneous combustion. On the contrary, much prolonged and careful planning went into the enterprise."[1724]

When their efforts to raise up the messiah failed and no such promised inheritance was forthcoming, in order to save Judaism and achieve its goals of world domination, zealous "Jews," i.e., "the Chosen," worked to concoct a story to demonstrate that their new covenant had

---

1721 Larson, 205.
1722 Larson, 206.
1723 Graham, 285.
1724 Baigent & Leigh, 209.

indeed been kept by "the Lord." Just as a Moses was created to give divine authority to "his people" and to make them the elect of God, so Jesus was devised to prove that the Lord had indeed sent his long-awaited redeemer to his chosen as part of the new covenant. However, it could not be demonstrated that such a redeemer was a great warrior who physically usurped the enemies of Israel, because Israel had been destroyed; therefore, the messiah's advent was made solely into a spiritual usurpation. As Higgins says, "It has ... always ... been the object of Jesus to open the Jewish religion to the whole world."[1725] For, as it says at John 4:22, "salvation is from the Jews." Translated differently, that passage would read, "Jesus is from the Jews."

With the final destruction of Israel, which drove out of Palestine not only the Jews but also the Samaritans, and with their subsequent entrance into the mystery schools, in particular at Alexandria, the push for the Judaizing of the Gnostic/Therapeutan Jesus sayings and narratives began in earnest. As Wheless says:

> It was at this critical juncture, to revive and stimulate the jaded hope of Jewish believers and to spread the propaganda amongst the all-believing Pagans, that the written Christ-tales began to be worked up by the Christian propagandists. Before their admiring eyes they had for models the "whole literature" of Jewish apocryphal or forged writings, plus the Pagan Oracles.[1726]

Any number of the Jewish aspects in the canonical gospels and epistles betray that the writers were ex-Jews, half-Jews or non-Jews who were not expertly familiar with Jewish rituals and practices, did not know the geography of Palestine, and certainly did not write in the language of the Jews. However, the historicizing conspirators were also doubtless aware that Judea was a perfect place to set the story, since, as Andrew Laird says, "Set a story in a distant time, or clime, or both, and you are more likely to be believed."[1727] And, since Judea was destroyed and its people scattered, it would be harder to disprove the tale.

In reality, much of the information about the Jews found in the New Testament was derived from the study of the Old Testament and other Jewish books, such as Josephus's histories, and not from any actual experiences of their own. These inaccuracies serve as evidence that the gospel writers were simply sitting around with books, studying and copying passages, and throwing in an original phrase or two to link them all together.

1725 Higgins, II, 253.
1726 Wheless, *FC*, 96.
1727 www.christianism.com

The Library and University of Alexandria

In their creation of Christianity, the Therapeuts had at their disposal the university and library at Alexandria, which had been established by Alexander the Great as an international center of learning. Indeed, in its heyday the Alexandrian Library was a vast repository of some 500,000–700,000 manuscripts collected from around the world. Doane stresses the importance of Alexandria:

> In Alexandria in Egypt, there was an immense library, founded by the Ptolemies.... *There flocked to this great intellectual centre, students from all countries*. It is said that at one time not fewer than fourteen thousand were in attendance. Subsequently even the Christian church received from it some of the most eminent of its Fathers, as Clemens Alexandrinus, Origen, Athanasius, etc.[1728]

Taylor describes the nature and climate of the library and university of Alexandria:

> The first and greatest library that ever was in the world, was at Alexandria in Egypt. The first of that most mischievous of all institutions-universities, was the University of Alexandria in Egypt; where lazy monks and wily fanatics first found the benefit of clubbing together, to keep the privileges and advantages of learning to themselves, and concocting holy mysteries and inspired legends, to be dealt out as the craft should need, for the perpetuation of ignorance and superstition, and consequently of the ascendancy of jugglers and Jesuits, holy hypocrites, and revered rogues, among men.
>
> All the most valued manuscripts of the Christian scriptures are Codices Alexandrini. The very first bishops of whom we have any account, were bishops of Alexandria. Scarcely one of the more eminent fathers of the Christian church is there, who had not been educated and trained in the arts of priestly fraud, in the University of Alexandria—that great sewer of congregated feculencies ["foul impurities"] of fanaticisms.[1729]

Of the creation of Christianity by the Therapeutan brotherhood, Taylor says:

> The Therapeutae of Egypt, from whom are descended the vagrant hordes of Jews and Gypsies, had well found by what arts mankind were to be cajoled; and as they boasted their acquaintance with the sanative qualities of herbs of all countries; so in

1728 Doane, 438–40.

1729 Taylor, R., 61.

their extensive peregrinations through all the then known regions of the earth, they had not failed to bring home, and remodel to their own purposes, those sacred spells or religious romances, which they found had been successfully palmed on the credulity of remote nations. Hence the Indian Chrishna might have become the Therapeutan head of the order of spiritual physicians.

> No principle was held more sacred than that of the necessity of keeping the sacred writings from the knowledge of the people. Nothing could be safer from the danger of discovery than the substitution, with scarce a change of names, "of the incarnate Deity of the Sanscrit Romance" for the imaginary founder of the Therapeutan college. What had been said to have been done in India, could be as well said to have been done in Palestine. The change of names and places, and the mixing up of various sketches of Egyptian, Phoenician, Greek, and Roman mythology, would constitute a sufficient disguise to evade the languid curiosity of infant skepticism. A knowledge within the acquisition of a few, and which the strongest possible interest bound that few to hold inviolate, would soon pass entirely from the records of human memory. A long continued habit of imposing upon others would in time subdue the minds of the imposers themselves, and cause them to become at length the dupes of their own deception, to forget the temerity in which their first assertions had originated, to catch the infection of the prevailing credulity, and to believe their own lie.[1730]

Taylor further summarizes the gospel work of the Therapeuts:

> Some entire scenes of the drama have been rejected, and some suggested emendations of early critics have been adopted into the text; the names of Pontius Pilate, Herod, Archelaus, Caiaphas, etc., picked out of Josephus's and other histories, have been substituted in the place of the original *dramatis personae*; and since it has been found expedient to conceal the plagiarism, to pretend a later date, and a wholly different origination, texts have been introduced, directly impugning the known sentiments and opinions of the original authors.... [T]hough they are to be received as the composition of Jews, contemporaries, and even witnesses of the scenes and actions they describe; those compositions do nevertheless betray so great a degree of ignorance of the geography, statistics, and circumstances of Judea at the time supposed, as to put it beyond all question, that the writers were

1730 Taylor, R., 63–64.

> neither witnesses nor contemporaries—neither Jews, nor at any time inhabitants of Judea.... The Therapeutae, we see, though not Jews, nor inhabitants of Palestine, were, says Eusebius, "likely *descended from Hebrews*, and therefore were wont to observe many of the customs of the ancients, after a more Jewish fashion."[1731]

In creating their myth, the Hebrew/Israelite conspirators took one more Baal, Baal Jehoshua, the Savior, and carnalized him anew. Like his predecessor Joshua, Jesus was made to be an Israelite/Galilean/Samaritan, not a Judean, with his Bethlehem birthplace added later to "fulfill scripture." The Samaritan influence on, and origins of, the gospel tale is evident, firstly because its early contributors, the Gnostics Apollonius and Marcion, were considered "Samaritans," as was Antioch. Furthermore, although Jesus is also made to call Samaritans "dogs," he himself is declared by the Jews a "demon-filled Samaritan," to which he is made to respond that he does not have a demon, without denying he is a Samaritan. In reality, the gospels elevate the Samaritans above the Jews. For example, the most lasting memory of the Samaritans is the New Testament story of the "Good Samaritan," in which Jews are made to look bad. Also, in the Gospel of John, Jesus is made to go against the Jews by welcoming a Samaritan woman, who, although she claims to have no husband, is told by Jesus that she has had in fact five, and "he whom you now have is not your husband." This "woman" with the "five husbands," however, is not a person but the northern kingdom of Israel, and these "husbands" are "her" foreign occupiers, Assyria, Persia, Egypt, Greece and Rome, none of whom, however, is Samaria's true "husband," or "baal," or "lord."

In the Gospel of John the Samaritans accept Jesus as the Messiah and "Savior of the world," but the Jews plot to kill him. John is an anti-Jewish text, with aspersions cast *only* against the Pharisees, "priests and Levites," as well as "the Jews," but with *no mention* by name of the Sadducees, who constituted in large part the Samaritan priesthood. In fact, in the New Testament the Sadducees are mentioned by name only about a dozen times, while the Pharisees are named 100 times and bear the brunt of the blame for Jesus's death. In addition, the Pharisees disparaged the Samaritans for being "adherers to the Bible" and for interpreting it in a literal manner, just as Christians do to this day.[1732] In the Talmud, the Samaritans are lumped together with the Sadducees, "followers of Jesus" and other "Gentiles." Indeed, the Talmudic code

1731 Taylor, R., 78–81.

1732 History of the Talmud, Rod Kinson, 1.

word "Sadducees" refers to Gentiles.

It is clear that the individuals who Judaized the Gnostic/Therapeutan efforts were in the main not Pharisaic but Hellenizing "Jews" or Israelites, i.e., Samaritan Zadokites/ Sadducees. Thus the gospel story serves to elevate not only "the Jews" as God's chosen but also the northern kingdom over the southern kingdom, with the southern actually being castigated for its interpretation of the law. In this regard, the Samaritan Jesus's character is patterned after a Pharisee so that he can debate "the Jews" and usurp their power. Orthodox, Pharisaic Jews, in fact, have rejected the fallacious gospel tale for 2,000 years, acknowledging in their Talmud that it was the Zadokites/Sadducees who created it and Judaized the books of the New Testament.[1733] Regardless of the internecine fighting, the Christian myth was an outgrowth of "Jewish" thinking; it was the logical extension, in fact, of the group belief that "the Jews" or Israelites were the spiritual leaders of mankind, that their god and religion were superior to all others, that their land was blessed above all others, and that their history and destiny, and theirs alone, were guided and directed by God. The Israelite version of the savior religion and solar myth did indeed usurp all others in the West, as those others were consigned to their proper status as myths, while the Judeo-Christian version was, through centuries of violence and slaughter, eventually maintained as fact.

While Christianity "sprang up in a thousand places," its seed germinated in Antioch and grew to strength at Alexandria. But it would not become a force to be reckoned with until its roots took hold at Rome.

1733 Talmud, Sanhedrin 100a-100b, fn 9, Soncino ed., p. 680.

Enter Rome

"It is one of our civilization's great archaeological and historical challenges to explain how a practice rooted in the low-magic of the Panhellenic world, syncretized with Neoplatonism and the mystery religions of the Roman East around the figure of Jesus Christ, to become a world religion."

—David of HHI, "Acts of the Chresmologoi: The Role of Oracles and Chronicles in the Creation of Divine Men"

"The emperor comes to be regarded as 'illuminating' his empire in the same way as the sun illuminates the world. There were precedents for such a conception. The Emperor Nero, a century and a half before, had erected a colossal image of the Sun.... In them we can trace a solar monotheism which sanctions what may be called a solar autocracy: 'one God, one empire, one emperor—that was the goal which Aurelian sought'; and his one god the Sun is sometimes figured on his coins as giving him a globe in token of his power over all the world."

— Ernest Barker, *From Alexander to Constantine*

Christianity was not created by a god who came to Earth 2,000 years ago but is a patchwork quilt of ancient motifs found in many parts of the world eons before the Christian era and spread mainly through fraud, fanaticism and force, as a deliberately contrived ideology. Christianity's earliest proponents, the Gnostics, were non-historicizers and non-Judaizers who were attempting to amalgamate the many religions of the Roman Empire and beyond. When the might of Rome crushed Palestine, into this Gnostic-Therapeut soup fell a multitude of Jews and Samaritans, including the Zadokites, who insisted upon supremacy and dominance, so that the allegorical and astrotheological Jesus became "Jewish." It was not until the Antiochan-Alexandrian efforts hit Rome, however, that they became locked into history, the result of the labors of the infamous church fathers, who were known liars, forgers and psychotics whose brains were apparently afflicted by the lead in Roman pipes.

Why Carnalize and Historicize the Solar Myth?

As the Christian myth was being formulated its proponents were ridiculed and rejected by the Pagan intelligentsia, compelling them to create forged texts and long rebuttals to the various imputations against them. In this way, the Christian product became increasingly historicized for a variety of reasons, one of which was that the conspirators had simply plagiarized older myths and legends. Indeed, historicizing their godman allowed the Christians to distinguish him from these more ancient mythological characters. For instance, when confronted with the fact that the various gods such as Krishna, Horus, et al., had the identical story as Jesus in many respects, Christian apologists argued that, while devilish "living realities," these "gods" were not flesh-and-blood incarnations and could thereby be dismissed, whereas Christ was historical and therefore must be accepted as who he said he was. An example of this usurpation is provided by the history of Mithraism, which was so important to Rome that in 307 the emperor designated Mithra the protector of the empire. Yet, Mithraism could not withstand the assault from Christianity. As Larson says:

> The power of Mithraism lay in its syncretism, its flexibility, its universality, its attractiveness to various classes. Its weakness lay in the fact that it could not point to an historical god-man savior.[1734]

Because he really came in the flesh, the argument went, Jesus was the only valid one of these godmen, while the others were but phantoms, planted in the heads of the ignorant masses, centuries and millennia before Christ's advent, in order to befuddle them and trick them into rejecting him. Of course, this argument is patently ridiculous special pleading, but it has worked for those who have been bedazzled by the biblical tale. The core myth of Christianity is that the events described in the Gospels actually happened. It should be remembered that, over the millennia, Krishna, Buddha and others have also been considered by a great number of people to have been real persons, so this debate also begs the question of why Christian believers do not follow these other "historical" characters, since they, too, claimed to be the "alpha and omega," the "way, truth and light," etc. Indeed, as Massey says:

> The doctrine of the incarnation had been evolved and established in the Osirian religion at least 4,000 and possibly 10,000 years before it was purloined and perverted in Christianity.[1735]

And Wells says:

> Osiris worshippers of ancient Egypt believed, as did the early Christians (Hebrews 4:14–15) that "man cannot be saved by a remote omnipotent deity but by one who has shared the experience of human suffering." … Initiation into the pagan mystery religions involved a "personal meeting with the god."[1736]

In fact, while the mystical and supernatural apparition of Jesus to

1734 Larson, 185.
1735 Massey, EBD, 91.
1736 Wells, DJE, 66.

Paul on the road to Damascus is portrayed as a unique experience, it is not, either then or now, as over the millennia and during the era in question, many gods commonly appeared mystically to their followers. As Fox relates:

> The "presence" of Isis was invoked to help mortals in lawsuits and on journeys, and was experienced by adherents who gazed fondly on her statue. Very soon after his creation, the god Serapis had spread widely because he was accessible in dreams and appeared and gave commands to people of all classes. Evidence for gods being thought to attend their own banquets and sacrifices is known from the sixth to fourth centuries BC, yet it surfaces again for us in the small invitation tickets to the "couch" of Serapis, known to us from the second century BC onwards.[1737]

Walker further explains the necessity for the incarnation:

> From the Christians' viewpoint, a real historical Jesus was essential to the basic premise of the faith: the possibility of immortality through identification with his own death and resurrection. Wellhausen rightly said Jesus would have no place in history unless he died and returned exactly as the Gospels said: "If Christ hath not been raised, your faith is vain" (1 Corinthians 15:17). Still, despite centuries of research, no historical Jesus has come to light. It seems his story was not merely overlaid with myth; it was mythical to the core.[1738]

In addition, Allegro states:

> The canonisation of the Joshua/Jesus legends focused so much popular piety and theological speculation on its central figure, that it became essential to historicize the myth, and successive generations of a largely non-Jewish Church were led to believe as fact the absurdly anachronistic and slanderously inaccurate picture painted in the Gospels of Jewish institutions in a Roman-dominated Palestine of the first century. Before long, pious pilgrims were scouring the Holy Land for relics of the Nazarene Master's life on earth, and erecting shrines to commemorate his activities and death in the most improbable places.[1739]

He continues:

> Unlike other eastern faiths, Christianity could "prove" by such relics the validity of its claim that God had entered history in the person of His Son, and had "so loved the world" that He

---

1737 Fox, 124.
1738 Walker, B. (1983), 470.
1739 Allegro, DSSCM, 139.

had given His own Substance that He might redeem mankind.[1740]

Furthermore, as noted, it was maintained by Irenaeus and other Christians that the belief was that "men" could not really "partake in salvation" if Jesus was merely imaginary. The author of the Epistle of Barnabas further illustrates this need for the carnalized Christ: "Then he clearly manifested himself to be the Son of God. For had he not come in the flesh, how should men have been able to look upon him, that they might be saved?"[1741] "Barnabas" also gives a hint as to the identity of Christ in his next sentence: "Seeing if they beheld only the sun, which was the work of his hands, and shall hereafter cease to be, they are not able to endure steadfastly to look against the rays of it." In other words, looking at "Christ," some have seen "only the sun, which … shall hereafter cease to be." And this was the charge of the conspirators: To make the "sun of God" disappear, so that its mythos would not be remembered and the person of "Jesus Christ" could be inserted in its place.

In *Against Heresies* V, Irenaeus expounds upon the need for the incarnation:

> Christ alone is able to teach divine things, and to redeem us: he, the same, tool flesh of the Virgin Mary, not merely in appearance, but actually, by the operation of the Holy Spirit, in order to renovate us … for in no other way could we have learned the things of God, unless our Master, existing as the Word, had become man. For no other being had the power of revealing to us the things of the Father, except His own proper Word.… Again, we could have learned in no other way than by seeing our Teacher, and hearing His voice with our own ears, that, having become imitators of His works as well as doers of His words, we may have communion with Him, receiving increase from the perfect One, and from Him who is prior to all creation.

The incarnation was established as doctrine in one of the most important of "Christian" councils, evidently held at Alexandria in the year after the Gnostic-Christian leader Marcion's death, 161, at which "Docetism," or the disbelief in the "historical" Jesus, was condemned as heresy.

As stated, many cultures were waiting for the mythos to become carnalized, just as people around the world today pray for any number of avatars, messiahs, maitreyas, mahdis and assorted other incarnations. In reality, this expectation can be found around the globe where the deep meaning of the mythos has been lost, as "the vulgar were taught to ex-

1740 Allegro, DSSCM, 230.
1741 Chapt. IV, 13.

pect a new incarnation every 600 years."[1742] As noted, in addition to the 2,150-year cycle of the precession of the equinoxes, there was this cycle of 600, the reason Christ himself was compared to a phoenix, who rises from the ashes every 600 years, and why Mohammed appeared on the scene some 600 years later. The expectation of the incarnation, in fact, allowed for some places to be more easily conquered by Christian armies. Because of this past experience with the ongoing cycles and "incarnations," the ancient priest-astrologers were well aware that in order to create a new "faith" there had to be an obvious break from the past, which was rife with cults, sects and religions, with "someone" new to come along to found it, alleged to have been sent by the "Almighty Himself." The race was on as to who would produce this incarnation, one in a long line on a recurring theme.

The cult was backdated also to make it appear as if its spread in the Roman Empire preceded Mithraism, whereas the reverse is the case.

Enter the Romans

While the Israelite Therapeuts had won the race and were seemingly in opposition to the Romans, having been displaced from Palestine, their efforts were eventually combined with those of Rome. Indeed, in the decades between 170–90 the push for Roman supremacy in the Gnostic-Therapeut-Christian Church began, and the various gospel texts and epistles were reworked on behalf of the vested interests at Rome, producing the four gospels, based on manuscripts from the Alexandrian school and other branches/churches of the network. As Walker says, "The Gospels themselves were forged as required to uphold privileges and practices of the early church."[1743] The Romanized gospels were thus slanted to bring the Jews into the fold by making them believe that their "Messiah" had bestowed his authority upon the Church, which would mean that the Jews were to follow the dictates of Rome.

It was also during this period that the canonical Book of Acts was written, to invest the Roman church with hierarchical supremacy. In addition, the "lost" Gospel of Peter, purportedly the favorite of the Nazarites/Nazarenes, was clearly written to exonerate Pilate and, therefore, the Romans for the crucifixion and to cast the onus upon Herod and the Jews instead. This gospel was once considered as important as the canonical gospels—or, in the words of Rev. D.H. Stanton, "perhaps even higher than some of them"[1744]—but it fell out of favor and was discarded. Furthermore, as noted, the Nazarenes were Samaritans and

---

1742 Higgins, I, 558.
1743 Walker, B. (1983), 320.
1744 The Lost Books of the Bible, 283.

enemies of the strictly Yahwistic Jews, or Pharisees, and were obviously in cahoots with Rome at this point at least.

The Acts of Pilate was also written to place the onus of Jesus's death upon the Jews and to remove the guilt from the Romans. In this book, Pilate is even represented as making a pitch for the Jews to follow Christ, comparing him to Moses.

Rome's grab at supremacy, however, was not pleasing to the other Gnostic-Therapeut-Christian factions. Nor were the priests of other religions and cults thrilled by the "new superstition" of Christianity. Potter describes the religious climate in Rome at the time:

> In the century before the birth of Christ and in the century or two after, so many Eastern religions and mysteries entered Rome that very little was left of the original Roman religion. The great city was simply a hotbed of cults of all possible sorts which vied with one another for supremacy. From Egypt came the worship of Isis and Osiris, from Phrygia the cult of Attis, and from Persia via Asia Minor the powerful soldier religion of Mithra, dominant in the second century AD.[1745]

As noted, Christianity from the beginning was marked by warring priestly factions and endless bloodshed, as it expanded to engulf these various other cults. To unite these religions, sects, cults and mystery schools and to establish the doctrine of the new superstition, hundreds of texts were produced and various councils were called in different cities of the brotherhood.

The Council of Nicea

Rather than the advent and death of a "historical" Christ, the most important events in the history of Christianity were the "conversion" of the Pagan Emperor Constantine and his convening of the raucous Council of Nicea in 325, which in fact marked the true birth of Jesus Christ. Constantine "converted" to Christianity partly because it offered a "quick fix" to all of his heinous crimes, including the murder of several family members, removed simply by confession and "believing unto the Lord," absolutions he could not procure from other religions such as Mithraism, which did not cater to murderers.

At the Council of Nicea there were not only Christian leaders from Alexandria, Antioch, Athens, Jerusalem and Rome but also leaders of many other cults, sects and religions, including those of Apollo, Demeter/Ceres, Dionysus/Bacchus/Iasios, Janus, Jupiter/Zeus, Oannes/Dagon, Osiris and Isis, and "Sol Invictus," the Invincible Sun, the object of Constantine's devotion. The purpose of this council was to unify the var-

---

1745 Potter, 464.

ious competing cults under one universal or "catholic" church, which, of course, would be controlled by Constantine and Rome as a tool of imperial security and stability. Rome claimed the ultimate authority because it purported to be founded upon the "rock of Peter." Thus, the statue of Jupiter in Rome was converted into "St. Peter," whose phony bones were subsequently installed in the Vatican. In a typical religion-making move, the gods of these other cults were subjugated under the new god and changed into "apostles" and "saints."

During the Nicene Council the names Jesus and Christ were put together possibly for the first time in the phrase "Jesus Christ" or "Christ Jesus," uniting two of the major factions, with Jesus representing the Hesus of the Druids, Joshua/Jesus of the Israelites, Horus/Iusa of the Egyptians and IES/Iesios of the Dionysians/Samothracians, and Christ representing the Krishna/Christos of India, the Anointed of the Jews and KRST of Egypt, among others. The phrase "Jesus Christ," which had never been a name, does not appear in Greek or Latin authors prior to the first Council of Nicea. Hence, just as the name "Hermes Trismegistus" "represents a tradition rather than a single man,"[1746] so does "Jesus Christ." It is also purported that one Bishop Eunomius charged fraud and blew the whistle on the Council of Nicea, the record of which was never published, even though it was supposedly made and may be in the Vatican vault to this day.

Regarding the compilation of the Bible and the creation of Christianity, Roberts says:

> Every rational person might have known that the writings of the New Testament were the works of a man or a school of men who sought to blend such portions of the preceding creeds, doctrines, ceremonies, practices and religious formulas into a single religion, that would serve to harmonize and unite mankind in one common effort to advance the welfare of all.... The religious systems of China, India, Persia, Egypt, Greece, Rome, Palestine, and even the Druidical system of Northern and Western Europe, were largely drawn from to make up the Eclectic system of religion.[1747]

Walker states:

> Far-Eastern traditions were utilized too. The Roman empire was well aware of the teachings and myths of Buddhism. Buddha images in classic Greek style were made in Pakistan and Afghanistan in the first century AD. Buddhist ideas like the "footprints

1746 Barnstone, 568.
1747 Roberts, 71.

> of Buddha" appeared among Christians. Bishop Sulpicus of Jerusalem reported that, as in India, "In the dust where Christ trod the marks of His step can still be seen, and the earth still bears the print of His feet." Buddhist metaphors and phrasing also appeared in the Gospels.[1748]

And Wheless relates:

> Cardinal Newman ... says that Milman arrays facts "admitted on all hands," to wit: "that the doctrine of the Logos is Platonic; that of the Incarnation Indian; that of a divine Kingdom Judaic; that of angels and demons (and a Mediator) Persian; that the connection of sin with the body is Gnostic; the idea of a new birth Chinese and Eleusinian; that of sacramental virtue Pythagorean; that of Trinity common to East and West; and that of the rites of baptism and sacrifice equally ubiquitous"![1749]

During the centuries after the purported advent of the Christian savior, at least 21 councils were convened to establish Church policy and doctrine, many of which were bloody melees. It was a long, slow process that eventually unified the numerous warring factions to a large extent. The following is a partial list of the various religions, cults, sects, secret societies and mystery schools that contributed to the formation of the state religion called Christianity:

1. Buddhist/Gymnosophic
2. Cabirian/Phrygian/Syrian
3. Dionysian/Bacchanal/Orphist/Samothracian
4. Druidic/Gallic/Teutonic
5. Egyptian/African
6. Essene/Nazarene/Nazarite/Ebionite/Therapeut
7. Greek/Eleusinian
8. Indian/Brahmanical
9. Mandaean/Manichaean
10. Marcionite/Valentinian
11. Mithraic/Zoroastrian
12. Neoplatonist/Stoic/Cynic/Eclectic/Peripatetic
13. Phoenician/Canaanite/Israelite/Samaritan
14. Yahwhist/Kabbalist/Pharisaic

1748 Walker, B. (1983), 469.
1749 Wheless, 29.

15. Roman/Etruscan
16. Samanean/Magusean/Sampsaean
17. Sethian/Ophite
18. Zealot/Zadokite/Sadducean

In addition to these groups, many of which obviously overlap, there were many other branches and even more esoteric designations such as the "Followers of the Eight-Pointed Red Cross," the "Sons of the Sun," the "Order of the Black Hand," the "Order of the Red Hand," and the famed "Order of Melchizedek." Other groups, such as the Marianites, or followers of the Goddess, were either excluded or given little empowerment at these councils.

The brotherhoods who were really in charge of the Therapeutan "churches" addressed in the Pauline epistles are as follows: Antioch was the seat of the Adonis cult; Ephesus was that of the Attis cult; Corinth represented the Greek gods and Eleusinian mysteries; Galatia was the locale of the Dionysian cult; and Rome had everything. The first Christians at Antioch were actually Gnostic Nazarenes, also Carmelites, who represented one of the oldest seats of the brotherhood and who were originally Egyptians/Canaanites/Phoenicians and later "Samaritans." These Nazarites/Nazarenes were also priests of Dionysus/Bacchus, who was the same as Joshua, Iasius, Iesius or Jesus, whose temple was found atop Mt. Carmel.

The Role of Masonry

As demonstrated, the Gnostic and Catholic endeavors in creating Christianity were eclectic and multinational, incorporating elements from around the world. Such a religion—and nationality—transcending group could only occur in one stratum of fraternity: that which is called Masonry.

Although the brotherhood of Masonry appears to be relatively new, it is in reality the oldest continuous network on the planet, dating back many thousands of years, beginning when stones were first dressed. Masonry today has a somewhat sinister reputation, because people suspect that this powerful brotherhood has been manipulating and exploiting them. However, the average Mason has never been "in the know" and is, therefore, merely a member of a social club. Nevertheless, the higher-ups have indeed had their hand in creation on this planet on a large scale for a long time.

Ancient peoples considered God to be the Grand Architect of the Universe; thus, the Masons viewed themselves as imitators of God. Obviously, it is Masons who build the temples, cathedrals and sacred monuments around the globe, and it was Masons who developed writing, as they were fond of inscribing their monuments and buildings. Hence, Masonry and the creation of religions go hand-in-hand.

Where were these ubiquitous Masons when Christianity was being formed? Why is there so little mention of them in the texts of the time? The Masons are there, perpetually hidden behind the scenes, leaving clues to their existence as a brotherhood, some of which are evident yet still not seen. For example, the biblical Nimrod, the king who built the tower of Babel ("Bab-el"—"gate of God"), is considered the first Mason. Like so many other biblical characters, Nimrod is found in older tales, as the Assyrian god of war and the hunt, serving as a personification of the Assyrian empire. Another biblical character, Hiram, king of Tyre, is revered as a great mason for building "Solomon's Temple," although the temple actually is in the skies. In addition, the mysterious Urim and Thummim are Masonic symbols, as are the pillars Jachin and Boaz.

Jesus is called the "very stone which the builders rejected … the head of the corner." Furthermore, this comment is prefaced by reference to the scripture where it is first written, Psalm 118:21: "I thank thee that thou … hast become my salvation. The stone which the builders rejected has become the head of the corner." As "Jesus" means "salvation," this Old Testament passage could read, "I thank thee that thou has become my Jesus. The stone which the builders rejected." The "chief cornerstone that the builders rejected" is an obvious Masonic symbol, referring to the peak of a pyramid, which is also the "all-seeing eye of Horus," the symbol of the sun who looks down upon the world, and which can be found on the back of an American dollar bill.

In addition, Peter "the Rock" and his keys are Masonic symbols. Church doctor/Therapeut Jerome relates that the man with the withered hand in Matthew 12 was "said to be a mason" and thus needed his hand for his livelihood.[1750] When at 1 Corinthians Paul calls himself a "skilled master builder," "he is using a word pre-eminently kabalistic, theurgic, and Masonic."[1751] At Hebrews 3:3–4, a Masonic calling card is left with the following passage (and notation), which was evidently interpolated: "Yet Jesus has been counted worthy of as much more glory than Moses as the builder of a house. (For every house is built by some one, but the builder of all things is God.)" In addition, Jesus is called "the rose of Sharon," also known as "Nazir," which, according to Higgins, who was a magistrate and a Mason, refers to "the schools of the prophets which

1750 Eusebius, 70.

1751 Blavatsky, IU, II, 91.

were on the mount of Carmel or the vineyard of God."[1752] Carmel, to repeat, was one of the earliest brotherhood strongholds and the site of a temple of Jupiter, Melchizedek, and Joshua, from which emanated the monkishness that became the Nazarene brotherhood. As real or fictional Nazarenes, Jesus and Paul were Masons as well. Furthermore, the "carpenter" label, also found in the stories of other solar heroes, is a Masonic designation, reflecting the sun's role as the great builder and designer.[1753]

The Indian-Gnostic Nazarene-Carmelites were also Nestorians, Manichaeans, Samanaeans and Buddhists, Templars and Rosicrucians, "or followers of the eight-pointed Red Cross and Rose of Sharon, all the same under different names,"[1754] serving to illustrate the complexity and pervasiveness of the international brotherhood of Masonry. The Masons were also Essenes, Therapeuts and Gnostics, and they are now Christians, Jews and Muslims. The Mithraites were also Masons, and the Kabbalists and Chaldeans were Master Masons. In fact, the Scottish Rite Masonry can be traced to the Chaldeans.[1755] The Chaldeans, then, were also closely linked to the Druids, who were likewise Masons. The Knights Templar were also linked to Chaldean traditions, the same as the Culdees of India and as the Gnostic Manichaeans, who were followers of Bel/Baal.[1756] The Culdees/Masons were the judicial astronomers of Rome,[1757] and, as we have seen, the followers of Baal/Molech constituted the Order of Melchizedek, whose members were also Gymnosophs, as well as Zadokites. The fortress at Qumran was likely a Masonic enclave, since masons built it, particularly its large tower, a strong Masonic symbol. Likewise, the Dead Sea Scrolls are abundant in "architectural metaphors," demonstrating their writers were Masons. Furthermore, the mysteries of Isis and Serapis, which were models of those of Eleusis and Samothrace, are part of Masonry.[1758]

The historian Josephus certainly knew of the Masons and allegedly was one, as well as being a member of the secret order called the "Sons of the Sun," to which also purportedly belonged Apollonius and the Emperors Claudius, Vespasian, Titus, Domitian, Nerva and Trajan.

Two centuries ago, no less an authority than the great Anglo-Amer-

1752 Higgins, I, 713.

1753 The importance of the mason and carpenter, and their conspicuous presence in society, is emphasized by their repeated mention in the Sumerian sacred poem "Inana's Descent into the Underworld" (41-47, etc.).

1754 Higgins, I, 809.

1755 Higgins, I, 717.

1756 Higgins, I, 745.

1757 Higgins, I, 768.

1758 Higgins, I, 719.

ican philosopher, revolutionary statesman and lover of truth Thomas Paine clearly outlined the origins of Christianity and its connection to Masonry. Paine himself apparently was a Mason, as were his associates, George Washington, Ben Franklin and other American Founding Fathers. Why Paine's truthful admissions have been ignored by religionists, politicians and scholars alike can only be explained by the remarkably effective and disturbing system of concealment for profit that has been in place for thousands of years. In his treatise, "Origin of Freemasonry," Paine writes:

The Christian religion and Masonry have one and the same common origin: Both are derived from the worship of the Sun. The difference between their origin is, that the Christian religion is a parody on the worship of the Sun, in which they put a man whom they call Christ, in the place of the Sun, and pay him the same adoration which was originally paid to the Sun....

In Masonry many of the ceremonies of the Druids are preserved in their original state, at least without any parody. With them the Sun is still the Sun; and his image, in the form of the Sun is the great emblematical ornament of Masonic Lodges and Masonic dresses. It is the central figure on their aprons, and they wear it also pendant on the breast in their lodges, and in their processions. It has the figure of a man, as at the head of the Sun, as Christ is always represented.

At what period of antiquity, or in what nation, this religion was first established, is lost in the labyrinth of unrecorded time. It is generally ascribed to the ancient Egyptians, the Babylonians and Chaldeans, and reduced afterwards to a system regulated by the apparent progress of the Sun through the twelve signs of the Zodiac by Zoroaster the law giver of Persia, from whence Pythagoras brought it into Greece.

The worship of the Sun as the great visible agent of a great invisible first cause, "Time without limits," spread itself over a considerable part of Asia and Africa, from thence to Greece and Rome, through all ancient Gaul, and into Britain and Ireland....

As the study and contemplation of the Creator in the works of the creation, the Sun, as the great visible agent of that Being, was the visible object of the adoration of Druids; all their religious rites and ceremonies had reference to the apparent progress of the Sun through the twelve signs of the Zodiac, and his influence upon the earth. The Masons adopt the same practices. The roof of their Temples or Lodges is ornamented with a Sun, and the floor is a representation of the variegated face of the earth either by carpeting or Mosaic work....

The Masons, in order to protect themselves from the persecution of the Christian church, have always spoken in a mystical manner of the figure of the Sun in their Lodges.... It is their secret, especially in Catholic countries, because the figure of the Sun is the expressive criterion that denotes they are descended from the Druids, and that wise, elegant, philosophical religion, was the faith opposite to the faith of the gloomy Christian church.

The high festival of the Masons is on the day they call St. John's day; but every enlightened Mason must know that holding their festival on this day has no reference to the person called St. John, and that it is only to disguise the true cause of holding it on this day, that they call the day by that name....

The case is, that the day called St. John's day, is the 24th of June, and is what is called Midsummer-day. The Sun is then arrived at the summer solstice ... and it is in honor of the sun, which has then arrived at his greatest height in our hemisphere, and not anything with respect to St. John, that this annual festival of the Masons, taken from the Druids, is celebrated on Midsummer-day....

As to what Masons, and books of Masonry, tell us of Solomon's Temple at Jerusalem, it is no wise improbable that some Masonic ceremonies may have been derived from the building of that temple, for the worship of the Sun was in practice many centuries before the Temple existed, or before the Israelites came out of Egypt. And we learn from the history of the Jewish Kings, 2 Kings xxii-xxiii, that the worship of the Sun was performed by the Jews in that Temple. It is, however, much to be doubted if it was done with the same scientific purity and religious morality with which it was performed by the Druids, who, by all accounts that historically remain of them, were a wise, learned, and moral class of men. The Jews, on the contrary, were ignorant of astronomy, and of science in general, and if a religion founded upon astronomy fell into their hands, it is almost certain it would be corrupted.... But to return to the worship of the Sun in this Temple.... [The] description that Josephus gives of the decorations of this Temple, resembles on a large scale those of a Mason's Lodge. He says that the distribution of the several parts of the Temple of the Jews represented all nature, particularly the parts most apparent of it, as the sun, the moon, the planets, the zodiac, the earth, the elements; and that the system of the world was retraced there by numerous ingenious emblems. These, in all probability, are, what Josiah, in his ignorance, calls the abominations of the Zidonians.... Everything, however, drawn from this Temple and applied to Masonry, still refers to the worship of the Sun, however corrupted or misunderstood by the Jews, and consequently to the religion of the Druids....

The religion of the Druids, as before said, was the same as the religion of the ancient Egyptians. The priests of Egypt were the professors and teachers of science, and were styled priests of Heliopolis, that is, of the City of the Sun. The Druids in Europe, who were the same order of men, have their name from the Teutonic or ancient German language; the Germans being anciently called Teutones. The word Druid signifies a wise man. In Persia they were called Magi, which signifies the same thing.

"Egypt," says Smith, "from whence we derive many of our mysteries, has always borne a distinguished rank in history, and was once celebrated above all others for its antiquities, learning, opulence, and fertility. In their system, their principal hero-gods, Osiris and Isis, theologically represented the Supreme Being and universal Nature; and physically the two great celestial luminaries, the Sun and the Moon, by whose influence all nature was actuated." ... In speaking of the apparel of the Masons in their Lodges, part of which, as we see in their public processions, is a white leather apron, he says, "the Druids were appareled in white at the time of their sacrifices and solemn offices. The Egyptian priests of Osiris wore snow-white cotton. The Grecian and most other priests wore white garments...."

"The Egyptians," continues Smith, "in the earliest ages constituted a great number of Lodges, but with assiduous care kept their secrets of Masonry from all strangers. These secrets have been imperfectly handed down to us by oral tradition only, and ought to be kept undiscovered to the laborers, craftsmen, and apprentices, till by good behavior and long study they become better acquainted in geometry and the liberal arts...."

I come now to speak of the cause of secrecy used by the Masons. The natural source of secrecy is fear. When any new religion over-runs a former religion, the professors of the new become the persecutors of the old. We see this in all instances that history brings before us. When Hilkiah the priest and Shaphan the scribe, in the reign of King Josiah, found, or pretended to find, the law, called the law of Moses, a thousand years after the time of Moses, (and it does not appear from 2 Kings, xxii-xxiii, that such a law was ever practiced or known before the time of Josiah), he established that law as a national religion, and put all the priests of the Sun to death. When the Christian religion over-ran the Jewish religion, the Jews were the continual subject of persecution in all Christian countries. When the Protestant religion in England over-ran the Roman Catholic religion, it was made death for a Catholic priest to be found in England. As this has been the case in all the instances we have any knowledge of, we are obliged to admit it with respect to the case in question, and that when the Christian religion over-ran the religion of the Druids in Italy, ancient Gaul, Britain, and Ireland, the Druids became the subject of persecution. This would naturally and necessarily oblige such of them as remained attached to their original religion to meet in secret, and under the strongest injunctions of secrecy. Their safety depended upon it. A false brother might expose the lives of many of them to destruction; and from the remains of the religion of the Druids, thus preserved, arose the institution which, to avoid the name of Druid, took that of Mason, and practiced under this new name the rites and ceremonies of Druids.

Thus, we have seen the remarkable history of Christianity and Masonry. Both are "brotherhoods of the Sun," the former exoteric and vulgar, and the latter esoteric and refined.

As Higgins says:

> Every part of Christianity refers back to Abraham, and it is all Freemasonry. Jesus Christ at table, at the head of the twelve, offering the sacrifice of Bread and Wine, is Abraham and Melchizedek over again; such, in fact, it is acknowledged to be by the Romish Church; such is its esoteric religion.[1759]

Doane further illustrates the connection between Masonry and Christianity:

> Masons' marks are conspicuous among the Christian symbols. On some of the most ancient Roman Catholic cathedrals are to be found figures of Christ Jesus with Masons' marks about him.[1760]

Masonry originally held, and still does at the higher levels, the knowledge that the Christ character was *the sun*. This knowledge has obviously been hidden from all but the few. In addition, the heliocentricity of the solar system and the roundness of the earth were known to the ancients eons prior to the Christian era, but these two facts, among innumerable others, were suppressed so that no one would apprehend the sublimation of the solar and celestial mythos. We must ask why the solar mythos, so significant and ubiquitous in cultures around the world for thousands of years, is now unknown, particularly when it is well understood that without the knowledge of the heavens we could scarcely function on Earth, time as we know it would not exist, and we would be unable to figure out when to plant and harvest our food, for one important example. What has happened to the ubiquitous celestial mythos? How is it that this information, so widely known in ancient times, is almost completely hidden from the masses today? The answer is that it

1759 Higgins, I, 791.
1760 Doane, 358.

has been *deliberately* suppressed, so that the masses would never realize the connection between their cherished gods and the celestial bodies.

As demonstrated by Paine, the Masons have known very well the true meaning and importance of astrology, which was considered a sacred science. Anderson explains this ages-old science and its relationship to Masonry and Catholicism:

> [Astrology] is the Word, and written from the beginning … an exact science, sublime and holy, which has existed longer than we have at present any history, and handed down by the great and wise of the past, those builders of the temples of the sun, or universe, until in its old age its ashes are buried in Roman Catholicism but yet burn in Freemasonry.… [The] astrology of the ancients is the base of all and every science, either of the past or the future, and that it was at one time a universal religion, science, and language, the remnants of the sign language still held by the Masonic bodies, to whom it is as "shining in the darkness and the darkness comprehending it not."[1761]

Astrology and astrotheology were not only known in the ancient world but have constituted an enormous portion of human civilization. Time and again, massive edifices around the globe have been built that are encapsulations of the heavenly story, serving as stellar "computers." But this astrotheological Masonry was corrupted, as the power-mongering historicizers drove its true meaning and religion underground in a vicious quest to subjugate the world and acquire its wealth.

The Motive

It is obvious the conspirators were after power and money, and, as Pope Leo X quipped, they certainly have become wealthy from the fable of Christ. In fact, during the 500-year period of the Inquisition, which Walker calls, "a standing mockery of justice—perhaps the most iniquitous that the arbitrary cruelty of man has ever devised,"[1762] the Church grew extremely rich. In reality, there is no other way to explain why the Romans would willingly worship a Jewish man as a god incarnate, a title and honor usually reserved for Caesars. As the Romans themselves said and as was admitted by Christians, they did not believe the tale, immediately recognizing it as a rehash of pre-existing myths, legends and rituals. Nor were they fond of the troublesome Jews, so as to have exalted one in such a manner. The Romanized Jesus, in fact, was designed to castigate the Jews and, as noted, to give the Romans authority over them.

1761 Anderson, iii-iv.

1762 Walker, B. (1983), 436.

The gospel story was also designed to put the onus on the Jews for the destruction of their nation, which is why the story was placed at the time it was. The tale had to occur before the destruction of the temple in 70 CE, obviously, or the play would not have had a stage on which to set it. In fact, Church historian Eusebius makes it clear that Christ's advent had to take place before the destruction of Jerusalem so that his Passion might be utilized as justification for that deed:

> To Pella those who believed in Christ migrated from Jerusalem; and as if holy men had utterly abandoned the royal metropolis of the Jews and the entire Jewish land, the judgment of God at last overtook them for their abominable crimes against Christ and His apostles, completely blotting out that wicked generation from among men.... Such was the reward of the Jews' iniquitous and wicked treatment of God's Christ.[1763]

Eusebius, it should be noted, was from Caesarea, which would essentially make him a Samaritan, although not necessarily of "Jewish" blood. It is obvious that, while he considers Christ from the house of Judah, he is not fond of "Jews"; nor were many others in the Roman Empire. The author of the Epistle of Ignatius to the Magnesians says, "To profess Jesus Christ while continuing to follow Jewish customs is an absurdity. The Christian faith does not look to Judaism, but Judaism looks to Christianity, *in which every other race and tongue that confesses a belief in God has now been comprehended.*"[1764] Thus, Ignatius's statements constitute an admission that orthodox Christianity was formulated to abrogate the Judean religion and to roll all the competing religions into one.

The motives of those who composed and spread the gospel story included the termination of the recurrent sacred king sacrifice/ scapegoat ritual with the final blood atonement prescribed in the Christian myth, as is stated in the Letter to the Hebrews, for example. As Dujardin says, "The sacrifice was in decadence in the first century in the official cults, scorned by Graeco-Roman society, and disparaged by the Rationalism of the intellectuals."[1765]

The results of this effort to end human sacrifice have been far from satisfactory, as millions of humans have been sacrificed in the name of Christianity. In addition, the dreary image of the suffering Jesus has served as a constant reminder of gloom and doom, casting a somber pall across the world. It would have been much better for the world if the

---

1763 Eusebius, 68–73.

1764 Early Christian Writings, 73.

1765 Mead, DJL, 10.

gnosis, or esoteric knowledge, had been made known in the first place.

When the Romans pulled together their state religion, they no doubt had in front of them the words of Josephus regarding Moses: "Now when once he had brought them to submit to religion, he easily persuaded them to submit in all other things."[1766] In addition, a favorite Roman adage was, "The common people like to be deceived—deceived let them be."[1767] Thus we see that the Romans were not mindlessly falling down to worship the Jesus character as an incarnation of God when they adopted the nascent religion, which they then changed for centuries to suit their own interests.

In order to pass off this doctrine of submission to the new faith, there had to be inculcated a fervent belief in the "One God," in order for it to be believed he had sent a messenger, prophet, son or other representative. This belief in an omnipotent supernatural being has not been difficult to sell, since it has existed from virtually the first moment man became cognizant of his surroundings. However, as Margaret Sanger said, "No God, no Master," and numerous freethinkers over the centuries have noted how the concept of an all-powerful, all-controlling god is used to create despotism, tyranny and fascism, which is, in the end, the motive for creating Christianity. Anderson describes the foundation of Christianity and its results:

> The Romans at that time were the worst of pagans or idolaters; but knowing well the power of state religion, strove to make from their original sun worship a religion which should embody Trinity; and so from the story of Buddha and Osiris, Isis and Horus, and the zodiacal signs, clothed the stories in new garments, and personified the sun into a *living* man, and the moon into a virgin mother, and the cross ✟ as the life-saving symbol, and then *forced the slaves of Rome by sword and wild beast, by inquisition and torture and auto-da-fe, to acknowledge as truth that which their souls abhorred*; forcing them to teach this to their children, established that abomination, the confessional, making spies and traitors in every household till, sinking deeper and deeper in despair and forced ignorance, generation after generation dared no longer even to think their soul was their own and given by God, but were led to believe that God the Father damned them from the beginning and delivered them over to the devil, to be saved (no matter how abominable their crimes) by this man called the Son of God.... In fact, the whole story is in-

1766 Josephus, Antiquities.
1767 Doane, 271.

> comprehensible; and as no one could explain it, the priests when questioned at once forbid such sacrilege as questions; and "It is a mystery" sufficed to stay all inquisitive minds.[1768]

And Wheless says:

> Thus was the ultimate merger and total identity of Paganism with "the new Paganism called Christianity" finally established by law and Imperial policy of "One State and One Religion," to which conformity was enforced by laws of confiscation and death; all the other religions of the Empire were fused by fire and sword into a bastard Christianity.[1769]

It was unquestionably these selfsame Roman authorities who put into the mouth of the fictitious Paul the exhortations that Christians obey the authorities "in everything." The honor that he exhorts them to give "to whom honor is due" is, of course, that due to the Emperor, as are the taxes Paul also tells his followers to hand over. It makes little sense that Paul and other Christians would be persecuted as claimed if they were obeying these injunctions. Why would the authorities seize and execute Paul, when he was preaching to the Romans that they should give their money to, and obey in everything, those same authorities? And why would Paul then grouse about being held prisoner, when he told his followers to submit to the authorities, for they are "from God?"

Furthermore, Christ himself is made to exhort his followers to despise "mammon," i.e., money, and to "render unto Caesar." When sought for his sage advice by Roman soldiers, John the Baptist tells them to "be content with their wages" (Luke 3:14). This injunction against money by the "rebellious" Jesus and his cohorts served the state and its religion very nicely, since it was they who ended up with the money. Such exhortations by "Jesus" beg the question as to why an omniscient and compassionate god would advise his followers to give away all their money and potentially starve to death. Such a god would not behave in this callous manner, but those who were to get the money would. Nor would any god need people to tithe to his priests and church if he were real and all-powerful, therefore having no need for the back-breaking labor of human beings to sustain him.

It is quite obvious who really wrote these passages, yet people still blindly submit to the authorities because of them, believing that there is indeed a single, omniscient, omnipresent and omnipotent being in charge at all times and that "he" has given the authorities their power.

After centuries of killing millions around the globe and stealing

1768 Anderson, 52.
1769 Wheless, 31.

their wealth, the Catholic Church became more "refined" in its extortionist policy, sending out its financial missionaries, the Jesuits. The Jesuits are the most effective proselytizers of Catholicism worldwide, for centuries envied by the other orders for their ability to acquire vast fortunes and properties. Over the past couple of centuries, the Jesuit handbook, "Secret Instructions of the Society of Jesus," has found its way into the hands of outsiders who have published it. This guidebook, or *Monita,* focuses on how to defraud old ladies by telling them that they will receive grace if they submit to the confessor, who will then oversee how every penny of theirs is spent and make sure their wills are made out to the Order. The *Monita* also describes how to convince the rich that donating to the Church will "relieve the pains of purgatory." In order to secure these fortunes, the Jesuits appeal to the vanity of the donor by insuring that he or she will have his or her name on a college or university building. The *Monita* was written in Latin, of course, so that only the educated would have any chance of knowing what it contained and that it would therefore remain secret. One outsider who published the book was a Scottish Rite Mason, demonstrating how these societies compete with each other even though they are intimately linked, growing, in fact, from the same root.[1770]

In reality, if we peek far behind the curtain of the secret societies and fraternities, we find traditional enemies working together to slice up the world for the benefit of the elite, creating nations and exploiting the masses. We discover they concoct conflict for profit, as many members have been weapons manufacturers—and there is no more contentious a weapon for them to wield than religion. Christianity, in effect, was a state religion devised to enrich and empower certain individuals and groups, who have since become among the most powerful on the planet.

The Making of a Myth

In creating their state religion, the Christian conspirators not only founded the world's greatest forgery mill but also went on a censorship rampage that silenced millions of dissident voices by murder and destroyed books, temples, statues, inscriptions and other traces of the previous cultures, eventually leading to immense ignorance and the virtual illiteracy of the Western world. As Roberts says:

> To get rid of the damning fact that there is no historical basis for their theological fictions, the Christian priesthood have been guilty of the heinous crime of destroying nearly all traces of the concurrent history of the first two centuries of the Christian era. What little of

1770 The *Monita* is almost certainly a rabid anti-Catholic hoax analogous to the anti-Semitic *Protocols of the Elders of Zion.*

it they have permitted to come down to us, they have so altered and changed, as to destroy its historical value.

Walker relates the Church's *modus operandi*:

It was always important for religious authorities to control literature, and to gain the legal right to destroy books that contradicted their own teachings. Few people were so assiduous in this endeavor as Christians. In the third to sixth centuries, whole libraries were burned, schools and universities destroyed and citizens' books confiscated throughout the Roman world, on the pretext of defending the church against paganism. Under the early Christian emperors, people were framed by ecclesiastical investigators who planted "magical writings" in their houses, then legally confiscated all possessions.[1771]

After the Council of Nicea, per the murderous Constantine's orders, the Christians turned up the heat on censorship, leading to the centuries-long orgy that obliterated millions of texts. One of the greatest crimes in human history was the destruction in 391 of the library at Alexandria perpetrated by Christian fanatics,[1772] some possibly bent on hiding the truth about their religion and its alleged founder. Because of this villainy, we have lost priceless information as to the true state of the ancient world, such desolation also setting back civilization at least 1,000 years. The portion of the Alexandrian library placed in the Temple of Serapis also perished, "as this very valuable library was willfully destroyed by the Christian Theophilus, and on the spot where this beautiful temple of Serapis stood, in fact, on its very foundation, was erected a church in honor of the 'noble army of martyrs,' who never existed."[1773] Of this nefarious demolition of the Serapion, Roberts asks:

Will any Catholic or Protestant prelate, priest or clergyman tell us why the Christian emperor, Theodosius the First, should have

1771 Walker, B. (1983), 122.

1772 In fact the Library of Alexandria was accidentally destroyed by Julius Caesar's troops when a fire set to engulf the Egyptian navy spread out of control.

1773 Walker, B. (1983), 440. Herbermann (1.303) relates the contention that the "small library in the Serapeum is supposed to have perished when the temple of Serapise was destroyed by Theophilus [Pope of Alexandria, d. 412]," but remarks that "there is no definite statement [from antiquity] to that effect." There is, however, an image from the fifth century of "Bishop Theophilus of Alexandria, Gospel book in hand, stand[ing] triumphantly atop the Serapeum in 391." (*P. Goleniscev 6 verso*; Bauer, A., and J. Strygowski, "Eine alexandrinische Weltchronik," *Denkschriften der Kaiserlichen Akademie der Wissenschaften*: Vienna, 1906; 1-204, fig. 6 verso.)

ordered the destruction of the Serapeum Library of Alexandria, if not to destroy the evidence it contained of the spurious nature of the Christian religion and its heathen philosophical origin?[1774]

Some decades later, the Christian patriarch of Alexandria, Cyril, instigated mobs to terrorize Jews and to hideously torture and murder the exalted female Pagan philosopher Hypatia (c. 370–415) by scraping the flesh from her bones with oyster shells. For his evil acts, Cyril was later canonized by the "infallible" Church. Hypatia was so esteemed and renowned for her wisdom and brilliance that her murder has been considered the "death of the Pagan world."

The destruction did not end there, however, as the ruination of literacy and history became an all-consuming Christian pursuit. As Graham states, "By the fifth century the destruction was so complete Archbishop Chrystostom could boast of it thus: 'Every trace of the old philosophy and literature of the ancient world has vanished from the face of the earth.'"[1775]

At some point, a death penalty was enacted for reading unapproved books (e.g., those who demonstrated the faith was a sham). Pope after pope continued the assault on books and learning. Gregory, Bishop of Constantinople (@ 540–604), the last of the "doctors" of the Church, actively engaged in book-burning. In the eleventh century, "Saint" Gregory had the Library of Palatine Apollo burned, and the Council of Trent (1545–63) reconfirmed the policy against "heathen" learning.

Where the Christians did not destroy the works of the ancient authors, they corrupted and mutilated them. Indeed, in order to preserve their texts from these violent hands, the Gnostics had to Christianize them and historicize their mythical characters.[1776] So extensive was this practice of fraud that evidently no ancient author's work maintains its original integrity.[1777] Walker elaborates upon the extent of the fraud:

> After burning books and closing pagan schools, the church dealt in another kind of forgery: falsification by omission. All European history was extensively edited by a church that managed to make itself the sole repository of literary and historical records. With all important documents assembled in the monasteries, and the lay public rendered illiterate, Christian history could be forged with impunity.[1778]

1774 Roberts, 267.
1775 Graham, 281.
1776 Doresse, 311.
1777 Higgins, I, 593.
1778 Walker, B. (1983), 320.

The erection of Christian churches on the ruins of pagan temples and sacred sites was not only common but *de rigeur*, serving to obliterate the evidence of the previous deities and worship. Walker relates the typical procedure used by Christians to usurp Pagan sacred sites: "After temples were destroyed, monks and hermits were settled in the ruins to defile the site with their excrement, and to prevent reconstruction."[1779]

Such were the efforts the "classy" Christians had to make for centuries to cement their fictions. The devastation of art and culture was appalling, yet some of the despoilers' efforts assisted in preserving evidence of the fraud:

> In some of the ancient Egyptian temples the Christian iconoclasts, when tired of hacking and hewing at the symbolic figures incised in the chambers of imagery, and defacing the most prominent features of the monuments, found they could not dig out the hieroglyphics, and took to covering them over with plaster; and this plaster, intended to hide the meaning and stop the mouth of the stone word, has served to preserve the ancient writings as fresh in hue and sharp in outline as when they were first cut and colored. In a similar manner the temple of ancient religion was invaded and possession gradually gained by connivance of Roman power; and that enduring fortress, not built but quarried out of solid rock, was stuccoed all over the front and made white awhile with its look of brandnewness, and reopened under the sign of another name—that of the carnalized Christ.[1780]

Thus, these hieroglyphs have revealed the truth, because they contain the celestial mythos and ritual, and demonstrate that the Christian story is in large part Egyptian.

In addition to this odious Christian behavior was the Inquisition, the most ghastly period in all of human history, in which millions were tortured and murdered over centuries to frighten the survivors and their descendants into conforming to the dogma of the Catholic Church. During those many centuries, no dissenter was allowed to flourish and few to live at all. Anyone who dared to question the fairytales now being forced upon them—in other words, all the *honest* people—were forced to convert or die. Either way, the people would then become fiscally beneficial to the greedy, deceitful Church, by serving as slaves, tithing or forfeiting their assets through death, natural or otherwise.

Of this endless destruction, Doane remarks:

> Besides forging, lying, and deceiving for the cause of Christ,

1779 Walker, B. (1983), 208.

1780 Massey, HJMC.

> the Christian Fathers destroyed all evidence against themselves and their religion, which they came across. Christian divines seem to have always been afraid of too much light.[1781]

Fortunately, they will not be able to escape the light today, as it is too bright. As Higgins says:

> Notwithstanding the strenuous exertions of the priests, for the last two thousand years, to eradicate every trace of the means by which their various doctrines, rites, and ceremonies have been established; yet they have not entirely succeeded.[1782]

A number of important texts fortunately survived the purges sufficiently intact to make it possible for us to trace how Christianity was created and shaped. To recap, the early contributors to the Christian version of the ubiquitous celestial mythos were the Syrian Gnostics, who were attempting to create a syncretistic religion that would encompass the wide variety of cultures from around the "known world." By the end of the first century CE, at Antioch, for one, the Gnostics were already involved in committing to writing the various sayings and deeds of the characters of the celestial mythos and savior cult that had been transmitted orally within the brotherhood for millennia. Eventually, as Doresse says, "In the time of Hadrian (AD 110–38), Gnosticism passes over from Syria into Egypt."[1783]

Meanwhile, in Palestine, possibly emanating out of Galilee and/or the ancient monastery on Carmel, with an outpost at Qumran, the Jewish/Samaritan priesthood of Masons and astrologers, the Zadokites/Sadducees, had been anticipating the Great Year's end and promoting themselves as the Elect, the inheritors of "the Lord's" kingdom on Earth, which would be brought about by a "wondrous child" and "restorer." After the destruction of Palestine, this group and others dispersed into various other brotherhood branches, including those at Antioch and Alexandria. The new influx reignited the centuries-old internecine struggle for supremacy over each other and the Gentiles. Thus began the conspiracy to set the ubiquitous solar hero sayings and narratives in Judea, with Jews as both protagonists and antagonists.

In the middle of the second century, the original Gnostic schools began to dissent from the Judaizing and historicizing activity, objecting that their work was not meant to be taken literally. At the end of the second century, the historicizing push increased with the success of the Roman play for domination, and the canonical gospels were composed,

1781 Doane, 438.
1782 Higgins, II, 107.
1783 Doresse, 12.

although they were continuously reworked to agree at least superficially with other newly forged manuscripts. This tinkering went on for centuries at the hands of numerous councils until relative uniformity was achieved. In fact, the mutilation of the texts continues to this day in translations that obfuscate original meanings.

The Intertestamental Literature and Christian Apocrypha

The Dead Sea Scrolls dating to the centuries before and after the beginning of the Christian era survived unknown and untouched by the forgers, and thus they reveal the Palestinian contributors to the Christian myth. In addition to the Samaritan Gnostic Marcion's New Testament, other texts utilized by the Christian conspirators included the intertestamental literature such as the Jewish Apocrypha and Pseudepigrapha, as well as the Christian Apocrypha. Many of these books were originally considered canonical but were later removed and condemned, demonstrating how often "God's infallible Word" has been changed. A number of the Jewish Apocrypha, however, have been retained in the Catholic Bible, but not in the Protestant canon, illustrating that the latter is a corruption of the former and not a "return to primitive Christianity." Moreover, in the various texts either removed or kept out of the biblical canon may be found more truth about the origins of Christianity than in those made canonical. As the editor of *The Other Bible* says:

> Deprived of all scriptures between the Testaments, the common reader is left with the impression that somehow Christianity sprang self-generated like a divine entity, with no past, into its historical setting. Yet a reading of the texts between the Testaments shows how major eschatological themes of the New Testament—the appearance of the Son of Man, the imminence of the End, the apocalyptic vision in the Book of Revelation, the notion of salvation through the messiah—are all preoccupations of intertestamental literature.[1784]

Indeed, the impression of mysterious self-generation is contrived to cover up the ruse, yet there are enough of these ignored texts that a thorough exegesis could fill a volume in itself.

The Book of Enoch

Among these texts was "The Book of Enoch," which was given scriptural recognition in the New Testament Letter of Jude and which remains ensconced in the canon of the Ethiopian Orthodox Church still today. Copies of Enoch were found at the Dead Sea, demonstrating that the Scrolls were not the writings of an isolated sect and that the Sadducean originators of Christianity used Enoch, which contained much of

1784 Barnstone, xix.

the story of "Jesus Christ" and which predated the alleged advent of the Jewish godman by centuries. Of this book Wheless says:

> The Book of Enoch, forged in the name of the grandson of Adam, is the fragmentary remains of a whole literature which circulated under the pretended authorship of that mythical Patriarch.... This work is a composite of at least five unknown Jewish writers, and was composed during the last two centuries BC.... In this Book we first find the lofty titles: "Christ" or "the Anointed One," "Son of Man," "the Righteous One," "the Elect One,"—all of which were boldly plagiarized by the later Christians and bestowed upon Jesus of Nazareth.... [The Book] abounds in such "Christian" doctrines as the Messianic Kingdom, Hell, the Resurrection, and Demonology, the Seven Heavens, and the Millennium, all of which have here their apocryphal Jewish promulgation, after being plagiarized bodily from the Persian and Babylonian myths and superstitions, as we have seen confessed. There are numerous quotations, phrases, clauses, or thoughts derived from Enoch, or of closest of kin with it, in several of the New Testament Gospels and Epistles.[1785]

And Carpenter states:

> In *The Book of Enoch*, written not later than BC 170, the Christ is spoken of as already existing in heaven, and about to come as Judge of all men, and is definitely called "the Son of Man." The Book of Revelations is *full* of passages from *Enoch*; so are the Epistles of Paul; so too are the Gospels.[1786]

The Book of Enoch relates that the messiah will come and establish supremacy: "The Chosen One will have the sinners destroyed."[1787] Of this judgment day, Wells says:

> Enoch's picture of the final judgement is strikingly paralleled at Matthew 25:31–46. Enoch says that "the Lord of Spirits seated the Elect One on the throne of his glory"; Matthew reads: "When the Son of man shall come in his glory ... then shall he sit on the throne of his glory." Both writers go on to describe how the righteous are vindicated while the rest are banished to flame and torment.[1788]

Enoch, of course, is not a historical character but is part of the

1785 Wheless, 85–7.
1786 Carpenter, 203.
1787 Book of Enoch, 37–38; Wells, WWJ, 169.
1788 Wells, WWJ, 170.

mythos. As Massey says, "In the *Book of Enoch* [61:9] one form of the Messiah is the '*Son of Woman'*; this was Enoch or Enos, the Egyptian SutAnush [Set], who had been twin with Horus but was superseded by him."[1789] Hazelrigg elaborates:

> Then came Enoch, or Anûsh, words which mean knowledge; he was known as Ur-anous, and, according to a Hebrew manuscript, as Hermes, the inventor of astronomy, mathematics, and of divine worship. Aonac, an Irish word (pronounced Enoch), signifies a cycle of the sun. He was also known as Atlas, whence Atlantis, of which country he was the Supreme Pontiff. His symbol was the Bull, emblematic of the shepherd age.[1790]

In actuality, the bull was the emblem of the *Taurean* age, which would mean that the book reflects a tradition 4,000 or more years old; the "Bull of Heaven, called "Gugalana," can be found in the *Epic of Gilgamesh*, which dates to the second or possibly third millennium BCE.[1791] The book is in fact highly astrological, as is to be expected. Higgins relates:

> Here are all the leading doctrines which I have been contending for clearly maintained. The residence or birth-place of the theology, Upper India; the signs of the Zodiac; the change of the Equinox from Taurus to Aries ... the Hindoo Trinity, than which nothing can be more clear ... and a history similar to the Jewish, but not copied from it; the prophecy of an *elect one* as described by all the prophets, including the prophecy of Virgil, and the elect one put to death, noticed by me in the cases of Buddha, Cristna, and him of the Apollo of Miletus.... It has been the subject of this work to show that an universal system extended over the whole of the old world; and the principal facts for which I have contended are supported by this curious and unquestionably genuine document.[1792]

Higgins avers that, based on the astrology Enoch reflects, it was originally composed around 2400 BCE in the latitude of Northern India.[1793]

Another pseudepigraphic writing attributed to Enoch is the Book of the Secrets of Enoch, one of the "366 books" allegedly written by him, a number symbolic for the 365+ days of the year. As in the Old Testament,

---

1789 Massey, HJMC.
1790 Hazelrigg, 96.
1791 Interestingly, in "Inana's descent," the goddess invokes "lord Gud-gal-ana," who is the "husband of my elder sister" who dies and is lamented.
1792 Higgins, I, 551-2.
1793 Higgins, I, 544–5.

in the Secrets it was said that Enoch lived to be 365 "years"; in other words, he is the sun, and his "life" is the length of a year. In the Secrets, Enoch continues the solar imagery when he describes how the "angels," or *angles of the zodiac*, "bore me away to the east, and placed me at the sun's gates, where the sun goes forth according to the regulation of the seasons and the circuit of the months of the whole year, and the number of the hours of day and night."[1794] This Enochian text is thus astrotheological, no doubt the reason it was eventually considered "apocryphal."

The Testaments of the Twelve Patriarchs

Although they are purported to be the products of the mythical "sons of Jacob," the Jewish Pseudepigraphon "The Testaments of the Twelve Patriarchs" was written likely between 137 to 107 BCE. Of the Testaments, the editor of *The Forgotten Books of Eden* says:

> When you look beyond the unvarnished—almost brutally frank—passages of the text, you will discern a remarkable attestation of the expectations of the Messiah which existed a hundred years before Christ.... The instances of the influence of these writings on the New Testament are notable in the Sermon on the Mount which reflects the spirit and even uses phrases from these Testaments. St. Paul appears to have borrowed so freely that it seems as though he must have carried a copy of the Testaments with him on his travels.[1795]

Like the Dead Sea Scrolls, these texts contain the blueprint for Christianity; however, some of them have been interpolated by conspiring Christians to give a semblance of "prophecy" of their pretended godman. As Barnstone says,

Indeed, because of the messianic nature of Jewish Pseudepigrapha, they were favorite readings of the early Christians and many of them were altered and "Christianized," falsified if you will, to make them reveal Christian truths.[1796]

In their cunning priestcraft, the mutilating Christians later accused the Jews of removing material from the originals. Nevertheless, some of the Christian-like passages are apparently genuine, implying that the forgers of Christianity were of the same school as the Testaments writers and used their texts.

These Testaments were written and/or interpolated for the express purpose of: 1. raising the Semites over the other "sons of Noah"; 2. uniting the tribes of Levi and Judah as the rulers over other Israelites

1794 The Forgotten Books of Eden, 85.
1795 The Forgotten Books of Eden, 220.
1796 Barnstone, 202.

and over the Gentiles; and 3. laying the foundation for the coming king, who, in anticipation of the destruction of Jerusalem/Judea, was to be made into a spiritual "son of God" as well.

The Testament of Simeon, for example, seeks to raise the "sons of Shem," over the Japhethites and Hamites. This book states: "Then the Mighty One of Israel shall glorify Shem. *For the Lord God shall appear on earth, and Himself save men*." Thus, the Semites will subjugate all other races, and God Himself will incarnate ostensibly *as a Semite*, according to the latter sentence, which is a Christian interpolation. As such, the Semitic godman will represent the tribes of Levi and Judah over the other Israelites, and provide salvation for all the nations, as Simeon also says:

> And now, my children, obey Levi and Judah, and be not lifted up against these two tribes, for from them shall arise unto you the salvation of God. For the Lord shall raise up from Levi as it were a High Priest, and from Judah as it were a King, *God and man*, He shall save all the Gentiles and the race of Israel.[1797]

In this union of Levi and Judah is the spiritual "savior" plus the temporal "messiah," which is equivalent to "Jesus the Christ."

Furthermore, in the Testament of Levi, dated to between 109–107 BCE, appears this stunning blueprint for Christianity:

> And behold I am clear from your ungodliness and transgression, which ye shall commit in the end of the ages against *the Savior of the World, Christ*, acting godlessly, deceiving Israel, and stirring up against it great evils from the Lord. And ye shall deal lawlessly together with Israel, so He shall not bear with Jerusalem because of your wickedness; but the veil of the temple shall be rent, so as not to cover your shame. And ye shall be scattered as captives among the Gentiles, and shall be for a reproach and for a curse there. For the house which the Lord shall choose shall be called Jerusalem, as is contained in the book of Enoch the righteous.[1798]

If this passage is not a shameless Christian interpolation, forged after the fall of Jerusalem, it is quite obviously a seed from which the Christ myth sprouted. It also verifies the importance of the Book of Enoch.

The Jewish Apocrypha and Pseudepigrapha provide a connection between not only Judaism and orthodox Christianity but also Judaism and Gnosticism, evidenced in such texts as the Wisdom of Solomon, the Haggadah, and the Wisdom of Jesus.

1797 The Forgotten Books of Eden, 226.
1798 The Forgotten Books of Eden, 230.

The Wisdom of Jesus, Son of Sirach, or Ecclesiasticus

For obvious reasons, the title of the pre-Christian "Wisdom of Jesus" is often represented without the "Jesus," as "Wisdom of Sirach" or "Ecclesiasticus." Thought to have been written around 180 BCE. by "Jesus" and translated into Greek by his grandson "Jesus," the text evidently represents the lineage of the pre-Christian Joshua/Jesus cultists. The Wisdom of Jesus contains hundreds of wisdom sayings, including Old Testament aphorisms such as, "To fear the Lord is the source of wisdom." Here, as in Gnosticism, wisdom is identified as a female entity (Hokmah/ Sophia). This lengthy book also contains several New Testament Sayings of Jesus, or *Logia Iesou*, and is without a doubt Therapeutan, in that it prescribes the putting of oneself in the hands of a spiritual physician in order to "cleanse one's heart from sin."

Like the gospel Jesus, the pre-Christian or Wisdom Jesus exhorts "faith and meekness" to win the approval of the Lord, excoriates hypocrites and admonishes readers not to exalt themselves. The pre-Christian Jesus also exhorts would-be servants of the Lord to "prepare yourself to be tried. Set your heart right and be firm … hold fast to him, and do not forsake him, so that you may be honored when your life ends," exactly as the followers of the gospel Jesus were told to be as "martyrs for the faith."

Like the gospel Jesus, who entreats his followers to give away their belongings, the Wisdom Jesus says, "So charity will atone for sin" and urges his followers to do good works for those less fortunate, so that they may become like "sons of the Most High" (El Elyon). The Wisdom Jesus is also very similar to Paul in his sexist attitudes, saying, "A silent wife is a gift from the Lord," among other noxious and repressive comments. Of the Wisdom of Jesus, Massey says:

> [The] Book of Ecclesiasticus contains the logia of a pre-Christian Jesus. Here are two of *his* sayings: "Forgive thy neighbor the hurt that he hath done unto thee, so shall thy sins also be forgiven when thou prayest." "Lay up thy treasures according to the commandments of the Most High, and it shall bring thee more profit than gold." These are assigned to the Jesus of Matthew's gospel.[1799]

Furthermore, the pre-Christian Jesus, like the gospel Jesus, calls God "Father" and says:

> He created me from the beginning before the world, and I shall never fail.… They that eat me shall yet be hungry, and they that drink me shall yet be thirsty. He that obeyeth me shall never

1799 Massey, HJMC, 152.

be confounded, and they that work by me shall not do amiss.[1800]

Obviously, either this text is interpolated, which would yet again demonstrate Christian fraud, or it serves as proof of the pre-Christian Jesus, eucharist and all.

Many of the exhortations in this book are for initiates into the brotherhood and are Buddhistic/Gymnosophic in nature. In fact, the Wisdom Jesus reveals his solar cult affiliation with his long homage to the sun, in which he states that the sun "has not permitted the saints of the Lord to recount all his wonders," i.e., to record in writing the mysteries of the solar mythos:

> The light-giving sun looks down on everything, and his work is full of the glory of the Lord. He has not permitted the saints of the Lord to recount all his wonders, which the Lord, the Almighty, has firmly established, so that the universe might stand fast through his glory.... The glory of the height is the firmament in its purity; the sight of the heavens with the spectacle of their splendor. The sun, when he appears, making proclamation as he goes forth, is a wonderful instrument, the work of the Most High; at noonday he dries up the country, and who can withstand his burning heat? ... He breathes out fiery vapors, and shoots forth his beams, blinding men's eyes. (42:16–43:5)

In fact, the Wisdom Jesus's paean to the sun is about as close to Pagan sun-worship as it gets. Moreover, these sayings constitute one of several places where the pre-Christian Jesus exalts the sun, moon and stars, displaying astrological/ astrotheological knowledge.

The Teachings of the Twelve Apostles, or The Didache

The early Christian apocryphon "The Teachings of the Twelve Apostles," also called the "Didache," was possibly utilized in the manufacture of the canonical gospels. Ben Yehoshua states it was based on writings concerning the "12 tribes," and Larson says it combines the *Logia Iesou*, or Sayings, with the Manual of Discipline found at the Dead Sea. The Didache does not contain a narrative but provides explanation and instructions concerning baptism, the eucharist, tribulation and parousia, or arrival of "the Lord in the clouds."

The Gospel of the Hebrews and Syrians

Dating to around 115–125 CE, the Gospel of the Hebrews was reputedly used first and almost exclusively by the early Jewish-Christian church, and was also called by Eusebius the "Gospel according to the Hebrews and Syrians," "by which he meant it was used by the Jews in Syria, as elsewhere," a view confirmed by Jerome, who also affirmed

1800 The Missing Books of the Bible, II, 279–80.

that "the Gospel of the Hebrews was written 'in the Chaldee and Syriac languages.' It appears it was used by the Nazarenes residing in Berea, Syria."[1801] The Gospel of the Hebrews was sometimes confused with the Gospel of Matthew, possibly because it represented the Egyptian "Oracles of Taht-Matiu." The Gospel of the Hebrews contained the *Logia Iesou* or Sayings of Jesus and was non-historicizing, containing no immaculate conception, genealogy "from Abraham to Christ" or childhood history.

The Gospel According to the Egyptians or Diegesis

Another text utilized in the creation of Christianity was the "Gospel of the Egyptians," which predated the canonical gospels and was written by the Therapeuts. Of the Gospel of the Egyptians, Waite says:

> The original of this gospel may have been in use among the Therapeutae of Egypt, a long time before the introduction of Christianity, the passages related to Christ being afterward added. Or it may have been written in another country, and brought into Egypt, with the Christian religion. In either case it may be dated as early as AD 110 to 115.... The story of Joseph and Mary appears not to have been known when this gospel was written. Neither is anything said, so far as we have information of its contents, of the miracles of Christ, or of the material resurrection.[1802]

Taylor states that the "narrative" mentioned by Luke, i.e., the Diegesis, was the Gospel of the Egyptians:

> The first draft of the mystical adventures of Chrishna, as brought from India into Egypt, was the Diegesis; the first version of the Diegesis was the Gospel according to the Egyptians; the first renderings out of the language of Egypt into that of Greece, for the purpose of imposing on the nations of Europe, were *the apocryphal gospels*; the corrected, castigated, and *authorised* versions of these apocryphal compilations were the gospels of our four evangelists.

The Gospel of Truth, the Gospel of Thomas and the Acts of Thomas

In addition, a number of the Gnostic gospels barely mention "Jesus" or "Christ," referring instead to the abstract "Savior," such as the Gospel of Truth (150 CE) and the Gospel of Thomas, which was composed primarily of the *Logia Iesou* and written in Aramaic/Syriac, representing

1801 Waite, 63.
1802 Waite, 86.

the Tammuz faction. Furthermore, the apocryphal Acts of Thomas were likely forged to explain how the "Christians of St. Thomas" ended up in India; however, as demonstrated, these "Christians" were Tammuz followers already in India possibly millennia before the Christian era.

The Protevangelion, or Book of James

Used by the forgers of Matthew and Luke, the Protevangelion is one of the oldest Judaized narratives, written by a Hellenic Jew around 120–130 CE. The text was originally Indian and Egyptian, with the myth of Isis-Mari and Seb becoming Mary and Joseph, and was somewhat "historicized" with the mythical persecution by Herod, who is made to take the role of both the Indian Kansa and the Egyptian Set-Typhon.

Furthermore, into the portions of the Protevangelion used by the evangelists were interpolated phrases to "fulfill prophecy": For example, the verses at Matthew 1:22–23 about the "virgin" conceiving and bearing a son called Emmanuel are not found in the earlier Protevangelion. Also missing is Luke 4:24: "And he said, 'Truly, I say to you, no prophet is acceptable in his own country.'" This interpolation was made to make Jesus, the ubiquitous solar savior and wisdom genius, appear to be a Jewish male.

The Gospel of the Infancy

Dating to around 120–130, the Gospel of the Infancy was attributed by Jerome to "Matthew" but was "received by the Gnostics," thus not taken literally. The original Gospel of the Infancy was based on the Hindu story of Krishna's childhood, the *Bhagavat Purana*, apparently procured from the Indian Nazarene brotherhood, with Zoroastrian influence. This and other infancy gospels were used to construct the brief gospel accounts of Jesus's childhood. One interesting phrase may have been inserted as a clue to its allegorical nature, in a passage (vi. 18) following a description of the infant Christ's miraculous healing powers: "The people therefore said, 'Without doubt Joseph and Mary and that boy are Gods, for they do not look like mortals.'" Indeed not.

This book is quite obviously fiction, so much so that much of it was not included in the canon. Matthew and Luke have cut the overt treatment of Mary and Joseph as deities and omitted the fantastic tales depicting Jesus as a vicious brat and a pint-sized sorcerer who changes other boys into goats so he can be their "shepherd," and strikes dead a Jewish boy who destroyed the young "savior's" fish pools because they had been built on the sabbath.

The Gospel of Luke

We have already seen that the Gospel of Luke was based on Marcion's gospel, with interpolations to historicize and Judaize it. In addition, the entire story of Jesus's entry into Jerusalem at Luke 19:29–48 is missing from Marcion; as demonstrated, this story is a part of the ancient mythos. The writer(s) of Luke also interpolated the Masonic phrases describing Jesus being "the head cornerstone the builders rejected" at 20:9–18, verses not found in Marcion. Furthermore, a number of passages were added "to fulfill prophecy."

Luke was not only interpolated but also expurgated to remove hints of the brotherhood. For example, at Luke 24, the "two men in dazzling apparel" were originally said to be "those in white clothing," i.e., monks or priests of the solar cult, or "Brotherhood of the Sun."

The Life of Apollonius

Accounts of the life of the Greek/Samaritan Nazarene/ Therapeut/ Gnostic miracle worker Apollonius (c. 2 BCE–c 102 CE) purportedly existed during the second century, prior to Philostratus's composition in 210 at the request of Empress Julia Domna. One or more of these accounts was used in the creation of the New Testament narrative, as alleged by a number of accusers, including Hierocles, the pro-consul under Diocletian (284–305), who wrote the "Philalethes" (303) exposing the Apollonius-Jesus connection. It should be noted that Philostratus's account makes no mention of any Jesus Christ, not even as a rival to Apollonius, who purportedly lived precisely at the time alleged of Jesus.

Other Texts

Other texts originally non-Christian but later Christianized include the Apocalypse of Adam and the Paraphrase of Shem, as well as the Apocryphon of John, as Barnstone states:

> The *Apocryphon of John* (here called *The Secret Book of John*) was "originally composed as a non-Christian text" whose Christian thrust was added by a later Christian editor.[1803]

The historicizers also used the works of Josephus and the teachings of the Gnostics Menander, Saturninus and Carpocrates, as well as those of the Neoplatonist Ammonius Saccas and others already mentioned.

In this mythmaking effort and religious conspiracy, hundreds of new texts were created, and these compositions produced turmoil among the warring priesthoods. The books of the New Testament, in fact, reveal how the rival factions developed and were counteracted. For example,

1803 The Other Bible, 52.

the synoptic gospels represent the synthesis between the solar gods of the East and the West. The Gospel of John was compiled to debunk the second-century Gnostics and to correct the errors of the other gospels as revealed by Pagan critics. The Epistles of John served to excoriate those who claimed Christ never existed. In Acts, the battle between Simon Peter and Simon Magus represents the break between the Roman and Syrian Gnostic churches. Indeed, the confusion and fighting over Christ's life and doctrine within the Church has existed because the Christian plagiarists over the centuries were attempting to amalgamate and fuse practically every myth, fairytale, legend, doctrine or bit of wisdom they could pilfer from the innumerable different mystery religions and philosophies that existed at the time. In doing so, they forged, interpolated, mutilated, changed, and rewrote these texts for centuries.

The Epistle of Barnabas

The Epistle of Barnabas provides several examples of the mythmaking obfuscation of texts. In the Latin version of Barnabas, for instance, we find the obligatory "our Lord Jesus Christ" interpolated at the beginning, yet in the Codex Sinaiticus, there is no such phrase. In this epistle, references to "Jesus" are in reality to "Joshua," the northern Israelite solar hero, also called the "Son of God." The verse in Barnabas regarding the Lord "delivering up" his body "to sanctify us by the remission of our sins; which is effected by the sprinkling of His blood," reflects the old sacred king drama, as performed by followers of Joshua in Palestine. In Christian scriptures, it was always a challenge to determine whether to translate "Joshua" as "Joshua" or "Jesus," and the identification between the two characters is clear, particularly in this epistle. For example, the following passage in the Codex Sinaiticus version is translated thus:

> Again, what has that other prophet, Moses, to say to them? Look, this is what the Lord God says: Enter into the good land which the Lord vowed he would give to Abraham and Isaac and Jacob.... What it is, in fact, saying is, "*Put your hopes in that Joshua who shall be shown to you in mortal guise.*"[1804]

The Latin version is translated thus:

> Moses also in like manner speaketh to them; Behold thus saith the Lord God; Enter ye into the good land of which the Lord hath sworn to Abraham, and Isaac, and Jacob.... It is as if it had been said, *Put your trust in Jesus, who shall be manifested to you in the flesh.*[1805]

1804 Early Christian Writings.

1805 The Lost Books of the Bible, 150.

The editor of the Sinaiticus version notes in reference to this Jesus/Joshua confusion: "Joshua, who led the Israelites into the Promised Land, is a *well-known type of Jesus*. In Hebrew the two names are the same."[1806] Also, references in the Barnabas epistle to "God's Son" are to Adam, not Jesus, but this fact is conveniently overlooked, with the excuse that Adam is also a "type of Jesus."

The Epistle of Barnabas serves as an illustration of the recurrent sacred king drama or "Passion" that preceded the Christian Era, complete with reenactment of the "blood upon us" ritual using scarlet wool on "wood," or branches that were then "sprinkled" on the faithful, a ritual also reflected in the canonical Letter to the Hebrews, as well as at Numbers 19:2–10. The Epistle of Barnabas, then, represented the Joshua cult, not the "historical" Jesus Christ, and served as instructions into the ages-old mysteries. As an initiate into those mysteries, Barnabas also admits that "IE," the designation of Apollo, is the same as "Jesus."

Barnabas further demonstrates his affiliation with the northern kingdom of Israel/Ephraim/Samaria when he mentions the story of Jacob's blessing of Joseph's son Ephraim, raising him above Manasseh. Says Barnabas, "So you can see who is meant by His decree that 'this People shall have the primacy, and inherit the Covenant.'"

The Shepherd of Hermas

An even earlier example of how "Christian" texts originally had nothing to do with "Jesus" or "Christ" is the noncanonical book "The Shepherd of Hermas," which was considered by Irenaeus and Origen to be divinely inspired and which was widely read in churches. As such, the book was included in the New Testament until the fourth century and deemed "apocryphal" thereafter.

Although the book is attributed to the "Hermas" who purportedly flourished around 140 CE, it is certainly an older writing and was asserted by Origen, Eusebius and Jerome to be the product of the "Hermas" referred to in the Pauline Epistle to the Romans. The *Encyclopedia Biblica* places the book to around 150 CE, and Fox to 90 CE. In any case, the book contains numerous Masonic and astrological references, indicating it was possibly a *Hermetic* writing belonging to the *tradition* of Hermes Trismegistus. This lengthy text speaks many times of "God," "the Lord," "the Holy Spirit" and "the Holy Church," as well as a number of times about "the devil," "salvation," and "sin," but, *in several dozen pages*, makes no reference whatsoever to "Jesus" or "Jesus Christ," names no apostle, and makes only one reference to Christians, an evident inter-

1806 Early Christian Writings, 183.

polation. Only twice, at the very end, is the word "Christ" used, also apparent interpolations. The book even refers to the "Son of God," who was the "rock" and "gate"—Masonic terms—but mentions no name. In fact, there are few if any references to a "historical" life of Jesus and no quotes from either the Old or New Testaments. In comparison, the later Epistles of Ignatius, for example, make reference in nearly every other sentence to "our Lord Jesus Christ." How Hermas escaped massive Christian interpolation can only be explained by the fact that it was so well-known and publicly read in churches. Other prominent Masonic symbols in the Shepherd are the tower and vineyard, emblem of Carmel.

Why Place the Christian Myth at this Time?

We have already seen reasons for placing the gospel tale at the time alleged. One was that it was a period of tremendous unrest and that the advent had to take place before Jerusalem's destruction, as asserted by Eusebius. In dating the gospel tale, in fact, Eusebius insists upon what should have been widely known, had it actually occurred:

> Herod, as I have said, was the first foreigner to be entrusted by the Roman senate and the Emperor Augustus with the Jewish nation. It was without question in his time that the advent of Christ occurred.[1807]

This insistence is odd, because the gospel story was supposedly written down long before the fourth century, when Eusebius wrote, and the date of Christ's advent should not have been a factor that needed to be addressed. Furthermore, if it was "without question," why did Eusebius need to state it so definitively? As we have seen, many people *were* questioning it.

Eusebius further explains that the gospel story had to occur at that particular time in order to fulfill the prophecy at Genesis 49:10: "The scepter shall not depart from Judah, nor the ruler's staff from between his feet, until he comes to whom it belongs," i.e., "Shiloh," or the Messiah, who, according to the next passage, would have garments washed in wine and eyes "red with wine." Eusebius states that Herod was the "first foreigner to become king of the Jewish nation," thus fulfilling this prophecy and ending the rule of Jewish leaders. This deposal, of course, spurred messianic fever, since it meant "Shiloh" would come. In fact, Eusebius is superimposing Jesus over the history of Herod, because Herod himself was thought to be the long-awaited Shiloh. As Larson says, "Galilee teemed with fanatics, including Essenes, Pharisees, and Zealots, as well as Herodians, who believed Herod was himself the

1807 Eusebius, 19.

Christ."[1808] Obviously, Herod was not the messiah, but the historicizers in hindsight determined that Christ must appear to have come during his rule. In fact, the Shiloh passage refers to no "prophecy" at all, as Judah, the "lion's whelp," is in reality the constellation of Leo, and the wine-drenched ruler to whom Judah passes his scepter is that of Virgo, the time of the grape harvest.

Moreover, in attempting further to affix Christ's advent to this era, Eusebius later admits that there was a debate as to when it really occurred. What is the need of such debate and attestation if the tale found in the gospel depicted real history? Why so much confusion and murkiness, particularly after three centuries of alleged continuous apostolic lineage? Had Eusebius, the keeper of records, no testimonies of the many purported eyewitnesses who surely would have repeatedly talked about Herod's and Pilate's dreadful actions? At the time of Eusebius, it was claimed that the Church had immediately sprung up with established hierarchies, a great deal of money and power, and a continuous lineage to his era, yet the Church's own historian evidently had no records at all except for the gospels, which were not sufficient to demonstrate when—and if—Christ's advent occurred. In his writings, Eusebius in actuality was fulfilling his task of creating the bogus history not only of Christ himself but of the Church. As Walker says, "The church never did have any continuous record of popes or 'bishops of Rome' from the beginning; most of the early popes were fictitious."[1809] Regarding his forged history of the Church, Eusebius says, "As for men, I have failed to find any clear footprints of those who have gone this way before me; only faint traces, by which in differing fashions they have left us partial accounts of their own lifetimes."[1810] Could there be any clearer admission that there was no "apostolic lineage" representing a "historical" savior?

Where the Bodies Are Buried

We have already seen a tremendous amount of evidence as to the mythological nature of Christianity and its founder. Further proof may be found in a variety of places, although it may not be wise to make them public, because fanatics have forever destroyed such evidence, burning and looting temples and libraries, and desecrating and defacing sacred images and symbols. A number of these sites may also have been destroyed in various wars, including the two World Wars. In addition, some areas are so forbidding that it will even today be difficult both

1808 Larson, 319.
1809 Walker, WDSSO, 60.
1810 Eusebius, 2.

to access them and to convince the keepers of their secrets to release them. Priests, high-ranking Masons and members of other such brotherhoods may well be informed about the real origins of Christianity but are sworn to a blood oath against revealing the truth. Perhaps some of these individuals will be encouraged that others not thus bound are exposing this all-important information.

The evidence of the Christian myth may still be found in libraries in many parts of the world, clandestine and public, such as the Library of Ambrose at Milan, the Florentine library, and the library of Mt. Athos, the mysterious mountain of monasteries in Macedonia, although it would be very difficult to gain the evidence from such a place. It may also be difficult to obtain evidence from the Maronite monastery of Mt. Lebanon in Syria, but we are told that it is, or was, there. Such evidence in the form of texts may also be obtained, we are informed, in monasteries in what was Armenia, in the locale of Mt. Ararat. Evidence may also be procured from the "Cluny Abbey" and from "Mor Gabriel" in Turkey. The Vatican Library and the miles of tunnels of booty under the Vatican, of course, could also provide a treasure trove of proof of the artifice. The churches of Russia likewise hold ancient manuscripts that would be valuable in our quest. Also, there may still be hidden texts in Jerusalem and other parts of Israel and Palestine, such as Mt. Carmel.

Such evidence can also be discovered in the ruins and statuary of pre-Christian cultures such as in Ireland, in the county of Armagh, or at Padua, Florence, Venice, Geneva and Rome, where there are, or were, statues of "the apostles" that were in reality Pagan gods made over. Such archaeological evidence may likewise be found at Heliopolis, the "City of the Sun," in Egypt, and in the sunken Phoenician city of Tyre, if it has not already been discovered and hidden or destroyed. Proof of the mythos also may be found in Upper Egypt, where arose one of the most ancient cultures. India, of course, is rife with the mythos, and evidence of the life of Krishna/Christos can be found in the caves at Elephanta, for example.

Regardless of whether this evidence is extant in these places, there are many sites already well-known that provide proof of the ubiquitous solar and celestial mythos that was carnalized, historicized and personified in Jesus Christ. That the mythos once extended around the world in much the same form is *a fact* that cannot be disputed. Again, what happened to the ubiquitous solar mythos? Where is it? Why did it disappear? The answer is, of course, it has been obscured; it is not gone but is simply concealed beneath a surface of subterfuge and deception developed to enrich and empower a relative handful, providing them with dominion over the "sheep."

Conclusion

After becoming aware of such "mysteries" revealed herein concerning Christianity and its alleged founder, many may find the standard scholarship on this subject unsatisfactory, to say the least, as it becomes clear that much of this information may be known by the scholastic elite. This becomes evident from admissions such as the following, which appears in *Fiction as History* by G.W. Bowersock, a professor of Ancient History at Princeton University in New Jersey. Says he:

> [In] a series of Norton lectures, Frank Kermode also turned to the Bible, and in particular to the New Testament, to develop a sophisticated analysis of novelistic elements in the Gospels. He argued that the problem of historical truth is so elusive in the Gospel narratives that those accounts are better viewed *simply as fiction* with a semblance of truth. The meaning, and obviously, the inspirational value of works of this kind *do not depend upon their historical veracity*, although apprehension of that meaning nonetheless does depend upon a provisional or temporary belief in their veracity. This is, in Kermode's words, a "*benign deceit*" that readers even today continue to countenance.[1811]

Here we have professor Kermode admitting that the New Testament is fiction, and professor Bowersock suggesting that such "benign deceit" does not matter, because the book has "inspirational value." First of all, this deceit has not been benign but utterly malignant for almost 2,000 years, contributing to endless genocide and the killing of both spirit and mind. Secondly, how do deception and lying have any value in a spiritual quest or religious life? Is it not the complete opposite of such an experience? Is it not the goal in becoming a mature, spiritual human being to be rid of deceit and mendacity? It is clear that scholars have known about the mythological nature of the Bible, yet they have gone to immense lengths to hide it, including the use of sophisticated language, like their priestly counterparts who have utilized the dead language Latin to go over the heads of the uneducated masses. It is possible that any number of these scholars are also Masons or members of some such secret brotherhood who are under the blood oath. Or they may merely be products of their occupation, in that many universities and colleges are under the dominion of the fraternities and the Catholic Church. In any case, they have been pawns, unwitting or otherwise, in the Christ conspiracy.

1811 Bowersock, 123.

Conclusion

For nearly 2,000 years hundreds of millions of people have been taught that a historical "son of God" called Jesus Christ lived, did miracles, suffered and died as a blood-atonement especially established once and for all by God Himself, the Creator of the entire cosmos. In reality, the gospel story of Jesus is not a factual portrayal of a historical "master" who walked the earth 2,000 years ago but a myth built upon other myths of godmen, who in turn were personifications of the ubiquitous solar mythos and ritual found in countless cultures around the world thousands of years before the Christian era. As such, the tale served to amalgamate the numerous religions, cults and sects of the Roman Empire and beyond, to create a state religion that was promulgated through forgery, fraud and force.

Nevertheless, countless believers have insisted that the gospel tale happened, not because of any evidence, but merely because they have been told it was so and blindly accepted it, against common sense and better judgment. Furthermore, historicizing scholars and other evemerists, funded by the same agencies who created the myth, have thrown their scientific minds out the window and dishonestly begun their desperate work with the wrong premise, thereafter constantly trying to shore up the impossible, with endless tortured speculation where there are no facts at all. The actuality is that, had Jesus been real, the world would have developed differently than it did, particularly immediately after his alleged miraculous advent; yet, the world went on as if nothing had ever happened. Earl Doherty summarizes the problem with the gospel "history":

> If this man Jesus had had the explosive effect on his followers that is said of him, and on the thousands of believers who responded so readily to the message about him, such a man would have had to blaze in the firmament of his time. That impact would have been based on the force of his personality, on the unique things he said and did. There is no other way. And yet the picture we see immediately after Jesus' death, and for the next two generations in every extant document, flatly contradicts this. The blazing star immediately drops out of sight. No contemporary historian, philosopher or popular writer records him. There is no sign of any tradition or phenomenon associated with him. For over half a century Christian writers themselves totally ignore his life and ministry. Not a saying is quoted. Not a miracle is marvelled at. No aspect of his human personality, anchored within any biographical setting, is ever referred to. The details of his life, the places of his career: they

raise no interest in any of his believers. This is an eclipse that does not even grant us a trace of a corona! If, on the other hand, Jesus was simply an ordinary human man, an unassuming (if somewhat charismatic) Jewish preacher, who really said little of what has been imputed to him, who performed no real miracles, and who of course did not rise from the dead—all of which might explain why he attracted no great attention and could have his life ignored as unimportant by his later followers—what, then, is the explanation for how such a life and personality could have given rise to the vast range of response the scholars postulate, to the cosmic theology about him, to the conviction that he had risen from the dead, to the unstoppable movement which early Christianity seems to have been? This is an unsolvable dilemma.

When pressed, scholars and clergy alike will admit that the founding of the Christian religion is shrouded in centuries of intrigue and fraud. They will confess that there is not a single mention of Jesus by any historian contemporaneous with his alleged advent and that the biblical accounts are basically spurious, not written by their pretended authors and riddled with tens of thousands of errors, impossibilities and contradictions. They will even admit that such texts had been forged by the hundreds and later interpolated and mutilated. Such "experts" may even go so far as to concede that the historicity of Christ has been called into question from the beginning, with that fact itself being cloaked in euphemism and deceit. They may further confess that there is absolutely no physical evidence of the event or the man, and that the numerous relics, including the infamous Shroud of Turin, are fakes, as are the tourist traps where the drama allegedly took place. These scholars may even have the courage to admit that the Jewish religion, upon which Christianity claims to be based, is itself not what it is asserted to be but is basically a rehash of older myths and theologies, as, in the end, is Christianity.

In other words, like the Christian fathers, these scholars and experts will concede that the gospel tale and Christian ideology constitute a direct lift from so-called Paganism. They will even admit that the gospel story is fiction, cagily calling it "benign deceit." Yet, these scholars and researchers will continue in their quest to find a "historical" Jesus, endlessly pumping out tomes that would be better off as trees. Waite describes their futile endeavors:

> Many attempts have been made to write the life of Christ. But it is difficult to see where, outside of the gospels, the material for such a work is to come from; while, if the gospels are to be taken as a basis, it is equally difficult to understand what is to be

> gained by rewriting what is contained in them. Any such attempt only brings out, in plainer light, the discrepancies in those accounts, and finally results in a mere display of ingenuity on the part of the biographer, in his efforts to reconcile them; or, as in the case of some writers, in a sublime unconsciousness of any discrepancies whatever.[1812]

Indeed, the efforts to find a historical Jesus have been pitiful and agonizing, based mainly on what he was *not*: To wit, the virgin birth is not history, and Jesus's parents were not called Mary and Joseph. Jesus was not from Nazareth, which didn't exist at the time, and the magi, star, angels and shepherds did not appear at his birth. He didn't escape to Egypt, because Herod was not slaughtering children, and he didn't amaze the priests with his teaching at age 12 in the temple. He did not suddenly at 30 reappear out of nowhere to mystify people who, if the birth stories had been true, would have already known him. The "historical" Jesus didn't do miracles or raise the dead. The sayings and sermons weren't originally his. He wasn't betrayed by Judas, since that would be illogical if he were already "world famous." There was no trial, no crucifixion and no resurrection.

Such are some of the numerous parts of the gospel story that have been thrown out by "skeptical" historicizers and evemerists over the centuries. All these purported events represent elements found ubiquitously in the myths of the solar heroes and in mystery rites. Tossing all these parts out, we might wonder, even more skeptically, where is the historical Jesus Christ? Have we found the core in the onion? The leap of faith even among evemerists is mindboggling. If 99 percent of this story is based on the myths and only one percent on any "history," what are people admiring and worshipping?

Although they are taught that "Jesus" represented a stunning break from the "old Pagan world," believers are worshipping basically the same deity or deities as the Pagans—in fact, practically all of them rolled into one. Yet, not knowing this, the faithful smugly set themselves apart in an atmosphere of superiority and pity, if not outright hatred, for so-called Heathens and Pagans, i.e., "those not of the faith." As Jackson says, "Many Christians denounce Paganism as a false religion. If this is correct, then Christianity is also false, for it is of pagan origin, and if one is not true, then neither is the other."[1813]

To reiterate, as Robertson says, "There is not a conception associated with Christ that is not common to some or all of the Savior cults

1812 Waite, 22.
1813 Jackson, 213.

of antiquity."[1814] And Carpenter states that "the doctrine of the Saviour is world-wide and world-old, and that Christianity merely appropriated the same (as the other cults did) and gave it a special flavor."[1815] He also remarks:

> The main Christian doctrines and festivals, besides a great mass of affiliated legend and ceremonial, are really quite directly derived from, and related to, preceding Nature worships; and it has only been by a good deal of deliberate mystification and falsification that this derivation has been kept out of sight.[1816]

It has often been said that the gospel tale is the "greatest story ever told." Of this greatest story ever *sold*, Massey states:

> In this way it can be proved that our Christology is mummified mythology, and legendary lore, which have been palmed off upon us in the Old Testament and the New, as divine revelation uttered by the very voice of God. We have the same conversion of myth into history in the New Testament that there is in the Old—the one being effected in a supposed fulfillment of the other! Mythos and history have changed places once, and have to change them again before we can understand their right relationship, or real significance.[1817]

The gospel story, fought so widely from the beginning because it was misrepresented as true, has now become through constant force and proselytizing unhealthily lodged in the human psyche, a meme that has caused a large proportion of the human race to live in a world of awful fantasy and endless waiting for the miraculous, for the divine to step in, like "he" purportedly did 2,000 years ago. Yet this alleged "miracle" of Jesus's advent was no more factual than that of Osiris, Krishna, Horus, Quetzalcoatl or any of the numerous other myths and savior gods upon which the Christ character is predicated. To believe that the mythical is the historical is not only to be dishonest but also to destroy the meaning of the mythical and to ruin its real miracle. Indeed, the historicizing of the mythos removes its value and makes the mind idiotic; but, to understand the gnosis behind it is to become wise.

As Massey also says:

[I]t is the miraculous that shows the mythical nature of the history; the identical miracles of Christ the healer that proves him to have been the same character as the healer Iu-em-hept, or Aesclapi-

1814 Robertson, 52.
1815 Carpenter, 130.
1816 Carpenter, 19.
1817 Massey, Lectures on the Moon.

us, and the caster-out of demons, Khunsu. It was the human history that accreted round the divinity, and not a human being who became divine. On the theory of an historic origin and interpretation the discrepancies may be paralleled for ever with no possibility of attaining the truth; the matter can never be molded into coherent consistency. But the mythical origin explains all.... The mythical origins only can explain why there are two Marys both of whom are described as being the mother of Jesus. The mythical origins only can explain why Jesus should have been rebegotten as the anointed son at thirty years of age.... The mythical origins only can explain why there is no history furnished from the time when the child-Christ was about twelve years of age to that of the adultship of thirty years. The mythical origins only can show how the Word, or Manifestor, from the first could be said to be made flesh.... The mythical Christ could have two birthdays like the dual-natured Horus, one at the solstice and one at the equinox.[1818]

Massey further states:

> The Christ of the gospels is in no sense an historical personage or a supreme model of humanity, a hero who strove, and suffered, and failed to save the world by his death. It is impossible to establish the existence of an historical character *even as an impostor*. For such an one the two witnesses, astronomical mythology and Gnosticism, completely prove an *alibi*. The Christ is a popular layfigure that never lived, and a layfigure of Pagan origin; a layfigure that was once the Ram and afterwards the Fish; a layfigure that in human form was the portrait and image of a dozen different gods.

As to the hackneyed evemerist arguments in favor of these "dozen different gods" and any others beginning as legendary heroes of old, rather than aspects of the celestial mythos, Higgins demonstrates their error and its consequences, obviously understood in his time over 180 years ago but suppressed:

> The following is the state of ancient history given by Mr. Bryant, and nothing can be more true: "… it is evident that most of the deified personages never existed: but were mere titles of the Deity, the Sun; as has been in great measure proved by Macrobius. Nor was there ever anything of such detriment to ancient history, as supposing that the Gods of the Gentile world had been natives of the countries where they were worshipped. They have been by these means admitted into the annals of times: and it

1818 Massey, HJMC, 182.

has been the chief study of the learned to register the legendary stories concerning them: to conciliate absurdities, and to arrange the whole into a chronological series—a fruitless labor, and inexplicable: for there are in these fables such inconsistencies and contradictions as no art, nor industry, can remedy."[1819]

The Age of Darkness

There is indeed nothing new under the sun. And "Jesus" is, basically, the same old sun, the Hellenized Joshua, the Judaized Horus and Krishna, thought by the deceived masses to have been a native of the country in which he was worshipped. Is it mere coincidence that, after the celestial mythos and astronomical knowledge had become completely eclipsed and subverted, the Western world was plunged into the Dark Ages?

Jackson describes the results of extinguishing the light of the sun:

> The Gnostic wisdom was not wholly lost to the world but its great, universal educational system was supplanted. It is a well-established historical fact, not denied by the church that it required about 500 years to accomplish this submersion of Gnosticism, and to degrade the new generations in ignorance equal to the state of imbecility. History again points its accusing finger at the living evidence. The horrible results of such a crime against nature and mankind are pictured in the Dark Ages.... Not even priests or prelates were permitted to learn to read or write. Even bishops could barely spell out their Latin. During this period of mental darkness, the ignorant masses were trained in intolerance, bigotry, fanaticism, and superstitious fear of an invisible power secretly controlled by the church; all of which begat a state of hysteria and imbecility.[1820]

Robertson explains why Christianity arose and what its purpose was:

> Religions, like organisms and opinions, struggle for survival and the fittest survive. That is to say, those survive which are fittest for the actual environment, not fittest from the point of view of another higher environment. What, then, was the religion best adapted to the populations of the decaying Roman Empire, in which ignorance and mean subjection were slowly corroding alike intelligence and character, leaving the civilized provinces unable to hold their ground against the barbarians? ... Christianity ... This was the religion for the Dark Ages.[1821]

1819 Higgins, I, 371.
1820 Jackson, 122.
1821 Robertson, 128–9.

And Larson states:

> We believe that, had there been no Christianity, Greek enlightenment would, after a fierce struggle with Mithraism and its offspring Manichaeism, have emerged victorious. There would have been no Dark Ages.[1822]

During this appalling Age of Darkness without the Sun, learning and literacy were all but destroyed. Libraries were burned, in order to hide the horrible secret of the Christian religion, and a world that had been reaching for the stars, with great thinkers appearing in numerous places, was now subjugated in darkness falsely portraying itself as the "light of the world." As Pike says:

> The Church of Rome claimed despotism over the soul, and over the whole life from the cradle to the grave. It gave and sold absolutions for past and future sins. It claimed to be infallible in matters of faith. It decimated Europe to purge it of heretics. It decimated America to convert the Mexicans and Peruvians.... The history of all is or will be the same—acquisition, dismemberment and ruin.... To seek to subjugate the *will* of others and to take the *soul* captive, because it is the exercise of the highest power, seems to be the highest object of human ambition. It is at the bottom of all proselytizing and propagandism.[1823]

And, as Wheless declares,

> Holy Fraud and Forgery having achieved their initial triumph for the Faith, the "Truth of Christ" must now be maintained and enforced upon humanity by a millennial series of bloody brutal Clerical Laws of pains and penalties, confiscations, civil disabilities, torture and death by rack, fire and sword, which constitute the foulest chapter of the Book of human history—the History of the Church![1824]

The Origins of Cultural Bigotry and Racism

One of the most unfortunate aspects of the historicizing of this "oldest story ever sold" was that one particular ethnic group, and that one only, became esteemed above all others for being "God's chosen people," the "priestly nation" and the spiritual masters of mankind. Another calamitous aspect has been the vilification of these same people as "Christ killers" and murderers of the Almighty Lord God himself. Thus, in believing the gospel tale Christians have been forced into a love-hate relationship with the Jews, who are to be perceived as "God's chosen" and "Christ killers"

1822 Larson, 416.
1823 Pike, 74.
1824 Wheless, FC, 303.

at the same time. Not only is this schizophrenic salvation plan and legacy not the product of any good god, it is utterly divisive, setting people against each other all over the world.

Furthermore, not a few people have wondered why these identical stories found outside of the Bible and revolving around "Gentile" or "Pagan" characters are "myths," while the biblical tales told about Hebrews and Jews are "history." As Jacolliot remarks:

> We have repudiated Greek and Roman mythologies with disdain. Why, then, admit with respect the mythology of the Jews? Ought the miracles of Jehovah to impress us more than those of Jupiter? … I have much more respect for the Greek Jupiter than for the God of Moses; for if he gives some examples not of the purest morality, at least he does not flood his altar with streams of human blood.[1825]

The gospel story constitutes cultural bigotry and does a disservice to the history of humanity. Contrary to popular belief, the ancients were not an ignorant and superstitious lot who actually believed their deities to be literal characters. Nor were they as a whole immoral or unenlightened. This propaganda has been part of the conspiracy to make the ancients appear as if they were truly the dark and dumb rabble that was in need of the "light of Jesus." As Massey says:

> The picture of the New Beginning commonly presented is Rembrandtlike in tone. The whole world around Judea lay in the shadow of outer darkness, when suddenly there was a great light seen at the centre of all, and the face of the startled universe was illuminated by an apparition of the childChrist lying in the lap of Mary. Such was the dawn of Christianity, in which the Light of the World had come to it at last! That explanation is beautifully simple for the simpleminded; but the picture is purely false—or, in sterner words, it is entirely false.[1826]

And Pike asks, "Did the Deity leave the whole world without Light for two score centuries, to illuminate only a little corner of Palestine and a brutal, ignorant, and ungrateful people?"[1827] The reality is that the ancients were no less advanced in their morals and spiritual practices, and in many cases were far more enlightened, than the Christians in their own supposed morality and ideology, which, in its very attempt at historicity, is in actuality a degradation of the ancient celestial and terrestrial religion. Indeed, unlike the Christians, the true intelligentsia among the ancients

1825 Jacolliot, 119.
1826 Massey, GHC, 2.
1827 Pike, 102.

were well aware that their gods were astronomical and atmospheric in nature. Even the much vilified Babylonians declared that their gods and those of other cultures and ages were the sun, moon, stars and planets, demonstrating that they were not only advanced but honest in this matter. In addition, the eminent Greek philosophers Socrates, Plato and Aristotle clearly knew that their gods, such as Zeus, the sky-god father-figure who migrated to Greece from India and/or Egypt, were never real people.

These three great Greek luminaries were, oddly enough, highly esteemed by early Christian conspirators, who, as they had with so many preceding purveyors of wisdom and ideologies, falsely presented these savants' known accomplishments in philosophy as divine revelation to the Church. Such appropriation was recognized by the ancients themselves. For instance, Amelius, a Platonist of the third century, "upon reading the first verse of St. John the Evangelist, exclaimed, 'By Jove, this barbarian agrees with our Plato.'"[1828] Cardinal Palavicino is quoted as saying, "Without Aristotle we should be without many Articles of Faith."[1829] It is amusing to consider that the omniscient "Lord," who came to deliver a "New Dispensation," needed the writings of Aristotle to determine doctrine for "his" Church. It is likewise interesting that, by constantly "borrowing from" and aligning themselves with exalted philosophers who were recognized as having penetrated the mysteries of the cosmos, the Christians themselves admitted just how advanced were their predecessors.

Rather than serving as an improvement, Christianity has been a psychic trauma, uprooting ideas and deities that were worshipped since Neolithic times, particularly nature gods and goddesses. The sexist Judeo-Christian-Islamic ideology has been at war with all things female, including Nature and Mother Earth. The patriarchal age has represented the military campaign of the sky-god father-figure against the earth-goddess mother-figure. In the process, the Goddess's groves—so sacred to the ancients that to cut them down was sometimes a capital offense—have been plowed under and her creatures butchered in a vicious quest for riches and "heaven," as enjoined in the first of the replacement Ten Commandments at Exodus 34:13 "You shall tear down their altars, and break their pillars, and cut down their Ashe'rim." The current culture is now headed for environmental cataclysm, because this ideology has served to disconnect human beings from the earth, to constantly focus their attention not on this life and this reality but on an imaginary afterlife.

Furthermore, as Graham says, "Such a story as the Gospels tell us is unworthy of man's respect; it is, we repeat, the greatest fraud and hoax

1828 Wheless, FC, 33.
1829 Wheless, FC, 33.

ever perpetrated upon mankind."[1830] No human culture can survive that bases its fundamental beliefs and perceptions on a hoax, particularly one in which the result has been the needless torture and slaughter of millions around the globe.

In reality, Christianity was the product of a multinational group composed of members of a variety of brotherhoods, secret societies and mystery schools, and was designed to empower and enrich such individuals and to unify their empire. To do so, these conspirators took myriad myths and rituals of virtually all the known cultures and combined them into one, producing a godman to beat them all. This unreachable fictional character has since been considered the "greatest man who ever walked the earth," to whom no one else can compare and besides whom nobody else deserves much recognition and appreciation. All others are, in fact, pathetic, born-in-sin wretches. But he did not walk the earth, and we must hereafter allow the dignity of sanctity to be bestowed upon not just one "man" but all of creation.

The prejudice and bigotry promulgated by Christianity and other monolithic yet divisive ideologies have caused an atrocious amount of destruction of cultural diversity. It has been demonstrated what a wonderfully colorful and varied world it is in which we live. Around the globe for millennia a mythos has thrived, a core of understanding that is cosmic and eternal in nature. It once had an infinite variety of flavors and incorporated much of creation in a divine and respectful play. To reduce all this glory to a handful of characters of a particular ethnicity who allegedly played out the cosmic drama in one time in history robs us not only of the truth but also of our diversity and universality as well. Furthermore, by removing our ability to question "authority" and to develop our own individuality, this ideology homogenizes us in a way that is not beneficial but is ugly and cowardly. By understanding the terrestrial and cosmic mythos conveyed for millennia, we can move ourselves at last into an age of enlightenment and enjoy the multiplicity of human thought, unfettered by controlling concepts and "thought police" that limit creativity and wisdom.

The New Era

The term "New Age" has been sullied in the eyes of many because of the excesses and the superficiality of the "New Age Movement." However, it is an ancient and venerated term with parallels in the New Testament (Matt. 19:28; 2 Cor. 5:17). Indeed, in antiquity the divine revelation of Christianity itself was considered the dawning of a new age, predicted by the ancient Greek Sybil.

1830 Graham, 356.

It has been demonstrated that Christianity pretty much got it all wrong—except the end to its erroneous means: it succeeded in enriching and empowering its most effective proponents many times over. According to the same astrological system used to create Christianity, the age for such divisiveness, fascism and hierarchical exploitation is now drawing to a close, and lying, deceit, cheating and stealing will fall by the wayside. Included in this age in which "the truth will be shouted from the rooftops" is the exposure of Earth's "dirty little secret." As Jacolliot says:

> Apostles of Jesus, you have counted too much upon human credulity, trusted too much that the future might not unveil your manoeuvres and your fabricated recitals—the sanctity of your object made you too oblivious of means, and you have taken the good faith of peoples by surprise in re-producing the fables of another age, which you believed buried for ever.[1831]

But the future is now, and the maneuvers are being unveiled. As far as Christianity's role in this "New Age," Carpenter states:

> Christianity therefore, as I say, must either now come frankly forward and, acknowledging its parentage from the great Order of the past, seek to rehabilitate *that* and carry mankind one step forward in the path of evolution—or else it must perish. There is no alternative.[1832]

The fact is that we *are* entering into a new age. "I am with you always to the close of the age"—so ends the Gospel of Matthew 28:20. What does this mysterious statement mean, and why was this all-important book concluded with it? The age referred to in the gospel tale is that of Pisces, and, through contrivance and duplicity, coercion and slaughter, the fish-god "Jesus," the Piscean Solar Avatar, has indeed been with us, but now it is the close of the age, and his time is over.

As Hancock says, "We live today in the astrological no man's land at the end of the 'Age of Pisces,' on the threshold of the 'New Age' of Aquarius. Traditionally these times of transition between one age and the next have been regarded as ill-omened."[1833] Ill-omened indeed, as the ongoing destruction of the earth and the endless warfare over ideology are on track toward the "Armageddon" so long awaited and planned for by those who cannot live for today but must look towards an afterlife. By realizing the cultural unity revealed behind the Christ conspiracy, however, humanity can pull together and prevent this fall, to create a better world.

1831 Jacolliot, 304.
1832 Carpenter, 264.
1833 Hancock, 240.

Bibliography

"2 Esdras." en.wikipedia.org/wiki/2_Esdras
"Adolf Hitler." en.wikiquote.org/wiki/Adolf_Hitler
"Ancient Mysteries: Astrology—Secrets in the Stars." A&E Video Documentary
"Apostles' Creed." en.wikipedia.org/wiki/Apostles'_Creed
"Archaeology in Australia." www.treasureenterprises.com/Miscellaneous/Archaeology_in_australia.htm
"Babylonian star catalogues." en.wikipedia.org/wiki/Babylonian_zodiac
"Bhagavad Gita." en.wikipedia.org/wiki/Bhagavad_Gita
"Bhagavata Purana." en.wikipedia.org/wiki/Bhagavata_Purana
"Descent to the underworld." en.wikipedia.org/wiki/Descent_to_the_underworld
"Development of the New Testament canon." en.wikipedia.org/wiki/Development_of_the_New_Testament_canon
"Dying God." en.wikipedia.org/wiki/Life-death-rebirth_deity
"Earliest Reference Describes Christ as 'Magician.'" www.msnbc.msn.com/id/26972493/#.TodpVOyyyO4
"*Epic of Gilgamesh*." en.wikipedia.org/wiki/Epic_of_Gilgamesh
"Epistulae (Pliny)." en.wikipedia.org/wiki/Epistulae_(Pliny)
"First Epistle to Timothy." en.wikipedia.org/wiki/First_Epistle_to_Timothy
"Flavius Vegetius Renatus." *Encyclopedia of the Ancient World*. www.enotes.com/flavius-vegetius-renatus-salem/flavius-vegetius-renatus
"From Jesus to Christ: Searching for Jesus." *Frontline* (4/7/1998), www.pbs.org/wgbh/pages/frontline/shows/religion/jesus/searching.html
—"What are the Gospels?" www.pbs.org/wgbh/pages/frontline/shows/religion/story/gospels.html
"Genetic Anthropology, Ancestry, and Ancient Human Migration." www.ornl.gov/sci/techresources/Human_Genome/elsi/humanmigration.shtml#3
"Genetic History of Indigenous Peoples of the Americas." en.wikipedia.org/wiki/Indigenous_Amerindian_genetics
"Harivamsa." en.wikipedia.org/wiki/Harivamsa
"Have 250 Million Been Killed in the Name of Christianity?" freethoughtnation.com/forums/viewtopic.php?p=19748
"Historias Fundadas y Ligadas Con la Verdad del Cenote Zací." mexicotravelclub.com/turismo/Yucatan/Valladolid/Leyendas-llenas-de-verdad
"Hitler Jewish? DNA Tests Show Dictator May Have 'Had Jewish And African Roots.'" www.huffingtonpost.com/2010/08/25/hitler-jewish-dna-tests-s_n_693568.html
"Iasion, the Pre-Homeric pagan Jesus." kahalyahweh.net/Articles/Iasius/Iasius-PreHomericJesus.htm
"Inana's Descent to the Nether World: Translation." etcsl.orinst.ox.ac.uk/section1/tr141.htm
"Inanna." en.wikipedia.org/wiki/Inanna
"Irenaeus." en.wikipedia.org/wiki/Irenaeus
"Is Tacitus Reference an Interpolation?" www.fromchristtojesus.org/English/DrillDown/Tacitus.htm
"Isaac Vossius." en.wikipedia.org/wiki/Isaac_Vossius
"Josephus on Jesus." en.wikipedia.org/wiki/Josephus_on_Jesus
"Keshava." en.wikipedia.org/wiki/Keshava
"Krishna." en.wikipedia.org/wiki/Krishna

"Krishna and the Cowherd." www.forumforhinduawakening.org/articles/id/understanding/stories/Krishna-and-the-Cowherd
"Life-Death-Rebirth Goddesses." en.wikipedia.org/wiki/Category:Life-death-rebirth_goddesses
"Lost City Revealed Under Centuries of Jungle Growth." news.nationalgeographic.com/news/2011/04/110426-maya-lost-city-holtun-science-guatemala-ancient/
"Mandaeism." en.wikipedia.org/wiki/Mandaeism
"Mathura." en.wikipedia.org/wiki/Mathura
"Mitochrondrial Eve." en.wikipedia.org/wiki/Genetic_Eve
"Moses of Chorene." en.wikipedia.org/wiki/Moses_of_Chorene
"MUL.APIN." en.wikipedia.org/wiki/MUL.APIN
"Multiregional Origin of Modern Humans." en.wikipedia.org/wiki/Multiregional_hypothesis
The Naked Truth, video series, IRES, 1990
"Narada's Cleverness," *The Hindu*. Sep 07, 2009; www.hindu.com/2009/09/07/stories/2009090755381200.htm
"Native Americans Descended from a Single Ancestral Group, DNA Study Confirms." *ScienceDaily*, April 29, 2009; www.sciencedaily.com/releases/2009/04/090428223836.htm
"Orosius." en.wikipedia.org/wiki/Orosius
"Osiander, Lucas, Sr." www.gameo.org/encyclopedia/contents/O825.html
"Pre-Columbian Trans-Oceanic Contact." en.wikipedia.org/wiki/Pre-Columbian_trans-oceanic_contact
"Priestly Blessing." en.wikipedia.org/wiki/Priestly_Blessing
"Pururavas." en.wikipedia.org/wiki/Pururavas
"Religion Among the Ainu People of Hokkaido Japan." www.suite101.com/content/religion-among-the-ainu-people-of-hokkaido-japan-a187473
"Resurrection." en.wikipedia.org/wiki/Resurrection
"Roman Naming Conventions." en.wikipedia.org/wiki/Roman_naming_conventions
"Satirical Parallels Between Josephus and the NT." altbibleschol.freehomepage.com/Josephus Parallels.html
"Shingō, Aomori." en.wikipedia.org/wiki/Shingō,_Aomori
"Tacitus on Christ." en.wikipedia.org/wiki/Tacitus_on_Christ
"Tammuz." en.wikipedia.org/wiki/Tammuz_(deity)
"Tears of Jihad." www.politicalislam.com/tears/pages/tears-of-jihad/
"Tecaxic-Calixtlahuaca Head." en.wikipedia.org/wiki/Tecaxic-Calixtlahuaca_head
"Tetragrammaton." en.wikipedia.org/wiki/Tetragrammaton#Loss_of_the_Tetragrammaton_in_the_Septuagint
"The Roman Head from Tecaxic-Calixtlahuaca, Mexico: A Review of the Evidence (1)." 66th Annual Meeting of the Society of American Archaeology in New Orleans, LA, April 22, 2001; www.unm.edu/~rhristov/calixtlahuaca.html
"The William Robertson Smith Website." www.william-robertson-smith.net/en/e010homeEN.htm
"Theophilus of Antioch," en.wikipedia.org/wiki/Theophilus_of_Antioch
"Vishnuparva." *Harivamsa*, 2.4. mahabharata-resources.org/harivamsa/vishnuparva/hv_2_004.html
"Vishvakarman." en.wikipedia.org/wiki/Vishvakarman
"Votan." en.wikipedia.org/wiki/Votan
"Vyasa." en.wikipedia.org/wiki/Vyasa

"White Horse." en.wikipedia.org/wiki/White_horse_%28mythology%29

"Yuz Asaf." en.wikipedia.org/wiki/Yuz_Asaf

"Zodiac." en.wikipedia.org/wiki/Zodiac

A Handy Concordance of the Septuagint. London: S. Bagster & Sons, 1887.

Aarons, Mark, and John Loftus. *Unholy Trinity*. New York: St. Martin's Press, 1991

Abhedānanda, Swami. *Great Saviors of the World*, v. 1. New York: The Vedanta Society, 1911.

Abrahams, Israel. *Studies in Pharisaism and the Gospels*. Cambridge: Cambridge University Press, 1917.

Acharya S. (See also D.M. Murdock). *The Christ Conspiracy: The Greatest Story Ever Sold*. Illinois: Adventures Unlimited Press, 1999.—*Suns of God: Krishna, Buddha and Christ Unveiled*. Illinois: Adventures Unlimited Press, 2004.

Acker, William R.B. *Some T'ang and Pre-T'ang Texts on Chinese Painting*. Leiden: E.J. Brill, 1954.

Adrados, Francisco Rodriguez. *Festival, Comedy and Tragedy: The Greek Origins of Theatre*. Tr. Christophor Holme. Leiden: E.J. Brill, 1975.

Agrawala, Prithvi Kumar. *Goddess in Ancient India*. New Delhi: Abhinav Publications, 1984

Aiyar, Indira Shankar *Durgā as Mahiṣāsuramardinī: A Dynamic Myth of Goddess*. Gyan Pub. House, 1997.

Akerley, Ben. *The X-Rated Bible*. Austin, TX: American Atheists, 1989.

Allegro, John. *The Dead Sea Scrolls and the Christian Myth*. Buffalo, NY: Prometheus, 1992. —*The Sacred Mushroom and the Cross*. Garden City, NY: Doubleday, 1970.

Allen, Don Cameron. *Mysteriously Meant: The Rediscovery of Pagan Symbolism and Allegorical Interpretation in the Renaissance*. Baltimore: Johns Hopkins Press, 1971.

Allert, Craig D. *Revelation, Truth, Canon and Interpretation: Studies in Justin Martyr's Dialogue with Trypho*. Leiden: Brill, 2002.

American Anthropologist, vol. 43. Berkeley, CA: American Anthropological Association, 1941.

Amir-Moezzi, Mohammed Ali, *La religion discreete: Croyances et pratiques spirituelles dan l'islam shi'ite*, Libr. Philosophique Vrin, Paris, 2006

Anand, Ram Prakash. *Origin and Development of the Law of the Sea: History of International Law*. Leiden: Brill, 1983.

Anderson, Karl. *The Astrology of the Old Testament*. Health Research, 1970, 1996.

Ankerberg, John, and John Weldon. *Handbook of Biblical Evidences: The Facts on Jesus, Creation and the Bible*. Eugene, OR: Harvest House Publications, 1997.

Apollodorus. *The Library*, v. 2. tr. James George Frazer. New York: G.P. Putnam's Sons, 1921.

Apollonius Rhodius. *The Voyage of Argo: The Argonautica*. tr. E.V. Rieu. Harmondsworth/Middlesex/Baltimore: Penguin Books, 1959.

Arnold, Edwin. *The Song Celestial or Bhagavad-Gita*. Boston: Roberts Brothers, 1888.

Art and Archaeology, vols. 11–12. Archaeological Institute of America, 1921.

Astour, Michael C. *Hellenosemitica*. Leiden: E.J. Brill, 1967.

Aśvaghosha. *The Fo-Sho-Hing-Tsan-King: A Life of Buddha*. tr. Samuel Beal. Oxford: Clarendon Press, 1883.

Athanasius. *The Incarnation of the Word of God, being the Treatise of St. Athanasius, De incarnatione Verbi Dei*. tr. Penelope Lawson. New York: Macmillan, 1946.

Athanassiadi-Fowden, Polymnia, and Michael Frede, eds. *Pagan Monotheism in Late*

Antiquity. Oxford: Clarendon Press, 2001.
Augustine. *City of God*. tr. Marcus Dods. Montana: Kessinger Publishing, 2004.
—*Retractiones*. ed. and tr. J.H.S. Burleigh. London: Westminster John Knox Press, 1953.
—*Writings in Connection with the Manichaean Controversy*. tr. Richard Stothert. Montana: Kessinger Publishing, 2004.
Augustsson, Oskar Z. "Who was Chrestus?" *Förnuftets Försvarare*. Vadstena, 2008.
Aune, David Edward, ed. *Studies in New Testament and Early Christian Literature*. Leiden: E.J. Brill, 1972.
Aurobindo, Sri. *The Secret of the Veda*. Pondicherry: Sri Aurobindo Ashram Press, 2003.
Avery-Peck, Alan, and Jacob Neusner. *Judaism and Christianity: New Directions for Dialogue and Understanding*. Leiden: Brill, 2009.
Awad, Luwis. *The Theme of Prometheus in English and French Literature*. Cairo: Ministry of Culture, 1963.
Bacchiocchi, Samuele. "From Saturday to Sunday." *Signs of the Times*. Nampa, ID: Pacific Press Publishing, June 2010; www.signstimes.com/?p=article&a=40064025600.786
Badiozamani, Badi. *Iran and America: Rekindling A Love Lost*, 2005.
Baigent, Michael, and Richard Leigh. *The Dead Sea Scrolls Deception*. New York: Simon & Schuster/Summit Books, 1991.
Bakola, Emmanuela. *Cratinus and the Art of Comedy*. Oxford: Oxford University Press, 2010.
Baldwin, Charles N., and Henry Howland Crapo. *A Universal Biographical Dictionary, Containing the Lives of the Most Celebrated Characters of Every Age and Nation*. New York, 1825.
Balfour, Edward, ed. *Cyclopaedia of India and of Eastern and Southern Asia*, v. 1. Madras: The Scottish and Adelphi Presses, 1871.—*The Cyclopedia of India and of Eastern and Southern Asia*, v. 2. London: Bernard Quaritch, 1885.
Bancroft, Hubert Howe. *The Native Races of the Pacific States of North America, III: Myths and Languages*. Hubert H. Bancroft, 1875.
Banerjee, Sreechandra. "When Lord Krishna Was Born." sreechandrab.sulekha.com/blog/post/2009/08/when-lord-krishna-was-born.htm
Baring-Gould, Sabine. *The Lost and Hostile Gospels: An Essay on the Toledoth Jeschu, and the Petrine and Pauline Gospels of the First Three Centuries of Which Fragments Remain*. London: Williams and Norgate, 1874.—*Legends of the Patriarchs and Prophets and Other Old Testament Characters from Various Sources*. New York: American Book Exchange, 1881.
Barker, Ernest. *From Alexander to Constantine*. Oxford: Clarendon Press, 1956.
Barnes, Harry Elmer. *The Twilight of Christianity*. Richard R. Smith, 1931.—*The Twilight of Christianity*. New York: The Vanguard Press, 1929.
Barnstone, Willis, ed. *The Other Bible*. San Francisco, Harper & Row, 1984.
Bart Ehrman and the Quest of the Historical Jesus of Nazareth: An Evaluation of Ehrman's Did Jesus Exist. American Atheist Press, 2013.
Barth, Auguste. *The Religions of India*. tr. J. Wood. London: Kegan Paul, 1891.
Bartram, John. "Archaeology of 'Chrest.'" historyhuntersinternational.org/about/
—"Chrest Magus." historyhuntersinternational.org/2010/05/31/christ-magus/
—"Chrestians and the lost history of Classical Antiquity." historyhuntersinternational.org/2010/06/05/chrestians-and-the-lost-history-for-classical-antiquity/
—"Josephus as a primary source for the New Testament." historyhuntersinternational.

org/2010/05/09/titus-flavius-josephus-as-a-primary-source-for-the-nt-gospels/all/1/
—"Mani and Authorship of the Canonical Gospels." historyhuntersinternational.org/2011/06/18/canonical-gospels-fourth-century/
—"Pliny correspondence with Trajan: Christians or Chrestians?" historyhuntersinternational.org/2011/05/25/pliny-correspondence-with-trajan-christians-or-chrestians/
—"The vacuum of evidence for pre-4th century Christianity." historyhuntersinternational.org/2011/03/06/the-vacuum-of-evidence-for-pre-4th-century-christianity/
Baumgarten, Albert I. *Elias Bickerman as a Historian of the Jews*. Tübingen: Mohr Siebeck, 2010.
—*The Phoenician History of Philo of Byblos*. Leiden: E.J. Brill, 1981.
Beal, Samuel, tr. *Si-Yu-Ki: Buddhist Records of the Western World: Translated from the Chinese of Hiuen Tsiang [Xuanzang] (AD 629)*, v. 1. London: Kegan, Paul, Trench, Trübner & Co., 1906.
Beane, Wendell Charles. *Myth, Cult and Symbols in* Śālta Hinduism. Leiden: E.J. Brill, 1977.
Beard, Mary. "Scrolling Down the Ages." *New York Times* (4/16/2006); www.nytimes.com/2009/04/19/books/review/Beard-t.html
Beausobre, Jacques de. *Histoire critique de Manichée et du manichéisme*, vol. 2. Amsterdam: Chez F. Frederic Bernard, 1809.
Bellamy, Francis Rufus, ed. *The Outlook: A Family Paper*, v. 50, pt. 2. October, 1894.
ben Yehoshua, Hayyim. "The Myth of the Historical Jesus." *mama.indstate.edu/users/nizrael/jesusrefutation.html*
Ben-Jochannan, Yosef A.A. *Black Man of the Nile and His Family*. Baltimore, MD: Black Classic Press, 1972.
Benko, Stephen. *The Virgin Goddess: Studies in the Pagan and Christian Roots of Mariology*. Leiden: E.J. Brill, 2004.
Bennett, DeRobingne Mortimer. *The Gods and Religions of Ancient and Modern Times*, v 2. New York: Liberal and Scientific Publishing, 1881.
Bernard, Raymond, PhD, *Apollonius the Nazarene*, Health Research, 1956.
Berry, Gerald L. *Religions of the World.* New York: Barnes and Noble, 1955.
Bhat, M. Ramakrishna. *Varahamihira's Bṛhat Samhitā, Part 1*. Delhi: Motilal Banarsidass Publishers Private Limited, 1997.
Bhattacharya, Sunil Kumar. *Krishna-Cult in Indian Art*. New Delhi: M.D. Publications, 1996.
Bhavan, Bharatiya Vidya. *Bhāratīya vidyā*. Bombay: Bharatiya Vidya Bhavan, 1978.
Biblical Archaeology Review, September/October 1994.
*Bibliothèque de L'*Ècole des Hautes Études, v. 29, F. Vieweg, 1877.
Biedermann, Hans, *Dictionary of Symbolism*, Facts on File, 1992
Bierlein, J.F., *Parallel Myths*, Random House, 1994.
Birrell, Anne. *Chinese Mythology: An Introduction*. Baltimore, MD: The Johns Hopkins University Press, 1993.
Blank, Jonah, *Arrow of the Blue-Skinned God: Retracing the Ramayana Through India*, Grove Press, 2000.
Blavatsky, Helena. *Isis Unveiled.* Point Loma, CA: Theosophical University Press, 1988.
—*The Secret Doctrine*. Point Loma, CA: Theosophical University Press, 1988.
—*Studies in Occultism*, v. 4. Point Loma, CA: The Aryan Theosophical Press, 1910.
Bleeker, C. Jouco, and Geo Widengren. *Historia Religionum: Religions of the Past*, v. 1. Leiden: E.J. Brill, 1969.
Blondel, David. *Des Sibylles Célébrées Tant Par l'Antiquité Payenne que Par le Saincts*

Pères. Paris: L. Perier & N. Perier, 1649.
Blue Letter Bible, www.blueletterbible.org
Bolle, Kees W. *The Persistence of Religion*. Leiden: E.J. Brill, 1971.
Boman, Thorleif. *Hebrew Thought Compared with Greek*. tr. Jules L. Moreau. New York: W.W. Norton & Company, 1960.
Bonnefoy, Yves. *Greek and Egyptian Mythologies*. Trans. Wendy Doniger. Chicago: University of Chicago, 1992.
Book of Enoch, The, Artisan Sales, 1980
Book of Jasher, The, J.H. Parry Publishers, 1887
Botterweck, G. Johannes, and Helmer Ringgren, eds. *Theological Dictionary of the Old Testament*, v. 1. Grand Rapids, MI : William B. Eerdmans Publishing Co., 1974.
— *Theological Dictionary of the Old Testament*, v. 11. Grand Rapids, MI: William B. Eerdmans Publishing Co., 2001.
Böttrich, Christfried. *Josephus und das Neue Testament*. Tübingen: Mohr Siebeck, 2007.
Böttrich, Thomas, *Josephus und Das Neue Testament*, Mohr Siebeck, 2007.
Bowerstock, GW, *Fiction as History: Nero to Julian*, University of California, 1994
Brake, Laurel, and Marysa Demoor. *Dictionary of Nineteenth-Century Journalism in Great Britain and Ireland*. Ghent: Academia Press, 2009
Bramley, William, *The Gods of Eden*, Dahlin Family Press, 1990.
Bremmer, Jan N. *Greek Religion and Culture, the Bible and the Ancient Near East*. Leiden: Brill, 2008.
Brinton, Daniel G. *The Myths of the New World*. New York: Leypoldt & Holt, 1868.
—*American Hero-Myths: A Study in the Native Religions of the Western Continent*. Philadelphia: H.C. Watts & Co., 1882.
Brockington, John L. *The Sanskrit Epics*. Leiden: Brill, 1998.
Bromiley, Geoffrey William. *International Standard Bible Encyclopedia: A-D*. Grand Rapids, MI: Wm. B. Eerdmans Publishing Co., 1979.
—*Theological Dictionary of the New Testament*. eds. Gerhard Kittel and Gerhard Friedrich. Grand Rapids, MI: William B. Eerdmans, 1985.
Brown, John Pairman, *Israel and Hellas*, III, Walter de Gruyter, Berlin, 2001.
Brown, Pete. "Chronological Summary of the 'Testimonium Flavianum' and its Censure." www.mountainman.com.au/essenes/Censure_of_the_TF.htm
Browne, Lewis. *This Believing World: A Simple Account of the Great Religions of Mankind*. New York: Macmillan, 1933.
Bryant, Edwin F., Bryant, *Krishna: The Beautiful Legend of God*, Penguin Classics, 2003.
—ed., *Krishna: A Sourcebook*, Oxford University Press, 2007.
Bryant, Jacob. *A New System; or, an Analysis of Ancient Mythology*, v. 3. London: J. Walker, 1807.
Budge, E.A. Wallis. *The Egyptian Book of the Dead*. New York: Dover Publications, 1967.
—*The Gods of the Egyptians or Studies in Egyptian Mythology*, v. 2. London: Methuen & Co., 1904.
—*A Guide to the Egyptian Collections in the British Museum*. London: Harrison and Sons, 1909.
—*A Hieroglyphic Vocabulary to the Book of the Dead*. New York: Dover, 1991.
Buitenen, Johannes Adrianus Bernardus, *The Mahābhārata*, University of Chicago Press, 1981.
Burckhardt, Jacob. *The Age of Constantine the Great*. Berkeley/Los Angeles: University of

California Press, 1983.
Burkert, Walter. *Greek Religion*. Cambridge: Harvard University, 2006.
Butler, Samuel, tr. *Homer's The Odyssey*. London: A.C. Fifield, 1900.
Cambridge Archaeological Journal, v. 4. Cambridge: Cambridge University Press, 1994.
Campbell, John. "The Ancient Literature of America." *Mémoires et Comptes Rendus de la Société Royale du Canada*, II. Ottawa: John Durie et Fils, 1896.
Campbell, Joseph. *In All Her Names*. New York: HarperSanFrancisco, 1991a.
—*Creative Mythology: The Masks of God*, Penguin, 1976.
—*Masks of God: Creative Mythology*. New York: Arkana, 1991.
—*Flight of the Wild Gander: Explorations in the Mythological Dimension*. Novato, CA: New World Library, 2002.
—*The Hero with a Thousand Faces*. Princeton: Princeton University Press, 1968.
—*The Hero with a Thousand Faces*, New World Library, 2008.
Cancik, Hubert, and Helmuth Schneider, David E. Orton. *Brill's New Pauly*, vol. 8. Leiden: E.J. Brill, 2006.
Cappelletti, Silvia. *The Jewish Community of Rome: From the Second Century BC to the Third Century CE*. Leiden: Brill, 2006.
Carlson, Stephen. *The Gospel Hoax: Morton Smith's Invention of Secret Mark*. Waco, TX: Baylor University Press, 2005.
Carpenter, Edward, *Pagan and Christian Creeds*, Health Research, 1975
Carpenter, Joseph Estlin, "Obligations of the New Testament to Buddhism," *The Nineteenth Century*, VIII, July-December 1880.
Carrier, Richard. "Luke and Josephus." www.infidels.org/library/modern/richard_carrier/lukeandjosephus.html
Carus, Paul, ed. *The Open Court*, v. 21, no. 1. Chicago: The Open Court Publishing Company, 1907.
—*The Open Court*, v. 29. Chicago: The Open Court Publishing Company, 1915.
—*The Open Court*, v. 35. Chicago: The Open Court Publishing Company, 1921.
Casey, P.J. *Understanding Ancient Coins An Introduction for Archaeologists and Historians*. London: B.T. Batsford, 1986.
Cashford, Jules. *The Moon: Myth and Image*. New York: Four Walls Eight Windows Press, 2003.
Catholic Encyclopedia, "Flavius Josephus," www.newadvent.org/cathen/08522a.htm
—I, The Catholic Encyclopedia Inc., 1913.
—II, The Encyclopedia Press, NY, 1907.
—X. New York: Robert Appleton Company, 1911.
—XIV, Robert Appleton Company, 1913.
Chadwick, John White. *The Bible of Today: A Course of Lectures*. New York: G.P. Putnam's, 1878.
Chalmers, Thomas. *The Works of Thomas Chalmers*. Philadelphia: Hogan & Thompson, 1833.
Chandra, Suresh. *Encyclopaedia of Hindu Gods and Goddesses*. New Delhi: Sarup & Sons, 2001.
Charlesworth, James. *Jesus and the Dead Sea Scrolls*. New York: Doubleday, 1995.
Cheyne, T.K., and J. Sutherland Black, eds. *Encyclopedia Biblica: A Critical Dictionary of the Literary, Political and Religious HIstory, the Archaeology, Geography and Natural History of the Bible*, v. 1. New York: The Macmillan Company, 1899.

Child, Lydia Maria. *The Progress of Religious Ideas, Through Successive Ages*, v. 2. New York: C.S. Francis & Co., 1855.
Chisholm, Hugh, ed. *The Encyclopaedia Britannia*, v. 8. Cambridge: Cambridge University Press, 1910.
—*The Encyclopedia Britannica*, v. 13. New York: The Encyclopedia Britannia Company, 1910.
—*The Encyclopedia Britannica*, v. 15. New York: The Encyclopedia Britannica Company, 1911.
Churchward, Albert, *The Origin and Evolution of Religion*
Clasby, Nancy Tenfelde. *New Jerusalem: Myth, Literature and the Sacred*. Scranton: University of Scranton Press, 2000.
Clement of Alexandria. *The Exhortation to the Greeks*. tr. G.W. Butterworth. London: William Heinemann, 1919.
Clough, Benjamin. *Clough's Sinhala English Dictionary*. New Delhi: Asian Educational Series, 1997.
Collins, Adela Yarbro, and John J. Collins. *King and Messiah as Son of God: Divine, Human and Angelic Messianic Figures in Biblical and Related Literature*. Grand Rapids, MI: William B. Eerdmans Publishing Co., 2008.
Comfort, Philip. *Encountering the Manuscripts: An Introduction to New Testament Paleography & Textual Criticism*. Nashville, TN: Broadman & Holman Publishers, 2005.
Conybeare, Fred Cornwallis. *Myth, Magic and Morals: A Study of Christian Origins*. London: Watts & Co., 1910.
Cook, John Granger. *Roman Attitudes Toward the Christians*. Tübingen: Mohr Siebeck, 2011
Coomaraswamy, Ananda Kentish, *Elements of Buddhist Iconography*, Munshiram Manoharlal, New Delhi 1972. (Originally published 1935 by Harvard University Press)
Cooper, Robert. *The Bible and Its Evidences*. London: E. Truelove, 1858.
Cooper, William R. *The Horus Myth in Its Relation to Christianity*. London: Hardwicke & Bogue, 1877.
Crombie, Frederick. *Ante-Nicene Fathers*, vol. 4. eds. Alexander Roberts, James Donaldson, and A. Cleveland Coxe. Buffalo, NY: Christian Literature Publishing Co., 1885. Revised and edited by Kevin Knight; www.newadvent.org/fathers/0416.htm
Crossan, John Dominic, and Richard G. Watts. *Who Is Jesus? Answers to Your Questions about the Historical Jesus*. Louisville, KY: Westminster John Knox Press, 1999.
Cummins, Thomas B.F. *Toast with the Inca: Andean Abstraction and Colonial Images on Quero Vessels*. Ann Arbor, MI: Univ. of Michigan Press, 2002.
Cumont, Franz. *The Mysteries of Mithra*. tr. Thomas J. McCormack. Chicago/London: The Open Court Publishing Company, 1903.
Curtis, David B. "Gospel Preached to all the World? (Matthew 24:4–14)." ecclesia.org/truth/mat03.html
Cutner, Herb. *Jesus: God, Man or Myth?* Escondido, CA: The Book Tree, 2000.
Dahlquist, Allan, *Megasthenes and Indian Religion*, Motilal Banarsidass Publ., 1996.
Dahn, L.T. "Identifying Theophilus." *The Gospel of St. Luke*. 2006; ltdahn-stluke.blogspot.com/2006/11/identifying-theophilus.html
Dalal-Clayton, Diksha. *The Adventures of Young Krishna*. Cambridge: The Lutterworth Press, 1991.
Dameron, James P. *Spiritism; the Origin of All Religions*. San Francisco,1885.
Darlison, Rev. Bill. *The Gospel and the Zodiac*. Gerald Duckworth & Co Ltd, 2008.

Dās, Bhagavān. *Krishna: A Study in the Theory of Avataras*. Bharatiya Vidya Bhavan, 1962.
Das, Subhamoy. "Christ-Krishna Connection." hinduism.about.com/od/lordkrishna/a/christ_krishna.htm
Davis, Richard H. *A Priest's Guide for the Great Festival*. New York: Oxford University Press, 2010.
Davis, Samuel. "On the Indian Cycle of Sixty Years." *British Critic and Quarterly Theological Review*, v. 3.
Davutoğlu, Ahmet. *Alternative Paradigms: The Ompact of Islamic and Western Weltanschauungs on Political Theory*. Lanham, MD: University Press of America, 1993.
Dawkins, Richard. *The God Delusion*. Boston/NY: Houghton Mifflin Company, 2006.
Dayagi-Mendels, Michal. *Drink and Be Merry: Wine and Beer in Ancient Times*. Jerusalem: Israel Museum, 2000.
de Acosta, Joseph/José. *The Natural & Moral History of the India*, v. II. tr. Edward Grimston (1604). London: Hakluyt Society, 1880.
de Boufflers, Stanislas Jean. *Oeuvres du Chevalier de Boufflers*. Paris: Chez Lelong, Libraire, 1823.
de Goeje, C.H. *Philosophy, Initiation and Myths of the Indians of Guiana and Adjacent Countries*. Leiden: E.J. Brill, 1943.
de Harlez, C., tr. *Avesta: Livre Sacré du Zoroastrisme*, v. 1. Liege: L. Grandmont-Donders, 1875.
Del Mar, Alexander. *The Worship of Augustus Caesar*, New York: The Cambridge Encyclopedia Co., 1900.
Deschner, Karlheinz. *Der gefälschte Glaube: eine kritische Betrachtung kirchlicher Lehren und ihrer historischen Hintergründe*. München: Knesebeck & Schuler, 1988.
Dhavamony, Mariasusai. *Classical Hinduism*. Rome: Universita Gregoriana Editrice, 1982.
Diamond, Jared. *Guns, Germs and Steel: The Fates of Human Societies*. New York: W.W. Norton & Company, 1997.
Didron, Adolphe Napoléon. *Christian Iconography; or, the History of Christian Art in the Middle Ages*, v. 1. tr. E.J. Millington. London: Henry G. Bohn, 1851.
Dīkshita, Pattamadai Appaya. *Third Book of Practical Vedanta: Being a Handbook of the Ancient Vaidika Sankhya-Yoga*. tr. Pandit G. Krsna Sastri. Mylapore: Oriental Publishing Co., 1911.
Dill, J. Gregory. *Myth, Fact and Navigators' Secrets: Incredible Tales of the Sea and Sailors*. Connecticut: Lyons Press, 2006.
Dixon-Kennedy, Mike. *Encyclopedia of Greco-Roman Mythology*. Santa Barbara, CA: ABC-CLIO, 1998.
Doane, Thomas W. *Bible Myths and Their Parallels in Other Religions*. New York: The Truth Seeker, 1882.
—*Bible Myths and Their Parallels in Other Religions*. Mokelumne Hill, CA: Health Research, 1985.
Dobbins, Frank S. *Error's Chains: How Forged and Broken*. Standard Publishing House, 1883.
Dobranski, Stephen B. "*Children of the Mind: Miscarried Narratives in* Much Ado about Nothing. Studies in English Literature, v. 38, 1–2. Baltimore, MD: Rice University, 1998.
Doherty, Earl, "Josephus Unbound," jesuspuzzle.humanists.net/supp10.htm
—*The Jesus Puzzle*. Ottawa: Canadian Humanist, 1999.
—*Jesus: Neither God Nor Man*. Ottawa: Age of Reason Publications, 2009.

Domarus, Max. *The Essential Hitler Speeches and Commentary*. Wauconda, Ill: Bolchazy-Carducci, 2007.

Donaldson, Thomas E. *Hindu temple art of Orissa*, v. 12, pt. 3. Leiden: E.J. Brill, 1990.

Doniger, Wendy. *The Hindus: An Alternative History*. New York: Penguin, 2009.

Doresse, Jean, *The Secret Books of the Egyptian Gnostics*, Inner Traditions International, 1986

Doughty, Darrell. "Tacitus' Account of Nero's Persecution of Christians." www.courses.drew.edu/sp2000/BIBST189.001/Tacitus.html; michaelturton2.blogspot.com/2011/06/darrell-doughty-on-tacitus-recovery.html

Dowling, Levi, *The Aquarian Gospel of Jesus the Christ*

Dowson, John. *A Classical Dictionary of Hindu Mythology and Religion, Geography, History and Literature*. London: Trübner & Co., 1879.

Draper, Jonathan. *Orality, Literacy and Colonialism in Antiquity*. Leiden: E.J. Brill, 2004.

Drews, Arthur. *The Witnesses to the Historicity of Jesus*. New York: Arno Press, 1972.

—*The Christ Myth*. Amherst, NY: Prometheus Books, 1998.

—*The Christ Myth*. London: T.F. Unwin, 1910.

Driver, Samuel Rolles. *Studia Biblica: Essays in Biblical Archaeology and Criticism*. London: Henry Frowde/Oxford University Press, 1885.

du Pin, Lewis Ellies. *A New History of Ecclesiastical Writers*, v. 1. London: Abel Swalle and Tim. Childe, 1693.

Dujardin, Edouard. *Ancient History of the God Jesus*. Health Research Books, 1993.

—*Ancient History of the God Jesus*, Watts & Co., 1938.

Dunlap, Samuel Fales. *The Ghebers of Hebron*. London: J.W. Bouton, 1898.

Dupuis, Charles. *The Origin of All Religious Worship*. C.C.W. Müller, 1871.

Dyer, Louis. *Studies of the Gods in Greece at Certain Sanctuaries Recently Excavated*. London: Macmillan and Co., 1891.

Early Christian Writings, Penguin, 1987.

Ebrard, Johannes Heinrich August. *Apologetics; or, the Scientific Vindication of Christianity*, III. tr. John Macpherson. Edinburgh: T&T Clark, 1887.

Eck, Diana L. *Banaras: City of Light*. New York: Columbia University Press, 1999.

Ehrman, Bart D., *Lost Christianities: The Battle for Scripture and the Faiths We Never Knew*, Oxford University Press, 2005.

—*Forged: Writing in the Name of God*. New York: HarperOne, 2011.

—*Why the Bible's Authors are Not Who We Think They Are*. New York: HarperOne, 2011.

Eisenman, Robert. *James the Brother of Jesus*. New York: Penguin, 1997.

—"Redemonizing Judas: Gospel Fiction or Gospel Truth?" www.huffingtonpost.com/robert-eisenman/redemonizing-judas-gospel_b_285093.html

Eisler, Riane T. *The Chalice & the Blade: Our History, Our Future*. San Francisco: HarperCollins, 1995.

Encyclopedia Biblica, v. 1. New York: The Macmillan Company, 1899.

—v. 3. New York: The Macmillan Company, 1902.

Encyclopedia Britannica, v. 3. Philadelphia: Maxwell Sommerville, 1894.

—v. 13. New York: The Werner Company, 1903.

—v. 23. New York: The Encyclopedia Britannica Company, 1911.

Entick, John. *Tyronis Thesaurus; or, Entick's Latin-English Dictionary, with a Classical Index of the Preterperfects & Supines of Verbs*. Baltimore: W. & J. Neal, 1834.

Eusebius, *History of the Church*, Penguin, 1989

—*Eusebii Pamphili Evangelicae Praeparationis*, Libri XV, Tomus III. ed. E.H. Gifford.

Oxford: E Typographeo Academico, 1903.
Evans, James, and J. Lennart Berggren. *Geminos's Introduction to the Phenomena*. New Jersey: Princeton University Press, 2006.
Fallows, Samuel, et al., eds. *Universal History: A Course of Lessons on the History of the World from the Earliest Date to the Present Time*, v. 1. Chicago: The University Association, 1895.
Farnell, Lewis Richard. *The Cults of the Greek States*, v. 4. Oxford: Clarendon Press, 1907.
Farrar, Frederic William. *The Life of Christ*. London: Cassell, Petter & Galpin, 1874.
—*The Early Days of Christianity*, v. 1. London: Cassell, Petter, Galpin & Co., 1882.
Fawcett, Fred. "On some Festival to Village Goddesses." *The Journal of the Anthropological Society of Bombay*, v. 2, no. 1. Bombay: Education Society's Press, 1890.
Feldman, Louis H. *Josephus: Jewish Antiquities*, v. 12. Cambridge: Harvard University Press, 1965.
—*Josephus and Modern Scholarship (1937–1980)*. Berlin/New York: Walter de Gruyter, 1984.
—*Studies in Hellenistic Judaism*. Leiden: E.J. Brill, 1996.
Feldman, Louis H., and Gohei Hata, eds. *Josephus, the Bible and History*. Detroit: Wayne State University Press, 1989.
—*Josephus, Judaism and Christianity*. Leiden: Brill, 1987.
Feldman, L.H., and J.R. Levison. *Josephus' Contra Apionem: Studies in its Character and Context*. Leiden: E.J. Brill, 1996.
Fideler, David. *Jesus Christ, Sun of God: Ancient Cosmology and Early Christian Symbolism*. Wheaton, IL: Theosophical Publishing House, 1993.
Finkelstein, Israel and. Neil Silberman. *The Bible Unearthed*. New York: The Free Press/ Simon & Schuster, 2001.
Fitzgerald, David. *Jesus: Mything in Action*, Vol. III (*The Complete Heretic's Guide to Western Religion*, Book 4). CreateSpace Independent, 2017.
Flavin, Richard D. "The Karanovo Zodiac and Old European Linear." *Epigraphic Society Occasional Papers*, v. 23. San Diego, CA: Epigraphic Society, 1998; www.flavinscorner.com/kz2.htm
Fleetwood, John. *Star of Bethlehem or the Heavenly Dawn Embracing the Life of Our Lord and Saviour Jesus Christ and the Lives of the Holy Apostles and Evangelists*. Chicago: National Publishing Company, 1890.
Foote, George William, and Edward Bibbins Aveling, J. M. Wheeler, eds. *Freethinker*, v. 15, part 2. G.W. Foote & Co., 1895.
Forbes, Jack D. *The American Discovery of Europe*. Urbana: University of Illinois Press, 2007.
Forlong, James George Roche. *Faiths of Man: Encyclopedia of Religions*, v. 1. London: B. Quaritch/University Books, 1906.
Forster, Nathaniel. *A Dissertation upon the Account Suppos'd to have been given of Jesus Christ by Josephus*. Oxford: James Flether, 1749.
Fox, Robin Lane, *Pagans and Christians*, Alfred A. Knopf, 1989
Frankfort, Henri. *Kingship and the Gods: A Study of Ancient Near Eastern Religion*. Chicago: University of Chicago Press, 1978.
Franklin, Michael John, ed. *Representing India: Institutes of Hindu Law, or the Ordinances of Menu*. Routledge, 2000.
Frawley, David. "Vedic Origins of the Zodiac: The Hymns of Dirghatamas in the Rig Veda."

www.archaeologyonline.net/artifacts/origins-zodiac.html
Frazer, Sir James, *The Golden Bough*, MacMillan, 1963.
—*The Golden Bough*, v. 5., pt. 1. London: Macmillan and Co., 1912.
—*Adonis, Attis, Osiris: Studies in the History of Oriental Religion*, v. 1. London: Macmillan and Co., 1906, 1914.
—*The Golden Bough: A Study in Magic and Religion*, 4, *Adonis Attis Osiris*, v. 1. London: Macmillan and Co., 1919.
Friedman, Richard. *Who Wrote the Bible?* Simon & Schuster, 1989.
Fuller, Christopher John. *The Camphor Flame: Popular Hinduism and Society in India*. New Jersey: Princeton University Press, 2004.
Ganguli, Kisari Mohan, tr. *The Mahabharata of Krishna-Dwaipayana Vyasa*, v. 1. ed., Pratāpacandra Rāya/Pratap Chandra Roy. Calcutta: Bharata Press, 1883.
—v. 2. Calcutta: Oriental Publishing Co.
—*The Mahabharata of Krishna-Dwaipayana Vyasa*, v. 13. ed., Pratāpacandra Rāya/Pratap Chandra Roy. Calcutta: Bharata Press, 1894.
Garbe, Richard. "Christian Elements in the Bhagavadgita." *The Monist*, v. 23. Chicago: The Open Court, 1913.
—"Christian Elements in Later Krishnaism and in Other Hinduistic Sects." *The Monist*, v. 24. Chicago: The Open Court, 1914.
—"Christian Elements in the Mahabharata." *The Monist*, v. 23. Chicago: The Open Court, 1913a.
—*India and Christendom: The Historical Connections between Their Religions*, Open Court, 1959.
Garland, Robert. *The Greek Way of Death*. New York: Cornell University Press, 2001.
Garnier, Colonel J., *The Worship of the Dead*, London: Chapman & Hall, 1904.
Gaster, Theodore, *The Dead Sea Scriptures*, Doubleday, 1976
Gesenius's Hebrew and Chaldee Lexicon to the Old Testament Scriptures. tr. Samuel Prideaux Tregelles. New York: John Wiley & Sons, 1893.
Gibbon, Edward. *The History of the Decline and Fall of the Roman Empire*, I. New York: P. Fenelon Collier, 1900–01.
—*History of the Decline and Fall of the Roman Empire*, v. 2. Dublin, William Hallhead, 1781. [fix]
—*History of the Decline and Fall of the Roman Empire*, v. 2. New York: Harper & Brothers, 1850.
—*The Miscellaneous Works of Edward Gibbon*, ed. Lord Sheffield John. London" B. Blake, 1837.
Gieseler, John C.L. *A Textbook of Church History*, v. 1. tr. Samuel Davidson. New York: Harper & Brothers Publishers, 1857.
Giles, John Allen. *Hebrew and Christian Records: An Historical Enquiry Concerning the Age and Authorship of the Old and New Testaments*, v. 2. London: Trübner & Co., 1877.
Gilman, Daniel Coit, Harry Thurston Peck, and Frank Moore Colby, eds. *The New International Encyclopaedia*, v. 19. New York: Dodd, Mead and Company, 1905.
Gitelman, Zvi, ed. *Jewish Life after the USSR*. Bloomington, IN: University of Indiana Press, 2003.
Golb, Norman, *Who Wrote the Dead Sea Scrolls?*, Scribner, 1995.
Gonda, J. *India Maior*. Leiden: E.J. Brill, 1972.
Goodspeed, Edgar Johnson. *Famous Biblical Hoaxes*. Grand Rapids, MI: Baker Books, 1956.

—tr. *The Apocrypha*, Vintage, 1989
Gopal, Balakrishnan Raja. *The Chalukyas of Kalyana and the Kalachuris*. Dharwad: Prasārānga, Karnatak University, 1981.
Gordon, Bruce. *Calvin*. New Haven/London: Yale University Press, 2009.
Gould, Andrew P. "Review of *The New Testament Code* by Robert Eisenman." www.roberteisenman.com/articles/ntc_review-gould.pdf
Graetz, Heinrich. *Geschichte der Juden von den ältesten Zeiten bis auf die Gegenwart*, v. 3. Leipzig: Leiner, 1905.
Graham, Lloyd, *Deceptions and Myths of the Bible*, Citadel, 1991
Grant, Michael, and John Hazel. *Who's Who in Classical Mythology*. New York: Routledge, 2002.
Grant, Robert. *The White Goddess*. New York: Farrar, Straus and Giroux, 1966.
Grant, Robert M. *Augustus to Constantine: The Rise and Triumph of Christianity in the Roman World*. Louisville: Westminster John Knox Press, 2004.
Graves, Kersey. *The Biography of Satan*. The Book Tree, 1995.
—*The World's Sixteen Crucified Saviors*, University Books, 1971.
—*The World's Sixteen Crucified Saviors*, AUP, IL, 2001.
Graves, Robert. *The White Goddess*. New York: Farrar, Straus and Giroux, 1966.
Green, Joel B., et al., eds. *Dictionary of Jesus and the Gospels*. Downers Grove, IL: InterVarsity Press, 1992.
Grethenbach, Constantine. *Secular View of the Bible: From Studies of the Hebrew; with the Evidences as to Jesus*. New York: Peter Eckler, 1902.
Griffith, Ralph T.H. *The Hymns of the Rigveda*, v. 1. Benares: E.J. Lazarus and Co., 1896.
Guignebert, Charles. *Jesus*. K. Paul, Trench, Trubner & Co., 1935.
—*Ancient, Medieval and Modern Christianity*. New Hyde Park: University Books, 1961.
Gupta, Om, *Encyclopaedia of India, Pakistan and Bangladesh*, Gyan Publishing House, 2006.
Gupta, Sanjukta. *Lakṣmī Tantra: A Pāñcarātra Text*. Leiden: E.J. Brill Archive, 1972.
Haase, Wolfgang, and Hildegard Temporini. *Aufstieg und Niedergang der römischen Welt: Geschichte und Kultur Roms im Spiegel der neueren Forschung*. Berlin: Walter de Gruyter, 1997.
Hachlili, Rachel. *Ancient Mosaic Pavements: Themes, Issues and Trends*. Leiden: Brill, 2009.
—*The Menorah, the Ancient Seven-armed Candelabrum: Origin, Form & Significance*. Leiden: Brill, 2001.
Haliburton, Robert Grant. *New Materials for the History of Man: Derived from a Comparison of the Calendars and Festivals of Nations*. Toronto: Royal Astronomical Society of Canada, 1920.
Hallion, Richard P. *Taking Flight: Inventing the Aerial Age from Antiquity through the First World War*. Oxford: Oxford University Press, 2003.
Hallo, William H. *Origins: The Ancient Near Eastern Backgrounds of Some Modern Western Institutions*. Leiden/New York: E.J. Brill, 1996.
Halsberghe, Gaston H. *The Cult of Sol Invictus*. Leiden: E.J. Brill, 1972.
Hamilton, Alexander, ed. *A Key to the Chronology of the Hindus; in a Series of Letters*, v. 2. Cambridge: J. Smith, for F.C. & J. Rivington, London, 1820.
Hamilton, Edith, *Mythology*, Penguin Books, 1969.
Hancock, Graham, *Fingerprints of the Gods*, Crown, 1995
Handy, Lowell K., ed. *The Age of Solomon: Scholarship at the Turn of the Millennium*.

Leiden: Brill, 1997.
Hanna, Ralph, ed., *Jankyn's Book of Wikked Wyves*, University of Georgia Press, 1997.
Harari, Josue V. *Textual Strategies: Perspectives in Post-Structural Criticism*. Ithaca, NY: Cornell University Press, 1979.
Hardwick, Michael E. *Josephus as an Historical Source in Patristic Literature through Eusebius*. Atlanta: Scholars Press, 1989.
Hardwicke, William Wright. *The Evolution of Man: His Religious Systems and Ethics*. London: Watts & Co., 1899.
Hardy, R. Spence. *A Manual of Buddhism*. Chowkhamba, India: Sanskrit Series, 1967.
Harivamsa/Harivamsha/Harivaṃśa. mahabharata-resources.org/harivamsa
Harper's New Monthly Magazine, v. 86, no. 511. "A New Light on the Chinese." December, 1892.
Harris, J. Rendel. *Boanerges*. Cambridge: Cambridge University Press, 1913.
—*The Diatessaron of Tatian: A Preliminary Study*. London: C.J. Clay and Sons, 1890.
Harris, Roberta. *The World of the Bible*. Thames and Hudson, 1995.
Harwood, William. *Mythology's Last* Gods*: Yahweh and Jesus*. Amherst, NY: Prometheus, 1992.
Haslam, C.J. *Materials for Deciding the Question, Whether or Not the Bible is the Word of God?* Salford: C.J. Haslam, 1840.
Hastings, Charles. *The Theatre: Its Development in France and England, and a History of its Greek and Latin Origins*. tr. Frances Alice Welby. London: Duckworth and Co., 1901.
Hastings, James, ed., *Encyclopaedia of Religion and Ethics*, XVI, Charles Scribner's Sons, NY, 1916.
—*Dictionary of the Apostolic Church*, v. 1. Edinburgh: T&T Clark, 1915.
Haught, James A. *Holy Horrors: An Illustrated History of Religious Murder and Madness*. Buffalo, NY: Prometheus Books, 1990.
Hazelrigg, John, *The Sun Book*, Health Research, 1971
Hegde, Gurupad K. *Pun in Sanskrit Literature: A New Approach*. Mysore: Prasaranga, University of Mysore, 1982.
Helms, Randel, *Gospel Fictions*, Prometheus, 1988
Hengel, Martin, *Crucifixion in the Ancient World and the Folly of the Message of the Cross*, tr. John Bowden, Fortress Press, 1977.
Henry, Carl F.H. *God, Revelation and Authority*, v. 3. Wheaton, IL: Crossway Books, 1999.
Henry, Jules. *Pathways to Madness*. New York: Random House, 1971.
Henry, Matthew. *An Exposition of the Old and New Testaments*, v. 3. London: Joseph Ogle Robinson, 1828.
Herbermann, Charles G., ed., et al. *The Catholic Encyclopedia*, v. 5. New York: Robert Appleton Company, 1909.
—v. 9. New York: Encyclopedia Press, 1910.
—v. 8. New York: The Universal Knowledge Foundation, 1913.
Herbermann, Charles G., et al., eds. The Catholic Encyclopedia, v. 1. New York: The Encyclopedia Press, 1907.
—*The Catholic Encyclopedia*, v. 9. New York: The Encyclopedia Press, 1910.
Herbert, Algernon. *Nimrod: Discourse on Certain Passages of History and Fable*, v. 1. London: Richard Priestley, 1828.
Herodotus. *The History*, v. 3. tr. George Rawlinson. London: John Murray, 1859.
Herrero de Jáuregui, Miguel. *Orphism and Christianity in Late Antiquity*. Berlin/New York:

Walter de Gruyter, 2010.
Higgins, Godfrey, Esq., *Anacalypsis*, A&B Books, 1992
Hiltebeitel, Alf. *The Cult of Draupadi*, v. 1. Chicago: The University of Chicago, 1988.
Hinduism Today, Vol. 17, No. 6, June, 1995
Hinnells, John R., ed., *Proceedings of the First International Congress of Mithraic Studies*, I, Manchester University Press, 1975.
—*Proceedings of the First International Congress of Mithraic Studies*, II, Manchester University Press, 1975.
Hislop, Alexander: *The Two Babylons*. Neptune, NJ: Loizeaux Brothers, 1959.
Historical Atlas of the World, Barnes & Noble, 1972
Hitler, Adolf. *Mein Kampf*. tr. James Murphy. London: Hurst and Blackett, 1939; gutenberg.net.au/ebooks02/0200601.txt
Hjelde, Sigurd. *Man, Meaning and Mystery: Hundred Years of History of Religions in Norway*. Leiden: E.J. Brill, 2000.
Hobgood-Oster, Laura. *Holy Dogs & Asses: Animals in the Christian Tradition*. Urbana: University of Illinois Press, 2008.
Hock, Hans Heinrich, and Brian D. Joseph. *Language History, Language Change, and Language Relationship: An Introduction to Historical and Comparative Linguistics*. Berlin: Mouton de Gruyter, 1996.
Hoffman, R. Joseph. *Jesus Outside the Gospels*. Buffalo, NY: Prometheus Books, 1984.
Holding, James Patrick, ed. *Shattering the Christ Myth: Did Jesus Not Exist?* Xulon Press, 2008.
Holley, Vernal, "Christianity: The Last Great Creation of the Pagan World," 1994
Homer. *The Odyssey*. tr. R.L. Eickhoff, R.L. New York: Forge, 2001.
Hopkins, Edward Washburn, *India Old and New, with a Memorial Address*, Charles Scribner's Sons, London, 1901.
Hornung, Erik. *The Ancient Egyptian Books of the Afterlife*. tr. David Lorton. New York: Cornell University Press, 1999.
—*Conceptions of God in Ancient Egypt*, tr. John Baine, Cornell University Press, NY, 1982.
Horstmanshoff, H.F.J., et al., eds. *Kykeon: Studies in Honour of H.S. Versnel*. Leiden: E.J. Brill, 2002.
Hotema, Hilton. *Secret of Regeneration*. Health Research, 1998.
Houtsma, M. *E.J. Brill's First Encyclopedia of Islam*. Leiden: E.J. Brill, 1987.
Hristov, Romeo H., and Santiago Genovés T. "The Little 'Roman' Head of Calixtlahuaja, Mexico: Some Reflections." *NEARA Journal*, vol. 28, #3 &4, 1994; www.neara.org/CARLSON/romehead.htm
—"The 'Phoenician' head from Las Balsas, Mexico." www.antiquity.ac.uk/ProjGall/hristov/
—"Reply to Peter Schaaf and Günther A. Wagner's 'Comments on "Mesoamerican Evidence of Pre-Columbian Transoceanic Contacts."'" *Ancient Mesoamerica*, v. 12, no. 1. Cambridge: Cambridge University Press, 2001.
Humboldt, Alexander de/von. *Researches, Concerning the Institutions & Monuments of the Ancient Inhabitants of America*. London: Longman, Hurst, Rees, Orme & Brown, 1814.
—*Vues des Cordillères et Monumens des Peuples Indigènes de l'Amérique*, I. Paris: La Librairie Grecque, 1816.
Humphreys, Kenneth. "The Buddhist Influence in Christian Origins." www.jesusneverexisted.com/buddha.html
—"Circus Circus! The Jesus Parade is Always in Town." www.jesusneverexisted.com/circus.

html
—"The End is Nigh—for Jesus, That is." www.jesusneverexisted.com/scholars.html
—"Philo of Alexandria." www.jesusneverexisted.com/philo.html
—*Jesus Never Existed.* East Sussex, UK: Iconoclast Press, 2005.
Hyde, William, and Howard L. Conard, eds. *Encyclopedia of the History of St. Louis*, v. 4. New York: The Southern History Company, 1899.
Indian Studies, v. 10, Ramakrishna Maitra, 1968.
Ingersoll, Robert G. *Trial of C.B. Reynolds for Blasphemy at Morristown, N.J., May 19th and 20th, 1887: Defence*. New York: C.P. Farrell, 1888.
Ioffe, Olympiad S. *Soviet Law and Soviet Reality*. Hingham, MA, USA: Kluwer Academic Publishers, 1985.
Irenaeus. *The Third Book of St. Irenaeus*. ed. Henry Deane. Oxford: Clarendon Press, 1874.
—*Libros quinque adversus Haereses*, v. 1 & 2. ed. W. Wigan Harvey. Cantabrigiae: Typis Academicis, 1857.
Jackson, John G. *Man, God and Civilization*. New York: Citadel Press, 1972.
—*Christianity Before Christ*, American Atheists, 1985
Jackson, Samuel M., *The New Schaff-Herzog Encyclopedia of Religious Knowledge*, VII, Funk and Wagnalls Company, NY/London, 1910.
Jackson, Samuel Macauley, and George William Gilmore, eds. *The New Schaff-Herzog Encyclopedia of Religious Knowledge*, VII. New York/London: Funk and Wagnalls Company, 1910.
Jackson, Samuel Macauley, Charles Colebrook Sherman, and George William Gilmore, eds. *The New Schaff-Herzog Encyclopedia of Religious Knowledge*, v. 1.: Funk and Wagnalls Company, 1908.
—*The New Schaff-Herzog Encyclopedia of Religious Knowledge*, v. 7. New York/London: Funk and Wagnalls Company, 1910.
Jackson, Samuel Macauley, Talbot Wilson Chambers, and Frank Hugh Foster, eds. *Concise Dictionary of Religious of Knowledge: Biblical, Doctrinal, Historical and Practical*. New York: The Christian Literature Company, 1889.
Jacolliot, Louis. The *Bible in India: Hindoo Origin of Hebrew and Christian Revelation.* Santa Fe: Sun Books, 1992.
Jaini, Padmanabh S. *Collected Papers on Buddhist Studies.* Delhi: Motilal Banarsidass Publ., 2001.
James, Edwin Oliver. *Comparative Religion: An Introductory and Historical Study*. Taylor & Francis, 1961.
—*The Cult of the Mother-Goddess*. New York: Barnes & Noble, 1961a.
—*The Tree of Life*. Leiden: E.J. Brill, 1966.
Janku, Lumir G. "Airplane Models." www.world-mysteries.com/sar_7.htm
Janus: Revue internationale de l'histoire de sciences. Leiden: E.J. Brill, 1960.
Jarus, Owen. "World's Earliest Christian Engraving Shows Surprising Pagan Elements." www.livescience.com/16319-earliest-christian-inscription-pagan-artifacts.html
Jastrow, Morris. "Sun and Saturn." *Revue D'Assyriologie et d'Archéologie Orientale*, v. 7. Paris, 1910; www.catastrophism.com/texts/sun-and-saturn
Jeffrey, Grant R. *The Signature of God: Astonishing Bible Codes*. Colorado Springs, CO: WaterBrook Press, 2002.
Jeffries, Peter. *The Secret Gospel of Mark: Imagined Rituals of Sex, Death and Madness in a Biblical Forgery*. New Haven, CT: Yale University Press, 2007.

Jerome. *De Viris Illustribus*. www.newadvent.org/fathers/2708.htm
—"Letter 46: Paula and Eustochium to Marcella." www.newadvent.org/fathers/3001046.htm
Jochmans, Joseph. "Top Ten Out-of-Place Artifacts." *Atlantis Rising*, #5.
John Rylands Library Bulletin, v. 21. Manchester University Press, 1937.
Johnston, Charles, tr. *Bhagavad Gita: The Songs of the Master*. Kessinger, 2006.
Jones, Jeremiah. *A New and Full Method of Settling the Canonical Authority of the New Testament*, v. 3. Oxford: Clarendon Press, 1827.
Joseph, Martin P. *The Mahabharata in the Light of Bible* [sic], v. 2. Tamil Nadu: Franciscan Brothers, 1988.
Journal of Anthropological Research, v. 20. University of New Mexico, 1964.
Journal of the North China Branch of the Royal Asiatic Society, v. 8. Shanghai: A.H. De Carvalho, 1874.
Journal of the Transactions of the Victoria Institute, v. 21. London: The Victoria Institute, 1886.
Julian. *The Works of Emperor Julian*, vol. 1. ed. Wilmer Cave France Wright. Cambridge, MA: Harvard University Press, 1949.
Justin Martyr. *Dialogue with Trypho*. tr. Thomas B. Falls. Washington, DC: Catholic University of America Press, 2003.
Kavanagh, Morgan Peter. *Origin of Language and Myths*, v. 2. London: Gilbert and Rivington, 1871.
Keable, Robert. *The Great Galilean*. London: Cassell and Company, 1929.
Keary, Charles Francis. *Outlines of Primitive Belief: Among the Indo-European Races*. New York: Charles Scribner's Sons, 1882.
Keel, John, *Disneyland of the Gods*, Amok, 1988
Keeler, Bronson C. *A Short History of the Bible*, Health Research, 1965.
—*A Short History of the Bible*, 1881.
Keim, Theodor. *The History of Jesus of Nazara*, v. 1. London: Williams and Norgate, 1873.
Kelle, Brad E. *Hosea 2: Metaphor and Rhetoric in Historical Perspective*. Leiden: E.J. Brill, 2005.
Keller, Werner, *The Bible as History*, Bantam, 1982
Kelly, Joyce. *An Archaeological Guide to Central & Southern Mexico*. Norman, OK: University of Oklahoma Press, 2001.
Kelso. "Victims of the Christian Faith." 1996; www.truthbeknown.com/victims.htm
Kennedy, J.H., "The Problem of Second Corinthians," *Hermathena: A Series of Papers on Literature, Science, and Philosophy*, XXIX. Dublin: Hodes, Figgis & Co., 1903.
Kenrick, William, et al. *The London Review of English and Foreign Literature*. London: T. Evans, Pater-Noster-Row, 1779.
Kerenyi, Carl. *Dionysos: Archetypal Image of Indestructible Life*. Princeton, NJ: Princeton University Press, 1996.
Ketkar, Shridhar V., *The History of Caste in India*, I, Taylor & Carpenter, 1909.
King, Charles William. *The Gnostics and Their Remains, Ancient and Mediaeval*. London: Bell and Daldy, 1864.
—tr. *Julian the Emperor, containing Gregory Nazianzen's Two Invectives and Libanius' Monody*. London: George Bell and Sons, 1888.
Kingsborough, Lord. "Extracts from Kingsborough's Mexican Antiquities." www.olivercowdery.com/smithhome/1880s-1890s/89-90_AL.htm#1889-117
Kippenberg, Hans G., and Guy G. Stroumsa, eds. *Secrecy and Concealment: Studies in the*

History of Mediterranean & Near Eastern Religions. Leiden: E.J. Brill, 1995.
Kirby, Peter. "Testimonium Flavianum." www.earlychristianwritings.com/testimonium.html
Kloppenborg, Ria, *The Sūtra on the Foundation of the Buddhist Order*. Leiden: E.J. Brill, 1973.
Knapp, Stephen, *Proof of Vedic Culture's Global Existence*, World Relief Network, 2000.
Knight, Christopher, and Robert Lomas. *The Hiram Key: Pharaosh, Freemasons and the Discovery of the Secret Scrolls of Jesus*. Gloucester, MA: Fair Winds Press, 1996.
Knight, Richard Payne. *The Symbolical Language of Ancient Art and Mythology*. New York: J.W. Bouton, 1876.
Knott, Kim. *The Location of Religion: A Spatial Analysis*. London: Equinox Publishing, 2005.
Krauss, Samuel. *Das Leben Jesus nach Jüdischen Quellen*. Berlin: S. Calvary & Co., 1902.
Krupp, Edwin C. *In Search of Ancient Astronomies*. New York: McGraw-Hill, 1979.
Kuhn, Alvin Boyd, *Lost Light: An Interpretation of Ancient Scriptures*, Filiquarian Publishing, 2007.
Kuhn, Alvin Boyd. *The Great Myth of the SunGods*. magna.com.au/~prfbrown/ab_kuhn.html
Lactantius. *Divine Institutes*. tr. Anthony G. Bowen. Liverpool: Liverpool University Press, 2003.
Laërtius, Diogenes. *The Lives and Opinions of Eminent Philosophers*. tr. C.D. Yonge. London: George Bell and Sons, 1901.
—Βίοι καὶ γνῶμαι τῶν ἐν φιλοσοφίᾳ εὐδοκιμησάντων. ed. H S Long. Oxford, 1964; www.mikrosapoplous.gr/dl/dl01.html
Lal, Braj B. *The Earliest Civilization of South Asia: Rise, Maturity and Decline*. Delhi: Aryan Books International, 1997.
Lancellotti, Maria Grazia. *Attis, Between Myth and History: King, Priest and God*. Leiden: Brill, 2002.
Landseer, John. *Sabaean Researches, in a Series of Essays on the Engraved Hieroglyphics of Chaldea, Egypt and Canaan*. London: Hurst, Robinson and Co., 1823.
Lane, Eugene N. *Cybele, Attis and Related Cults*. Leiden: E.J. Brill, 1996.
Langer, Walter C. *The Mind of Adolf Hitler*. New York: Basic Books, 1972.
Lardner, Nathaniel. *A Large Collection of Ancient Jewish and Heathen Testimonies to the Truth of the Christian Religion*, v. 1. London: J. Buckman and T. Longman, 1764.
—*The Credibility of the Gospel History, Part II*, v. 6. London: A. Millar, 1745.
—*The Works of Nathaniel Lardner*, v. 1. London: J. Johnson, 1788.
—*The Works of Nathaniel Lardner*, v. 3. London: Thomas Hamilton, 1815.
—*The Works of Nathaniel Lardner*, v. 4. London: Thomas Hamilton, 1815.
—*The Works of Nathaniel Lardner*, v. 5. London: J. Johnson, 1788.
—*The Works of Nathaniel Lardner*, v. 6. London: William Ball, London, 1838.
—*The Works of Nathaniel Lardner*, v. 8. London: William Ball, London, 1838.
Larson, Martin A., *The Story of Christian Origins*, Village, 1977
Lataster, Raphael. *Questioning the Historicity of Jesus* (Book 336). Brill Publishing, 2019.
Latham, Robert G. *The Natural History of the Varieties of Man*. London: John van Voorst, 1850.
Le Plongeon, Augustus. *Queen M'oo and the Egyptian Sphinx*. London: Kegan, Paul, Trench, Trübner & Co., 1896.
—*Vestiges of the Mayas or, Facts tending to prove that Communications and Intimate Relations must have existed, in very remote times, between the inhabitants of Mayab and those of Asia and Africa*. New York: John Polhemus, 1881.

Lebow, Richard Ned. *The Tragic Vision of Politics*. Cambridge: Cambridge University Press, 2003.

Lee, J. Fitzgerald. *Great Migration*. Montana: Kessinger Publishing, 2003.

Leedom, Tim, ed., *The Book Your Church Doesn't Want You to Read*, Kendall/Hunt, 1993

Leeming, David Adams. *Mythology: The Voyage of the Hero*. New York/Oxford University Press, 1998.

—*The Oxford Companion to World Mythology*. New York; Oxford: Oxford University Press, 2005.

Leighton, Taigen Daniel, *Visions of Awakening Space and Time: Dōgen and the Lotus Sutra*, Oxford University Press, NY, 2007.

Lemche, Niels Peter. *The Old Testament Between Theology and History: A Critical Survey*. Louisville: Westminster John Knox Press, 2009.

Lemprière, John. *Bibliotheca Classica*, v. 1. New York: G. and C. and H. Carvill, 1831.

Leslie, Elmer Archibald. *The Prophets Tell Their Own Story*. Nashville: Abingdon-Cokesbury Press, 1939.

Levine, Amy-Jill, Dale C. Allison, and John Dominic Crossan, eds. *The Historical Jesus in Context*. Princeton, NJ: Princeton University Press, 2006.

Lewis, Naphtali, ed. *Samothrace: The Ancient Literary Sources*. New York: Pantheon/ Bollingen Foundation, 1958.

Lewis, Naphthali, and Meyer Reinhold, eds. *Roman Civilization: The Empire*, v. 2. New York: Columbia University Press, 1990.

Lewis, Robert E., ed. *Middle English Dictionary*. Ann Arbor: University of Michigan Press, 1986.

Liddell, Henry George, and Robert Scott. *A Greek-English Lexicon*. New York: Harper & Brothers Publishers, 1852.

Lillie, Arthur, *Buddha and Buddhism*, T&T Clark, 1900.

—*Buddhism in Christendom: Or Jesus, the Essene*, Kegan Paul, London, 1887.

Lima, Robert. *Stages of Evil: Occultism in Western Theater and Drama*. Lexington: University Press of Kentucky, 2005.

Linck, Kurt, ed. *De Taciti quod ad Christianos spectat testimonio*. Numburgi, Salam, Typis Lipperti, 1913.

Lindemann, Albert S. *Esau's Tears: Modern Anti-Semitism and the Rise of the Jews*. Cambridge: Cambridge University Press, 1997.

Lindow, John. *Norse Mythology: A Guide to the Gods, Heroes, Rituals and Beliefs*. New York: Oxford University Press, 2002.

Lindtner, Christian, "Jesus Is Buddha," jesusisbuddha.com

—*Geheimnisse um Jesus Christus: Das Neue Testament Ist Buddhas Testament*, Lühe-Verlag, 2005.

Lingat, Robert. *The Classical Law of India*. tr. J. Duncan M. Derrett. Berkeley/Los Angeles/ London: University of California Press, 1973.

Littlewood, R. Joy. *A Commentary on Ovid's* Fasti, *Book 6*. New York: Oxford University Press, 2006.

Lockhart, Douglas, *Jesus the Heretic*, Element, 1997.

Lockhart, James. *The Nahuas after the Conquest: A Social and Cultural History of the Indians of Central Mexico, Sixteenth through Eighteenth Centuries*. Stanford: Stanford University Press, 1992.

Lockwood, Michael. *Buddhism's Relation to Christianity*. Tambaram, Chennai, India:

Sudarsan Graphics, 2010.
Long, Thomas G., and Cornelius Platinga. *A Chorus of Witnesses: Model Sermons for Today's Preacher*. Grand Rapids, MI: Wm. B. Eerdmans, 1994.
The Lost Books of the Bible. Crown, 1979
Lowder, Jeffery Jay. "Josh McDowell's 'Evidence' for Jesus: Is it Reliable?" www.infidels.org/library/modern/jeff_lowder/jury/chap5.html
Lucian. *The Works of Lucian of Samosata*, v. 2. tr. H.W. Fowler and F.G. Fowler. Oxford: Clarendon Press, 1905.
Lucian. *Lucian*, v. 3. tr. A.M. Harmon. New York: G.P. Putnam's Sons, 1921.
—*A Second-Century Satirist; or, Dialogues and Stories from Lucian of Samosata*. tr. ed. Winthrop Dudley Sheldon. Philadelphia: Drexel Biddle, 1901.
—*The Works of Lucian of Samosata*, v. 2. tr. H.W. Fowler and F.G. Fowler. Oxford: Clarendon Press, 1905.
Maccoby, Hyam, *The Mythmaker: Paul and the Invention of Christianity*, Harper, 1987
MacDonald, Dennis R. *The Homeric Epics and the Gospel of Mark*. New Haven, CT: Yale University Press, 2000.
—*Does the New Testament Imitate Homer? Four Cases from the Acts of the Apostles*. New Haven, CT: Yale University Press, 2003.
Macdonnell, Arthur A. *A Sanskrit-English Dictionary*. London/New York: Longmans, Green, 1893.
Mack, Burton, *The Lost Gospel of Q: The Book of Christian Origins*, Harper, 1993
Mackay, Robert William. *The Progress of the Intellect*, v. 2. London: John Chapman, 1850.
Mackey, Albert G, ed. *The American Quarterly Review of Freemasonry*. New York: Robt. Macoy, 1858.
MacMullen, Ramsay, *Paganism in the Roman Empire*, Yale University Press, NY/London, 1981.
Macnicol, Nicol. *The Religious Quest of India: Indian Theism from the Vedic to the Muhammadan Period*. London: Oxford University Press, 1915.
Macrobius. *The Saturnalia, Books 1–2*. ed. and tr. Robert A. Kaster. Cambridge, MA: Harvard University Press, 2011.
—*The Saturnalia*. tr. Percival Vaughan Davies. New York: Columbia University Press, 1969.
Mafico, Temba L.J. "The Biblical God of the Fathers and the African Ancestors." *The Bible in Africa: Transactions, Trajectories and Trends*. eds. Gerald O. West, Musa W. Dube Shomanah. Leiden: Brill, 2000.
Mahābhārata online. fiindolo.sub.uni-goettingen.de/gretil/1_sanskr/2_epic/mbh/sas/b05/b05c187.htm
Maier, Paul L., ed. *The New Complete Works of Josephus*. tr. William Whiston. Grand Rapids, MI: Kregel, 1999.
Maitland, Edward. *The Keys of the Creeds*. London: Trübner & Co., 1875.
Mangasarian, Mangasar Mugurditch. *The Truth about Jesus: Is He a Myth?* Chicago: Independent Religious Society, 1909.
Manuel, Frank E. *A Requiem for Karl Marx*. Cambridge, MA: Harvard University Press, 1997.
Marshack, Alexander. *The Roots of Civilization: The Cognitive Beginnings of Man's First Art, Symbol and Notation*. Mt. Kisco, NY: Moyer Bell, 1991.
Marshall, L. Howard, ed. *Moulton and Geden: Concordance to the Greek New Testament*. London/New York: T & T Clark, 2002.

Massey, Gerald, *Ancient Egypt: Light of the World*, I, T. Fisher Unwin, London, 1907.
—*Ancient Egypt: Light of the World*, II, T. Fisher Unwin, London, 1907.
—*Egyptian Book of the Dead and the Mysteries of Amenta*, T. Fisher Unwin, London, 1907.
—*The Historical Jesus and the Mythical Christ*, The Book Tree, 2000.
—*The Natural Genesis*, v. 2. London: Williams and Norgate, 1883.
—*A Book of the Beginnings, II: Egyptian Origins in the Hebrew, Akkado-Assyrian and Maori*. London: Williams and Norgate, 1881.
—*The Egyptian Book of the Dead and the Mysteries of Amenta*. Originally published in a private edition, c. 1900.
—*Gnostic and Historic Christianity*, Sure Fire Press, 1985.
—*The Historical Jesus and the Mythical Christ*, The Book Tree, 2000.
—*The Natural Genesis*, II, Williams and Norgate, London, 1883.
Mathah, Sri Ramakrishna. *The Vedanta kesari*, v. 76. Madras, 1989.
McClintock, John, and James Strong. *Cyclopaedia of Biblical, Theological, and Ecclesiastical Literature*, I. New York: Harper & Brothers, 1891.
McDonald, Heather. *Blood, Bones and Spirit: Aboriginal Christianity in an East Kimberley Town*. Victoria: Melbourne University Press, 2001.
McGiffert, Arthur Cushman. *A History of Christianity in the Apostolic Age*. New York: Charles Scribner's Sons, 1897.
McGlew, James F. *Citizens on Stage: Comedy and Political Culture in the Athenian Democracy*. University of Michigan Press, 2005.
McGowan, Andrew, Brian E. Daley, and Timothy J. Gaden. *God in Early Christian Thought*. Leiden: Brill, 2009.
McIntyre, Kellen K., and Richard E. Phillips. *Woman and Art in Early Modern Latin America*. Leiden: Brill, 2007.
Mead, George R.S. *Did Jesus Live 100 BC?*, Health Research, 1965.
—*Fragments of a Faith Forgotten: Some Short Sketches Among the Gnostics Mainly of the First Two Centuries*. London: Theosophical Publishing Society, 1906.
—*The Gospels and the Gospel*. London: Theosophical Publishing, 1902.
—*The Gospels and the Gospel*, Health Research, 1972
—*Pistis Sophia*, Garber Communications, 1989.
—*Pistis Sophia: A Gnostic Gospel*. San Diego: The Book Tree, 2003.
Megged, Amos. *Exporting the Catholic Reformation: Local Religion in Early Colonial Mexico*. Leiden: E.J. Brill, 1996.
Meier, John P. *A Marginal Jew: Rethinking the Historical Jesus*, v. 1 & 2. New York: Doubleday, 19914 & 1994.
Men, Hunbatz. *Secrets of Mayan Science/Religion*. Rochester, VT: Bear & Company, 1990.
Mettinger, Tryggve N D. *The Riddle of Resurrection: "Dying and Rising Gods" in the Ancient Near East*. Stockholm: Almqvist & Wiksell International, 2001.
Metzger, Bruce M. *The New Testament: Its Background Growth and Content*. Nashville: Abingdon Press, 2006.
Meyer, Marvin W. *The Ancient Mysteries: A Sourcebook of Sacred Texts*. Philadelphia: University of Pennsylvania Press, 1999.
Meyer, Marvin W., ed. *The Nag Hammadi Library in English*. tr. James M. Robinson. Leiden: E.J. Brill, 1977.
Middleton, Conyers. The *Miscellaneous Works of the Late Reverend and Learned Conyers Middleton, D.D.* London: Richard Manby, 1752.

Migne, Jacques-Paul, ed. *Patrologiae cursus completes: Eusebius Pamphili Caesariensis Episcopus*, v. 21. Paris: J.P. Migne, 1857.

Miller, Joseph Dana, ed. *The Single Tax Review: A Bi-Monthly Record of the Progress of Single Tax and Tax Reform throughout the World*, v. 10. New York, 1910.

Milman, Henry Hart. *The History of Christianity: From the Birth of Christ to the Abolition of Paganism*, v. 3. London: John Murray, 1840.

Minns, Denis, and Paul Parvis, trs. *Justin, Philosopher and Martyr: Apologies*. ed. Henry Chadwick. Oxford: Oxford University Press, 2009.

Mirecki, Paul, and Jason Beduhn, eds. *Emerging from Darkness: Studies in the Recovery of Manichaean Sources*. Leiden: Brill, 1997.

—*The Light and the Darkness: Studies in Manichaeism and its World.* Leiden: Brill, 2001.

Mishra, Krishna Chandra. *Tribes in the Mahabharata: A Socio-Cultural Study*. New Delhi, India: National Pub. House, 1987.

Missing Books of the Bible, The, Halo, 1996

Mitchell, Logan. *The Christian Mythology Unveiled.* Printed privately, 1842?

Monier-Williams, Monier. *A Sanskrit English Dictionary*. Delhi: Motilal Banarsidass, 2005.

Moreschini, Claudio, and Enrico Norelli. *Early Christian Greek and Latin Literature: From the Council of Nicea to the Beginnings of the Medieval Period.* Peabody, MA: Hendrickson Publishers, 2005.

Mosheim, John Lawrence von. *Institutes of Ecclesistical History*, v. 1. New Haven: A.H. Maltby, 1832.

Moss, Candida. *The Myth of Persecution: How Early Christians Invented a Story of Martyrdom*. HarperOne, 2014.

Muck, Otto, *The Secrets of Atlantis*, Time Books, 1978.

Muir, John. "Contributions to a Knowledge of the Vedic Theogony and Mythology." *Journal of the Royal Asiatic Society of Great Britain and Ireland*, v. 1. Cambridge: Cambridge University Press, 1865.

—*The Oriental Studies*. Calcutta: Ghosha and Brother, 1878.

Original Sanskrit Texts on the Origin and History of the People of India, 4. London: Trübner & Co., 1863.

Mullick, Promatha Nath. *The Mahabharata As It Was, Is And Ever Shall Be*. Calcutta: The Pioneer Press/Kessinger Publishing, 1934, 2004.

Müller, F. Max. *Chips from a German Workshop*, vols. 2–3. Charles Scribner's Sons, 1890.

—*Contributions to the Science of Mythology*, v. 2. London: Longmans, Green and Co., 1897.

—*Theosophy or Psychological Religion*. London: Longmans, Green and Co., 1893.

Murdock, D.M., Acharya S. "Beddru is Beddou is Buddha." www.truthbeknown.com/beddru.html

—"Bone Box No Proof of Jesus." www.truthbeknown.com/ossuary.htm

—"Cruciforms/Gods on Crosses." freethoughtnation.com/forums/viewtopic.php?f=16&t=3014

—*Did Moses Exist? The Myth of the Israelite Lawgiver*. Stellar House Publishing, 2014.

—"Early Critic Contends Christianity an Eclectic Mishmash of Earlier Philosophies and Religions." *Freethought Nation Forums*. freethoughtnation.com/forums/viewtopic.php?p=27359#p27359

—"Jesus as the Sun throughout History," www.stellarhousepublishing.com/jesussunexcerpt.html

—"Jesus the Druid." www.truthbeknown.com/christ-great-britain.html

—"Jesus in India? The Myth of the Lost Years." www.truthbeknown.com/jesus_in_india.htm
—"Dating of Krishna." freethoughtnation.com/forums/viewtopic.php?f=16&t=2930
—"Rebuttal to Dr. Chris Forbes." www.truthbeknown.com/chrisforbeszeitgeist.html
—"Was Krishna's Mother a 'Virgin?'", www.freethoughtnation.com/forums/viewtopic.php?f=16&t=1597
—"What Is a Mythicist?" stellarhousepublishing.com/mythicist.html
—"What Is Mythicism?" stellarhousepublishing.com/mythicism.html
—*The Astrotheology Calendar Guide*. Stellar House Publishing, 2010.
—*Christ in Egypt: The Horus-Jesus Connection*. Stellar House Publishing, 2009.
—*The Gospel According to Acharya S*. Stellar House Publishing, 2009.
—*Who Was Jesus? Fingerprints of The Christ*. Stellar House Publishing, 2007.
Muss-Arnolt, William. *A Concise Dictionary of the Assyrian Language*. Reuther & Reichard, 1905.
Mysteries of the Past. American Heritage, 1977
Nabarz, Payam, Israel Campos Mendez (Contributor), and D.M. Murdock (Contributor). *Anahita: Ancient Persian Goddess & Zoroastrian Yazata*. Avalonia, 2013.
Nabarz, Payam. *The Mysteries of Mithras: The Pagan Belief that Shaped the Christian World*. Inner Traditions, 2005.
Narayan, Aiyangar. *Essays on Indo-Aryan Mythology*. New Delhi: Asian Educational Services, 1987.
Naville, Edouard. "The Book of the Dead." *Proceedings of the Society of Biblical Archaeology*, v. 24. Bloomsbury: Harrison and Sons, 1902.
Nefesh, Zion. "Zohar 70—Three Letter יהו, Six Directions, Now Shake!" dailyzohar.com/?p=604
Neusner, Jacob. *Early Rabbinic Judaism: Historical Studies in Religion, Literature and Art*. Leiden: E.J. Brill, 1975.
New Larousse Encyclopedia of Mythology, Hamlyn, 1983
Newbery, George Harkness, and Diego Newbery. *Pampa grass: The Argentine Story as Told by an American Pioneer to His Son, Diego Newbery*. Buenos Aires: Editorial Guarania, 1953.
Nielson, Paula I. "Japanese DNA Testing Shows Links to Native Americans." www.suite101.com/content/japanese-origins-from-dna-testing-shows-links-to-native-americans-a234745
Nimoy, Leonard. *I Am Not Spock*. Cutchogue, NY: Buccaneer Books, 1997.
Nixey, Catherine. *The Darkening Age: The Christian Destruction of the Classical World*. Houghton Mifflin Harcourt, 2018.
Nongbri, Brent. "The Use and Abuse of P52: Papyrological Pitfalls in the Dating of the Fourth Gospel." *Harvard Theological Review* 98:23–52. Cambridge, MA: Harvard Divinity School, 2005.
North American Review, v. 17; New Series, v. 8. Boston: O. Everett, 1823.
Notes and Queries: A Medium of Inter-Communication for Literary Men, General Readers, etc., ser. 3, v. 4. London, 1863.
Notovich, Nicholas, *The Unknown Life of Jesus Christ*, Tree of Life, 1980
Numen, v. 28–30. ed. International Association for the History of Religions. Leiden: E.J. Brill, 1981.
O'Flaherty, Wendy Doniger. *Hindu Myths: A Sourcebook*. New York: Penguin Classics, 1975.
O'Hara, Gwydion, *Sun Lore*, Llewellyn, 1997
Ober, Josiah. *Mass and Elite in Democratic Athens*. Princeton: Princeton University Press, 1989.

Oberman, Heiko Augustinus, and Donald Weinstein, eds. *The Two Reformations: The Journey from the Last Days to the New World*. New Haven, CT: Yale University Press, 2003.
Obeyesekere, Gananath. *The Cult of the Goddess Pattini*. Chicago: University of Chicago Press, 1984.
Ogilvie, John. *The Imperial Dictionary of the English Language*, v. 1. London: Blackie & Son, 1885.
Oldenburg, Ulf. *The Conflict Between El and Baal in Canaanite Religion*. Leiden: E.J. Brill, 1969.
Olson, Carl. *The Many Colors of Hinduism*. Rutgers University Press, 2007.
Olson, Ken A. "Eusebian fabrication of the Testimonium." groups.yahoo.com/group/JesusMysteries/message/1126
—"Eusebius and the Testimonium Flavianum." *Catholic Bible Quarterly*, v. 61. 1999.
Oort, Henricus, Isaac Hooykaas, and A. Kuenen. *The Bible for Learners*, v. 3. Boston: Roberts Brothers, 1880.
Orr, James, ed. *The International Standard Bible Encyclopaedia*, v. 1. Chicago: The Howard-Severange Company, 1915.
Osho. *The New Freedom: On Love, Meditation and the Search*. New Delhi: Sterling Publishers, 2008.
Ovid. *Metamorphoses*. tr. Stanley Lombardo. Indianapolis, IN: Hackett Pub. Co., 2010.
—*Metamorphoses*, v. 2. tr. Frank Justus Miller. New York: G.P. Putnam's Sons, 1916.
Owen, Robert, and Alexander Campbell. *Debate on the Evidences of Christianity*. London: R. Groombridge, 1839.
Oxford English Dictionary. Oxford: Oxford University Press, 1999.
Oxley, William. *The Medium and Daybreak*, no. 770, vol. XVI. London: J. Burns, 1885.
Pagels, Elaine, *Adam, Eve and the Serpent*, Vintage, 1989.
—*The Gnostic Gospels*. Vintage, 1989.
Paine, Robert T. *The Art and Architecture of Japan*. New Haven: Yale University Press, 1981.
Pape, William. *Handwörterbuch der griechischen Sprache*. ed. von Max Sengebusch. Braunschweig: Vieweg & Sohn, 1849.
Park, Roswell, *An Epitome of the History of Medicine*, F.A. Davis Company, 1901.
Parker, Julia and Derek, *Parker's Astrology*, Dorling Kindersley, 1991
Parmeshwaranand, Swami, *Encyclopaedic Dictionary of Purānas*, Sarup & Sons, 2001.
Pärssinen, Martti, and Denise Schaan and Alceu Ranzi. "Pre-Columbian Geometric Earthworks in the Upper Purús: A Complex Society in Western Amazonia." *Antiquity*, v. 83, no. 322, pp. 1084–95. antiquity.ac.uk/ant/083/ant0831084.htm
Past Worlds: Atlas of Archaeology. London: HarperCollinsPublishers/Borders Group, 1997.
Patton, Kimberley Christine. *Religion of the Gods: Ritual, Paradox and Reflexivity*. Oxford: Oxford University Press, 2009.
Pausanias. *Description of Greece*, v. 5. tr. J.G. Frazer. London: MacMillan & Co., 1913.
—*Description of Greece*, v. 1 & 2. tr. W.H.S. Jones. New York: G.P. Putnam's Sons, 1917.
—*Description of Greece*, v. 1. tr. Arthur Richard Shilleto. London: George Bell and Sons, 1886.
Pearse, Roger. "C. Plinius Secundus (Pliny the Younger): Letters: Manuscripts and Transmission." www.tertullian.org/rpearse/pliny/pliny_mss.htm
—"Tacitus and His Manuscripts." www.tertullian.org/rpearse/tacitus/index.htm
Perry, John T., *Sixteen Saviours or One? The Gospels Not Brahamanic*, P.G. Thomson, 1879.
Philostratus. *The Life of Apollonius of Tyana*, v. 1. tr. F.C. Conybeare. New York: The

Macmillan Co., 1912.
Pike, Albert, *The Morals and Dogma of Scottish Rite Freemasonry*, LH Jenkins, 1928
Pinch, Geraldine. *Handbook of Egyptian Mythology*. Santa Barbara: ABC-CLIO, Inc., 2002.
Platt, Rutherford, ed., *The Forgotten Books of Eden*, Crown, 1981
Platts, John. *A New Universal Biography, Chronologically Arranged*, v. 5. London: Sherwood, Gilbert and Piper, 1826.
Pliny the Younger. *Epistulae ad Traianum Imperatorem cum Eiusdem Responsis*. ed. Ernest George Hardy. London: MacMillan and Co., 1889.
Plumptre, Constance E. *General Sketch of the History of Pantheism*. Cambridge: Cambridge University Press, 2011.
Poorthuis, Marcel, Joshua Schwartz and Joseph Turner, eds. *Interaction between Judaism and Christianity in History, Religion, Art and Literature*. Leiden: Brill, 2009.
Pope, Marvin H. *El in the Ugaritic Texts*. Leiden: E.J. Brill, 1955.
Popkin, Richard H., and Arjo Vanderjagt, eds. *Scepticism and Irreligion in the Seventeenth and Eighteenth Centuries*. Leiden: E.J. Brill, 1993.
Popley, Herbert Arthur, tr. *The Sācred Kural: or, The Tamil Veda of Tiruvaḷḷuvar*. Calcutta: YMCA Publishing House, 1958.
Porter, Stanley E. *Reading the Gospels Today*. Grand Rapids, MI: Wm. B. Eerdmans Publishing Co., 2004.
Potter, Charles Francis, *The Great Religious Leaders*, Simon & Schuster, 1958.
Potter, Stephen, and Laurens Christopher Sargent. *The New Naturalist Pedigree: Essays on the Etymology of Words from Nature.* New York: Taplinger Pub. Co., 1974.
Prabhupada, A. C. Bhaktivedanta Swami. *Bhagavad-Gita as It is*. Los Angeles: The Bhaktivedanta Book Trust, 1976.
—*Srimad-Bhagavatam: Tenth Canto*, v. 1. New York: Bhaktivedanta Book Trust, 1977.
Prange, Gordon W., ed. *Hitler's Words*. Washington: American Council on Public Affairs, 1944.
Price, Christopher. "Did Josephus Refer to Jesus? A Thorough Review of the Testimonium Flavianum." www.bede.org.uk/Josephus.htm
Price, Robert M. "A Review of Gerd Lüdemann's *Paul: The Founder of Christianity*." www.robertmprice.mindvendor.com/rev_ludetwo.htm
—*Deconstructing Jesus*. Buffalo: Prometheus Books, 2000.
—*The Pre-Nicene New Testament*. Salt Lake City: Signature Books, 2006.
Price, Robert M. *The Pre-Nicene New Testament*. Salt Lake City: Signature Books, 2006.
Purohit, Shri Swami, tr. *The Bhagavad Gita: Annotated and Explained*. ed. Kendra Crossen Burroughs. Woodstock, VT: SkyLight Paths, 2007.
Radhakrishnan, Sarvepalli. *The Bhagavadgītā*. New York: Harper & Row, 1974.
Ragozin, Zénaïde Alexeïevna. *The Story of Media, Babylon and Persia*. New York: G.P. Putnam's Sons, 1888.
Raheja, Gloria Goodwin. *Poison in the Gift: Ritual, Prestation and the Dominant Caste in a North Indian Village*. Chicago: University of Chicago Press, 1988.
Rahner, Hugo. *Greek Myths and Christian Mystery*. New York: Harper & Row, 1971.
Rajagopalachari, Chakravarti, tr. *Ramayana*. Bombay: Bharatiya vidya bhavan, 1957.
Ramacharaka, Yogi. *The Bhagavad Gita or the Message of the Master*. Chicago: The Yogi Publication Society, 1907.
Rank, Otto, Lord Raglan, and Alan Dundes. *In Quest of the Hero*. Princeton: Princeton University Press, 1990.

Raymond, Robert. *Out of the Fiery Furnace: The Impact of Metals on the History of Mankind*. Pennsylania State University Press, 1986.
Read, Kay Almere, and Jason J. Gonzalez. *Mesoamerican Mythology: A Guide to the Godes, Heroes, Rituals and Beliefs of Mexico and Central America*. Oxford: Oxford University Press, 2000.
Reardon, B.P., ed. *Collected Ancient Greek Novels*. Berkeley/LA: University of California Press, 1989, 2008.
Record of Christian Work, v. 39, no. 4. East Northfield, MA: Record of Christian Work Co., 1920.
Reed, Elizabeth A. *Hindu Literature; or, the Ancient Books of India*. Chicago: S.C. Griggs and Company, 1891.
Reinach, Salomon. *Orpheus: A General History of Religions*. tr. Florence Simmonds. New York: G.P. Putnam's Sons, 1909.
Remsburg, John Eleazer. *The Christ: A Critical Review and Analysis of the Evidences of His Existence*. New York: Truth Seeker, 1909; BiblioBazaar, 2009.
Reynolds, Larry J. *Righteous Violence: Revolution, Slavery and the American Renaissance*. Athengs, GA: University of Georgia Press, 2011.
Riddle, John M. *The History of the Middle Ages*. Rowman & Littlefield, 2008.
Rigoglioso, Marguerite. *The Cult of Divine Birth in Ancient Greece*. New York: Palgrave Macmillan, 2009.
—*Virgin Mother Goddesses of Antiquity*. New York: Palgrave Macmillan, 2010.
Ritter, Carl, *The Comparative Geography of Palestine and the Sinaitic Peninsula*, tr. William L. Gage, III, New York: D. Appleton and Co., , 1866.
Roberts, Alexander, and James Donaldson. *The Ante-Nicene Fathers*, v. 1. New York: Charles Scribner's Sons, 1903, 1905.
—*Ante-Nicene Fathers*, v. 1. Buffalo: The Christian Literature Publishing Co., 1885.
—*Ante-Nicene Fathers*, v. 2. Buffalo: The Christian Literature Publishing Co., 1885.
—*Ante-Nicene Fathers*, v. 2. Edinburgh: T&T Clark, 1879.
—*Ante-Nicene Fathers*, v. 3. New York: Charles Scribner's Sons, 1903.
—*Ante-Nicene Fathers*, v. 4. New York: Charles Scribner's Sons, 1926.
—*Ante-Nicene Fathers*, v. 6. New York: Charles Scribner's Sons, 1903.
—*Ante-Nicene Fathers*, v. 6. New York: The Christian Literature Company, 1890.
—*Ante-Nicene Fathers*, v. 7. Buffalo: The Christian Literature Publishing Co., 1886.
—*Ante-Nicene Fathers*, v. 8. New York: The Christian Literature Publishing Co., 1903.
—*Ante-Nicene Fathers*, v. 9. New York: The Christian Literature Company, 1896.
Roberts, J.M., *Antiquity Unveiled*, Oriental Publishing Company, 1912.
Robertson, John M., "Mithraism," *Religious Systems of the World*, Swan Sonnenschein & Co., London, 1902.
—*Christianity and Mythology*, Watts & Co., London, 1900.
—*Christianity and Mythology*, Kessinger, 2004.
—*Pagan Christs*. New York: Dorset Press, 1966. 1987.
—*Pagan Christs: Studies in Comparative Hierology*. Kessinger, 2003.
Rolfe, J.C. *Suetonius: With an English Translation*, v. 2. eds. T.E. Page, W.H.D. Rouse. New York: The Macmillan Co., 1914.
Rollin, Charles, *The Ancient History of the Egyptians, Carthaginians, Assyrians, Babylonians, Medes and Persians, Macedonian and Grecians*, II, J.B. Lippincott & Co., Philadelphia, 1869.

Rollin, Charles, *The Ancient History of the Egyptians, Carthaginians, Assyrians, Babylonians, Medes and Persians, Macedonian and Grecians*, II, J.B. Lippincott & Co., Philadelphia, 1869.
Roscoe, William. The *Life and Pontificate of Leo the Tenth*, v. 3. Joseph Engelmann, 1828.
Rose, Hugh James. *A New General Biographical Dictionary*. London: B. Fellowes, et al., 1848.
Ross, John Wilson. *Tacitus and Bracciolini: The Annals Forged in the XVth Century*. London: Diprose & Bateman, 1878.
Rousseau, John J., and Rami Arav. *Jesus and His World: An Archaeological and Cultural Dictionary*. Minneapolis, MN: Augsburg Fortress, 1995.
Ruggles, Clive N. *Ancient Astronomy: An Encyclopedia of Cosmologies and Myth*. Santa Barbara, CA: ABC-CLIO, Inc., 2005.
Ruiz de Alarcón, Hernando. *Treatise on the Heathen Superstitions that Today Live Among the Indians Native to This New Spain, 1629*. tr. J. Richard Andrews and Ross Hassig. Norman, OK: University of Oklahoma Press, 1984.
Runia, David T. *Philo of Alexandria and the Timaeus of Plato*. Leiden: E.J. Brill, 1986.
Ryan, Patrick John, et al., eds. *The American Catholic Quarterly Review*, v. 24. Philadelphia, January-October, 1899.
Saladin, *The Secular Review: A Journal of Agnosticism*, v. 18, no. 24. London: W. Stewart, 1885.
Sale, George, tr. *The Koran: Commonly Called The Alcoran of Mohammed*. Philadelphia: J.B. Lippincott & Co., 1871.
Salsitz, Norman. *Three Homelands: Memories of a Jewish Life in Poland, Israel and America*. Syracuse, NY: Syracuse University Press, 2002.
Sanchez, Lino. "Christianism ('Christianity'), etc." www.christianism.com/articles/article2.html
Sandy, Gerald, ed. *The Classical Heritage in France*. Leiden: Brill, 2002.
Sankarananda, Swami. *The Rigvedic Culture of the Pre-Historic Indus*, v. 1 & 2. Abhedananda Academy of Culture, 1946?
Schäfer, Peter. *Judeophobia: Attitudes toward the Jews in the Ancient World*. Cambridge, MA: Harvard University Press, 1997.
Schäfer, Peter, and Mark R. Cohen. *Toward the Millennium: Messianic Expectations from the Bible to Waco*. Leiden: E.J. Brill, 1998.
Schaff, Philip. *A Select Library of Nicene and Post-Nicene Father of the Christian Church*, v. 1. New York: The Christian Literature Company, 1890.
—*A Select Library of Nicene and Post-Nicene Father of the Christian Church*, v. 6. New York: The Christian Literature Company, 1893.
Scherer, Burkhard, "The Secrets about Christian Lindtner," www.jesusisbuddha.com/scherer.html
Schleiermacher, Friedrich. *A Critical Essay on the Gospel of St. Luke*. London: John Taylor, 1825.
Schmiedel, Otto M. *Die Hauptprobleme der Leben-Jesu-Forschung*. Tübingen: J.C.B. Mohr (P. Siebeck), 1906.
Schmieke, Marcus. "Were the Maya's Pyramids Built by the Vedic Architect Maya?" www.vedic-academy.com/articles/vasati/mayas_pyramids.htm
Schneemelcher, Wilhelm, ed. *New Testament Apocrypha, Volume One: Gospels and Related Writings*. tr. R. McL. Wilson. Louis: Westminster John Knox Press, 2003.

Schuddeboom, Feyo L. *Greek Religious Terminology: Telete & Orgia*. Leiden: E.J. Brill, 2009.
Schürer, Emil. *History of the Jewish People in the Time of Jesus Christ*, v. 1. eds. Geza Vermes and Fergus Millar. Edinburgh: T&T Clark, 1973.
—*Geschichte des jüdischen Volkes im Zeitalter Jesu Christi*, v. 1. Leipzig: J.C. Hinrichs, 1890
Scott, George Ryley. *Phallic Worship*. Westport, CT: Associated Booksellers, 1949?
Scrivener, Frederick H. *An Exact Transcript of the Codex Augiensis: A Graeco-Latin Manuscript of S. Paul's Epistles, Deposited in the Library of Trinity College, Cambridge*. Cambridge: Deighton, Bell and Co., 1859.
Sedlar, Jean W. *India and the Greek World*. Totowa, NJ: Rowman & Littlefield, 1980.
Seidel, Andrew L. *The Founding Myth: Why Christian Nationalism Is Un-American*. Sterling, 2019.
Seiss, Joseph Augustus. *The Gospel in the Stars*. Kregel Publications, 1884.
Sen, Dineschandra. *The Ballads of Bengal*, v. 1. Delhi: Mittal Publications, 1928/1988.
Senart, Emile. *Essai Sur La Légende du Buddha: Son Caractère et Ses Origines*. Paris: Impremerie Nationale, 1875.
Seward, A.C., ed. *Darwin and Modern Science: Essays in Commemoration of the Centenary of the Birth of Charles Darwin and of the Fiftieth Anniversary of the Publication of The Origin of Species*. Cambridge: Cambridge University Press, 1909.
Sharma, Arvind. *Studies in "Alberuni's India."* Wiesbaden: Otto Harrassovitz, 1983.
Shashi, Shyam Singh, ed. *Encyclopaedia Indica: India, Pakistan, Bangladesh*, v. 20. New Delhi: Anmol Publications, 1997.
Sheridan, Daniel P. *The Advaitic Theism of the Bhagavata Purana*. Delhi: Motilal Banarsidass Publ., 1986.
Shipp, R. Mark. *Of Dead Kings and Dirges: Myth and Meaning in Isaiah 14:4b-21*. Leiden: Society of Biblical Literature/Brill, 2002.
Sider, Robert D. *Christian and Pagan in the Roman Empire: The Witness of Tertullian*. Washington, DC: Catholic University of America Press, 2001.
Sitchin, Zecharia, *The Lost Realms*, Avon, 1990
—*When Time Began*, Avon, 1993.
Smallwood, E. Mary. *The Jews Under Roman Rule: From Pompey to Diocletian*. Leiden: E.J. Brill, 1981.
Smedley, Edward, Hugh James Rose, and Henry John Rose. *Encyclopaedia Metropolitana or, Universal Dictionary of Knowledge*, v. 11. London: B. Fellowes, et al., 1845.
Smith, Evans Lansing. *The Hero Journey in Literature: Parables of Poesis*. Lanham, MD: University Press of America, 1997.
Smith, Mark S., and Wayne Thomas Pitard. *The Ugaritic Baal Cycle*. Leiden: E.J. Brill, 1994.
Smith, Rowland. *Julian's Gods: Religion and Philosophy in the Thought and Action of Julian the Apostate*. London/New York: Routledge, 1995.
Smith, R. Scott, and Stephen M. Trzaskoma, trs. *Apollodorus' Library and Hyginus' Fabulae: Two Handbooks of Greek Mythology*. Indianapolis/Cambridge: Hackett Publishing Company, 2007.
Smith, William, ed. *Dictionary of Greek and Roman Biography and Mythology*, v. 2. London: Taylor and Walton, 1846.
—*Dictionary of Greek and Roman Biography and Mythology*, vol. 1. London: Taylor, Walton and Maberly, 1850a.
—*New Classical Dictionary of Biography, Mythology and Geography*. London: John Murray,

1850.

Snyder, Louis L. *Hitler's Third Reich: A Documentary History*. Chicago: Nelson-Hall, 1981.

Sorenson, John L. "New Light: The Problematic Role of DNA Testing in Unraveling Human History." *Journal of Book of Mormon Studies*, vol. 9, no. 2, pp. 66–74. Provo, UT: Maxwell Institute, 2000; maxwellinstitute.byu.edu/publications/jbms/?vol=9&num=2&id=231

—*Pre-Columbian Contact with the Americas across the Oceans*, v. 2. Provo, UT: Research Press, 1996.

Spoer, Hans H. *The Origin and Interpretation of the Tetragrammaton*. Chicago: University of Chicago Press, 1901.

Spong, John Shelby. *Resurrection: Myth or Reality? A Bishop's Search for the Origins of Christianity*. New York: HarperCollins, 1995.

Squier, Ephraim George. *American Archaeological Researches, No. I: The Serpent Symbol and the Worship of the Reciprocal Principles of Nature in America*. New York: George P. Putnam, 1881.

St. *Chrysostom's Picture of the Religion of His Age*. London: Society for Promoting Christian Knowledge, 1876.

Staniforth, Maxwell. *Early Christian Writings: The Apostolic Fathers*. ed. Betty Radice. London: Penguin Group, 1988.

Stavrakopoulou, Francesca, and John Barton. *Religious Diversity in Ancient Israel and Judah*. London: T&T Clark International, 2010.

Steele, John. "Was Jesus a Taoist?" California: Privately Published, 1978.

Stein, Gordon. "The Jesus of History: A Reply to Josh McDowell." www.infidels.org/library/modern/gordon_stein/jesus.html

Steiner, Rudolf. *Christianity as Mystical Fact*. Anthroposophic Press, 1972

Stone, Merlin. *When God Was a Woman*. New York: Dial/Dorset, 1976.

Stoyanov, Yuri. *The Other God: Dualist Religions from Antiquity to the Cathar Heresy*. New Haven: Yale University Press, 2000.

Strange, Thomas Lumisden. *The Sources and Development of Christianity*. London: TrUbner & Co., 1875.

Stray, Christopher. *The Classical Association: The First Century*, 1903–2003, v. 56–60. Oxford: Oxford University Press, 1959.

Strobel, Lee. *The Case for Christ*. Grand Rapids, MI: Zondervan, 1998.

Strong's Concordance, www.blueletterbible.org

Śūdraka. *Mrcchakatikā, The little clay cart*. ed. Revilo P. Oliver. Urbana: University of Illinois Press, 1938.

Sykes, Egerton. *Who's Who in Non-Classical Mythology*. ed. Alan Kendall. London/New York: Routledge, 2002.

Tabor, James D. *The Jesus Dynasty*. New York: Simon & Schuster, 2006.

Tacey, David John. *Patrick White: Fiction, and the Unconscious*. Melbourne/New York: Oxford University Press, 1988.

Tacitus. *The Annals of Tacitus*, v. 1–6. ed. William Francis Allen. Boston and London: Ginn & Company Publishers, 1890.

—*The Histories* v. 1 & 2. tr. W. Hamilton Fyfe. Oxford: Clarendon Press, 1912.

Tanabe, George, ed. *Writings of Nichiren Shōnin, Doctrine 2*. Honolulu: University of Hawai'i Press, 2002.

Tavard, George H. *The Thousand Faces of the Virgin Mary*. Collegeville, MN: Liturgical Press, 1996.

Taylor, Jeremy. *The Life of Our Blessed Lord and Savior Jesus Christ*. Pittsburgh, PA: Cook and Schoyer, 1834.

Taylor, J. Glen. *Yahweh and the Sun: Biblical and Archaeological Evidence for Sun Worship in Ancient Israel*. Continuum International Publishing Group, 1993.

Taylor, Robert, *The Diegesis*, Abner Kneeland, Boston, 1834.

Taylor, Robert. *The Diegesis; being a Discovery of the Origins, Evidences and Early History of Christianity*. London: Richard Carlile, 1829.

—*The Diegesis*. Boston: Abner Kneeland, 1834.

—*The Diegesis*. CA: Health Research, 1977.

te Nijenhuis, Emmie. *Indian Music: History and Structure*. Leiden: E.J. Brill, 1974.

Teixidor, Javier. *The Pantheon of Palmyra*. Leiden: E.J. Brill, 1979.

Tenney, Merrill C. *New Testament Survey*. Grand Rapids, MI: Wm. B. Eerdmans Publishing Co., 1985.

Tertullian. *Adversus Marcion*, v. 1. tr. Ernest Evans. Oxford: Clarendon Press, 1972.

Thackeray, H. St. J., tr. *Josephus: Jewish Antiquities, v. 1: Books 1–3*. Cambridge: Harvard University Press, 1998.

The Atlantic Monthly, v. 292. Boston, MA: Atlantic Monthly Co., 2003.

The Christian Remembrancer Quarterly Review, vol. 41. London: J.&C. Mozley, 1861.

The Classical Journal, XXIX. London: A.J. Valpy, 1824.

The Gift of Scripture: Catholic Bishops' Conferences of England and Wales, and of Scotland. London: The Catholic Truth Society, 2005; www.catholic-ew.org.uk/content/download/3999/27399/file/Gift%20of%20Scripture%20text.pdf

The London Quarterly, v. 6. London: Alexander Heylin, 1856.

The Monthly Repository of Theology and General Literature, v. 5. London: C. Stower, 1810.

The New International Encyclopedia, v. 1. New York: Dodd, Mead and Company, 1914.

The New Strong's Concordance of the Bible. Nashville: T. Nelson, 1985; www.blueletterbible.org/lang/lexicon/lexicon.cfm?Strongs=H4216&t=KJV

The Pocket Oxford Classical Greek Dictionary. Oxford: Oxford University Press, 2002.

The Southern Review, IV, A.E. Miller, Charleston, 1829.

Theissen, Gerd, and Annette Merz. *The Historical Jesus: A Comprehensive Guide*. Minneapolis: Fortress Press, 1998.

Thierens, A.E. *Astrology in Mesopotamian Culture*. Leiden: E.J. Brill, 1935.

Thomassin, Louis. *La méthode d'*étudier et d*'enseigner Chrétiennement*. Paris: Chez François Muguer, 1682.

Thorburn, Thomas James. *The Mythical Interpretation of the Gospels: Critical Studies in the Historic Narratives*. New York: Charles Scribner's Sons, 1916.

Thundy, Zacharias P., "The Sanskrit Sources of the Gospel Narratives of the Trial and Death," www.jesusisbuddha.com/thundy.html

—*Buddha and Christ: Nativity Stories and Indian Traditions*, E.J. Brill, Leiden, 1993.

Titcomb, Sarah. *Aryan Sun Myths*. Escondido, CA: Book Tree, 1999.

Tod, James. *Annals and Antiquities of Rajasthan*, v. 1. London: Routledge & Sons, 1914.

—*Annals and Antiquities of Rajasthan*, v. 2. London: Oxford University Press, 1920.

Torrey, Reuben Archer, and John Canne, eds. *The Treasury of Scripture Knowledge: Five-Hundred Thousand Scripture References and Parallel Passages*. London: Samuel Bagster & Sons, 1971.

Toulson, Shirley. *The Winter Solstice*. London: Jill Norman & Hobhouse, 1981.

Tripathy, Ajit Kumar. "The Real Birth Place of Buddha: Yesterday's Kapilavastu, Today's

Kapileswar." *OHRJ*, 47.1. orissa.gov.in/e-magazine/Journal/jounalvol1/pdf/orhj-3.pdf

Turcan, Robert. *Mithras Platonicus*. Leiden: E.J. Brill, 1975.

Turner, Patricia, and Charles Russell Coulter. *Dictionary of Ancient Deities*. Oxford: Oxford University Press, 2000.

Tylor, Edward Burnet. *Researches into the Early History of Mankind and the Development of Civilization*. London: John Murray, 1865.

Tyson, Joseph B. *Marcion and Luke-Acts: A Defining Struggle*. Columbia, S.C.: University of South Carolina Press, 2006. Ulansey, David, *The Origins of the Mithraic Mysteries*, Oxford University Press, 1991.

Ulansey, David, *The Origins of the Mithraic Mysteries*, Oxford University Press, 1991.

Vallabhācārya. Śrīsubodhinī—*Sri Subodhini: Text with English Translation*, v. 7. Delhi: Sri Satguru Publications, 2003.

van den Berg, R.M. *Proclus' Hymns: Essays, Translations, Commentary*. Leiden: Brill, 2001.

van der Loos, H. *The Miracles of Jesus*. Leiden: E.J. Brill, 1965.

van der Toorn, Karel, Bob Becking, and Pieter W. van der Horst, eds. *Dictionary of Deities and Demons in the Bible*. Leiden: E.J. Brill, 1999.

van Kooten, Geurt Hendrik. *The Revelation of the name YHWH to Moses*. Leiden: Brill, 2006.

Vanstiphout, Herman. *Epic of Sumerian Kings: The Matter of Aratta*. ed. Jerrold S. Cooper. Leiden: Society of Biblical Literature/Brill, 2003.

Van Voorst, Robert E. *Jesus Outside the New Testament: An Introduction to the Ancient Evidence*. Grand Rapids, MI: Wm. B. Eerdmans Publishing Co., 2000.

Vemuri, V. Rao. *Telugu-English Dictionary and Thesaurus*. New Delhi: Asian Educational Services, 2002.

Vermaseren, Maarten Jozef. *Corpus Cultus Cybelae Attidisque*. Leiden: E.J. Brill, 1977.

—*Cybele, Attis, and Related Cults: Essays in Memory of M. J. Vermaseren*. Leiden/New York: E.J. Brill, 1996.

Vermes, Geza, *The Dead Sea Scrolls*, Penguin, 1987

Vetterling, Herman. *Illuminate of Gorlitz or Jakob Bohme's Life and Philosophy, Part 3*. Kessinger Publishing, 2003.

Viegas, Jennifer. "Neanderthals, Humans Interbred, DNA Proves." *Discovery News*, May 6, 2010; news.discovery.com/human/neanderthal-human-interbreed-dna.html

—"All Non-Africans Part Neanderthal, Genetics Confirm." *Discovery News*, July 18, 2011;

Viklund, Roger. "Alice Whealey." rogerviklund.wordpress.com/category/alice-whealey/

—"The Jesus Passages in Josephus—a Case Study: Excursus—'The Emmaus Narrative in Luke.'" rogerviklund.wordpress.com/2011/04/16/the-jesus-passages-in-josephus—a-case-study-excursus—"the-emmaus-narrative-in-luke"

—"Tacitus as a Witness to Jesus." rogerviklund.wordpress.com/2010/10/02/tacitus-as-a-witness-to-jesus—an-image-illustration-of-what-the-original-might-have-looked-like/

Viladesau, Richard R. *The Beauty of the Cross: The Passion of Christ in Theology and the Arts, from the Catacombs to the Eve of the Renaissance*. Oxford: Oxford University Press, 2006.

Vitsaxis, Vassilis. *Hindu Epics, Myths and Legends in Popular Illustrations*. Oxford: Oxford University Press, 1977.

Voltaire, François-Marie Arouet. *A Philosophical Dictionary*, v. 2. London: John and H.L. Hunt, 1824.

von Albrecht, Michael. *A History of Roman Literature: From Livius Andronicus to Boethius*,

v. 1. Leiden: E.J. Brill, 1997.
Vyas, Ramnarayan. *The Bhāgavata Bhakti Cult and Three Advaita ācāryas, Śaṅkara, Rāmānuja and Vallabha*. Nag Publishers, 1977.
Vyasa, et al., *Srimad Bhagavatam of Sri Krishnadvaipayana Vyasa*, Sree Gaudiya Math, 1986.
Waite, Charles, *History of the Christian Religion to the Year Two Hundred*, Caroll Bierbower, 1992
Walker, Barbara. *The Woman's Dictionary of Symbols and Sacred Objects*. HarperSanFranciso, 1988, 1991.
—*The Woman's Encyclopedia of Myths and Secrets*. HarperSanFrancisco, 1983.
Walker, James. *The Dark Bible*. CreateSpace, 2009; www.nobeliefs.com/DarkBible/DarkBibleContents.htm
Walker, William O. *Interpolations in the Pauline Letters*. London: Sheffiled Academic Press, 2001.
Wallbank, Thomas Walter. *Civilization Past and Present*, v. 1. Scott, Foresman, 1960.
Walsh, Peter G., tr. *Pliny the Younger: Complete Letters*. Oxford: Oxford University Press, 2006.
Warburton, William. *The Works of the Right Reverend William Warburton*, v. 2. London: Luke Hansard & Sons, 1811.
Warrier, A.G. Krishna. *The Sāmānya Vedānta Upaniṣad-s*. Madras: Adyar Library and Research Centre, 1991.
Waterhouse, Joseph. *The King and People of Fiji: Containing a Life of Thakombau*. London: Wesleyan Conference Office, 1866.
Waugh, Alexander. *GOD*. New York: Thomas Dunne Books, 2004.
Weber, Albrecht Friedrich. Über die Krishnajanmâshtamî (Krishna's *Geburtsfest)*. Berlin: Harrwitz und Gossmann/G. Vogt, 1868.
Websters II New College Dictionary. Boston: Houghton Mifflin Company, 2005.
Weigall, Arthur. *The Paganism in Our Christianity*. New York/London: G.P. Putnam's Sons, 1928.
Welburn, Andrew J. *Mani, the Angel and the Column of Glory*. Edinburgh: Floris, 1998.
Wells, George A. Wells, *Did Jesus Exist?* London: Elek, 1975.
—*Did Jesus Exist?* Pemberton, 1986.
—*The Historical Evidence for Jesus*. Prometheus, 1988.
—*Who Was Jesus?* Open Court, 1991.
Westcott, Brooke Foss. A *General Survey of the History of the Canon of the New Testament*. London: Macmillan and Co., 1875.
Westerman and Lessing, *The Bible: A Pictorial History*, Seabury Press, 1977.
Westervelt, William Drake. *Legends of Ma-Ui, A Demi God of Polynesia, and of His Mother Hina*. Hawaii: The Hawaiian Gazette Co., 1910.
Wharton, Annabel Jane. *Selling Jerusalem: Relics, Replicas, Theme Parks*. Chicago: University of Chicago Press, 2006.
Whealey, Alice. *Josephus on Jesus: The Testimonium Flavianum Controversy from Late Antiquity to Modern Times*. New York: Peter Lang, 2003.
Wheeler, J. Talboys. *The History of India From the Earliest Ages*, v. 1. London: N. Trübner & Co., 1867.
Wheen, Francis. *Karl Marx: A Life*. W.W. New York: Norton & Company, 2001.
Wheless, Joseph. *Forgery in Christianity*. Health Research, 1990.

—*Is It God's Word?* Montana: Kessinger Publishing, 1992.
Whiston, William, tr. *The Complete Works of Josephus*. Kregel, 1981.
Whitehouse, David. "Ice Age star map discovered." *BBC News*. news.bbc.co.uk/2/hi/871930.stm
Whitney, Loren Harper. *A Question of Miracles: Parallels in the Lives of Buddha and Jesus*, Chicago: The Library Shelf, 1908.
Willard-Archer, B. *Characteristics of the Romish Church*. London: Swan Sonnenschein & Co., 1904.
William, Alexander. *The Creed of Japhet, That Is of the Race Popularly Surnamd Indo-Germanic or Aryan*. London: W. Clowes and Sons, 1891.
Williams, Sandra. "Sadducean Origins of the Dead Sea Sectarians." ddi.digital.net/~billw/Scrolls/scrolls.html
Wilson, Horace Hayman.
Wilson, Ian. *Jesus: The Evidence*. Harper, 1988.
Wilson, Robert Anton. *Everything is Under Control: Conspiracies, Cults and Cover-ups*. Harper, 1998.
Winter, Irene J. *On Art in the Ancient Near East, Volume 2: From the Third Millennium BCE*. Leiden: Brill, 2010.
Wise, Michael, Martin Abegg, Jr. and Edward Cook. *The Dead Sea Scrolls: A New Translation*. New York: HarperCollins, 1996, 2005.
Wood, Joyce Rilett, John E. Harvey, and Mark Leuchter, eds. *From Babel to Babylon*. New York: T&T Clark, 2006.
Wright, F. Warren. *Studies in Menander: A Dissertation Presented to the Faculty of Princeton University*. Baltimore: The Waverly Press, 1911.
Wright, J. Edward. *The Early History of Heaven*. Oxford: Oxford University Press, 2000.
Wright, G. Ernest, ed. *The Bible and the Ancient Near East: Essays in Honor of William Foxwell Albright*. Winona Lake, ID: Eisenbrauns, 1979.
Xiaochun, Sun, and Jacob Kistemaker. *The Chinese Sky During the Han: Constellating Stars & Society*. Leiden: Brill, 1997.
Yin-shun, Venerable. *The Way to Buddhahood: Instructions from a Modern Chinese Master*. tr. Wing H. Yeung. Somerville, MA: Wisdom Publications, 1998.
Yogananda, Sri Sri Paramahansa. *God Talks with Arjuna: The Bhagavad Gita*. India: Yogoda Satsanga Society, 1999.
Yu, Anthony C. *Journey to the West*. Chicago/London: University of Chicago Press, 1984.
Zara, Erik. "The Chrestianos Issue in Tacitus Reinvestigated." www.textexcavation.com/documents/zaratacituschrestianos.pdf
—"Tacitus' sentence about Christus—a marginal gloss?" groups.yahoo.com/group/JesusMysteries/message/53632
Zeitlin, Solomon. "The Halak in the Gospels and Its Relation to the Jewish Law at the Time of Jesus," *Hebrew Union College Annual*, v. 1.
—*The Rise and Fall of Judaean State: 37 BCE–66 CE*. Philadelphia: Jewish Publication Society of America, 1978.
Zorach, Rebecca. *Blood, Milk, Ink, Gold: Abundance and Excess in the French Renaissance*. Chicago: University of Chicago Press, 2005.
Zondervan Illustrated Bible Dictionary. eds. J.D. Douglas, Merrill C. Tenney and Moises Silva. Zondervan, 2011